Survival and Consolidation provides an intriguing and detailed examination of the new political realities that emerged in eastern Europe out of the chaos left in the wake of the First World War. Uncovering the reasons for the victory of V.I. Lenin's Bolshevik government in the Russian civil war, Richard Debo demonstrates that Bolshevik political and diplomatic skills were far superior to those of either their indigenous opponents or their many foreign enemies. For much of 1919, enemies of the Soviet government were more interested in fighting amongst each other than with the Bolsheviks, and although foreign powers sought influence among competing anti-Bolshevik generals, they contributed little to the defeat of the Red Army. Meanwhile, the Bolsheviks found they could establish realistic priorities, formulate flexible policies, and make political sacrifices unimagined by their enemies. As a result they were able to find allies and divide opponents.

As victory for the Bolsheviks neared, they turned their attention to the consolidation of power within the former Russian empire. When they took power in 1917 the Bolsheviks had said that their revolution would spread beyond Russia or perish. Neither happened; in the spring of 1921, at the end of hostilities, they stood alone in the wreckage of the former empire. The Bolsheviks had, in Lenin's words, "won the right to an independent existence." This entirely unforeseen situation surprised both them and their enemies.

Debo shows that nothing predetermined that Soviet Russia would, at the end of the civil war, enjoy an "independent existence" – or even exist at all. After close examination of the evidence, he suggests that a wide range of circumstances contributed to the eventual outcome of the war, which could have ended indecisively. In his evaluation of the Soviet diplomatic achievement, Debo describes the successes with Britain, Poland, and Germany, the continuing difficulties with Romania, France, and the United States, and the threat from the Far East. Diplomatic achievements, he maintains, were the result of Soviet victory in the civil war and the patient pursuit of realizable objectives.

RICHARD K. DEBO is a professor in the Department of History, Simon Fraser University.

SURVIVAL AND CONSOLIDATION

The Foreign Policy of Soviet Russia, 1918–1921

Richard K. Debo

McGill-Queen's University Press
Montreal & Kingston • London • Buffalo

© McGill-Queen's University Press 1992
ISBN 0-7735-0828-7

Legal deposit third quarter 1992
Bibliothèque nationale du Québec

Printed in Canada on acid-free paper

This book has been published with the help of
a grant from the Social Science Federation
of Canada, using funds provided
by the Social Sciences and Humanities
Research Council of Canada.
Publication has also been assisted
by a grant from the Simon Fraser
University Publications Committee

Canadian Cataloguing in Publication Data

Debo, Richard K., 1938–
Survival and consolidation
Includes bibliographical references and index.
ISBN 0-7735-0828-7
1. Soviet Union – Foreign relations – 1917–1945.
I. Title.
DK265.D32 1992   327.47   C92-090093-3

This book was typeset by Typo Litho composition inc.
in 10/12 Baskerville.

To Tonie and Natasha

Contents

Acknowledgments

In completing a study of this nature the historian is made aware of how much is owed to others. The list is endless. To begin I am glad to have a further opportunity to express my thanks to Albin T. Anderson, whose original inspiration has proved so strong and lasting. I must also thank my colleagues at Simon Fraser University, in particular Michael Fellman, Richard Boyer, Charles Hamilton, John Hutchinson, Edward Ingram, Robert Koepke, Martin Kitchen, and Lenard Cohen. All have cheerfully endured my enthusiasm for this subject and been willing to discuss it at length. A special tribute is due to the late Richard Sullivan, whose nimble mind and fertile curiosity, nurtured by the wonders of his beloved classical antiquity, never ceased to amaze me. Successive chairpersons of the Department of History have aided my research. Robert Brown, Dean of Arts, has been equally supportive. Colleagues elsewhere also deserve special mention. Michael J. Carley, T. R. Ravindranathan, Rex Wade, Donald Raleigh, Ted Uldricks, Timothy O'Connor, and Keith Neilson all contributed in many different ways to the completion of this work. Philip Amos has been a constant source of intellectual stimulation.

I owe gratitude to the many institutions where I conducted the research for this book. I am indebted to the librarians and archivists of Simon Fraser University; the University of British Columbia; the University of Washington; the University of Hawaii, Manoa; the French Ministry of Foreign Affairs; the French Ministry of War; the British Library; the House of Lords; the Public Record Office, Kew; the United States National Archives; the Library of Congress; the Hoover Institution; and the Sterling Memorial Library, Yale University.

The manuscript could never have been completed and prepared for publication without the co-operation and valued assistance of Joanna Koczwarski, Joan MacDonald, Maylene Leong, Peggy Mitchell, and Anita Mahoney. Diane Mew has been an understanding and perspicacious copy-editor. Derek Oye prepared the map. Stephen and Rachael Fleming compiled the index. All errors are mine.

All dates in this work are given according to the Gregorian or Western calendar. Transliteration from Russian is based on the Library of Congress system but diacritical marks have been omitted.

Preface

In the spring of 1920 the government of Soviet Russia prepared for negotiations with the foreign powers which had intervened in the civil war then coming to an end. A settlement with Great Britain was especially important to the restoration of peace, and Georgii Chicherin, the foreign commissar, prepared the instructions for these talks himself. He wrote to Leonid Krasin who would represent Moscow in London:

We must not appear in the role of the pitiful suppliant. Once the Russian foreign minister Gorchakov said: "Great powers do not need recognition, they declare their own existence." In 1917 we declared our own existence, year by year we grow stronger and the day is not far off when we will be recognized. History itself will force the imperialists to do this.[1]

This declaration clearly reflected the commissar's bitter experience, over two years, in dealing with far stronger powers from a position of great weakness and gave clear voice to the anguish felt by so many (even Bolshevik) *intelligenty* at the collapse of Russia as a great power. Chicherin, who had graduated in history from St Petersburg University, had served in the archives of the imperial foreign ministry. There he had written a biography of Alexander M. Gorchakov, the foreign minister of Alexander II in the years following defeat in the Crimean War when Russia had suffered an earlier, if less precipitous, fall from greatness. Now Chicherin invoked Gorchakov, in some ways his posthumous mentor, to make the point that this fall was only temporary and Russia would once more be great. Greatness required no external validation, only the power and determination to make its will felt in the world. In March 1920 this was a novel point of view. Throughout much of the previous two years the Soviet government had been thankful to survive on a day-to-day basis; its fall had been routinely announced in the foreign press. By the end of 1919 this precarious existence had come to an end, and Moscow was able to think in terms of a more elaborate foreign policy. Survival made way for consolidation.

Survival and consolidation, in fact, characterized the fundamental foreign policies of the Soviet government between 1918 and 1921. This work will focus on both. First it seeks to identify the political, especially international, reasons for Bolshevik victory in the Russian civil war, setting them apart as far as possible from the purely military aspects of this achievement. As the Russian civil war was essentially a political struggle, the Bolsheviks enjoyed an enormous advantage. Bolshevism was politics writ large while the political skills of the Whites, as their conservative Russian opponents were called, were primitive, and this contributed to the frittering away of their initial military advantage. But it was not merely the Whites who were politically deficient; in coping with eastern Europe their foreign supporters exhibited similar limitations. An odd feature of the civil war was that the intervening powers, while genuinely hostile to Soviet Russia, were not primarily concerned with defeating the Bolsheviks. Many foreign representatives, some specific agencies, and the occasional minister understood the importance of events unfolding in eastern Europe, but in 1919, at the height of the civil war, western governments were distracted by other problems and assigned a low priority to the Russian problem. Even the French, who wished to regain a valued ally and redeem their huge pre-war investment in Russia, first had to influence Great Britain and restrain Germany. After being forced to withdraw the large expeditionary force sent to Ukraine in late 1918, the French had to join the other intervening powers in leaving the actual task of fighting the Bolsheviks to the White generals. To be sure, each power wanted to back the winning general, but this only served to promote rivalry and distract attention from the necessity of first defeating the Red Army. How did these circumstances arise and develop? In what ways were the Bolsheviks able to exploit them for their own advantage? The answer to the second question relates in part to the Bolshevik ability to contemplate politically advantageous sacrifices which their enemies – foreign and domestic – could not even imagine. This in turn reflects the Bolshevik ability to establish priorities. This work will examine those priorities as well as how and why they changed over the course of time. In particular it will focus on the manner in which the Foreign Commissariat promoted these priorities abroad and contributed to winning for Soviet Russia, as Lenin said in March 1921, "the right to an independent existence."[2]

No one, least of all the Bolsheviks, had expected this outcome. Time and again they had told themselves that the revolution would spread beyond Russia or surely perish. And yet at the end of hostilities, while they had won the right to an independent existence, they were isolated in the wreckage of the tsarist empire and held tightly in the jaws of "capitalist encirclement."[3] When did the possibility of this enormity begin to materialize? How and why did it take shape? To what degree did it develop independently of Moscow? How did the Bolsheviks contribute to its eventual realization? Nothing predetermined that Soviet Russia would enjoy an independent existence or, for that matter, exist at all at the end of the civil war. Close examination suggests that the war could have ended differently, perhaps continuing for a longer time or even ending indecisively. It did not, and as soon as the Bolsheviks realized they had won decisively they moved quickly to consolidate their victory. How did the Bolsheviks shift their policy from survival to consolidation and how did they decide which parts of the former empire were to be included in the Soviet state? These were painful decisions, and they were reviewed repeatedly from 1919 to 1921. Nothing predetermined the final territorial settlement. The Soviet state which emerged from the civil war could easily have been somewhat larger or smaller had circumstances changed even marginally.

Soviet policy towards Poland occupies a special place in the second half of this study. Originally Bolshevik leaders viewed Poland little differently from other parts of the western borderlands, but the unexpected opportunities opened by Pilsudski's invasion of Ukraine soon led them to re-examine their earlier priorities. In the summer of 1920 they abandoned the cautious realism that had characterized their foreign policy since the treaty of Brest-Litovsk and began to define new and far more ambitious aims. Was this a reversion to revolutionary romanticism or something quite different? Would Soviet Russia even have benefited from the annihilation of Pilsudski's Poland in late August 1920? One of the arresting features of these events is the rapidity with which the Bolsheviks' immodest aims in the summer of 1920 were abandoned following the defeat of the Red Army on the approaches to Warsaw. Why did this happen so abruptly and what aims were put in the place of the discredited goals?

The fall of 1920 was a period of both military and political retrenchment, which encouraged Soviet leaders to think realistically about the future. Aims enunciated at that time became the basis for the agreements with Afghanistan, Persia, Nationalist Turkey, Poland, Great Britain, and Germany that were concluded between February and May 1921. What was the significance of these agreements for Soviet Russia? Although early 1921 was a period of great weakness for the Soviet government, its most immediate adversaries chose to leave the field of battle and come to terms with Moscow. Why did they do this and what did their action suggest about the changing role of Soviet Russia in international affairs? These are the questions I will seek to answer.

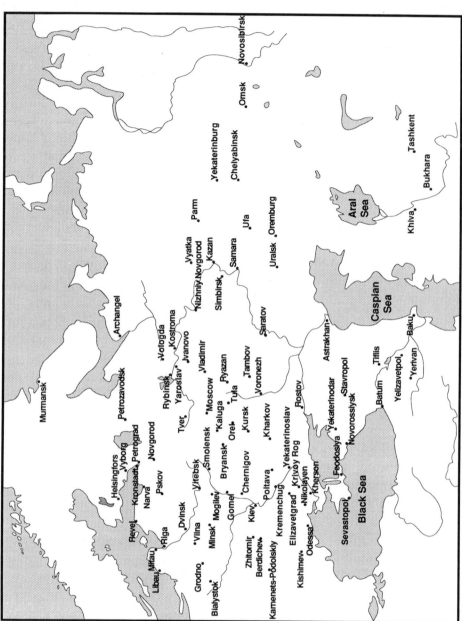

Russia, 1918

Survival and Consolidation

Nec Pluribus Impar

CHAPTER ONE

Introduction

On 11 November 1918 the armistice between Germany and the allied powers took effect. Fighting in the Great War came to an end, and the guns fell silent along a line from the North Sea to Switzerland. In eastern Europe, however, hostilities continued. The civil war in Russia, already more than six months old, blazed even more brightly, for the armistice left the fate of eastern Europe unsettled. Since March Germany had exercised an iron-fisted hegemony over this region but, as German power began to ebb, all of eastern Europe was drawn into the vacuum left by the collapse of the Reich.

War, revolution, and military occupation had left eastern Europe a shambles. The old order, regulated before 1914 by the courts of Berlin, St Petersburg, and Vienna, had been smashed; a new one had not yet taken its place. Tentative and diverse efforts to create a new order had begun with the fall of the Romanov dynasty but had been crushed by the German army as it moved forward to occupy much of eastern Europe. Everywhere the Germans had provided protection for the conservative elements of society but had given them no real power to order local affairs. Now, with the German army about to leave, these remnants of the old order were unable to stand on their own feet. They were destined to depart with the Germans and end their days in exile.

Rival national aspirations added to the problem of social disorder. Eastern Europe was a tangle of nations small in size and power but great in pride and imagination. Each aspired to independent statehood and aggrandizement at the expense of neighbouring peoples. The old imperial order had held these rival forces in check and the German army ruthlessly repressed any outburst of national hostility. But with the armistice the many nationalities of eastern Europe were freed to pursue their conflicting aspirations in any way they thought best. From Finland to Azerbaijan spokesmen for rival national movements emerged to put forward the most far-reaching claims against the territory and economic resources of their neighbours. The basis existed in eastern Europe for a truly Hobbesian *bellum omnium in omnes*.

Soviet Russia was the only centre of real power in eastern Europe. During most of 1918 it, too, had been reduced to the status of a German client state, but had not been subjected to military occupation. Even after the terrible losses suffered as a result of defeat in the Great War and the civil conflict that followed, Soviet Russia retained a greater territory, larger population, and more substantial resources than its neighbours. Although total economic activity declined throughout 1918, the resources available to the Soviet state increased. Such circumstances, and the steadily worsening position of Germany on her western borders, had allowed Soviet Russia to obtain German protection primarily on the basis of promises. The Bolsheviks had made good use of the breathing space purchased at Brest-Litovsk. Virtually powerless in March 1918, Soviet Russia emerged as the strongest surviving member of the system of German client states that collapsed with the Reich in November 1918.

Having seized power in November 1917, V.I. Lenin and the Bolsheviks had used the following year to enlarge their party, restructure the Soviet state, and build a new army. By the end of 1918 they had created an efficient government machine and expanded the party to include a quarter of a million members. Both party and state were highly centralized. The Bolsheviks had initially vested executive authority in a central committee and, after March 1919, a much smaller political bureau (Politburo). The Soviet government was directed by the Council of People's Commissars (Sovnarkom) of whom V.I. Lenin was chairman. Lenin coordinated the Politburo and Sovnarkom, giving him great but not unlimited authority in the revolutionary regime. By the end of 1918 party and state were primarily concerned with revolutionary defence. They had transformed the Red Guard, originally a revolutionary militia, into the Red Army, a fighting force of more than one and a half million men, organized into regular divisions commanded by professional soldiers drawn from the pre-revolutionary Russian officer corps. It comprised forty-two rifle and three cavalry divisions, organized into thirteen separate armies defending five fronts.[1] With the departure of the Germans the Red Army represented the paramount military force in eastern Europe.

The Soviet government could also deploy a popular ideology. With all traditional institutions and values discredited, the day of revolutionary social democracy had arrived. The simple message of social justice, class warfare, and an end to imperialism appealed deeply to peoples weary of war and oppression. Land to the peasants, factories to the workers and self-determination for all peoples were slogans which could not be matched by other parties. Peace and prosperity with social justice, the Bolsheviks said, could be attained through proletarian internationalism, the mutual assistance and solidarity of all revolutionary social-democratic parties and groups. Bolshevik disciples spread this message throughout eastern Europe, with the party faithful toiling tirelessly to bring their localities within the frontiers of the revolutionary Soviet state.[2]

Soviet Russia threatened the existence of all other German client states in the region. Once the German army left, nothing would stop the local Bolsheviks from seizing power. For months they had been restrained by Moscow from rebelling against the Germans but now the Soviet government also wanted to establish Bolshevik rule in the borderlands.[3] The Bolsheviks did not conceal their intentions; as a result, their opponents in eastern Europe were aware they would soon have to confront a determined revolutionary assault backed by the Red Army. This led the neighbours of Soviet Russia to seek help from the victorious allies. It was clear that authorities as diverse as the governments of Finland, Georgia, Azerbaijan, and Ukraine as well as the national committees formed in Estonia, Latvia, and Poland did not consider themselves capable of withstanding a political and military struggle against Soviet Russia. Their fears were an accurate reflection of the east European balance of power.

The allied powers were delighted to witness the end of German hegemony in the region, but none wished to see any of the territory evacuated by the Germans fall into Bolshevik hands. The Bolsheviks had collaborated with Berlin through most of 1918 and were considered much too dangerous to be left in control of Russia. Lord Robert Cecil, assistant secretary of state for foreign affairs and a major figure in shaping British policy in Russia, wrote: "Now that our enemies are defeated, the chief danger to this country is Bolshevism."[4] The French view was similar. Fernand Grenard, former consul general in Moscow, described the Soviet regime as an 'unlimited despotism ... more contrary to a peaceful and healthy organization of Europe than Prussian despotism."[5] A French Foreign Ministry memorandum foresaw "a terrible recrudescence of Bolshevism in the Ukraine, Lithuania and Poland with a jacquerie, the massacre of estate owners, pillage, etc."[6] The British war cabinet received the same warning from the Foreign Office.[7]

But allied action was limited by constraints of geography and circumstances. Germany had been able to act effectively against Soviet Russia because her army occupied territories adjacent to Petrograd and Moscow and could have toppled the Bolsheviks at any time. The allies had no such advantage. They had landed small forces in Russia, but these were too weak and dispersed to pose the same threat to Moscow. Nor was it likely that the allies would be able to land a major force in Russia. With the armistice their tired soldiers wished only to return home. Furthermore, the war was not over. Peace had not been made, and hostilities could resume at any time. It would be dangerous for the allies to mount a major campaign in Russia with Germany still poised on their flank and ready to take advantage of any reverse suffered against the Bolsheviks.

The most effective way for the allies to act against the Bolsheviks was in concert with Berlin. This would reduce the possibility of further hostilities with Germany. But cooperation carried a price, which included a more lenient peace and inclusion in whatever order emerged in eastern Europe after the fall of the Bolsheviks. For the French, at least, this was too great a price to pay. When the Germans let it be known that they were ready to consider cooperation with the allies in Russia, Georges Clemenceau, the French premier, rejected the suggestion out of hand. All the same, he did agree to the inclusion in the armistice of a clause which specified that the German evacuation of eastern Europe was to be delayed until "the Allies think the moment suitable, having regard to the internal situation of these territories."[8]

Disunity was a further factor limiting allied ability to act in Russia. Throughout late 1917 and early 1918 the danger of defeat by Germany had imposed an uneasy unity upon allied policies in Russia. In early summer, when Ludendorff menaced Paris, even President Wilson of the United States had reluctantly joined his policy to that of the allies and had agreed to send American troops to Russia. This had been an act of solidarity with his hard-pressed associates in Europe at a moment when he was unable to offer any other assistance in redressing the deplorable military situation in France. Action in Russia was necessary, London and Paris had argued, in order to draw the Germans away from the western front. Wilson was so suspicious of allied motives, however, that he placed strict limits on intervention in Russia. Indeed, he claimed not even to be intervening at all, but merely helping an allied force, the Czech Legion, which was trying to leave Russia by way of Vladivostok. In addition, he said, the United States would seek "to steady any efforts at self-government or self-defence in which the Russians themselves may be willing to accept assistance." In pursuit of these aims Wilson sent small American forces to Vladivostok and Archangel to join other allied forces already there.[9]

The American experience in Russia only served to deepen Wilson's suspicion. At Vladivostok he found his troops alongside seventy thousand Japanese troops who quickly displayed a keen interest in promoting more far-reaching aims than those he defined. At Archangel the British involved the newly arrived Americans in fighting against the Bolsheviks and gave the appearance of seeking to establish a reactionary government. As a consequence, when the allies asked him to send more troops, Wilson refused. On 7 October 1918 he informed them officially of his decision not to become further involved in Russia.[10] Although Wilson denied that he was trying to force the allies to accept his policy, it was clear that American abstention would greatly limit any action. Only the United States had the resources to mount a major intervention in Russia. Not much could be done there, the British director of military operations informed the war cabinet, without whole-hearted American support.[11]

Anglo-French cooperation soon ended as well. During most of 1918 the Supreme War Council had coordinated intervention in Russia. This role ceased when Wilson withdrew the authority of the American representative to participate in these deliberations. No other institution took up this function and, as a result, planning for action in Russia devolved upon the individual allied governments. No consultation occurred, and little information was exchanged. Each government acted independently within the framework of earlier agreements dividing

Russia into "zones of influence." Britain was free to direct action in north Russia, south Russia, and the Caucasus; France was to focus on Bessarabia, Ukraine, and the Crimea. Primary responsibility for action in the Baltic, Poland, and Siberia remained unassigned.[12] In November 1918, therefore, the British decided to remain in occupation of north Russia, support the Omsk directorate, secure the rail line from Baku to Batum, and assist the Baltic states.[13] The French decided to send six divisions to occupy Odessa and Sebastopol, then advance into the Dneiper and Donetz basins "to assure protection for allied interests," and "assist local governments to maintain internal order and give them the time and means to organize their own army."[14]

Allied action in Russia was greatly influenced by the existence of a number of anti-Bolshevik centres located around the periphery of the Soviet state. In November 1918 the most important of these were the government of N.V. Chaikovsky in north Russia, the All-Russian Provisional Government (itself composed of the socialist-revolutionary centre at Samara and the bourgeois Siberian Provisional Government) at Omsk, the Cossacks of Ataman Krasnov on the Don, and the Volunteer Army of General Denikin. Anton I. Denikin had assumed command of the Volunteer Army in April of that year. It was the largest White army in European Russia and at that time was based in the North Caucasus. With the exception of Krasnov, all had "kept faith" with the allies and had remained in a technical state of war with Germany. None had actually fought the Germans, but they had fought the Bolsheviks, and in allied minds this was the same thing. Those western leaders who wished to continue the war against Soviet Russia, therefore, were able to claim that the allies owed the anti-Bolsheviks a debt of gratitude and the Whites should be supported in their attempt to crush the Bolsheviks. Some felt this debt more deeply than others, and by the end of 1918 the first voices had begun to ask how long it would be necessary to honour it.[15]

By the end of 1918 the Whites were virtually the only hope the allies had of installing an anti-Bolshevik regime in Moscow. The Germans could do it, but the allies would not let them. The Americans could probably do it but did not want to. The Japanese could probably do it also, but did not want their troops west of Irkutsk even if the Americans would agree. The British and French wanted to, but did not have the resources to conduct a major campaign in Russia. This left only the Whites, who were few in number, badly dispersed, ill equipped, and frightfully disorganized.[16] Yet if the allied desire to restore their version of order in Russia was to be realized, it would depend upon such men as Chaikovsky, Denikin, and the All Russian Provisional Government at Omsk. This was acknowledged in the British decision of 14 November to recognize the Omsk regime as the legitimate government of all Russia and provide it and other groups such as the Volunteer Army with arms and munitions.[17] How effective this aid would be remained an open question. The seriousness of the situation can be seen in the short lifespan of the All-Russian Provisional Government, which was overthrown on 17 November by its minister of war, Admiral Alexander V. Kolchak. Kolchak, who had no use for his socialist colleagues, proclaimed himself Supreme Ruler of All Russia. [18]

The Omsk fiasco was simply one more page in the long saga of allied failure in Russia. Since March 1917 they had repeatedly backed losing politicians. This pattern was being repeated, for while allied leaders thought in terms of aiding the Whites to fight the Bolsheviks, the Whites thought in terms of the allies sending a large army to Russia to do this fighting. The more level-headed White leaders were well aware of their weakness and were quite certain they could not defeat the Bolsheviks. Chaikovsky had informed the British of this in October and it was repeated shortly thereafter by M.I. Tereshchenko, a former Russian foreign minister under Kerensky, and Prince Lvov, the first prime minister of the 1917 Provisional Government. Reports from highly qualified allied and neutral observers confirmed this pessimistic picture but did not alter either British or French policy. [19] Both continued to develop with little reference to actual circumstances in Russia.

The incoherence of allied policy allowed Lenin and the Soviet government to strengthen their position in Russia. Continued intervention provided the Bolsheviks with the opportunity to broaden the base of their government and enlist the active cooperation of many individuals, intellectuals in particular, who had previously opposed the Soviet regime. As the Great War came to an end, Lenin hastened to make a virtue of necessity and take credit for developments which would have occurred in any case. Thus, having lost the protection of Germany which he had so avidly sought through all of the previous year, he now annulled the treaty of Brest-Litovsk and its supplements. [20] By this action Lenin was able to launch an appeal to all socialists who had been alienated by his policy of collaboration with Germany. He used the example of Pitrim Sorokin, a member of the Socialist-Revolutionary party, who had chosen to withdraw from politics to avoid further obstruction of the Soviet government. Sorokin's action, Lenin claimed, was of great significance, because he was "representative of the Menshevik-Socialist Revolutionary trend" which had proved irreconcilable in its opposition to Soviet foreign policy the previous year. This opposition had grown from the petit-bourgeois nature of these parties. They claimed to be socialist but in reality represented the middle peasantry, clerical employees, and many intellectuals. These layers of Russian society were deeply infused with patriotism and reacted with "bitterness, resentment and violent indignation" to the sacrifice of Russian national interests to preserve the revolution. A major problem of the proletarian revolution, he said was "that it was obliged to pass through a phase of extreme departure from patriotism, the phase of the Brest-Litovsk peace."

That phase, however, was at an end. Current circumstances, as Sorokin showed, were moving the petit-bourgeoisie in the direction of the Soviet government. The allied powers, by imposing crushing terms on Germany, were behaving exactly as the Bolsheviks had predicted and appeared intent on validating the entire Soviet analysis of international relations. Not simply Bolshevism but the revolution as a whole was threatened by allied imperialism. "In spite of their hatred of Bolshevism," Lenin said, the petit-bourgeois democrats of Russia were turning "first to neutrality and then to support of Bolshevism ... The objective conditions existing in the world now compel them to turn to us."[21]

This movement was in fact under way, and throughout the final months of 1918 several splinters of Menshevik and Socialist Revolutionary parties passed resolutions denouncing foreign intervention in the Russian civil war and expressing solidarity with the Soviet government in the armed struggle against it. They also rejected any form of coalition or cooperation with bourgeois parties anywhere in Russia.[22] Iuri Martov testified that the Menshevik Central Committee took this action because "there is talk that the socialist world revolution is evidently" 'bypassing democracy' and taking the Bolshevik road, and that it is dangerously doctrinaire to oppose this process – one must look for some kind of 'bridge' with bolshevism."[23]

Many Bolsheviks were less impressed by this movement than Lenin. Iuri Steklov, editor of *Izvestiia*, for example, kept up a steady polemic against the moderate socialists, criticizing them for their tardy and hesitant renunciation of opposing Bolshevik rule.[24] Lenin found it necessary to return to this theme on several occasions and lecture his followers on elementary political tactics. To win the support of millions of peasants and tens of thousands of skilled workers and intellectuals it was necessary, he said, to abandon past slogans of terror and suppression of the petit-bourgeoisie. This did not mean that Lenin was suggesting that the Bolsheviks should move in the direction of their socialist adversaries. He believed they were moving in his direction, not he in theirs. He did not expect them to become communists. It was sufficient that they, like Sorokin, become politically neutral. This was in itself a highly political act and could only benefit the Bolsheviks. "You maintain good-neighbourly relations with us," said Lenin, "and we shall keep state power."[25] Martov understood this perfectly. "No bridge is possible," he wrote, "except outright surrender, since bolshevism does not admit the idea of an opposition party, even if it is ultraloyal and accepts the Soviet principle. The only 'reconciliation' they admit is for members of this or that opposition party to join them as 'individual guests.'"[26]

In this manner, with a somewhat broadened base of popular support, Lenin began to shape Soviet foreign policy in the second year of the revolution. On the one hand this policy was to be couched heavily in ideological terms stressing proletarian internationalism. The Soviet government would aid Bolsheviks and sympathizers in the borderlands and beyond who were prepared to take their directives from Moscow. Lenin would also seek help from radical groups in the capitalist world. Ideology, however, would not be the only guide for Soviet policy; the coldest calculation of relative power would also play its part. In the borderlands the Red Army would be used to smash weaker opponents; but it could not be expected, by itself, to fend off the allied powers. Political power would supplement that of the military, and Soviet diplomacy would identify, exacerbate, and promote differences among the powers hostile to Soviet Russia. Lenin was capable of reaching agreement with any or all of the allied powers, but any agreement would be based on the precise balance of power existing at the moment of its conclusion and would be subject to change should circumstances subsequently favour the Bolsheviks. Finally, there was the question of Germany. The Reich had been defeated, but German power had not been broken. She remained a key factor in east European politics and, of necessity, would be of prime concern in Lenin's policy as it developed.

CHAPTER TWO

"We are not accustomed to waiting": Soviet Russia, the German revolution, and eastern Europe

From its very beginning Russian social democracy had been deeply influenced by Germany. German culture had already left an indelible mark on the Russian intelligentsia, and as this alienated segment of the Russian intellectual world evolved towards Marxism, German influence grew much greater. Germany with its burgeoning industry, massive proletariat, disciplined socialist party, and galaxy of Marxist theorists became an irresistible magnet attracting the attention of Russian Social Democrats. Although Russian social democracy did not exert a reciprocal influence in Germany, it did attract attention largely because of the degree to which German social democracy was drawn into the factional quarrels of the Russian Marxists. The moderate majority of German Social Democrats tended to blame Lenin and the Bolsheviks for this factiousness. The Bolsheviks, for their part, had already begun to doubt the revolutionary sincerity of many German Social Democrats. For Lenin, German socialists such as Friedrich Ebert and Philipp Scheidemann ceased to be social democrats and had become social-traitors and social-chauvinists, socialists in word but chauvinists in deed. They had become the class enemies of the proletariat for they utilized the familiar rhetoric of socialism to advance the aims of the ruling classes.

The revolution in Russia hardened all these attitudes. The reality of the dictatorship of the proletariat and the violence of the Red Terror horrified the German Social Democrats. The Bolsheviks, on the other hand, could not comprehend the loyalty of the German Social Democrats to the Wilhelmine Reich. Bolshevik efforts to promote dissidence within socialist ranks in Germany simply made relations worse. The Bolsheviks viewed the moderate socialists as traitors; the moderate socialist saw the Bolsheviks as dangerous fanatics.[1]

Oddly enough, the Bolsheviks got along better with the civilian government of imperial Germany than with the Social Democrats. They expected the German government to act like a gang of heavily armed robbers and were never disappointed. Ideological dispute and failed expectation never interfered in relations between the Kremlin and the Wilhelmstrasse. Instead, the Bolsheviks based their relations on the pursuit of unalloyed self-interest. This was not an arrangement of equals, but one of master and vassal. Nor was it a smoothly functioning relationship, for if Russian commissars and German ministers understood one another, the same could not be said about the German high command. German generals hated Bolsheviks and were only barely restrained from unseating the Soviet government. In the late summer of 1918, however, a mutually advantageous (if extraordinarily fragile) arrangement was worked out between the two states. In effect the Bolsheviks agreed to allow the Germans unlimited access to the economic resources of the territories under their control in exchange for non-intervention in Russian internal affairs, aid in settling disputes with other German clients, and military protection from the allies. Unlike the treaty of Brest-Litovsk, these agreements were freely negotiated and gladly signed by the Soviet government. In them they received what they most needed from Germany – time to consolidate their hold on Russia.[2]

The Bolsheviks did not receive nearly as much time as they had expected. Even the most perceptive Bolsheviks had not gauged the speed with which the Reich actually fell apart. In mid-September A.A. Ioffe, the Soviet minister in Berlin, thought Germany might last another two years;[3] at the end of October Julian Marchleswki, long experienced in German political life and just returned from Berlin, foresaw the war continuing indefinitely; and as late as 3 November Karl Radek, director of central European affairs at the People's Commissariat of foreign Affairs (the Narkomindel), thought the crisis might still be postponed until the spring of 1919.[4] All three believed German generals would find it impossible to admit defeat and would fight to the bitter end.

Defeat released pent-up political frustration, and in October a revolutionary situation began to emerge in Germany. Lenin tried to put his propaganda machine in high gear and instructed Ioffe to spend freely in promoting revolution in Germany.[5] Ioffe, thinking of the many delicate questions he was negotiating with the imperial government, warned that a propaganda campaign "would spoil everything."[6] Lenin replied that while diplomacy could continue, he believed "its significance had decreased."[7] Chicherin later wrote that "the rising revolutionary wave in Germany gradually forced the technical diplomatic work into the background."[8] Ioffe did his best to assist the emerging revolution. He subsidized newspapers, collected information, paid for the printing of revolutionary literature, and provided several hundred thousand marks for the purchase of arms.[9] In all, he probably spent something in excess of a million marks attempting to promote a Bolshevik-style revolution in Germany.

It was too little too late. By early November imperial Germany had begun to disintegrate, but the revolution that gripped the country bore little resemblance to that desired by the Bolsheviks. Lenin had already lamented the absence of Bolshevik-style parties in western and central Europe,[10] and this was to prove critical in Germany. Power passed from the crippled regime of Prince Max von Baden to the Social Democratic party headed by Ebert and Scheidemann and the Independent Social Democratic party led by Hugo Haase. Although bitter rivals, the two parties were thrust together by the tumultuous events of early November. Neither wanted a Russian-style revolution in Germany or even collaboration with Moscow.[11] Only the Spartacists led by Rosa Luxembourg and Karl Liebknecht were sympathetic to the Bolsheviks. Although they were influential within the Independent Social Democratic party, they were too few to grasp the initiative from the well-organized and disciplined Social Democratic party.[12]

The German Social Democrats, in fact, struck the first blow against the Bolsheviks. While still members of the coalition government of Prince Max von Baden, they had agreed that Germany would have to play on the allied fear of Bolshevism to obtain a more lenient peace. They intended to portray the Reich as the last barrier of "civilization" against Bolshevik "barbarism." This required a complete break with the Bolsheviks.[13] Thus, on 5 November the Soviet legation was surrounded by police, and the next morning Ioffe and his staff were removed from Berlin.[14] Just days before the eruption of revolutionary violence in Berlin, Moscow lost most of its ability to influence events in Germany.

Soviet reaction took two forms. On the surface, the Bolsheviks said the events were of little consequence. Privately, however, Lenin warned that the rupture signalled the first step in forging an anti-Bolshevik alliance.[15] On the fall of the Hohenzollerns on 9 November, messages began to flow from Moscow in a steady stream, seeking to link the Bolsheviks with the German revolution. Almost at once, however, the Bolsheviks observed they were receiving nothing in return. Nor could they contact Ioffe. The German army was holding him and his party near the demarcation line but refused to allow Chicherin to communicate with him.[16]

This left Moscow very badly informed about the German revolution. Soviet leaders were misled by the terminology of the German revolution which so closely paralled their own: soviets of workers' and soldiers' deputies were reported as springing up all over Germany, an apparently ultra-radical soviet had been formed in Berlin, and the new government emerging from the revolution styled itself the Council of People's Representatives. Thus, when direct contact with Berlin was restored on 11 November, Chicherin's first messages reflected a very optimistic view of events there. The day before a "revolutionary workers' and soldiers' council" composed of German communists among prisoners of war in Russia had seized control of German diplomatic installations in Moscow and Petrograd, and these self-proclaimed German representatives were able to place him in contact with Oskar Cohn, the Reichstag deputy who had served as legal consul for the Soviet legation in Berlin. In their teleprinter conversation, Chicherin told Cohn that the Soviet government wanted to conclude an offensive and defensive alliance with revolutionary Germany.[17] Moscow had already decided

to send two trains loaded with grain to be put at the disposal of the struggle for
the dictatorship of the proletariat in Germany.[18] Chicherin said the Soviet government wanted to help in breaking the allied blockade of Germany. Cohn had
no authority to speak for anyone but undertook to convey Chicherin's message
to his associates in the Independent Social Democratic party.

Shortly after speaking to Cohn, Chicherin drafted another message for transmission to Germany. Here he recommended that German revolutionaries sympathetic to Soviet Russia should support "the revolutionary movement directed
by Liebknecht." As a practical program he suggested they work for "the evacuation of the occupied region, the conclusion of an offensive and defensive
alliance of the revolutionary socialist republics of soviets, [and] an active participation on the part of German troops against Krasnov's counter-revolutionary
bands."[19]

Neither this nor other Soviet messages sent during the first days of the German
revolution reached their intended recipients. They were intercepted by Rudolf
Nadolny who directed Russian affairs at the Auswärtiges Amt. The Council of
People's Representatives readily agreed when Nadolny suggested that the entire
question of Germany's relations with the Bolsheviks be dealt with in a "dilatory
manner."[20] The Council did not allow Ioffe to return to Berlin or accept delivery
of the two trainloads of Soviet grain. Already by 12 November the pace and
quality of the German revolution had diverged so greatly from the Russian model
that the Soviet government issued a warning that the situation in Germany might
only have reached the stage of "February" and not that of "October."[21]

Ebert and Scheidemann showed no inclination to enter into relations with
Soviet Russia. Instead the Auswärtiges Amt demanded the release of the German
diplomats and their exchange for Ioffe and his staff. Ioffe was a symbol of the
Russian revolution and his return to Russia would calm the allied fears that Berlin
had not broken completely with Moscow. But the Germans had to secure the
release of their diplomats. On the night of 14 November, therefore, Hugo Haase,
the People's Representative responsible for the supervision of foreign affairs in
the new German government, re-opened the teleprinter link with Moscow. Chicherin and Radek conducted the conversation for the Soviet government. It was a
moment of great suspense, and Radek later recalled that after Chicherin had
completed his first transmission there was total silence in the room. "Chicherin
and I stood there, our eyes not moving from the Hughes ribbon."[22]

The Bolsheviks were to be bitterly disappointed. They wanted to determine
if Germany and Soviet Russia could collaborate against the allied powers; Haase
sought only the release of the German diplomats. Nor would Haase agree to the
restoration of diplomatic relations. When Chicherin and Radek urged him to
allow the unhindered movement of Soviet troops into the borderlands, Haase
would not commit himself. At this point Radek burst out: "We are not accustomed
to waiting if the situation demands quick and energetic measures. In the event
the German government do not do everything to reach agreement with us

promptly ... we will be forced to do on our own initiative and responsibility whatever the situation demands."[23] And so it was to be. Political collaboration between revolutionary Germany and Soviet Russia was still-born. "As soon as I read the ribbon of my conversation with Haase to [Lenin]," Chicherin subsequently reported, "he said, 'nothing will come of it; this must be stopped.'"[24]

The Germans waited until 21 November before officially rejecting the Bolshevik overtures of the previous week. Prior to the restoration of diplomatic relations they required a clear statement from the Soviet government recognizing "the present German People's Government" and pledging "not to exert any influence on the German people for the formation of another government." They also demanded that all their diplomatic personnel be allowed to return immediately to Germany.[25] This was no problem; the German diplomats were exchanged for Ioffe and his party on 23 November. But the first requirement scandalized Lenin. "Will we recognize the German government?" he exclaimed, " *Will all* the [German] soviets *recognize* them?" He directed Chicherin to draft "a *very* detailed *poisonous* message" saying that if the Germans put forward their demand "*in an ultimative fashion*, then we *will not conduct agitation, nor,* because of this [demand] *rupture* [relations with them]."[26]

On 25 November Chicherin sent Berlin a radio message dripping with sarcasm and contempt. Moscow's repeated call for a "restoration of normal relations between Russia and Germany by themselves," he said, "presupposes recognition of the present German government on the part of the Russian government." "Recognition," he declared, was "a self-evident fact." As for the exertion of influence, if the new German government insisted on renunciation of agitation, then "the Russian government was prepared to accept even this demand." As this met all German requirements for the restoration of diplomatic relations he concluded by asking that Ioffe and his staff be allowed to return to Berlin. The message made no impression on the German government.[27]

The events of November showed that Soviet Russia had no friends within the German government. The Berlin Soviet was another matter, for here the Spartacists exerted considerable influence. Thus, when it was decided to summon an all-German Congress of Soviets to meet on 16 December, and Moscow asked to send a delegation, the Executive Committee of the Berlin Soviet tendered the requested invitation.[28] The Bolsheviks received the invitation on 4 December, and the next day their delegation, led by Ioffe and including Karl Radek, Julian Marchlewski, Christian Rakovskii, and Nikolai Bukharin, left for Berlin. They never reached Germany. On the way they were stopped and told by German authorities that "they would do well to cancel their trip in view of the German situation."[29]

"The German situation" nicely summarized the problem. Internally, the Spartacists were gathering strength, and Germany stood on the brink of civil war. Externally, allied hostility towards any Russian-German tie remained as great as ever. Karl Edler von Stockhammern, a leading official of the Auswärtiges

Amt, wrote in mid-December: "The enemy stands 60 kilometres from the West-falian coal-basin and is waiting only for a pretext to occupy it. If that happens all is lost ... The resumption of our connection with Russia would provide that pretext, for should Ioffe ... return ... Moscow would broadcast to the world: 'See, the Germans are taking up with us again.' Then ... the armistice would not be renewed. We must have peace at any price."[30]

The German government ordered the Bolshevik delegation returned to Russia. Only Radek persevered. With Moscow's permission he made his way in disguise through the German lines and reached Berlin illegally.[31]

RADEK HAD BEEN ABLE to cross the demarcation line because of the great confusion created by the withdrawal of the German army from eastern Europe. Article 12 of the Compiégne armistice had sought to avert this situation, but subsequent events had made it a dead letter. The Polish insurrection of mid-November virtually assured the precipitous withdrawal of the German army from the remainder of eastern Europe, for the collapse of German authority in Poland severed all direct transportation links with Russia and Ukraine. This left the Germans only one rail line running north from Kiev to Brest-Litovsk, Bialostok, and eventually East Prussia. All of Army Group Kiev would have to withdraw along this line, menaced in the west by the renascent Poles and in the east by the Bolsheviks. Accordingly the German War Ministry ordered the army to evacuate the entire area of eastern Europe immediately. From Rostov in Ukraine to Narva on the Gulf of Finland German troops began the long trek home, crossing the border into East Prussia at a rate of more than eight thousand a day.[32]

The Bolsheviks made preparations to occupy the territories which the Germans intended to abandon. There was no question of actually driving the Germans from the region.[33] A more or less peaceful occupation was intended, aided by whatever forces local Bolsheviks could provide. Estonian, Latvian, and Lithu-anian military units assigned to other Soviet fronts were hastily summoned to reinforce Red Army divisions to the Baltic provinces. On a political level, communists from these provinces resident in Russia prepared to form a soviet government for each province and proclaim it an independent republic. At the end of November these new republics came into existence. They had to contend immediately with the emergence of bourgeois nationalist governments in the western borderlands. Such regimes had been ruthlessly repressed (in Latvia and Estonia) or tightly controlled (in Lithuania and Ukraine) as long as the Germans dominated eastern Europe, but they now came self-assertively forward. They feared the Bolsheviks, but their first problem was to get free of the Germans. The latter were not all inclined to be helpful. They hoped eventually to restore their influence in eastern Europe, and the emergence of strong nation states did not figure in their calculations. At the moment they wanted to withdraw as quickly as possible, and this had nothing in common with aiding the nationalist forces. This would only provoke the Bolsheviks who might otherwise let them depart peacefully. The German army, therefore, rejected all nationalist pleas for help against the Bolsheviks.[34] Instead, they established a general government in Lithuania to protect the vital withdrawal corridor from Ukraine and concluded agreements with the Estonian and Latvian governments for the unhindered withdrawal of their troops from the region. They then withdrew, at their own pace, taking whatever they wanted with them.

The Soviet columns moved forward at the end of November. The Red Army had strict orders not to initiate hostilities and they were, for the most part, carried out. "[We] are acting in agreement with the Germans," reported a typical Soviet commander, "and follow after them step by step."[35] Nor were the Germans spoiling for a fight. Their armies were disintegrating, and they were barely able to maintain an orderly retreat to East Prussia. The Red Army moved forward, occupying Narva and Pskov in late November, Polotsk and Borisov in early December, Dvinsk, Minsk and Valk in mid-December, and Riga and Vilna early in the new year. As 1918 gave way to 1919 Soviet republics were functioning in Latvia, Lithuania, and Estonia. Their bourgeois rivals were confined to a steadily diminishing territorial base.[36] It appeared only a short while before revolutionary regimes organized by Moscow would exercise authority over the entire territory of the former Baltic provinces.

By the first days of 1919, however, the Bolshevik advance had reached its farthest limits. Behind the shattered German lines new forces were being organized to stop the Bolshevik offensive. The German government began to organize military units composed entirely of volunteers (Freikorps).[37] Recruiting began in Germany, extended into the Baltic region, and soon encompassed German assistance to the bourgeois Latvian government in the organization of its own volunteer armed force. Such assistance came, however, only after the Red Army had overrun much of Latvia and posed a threat to East Prussia itself. At the same time Finland sent a similar volunteer force to aid the bourgeois government of Estonia. By the end of the year a British naval squadron had also appeared in the eastern Baltic and delivered arms and munitions to the Latvian and Estonian governments. None of these actions was coordinated. The Germans and British were still at war with each other, and all parties involved viewed the others with the greatest suspicion. Nevertheless this combined force was sufficient to bring the advance of the Red Army to a halt. No reinforcement came from the centre to permit the establishment of viable Soviet republics in the western borderlands.

The political situation in Ukraine was chaotic.[38] What had started in 1917 as a rather straightforward struggle between Ukrainian nationalists and Great Russian centralists had blossomed into full-scale class warfare. In 1918 the German army had been drawn into this conflict on the side of the hard-pressed property-owning classes and had become hopelessly sunk in the morass of the Ukrainian civil war. The Germans overthrew the Rada, a regime uniting fierce nationalism with moderate socialism, and established a quasi-monarch, the Hetman Pavel Skoropadkii, in its place. The Ukrainian nationalists, so rudely ejected from Kiev in May, waited in the wings but were divided between fervent socialists such as V.K. Vinnichenko and less enthusiastic social engineers like Simon Petliura, who believed the salvation of Ukraine lay primarily in the organization of a large and well-equipped army. The local Bolsheviks also waited in the wings. They too were divided into two factions: the Kievans, ultra-internationalists barely able to contain their contempt for Ukrainian nationalism, and the Kharkov-Ekaterinsoslav group, ready to recognize the Ukrainian context in which they worked. Both had links with the parent party in Russia. The Kievans were sympathetic with the left-communists while the moderates were closely tied to Lenin. Anarchy gripped Ukraine. In the countryside the peasantry had begun to arm themselves in self-defence. The situation was so complicated that even Lenin was reluctant to plunge into it.

Part of Lenin's hesitation was due to the advice he received from the Revolutionary Military Soviet of the Republic, and I.I. Vatsetis, commander-in-chief of the Red Army. They had identified the Volunteer Army of A.I. Denikin as their most formidable opponent. Its destruction would provide Soviet Russia with the raw materials needed to bring the civil war to a victorious conclusion, and the Red Army high command were determined to resist the squandering of meagre resources on secondary fronts. So long as Germany exercised a protectorate over the hetmanate, those Bolsheviks, Lenin included, who opposed adventures in the south were able to block any rush into Ukraine. With the German revolution events in Ukraine accelerated at a dizzying pace. Already on 14 November, Vinnichenko and his colleagues had proclaimed the Directory, a governmental institution to rival that of the hetman. Petliura began to organize an armed force and within a short time real power began to flow from the Germans and Skoropadskii to the Directory. The Germans proclaimed their neutrality and prepared to leave the country. All this profoundly disturbed Ukrainian communists in exile in Russia, and their clamour for assistance to restore them to power grew louder by the day. Moscow responded by stepping up support for the communist bands active in eastern Ukraine, but the Kievans now demanded a provisional government and the opening of a Ukrainian front south of Kursk. Lenin did not want the former, and Vatsetis would not hear of the latter. The commander-in-chief would only agree, on 17 November, to the creation of an "army group of the Kursk line of advance" commanded by V.A. Antonov-Ovseenko, an old Bolshevik long familiar with Ukraine. The title of his command was ambiguous. As the name implied, it was to be a military force based on the city of Kursk, a short distance from the demarcation line. Seemingly the "line of advance" from Kursk would lead into Ukraine along the axis Belgorod-Kharkov-Ekaterinoslav. This is certainly what Ukrainian communists assumed. Vatsetis had other ideas. His first orders directed the new force to concentrate along the demarcation line but not to enter Ukraine. Its best units were to assist the adjacent Eighth Army of the southern front by striking in the direction of Millerovo, more than three hundred kilometres east of Kharkov.[39]

Antonov-Ovseenko received this order with shock and dismay. On 22 November he appealed directly to Lenin: "Help me, Vladimir Il'ich, they are calling us from the Ukraine. The workers everywhere salute the Bolsheviks and curse those who represent the Rada ... Under such conditions, I have decided to advance. It is now possible for the bold to take with bare hands that which we shall later have to go at head down."[40] The last sentence points to the crux of the argument between Antonov-Ovseenko and Vatsetis. The commander-in-chief was a professional soldier who thought in terms of classic military concepts; he viewed the Ukrainian problem as one of military conquest. Antonov-Ovseenko, despite his association with the military since the beginning of the revolution, remained a politician, keenly attuned to the demands of the moment. He was ready to plunge into Ukraine to "make" the revolution there in the same way it had been "made" elsewhere. Taking advantage of popular hatred of the status quo and a demoralized enemy, he was prepared to use whatever force he had at his disposal to impose the revolution on Ukraine. He knew that the "status quo" and the "enemy" were not fixed quantities. At the moment they were the Germans and the hetmanate, but once the former were gone the latter would fall. Who would rule after the Germans left depended on who moved fastest to pick up the pieces.

Lenin understood this doctrine; he had been its greatest teacher in the previous eighteen months. Here, however, his judgment differed from Antonov-Ovseenko's: he did not expect a rapid collapse of the Germans. Thus, while he and Vatsetis agreed to send small reinforcements,[41] they continued to rule out any far-reaching operation in Ukraine. Despite this warning, Antonov had sufficient troops to launch an attack, and on 23 November he advanced towards Kharkov. Permission to issue a manifesto announcing the existence of the "provisional Workers-Peasant Government of the Ukraine" was given by Moscow on 27 November.[42] As soon as a small corner of Ukraine had been occupied, the provisional government moved there and sent representatives to negotiate with the German army in Kharkov. Although Antonov commanded fewer than ten thousand men, the Germans, who did not want to fight their way out of eastern Ukraine, decided to come to terms with him. They agreed that in exchange for the right of unhindered departure no attempt would be made to prevent the movement of "revolutionary troops" into Ukraine. These troops were free to occupy any region not held by the Germans. The Germans said they hoped to be out of Ukraine by the end of the year. This agreement was ratified by the Central Committee of the Russian Communist Party with the admonition that the provisional government should keep in mind that it was "directly linked to the Central Committee of the Russian Communist Party, receiving directives from it."[43]

The quickening pace of German evacuation soon forced the Bolsheviks to accelerate the movement of their forces into Ukraine. Thus, on 11 December the Germans reached agreement with Petliura not to interfere in the Directory's assumption of power west of the Dnieper.[44] As a result they removed their protection from Skoropadskii, and on 14 December the hetmanate fell. The Bolsheviks had to act with equal resolution to validate their claim to eastern Ukraine. On 20 December nearly ten thousand Soviet troops advanced on Kharkov. A week later a popular insurrection placed Ekaterinoslav in Soviet hands, and, on 3 January 1919, Kharkov itself fell. Antonov-Orseenko's force, local Bolshevik bands, and a peasant force led by the anarchist Nestor Makhno had crushed the authority of the Directory in eastern Ukraine.[45] Understandably, the Directory were outraged and sent an angry protest to Moscow. Chicherin replied: "There is no army of the Russian Soviet Republic on Ukrainian territory. The military operations taking place on Ukrainian territory involve the army of the Directory and the army of Piatakov. Between the Ukraine and Soviet Russia there are at present no armed conflicts."[46] This was what a later generation would recognize as "socialist realism." A distracted audience of a less sophisticated age judged it more harshly. From the first days of its existence the Directory were at war with Soviet Russia.

Almost at once the Ukrainian campaign began to drain much needed resources from the southern front and still the supply of men and material was not enough to meet the needs of Antonov-Ovseenko. From the start he had to ally himself with the anarchist leaders of peasant bands which had sprung up spontaneously in Ukraine. These alliances were inherently unstable as they were based on nothing more than a mutual hatred of the status quo; the Bolsheviks and anarchists were fighting for radically different goals. Vatsetis saw all these problems before they developed and continued to oppose the campaign. Early in the new year he reprimanded Antonov-Ovseenko for describing his command as a "Ukrainian Army." Such a force did not exist. "Strategic tasks in the Ukraine," he said, "are so enormous that several armies are needed for their solution, and to these demands only the strength of the armies of the RSFSR will be equal." For the moment these armies were needed elsewhere, but when Denikin was defeated, "then all necessary Red Army forces will take part in the solution of the Ukrainian problem."[47]

The indispensable condition of the Bolshevik return to the western borderlands was the withdrawal of the German army. By the end of 1918 this withdrawal was nearly completed. The successful return of the army from the east marked the end of the paralysis and powerlessness suffered by the German authorities from the beginning of the revolution. Those opposed to revolutionary forces at home and abroad were now able to think in terms of resistance. Army, officials, and Social Democrats were all eager to regain control of Berlin and halt the withdrawal from the east short of the 1914 frontiers of Germany. Both civil and military authorities wished to hold Bolshevism as far from Germany as possible. This meant support for the bourgeois governments of Latvia and Lithuania and, with the arrival of the Freikorps, a continuing armed presence in the Baltic.

A NEW FEATURE WAS added to this configuration when in late December the Polish government, despite breaking off relations with Germany in mid-month, asked Berlin for help in fighting the Bolsheviks. Some German leaders were ready to agree; they preferred to have Poland fighting the Bolsheviks than the Reich. This was the view of the Social Democrats but not the Independents. Hugo Haase had not wanted to aid the Bolsheviks, but neither was he ready to take up arms against them. Any weapons delivered to the Poles, he said, would one day be used against Germany. "We are not obligated by the armistice agreement to enter into a struggle with the Bolsheviks," he argued. "The treaty of Brest-Litovsk is invalid, therefore, the Russians have the right to occupy their territories again."[48]

No aid was given Poland at this time, but events within Germany soon removed the barrier to a more hostile policy towards Soviet Russia. Relations between the majority and the Independent Social Democrats grew steadily worse, and on 29 December the Independents resigned from the cabinet. Ebert reformed his government to include only majority Social Democrats and a new foreign secretary, Count Ulrich von Brockdorff-Rantzau. Despite his earlier (and subsequent) ties with Russian revolutionaries, Rantzau was inclined to woo the Americans and repel the Bolsheviks.[49]

Karl Radek contributed to this rapid deterioration of relations with Moscow. After reaching Berlin in mid-December he had played an active role in the formation of the Communist Party of Germany.[50] Almost immediately the new party found itself in confrontation with the forces of German conservatism, who gladly accepted the communist challenge. This was a very dangerous development for Soviet Russia and all the Bolshevik leaders recognized this threat. "The greatest danger which can threaten the Russian revolution," Radek told the founding congress of the German Communist Party, "is that international capitalism can bring this war to an end by way of a compromise peace." If the rival imperialists could do that, they would then join to destroy the revolution in Russia. Radek believed the way to avoid this danger was to deepen the revolution in Germany, and this had been his aim since arriving in Germany.[51] This too was the policy of the Soviet government. It failed because the German revolution moved according to its own dynamic, and the Bolsheviks had few means to make much impact on events in Germany. The impact which they did make was mainly negative – anger, outrage, and fear engendered by Bolshevik interference in German affairs. With the formation of a purely majority socialist government the way was open for that anger, and the traditional German fear of Russia, to find expression in policies overtly hostile to the Bolsheviks.

CHAPTER THREE

Audiatur et altera pars:
The Soviets propose peace

The Soviet government had been seeking to engage the allied powers in negotiations since the previous November. The Bolsheviks had originally wanted to
draw the allies into negotiations for a general peace and, when this failed, to
use them as a counter-weight to their increasingly one-sided relationship with
Germany. Both ambitions were heavily laden with dire consequences for the
war aims and internal stability of the western states, and precisely for this reason
allied leaders refused to talk with the Bolsheviks. Allied policy was to wage war
against Germany and promote their own interests in Russia. Western leaders
saw the Soviet government as an obstacle to both. By the end of the war the
Bolsheviks were viewed as a greater danger than their German associates. The
allies wanted to exchange bombs and bullets, not words, with the Bolsheviks.
   Moscow still persisted. Even when the western powers opened armed hostilities, the Soviet government still clamoured for negotiation. Bruce Lockhart and
General Jean Lavergne, official allied agents left behind in Russia when the
regular diplomats withdrew, both returned to western Europe bearing Bolshevik
peace proposals.[1] Shortly afterwards the Soviet government released Paul Dufour, another French agent in their custody, bearing an even more detailed offer.
Chicherin had given Dufour documents declaring the Soviet government ready
to undertake the payment of prewar Russian debts. All foreign property nationalized the previous year would be retained by the Soviet state, but its former
owners would be reimbursed for their losses. The Russian state gold reserve in
its entirety would be delivered to the allies as a pledge that these debts would
be paid. Raw materials promised to Germany would be delivered to the allies
instead, and allied citizens would be granted concessions to operate profitable
enterprises inside Russia.[2] The proposal indicates the nature of the offer being
made to the allies. Earlier in the year Germany had been bought off by Moscow
agreeing to extortionate economic demands; the Bolsheviks clearly believed that
the allies could be enticed in the same way.[3]

The Soviet government received no reply to these overtures. On 11 October, therefore, Chicherin instructed his foreign representatives to try to enter into direct contact with allied agents.[4] A week later V.V. Vorovskii, Soviet representative in Sweden, acting through Ludwig Meyer, a Norwegian jurist sympathetic to the Bolsheviks, contacted Sir Mansfeldt Findlay, the British minister in Norway. Meyer said Vorovskii was ready to open negotiations with the British government and urged Findlay to accept the proposal as he believed it possible to arrive at an arrangement with the Bolshevik government "through which Russia might enter into a more peaceful phase of development." Findlay would not meet Vorovskii without the permission of London, and the Foreign Office rejected the proposal. "I cannot believe," wrote Sir Ronald Graham, "that any arrangement is possible with the Bolsheviks, now or in the future ... They are fanatics who are not bound by any ordinary codes."[5]

By early November the time for such an indirect approach was over. The magnitude of allied victory grew with every passing day, and the Soviet government had to accelerate their peace offensive. On 3 November Chicherin addressed a note to the Norwegian and Swedish ministers in Petrograd asking them to transmit peace proposals to the western states. In confidence, he asked the Norwegian minister to inform the western capitals that the Soviet government were "prepared to go very far with regard to concessions to the entente powers with a view of arriving at an understanding."[6] This proposal received a very cold reception in the West. At the lowest level of the Foreign Office, E. H. Carr was bold enough to suggest that "an understanding with the Bolsheviks could ... be reached on the basis of the present positions," but further up the official ladder there was no sympathy for any agreement with Soviet Russia.[7] Nor were the Italians, Americans, or French interested. The allied and associated powers quickly agreed that it was "premature to enter into any relationship with the Bolshevik Government in Russia, or, for the present to send any reply to the advances which they have made through the Norwegian Government."[8] The war against Russia would continue.

The Bolsheviks viewed the rejection of their peace proposals from a marxist perspective. The Great War, they believed, had arisen from the contradiction within capitalism between the world character of production and the national character of appropriation. That which was produced globally was consumed nationally and in no way proportionally to the actual contribution to production. The metropolitan homelands of the great empires consumed much more than their share and, because of the insistent demands of competition, investment, and armed protection, cried out for an ever greater percentage of world production. The bourgeoisie of each state had sought to enlarge its share of consumption at the expense of all other states and, finding this impossible, had turned to arms in an effort to take by force that which could not be obtained peacefully. Soviet publications frequently described the war as having been fought by two old pirates – Germany and Britain – who could not agree on how to divide the loot they had stolen from the rest of the world. They had fought each other to exhaustion. The intervention of the "son of the British pirate" – the United States – had been necessary to end the war. But even with this victory the fundamental contradiction remained, and a new struggle was sure to emerge. The victors would argue over the spoils and eventually resort to force to settle their quarrel. Russia was part of the spoils. First Germany and the western allies had fought over her; now the victorious allies would do the same. The ferocity of imperialist rivalry gave the Bolsheviks substantial reason to hope for survival.[9]

Marxist theory taught the Bolsheviks that rival ambitions and insatiable greed should prevent the allies from acting together. Yet in November several signs pointed in the opposite direction. One was the way in which Germany had broken all ties with Soviet Russia and was sincerely seeking peace with the western powers. Another was the seeming emergence of Woodrow Wilson and the United States as *primus inter pares* in the allied coalition. American power had grown enormously during 1918, and by November Wilson's influence had reached new heights within both allied and enemy states. Moreover, he was placing ever greater stress on the idea of a League of Nations which would regulate international relations in the postwar world. To Moscow this looked suspiciously like a modern-day "holy alliance," a league of imperialist states to crush Soviet Russia. The rapid acceptance of the League in Germany, especially among German Social Democrats, created further concern. If Wilson could create a League uniting victor and vanquished, Soviet security would be seriously compromised.[10]

This was a frightening possibility, but not one which paralysed the Bolsheviks. "An impossible task stands before Anglo-American imperialism," wrote Nikolai I. Bukharin, "on the one hand, the necessity of pacifying all of western and eastern Europe as well as being prepared to pacify Asia (India and the colonies); and, on the other – the impossibility of using the mass army raised to fight on the western front to accomplish this end." War weariness, especially if not relieved by immediate demobilization, might well promote the growth of revolutionary situations such as had emerged so suddenly in Germany. Bolshevik leaders believed the West was ripe for revolution and watched eagerly for its appearance. "We have now entered an epoch," Trotsky declared, "in which, revolution, the daughter of war, truly walks ... in iron sandals." Bukharin, at that time a leading member of the Central Committee, was of the same opinion. The western powers, he wrote, "are in no position to conduct a war in the previous sense of the word, a Great War. And a little war against a great revolution can not end in victory."[11] This suggested that the Red Army, growing with every day, would be able to mount a successful defence of Soviet Russia. Trotsky declared, "The army exists, is fighting and has become an international factor which our enemies must already take into consideration."[12]

The Red Army, however, was not to have everything its way. Victorious in the borderlands, it proved less successful elsewhere. Operations in the last months of 1918 against the army of the Cossack leader, Ataman Krasnov, on the southern front proved singularly unsuccessful. Trotsky blamed this failure on the incompetence of the command structure. He set about rebuilding the front, but that would take time, and the hope of eliminating Krasnov, and behind him Denikin, before the arrival of the allied forces, had to be abandoned.[13] The eastern front also failed. Due to its comparative stability and low priority, Vatsetis had begun to withdraw divisions from Siberia to reinforce the southern front. As a result, when Kolchak launched an offensive in Siberia in late November the Soviet Third Army collapsed. Its thirty-five thousand men had been in the field for nearly six months and were ready to drop from exhaustion. Within a month the Third Army retired more than three hundred kilometres, losing eighteen thousand men and surrendering Perm on 25 December 1918. Four thousand railway cars and the bridge over the River Kama were lost. This opened the road to Viatka, and the British at Archangel, to the victorious White army.[14]

In the southwest a potentially greater problem was shaping up for the Bolsheviks. In December French warships landed marines to hold the docks at Odessa until the arrival of a larger force. Shortly thereafter several thousand troops loyal to the Directory occupied the city. Local Bolsheviks were also active, but neither they nor Petliura's troops challenged the French marines. French commanders knew virtually nothing about Ukraine. General Borius, commander of the 156th division, was told not to anticipate any opposition; he would be greeted "with open arms, fêted and cheered." It was a risky venture, but initially the French were successful. They disembarked peacefully, drove the Petliurists from the city and by 29 December controlled Odessa. Other French troops occupied cities along the Black Sea coast and in the Crimea.[15]

IN THESE CIRCUMSTANCES it was clearly time for the Bolsheviks to resume the effort to open negotiations with the allies. On 2 December Chicherin addressed another radio message to the western powers informing them that the Soviet government was aware of their preparations to expand intervention in Russia and asking instead for a cessation of hostilities. At the same time, his deputy, Maxim Litvinov, was sent back to Scandinavia. He arrived in early December and, through the agency of friendly journalists, tried to place Soviet peace proposals in the hands of the allied ministers in Stockholm, who immediately rejected them.[16] The large allied intelligence community in Stockholm, however, took an immediate interest in Litvinov and his mission. Neither the British nor French secret services had any difficulty penetrating his mission and, in the face of the refusal of allied diplomats even to speak to him, it is not inconceivable that Litvinov may have facilitated their task as a means of bringing Soviet views to the attention of allied leaders. At any rate, on 9 December, only two days after the diplomats had refused to speak with him, the allied secret services began to forward accounts of his mission to London and Paris.[17]

After two weeks passed without any response to this new initiative, Litvinov addressed letters to each minister saying he had "been authorized by the Soviet government to enter into preliminary peace negotiations with representatives of the Allied countries."[18] The next day he directed a longer message to President Wilson who had just arrived in Europe. Wilson's prestige had risen to even new heights since the armistice, and he appeared certain to dominate the peace negotiations. Appealing directly to Wilson's liberalism, idealism, and pacifism – values it should be noted which the Bolsheviks themselves rejected as fraudulent – Litvinov submitted there were only two courses open to western leaders. One was "continued open or disguised intervention," while the other was

impartially to weigh and investigate the one-sided accusations against Soviet Russia, to come to an understanding with the Soviet Government, to withdraw the foreign troops from Russian territory, and to raise the economic blockade – soothing thereby the excited passions of masses – to help Russia to regain her own sources of supply, and to give her technical advice how to exploit her natural richness in the most effective way, for the benefit of all countries badly in need of foodstuffs and raw materials.

The Soviet government, he concluded, asked for an opportunity to place its case before the western powers. "I venture to appeal to your sense of justice and impartiality. I hope and trust, above all, that before deciding on any course of action you will give justice to the demand: *audiatur et altera pars* [let the other side also be heard]".[19]

The message was well timed. Wilson was scheduled to visit London at the end of December to confer with the British prime minister, Lloyd George, and Russia had to appear on their agenda. The Bolsheviks calculated that the two would have to take some notice of the constantly reiterated Soviet peace proposals. This, in fact, happened, and in preparation for this meeting the British government prepared its own position. On 23 December Lord Milner, the secretary of state for war, informed the imperial war cabinet that Litvinov "had for some days past been trying hard to offer us terms on behalf of the Bolsheviks." This sparked a wide-ranging discussion of the Russian question during which Winston Churchill, soon to replace Milner as war secretary, defined the alternatives facing the British. He declared "that we must make up our minds either to allow the Russians to murder one another without let or hindrance, or, in the name of order, to interfere and do it thoroughly." Churchill favoured the latter policy, but few of his colleagues agreed. Lloyd George, in particular, opposed it and came to the meeting armed with a sheaf of telegrams testifying to the Bolshevik readiness to negotiate. Lord Balfour, the foreign secretary, at first objected, reminding the meeting of the moral obligation Britain had assumed by encouraging the Whites to fight the Bolsheviks. Moreover, the allies had become protectors of the many small nationalities seeking to break away from Russia. Lloyd George brushed these objections aside. "Had we any right to support a minority against a majority because we happened to have political relations with the former?" The meeting decided to authorize the British minister in Stockholm to obtain, in writing, Litvinov's proposals for an understanding with the British government. Three days later, in a conversation with Lloyd George, President Wilson readily agreed with this position. [20]

Despite these decisions, the British minister did not meet with Litvinov. Balfour remained opposed and displayed no urgency in acting on the war cabinet decision. On 30 December he chose to ask Britain's allies if they approved a meeting with Litvinov. [21] In effect this meant asking the French, and as Balfour knew, Paris was adamantly opposed to consulting the Bolsheviks about anything. Stéphan Pichon, the French foreign minister, instructed his ambassador in London to see Balfour at once "to turn aside [this] unexpected proposal." [22] The Italians responded similarly, and the British found it expedient not to proceed with their plan to receive peace proposals from Litvinov.

This incident is instructive, for it points the way enemies of peace would block the opening of negotiations for nearly a year. Here it was the imperial war cabinet, subsequently it would be the much smaller British war cabinet and later still the normal British cabinet reconstituted after the conclusion of peace. In this instance advocates of continued intervention solicited the aid of the French government, a group of men known to be profoundly hostile to the very idea of peace with the Bolsheviks. Repeatedly the enemies of peace would look to France for assistance and never be disappointed. [23] But they would turn elsewhere as well, to Conservative backbenchers known as "diehards," as unflinching as the French in their hatred of Bolshevism; to the great British newspapers increasingly hostile to Lloyd George; and later to Washington, when Wilson's idealism had cooled somewhat. While waiting for assistance they would stall for time. In this they were well placed, for in the new government formed by Lloyd George in the aftermath of his great electoral victory, Lord Balfour remained at the Foreign Office with Lord Curzon as his deputy. Churchill became secretary of state for war. All three, for different reasons, opposed peace with the Bolsheviks and were supported in this by the senior staff of their departments. They were thus able to construct a formidable barrier to peace with Soviet Russia, and even Lloyd George, possessing all the powers of prime minister, found it impossible to remove it.

Lloyd George did not fail for want of trying. Fully aware of the necessity of securing peace in Russia, he seized on an idea discussed in the imperial war cabinet on 30 December. There Sir Robert Borden, the Canadian prime minister, had suggested that it might be possible to induce the various governments which had sprung up on the territory of the former Russian empire to send representatives to western Europe to confer with the allies and negotiate a peaceful settlement of their civil war. [24] This was the origin of what came to be called the "Prinkipo policy." [25] On 2 January 1919 telegrams went out from London to allied capitals suggesting that messages be sent to all de facto Russian regimes, including the Soviet government at Moscow, declaring that one of the first tasks of the peace conference about to assemble at Paris would be "an endeavour to bring about peace in Russia," and that if the governments contending there "should desire to send representatives to Paris to discuss with the Great Powers conditions of a permanent settlement, the Great Powers would be prepared to enter on such a discussion with them."[26]

This initiative elicited an even more hostile response than the suggested meeting with Litvinov. The French predictably led the way, declaring that the British proposal merely played into the hands of the Bolsheviks. In his response of 6 January 1919, Pichon described the Soviet government as a "criminal regime" based "solely on anarchic oppression." The French government, Pichon concluded grandly, "will enter into no agreement with crime."[27] This struck a resonant chord at the Foreign Office. "There is much to be said for the French attitude," minuted Sir Ronald Graham. "The French Government were certain to take this line and the US Government and Italian Government will probably follow suit," wrote another unsympathetic official. And so it was. The Italians and the American State Department, unaware of Wilson's position on this question, registered their disapproval. Lord Curzon placed the final minute on the Foreign Office docket. "The suggestion was, I fear, doomed to failure."[28]

Indeed it was, but not yet, for Lloyd George was not acting alone. He was acting in concert with Wilson, who now became fully involved in the negotiations question. In fact, he had decided to send his own representative to meet with Litvinov. W.H. Buckler, a secretary of the American embassy in London, was ordered to proceed to meet with Litvinov in Stockholm and determine the basis on which the Soviet authorities would make peace.[29]

But before Buckler could meet Litvinov, the façade of allied unity collapsed. On 11 January, one day before the peace conference was to open, L'Humanité, the organ of the French Socialist party, published virtually verbatim the French rejection of the proposal to negotiate with the Bolsheviks. The note made very interesting reading for the Bolsheviks. Litvinov immediately informed Moscow of its contents,[30] and Chicherin replied that the British proposal bore witness "to the existence of reasonable elements" among western leaders. To overcome French resistance Chicherin authorized Litvinov "to declare that [Soviet Russia is] prepared to open negotiations regarding [Russian state debts] and together with France find the means of reaching an agreement. For Russia the principle of annulment does not bear a general character."[31] The French would not talk. Neither this proposal nor one to send a "Red Cross" mission to France to negotiate an exchange of prisoners[32] could pry their jaws open. Litvinov, therefore had to content himself with cultivating his British contacts in Scandinavia. All the same, he told Chicherin that he did not think that "the moment of peaceful accord had yet been reached and that the allies will make one more attempt to reduce us to complete capitulation."[33]

To avert such an attempt the Bolsheviks turned again to Ludwig Meyer. At Litvinov's request Meyer wrote to Sir Mansfeldt Findlay enclosing a letter from the Soviet representative. Here he outlined Soviet peace terms. These included an amnesty for most opponents of the Soviet government, exclusion from "active citizenship" of only "an insignificantly small and ever diminishing part of the population," self-determination for the national minorities of the former Russian empire, and a willingness to "reconsider some [Soviet] decrees affecting the financial obligations of Russia towards other countries." Russia would desist from carrying on propaganda in allied countries. In return, Moscow asked that the allies "discontinue all direct or indirect military operations against Soviet Russia, all direct or indirect material assistance to Russian or other forces operating against the Soviet Government, and also every kind of economic warfare and boycott." Meyer volunteered to act as an intermediary through which the British and Soviet governments could communicate and asked to visit London. The Foreign Office refused. By then the allied powers had asked the Bolsheviks to attend a conference on the Prinkipo islands, and the Foreign Office hid behind this invitation. The Norwegian foreign minister was told that the "allied governments, having invited [the] Bolsheviks to attend the Prinkipo conference, see no reason for engaging in any other *pourparlers* with them." [34]

Meyer's services were not necessary. Four days after Litvinov wrote the Norwegian jurist, Buckler arrived in Stockholm and met with Litvinov. Buckler explained that he was "merely a private telephone" through which the Soviet representative could supplement his telegram of December 24. Litvinov was delighted to put the Bolshevik case before Buckler. "The Soviet Government," he began, detested "the military preparations and costly campaigns" which had been forced on Russia. "The only real question," he said, was "whether the Allies and the United States would allow the Soviet Government to exist. If they would, an agreement would not be difficult to reach." Was "the total destruction of the Bolshevik party an aim of the Allies and of the United States?" he asked. "If so, the present struggle must continue." If, however, the western powers wanted peace they could have it, "for the Soviet Government is prepared to make concessions on every point." This included payment of the Russian debt, protection for existing foreign enterprises, the granting of new concessions, supply of needed raw materials, and the purchase of western machinery and manufactured goods.

Litvinov denied that Soviet Russia had any "imperialist designs" on small states which had seceded from Russia. "So long, however, as foreign powers support the capitalist classes in those countries," he hastened to add, the Russians felt "just in supporting the laboring classes there." Nor would the Soviet government recognize "the purely autocratic and self-appointed regime of Koltchak" or any of the other governments functioning under allied protection in various parts of Russia. The Soviet government was prepared to extend an amnesty to most of those who had opposed them, while the small number of leaders "might be permitted to leave Russia for foreign countries." The issue of propaganda, he said, could also be settled easily. "The war declared by the allies has called forth this revolutionary propaganda as a measure of retaliation, just as it has produced violence and terror in other forms; but these will all cease as soon as the war stops."

The statement of Soviet peace terms represented the carrot Litvinov dangled in front of the allies. He also had a stick. Litvinov himself did not brandish it; he left this to Arthur Ransome, correspondent of the *Daily News* and a good friend of the Soviet government. Ransome, who was present at the last meeting with Litvinov, subsequently told Buckler that even if the allies succeeded in breaking Soviet power, their intervention in Russia would be unable to end there; instead it "would have to be continued on a still bigger scale." There was no political alternative to the Bolsheviks, and if they were crushed the allies "would be faced with a Russia seething with anarchy and requiring to be policed." This would place an enormous strain on the western countries and produce in Russia the very conditions that favoured the growth of Bolshevism. Many Bolsheviks, Ransome told Buckler, opposed compromise with the allies for this very reason, and continued intervention would play into their hands. On the other hand, Lenin and Chicherin were "more statesmanlike and intelligent" and preferred to reach their goals more slowly. Provided the Soviet form of government could be retained, they favoured an understanding with the allies. Litvinov could not come out and say it, Ransome told Buckler, but he believed the Soviets would agree to compromise virtually any question of territory, and with regard to Siberia "that the Ural frontier would probably satisfy them."[35]

Buckler summarized the results of his meetings with Litvinov in a long telegram sent on 18 January 1919. It reached Paris the following afternoon and was followed by a second telegram arriving on the morning of 20 January. Here he submitted his own recommendations on the question of peace with the Bolsheviks. These were based in part on the assumption, shared by the ambassador and military attaché in Stockholm, that "military intervention and occupation of Russia even if ultimately successful," could "only succeed at an indefinite date in the future." In the meanwhile the war against the Bolsheviks would promote their doctrine everywhere. "Agreement with Russia can take place at once," he concluded, and "if we do not greatly curtail Russian territory, we can make a fair bargain regarding foreign debt and foreign interests. If Russia loses Siberia and coal and oil fields, the terms granted as to debt will be proportionately less good."[36] Thus the full Soviet brief was available in Paris as the peace conference took up the fate of Russia in the postwar world.

WESTERN LEADERS HAD been discussing Russia since the armistice, entirely without result.[37] When the leaders, meeting as the Council of Ten, turned to the Russian question on 12 January 1919, all they could agree upon was that, for the moment at least, Russia should not be represented at the peace conference. The French and Italians wanted to listen to the views of the various anti-Bolshevik governments, but Lloyd George objected. To listen to them and not the Bolsheviks "would give the public the impression that we considered they represented Russia."[38]

Four days later Russia was again on the agenda. Lloyd George said there were three policies from which to choose. One was to seek to destroy Bolshevism. But "was anyone prepared to carry it out? ... Was anyone of the Western Allies prepared to send a million men into Russia?" A second policy was to erect a cordon sanitaire and try to starve the Bolsheviks into submission. A blockade, however, "would lead to the killing, not of the ruffians enlisted by the Bolsheviks, but of the ordinary population." Finally there was a proposal that the allied powers should meet with representatives of all governments in Russia, including the Bolsheviks. This suggestion, he said, had been misunderstood. There was no intention of recognizing the Bolsheviks "to the extent of offering them a seat at the Peace Conference." He only proposed that the warring factions conclude a truce and send representatives to Paris where the allies could aid them in "the accommodation of their differences." Wilson strongly supported Lloyd George. None of this sat well with the French and Italians. They asked that Joseph Noulens and Harald de Scavenius, only recently returned from Russia, be heard before the council reached a decision.[39]

Noulens had been French ambassador and Scavenius the Danish minister in Russia when the Bolsheviks had seized power. Both advocated prompt military intervention to destroy the Soviet government. They expressed precisely the views which the Whites would have put forward had they been allowed to address the council; their appearance, therefore, was Clemenceau's way of getting around the Anglo-American refusal to hear the Whites without the Bolsheviks. Neither man, however, made much impression on Wilson or Lloyd George. They were too shrill, denouncing the Bolsheviks in terms of criminality and depravity. Worse still, they gave their testimony on the very days on which Buckler's telegrams reached Paris, and Wilson did not hesitate to counter their views by reading the messages from Stockholm. The telegrams fell with special effect, for in his appearance before the council Noulens had declared flatly that "the Bolshevik Government was definitely imperialist. It meant to conquer the world, and to make peace with no Governments save Governments representing only the labouring classes."[40] Clearly the Bolsheviks were of a different stamp than that described by the former envoys.

Wilson now suggested a modification of the earlier British proposal. Rather than summoning Russian representatives to Paris, he proposed that they be called "to some other place, such as Salonica, convenient of approach, there to meet such representatives as might be appointed by the Allies, in order to see whether they could draw up a programme upon which agreement could be reached." Lloyd George agreed, as he knew that Clemenceau would not consent to Bolshevik representatives coming to Paris. Baron Sonnino, the Italian foreign minister, objected, however, to even holding such a conference. "All the Russian parties had some representatives [in Paris]," he said, "except the Soviets, whom they did not wish to hear." Lloyd George responded "that the Bolsheviks were the very people some of them wished to hear" as they were "the people who at the present moment were actually controlling European Russia." Buckler's report "showed that the Bolsheviks were not convinced of the error of their ways, but they apparently realized the folly of their present methods. Therefore they were endeavoring to come to terms."[41]

This was an argument which would be made time and again during the next two years by those who favoured an end to the war in Russia. It usually made no impact on those who wished to crush Bolshevism by force, but in this instance Clemenceau seized on it as a graceful way of yielding to Anglo-American insistence that the Bolsheviks be heard. The French premier agreed that Wilson should draft "a proclamation, for consideration at the next meeting, inviting all organized parties in Russia to attend a meeting to be held at some selected place, such as Salonica or Lemnos, in order to discuss with the representatives of the Allied and Associated Great Powers the means of restoring order and peace in Russia." At the last moment Lord Balfour indicated that in his view Bolshevik "abstention from hostile action against their neighbours should be made a condition of their sending representatives to this meeting." The council concurred.[42]

The next day Wilson presented the council with his draft proclamation. Unfortunately the minutes of this meeting are opaque, simply recording that the president's draft "was carefully considered, amended in one or two particulars, and accepted by all." Such economy of expression frequently conceals serious disagreement, and it would be surprising if such is not the case here. Clemenceau in particular, must have been most unpleasant and was probably responsible for whatever amendment which took place. The document which resulted was an unhappy amalgam of Wilsonian idealism and Machiavellian chicanery. Given the presence of allied troops in Russia and their support for the Whites, even the idealism sounded badly and could not help but appear as hypocrisy. Thus Wilson proclaimed that the single object the associated powers "had in mind in their discussions of the course they should pursue with regard to Russia has been to help the Russian people, not to hinder them, or to interfere, in any manner with their right to settle their own affairs in their own way." Nor would anyone familiar with the Russian scene find it easy to accept Wilson's assertion that the associated powers did not "wish or propose to favor or assist any one of the organized groups now contending for the leadership and guidance of Russia as against the other. Their sole and sincere purpose is to do what they can to bring peace and an opportunity to find her way out of her present troubles." To this end Wilson then tendered an invitation to these organized groups to send representatives "to the Prince's Islands, Sea of Marmora, where they will be met by representatives of the associated powers."

Here the chicanery began, for it is worth noting that the invitation was not tendered to specific governments or, indeed, governments at all, but to unspecified organized groups, civil and military, spread across two continents. Had such a meeting actually taken place with all eligible groups in attendance, a conference larger than that then meeting in Paris would have convened. But this was only a start, for the declaration then made the convening of the conference dependent on the provision that "in the meantime there is a truce of arms amongst the parties invited ... and aggressive military actions cease." Here was Balfour's concern of the previous day and Clemenceau's sly maliciousness writ large. Given the number of contestants and the fluid nature of warfare in the Russian conflict, such a prescription, even with the best of will, was impossible of fulfilment. So broad was this injunction that it could provide unlimited cover for the bad faith of any or all of the inviting powers. To give a final touch of unreality to the document, Wilson specified that, the allied conditions first having been met, the conference would begin on 15 February 1919, barely three weeks from the date of invitation.[43] The following day Sir Ronald Graham attached the startled reaction of an unprepared Foreign Office to this latest document from the peace conference: "I must say, with all respect, that his seems a remarkable proposal."[44]

CHAPTER FOUR

"Concessions to imperialism":
Soviet Russia and the Bullitt Mission

While the peace conference met in Paris the civil war continued in Russia. Despite checks in the south and actual reverses in the east, Soviet leaders could take considerable satisfaction with the progress of this war. In his new year's report to Lenin in January 1919 I.I. Vatsetis, the supreme commander of the Red Army, was able to declare proudly:

During the past months the territory of our Republic has almost doubled: from the cramped central regions, the narrow confines of Grand-Duchy Moscow our Republic, at the present time, has every right to claim the name Russian Federation. In the East, the Caucasus, the West and Baltic we have attained unforeseen results, and, in the Baltic, our success has brought us to the natural borders of the Baltic Sea. The same may, in a short period of time, be expected in the West when we reach the borders of Poland. [1]

At about the same time Trotsky underlined the significance of this success. Since August 1918 the Red Army had liberated no less than 130 districts in twenty-eight provinces of the old empire. This amounted to more than 1,300,000 square kilometres inhabited by nearly forty million people. [2] This gave the Soviet government access to important raw materials and sufficient grain to feed the starving cities of central Russia. Vatsetis nevertheless warned that this success had "been attained exclusively by arms. In no instance have negotiations or agreements succeeded in the enlargement of our territory, and, therefore, we must expect to have to hold by force of arms that territory which we have occupied." [3]

The Soviet government was determined to do just that. Nevertheless, it did not pursue a policy of simple military resistance and was quite prepared to make far-reaching concessions to its enemies in order to secure an end to the civil war. Having secured a solid territorial base with ample economic resources, the Bolsheviks were prepared to allow the remainder of the former Russian empire to remain for the moment beyond their grasp. They were convinced that in time these territories would revert to the central Russian core.

The Bolsheviks were also prepared to make economic concessions to the West. These included payment of old debts and reimbursement for properties nationalized during the revolution and also permission to originate and profit from new enterprises developed in Soviet Russia. Since late 1918 they had been attempting to negotiate a pilot project of such an economic concession with Norwegian entrepreneurs. The venture would have seen the construction of a new railway from the river Ob through Kotlas to a junction with the Baltic railway system at Petrograd. The Norwegian Company was to build and operate the line, which would revert to the Soviet state after forty-eight years. Lenin strongly supported the proposal. "It is better," he told the Petrograd Soviet early in 1919, "to pay tribute to foreign capitalists as long as they build railways. We shall not perish on account of that tribute, but if we do not organize railway transport we may perish because the people are hungry."[4] However the contract was never signed as the two sides could not agree on the details. Nevertheless Lenin continued to uphold this type of agreement as a way of seeking accord with western capitalists and their governments.[5]

The Bolsheviks were prepared to surrender territory, pay old debts, and accept the participation of foreign entrepreneurs in the development of the Russian economy. They would concede nothing, however, regarding their hold on state power. The Bolsheviks were sovereign within Soviet Russia, and fully intended to remain so. In February 1919 two Norwegian journalists were granted interviews with Chicherin and Lenin. They asked the foreign commissar "if the Entente made it a condition for peace that a democratic representation on the usual parliamentary basis should be formed, could the Soviet Government agree?" Chicherin responded that such a demand "would be a remarkable interference with Russian internal affairs" and "it would be impossible to accept," because "it would mean a return to a bourgeois condition of affairs." A parliament would pave the way for a restoration of middle class capitalism, because "without the Soviet system the masses cannot be politically educated and enlightened." Lenin made it clear there could be no truck with the other trappings of bourgeois democracy. Could there be freedom of the press, asked the correspondents. "We consider that the so-called freedom of the press," replied Lenin, "simply gives the [bourgeoisie] the right to stupify the people and lie to them ... Freedom of the press means simply freedom for capital, and we suppress capital ... Pure democracy is a lie, and merely a capitalistic phrase."[6]

These were not mere words; Lenin and the entire communist leadership recoiled in horror from the prospect of yielding even the smallest portion of power in Russia. No sooner had such a prospect been raised as possibly necessary to secure peace with the allies than they responded by further entrenching their dictatorship. Thus, in late 1918 various splinters of the moderate socialist parties outlawed the previous summer had been legalized and allowed to function openly within the Soviet system. As late as early February an effort had even begun to extend this toleration to certain portions of the Right Socialist-Revolutionary party in order to attract an even larger number of supporters to the Soviet government and further accentuate the reactionary nature of the anti-Soviet governments.[7] The limits of this wholly unwanted toleration were reached on 20 February when the newly reopened Menshevik newspaper published an article entitled "End the Civil War" which criticized the Soviet government for squandering the diminishing resources of the Russian people on the Red Army and being insufficiently zealous in the pursuit of peace. The result was a decree of 26 February closing the offending newspaper and an investigation by the Cheka to determine if treachery rather than simple indiscretion had motivated the article in question.[8] Lenin, who had argued so forcefully for the effort to win the support of the moderate-socialist rank and file, fully supported the campaign which was now waged against the Mensheviks and Socialist-Revolutionaries.[9] Parliamentary democracy, fundamental civil liberties, or any form of government other than the Bolshevik-dominated dictatorship of the proletariat, therefore, were simply not negotiable in the effort to secure an end to the civil war and foreign intervention in Russia. The perceptive Sir Esmé Howard, seconded to the British delegation in Paris from the Foreign Office, recognized this immediately. On reading the account of Lenin's interview with the Norwegian journalists, he wrote this meant "that no real peace with him can be hoped for. Any peace he and the Bolshevik leaders made with us will be only like Brest-Litovsk to gain breathing time. Otherwise it is war to the knife, underground if not above it."[10]

Soviet policy, therefore, was simultaneously unyielding and extraordinarily flexible: unyielding on questions of primary concern – ideology, real power, sovereignty; flexible in secondary matters – territory, gold and resources. Both tendencies were encouraged by the increasing awareness in Moscow that the allies could not formulate a common policy on Russia, and the Soviet press eagerly pounced on every report of disunity. "It is becoming more and more clear, that something is very wrong in the camp of the Allied imperialists," reported *Pravda* in December 1918. The allies had been able to defeat Germany, but at such an immense price that they too were ruined economically. To repair the devastation in their own countries they planned to levy a terrible indemnity on the vanquished. "The victorious bandit is robbing the defeated bandit" is how Lenin subsequently described it.[11] But the victors were unable to agree on how to split up the booty. "In no way can imperialism abstain from pillage," intoned *Pravda*, "least of all can it do this at the present time."[12] Soviet leaders concluded that they had been granted a second breathing space similar to that obtained from Germany in the past year, and that it might prove possible to lengthen that space still further. Lenin wrote that he saw nothing wrong with buying off the western powers: "While we were buying off the German bandits by paying them a few hundred million we strengthened our Red Army, but the

German bandits now have nothing left. That's what will happen to other imperialist bandits."[13]

Such was the frame of mind in Moscow when the Prinkipo proposals arrived.
Lenin wired Trotsky: "I am afraid that [Wilson] wants to establish his claim to
Siberia and part of the South, having otherwise scarcely a hope of retaining
anything. This factor ... obliges us in my opinion to exert every effort in order
to take Rostov and Cheliabinsk and Omsk within a month. The person to visit
Wilson will, to all appearances, have to be you."[14] Troksky responded the
following day: "We will of course strive to take Rostov and the Don ... As
regards Wilson there is, as it seems, no cause for haste on our part ... It would
be better to send Chicherin and Rakovskii. They are better equipped for this;
there will be no call for 'polemics' on this occasion, since everything has been
made clear already."[15]

But there was very little clarity about Wilson's message. In an effort to secure
further information, Chicherin sent identical telegrams to V.V. Vorovskii, his
only representative still abroad, and to Jean Longuet, editor of *Le Populaire*, a
French journal sympathetic to the Bolsheviks. The messages described Wilson's
proposal as "strange and implausible" but of great interest. "If, which is improbable, this information should be confirmed," wrote Chicherin, it would be
given the most serious consideration by the Soviet government. The choice of
Prinkipo, he said, "far-distant from European political centres, can only have
the aim either of surrounding it with impenetrable secrecy or creating for it an
artificial and prejudicial publicity." He also found it strange that the allies should
claim that they only wished to promote the pacification of Russia and had
proposed their arbitration as the best way of bringing the civil war to an end.
Each of the inviting powers was a party to the dispute and their armed forces
alone sustained the Whites. The call for an armistice was equally strange. There
had been no such request when Soviet armies were in retreat; now that the Whites
were in disarray the allies suddenly wanted an end to the fighting. The Soviet
government, he said, wanted clear information about allied intentions. Were
they, as their proposals suggested, "really pursuing annexationist goals in relation
to Archangel, Siberia, Baku, Ashkhabad and Rostov-on-Don?"[16]

Although neither recipient was able to provide Chicherin with useful information,[17] the telegram did receive careful examination in the allied chancelleries.
The Quai d'Orsay complained that the Soviet government appeared satisfied that
the allied proposal resembled "an indirect recognition of its power," while in
London the Foreign Office declared that the invitation had "given the Soviet
government an opportunity to score and make propaganda of which it is not
slow to take advantage."[18]

The representatives of the anti-Bolshevik governments gathered in Paris received the Prinkipo proposal with incredulous anger. Already rejected as equal
participants in the peace conference, they had now been invited to meet with
Bolsheviks. On 24 January their chief spokesman told Sir Esmé Howard "you

cannot really expect us to talk with these people at all ... They are the sort of pitch which we will not touch." The Whites threatened: "If this is the way it going to be then we will get together with the Germans."[19]

The Bolsheviks quickly agreed to attend Prinkipo. Trotsky was hesitant, Zinoviev urged caution, and certain elements in the party clearly feared a trap, but no articulate opposition emerged. Trotsky issued his warning, even before the allied invitation arrived, in a brief article entitled "Memorandum for any kind of newly-fledged Anglophilia." British policy, he said, could be summarized in the words of a tsarist general M. Dragomirov who, before the Great War, had declared it to be "tout prendre, rien rendre, toujours prétendre."[20] Zinoviev told the Petrograd Soviet much the same thing. Unable to obtain their aims through violence, the western powers had "to show the fox's tail instead of the wolf's teeth." All the same, he agreed that the Bolsheviks should send their representatives to Prinkipo.[21] In fact, as Lenin recorded, when the central committee discussed the question of participating in a conference there was not a single voice of protest among the proletariat or the party.[22]

There still remained the problem of precisely how the Soviet government would respond to Wilson. The fact that the Prinkipo conference had been announced by press release and that the Soviet government had not received a specific invitation was troubling. Chicherin informed Wilson on 28 January that since the Soviet government had not yet received a specific invitation, "the absence of a response on our part should not serve as a basis for incorrect interpretation." Two days later he asked his representative in Petrograd to sound the neutral consuls there to discover if they knew anything about the situation. Finally on 31 January Chicherin radioed Paris denying a French report that in response to the Prinkipo invitation he had demanded "guarantees and more precise information."[23]

This flurry of messages captured the attention of allied leaders but did not loosen their tongues. On 1 February Wilson brought Chicherin's message to the attention of the Council of Ten and "wished to know what action should be taken." The minutes of the meeting, unfortunately, have been thoroughly sanitized and only the absence of a decision reflects what must have been a rather warm exchange. "He was quite willing to ignore M. Tchicherin's request," Wilson is recorded as having said, "but the Great Powers were anxious to get these delegates together, and perhaps an answer should be sent to take away the excuse that they had received no invitation to attend the meeting." These alternatives probably represented the poles of the argument, with Wilson, and possibly Lloyd George, wanting to issue some further statement about the proposed meeting while the French and Italians would not hear of it. This division was then concealed by deciding "to adjourn the question for further consideration."[24]

While the peace conference considered, the Bolsheviks acted. On 4 February they broadcast their official response to the allies. It publicized the substance of the concessions which Moscow was prepared to make but which previously had only been conveyed to the allies in private. These proposals, said Chicherin, were directed to the western powers rather than the Whites, because the latter were entirely dependent on the former for existence, and therefore the allies were the true adversaries of Soviet Russia. To obtain peace Moscow was prepared to pay Russia's debts and offer raw materials, economic opportunities, and territory to the allies. "The Soviet Government," said Chicherin, did not "insist on excluding from these negotiations all consideration of the question of the annexation of Russian territories by the Allied Powers." In the opinion of the Soviet government, he added, "the maintenance in any part of the territory of the former Russian Empire, with the exception of Poland and Finland, of armed forces of the Entente or of forces which are maintained by the Allied Governments or receive financial, technical, military or any other kind of support from them, should also be classified as annexation." To benefit from these concessions, said Chicherin, the allies would have to act quickly, because with the exception of debt payment, their extent would depend on the Soviet "military situation in relation to the Allied Powers, and this situation is at present improving daily." The foreign commissar also reaffirmed the willingness of the Soviet government "to include in the general agreement with the Allied Powers an undertaking not to interfere in their internal affairs, observing, however, that it cannot limit the freedom of the revolutionary press." On this basis, he concluded, the "soviet government is ready to enter into immediate negotiations on Princes Island or in any other place with all the Allied Powers jointly or with individual Powers among their number or with any Russian political groups as the Allied Powers may wish." [25]

The Soviet message did not elicit any immediate response. This was due in part to the return of Lloyd George to Britain, but also to the design of Clemenceau, who hoped to postpone consideration of the Prinkipo question until Wilson, needed in Washington for the opening of Congress, also left Paris. On 11 February, Philip Kerr, Lloyd George's personal representative in Paris, warned the prime minister of Clemenceau's intentions. [26] Lloyd George replied the next day: "Your explanation is no doubt the correct one. The old tiger wants the grizzly bear back in the Rocky Mountains before he starts tearing up the German hog!" Lloyd George was determined, however, that the Russian question be decided upon one way or another before President Wilson left Paris. He still favoured Prinkipo but feared that the refusal of the Whites to attend would scuttle it. "[They] are behaving stupidly; so are the French and especially the Italians. Bolshevism cannot help winning with such poor material as that which is opposed to it. Now you can exact some terms which would guarantee better government in Russia; a few months hence the Bolsheviks may be triumphant and absent." Despite these views, Lloyd George had now changed his mind and was no longer ready to move forward in the teeth of White and French opposition. He informed Kerr that without the Whites there would be no conference, for he did not want to meet with the Bolsheviks alone. [27]

What had happened? It was not merely a hardening of French and White opposition; it was a major political storm in Britain. Tory backbenchers rebelled against a policy of negotiations with the Bolsheviks. Spurred on by mounting labour difficulties in the country, they objected bitterly to a policy which they saw as encouraging "Red revolution" at home and abroad.[28] Reeling before this unexpected storm, Lloyd George found it necessary to give ground on Prinkipo, especially when Churchill allowed the anti-Bolshevik wind to fill his political sails. Early in February Churchill promised the Whites he would continue to supply the anti-Bolshevik armies with munitions and military equipment. "'I will continue this supply,' he promised, 'as long as I do not receive a categorical order to stop.'"[29] This was not his preferred policy, which would have been to have the allied powers themselves wage full-scale war against the Bolsheviks, but it was a policy which he was able to pursue over the next year through his authority as secretary of state for war. As such he controlled enormous stocks of surplus military supplies which he wanted to make available to the Whites to continue the war against the Bolsheviks.

Churchill put this proposal directly to the prime minister in a meeting of 13 February.[30] He asserted that the Whites were not asking for British troops, but needed "the aid of aeroplanes and tanks, and skilled operators, who did not exist in Russia." To this Lloyd George responded that "he had no objection to supplying the Russians with ammunition and equipment, for which they could pay later when they had a stable Government." Sir Henry Wilson, chief of the Imperial General Staff, who also attended the meeting, pointed out that supplies by themselves were unlikely to do much good. "There was no chance of seriously damaging the Bolsheviks unless we put our backs into the effort. We had ample quantities of war material which could be sent to Russia, much of which would probably be lost." Lloyd George responded that he thought they "might run the risk of the loss. The Russians had a certain moral claim upon us, and we might see that they did not fail for lack of material." In short, this decision did not reflect the situation in Russia itself but only the realities of British politics and the careful balancing of power within the government.

Lloyd George, however, had only retreated, not surrendered. There could be no question of sending further British troops to Russia, and he remained committed to withdrawing those already there. Moreover, since Churchill had chosen to intervene so forcefully in the question, Lloyd George was more than willing to allow him to go to Paris to push this policy. Churchill could experience the difficulties of dealing with Wilson, and, in doing so, attract to himself some of the criticism which previously had accumulated only around himself. For the moment Lloyd George was content to take whatever shelter seemed available in the raging political storm.[31]

Churchill appeared before the Supreme War Council the following evening, February 14. The cabinet, he said, had asked him to obtain some decision concerning the Russian situation. Were the allies going to proceed with the

Prinkipo plan or adopt some other policy? Wilson expressed his personal opinion, first, "that the Allied and Associated Powers ought to withdraw their troops from all parts of Russia," and second, that the allies were not seeking rapprochement with the Bolsheviks, "but clear information." To that end, "he would be quite content that informal American representatives should meet representatives of the Bolsheviks." Here was the first hint of what would emerge as the Bullitt mission, but this was not the resolution of the Russian problem which Churchill had in mind, and he pointed out that the consequence of complete withdrawal of all allied troops would be the destruction of all non-Bolshevik armies in Russia. Wilson responded that unfortunately allied withdrawal from Russia would lead to the loss of many lives, "but some day or other the Allied troops would have to be withdrawn; they could not be maintained there forever and the consequences to the Russians would only be deferred." Churchill then put forward the plan approved by Lloyd George the previous evening. None of the allies "could send conscript troops to Russia," he said, but "volunteers, technical experts, arms, munitions, tanks, aeroplanes, etc. might be furnished." Wilson was not impressed, observing that the Whites had not made very good use of the weapons already supplied them, but Churchill continued to press him, wanting to know "whether the Council would approve of arming the anti-Bolshevik forces in Russia should the Prinkipo Conference prove a failure." Wilson refused to be pinned down, but just as he was leaving he added that "he would, however, cast in his lot with the rest."[32]

It was unclear what Wilson meant by this. He certainly did not mean that he would join in any military adventure in Russia; he had spoken too often against such a policy, and he was acutely aware that Congress would not appropriate money for such a venture. What he probably meant was that, within the well-known limits of his views on Russia, he would accept his share of responsibility for whatever policy his associates arrived at in his absence. Balfour had stressed the British concern that he do so,[33] and the president no doubt felt obliged to make this gesture. Churchill, however, took it to mean that the president would support "active assistance to the anti-Bolsheviks in the event of the Prinkipo proposal failing to produce a settlement." Such was the report which Kerr sent Lloyd George the next day. "Mr. Churchill gathered that the President said that he would agree to this," he wrote, "but the Minutes are not so definite."[34] Indeed they were not, and this led to great confusion in succeeding days.

Churchill lost no time in executing the imputed mandate from the prime minister and president. With their absence from the conference he must have thought that he would have a sympathetic audience for his views.[35] The next day he presented two proposals to the conference. The first called for a new message to the Bolsheviks, and the second proposed the establishment of a council for Russian affairs. He suggested that Moscow be told its response to the Prinkipo invitation was unacceptable. It did not mention a cessation of hostilities and, in fact, the Soviet government had intensified their military activity since receiving the invitation. This had to stop. Churchill proposed that the Bolsheviks be told that: "Unless within 10 days from the 15th instant the Bolshevik forces on all fronts have ceased to attack and have withdrawn a distance of not less than 5 miles from the present position of their adversaries' outpost lines, the Princes Island proposal will be deemed to have lapsed." His proposed council would have political, economic, and military sections. The military section, he said, should "be asked to draw up a plan for concerted action against the Bolsheviks" should the Prinkipo proposal fail. Surprisingly, the American representatives (Robert Lansing and Colonel House, acting for the United States in the absence of Wilson) accepted the idea of an ultimatum; they were less enthusiastic about the proposed council. The French and Italians rejected the proposed ultimatum while accepting, at least in principle, the idea of consultations regarding possible military action in Russia. They rejected the ultimatum out of fear that the Bolsheviks might accept it and that they would then be compelled actually to meet somewhere with Soviet representatives. They proposed, therefore, to say absolutely nothing to the Bolsheviks but, recognizing the failure of Prinkipo, direct their military advisers to "suggest other solutions" to the Russian problem.

This did not mean that they wished to go adventuring in Russia. Clemenceau was already aware of the precarious state of the French expeditionary force at Odessa, and he declared meaningfully that "he did not court defeat in Russia, after having been victorious on the Rhine." He spoke warmly of "encirclement: the policy of setting up a barrier around Russia." Churchill, in short, found himself in a most awkward situation. Like Lloyd George, he had the Americans by his side with the French and Italians in opposition. Clemenceau and Sonnino, the Italian foreign minister, called upon him to repudiate Prinkipo, but he had to tell them that "the British Cabinet would never agree, having gone so far, to break off the Prinkipo policy without making it quite clear to the world that the proposal had been sincerely put forward and sincerely pressed, as long as any chance of its succeeding existed." There was also the problem of left-wing public opinion. "The British Government," he declared, "wished it to appear that they had acted fairly by the Bolsheviks." The French and the Italians, however, had their own political problems, and they would have nothing further to do with anything associated with Prinkipo. Further consideration of the two questions was postponed until Monday, 17 February.[36]

Postponement allowed opposition to organize. Kerr warned Lloyd George that Churchill was bent "on forcing a campaign against Bolshevik Russia by using Allied volunteers, Polish and Finnish and any other conscripts that can be got hold of, financed and equipped by the Allies."[37] The American delegation also concluded that they could not support any proposals which would involve the United States in further military action in Russia.[38] Churchill, meanwhile, had given in to the French and Italian demand for an end to the entire Prinkipo venture. "Will you not send a telegram to the Prime Minister saying that we do not feel that Prinkipo can be kept alive after to-morrow's meeting?" he asked the foreign secretary.[39]

Balfour would not serve as a cat's paw for anyone. He loathed Bolshevism and had opposed Prinkipo but did not want to send a larger allied force to Russia. He doubted its practicality and was uncertain the allies could enforce their will in Russia. He did know that they could abstain from hindering the Whites or aiding the Bolsheviks – in short, a continuation of hostilities to exert pressure on Moscow. Balfour wanted the Bolsheviks to "be given the chance of tumbling into ruins under [their] own weight."[40] Thus, he told Churchill that he would have to take the lead himself in presenting his policy to the prime minister.[41]

Churchill cabled Lloyd George saying he intended to accept the French position and not to send a second telegram to Moscow. He proposed "to set up the Military Commission at once to take stock of the whole situation, to prepare out of the resources which are available a plan of war against the Bolsheviks, to submit the plan when completed to the Supreme War Council together with an expression of authoritative military opinion, as to whether it has a reasonable chance of success or not."[42] This telegram alarmed Lloyd George. He responded that the cabinet had "never authorized such a proposal. They have never contemplated anything beyond supplying armies in anti-Bolshevik areas in Russia with necessary equipment to enable them to hold their own and that only in the event of every effort at a peaceable solution failing." Churchill should "bear in mind the very grave labour position" in Britain. "Were it known that you have gone over to Paris to prepare a plan of war against the Bolsheviks it would do more to incense organized labour than anything I can think of." Churchill should disregard the French: they wanted nothing better "than to see us pulling the chestnuts out of the fire for them."[43] Lloyd George did not trust Churchill to act as instructed, and therefore cabled Kerr to inform not only the British delegation of his opposition to Churchill's plan but the Americans as well.[44]

With this background the Supreme War Council meeting of 17 February collapsed into acrimonious dispute. Churchill brought forward his proposals only to have them rejected by the Americans and disowned by Balfour. House would not agree to the establishment of a special military committee to examine the Russian problem. The American government would not contribute either men or material to a new military venture in Russia. This excited Clemenceau to exclaim that if this were the case then the other allies would discuss Russia without the United States. This was sheer bluff, as the other powers had neither the men nor the money to act without the Americans. The Bolsheviks knew that the allies were quarrelling, but not even they suspected the depths to which this dispute had sunk. The council could not even agree on a sanitized record of their proceedings; instead, they decided to suppress the complete record of the day's "discussion." No formal military commission was established, but allied military representatives were to consult informally and report separately to their respective governments regarding the feasibility of military action in Russia. That night Churchill left Paris in disgust.[45]

The adversaries had fought themselves to a standstill. Lloyd George had blocked Churchill and the French, but the latter had effectively put the knife to Prinkipo. Moreover, when Wilson learned of the interpretation which Churchill had placed on his parting remarks, he immediately informed Colonel House that the United States "are not at war with Russia and will not in circumstances that we can now foresee take part in military operations there against the Russian."[46] Thus, the far-reaching plan of Marshal Foch for vastly expanded intervention failed when submitted to the council at the end of the month.[47] It was equally impossible for advocates of peace to make any headway. Churchill soon had so much surplus war material on its way to Denikin that British shipping could not handle it all. In early March the cabinet decided to evacuate North Russia, but the only immediate result was to provide Churchill with an argument for the reinforcement of Archangel and Murmansk to insure the safe withdrawal of British troops already there.[48] Perhaps most important, conservative opinion in Britain and France remained as solid blocks to any public effort to revive negotiations.

A PUBLIC EFFORT WAS blocked; a secret one was not. Stalemate prompted advocates of both persuasions to act in ways they sought to conceal from the other. Such was the case with the mission of William Bullitt to Soviet Russia. In the wake of Churchill's abortive effort to enlarge the war in Russia, Colonel House decided to send William Bullitt, a young member of his staff, to Moscow. It is unknown if Wilson ordered the mission or even knew of it before he left Paris, but no sooner had he gone than House entered into negotiations with the anti-interventionists in the British delegation to determine their views on a mission to Russia. House told Kerr on 17 February that "he was in favour of keeping in touch with the Bolsheviks with the object of gradually bringing them to terms, restoring Allied influence in Russia and so composing the peace."[49] The two congratulated themselves for having put a spoke in Churchill's wheel but agreed that some other policy still had to be formulated. House asked what Kerr knew of Lloyd George's policy. Kerr replied that other than opposing an attack on the Bolsheviks and feeling "that we ought to stand by our friends until we could bring about some reasonable settlement of the Russian problem," he did not know. Pressed by House, Kerr said that he "personally would be willing to negotiate with the Bolsheviks provided that they sign an armistice suspending hostilities on all fronts." He would then want to "negotiate a settlement which would secure to Koltchak, Denikin, the Archangel group and the small nations on the Western border of Soviet Russia the free control of their own affairs and at the same time allow Allied agents to penetrate European Russia with full guarantees for life and property."[50] House agreed and this became the basis of the "peace terms" which Bullitt carried with him to Russia. These included "amnesty to all political prisoners on both sides," the "restoration of trade relations between Soviet Russia and the outside world," and an independent consideration of Russia's debts. Should the Soviet government agree to these broad principles, it was proposed that all allied troops should be withdrawn from Russia "as soon as Russian armies above [a] quota to be defined have been demobilized and their surplus arms surrendered or destroyed." These conditions were contained in a note from Kerr to Bullitt dated 21 February. Kerr described them as "the sort of conditions upon which I personally think it would be possible for the allied Governments to resume once more normal relations with Soviet Russia." He emphasized that they had "no official significance and merely represent suggestions of my own opinion."[51] The following day Bullitt left Paris carrying this note and official credentials empowering him to study "conditions, political and economic" in Russia on behalf of the government of the United States.[52]

Nearly everyone involved with this enterprise had a different conception of its purpose. For Wilson and Lansing the official purpose – the collection of reliable information of a general nature – was foremost. For Lloyd George and Kerr other considerations were paramount. While wishing a cessation of hostilities with the Bolsheviks, they also wanted to protect the anti-Soviet governments and small nations emerging from the former Russian empire. They needed to know, therefore, to what extent the Bolsheviks would tolerate the continued existence of these groups and peoples with whom they were currently at war. House, on the other hand, saw the mission as part of a lengthier process which would eventually result in "composing the peace" of eastern Europe. He therefore was able to mediate between the British and American principles at the conference while pursuing his own aim for the mission. The same was true of his relationship with Bullitt. Bullitt was a trusted member of his entourage who had developed a considerable interest in Russia. His primary concern, as contrasted with the aims of the major leaders, including House, was the prompt conclusion of peace with the Bolsheviks. No other official figure, British or American, shared his aspiration, and this was to contribute mightily to the ultimate failure of his mission. House, who clearly did not understand the ambition of his young assistant, unwittingly encouraged it by allowing Kerr and himself to be drawn by Bullitt into lengthy speculation about the "peace terms" to be carried to Russia. In the heady atmosphere generated amongst the anti-interventionists by Churchill's defeat, Bullitt clearly came to see himself as the chief agent for the negotiation of peace with Soviet Russia.

Bullitt was joined in his mission by Walter W. Petit, a captain in American military intelligence, and Lincoln Steffens, a journalist closely associated with House and "regarded as a friend of Russia." They travelled by way of Scandinavia and arrived in Petrograd on 8 March. As soon as Zinoviev learned they did not have full powers to negotiate with the Soviet government, he refused to speak with them. "He turned away abruptly," reports Steffens, "and we never saw him again." That was the only unpleasantness encountered by the Americans, for Chicherin and Litvinov soon arrived in Petrograd to take charge of the situation. They invited them to travel to Moscow to discuss their mission with Lenin.[53] The two made an excellent impression on Bullitt, and he agreed to meet Lenin. Before leaving for Moscow he sent House a telegram which reflected the mounting importance he attached to the mission. Within a week he expected to have "an exact detailed statement of the position of the Soviet Government on all points ... Suspend judgement on any action until then. I am certain from conversation already held that the Soviet Government is disposed to be reasonable and that I shall have a communication of the utmost importance to transmit."[54]

Bullitt spent three days in Moscow. He met not only with Lenin and other Bolshevik leaders but also with representatives of opposition parties recently legalized by the Soviet government. Mensheviks and Socialist-Revolutionaries alike told him the same thing; they had come to support the Bolsheviks "largely because Russia was being attacked from outside and threatened by more drastic intervention." The Soviet government, Bullitt reported, was "firmly established and the Communist Party [was] strong politically and morally." The only alternatives were chaos and anarchy, conditions which could be produced by continuing the current war against them but which would then leave the allied powers the necessity of establishment themselves "a form of government [the Russian people] do not want and against which they will revolt whenever strength returns to them."[55]

Bullitt said such a brutal policy was unnecessary. He had discussed with the Soviet government the "peace terms" worked out by House and Kerr in Paris, and they had readily accepted them as a basis for discussion and incorporated them in peace proposals of their own submitted to him at the time of his departure. These proposals had been approved by "the Executive Council of the Soviet Government,"[56] who considered themselves bound by them provided the allied and associated powers accepted them on or before 10 April 1919. The terms called for the cessation of hostilities on all fronts by all parties engaged in hostilities on the territory of the former Russian empire. One week after the cessation of hostilities a conference of all belligerents would open in a neutral country to be chosen by the allies. The armistice was to have an initial duration of two weeks but be renewable by mutual consent. The conference would discuss peace on the basis of seven principles which would *not* be subject to revision:

1 All existing *de facto* governments established on the territory of the former Russian empire were to remain in control of all territory held at the beginning of the armistice until such time as the peoples inhabiting these territories "[should] themselves determine to change their governments." The allied governments were "to undertake to see to it that the *de facto* Governments of Germany [did] not attempt to upset by force the *de facto* Governments of Russia."

2 The blockade of Russia was to be lifted.

3 Soviet Russia was to have the right of unhindered use of all railways and ports of the former Russian empire necessary for the "transportation of passengers and goods between [its] territories and the sea."

4 Reciprocal rights of free entry, sojurn, circulation, and security were to be extended to the citizens of all signatory governments "provided they [did] not interfere in the domestic politics" of the host states. Each signatory was entitled "to send official representatives enjoying full liberty and immunity" to all the others. The allies were to "see to it that Poland and all neutral countries [extended] the same rights" to the signatories.

5 A general amnesty was to be given to all political prisoners.

6 Immediately after the conclusion of peace, the allied and associated governments and other non-Russian governments were to withdraw all their troops from Russia and cease giving military assistance to anti-Soviet governments established on the territory of the former Russian empire.

7 All governments established on the territory of the former Russian empire were to "recognize their responsibility for the financial obligations of the former Russian Empire, to foreign states parties to this agreement and to nationals of such states."

Independent of these proposals, but submitted with them, was a statement on the part of the Soviet government that they were eager to receive "semi-official guarantees from the American and British Governments that they [would] do all that lies in their power to get France to observe the conditions of the armistice."[57] The extent of the concessions offered the allied powers was enormous but so, too, was the quid pro quo. In return for the recognition of their right to exist, the Soviet government was offering to give up their claim on the larger part of the territory of the former Russian empire and to repay the vast losses suffered by citizens of the victorious powers as a result of the Russian revolution. Clearly this did not go down well with many Bolshevik leaders, but unlike Soviet policy at the time of the conclusion of the treaty of Brest Litovsk, this peace proposal was not debated or seriously questioned in public. What was said privately can only be inferred from such bits of indirect evidence as Zinoviev's hostility to Bullitt and Trotsky's reference in a message of 17 March 1919 to the American mission as "eavesdroppers" sent "to assess whether we should hold firm or not."[58] We also know that Chicherin felt it necessary to plead with other Soviet leaders to accept the sacrifices foreseen by the agreement. "The decision is very important," he wrote. "If we don't try to get an agreement the policy of blockade will be pressed with vigor. They will send tanks ... to Denikin, Kolchak, Petlura, Paderewski."[59] Moreover, although not publicly challenged on the question, Lenin presented a forceful defence of his policy both in front of the Petrograd Soviet, Zinoviev's home base, and the Eighth Congress of the Russian Communist Party. In Petrograd on 12 March he asked if Soviet Russia was strong enough to launch an offensive war against world imperialism. He responded that this was "misplaced fantasy, today our country alone cannot overthrow world imperialism ... so ... we have to make concessions to imperialism."[60] In Moscow six days later he told the party congress that "in relation to Western Europe, in relation to the Entente countries, we have, or shall have, to repeat a good deal of what we did at the time of the Brest peace."[61]

The Bolsheviks were, in fact, offering a great deal for peace, but not nearly as much as it might first appear. Their proposal was a document of political genius, yet one more example of the "rotten compromise" for which Lenin was so justly famous. It might just as well have been headed "A Charter to Bolshevize Russia." Adoption, in whole or in part, would almost surely have led to the collapse of the anti-Soviet governments in Russia even more rapidly than was actually to take place. No one, least of all themselves, believed that they could long exist without substantial foreign assistance. The proposed agreement purported to secure them against the Soviet government and the Red Army. Even if it had, nothing protected them from the Bolshevik party, deeply rooted and active, in all the territories of the former Russian empire. Invigorated by the proposed amnesty, reinforced by added cadres from Soviet Russia, and aided by the instant demoralization which would have swept through the anti-Bolshevik forces once the Soviet government had received some form of allied recognition, local Bolshevik organizations would have made fast work of the bogus regimes they confronted. When the inevitable came, it would fall well within the agreement for, of course, it provided that no existing de facto governments were to be altered until such time as the peoples inhabiting their territories "shall themselves determine to change their governments." This was self-determination Bolshevik-style with a vengeance.

Confidently anticipating victory in the struggle against the Whites, Soviet leaders were careful to include features in the peace proposal which would facilitate their conduct of political and economic relations with the outside world. Special note should be taken of the Soviet request that the Allied Powers "see to it that the *de facto* governments of Germany do not attempt to upset by force the *de facto* governments of Russia." As will be shown, in March Germany had again come to pose a real threat to the Bolsheviks, and if the allies did as requested they would relieve Moscow of considerable anxiety. But the mere statement of this request was loaded with the greatest political meaning. It implied de facto recognition and acceptance of the unequal status of Germany in international affairs and the authority of the peace conference over the conduct of her foreign relations. It was an open invitation for both the peace conference and Berlin to reflect upon the meaning of such an admission. To Berlin it served as a warning to back away from policies injurious to Moscow or be faced by an effort to secure allied aid in terminating them. The previous year when Germany had exercised hegemony over eastern Europe, the Bolsheviks had gained substantial advantage by recognizing that hegemony and securing German aid in opposing allied encroachment in Russia. Now the reverse was suggested by this Soviet proposal. Other German clients had enlisted in the service of the allies and here was a suggestion that, if the price was right, Moscow might as well.

In much the same vein the Bolsheviks sought to exploit the split between the French and their Anglo-American allies. Bullitt's presence, bearing evidence of British but not French interest in his mission, openly invited Chicherin to attempt to widen this breach. He lost no time in doing so, telling Bullitt that he had "full confidence in the good will of the American Government but [had] the greatest distrust of the French Government and fear[ed] that it [would] employ the period of the armistice to send large supplies to anti-Bolshevik armies and to raise forces to operate against the various Soviet Governments."[62] He stressed that the Soviet Government would expect the United States and Great Britain "to get France to observe the conditions of the armistice."

The Bolsheviks also built into their document certain features clearly designed to draw the French into the peace negotiations. Russian bonds and securities were widely held throughout France, and Moscow believed that the collective anger of the French rentiers provided the political basis for the hostility of the French government towards Soviet Russia. As we have seen, the Bolsheviks had already signalled Paris repeatedly that they were prepared to pay compensation for French losses, and Chicherin, in his conversations with Bullitt, again stressed this readiness. The Bolsheviks cleverly proposed that "the Soviet Government and the other Governments which has been set up on the territory of the former Russian Empire and Finland shall recognize their responsibility for the financial obligations of the former Russian Empire, to foreign states parties to this agreement and to the nationals of such states." The final portion of this sentence is important because, while it extended the recognition of indebtedness to nationals as well as states – an obvious effort to interest French rentiers in the negotiations – it also implied that foreign states not party to the agreement, and consequently their nationals, would enjoy no such benefit. Carrot and stick, thus, appear side by side in the document. The first portion of this proposal is equally interesting, for here for the first time appears the Soviet contention, subsequently developed at great length, that all the successor states and not just Soviet Russia must bear a share of responsibility in the payment of the financial obligations of the former Russian empire. These successor states had drawn their very existence from the old empire and they would have to shoulder their portion of the debts as well as take its resources. This reflects the seriousness with which the Bolsheviks had begun to treat the problem of foreign indebtedness and their willingness to come to grips with it in an international form.

Indeed, the document reflects a Soviet readiness to negotiate all problems outstanding between themselves and the allies and should have served the purpose of getting negotiations started. This was not to happen because it was Bullitt, and not his principals, who was most interested in the opening of peace talks. He clearly had not perceived the casuistry lurking behind the seemingly reasonable proposals concerning an armistice among the several hostile Russian governments, but that was not his primary concern. He, like the Bolsheviks, was interested in peace between the Soviet and western governments, and that was clearly within reach. His principals would find the Soviet proposals much less satisfactory, because they were either less interested or wholly uninterested in peace with the Bolsheviks on any terms. Bullitt did not realize this and hence suffered great disappointment when the Soviet peace proposals were spurned.

His disillusionment came quickly. He reached Paris on 25 March and within days learned that nothing would come of his mission. Wilson, who had also returned to Paris, would not see him, and House was powerless to help. Bullitt took his cause to Lloyd George, but found no support there either. The prime minister, holding a copy of the *Daily Mail* in his hand, said "As long as the British press in doing this kind of thing how can you expect me to be sensible about Russia?"[63]

What had happened? In part it was, as Lloyd George suggested, the continued campaign of hatred against the Bolsheviks and anyone who would negotiate with them carried on by the conservative press in all allied nations. Lloyd George remained a prime target for such attacks, and was reluctant to act in any way that would further injure him politically. There was also the problem of Germany. The victorious powers were in no more agreement regarding her than about Russia, and much of the work of the peace conference now revolved around the effort to settle this problem. Little time was left for the Russian question. Most of all, however, the international environment had changed. When Bullitt left for Russia the allied powers still had a firm grip on their victory; by late March this was no longer the case. The existing social order in central Europe, seemingly secure in February, had been badly shaken by further disorders in Germany during March and the unexpected revolution in Hungary. Further east, the Red Army, having swept triumphantly through Ukraine, stood poised to drive the French out of south Russia. All of this had a profound impact on the peace conference and inclined allied leaders to exercise even greater caution than before.

THE WHITES HAD ALSO begun to show signs of life. In the south, Krasnov's Cossacks had finally joined with the Volunteer Army, and both had begun to receive substantial quantities of British supplies. But the major change was the unexpected success of Admiral Kolchak in Siberia. The supreme ruler had taken advantage of the concentration of the Bolsheviks on other fronts to push his own forces towards the Urals. The demoralized Bolshevik armies were forced to retreat along the entire eastern front. No serious effort was made to reinforce them, and Moscow clearly counted on the spring thaw to bring them to a halt. Trotsky visited the front and pronounced the situation serious but "not terrible, much less catastrophic."[64] All the same, reports received from Omsk confidently predicted that Kolchak would soon make further gains. On 22 March the British military mission in Siberia reported that a small detachment from Kolchak's army had made contact with a similar unit sent from Archangel by General Eugenii Miller, commander of the White armies in northern Russia.[65] All this was tenuous, but in the larger context of mounting allied failure in eastern Europe it was enough to enhance Kolchak's prestige.

In Ukraine the situation was vastly different, so serious as to threaten the French with disaster.[66] Circumstances there were so confused that it was not until the end of January that Paris satisfied itself that Petliura was not a Bolshevik and instructed the commander of the French expeditionary force to cooperate with him against the Bolsheviks.[67] By that time the Bolshevik tide had reached flood, Ukrainian socialists of all persuasions were deserting the Directory, and Moscow was demanding its capitulation pure and simple. On 23 January, Chicherin demanded that the Directory dissolve itself, join individually with the Ukrainian Soviet government, "and forgetting completely their separatist tendencies to create a unitary communist front against the aggression of the western imperialists."[68] In the last days of January something very similar to this happened. The nationalist elements which had supported the Directory rallied around Petliura while the socialist elements hastened to make peace with the rapidly advancing Red Army. First among the latter was the Ataman Grigoriev, who commanded a substantial number of partisans in southwestern Ukraine, immediately adjacent to French-occupied Odessa. His partisans now posed a serious threat to the French expeditionary force which clung to the Black Sea coast from Odessa to Bessarabia.[69]

The situation grew steadily worse. On 5 February Kiev fell to the Bolsheviks, and the Soviet Ukrainian government promptly invited the French to evacuate those parts of Ukraine they were then occupying.[70] With the Bolsheviks becoming more active in Odessa, General Berthelot, the French commander in south Russia, appealed urgently for reinforcement. The situation, he said, was grave, but still possible of redress if urgent measures were taken. Clemenceau promised reinforcements, but none reached Berthelot.[71] Instead, Grigoriev's partisans descended upon him with devastating fury. Early in March they launched their attack on Kherson while a general uprising took place in the city itself. After suffering severe casualties, on 10 March the French evacuated Kherson under the covering fire of their warships.[72] They also had to evacuate Nikolaev to avoid a repetition of events at Kherson. This was complicated by the presence of six thousand German troops left stranded in the city. The French left peacefully on 14 March followed two days later by the Germans who surrendered the city and port to Grigoriev intact, including its high-powered radio transmitter and substantial supplies of arms and munitions.[73]

All this came as a terrible shock to the French. Their adversary, reported General Franchet d'Esperey, the military commander in eastern Europe, was "no longer Bolshevik bands, without command," but an "army well commanded and perfectly disciplined, restoring order in place of disorder." This, of course, was not true, for the main body of the Red Army remained well to the north; the French were facing Grigoriev's partisans, but in such numbers and so well armed that they were mistaken for "a regular army manoeuvring in the German style."[74] In fact, the French were victims of their own propaganda which depicted the Bolsheviks, and by implication all Russian revolutionaries and increasingly all Russians, as agents of disorder incapable of disciplined military action. When confronted with a capably led superior force they more often than not blamed the Germans for their misfortune; March and April 1919 would give them ample scope to indulge this particular fantasy.

Franchet d'Esperey, viewing the developing catastrophe in south Russia from Constantinople, warned that failure at Odessa would damage French prestige in eastern Europe. He was particularly concerned by the "nearly unanimous hostility of the dissolute and xenophobic population which corrupts our soldiers and then shoots them in the back as soon as the Bolshevik army appears." He feared the mass rising which had occurred at Kherson would be repeated in Odessa whose nine hundred thousand inhabitants made the danger even greater.[75] Reporting from Bucharest, General Berthelot drew the logical conclusions. He recommended the immediate withdrawal of the French expeditionary force from south Russia. He had neither the men nor resources to reinforce Odessa, and those promised from France could not arrive in time to stave off disaster. With the hinterland in Bolshevik hands the city could not be fed, and the situation there would soon become untenable.[76]

Clemenceau first attempted to restore the confidence of his badly demoralized army. He ordered reinforcements and assured his commanders that Odessa could be supplied with food from abroad. The city was not to be surrendered, because "repercussions of all sorts" would follow its loss. Berthelot, who had asked to be relieved of his command of the troops at Odessa because of poor communications between that city and Bucharest, was granted his wish and the expeditionary corps was placed directly under Franchet d'Esperey.[77]

This sang froid did not last. Already on 16 March the director of Russian affairs at the Quai d'Orsay summed up the situation in one sentence: "The Ukraine is lost."[78] The government reluctantly accepted this conclusion. Odessa, it was decided, could only be held at a prohibitive cost. The French could not feed the city alone and their allies would not help them. President Wilson could see no reason to feed a city whose population was as hostile as that of Odessa. The French experience there, he said, only confirmed his own belief that the allies should evacuate all Russian territory as quickly as possible. The Council of Four, into which the primary allied leaders had now organized themselves, decided on 27 March to abandon the city. In early April the French forces there retreated along the rail line into Bessarabia. On 6 April 1919 the Bolsheviks occupied Odessa.[79]

As predicted, the evacuation of Odessa had far-reaching repercussions. The Romanians had watched with horror as the French position in south Russia collapsed. They had good reason to fear the consequences of this defeat, because in November, as the Great War was ending, they had hastened to occupy Bessarabia and claim the Dniester as their eastern frontier. The Romanian occupation was not popular in Bessarabia, and none of the regimes contending for power in the Ukraine would recognize the legitimacy of the seizure.[80] The Ukrainian Bolsheviks had warned both Bucharest and the allies that they would not tolerate the continued occupation of Bessarabia by Romania.[81] Now the Romanians described the situation on their frontier as "most alarming," proclaimed themselves to be the last rampart against Bolshevism, and submitted a long list of military equipment which they said they needed to defend themselves and Europe against invasion. This request was strongly backed by the allied representatives in Bucharest. The Council of Four heard this request on the same day they decided to abandon Odessa and agreed to provide the Romanians with needed military supplies. Clemenceau instructed d'Esperey: "Your mission on the Bessarabian as well as the Hungarian front consists exclusively in stopping any Bolshevik advance."[82]

The reference to the Hungarian front points to the final thorn in the allied crown. On 21 March the government of moderate socialists, who had held power in Hungary since the previous November, resigned and installed in their place a communist government headed by Bela Kun. Kun, who had only recently returned from Soviet Russia, had been apprehended and thrown in jail by the very men who now elevated him to power. They were no longer able to cope with the economic disruption caused by the allied blockade and the permission granted to neighbouring states, including Romania, to occupy large portions of Hungarian territory. They brought the startled Kun directly from prison to form a new government. The communists, they hoped, with their increasingly powerful friends in Soviet Russia and Ukraine, would be able to deal with the allies more forcefully and successfully than themselves.[83]

In Moscow the new Soviet republic was greeted with enthusiasm. Lenin conveyed his warmest greetings to Kun,[84] and the two governments entered into an exchange of views by radio. In the chaotic circumstances of central and eastern Europe the potential for cooperation between the two revolutionary governments was enormous. Unfortunately the territories of the two states were separated by several hundred kilometres by Galicia and Bukovina. In the coming months this territory would become a major focus of attention for all the states in this corner of Europe as well as the allies meeting in Paris. Already on 23 March the Red Army high command began to prepare a plan for the establishment of a direct connection with Soviet Hungary by way of Galicia and Bukovina.[85] Just as promptly western military leaders called the attention of the Council of Four to this area. General Foch recommended that Poland be instructed to occupy this region and establish a common front with Romania against the Bolsheviks. Wilson pointed out that this would prejudice the final disposition of Galicia which was claimed by both Poland and Ukraine. Furthermore, he said, the proposal sounded suspiciously like those made earlier by Foch in an effort to establish an offensive fighting front against the Bolsheviks in eastern Europe. That proposal had been rejected and so was this one. Franchet d'Esperey, however, lost no time in sending a special mission north into Bukovina to observe the road, rail, and telegraphic facilities in the region and to prevent if possible the establishment of direct links between Hungary and Ukraine.[86]

ALL THESE EVENTS PUT a final end to any possibility of the allies, or any one of them separately, entering into negotiations with the Bolsheviks. Allied authority had been severely shaken, and peace had not yet been made with Germany. Any move to negotiate with the Bolsheviks could easily be interpreted as a sign of further weakness and perhaps provoke in Germany, or elsewhere, a repetition of events in Hungary. *Le Temps* of Paris, neatly summed up the situation: "The Prinkipo policy has become obsolete, because at the time we invited Lenin to Prinkipo we were in a position to speak to him as with the vanquished; after the evacuation of Odessa and after the Hungarian revolution we must speak with him as the victor."[87]

CHAPTER FIVE

Defence against "disguised intervention": Soviet policy in the Baltic and Poland

In early 1919 Soviet leaders again peered anxiously at the western borderlands. During the previous two months they had enjoyed substantial success in this region but it was not an area they could afford to ignore. Petrograd and the Baltic coast remained dangerously exposed. Further south, along the roads and railways of Lithuania and Belorussia, the danger was still greater. Along them ran the most direct route to Moscow. Only weeks before the German army could have easily driven the Bolsheviks from their capital. Now Moscow was shielded by the anarchy which gripped eastern Europe, but how long would this disorder last? The Bolsheviks had advanced westward with negligible forces and against little resistance. Any equal force would stop this advance, and a larger one would immediately threaten the Soviet heartland.

Germany continued to be the key to Soviet security in the west, as only the Reich could mobilize the men and material needed to mount a major military operation east of its frontiers. It was doubly dangerous, therefore, that the political crisis in Germany of late December resulted in the formation of a cabinet whose key members were convinced, as were the permanent officials at the Auswärtiges Amt, that a loudly proclaimed anti-Bolshevism was the surest way for Germany to secure a lenient peace from the allies.[1] Their policy was clearly spelled out in a memorandum prepared by Rudolf Nadolny for Count Ulrich von Brockdorff-Rantzau, the new foreign secretary. In it Nadolny insisted that the Bolshevik regime would ultimately succumb to allied pressure. Thus, Germany should "make it clear to the Entente that the imposition of ruinous peace terms must drive us into the arms of Bolshevism. Furthermore, we must be seen to offer the greatest possible resistance to the Bolsheviks in their advance [westward]. In addition, we must also exercise the greatest possible discretion in keeping Bolshevism at a distance from Germany, and, for the future to acquire for ourselves as many friends as possible in the restored Russia."[2] The German government was to follow this policy for the next four months.

This coincided perfectly with the views of the German army high command[3] which, early in the new year, began to reassert its authority both in the Reich and in the eastern marches. First tacitly, then officially, the army was allowed to recruit volunteers to replace the last remnants of the old imperial army. Early in January the high command ordered an end to the withdrawal from the east and sent General Hans von Seeckt, one of their most able officers, to take charge of the situation. By mid-month he had re-established a front against the Bolsheviks extending from Libau to Kovno, Grodno, and Bialystok.[4] The Red Army, however, continued to advance, and on 12 January Vatsetis ordered his forces to occupy all of Lithuania and press on towards Memel and Tilsit in East Prussia. The Germans responded by reinforcing their troops in Lithuania.[5] Stung by this unexpected resistance Moscow warned the Auswärtiges Amt that a resumption of hostilities in the Baltic could only benefit local counter-revolutionaries and delay the final withdrawal of the German army from eastern Europe.[6]

Worse was to come, for in the first weeks of January the newly formed Communist Party of Germany attempted to seize power. Ironically, in view of the charges soon brought against him, Karl Radek opposed the action almost from the beginning. He urged the communists to end the popular action promptly and to portray it as a measure of proletarian defence against the gathering counter-revolutionary forces in Germany. He was not heeded; in mid-month the government, pleased to settle accounts with the unruly radicals and to establish their own anti-Bolshevik credentials, unleashed the new volunteer army on the insurgents. The Freikorps made short work of the radicals and, as a harbinger of things to come, murdered Karl Liebknecht and Rosa Luxemburg. Radek escaped into the Berlin underground but was captured and imprisoned the following month.[7] The German government hastened to portray the events of January as a Bolshevik enterprise. It promised to take the strictest measures against "all Russians guilty of supporting the insurrection movement or still continuing this activity."[8]

Soviet reaction took two forms. Lenin held Ebert and Scheidemann personally responsible for the murder of Liebknecht and Luxemburg. Officially, Chicherin denied there were any Russian government or Bolshevik party agents in Berlin. He allowed there was "one Soviet Russian official in Berlin, Comrade Radek," but claimed he had been "able to travel there as a consequence of not being a Russian citizen." The German protest was all the more inappropriate due to their own intervention in the affairs of the Soviet republics. In Latvia and Lithuania they were intervening actively on behalf of the "White-guardists" not by sending single agents, but militarily, with all the armed force they could muster.[9] Most of what Chicherin said was true, and he made a good argument for the Bolsheviks not accepting instruction in non-intervention from the German government, but the document, taken as a whole, was an exercise in unabashed casuistry. The reference to Radek's citizenship highlights this. Bolshevism was an internationalist creed which held traditional notions of nationality in contempt; the upper reaches of the Soviet Russian government included a galaxy of non-Russian luminaries. Their agents were drawn from countless nationalities and, except when it suited their purpose, they did not make any claim to "Russian citizenship." Indeed, Moscow had at its disposal thousands of agents genuinely possessing German citizenship. Two such Germans, Ernst Reuter and Felix Wolf, had accompanied Radek to Berlin, and in January they were followed by Julian Marchlewskii, a long-time collaborator of the Spartacist leaders. He arrived only three days after the murder of Liebknecht and Luxemburg and quickly assumed many of their functions.[10] Chicherin's claim of Soviet innocence, therefore, need not be taken seriously. The Soviet government only regretted that more could not be done to bring down the hated Social Democrats. "If we had been strong enough," Lenin told the Petrograd Soviet on 12 March, "we would not have allowed the Scheidemanns to mow down the Spartacists, but would have kicked them out."[11]

Soviet leaders were well aware that they lacked the strength to realize their ambitions in the west. "It is very important to transport arms from the West [to the southern and Ukrainian fronts]," Trotsky wrote to Lenin on 24 January, "and the new [Soviet] governments [in the Baltic] are hindering this."[12] Throughout 1919 the claims of the western front were consistently put below all others, and after the new year it proved impossible to pursue an active policy in that region. The initiative passed to the many enemies of the Bolsheviks, and Moscow could only react to each threat as it arose.

POLAND QUICKLY CAME to pose a threat to the Soviet western border second only to Germany. All the hostility latent in the Russo-Polish relationship received new expression in the vastly altered postwar structure of eastern Europe. Renascent Poland achieved independence under the auspices of the property-owning classes in alliance with the indigenous officialdom left in place by the expiring empires.[13] Such men loathed the Bolsheviks and were hated by them in return. Worse yet, the two immediately discovered a fat bone of contention: the territories between those inhabited by an overwhelmingly Polish population and those which were unquestionably Russian in character. These borderlands, inhabited by Lithuanians, Jews, and Belorussians, had formed part of the Polish Republic until the eighteenth century, but since then had been subject to substantial Russian cultural influence. The Bolshevik party had deep roots in this area, and this had certainly influenced the Soviet decision to plunge forward to Vilna, Minsk, and Baranowicze. Warsaw too claimed the region, and on 12 December decided to send its army into Lithuania to defend Polish interests there.[14] A clash between Poles and Bolsheviks, each rushing into the vacuum left by the Germans, was virtually certain.

The actual clash was delayed two months by the continued presence of German troops in the disputed territories. This did not stop Poland and Soviet Russia from opening verbal hostilities by way of long-distance radio transmitters. On

22 December Leon Wasilewski, the Polish foreign minister, filed an energetic protest with Moscow, "against the movement of Soviet troops toward the Polish frontiers." Chicherin replied the following day that Russian troops were "not only at a very great distance from the Polish frontier, but were indeed separated from it by Lithuania and adjoining parts of the Ukraine; in fact, at the moment, Poland and Russia do not even have any common frontiers." The Polish government may be excused for not being reassured by this message. Not only did Chicherin imply that Moscow had determined where the Polish eastern frontier was located, but he left the clear impression that the Red Army, then pushing westward through Lithuania and Belorussia, was not composed of "Russian troops" and consequently was not answerable to the authorities in the Kremlin. Warsaw was alarmed further two weeks later when, in response to a further Polish message, Chicherin confirmed that Moscow considered Polish claims to any part of the borderlands to be illegitimate. Only the large landowners of Polish origin wanted union with Poland, he said, the Lithuanian and Belorussian workers and peasants did not.[15]

Even before receiving this message the Polish authorities sought help from the western powers. No doubt events in Warsaw, as well as in Lithuania, prompted this appeal, for during the last days of 1918 communist-inspired civil unrest broke out in the Polish capital. The arrest of a Soviet Red Cross mission arriving unexpectedly in the city offered Bolshevik sympathizers an opportunity to demonstrate against the government. The police scattered the demonstrators and expelled the Red Cross mission,[16] but the Polish government, already unsteady, felt seriously threatened. Warsaw radioed Paris that a Bolshevik invasion of former Polish territories was under way and British, French, and American troops were needed at once "to stop [the] further progress of this barbarous movement."[17] Allied military officers who had just arrived in Warsaw quickly joined the chorus and submitted a lengthy shopping list of military supplies the Poles needed to stop the Bolsheviks. The British military representative informed the War Office that "unless help begins to arrive within five weeks Poles will be overwhelmed, and this will mean the disappearance of last barrier between Bolshevism and Western Europe."[18]

These reports were received sceptically in London and Paris. The Poles continued to press for allied assistance but with little success.[19] The Bolsheviks had proved unable to exploit their initial advantage, and in early February the Germans who had been hindering the Poles suddenly became cooperative. They were just completing the withdrawal of their army into northern Lithuania, and, as part of their broader anti-Bolshevik policy, were quite happy to facilitate the movement of Polish troops into the districts they were evacuating. On 5 February the Poles occupied Bialystok, and a few days later the Germans also turned over Brest-Litovsk to them.[20] Nothing now stood between the Poles and the Red Army.

The Bolsheviks did not want to fight Poland. They were already fully engaged elsewhere and were unable to reinforce their western front. Moreover, armed hostilities with Poland, a client of the western powers, could only complicate the effort to negotiate an end to allied intervention in the Russian civil war. As soon as Moscow learned that the Germans had stepped back to make way for the Poles, therefore, it sought to negotiate a peaceful settlement with Warsaw. In this it was aided by a change of Polish government. At the end of January the Moraczewski cabinet was replaced by one led by Ignacy Paderewski. Paderewski was inclined to seek a peaceful settlement with Soviet Russia, even suggesting that Moscow receive a Polish special delegate to open negotiations between the two countries. Chicherin responded with alacrity, replying that Alexander Wieckowski, the proposed delegate, should come to Moscow as soon as possible. He added that the proposed negotiations would touch on questions which also concerned the Soviet governments of Lithuania and Belorussia and, as a consequence, he would approach these states with the suggestion that they should make use of Soviet Russian good offices in settling their disputes with Warsaw. This did not go down well in either Vilna or Minsk, where the Soviet regimes were far more hostile to the existing order in Poland than was the government in Moscow, but they dutifully did as they were told and informed Warsaw on 16 February that they were prepared to form a mixed commission to define the political frontier between Poland and themselves. At the same time Moscow informed the western powers of this exchange of messages, but noted that, despite the Soviet initiative, Polish troops continued to mass for an attack on the Soviet republics. Chicherin asked the allies to use their influence to avert this attack and promote peace in eastern Europe.[21]

The allies, of course, would do no such thing. Their concern was that the Wieckowski mission might reflect a Polish inclination to conclude peace with the Bolsheviks, and the British representative in Warsaw was directed to ask Paderewski the purpose of the mission. The Polish premier replied that Wieckowski had no political mission but was going only "to discuss questions of Polish prisoners" held by the Bolsheviks in Russia.[22]

Paderewski's prevarication foreshadowed the ultimate failure of the mission. Although the Polish premier and many of his associates sincerely wanted peace, other important Polish leaders did not. Josef Pilsudski, chief of state and creator of the new Polish army, was foremost among the latter. Pilsudski hoped to build not merely a Polish nation state but a great federation of peoples under the aegis of Poland which would replace Russia as the great power of eastern Europe. Lithuania, Belorussia, and Ukraine were all to be included. His plan called for a truncated and vastly reduced Russia, a plan which excluded negotiation prior to military victory. Much preparation was required for such far-reaching plans, and in March 1919 Pilsudski was not ready to proceed with their realization. He could tolerate and even approve Paderewski's effort to negotiate with Moscow as it would serve to mask his own military preparations. He could not risk any possibility of the mission succeeding. In this he had the unwitting assistance of the western powers, for in their concern that Poland not engage in separate negotiations with Moscow they gave the Polish chief of state an irrefutable

argument against allowing Wieckowski any latitude in his talks with the Bolsheviks. He would go to negotiate for the release of Polish prisoners and no
other official purpose. This was contrary to Paderewski's original proposal but
corresponded with Polish and international political realities.

Wieckowski left for Moscow in early March. He carried no peace proposals
from the government of Poland, but he did convey a letter from the Central
Committee of the Polish Socialist Party to the Central Committee of the Russian
Communist Party. Even this was an unpromising document as it did not once
mention the word "peace" or how it might be achieved. Instead it demanded an
end to Soviet interference in the internal affairs of Poland. Moscow, it said, had
to end its support of the Communist Party of Poland and liquidate the Polish
communist government established at Vilna. It also demanded self-determination
for the people of Lithuania and Belorussia, which could only be guaranteed after
the withdrawal of all foreign troops and the establishment of full political
freedom.[23]

The Soviet government gave this unorthodox document careful attention. Despite its ambiguity, they decided to use it as a basis for further negotiations with
Poland. Lenin instructed Chicherin to draft a new note to the Polish government
answering the charges contained in the letter of the Polish Socialist Party and
proposing concessions to their position. Chicherin handed this document to
Wieckowski on 24 March. In it he denied that Soviet Russia intended to invade
Poland and explained that no Polish communist government existed at Vilna or
anywhere else. The suggestion of a plebiscite in Lithuania and Belorussia was
treated more favourably. Soviet Russia, he said, considered it entirely suitable
that the "working people" of these regions be polled following the withdrawal
of foreign troops and would recommend to the Soviet governments of Lithuania
and Belorussia that they also accept this proposal. Chicherin also agreed to allow
all Polish prisoners held by the Soviet government to return home.[24]

It must be noted that, strictly speaking, Chicherin was telling the truth in
denying any Soviet intent to invade Poland. Similarly, there was no Polish
communist government at Vilna. What did exist there was a Lithuanian communist government which included many Polish communists. This government
harboured the most far-reaching ambitions regarding Poland and was only restrained from acting on them by the short rations and tight leash administered
by Moscow. Warsaw had good reason to complain of this government and of
the aid given to the Polish communist party by Moscow. Here, it is worth noting
that Chicherin did not even deny that Moscow provided this support. Given the
publicity surrounding the recently completed first congress of the Communist
International, he must have assumed it was pointless to do so.[25] The proposals
concerning plebiscites in Lithuania and Belorussia, however, are the most interesting portions of this document. It is true that such plebiscites together with
preliminary withdrawal of foreign troops constituted an integral part of the original Bolshevik foreign policy unveiled at Brest-Litovsk in 1917,[26] but following

the failure of that ill-starred conference little had been heard of this proposal. Now it was accepted, at least in principle, as the basis for settling the fate of two regions in which Soviet authority was far from secure.

Unfortunately, no Soviet leader has left us an explanation of this seemingly risky concession. Several possible explanations suggest themselves. It may not have been a serious proposal. Lenin may have decided that the Poles were unlikely to engage in actual negotiations and that it was safe to accept the proposed plebiscite as the surest way of obtaining a propaganda advantage in the struggle with Poland. Yet he would have had to reckon with the outside chance that the Poles might accept his offer. His specific limitation of the franchise in the proposed plebiscites to the "working people" of the regions would seem to suggest such a calculation. This, of course, was both good propaganda and a very real limitation of the liability assumed in accepting the proposal. "Working people" was a wonderfully elastic phrase and could be defined in a variety of ways. The same could be said of the term "foreign troops." Given the heterogeneity of the population of the borderlands, it would be difficult to determine which troops were foreign to the region. But even if all armed forces – Soviet and otherwise – were withdrawn, the Bolsheviks, with their deeply rooted party organization, would still retain a substantial advantage over all possible contenders. Even so, acceptance of the Polish proposal was a very risky venture uncharacteristic of Leninist policy in general. To be understood, therefore, it must be viewed within the context of the broader outlines of Soviet foreign policy in early 1919, one of seeking a second Brest-Litovsk, of buying peace with the allies. This suggests that the Kremlin was quite prepared to sacrifice Lithuania and Belorussia to obtain peace, not so much with Poland, as with the western powers. In their response to the Prinkipo proposal the Bolsheviks had certainly displayed a readiness to give up far more to secure their objective. Lithuania and Belorussia were most likely considered as simply added parts of the ransom which would have to be paid, in this instance to Poland, for an end to allied intervention.

This miniature Prinkipo collapsed with the larger venture. Just as the primary allied powers never responded to the Bolshevik answer to their Prinkipo invitation, the Poles ignored Chicherin's bid to open negotiations with them. Instead Pilsudski reinforced his eastern front and moved steadily deeper into Lithuania and Belorussia. This did not deflect the Bolsheviks from their effort to negotiate with Warsaw. They turned repeatedly to Wieckowski, asking him to urge his government to respond in some way to their peace initiative. When the Polish advance and that of the Red Army in Ukraine threatened to add a new dimension to the conflict, Chicherin sought to put Kiev in touch with Warsaw for the purpose of defining a frontier between Poland and Soviet Ukraine. All was to no avail, and in late April when Pilsudski, by a military ruse, succeeded in snatching Vilna from the Bolsheviks, the Soviet government decided to end the talks with Wieckowski. On 25 April he was told that his presence in Moscow would no longer serve any useful purpose. At the same time, however, Chicherin reaffirmed the readiness of the Soviet government to resume negotiations once the Polish government had ended military operations against the Soviet republics.[27]

Chicherin's assertion of continued readiness to negotiate with Poland was not mere rhetoric. Soviet leaders were well acquainted with Pilsudski, knew his love of political intrigue and the depths of his hatred for the old order in Russia. Despite the hostility between the Bolsheviks and Pilsudski, they shared certain basic interests. Most important was a common enemy, the White generals seeking to restore Russia one and indivisible. Xenophobic Russian chauvinism was a greater threat to Pilsudski's dream of a greater Polish state than revolutionary communism, and he was unlikely to contribute even indirectly to a White victory. The Whites wanted to confine Poland to its ethnographic frontiers and exclude it from Lithuania, Belorussia, and Ukraine. Pilsudski rejected these limits and looked with contempt upon Polish conservatives who were willing to accept this boundary in exchange for further expansion in the west at the expense of Germany. The French, in particular, favoured this solution of the Polish problem, and Pilsudski feared the support which Paris would give to a victorious White government in Russia.[28] But if the Whites were to replace the Bolsheviks, most, if not all, the western powers would back Russia rather than Poland in settling the fate of eastern Europe. Whatever role Poland would play in such a settlement, she was certain to be subordinate to Russia. There was also the question of Germany. In April 1919 it was unclear exactly what role Germany would play in future east European affairs but, potentially at least, it was a large and important one. If at the moment it appeared that Germany was more likely to cooperate with Poland than Soviet Russia, that could change quickly. It was important for both Pilsudski and Soviet Russia to retain a certain flexibility in their relations.

Until late May this flexibility remained more theoretical than real. But with the allied decision to recognize Kolchak and the possibility that Germany might refuse the allied peace terms, the worst of all contingencies suddenly loomed before Pilsudski – the simultaneous recrudescence of German militarism and Russian ultra-conservative chauvinism. His army was already fully engaged along both the western and eastern frontiers of Poland and would have found it difficult to expand its operations against Germany if that proved necessary. In these circumstances the appearance in Warsaw of Julian Marchlewski assumed major importance. Marchlewski, who had been forced to flee Germany and was seeking to reach Russia by way of Poland, took advantage of the hostility generated by allied recognition of Kolchak to make his presence known to Pilsudski. Through the intermediary of Josef Beck, the vice-minister of internal affairs, and his superior, Stanislaw Wojcechowski, he said that a community of interest had arisen between Poland and Soviet Russia. Pilsudski needed to free his army for possible use against Germany; Soviet Russia needed to reinforce its armies fighting Kolchak and Denikin. The basis for an agreement, however tentative, existed, and it should be explored by competent representatives of the two governments. By mid-June it was decided that Marchlewski should travel to Moscow and inform Lenin that Pilsudski was ready to enter into further secret and unofficial negotiations. On 18 June Marchlewski crossed the front into Soviet-held territory. The first step towards a de facto Soviet-Polish armistice had been taken.[29]

TO THE NORTH, ALONG the German-held front in Latvia, the Red Army was engaged for the entire first half of 1919. At the end of December 1918 it had appeared as if Germany would withdraw completely from the Baltic provinces, but in the new year their evacuation ceased. On 13 January the weak German forces in southern Latvia were ordered "to hold Libau under all circumstances and with all available means." This was no easy task as the means available consisted of only three thousand volunteers. Moreover, the Latvian population of Courland was hostile to both the Germans and the Latvian government, which they protected from the Red Army. Not that the Germans liked the Ulmanis regime which had taken shelter in Libau; they were too anglophile and unwilling to cater to German interests in Latvia.[30] The Germans, however, did hold Libau. In February substantial reinforcements began to arrive and by the end of the month General Rüdiger von der Goltz, the new German commander in Latvia, had at his disposal more than thirty thousand volunteers. This was more than sufficient to overawe the local population and permit the Germans to think of establishing a puppet government in Latvia. It also allowed them to turn decisively against the Bolsheviks. By early March the Red Army was retreating towards Riga while fending off an attack by combined Latvian and Estonian forces striking south towards Dvinsk.[31]

The Bolsheviks had no reserves and could not obtain reinforcement from other fronts. The best they could do was to make the most of available resources. In early February they subordinated the previously autonomous Latvian Red Army to the neighbouring Soviet Russian Seventh Army and a few days later, in a major re-organization, created a continuous western front extending from Estonia to the northern boundary of Soviet Ukraine.[32] This did nothing to restore the offensive capacity of the Red Army in the west, but it did allow a more orderly retreat eastward. Chicherin protested the resumption of German military action but with no effect. Berlin said Germany was only acting in its own defence and that of the bourgeois governments of Latvia and Lithuania.[33]

A similar situation had developed further north in the Baltic. There the initial Soviet success in Estonia had been reversed during the first days of 1919, and, by the end of February, virtually the entire province had been cleared of Bolsheviks. This had been done with the aid of Finnish volunteers. Helsingfors, capital of the newly independent Finland, had become a major centre of White

Russian activity, and Marshal Mannerheim, commander-in-chief of the Finnish army, made no secret of his ambition to lead a military expedition against Petrograd. Reports from Finland alarmed Soviet leaders, and in February Chicherin demanded an explanation for the frequent violation of the Soviet frontier and the many signs of an impending attack on Petrograd.[34] Helsingfors did not respond directly to Chicherin, but Minister-President Lauri Ingman, in answer to a parliamentary question on 21 February, denied that Finland was planning to attack Soviet Russia.[35] In fact Mannerheim had already told the British military attaché in Stockholm that he "would be ready to attack Petrograd with some 50,000 troops if he could receive a definite indication that Great Britain and France approved." Neither the British nor French governments showed any interest in the operation at this time, but this did not prevent Mannerheim from continuing to press allied representatives for western support.[36] The White Russians in Helsingfors who detested Finnish national aspirations as much as Bolshevism, opposed Mannerheim's plan but sought to interest Berlin in the idea of Germany organizing the armed liberation of Petrograd.[37] Rumours of both schemes circulated freely in Helsingfors and easily reached Moscow, increasing apprehension regarding the safety of the Soviet western frontier.

This apprehension reached its height in March 1919. Polish, German, Latvian, Lithuanian, Estonian, and Finnish troops had all taken the offensive and threatened to break the Soviet western front in several locations. Although not actually coordinated, these separate initiatives gave the appearance of being directed by a single command. Most menacing was the German offensive in Courland which soon led to the fall of Frauenburg and Mitau. The situation in the Baltic was made to appear all the more menacing by the simultaneous German announcement of their willingness to align themselves with the allies' Prinkipo policy[38] and the failure of the western powers to open negotiations with Soviet Russia. Prinkipo, in short, was beginning to take on a character hostile to a negotiated settlement at exactly the time Germany appeared ready to embrace it. The general staff now concluded that the western front posed the greatest threat to Soviet security. They were not impressed by the military potential of the Baltic states but were deeply fearful of Germany. They recommended that the entire strategic reserve of over eighty thousand men be committed to the defence of the western front.[39] On 16 March Stalin, clearly speaking for the Central Committee, published a lead article in *Izvestiia* saying that the failure of their direct intervention had only caused the allies to adapt a new form of attack. This was a "disguised form of armed intervention," more complicated than open intervention, "but on the other hand more 'convenient' for the 'civilized' and 'humane' Entente." Only yesterday, he said, Russia's neighbours had been "at each other's throats on the pleas of 'national' interests and national 'liberty,' each waging a 'patriotic war' against the others." But what did the 'fatherland' count for in comparison to the financial wealth of the Entente, once the latter had ordered the cessation of 'internecine warfare!' Once the Entente had ordered the establishment of a united front against Soviet Russia, could they, the hirelings of imperialism do anything but 'spring to attention!'"[40]

Here then was the danger. On 20 March Vatsetis warned Lenin that Germany, Poland, Lithuania, and Petliurist Ukraine were acting together against the Bolshevik western front. All available forces, they said, would have to be mobilized to meet this challenge.[41]

A transfer of reserves did begin in mid-month but was ended almost at once. Kolchak's offensive, launched on 5 March, was the immediate cause of this change in policy. Moscow had not initially taken this threat seriously, but confronted by near disaster found it necessary to transfer all available reserves to the east. Fortunately for the Bolsheviks, Kolchak's attack was not coordinated with military operations in the west. The belligerents along the Soviet western front were acting independently, and in March had simply stepped up their military operations to take advantage of the few weeks of favourable weather between the rigour of winter cold and the cloying mud of early spring. The Bolsheviks soon determined that the attacks had only tactical, rather than strategic, objectives. They could be dealt with separately and territory traded for time to deal with the strategic problems posed by the eastern front. Further retreat, therefore, continued to guide Soviet policy in the west.[41]

GERMANY REMAINED THE focus of Soviet concern, because in early 1919 the German government allowed their Russian policy to be shaped largely by the wishes of the allied powers. The Hungarian revolution and French evacuation of Ukraine reinforced this policy, for these events seemed to demand that the western powers seek German aid against the rising tide of Bolshevism.[42]

Logic seemed to justify this expectation; reality did not. As late as 18 April Rantzau was excited by reports that allied agents in the Baltic were seeking German aid against the Bolsheviks. "Germany welcomes this suggestion of a common defence against the Bolshevik danger," he responded, "and is prepared to advance on the Baltic and Lithuanian fronts in the manner suggested."[43] His optimism proved unwarranted. But the allies had not sought German aid against the Bolsheviks; Clemenceau would never have stood for it. He was well informed about the motivation of Berlin's well-advertised anti-Bolshevism, and would not play the German game. Instead, through stubborn refusal to modify his own objectives and by playing on Wilson's Polonophilia, he was able to convince the allies to impose still harsher terms upon Germany. The Germans thought that time was working in their favour, but it was not.[44]

It took the Germans a long time to realize this. Evidence, however, continued to mount, the most serious being the support the allies gave to Poland in her quest to wrench Prussia's eastern provinces from the Reich. For Germany this was doubly disturbing, for it could only diminish still further the possibility of cooperation against the Bolsheviks while again posing the threat of a two-front war should the peace negotiations end in failure. Until the end of April, however, none of this caused the German government to consider what should be done in such a situation or whether, in the interest of greater political flexibility, it should not modify its policy of modulated belligerence against Soviet Russia.

Moscow answered hostility with hostility. The Soviet press highlighted German social disorder and greeted each revolutionary explosion with enthusiasm. Prominent Soviet leaders expressed their satisfaction in mid-April when a questionable Soviet republic was proclaimed in Bavaria. Zinoviev, speaking as president of the Executive Committee of the newly formed Communist International, sent his "warmest greetings" to the new republic and proclaimed "that the time is not far off when the whole of Germany will be a Soviet Republic."[45] This did not prevent the Soviet government from renewing its effort to interest Berlin in the opening of negotiations. The steadily worsening conflict between Poland and Germany led Moscow to believe the Germans might be more receptive to peace proposals in April than in February. Thus, on 17 April Chicherin again radioed Berlin, cataloguing his earlier efforts to initiate negotiations, protesting the German failure to take any notice of them and reaffirming that they still held good.[46]

This message struck a responsive note in the German government, especially among those ministers who had begun to sense that their original foreign policy was a failure. Foremost among these were August Winnig, the plenipotentiary for the Baltic states, and Matthias Erzberger, the chairman of the German Armistice Commission. Both favoured at least an armistice with Soviet Russia. On 24 April, with General Groener present, the German government debated the issue. Groener and Rantzau rehearsed all the arguments previously raised against the restoration of ties with Moscow, but the contrary proposition, previously unargued, now came forward. Erzberger said only the allies would benefit from a long struggle in the east. Winnig hoped an armistice with the Bolsheviks would turn the allies against Poland. Nevertheless, the impending departure of the German peace delegation for Versailles proved sufficient to prevent a change of policy. Rantzau insisted that "until the conclusion of peace the chief aim [of German policy in the East] had to remain the struggle against Bolshevism"; any other policy could only worsen the peace terms the allied powers would impose on Germany.[47]

Allied intentions were obvious when the Germans arrived at Versailles on 7 May. The hostility and courtroom-like proceedings to which they were subjected made it clear that the allies had prepared a punitive peace. Rantzau had come prepared. While remaining seated, to avoid the appearance of a prisoner in the dock, he read an uncompromising statement objecting to the way in which the allies were preparing to dictate peace. He then stalked from the room, only stopping at the door to light a cigarette. The statement and Rantzau's demeanour infuriated the allied leaders. Lloyd George was left speechless, while Clemenceau barely restrained himself from physically assaulting the count. Wilson kept repeating "Truly, these people are absolutely stupid." [48] A new and hermetic seal had been placed on the hatred and hostility dividing Germany from the western powers.

German minds turned to thoughts of resistance. Germany had been forced to demobilize, but the allied armies had been greatly diminished since November and, with the recruitment of volunteers, German numbers had begun to rise again. The immediate threat appeared to come from Pilsudski. Therefore, one day after receiving the proposed peace treaty, the German government decided to withdraw its troops from the Baltic so as to concentrate them against Poland. [49] This decision was laden with the most far-reaching implications. Military withdrawal meant an end to German political influence in the Baltic. Moreover, an agreement with Soviet Russia was the necessary concommitant of military withdrawal from the Baltic. None of this was wanted in Berlin and served to sap the resolve of the German government to implement their decision. Thus, Berlin agreed that German forces should merely be withdrawn from the front but need not be returned at once to the Reich. [50]

General von der Goltz was on the verge of launching a major offensive in Latvia against the Bolsheviks. He knew the Soviet position was weak, and expected to drive them from Riga and perhaps the Baltic as a whole. In mid-April, in preparing for this offensive, he had arrested the Latvian bourgeois government and replaced them with a puppet regime of German Balts. This had been done without the approval of the German government who, on allied insistence, had refused to recognize the new Latvian administration. Berlin, however, had not insisted on the restoration of the Ulmanis cabinet or interfered with the general's close association with ultra-conservative Russian military organizations in Latvia. Von der Goltz hoped to join with these groups in overthrowing Bolshevism in Russia. When he objected sharply to the withdrawal of his troops from Latvia, he was summoned to Berlin and bluntly told that Germany could not fight Poland, the allies, and Soviet Russia simultaneously. His troops were urgently needed to defend the territorial integrity of the Reich. This appeal to common sense and patriotism made little impact on him, and he returned to Latvia determined to accelerate his plans. On 22 May he launched his attack, occupying Riga the same day. [51]

The fall of Riga sowed panic throughout eastern Europe. Seen as recrudescent German militarism allied with Russian ultra-conservatism, it frightened every regime in the area. Lenin warned that it might be part of the "build-up of a determined general offensive along the entire western front," and urged Trotsky to accelerate Soviet military operations elsewhere so as to free troops for possible use in the Baltic. Bourgeois governments also felt threatened, especially that of Estonia, whose armed forces pushing south into Latvia soon clashed with those of von der Goltz north of Riga. Western leaders quickly came to view the German offensive as part of a larger plan to opppose the peace terms about to be imposed

on the Reich. In mid-June, therefore, the peace conference demanded the withdrawal of all German forces from Latvia and the restoration of the former Ulmanis
government in Riga.[52]

The German government had also been surprised by the arbitrary action of
von der Goltz. The day before the seizure of Riga, in fact, they had decided to
initiate armistice negotiations with the Bolsheviks to allow the rapid withdrawal
of their troops from Latvia. This was no longer possible, and Berlin was suddenly
confronted with widening warfare in the Baltic and the mounting anger of the
western powers. While the German government remained uncertain whether they
would accept the allied peace terms, they were reluctant to act forcefully against
von der Goltz. Only when they decided to sign the treaty and after the allies
made peace contingent on German withdrawal from Latvia did Berlin reinvoke
its authority. On 26 June an allied commission arrived in Libau and announced
the restoration of the Ulmanis government.[53] Von der Goltz and his troops soon
left Latvia, but a large number of German adventurers remained behind to bedevil
the tormented population.

ALLIED HOSTILITY VIRTUALLY compelled Berlin to turn to Soviet Russia.
Ironically, given allied fears of Russo-German cooperation, the insistence that
Germany evacuate Latvia simply facilitated the eventual rapprochement. German
withdrawal liquidated the armed conflict between the two and insulated them
against its imminent resumption. This left them free to contemplate the many
enemies they had in common. Yet rapprochement did not come easily. Even
when confronted by the draft treaty at Versailles, Rantzau would not turn to
Moscow. Previously he had feared alienating the western powers. Now he was
concerned about the situation in Russia. "So long as developments in Russia
can not be foreseen," he wrote on 17 May, official contact with the Bolsheviks
"must unconditionally be avoided."[54] If Kolchak defeated the Bolsheviks, Germany did not want to be on the side of the losers. Thus, when Rantzau learned
that the allied powers were preparing to recognize Kolchak's regime, he agreed
that trustworthy Russians sympathetic to Germany should be sent to Omsk. They
were to tell Kolchak that the German government possessed no ties with the
Bolsheviks and to report back to Berlin about the situation in Siberia.[55]

It was true that Berlin had no ties with the Bolsheviks, but following publication of the allied peace terms it began to listen carefully to the views of
the Soviet government. First contact was made on 12 May when Fritz Deck
of the *Frankfurter Zeitung* reported from Stockholm to Victor Naumann, chief
of the Auswärtiges Amt intelligence department, that he had been approached
by Karl Moor, who had just arrived in Sweden on his way home to Switzerland
from Russia. During the war Moor had been an active confidant of the German
Foreign Office, but since 1917 he had entered into an increasingly close relationship with the Bolsheviks.[54] He was, therefore, the ideal individual to convey
the views of the Soviet government to Berlin. Moor told Deck that the Soviet

government was eager to come to terms with Germany. Germany, he said, would have to recognize "that today there was only *one* country, Soviet Russia, where the Entente really had no influence." Germany's entire Russian policy, and especially the campaign in the Baltic, was nothing but "manifest folly." If Germany hoped to escape Versailles, she would have to work with Soviet Russia. Coming as this did at the height of Kolchak's success, Deck was clearly moved to inquire of the life expectancy of the Soviet regime. Moor responded that "no other Russians could compete with Lenin and his Bolsheviks, and there was no way the Entente could even begin to conquer Russia." Lenin and Chicherin, he concluded, were Russian statesmen with whom Germany could work successfully.[57] Naumann was not convinced by these assertions, but he advised Rantzau that it would be an error to leave the allies with the impression that under no circumstances would Germany turn to Moscow. The western powers feared a Russo-German alliance, and it was necessary to play on this fear. "It goes without saying," he concluded, "and I again emphasize this, that I am not thinking of an alliance, but only of a warning shot [einen vorläufigen Schreckschuss]."[58]

When Moor reached Berlin in early June Nauman gave him a three-hour interview. He urged Berlin to settle its differences with Soviet Russia. This would "strike terror in the hearts of the Entente," for "they feared nothing more than the formation of an eastern league of nations." It was not necessary to speak directly of such an alliance; it would be better "to send a skilled man to Lenin in order to discuss the future with him." Moor volunteered to accompany a German representative to Moscow. Naumann endorsed this proposal. "Truly, we have nothing to lose, and we could gain something," he concluded.[59]

Rantzau still hesitated. Only when he learned that Kolchak had suffered a serious defeat was he ready to explore the possibility of resumed relations with Moscow. Writing to the economics minister on 12 June, Rantzau endorsed the restoration of economic relations, saying this should be done "as soon and to the greatest extent possible," allowing even that such a restoration might pose the danger of "unwanted [read: revolutionary] elements' becoming active in Germany." As a first step he recommended that a commission be sent to Moscow to investigate conditions there and advise the government on how best to promote a restoration of commercial relations.[60]

This was the end of Rantzau's official role in the reversal of Germany's policy in Russia. Within a week the allied demand that Germany sign an only slightly altered peace treaty precipitated a cabinet crisis. Rantzau resigned when the government accepted the allied ultimatum. His proposed commission was never formed, and no German representative went to Moscow for the confidential talks recommended by Moor. Apparently realizing that the new government was unlikely to proceed in the manner he favoured, Rantzau decided to facilitate whatever efforts Soviet Russia might make towards the restoration of relations with Germany. Thus, before leaving office he unofficially sanctioned the arrival in Germany of Victor Kopp as a special agent of the Soviet government. Kopp had been a member of Ioffe's embassy in 1918 and now returned to promote the rapprochement of the two governments.[61] Rantzau also seems to have been instrumental in initiating the release of Karl Radek from prison. On 28 June, the day Germany signed the Versailles treaty, the Auswärtiges Amt informed Moscow that they were prepared to allow Radek to return to Russia.[60]

SIX MONTHS HAD PASSED since Germany had initiated an actively hostile policy against Soviet Russia and for most of these months Moscow was a spectator. The initial energy which she invested in the sweep through the borderlands could not be sustained; her resources were needed elsewhere. Throughout early 1919 her military position in the west deteriorated, and by the summer most of her territorial gains had been lost and she was faced with the prospect of losing still more. Paradoxically, her political position actually improved during this period, because allied policies or the absence of them promoted Bolshevik interests along the Soviet western frontier. The inability of the allies to formulate a common Russian policy not only crippled their own action but demoralized the successor states of eastern Europe and left them without guidance. The few clear-cut policies the allies managed to shape at Versailles also benefited the Bolsheviks. Every snub the allies administered to Germany and every punitive clause written into the peace treaty lessened the chance of the belligerents combining against Soviet Russia. Similarly, the belated recognition of Kolchak drove Pilsudski straight into Bolshevik arms. With both Germany and Poland neutralized, the Bolsheviks had little to fear in the west, and, precisely as in 1918, they were able to strip their western marches of troops to reinforce the dangerously im- perilled east.

The Bolsheviks, however, did not rely simply on allied ineptness to defend their western frontier. Despite their incessant hostile propaganda against the governments of Germany and Poland, they never closed the door to improved relations with either state. To the contrary, Chicherin stressed repeatedly that Soviet Russia was ready at any time to open negotiations with Berlin and Warsaw. Nor did the Soviet government withdraw these offers when provoked by such unexpected blows as the seizure of Vilna or the fall of Riga. The Soviet gov- ernment watched events unfold in the west and followed each allied blunder with a renewed bid to open negotiations. Success came only when Germany could hope for nothing but allied hostility and Pilsudski feared the western powers were preparing to abandon him for Kolchak. At mid-year the Germans had nowhere else to go but to Moscow; Pilsudski had other options but still felt it wise to open clandestine talks with the Bolsheviks. By the end of June it was clear that, in the near future, neither would be a part of an anti-Bolshevik crusade. This was of enormous value to the Bolsheviks, for without Germany and Poland it would be impossible to launch an attack against Soviet Russia from the west. At mid-year 1919, therefore, Moscow could breathe much easier than even two months before.

CHAPTER SIX

"The Intruder" : Soviet Russia
and the final months
of the Paris peace conference

Two months after convening, the Paris peace conference had made no progress toward the solution of the Russian problem. When President Wilson and Lloyd George returned to France they found the problem as intractable as ever. The allied powers were unable to agree on a common policy. Nor did they possess the resources to act effectively in the east. Events there continued to unfold independently of their will and in ways profoundly disturbing to them. Into this morass Bullitt returned on 25 March with Lenin's peace proposals. Bullitt believed these proposals would form the basis of peace in eastern Europe. They did not because, despite his extensive concessions, Lenin would not compromise on essential elements of his dispute with the western leaders. He would not recognize the moral authority of their power. Still less would he create a bourgeois democracy in Russia. He would recognize only the reality of their power. He was prepared to pay a very high price, in terms of territory and economic resources, to be left alone, but he would pay it only as a victim pays a criminal to spare his life. Allied leaders would not accept this. Only unqualified recognition of their moral authority and legitimate right to settle the peace would satisfy them. Lloyd George, more the realist than the others, would probably have tolerated Bolshevik insolence to obtain some semblance of peace. Neither Wilson nor Clemenceau would hear of it.[1]

In the void left by the rejection of Bullitt's plan, Herbert Hoover, director of the American Relief Administration, then feeding half of Europe, stepped forward to make his own proposals. When Wilson learned of Hoover's interest in the problem he instructed House to talk to him "and see whether we could get ships and food to Russia in the event we wished to do so." In a memorandum of 28 March Hoover proposed two lines of action: "First: We cannot even remotely recognize this murderous tyranny ... Second: That some neutral of international reputation for probity and ability should be allowed to create a

second Belgian Relief Commission for Russia." With allied help such an individual would "enter upon the humane work of saving life" in Russia through
the supply of food and medicine to her suffering people. The individual chosen
would be told "that we will raise no objection and would even help in his
humanitarian task if he gets assurances that the Bolsheviki will cease all militant
action across certain defined boundaries and cease their subsidizing of disturbances abroad." Hoover stressed that his plan did not "involve any recognition
of relationship by the Allies of the Bolshevik murderers" and if accepted by
Moscow would "at least give a period of rest along the frontiers of Europe and
would give some hope of stabilization."[2]

It is easy to see why these ideas appealed to Wilson. They allowed him to
step away from the Bullitt proposals without moving in the direction of military
intervention. They gave him a policy when he had none. They armed him with
a response to the importunate demand of his associates for a means of dealing
with the Russian question. Thus, he could continue to play for time in the hope
that the political circumstances of eastern Europe might soon take a turn favourable to the promotion of bourgeois liberalism.

Fridtjof Nansen, the Norwegian explorer long active in humanitarian affairs,
was the "neutral of international reputation" whom Hoover had in mind to head
his relief commission. He had already discussed the proposal with Nansen and
prepared a letter in which the Norwegian addressed an appeal to the major allied
leaders asking for their permission to establish "a purely humanitarian commission for the provisioning of Russia composed of Scandinavian and other neutral
representatives." If thus organized, he said, "it would raise no question of
political recognition or negotiations between the Allies with the existing authorities in Russia." Nansen sent the letters on 3 April.[3] Discussion within the
American delegation now centred on how to respond to their own request. The
more conservative delegates wished to require the Bolsheviks to suspend hostilities and place the Russian railway system under the control of the neutral
commission prior to receiving the promised aid. Bullitt warned House that the
Bolsheviks would not accept these conditions. He proposed a call for a general
armistice and a conference of representatives of all governments accepting it
with those of the allied powers to meet in Christiania on 25 April "to discuss
peace and the provisioning of Russia" on the basis of principles similar to those
contained in his own agreement with Lenin. This proposal was brushed aside,
but Bullitt's narrower objections were heeded. The final document, approved by
Wilson on 6 April, proposed that the allied powers inform Nansen that they
were prepared to guarantee transport of relief supplies to Russia but believed
that "the problem of distribution should be solely under the control of the people
of Russia themselves." Successful relief, the response concluded, would depend
upon "cessation of all hostilities within the territory of the former Russian
Empire." That cessation would include "a complete suspension of the transfer of
troops and military material of all sorts to and within these territories."[4]

The Americans had decided on a policy; now they had to secure its acceptance by the allies. The British and Italians readily agreed; the French found it wanting in every respect. It was impossible, they concluded, even for the Americans to feed all of Russia; if they could, ships were not available to carry the grain; if they should become available, finance would prove impossible. The conditions which the Americans attached to the offer were either unworkable or unacceptable. There was simply no way for all hostilities to cease in such a chaotic struggle as the Russian civil war and consequently the suspension of allied aid to the anti-Bolshevik armies "would result in the destruction of the only forces organized in Russia against anarchy."[5] On 14 April Hoover met privately with Pichon, the French foreign minister. He called his attention to the most recent reports from the Black Sea where the Romanians feared they were about to be overwhelmed by the Bolsheviks. "We must not reject arrangements," he said, "which despite certain inconveniences appear to offer a final hope of stability or at least a way of avoiding that the situation grows worse." Pichon complained that the proposal seemed to require an end to allied aid to the anti-Bolsheviks. Hoover agreed, but argued that since all military operations would cease neither side would suffer disadvantage. He also said that allied aid had not been effective. Ukraine had fallen, and the Crimea seemed about to be lost. Pichon replied heatedly that the French withdrawal from southern Russia had been "voluntary" and emphasized that the allies should avoid the appearance of abandoning their friends in Russia. He would offer no more than a conditional acceptance of the Nansen proposals.[6] Two days later, in a letter to Hoover, he specified that the operation had to be conducted only in the name of Nansen and that it not be permitted to work in any way against the vital interests of those Russians faithful to the allies. Pichon also insisted that Nansen undertake a tour of inspection in Russia to verify that he could fulfill the mission outlined in his letter.[7] He did this, a Quai d'Orsay memorandum tells us, "to play for time."[8] Delay, in fact, became the basis of the French response. Even after Clemenceau signed the document on 16 April the Quai d'Orsay refused to transmit the proposal to Russia; Hoover had to have it sent by a Dutch transmitter. Its adoption by the Council of Four, however, marked the end of earlier American peace initiatives. It represented "the total result of our efforts," Bullitt told one of his associates, "and I am rather ashamed of it."[9]

In Britain conservative opinion witnessed these developments with mounting alarm. Those who favoured a clear cut anti-Bolshevik policy were fewer than those who opposed intervention, but they were better placed to make their influence felt. Churchill was still first among those who urged a more vigorous Russian policy, and his views were shared by a large number of the Conservative members elected to the new Parliament in December. This gave him an important means of bringing pressure to bear on Lloyd George, especially when the Conservative press, *The Times* in the van, joined in the anti-Bolshevik refrain. For this reason Lloyd George took great care to deny all knowledge of Bullitt and his mission. When rumours of it reached the press tension mounted, and on 9 April more than two hundred furious Conservative back-benchers wired the prime minister demanding an explanation of his Russian policy. Lloyd George had to return to London and face the House of Commons.

The prime minister was equal to the task. When he rose to speak on 16 April he knew that he would have to give ground before the anger of the Conservative backbenchers, but he had no intention of surrendering to them. The Russian problem was far more complex than they could imagine and he barricaded himself in that complexity as his surest defence. His speech was rambling, illogical, and shot through with internal inconsistencies; it displayed great ignorance of Russia and made no effort to answer the more serious critics of his conduct in Paris. Yet, from a political point of view, it was a great success, because the Conservative backbenchers embraced no more logical or consistent policy than he did and knew even less about Russia. Lloyd George ignored logic and spoke to the deepest emotions of the House.

First he spoke of the horrors of Bolshevism and reassured his listeners that there was no question of recognizing the Soviet government. Then he built a back-fire of emotional arguments to stem the advance of those who wished to enlarge intervention. Not only was interference in the internal affairs of another nation, no matter how deplorable its government, against the "best tradition of British foreign policy," it was also, in the case of Russia, very dangerous. "Russia," he warned, "is a country which it is very easy to invade, but very difficult to conquer." As he spoke, the House could almost see the Grand Army of Napoleon limping back to France in the midst of a howling blizzard with the army of Hindenburg close behind. He warned of the cost of intervention. "I share the horror of all the Bolsheviks' teachings," he emphasized, "but I would rather leave Russia Bolshevik until she sees her way out of it than see Britain bankrupt. And that is the surest road to Bolshevism in Britain ... to attempt military intervention in Russia would be the greatest act of stupidity that any government could possibly commit." Russia, he asserted, could only be redeemed by her own sons. Britain would not abandon those Russians who were fighting the Bolsheviks, for they had stood by the allies in the last year of the war. All the anti-Bolsheviks asked was that they be provided with the weapons to continue their fight; Britain would not deny them these weapons. This he claimed with an absolutely straight face was "not in the least regard ... a departure from the fundamental policy of Great Britain not to interfere in the internal affairs of any land." Britain was merely helping her friends to protect themselves against a common enemy.

Lloyd George had one last hurdle to overcome before he could leave the House safely. In the question period he was asked directly about the newspaper reports concerning contact with the Bolsheviks. He met this challenge by denying all knowledge of any approach to the Bolsheviks.[10] But who was to call him a liar?

More importantly, who would openly call for the continuation of conscription and higher taxes to wage war in Russia? Profoundly suspicious of the prime minister and even more disappointed that they could not get a firm hold upon him, the Conservative majority had to content themselves with his statement.

In the next two months Lloyd George changed course. Whereas before he had favoured a modus vivendi with Soviet Russia, he now turned to their opponents and, despite his words about avoiding armed intervention, tolerated at least a temporary increase in the number of British troops in Russia. This was due in part to political expediency. Lloyd George was not one to stand rigidly in the midst of a political storm, and in mid-April he had weathered a genuine gale. But the situation in Russia had also changed. Until then the Bolsheviks possessed the only government exercising genuine authority over any significant extent of territory. The anti-Bolsheviks simply did not have credible governments able to inspire confidence in their life expectancy. In March this began to change. The regime at Omsk under Admiral Kolchak began to take on more characteristics of a real government and gain some control over the territory it claimed to rule. More important, it survived the Bolshevik military challenge and then took the offensive.[11] When this proved successful, Kolchak began to be taken seriously by Lloyd George and the other allied leaders. At last it appeared that the peace conference had a congenial alternative to the Bolsheviks. Lloyd George needed no urging; he turned gladly to Kolchak.

Wilson reacted similarly. He was even less inclined than Lloyd George to deal with the Bolsheviks but could not exclude the possibility as long as they remained the most substantial power in Russia. Now he began to receive information indicating that Kolchak might defeat the Bolsheviks. For Wilson it was important that Kolchak establish a regime compatible with his own liberal ideas. Thus, it was especially heartening that his representatives reported that "Kolchak seems sincerely committed to the good of Russia reorganizing policies of liberal character with possible personal preference for constitutional monarchy rather than for Republic, but not at all in favour of old type of government."[12]

The British were less interested in Kolchak's ideas, real or imaginary. They were delighted, however, by his victories, and as early as 5 April Sir Charles Eliot, their representative in Omsk, called for the recognition of Kolchak's regime as the "Provisional Government for Siberia."[13] The imperial general staff and the Foreign Office both agreed and advised Lloyd George that such recognition would encourage the admiral and enhance his prestige.[14] When Lloyd George did not respond promptly Churchill wrote him on 26 April, strongly recommending recognition. His only criticism was that recognition should be limited to Siberia. He wanted the Omsk regime recognized as the "National Provisional Government of all Russia." The word "national" was the key, for it drew "a clear distinction from the International character of the Bolshevik Government." Recognition, however, was the important thing, and "if the Prime Minister preferred 'National Provisional Government of Siberia' that would be better than nothing." Churchill urged Lloyd George to act promptly, adding meaningfully, "I need scarcely say how extremely advantageous the recognition of Kolchak's Government would be among the political forces in the House of Commons on which you are relying." [15]

The recognition of Kolchak's government was not the only ambitious aspect of Churchill's plans. In March he had reluctantly agreed to the evacuation of British forces from north Russia. Now he proposed to convert that evacuation into a triumphal offensive to link up with Kolchak's army. In April the far right wing of Kolchak's army was approaching Glazov, and he hoped to be in Kotlas by June. [16] The Imperial General Staff had prepared a plan for British forces at Archangel to reach Kotlas at about the same time. A junction there would link two of the three major anti-Bolshevik armies, open communication with Kolchak through northern Russia, and serve as a base for further operations against Vologda. Together with the continued advance of Kolchak's other forces in the direction of Kazan and Nizhni Novgorod, the junction in the north would pose a genuine threat to Moscow. Churchill, therefore, set about seeking approval for the operation. "Don't be vexed with me about my Kolchak," he wrote the prime minister on 28 April, "There really is a good chance of his pulling the chestnuts out of the fire for all of us." He sent the chief of the Imperial General Staff to Paris to discuss the proposal with the prime minister. Sir Henry Wilson reported on 2 May that if Kolchak's army reached Viatka and moved up the railway towards Kotlas, Lloyd George would not object to a British force from north Russia being sent up the Dvina river to join them. The cabinet would have to be consulted first. Churchill took this as sufficient warrant to authorize General Ironside on 4 May to make the necessary preparations to advance. Meanwhile he began to organize a strong relief force for north Russia. This force, composed entirely of volunteers, was to form the spearhead of the British assault on Kotlas.

In early May, as the peace conference moved towards recognition of Kolchak, the fate of the Nansen scheme had still not been decided. The Whites and their western supporters, however, did not find it attractive. Churchill said he was "utterly unable to understand how we can feed the Bolsheviks with the one hand and fight them with the other." [17] Kolchak expressed his uneasiness about the scheme and feared it was "directed against himself and his movement." [18] It was "absolutely impossible for any anti-Bolshevik government to accept an armistice," reported the British minister at Archangel. If food was available to feed Russia it should be stock-piled behind the front lines and distributed as soon as a region was cleared of the Bolsheviks. "Knowledge that these supplies existed," he said, "would have an immense effect on the population of districts in the rear of Bolshevist forces, and if it did not turn them into active supporters of Kolchak would ensure his and our men a warm welcome." [19] The Whites would have nothing to do with the Nansen proposal.

WHAT OF THE BOLSHEVIKS? They did not learn officially of the proposal until 4 May when it was finally broadcast from the Netherlands. They did, however, monitor unofficial radio broadcasts reporting the scheme and, as early as 23 April, informed foreign journalists in Moscow that they did not like what they heard. There was no mention of either peace negotiations or lifting the blockade. They were no more pleased with the official proposal when it arrived. Lenin instructed Chicherin to "use it *for propaganda*, because it is clear that we *can not* use it in any other way. Treat Nansen with utmost politeness while being *ultra-insolent* with Wilson, Lloyd George and Clemenceau ... that is the *only* proper tone with them." He suggested that the response be divided into sections, one dealing with the humanitarian aspect of the proposal and the other with its political implications. The first should be "grateful and complimentary to Nansen *personally* while making it clear that the portion of his proposal which called for an armistice in Russia was clearly political." "Explain to him," Lenin instructed Chicherin, "as to a 16 year old girl, why an armistice is *politics*." Lenin also wanted to use the Soviet response as a vehicle to expose the agreement recently concluded with Bullitt. Clearly, the Foreign Commissariat did not share his view, for Lenin added in the margin of his note that if they disagreed with this suggestion they could delete it. There could be no question of an armistice which confused political and humanitarian concerns and did not aim at the conclusion of peace.[20]

Chicherin constructed his response around this framework. He welcomed the proposal to feed the people of Russia but pointedly rejected the call for an armistice. "We need not explain to you," he told Nansen, "that military operations which obviously have in view to change external or internal conditions of the involved countries belong wholly to the domain of politics and that likewise cessation of hostilities which means preventing the belligerent who has every reason to expect successes from obtaining them is also a purely political act." The Soviet government sincerely wanted an end to hostilities but only within the context of being able to "discuss the whole question of our relations to our adversaries." The Soviet government had proved this willingness by agreeing to meet with the allies at Prinkipo. The only reference to Bullitt came at this point as Chicherin added mysteriously, "We responded in the same peace-loving sense to overtures made by one of the Great Powers." None of the Soviet peace proposals had been accepted, he continued, and thus the war, which was being conducted by the Soviet government "with ever growing success," had to continue. The Soviet government could not "make any concessions referring to these fundamental problems of our existence under the disguise of a presumably humanitarian work. The latter would have to remain purely humanitarian and non-political." As such a work, however, he expressed the willingness of the Soviet government to give Nansen every possibility of controlling the realization of his plan and would pay "all the expenses of the work and the cost of the foodstuffs." Nansen, he concluded, should set a time and place for Soviet representatives to meet him abroad to discuss the provisioning of Russia with food and relief supplies.[21]

The Soviet message reflected the considerable disappointment felt in Moscow that nothing had come of the Bullitt proposals. They had carried with them Bolshevik hopes for a quick end to allied intervention in the civil war. Moscow was confident that the end of intervention would lead to the collapse of the White armies. Thus allied failure to accept the Bullitt proposals meant the civil war would continue indefinitely. Such a prospect easily generated the desire, sharply expressed by Lenin, to make some use of the Nansen proposal if only for propaganda purposes. Chicherin did so, arraigning the allies as hypocrites and pointing again at the devious ways of western governments. The most interesting aspect of his response, however, was the evident confidence it reflected that the Soviet government, despite the military situation in Siberia, was actually winning the civil war. Throughout late March and much of April Soviet leaders had viewed Siberia with mounting concern, but as troops were shifted to the eastern front and counter-measures began to take shape, Moscow concluded the situation there would soon be brought under control. They learned that Kolchak's forces had no reserves, and, once the front was broken, it was likely to collapse entirely. The Kolchak offensive was a soap bubble waiting to be pricked.[22] The Soviet counter-attack had already begun when Chicherin penned his response to Nansen, and he could, therefore, write with some little confidence about Soviet military prospects.

Lloyd George was the only allied leader to grasp the significance of Chicherin's words. In a meeting of the Council of Four on 19 May he asked his colleagues if they had seen the Soviet telegram and what they thought of Kolchak's victories. "By refusing the armistice posed as a condition for relief Lenin gives us to understand that it is he who is advancing."[23] No one responded, perhaps because they did not wish even to consider the possibility that Lenin might yet defeat Kolchak. Virtually all western leaders shared a common relief that the Soviet rejection of the Nansen scheme freed them from further dealings with the Bolsheviks. When Hoover told the French that he considered the proposal to be "dead and buried" the Quai d'Orsay gleefully transmitted this good news to all their major diplomatic outposts throughout the world. Nansen created momentary consternation when he announced his intention to proceed to Petrograd to continue negotiations with the Soviet government, but Hoover hastily stepped in and warned him that he considered it "extremely inadvisable to arrange any meeting with Bolshevik representatives" until the question was further considered by the allied leaders.[24]

Throughout May the peace conference continued to give active consideration to the Russian question. Events in Siberia encouraged Churchill, and he applied steady pressure on the allied leaders in Paris. "I feel convinced that now is the time," he wrote Lloyd George on 7 May, "and that if the opportunity is lost Kolchak may either become too weak to be of any use or too strong to require our advice." The Whites clamoured for Kolchak's recognition, warned allied representatives of the increasing hostility of all Russians towards the entente, and boasted that Russia would "have lots of friends when Kolchak gets to Nizhni-Novgorod."[25] Lloyd George called his colleagues' attention to the pro-German sentiment rampant among the Whites and thought it wise to attach political conditions to any further aid given them. Wilson suggested that the Council of Four "should demand a programme of reforms and insist that our continued support depended on its being adopted." Lloyd George agreed heartily, saying that "the Allies should prevent Russia from becoming Imperial again. He himself feared that more than he did Bolshevism." Clemenceau spoke up to say that he was afraid of both, which led Wilson to explain what he thought was the essential difference between the two dangers. "Bolshevism must collapse," he said, "whereas an Imperial Russia might remain."[26]

When the Council of Four next turned to the issue on 20 May they first agreed that the Nansen proposal was dead and then proceeded to what must have been the frankest discussion of the Russian question during the entire peace conference. In the opinion of Clemenceau, now that the Whites were winning, it was time to base a policy on them. Wilson pointed out that the allies could cut off all aid to Kolchak if they wished, and in this way bring him to do their bidding. He proposed that "pledges could be exacted for further support." Clemenceau and Lloyd George agreed. They sent for Philip Kerr to draft a dispatch to be sent Kolchak specifying the conditions on which the allies would continue their support for him. Kerr was told they wanted assurances from Kolchak that he would summon the Constituent Assembly and create a democratic government in Russia after his army reached Moscow. Wilson declared he did not want a restoration of the autocracy or anything like tsarism. Kerr asked what promises could be given Kolchak to encourage him to give these undertakings. Lloyd George said "it was not a question of promising more, but of continuing the assistance which was now given," and Wilson added that the despatch "should intimate that without satisfactory guarantees no further help would be given."[27] The four undoubtedly felt great satisfaction that they could dictate terms to Kolchak rather than have to receive insults and implied bribes from Lenin.

Their satisfaction was short-lived. On 23 May they learned that the Japanese government, who had not been party to their discussions, was preparing to recognize the Kolchak regime as the provisional government of Russia. The allies had no wish to see the Japanese take the initiative in Russia, and therefore they decided to examine immediately the draft declaration prepared by Philip Kerr. It reaffirmed that the "cardinal axiom" of allied policy was "to avoid interference in the internal affairs of Russia" while seeking to aid the Russian people to restore "peace and order" in their land. Their experience of the past year had convinced them "that it was not possible to secure self-government or peace for Russia by dealings with the Soviet government of Moscow"; they were, therefore, disposed to assist Kolchak with munitions, supplies, food, and other help provided they received guarantees that his policy had the same ends as those of the allied powers. Kolchak was to accept seven major undertakings: to summon a freely elected constituent assembly when his armies reached Moscow; to allow free elections for local assemblies in areas he already controlled; not to attempt "to revive the special privileges of any class or order in Russia"; to recognize the independence of Finland and Poland; to submit the solution of unresolved relations between Estonia, Latvia, Lithuania, and the Caucasian and Transcaspian territories and Russia to the League of Nations; to join the League of Nations; and to recognize the responsibility of Russia to pay her past debts. This declaration was adopted and submitted to the Japanese who were urged to join the western powers in sending it to Kolchak. The Japanese agreed, and on 26 May the despatch was issued under the signature of the five allied leaders in Paris.[28]

THE ALLIES HAD FINALLY agreed upon a policy for Russia. Its success, however, depended upon Kolchak's ability to defeat the Bolsheviks. Would he win the Russian civil war? Lloyd George continued to doubt it. On 24 May he asked Lieutenant-Colonel F.H. Kisch, Britain's military intelligence specialist in Russian affairs, if there was any substance to Soviet claims of recent military victories near Samara. Kisch said these gains were insignificant. The Red Army lacked rolling stock and fuel, he said, and it would be impossible for them to move their troops eastward. "In the south it is possible that the Bolshevik advance will continue," he said, "but once the Siberian troops arrive at Viatka, the Bolsheviks will doubtlessly retire to the west of the line Viatka-Kotlas, and Kolchak will join the troops from Archangel at Kotlas." He thought this would lead to the fall of Vologda, which in turn would open direct communications between the Urals and the Baltic.[29]

This appreciation fitted perfectly with the plans of the British War Office but had nothing in common with reality. Even as Kisch spoke the Siberian army was in full retreat, hotly pursued by the Bolsheviks. Kolchak had no reserves and was unable to restore the front. The collapse assumed such proportions that Lenin at first found it difficult to grasp its magnitude. He had greeted earlier predictions of imminent success with great scepticism and as late as 29 May had remained pessimistic.[30] But on 9 June, with Kolchak's forces retiring from in front of Glazov and preparing to evacuate Ufa, Lenin too became a believer. He endorsed the request of the high command and approved the withdrawal of troops from the eastern front to reinforce other regions. At the same time he ordered the pursuit of Kolchak into the depths of Siberia. "The enemy has not to be beaten off but to be destroyed," he insisted.[31] By mid-June, well before the allied leaders had even left Paris, Kolchak was defeated.

News of the débâcle poured out of Siberia in early June. It was accompanied by searing criticism of Kolchak. "The failure of the western army," wrote General Knox, the chief British adviser in Siberia, "owing to the usual Russian

incompetent leading, makes it necessary to reconsider the whole position."
Nothing further could be expected of Kolchak, he said, only real military intervention would save the situation. He suggested further reinforcement of Archangel and the landing of fifty thousand allied troops at Narva to seize Petrograd
and strike at Moscow. The French were not so pessimistic but had to acknowledge
that "the march of the Siberian army in the direction of the Volga has been
momentarily suspended."[32]

Lloyd George called the attention of his colleagues to this bad news, but they
preferred to discuss Kolchak's response to their despatch of 26 May. The admiral
in his reply had given virtually every assurance they had asked from him. As a
consequence they decided to publish their own despatch and Kolchak's response,
announcing at the same time that as a result of his satisfactory declaration they
were "willing to extend to him and his associates the support set forth in their
original letter." As this foresaw nothing beyond that aid which they were already
providing him, it was not likely to be of much help in the circumstances in which
he found himself. The minutes of the June meetings of the Council of Four,
however, say nothing about this embarrassing detail. They had concluded their
consideration of the Russian problem and, with the peace conference about to
end, were not about to set forth on yet another divisive exploration of its maze.
The futility and bankruptcy of allied policy was embodied in this final decision
– a half-hearted cheer for a military regime already expiring in the depths of
far-distant Siberia. The only concession which the departing western leaders
made to harsh reality was to decide on 17 June to maintain their naval blockade
of Soviet Russia; with the conclusion of peace with Germany it would no longer
have any basis in law, but they agreed, for the moment, to ignore this formality.[33]

Churchill did not draw logical conclusions from the defeat of Kolchak. He
had built his entire plan for British evacuation of north Russia around a preliminary campaign to join forces with the Whites at Kotlas and despite Kolchak's
retreat was determined to get his north Russian operation under way. Lloyd
George insisted that he present his plan to the war cabinet who, on 11 June,
gave their approval as a measure to ensure the safe withdrawal of all British
forces from north Russia but reached their decision without full knowledge of
the extent of Kolchak's defeat. When Curzon learned of the true situation in
Siberia he wrote to Churchill asking if, in the new circumstances, he was "not
apprehensive of a fiasco." Lloyd George also began to jib. He insisted that
General Ironside be informed "first, that under no circumstances whatever was
he to get himself so embroiled that it would be necessary to send an expedition
to pull him out, because no expedition would be sent; and secondly, under no
circumstances whatever was he to run any chance of not being able to withdraw
the whole of his force from Archangel before the ice set in." The War Office
also found it necessary to inform Knox that there was no way the allies would
land fifty thousand men at Narva or anywhere else in Russia.[34] On 18 June the
war cabinet came close to scrapping the entire north Russian venture, but Church-

ill defended the operation vigorously saying that regardless of Kolchak, "it was first necessary ... to strike an effective blow on that front." Churchill received permission to continue his preparations for a blow at Kotlas, but the cabinet withheld final approval until the end of the month.[35]

Defeat in Siberia did not stop Churchill. When the end of June came and Kolchak was in even worse shape than before, he still argued that it was necessary to seize Kotlas before withdrawing from north Russia. It was far more dangerous not to undertake the operation than to do so, for if left unmolested the Bolsheviks might launch a sudden attack which could wipe out the British garrison entirely. This argument carried the day,[36] but events in North Russia soon intervened to terminate British military operations. When they eventually withdrew from north Russia the British had hoped to leave behind a Russian force capable of defending the region against the Bolsheviks and they had raised and trained a substantial number of men for this purpose. Important units of this force mutinied in July, killing their British officers and going over to the Bolsheviks. This led General Ironside to recommend that the operation against Kotlas be cancelled. On 23 July, with Lloyd George in the chair, the war cabinet decided that the evacuation of north Russia was to be "carried out with the least possible delay." Churchill finally agreed that there was no chance of Ironside linking up with Kolchak or saving the Archangel government. The situation in Siberia was so bad that he "thought it quite probable that in the course of the next two months the whole Kolchak movement would crumple to pieces." The cabinet were so alarmed about the safety of British forces in Archangel that further reinforcements were sent to bring out the garrison safely.[37] Two months later the British completed the military evacuation of the Archangel region, thus ending that portion of intervention begun in March 1918.

THE BOLSHEVIKS HAD GOOD reason to feel confident. The peace conference had adjourned without formulating any effective opposition to them. Short months before, the allied powers could easily have crushed the revolution, but they had failed to do so. They could have recruited Germany to do their dirty work, but again they had not. Instead they were virtually thrusting the Germans into the eager Soviet embrace. With Kolchak on the run and the British unable to make any strategic use of their base at Archangel, quarter of the iron ring forged around them in the previous year was broken, and it was possible to drain military resources from this region to reinforce other hard-pressed areas. The threat to Petrograd and the south did not permit any victory celebrations, but in mid-summer Lenin and Chicherin did not hesitate to heap scorn on the departing delegates of the Paris peace conference. Lenin mocked them openly: "You bought Kolchak. Why didn't you save him? You recently passed a resolution to the effect that the international League of Nations of the Allied Powers recognized Kolchak as the only authoritative Russian ruler. And after that nothing was seen of Kolchak but a pair of clean heels. Why did that happen?"[38]

Chicherin was more analytical and menacing. The imperialists of Europe, he said, had begun the Great War in an effort to halt the rise of revolutionary socialism and enrich themselves at the expense of their weakest competitors. The war, however, had actually given birth to the revolution they feared and impoverished them beyond their worst apprehension. Conscription, which had been meant to oppress the workers, provided the masses with arms, and they had turned their weapons against their masters. Revolution had made the war too dangerous to continue, and the imperialists had ended it. The ruling classes, however, still hoped to divert the masses by continuing to stoke the fires of national hatreds. The peace concluded at Paris was not a genuine peace but simply a prolongation of the war by other, supposedly safer, means. Dangerously large armies could be demobilized, the workers disarmed, and the most efficient weapons placed in the hands of a small number of well-paid hirelings. The victorious powers spoke of disarmament but really meant only the disarmament of the masses. They also spoke of a League of Nations to guarantee the peace, but it was nothing but a league of victors and a league of violence designed to police the new order sanctified at Versailles. Germany was to be bled white, the small nationalities enslaved, the workers suppressed in the name of peace and good order. The European concert of 1814 had become the all-world concert of 1919. Chicherin cast Clemenceau in the role of Metternich and Wilson as Alexander I. Metternich-Clemenceau tended to the realities of power; Alexander-Wilson justified the settlement with an all-embracing ideology. Just as the treaties of Vienna attempted to restore the aristocratic world shattered by the French Revolution, so that of Versailles tried to protect bourgeois imperialism from the Russian Revolution. Both treaties sought to satisfy the appetites of the great powers and establish their legal claim to the territories they had seized. Only Soviet Russia remained beyond the grasp of the victorious powers, and for this reason they had waged war against her. Although they had failed to crush her, Wilson was reported as saying that Soviet Russia would "soon knock at the door in order to be admitted to the League of Nations." To this Chicherin responded:

Yes, it will knock, but not to be admitted into the company of those who frankly reveal themselves to have the thieving nature of robbers. It will knock – the world workers' revolution will knock. It will knock as the intruder in the play of Maeterlinck whose unseen approach fills the heart with freezing terror, whose steps, accompanied by the sharpening of a scythe, can already be heard on the staircase. It will knock, it is already entering, it has already sat down at the table of the panic-stricken family; it is the intruder; it is invisible death.[39]

These responses clearly exhibit the contempt in which Soviet leaders held the new order just established at Versailles. They would never have acknowledged the moral authority or legitimacy of the system established there, but even two months before they would have gladly acknowledged the brute force at the disposal of the peace conference and ransomed themselves at whatever exorbitant price in territory and economic resources the western leaders might have demanded of them. By late June they were aware that the armed force at the disposal of allied leaders had largely disappeared and that which remained almost certainly could not be effectively brought to bear against them. In addition, the international order consecrated at Versailles institutionalizing allied-German hostility and leaving no great power along the marchlands of the Russian western frontier could only facilitate the future conduct of Soviet foreign policy. In June the Bolshevik international position was far from consolidated but the foundations of that consolidation had already been laid.

CHAPTER VII

"Don't halloo until you're out of the woods" : Soviet nationalities policy and the Baltic

A vast distance separated Archangel and Omsk, yet in the context of the Russian civil war their fate was decided together. Failure in Siberia rendered the allied position at Archangel meaningless and left little option but withdrawal. A similar, yet different, situation existed farther west, where the fate of Murmansk was directly tied to that of Reval. Murmansk and Archangel, although usually lumped together simply as northern Russia, in fact faced two different directions. Archangel faced east to Siberia; Murmansk faced west to the Baltic, linked to it by the railway built between Petrograd and the Arctic Ocean in the midst of the Great War. An axis drawn from Murmansk to Reval has a length of more than eleven hundred kilometres. Helsingfors nearly straddles this axis, and in 1919 was an integral part of the northwestern quadrant of forces opposed to Soviet Russia. The focus of all these forces was the city of Petrograd.

After its year of revolutionary glory, Petrograd had become a political backwater. All political, military, and administrative power had been transferred to Moscow. As Russia's transportation crisis deepened, the economic life of the city, already severely damaged by the disruption of the previous two years, declined still further. Food and fuel were in short supply, and the population of the city began to dwindle.[1] Politically and economically Petrograd was a mere shell, but it still retained great strategic and symbolic importance. Port and warehouse facilities made it a natural marshalling yard for the supplies necessary for any large undertaking in Russia and railways radiated from it in every direction to carry those supplies where needed. In particular they led east to Vologda and then on the Siberia and southeast to Moscow, the centre of Russia. Petrograd was an excellent base from which to strike at whoever controlled Moscow, Bolsheviks or otherwise. The fall of "Red Peter," the cradle of the revolution, would have a devastating psychological impact on revolutionaries everywhere.

Petrograd was not simply a Russian problem. Set at the very edge of the former empire, it was flanked by Finland on the north and Estonia to the west. Both viewed the nearby metropolis, with its reduced but still formidable resources, as a threat to their existence.[2] Many Finns and Estonians also observed that while Petrograd was a Russian city it was set in an environment of Karelians and Ingermanlanders, people very closely akin to themselves. Ultra-nationalist circles in Finland dreamed of creating a Greater Finland of still undetermined dimensions, which conceivably could have encompassed all the territory around the Gulf of Finland including the former imperial capital.[3] Against such aspirations Russians of all political persuasions rebelled, but the more conservative elements rejected even independence for Estonia and Finland. This was particularly disruptive, for in early 1919 many of the most conservative Russian émigrés had taken up residence in Reval and Helsingfors. There, *sotto voce*, they denied the right of their hosts to sovereignty while demanding full cooperation in crushing the Bolsheviks. Ironically the Bolsheviks, while threatening the social structure of the two neighbouring states, did not contest their claim to independence. The role of the allied and associated powers further internationalized the Petrograd problem. While wishing to promote the national aspirations of Finland and Estonia, they did not want to violate the territorial integrity of a future non-Bolshevik Russia. Least of all did they want to be seen by Russian nationalists as posing a threat to Petrograd, especially since western leaders believed that the Germans would take full advantage of any such Russian fear. Here, then, for those who wished to wrest Petrograd from the Bolsheviks, was the problem: how to secure a minimum of international cooperation in the midst of such violently conflicting national aspirations?

The Bolsheviks faced a somewhat similar problem, not merely in the Baltic but everywhere around the vast periphery of Soviet Russia. Lenin's followers, of course, were avowed internationalists and did not display the same violent nationalism as their enemies. Nevertheless, once the Bolsheviks achieved power they quickly came to exhibit a very real revolutionary patriotism. This was true not only of Russian-based Bolsheviks but also of those from the borderlands. The latter had chafed on the restraints imposed on them until the German collapse and then hurried forward to establish their own soviet socialist republics. They had established their own governments, administrations, and armies with the aid of Soviet Russia, to be sure, but with a great deal of autonomy in their everyday activities. They soon developed priorities which did not always correspond with those of Moscow. While eastern Europe remained a vacuum, borderland Bolsheviks as a rule wanted to move forward more aggressively than their more cautious Moscow comrades; when the international climate worsened they sought to defend their newly won territories more tenaciously than Moscow felt was necessary. In both expansion and contraction, conflict characterized relations between Moscow and regional Bolshevik centres. The problem for those seeking to defend the Soviet republics was how to minimize this conflict and use the sparse resources available in the most efficient manner.

The struggle which developed in the Baltic during the spring and early summer of 1919 must be seen within the larger context of the Russian civil war. It burst into flame with the first success of Kolchak in Siberia; it sputtered out as the admiral showed his heels to the Bolsheviks. It was a phenomenon directly related to the generally accepted belief that the Bolsheviks would fall with the first hard blow they received, a belief which Kolchak's rapid advance in April seemed to confirm. Everyone in the Baltic wanted to be in on the kill. None of the forces arranged along the Murmansk-Reval axis, singly or collectively, could topple the Bolsheviks. If Kolchak did that for them, however, it would be simple to seize Petrograd. Moreover, with the admiral's grip on power not yet secure, the various forces to the north and west of Petrograd would have every reason for wanting to seize control of this strategically important corner of Russia. It would provide the White Russians of Finland and Estonia with a base from which to bring their influence to bear on Kolchak; it might, perhaps with some German help, allow them to challenge him for control of all Russia. In the hands of Finland, with Estonia perhaps occupying adjacent Ingermanland, Petrograd would provide surety that Kolchak would recognize the independence of the new Baltic republics. For the allies, and Britain especially, control of the city would ensure a restoration of influence in the new anti-Bolshevik Russia. In April and May, with the peace conference going badly and the Germans displaying disconcerting truculence, such influence appeared especially important. During the months of Kolchak's ascendency, therefore, all parties involved in the struggle for Petrograd augmented their activity and prepared for further action. Each acted independently, however, and frequently showed more concern about the intentions of the other anti-Bolshevik forces than those of the Soviet government. Everyone called for cooperation, in so far as it benefited themselves, but withheld it in all circumstances in any way compromising their own objectives.[4]

EAST KARELIA PROVIDED one theatre for this clash of interest. The region extends more than seven hundred kilometres from Lake Ladoga to the White Sea. It was a land of relatively minor economic importance but of great strategic significance, for through its endless marshes and forests ran the only railway connecting Murmansk with Petrograd. Whoever controlled the railway controlled the territory through which it passed and perhaps much more, for the region constituted the best available base for exerting influence over the northern lands further to the east. The Karelians who lived here were related ethnically to the Finns as were, less directly, many tribes in northern Siberia. In an age of flaming nationalism, this relationship gave the Finns a certain claim to the region or at least the right to demand self-determination for their eastern kinsmen. Advocates of a greater Finland cherished dreams of a state extending almost indefinitely into the depths of Siberia. Realization of their dream depended on the total disintegration of Russia, but in early 1919 this seemed a real possibility and advocates of a greater Finland conducted a noisy campaign to win public support for their aspirations. The bourgeois parties, in general, lent their support to the claim for East Karelia, and expansionists had numerous friends in the government and army. Most important, the regent and commander-in-chief of the army, Karl Gustav von Mannerheim shared their dream.

The Karelian question, however, was complicated by important international considerations. Although the Bolsheviks had recognized Finnish independence on 31 December 1917, the Whites refused to do so. Consequently the allies withheld recognition of the independence of Finland and were known to oppose Finnish expansion. The Finns were tainted by their earlier association with Germany, and many in the west still saw them as working for Berlin. Eastern expansion by Finland, therefore, could be construed as part of Germany's effort to escape the consequences of defeat. Finnish representatives in London and Paris, while seeking to deny this construction, strongly advised their government not to pursue an expansionist policy in East Karelia. The Kolchak offensive, however, forced a decision on Helsingfors. If Finland was ever to stake its claim to Karelia she would have to do it before Kolchak or some other Russian acceptable to the allies reached Moscow. As long as the Soviet regime held power, Finland could portray military operations in Karelia as part of the war against Bolshevism. But once the Whites were established in Moscow they would demand the evacuation of Russian territory and were likely to receive allied support. Even with the Bolsheviks in Moscow the allies were reluctant to see Finland occupy Russian territory.

With this in mind, Mannerheim proceeded cautiously. Rather than using his regular army to seize East Karelia, he allowed volunteers to attack the Bolshevik-held southern portion of the region. They received their arms and equipment from the Finnish army but were paid by the Karelian Committee, a private group seeking Finnish annexation of East Karelia. Nothing was said of annexation; liberation from Bolshevism and Karelian self-determination were proclaimed as their goals. In secret, however, the Finnish general staff gave the mission commander quite different instructions. He was told that although the government would try to obtain British cooperation, it was "unconditionally important" that he occupy Petrozavodsk before they did. If he succeeded Finland could then block the British and Russian forces at Murmansk from making further progress toward Petrograd, secure a key position for future military operations, enhance the need for Finnish cooperation in such a venture, and obtain a base for an advance northward along the Murmansk railway to enforce her claim to Karelia, the Kola Peninsula, and who knew what else.[5]

The British observed these preparations with dissatisfaction. Their White Sea front, commanded by Major-General Charles Maynard, was anchored at Segeja, 640 kilometres south of Murmansk and 240 kilometres north of Petrozavodsk.

It had been stationary and largely quiet since early in the year and, prior to receiving information about the Finnish preparations, there had been no intention to activate it in the spring. All the action in northern Russia was taking place on the Archangel front, and the British really did not need the distraction of further operations south of Murmansk. Both Maynard and the local Russian government he kept in power, however, were disturbed by the information from Helsingfors and wanted to guard against the Finns helping themselves to Karelia. In mid-April he tested his front and caught the Bolsheviks napping; he drove them a farther twenty-five kilometres south along the railroad to Urosozero. He wanted to proceed farther south to the northern shore of Lake Onega, but he had strict orders not to undertake any serious offensive action without permission from London. When the Finns began their offensive in Karelia on 21 April and captured Olonets three days later, however, Maynard appealed to the War Office, "requesting sanction for an immediate advance." On 29 April he received approval; two days later he began his push towards Lake Onega.[6]

The Bolsheviks were now engaged on two fronts in Karelia and gave way steadily before the British offensive. Within three weeks Maynard had reached the shores of Lake Onega. In the south, however, the Bolsheviks reversed the Finnish advance. The Red Army regained Olonets and prepared to drive the Finns out of Karelia. Military logic demanded close cooperation between the two anti-Bolshevik forces; political logic produced a different result. If Maynard and the Finns coordinated their military operations and defeated the Bolsheviks, it appeared as if the Finns would be the first to reach Petrozavodsk. All White Russian leaders – in Siberia, north Russia, and the Baltic – deplored such a possibility. They demanded that Finland renounce all annexationist intentions regarding Karelia and declare that her military operations were directed only against the Bolsheviks. The Finns, of course, were quite prepared to give such an undertaking. But the Whites also insisted that the Finns agree, should they reach Petrozavodsk first, to turn it over immediately to a Russian administration appointed by the government at Murmansk. The British liked this proposal, and when Finnish officers arrived at Maynard's camp at the end of May he asked that they accept these terms. At first the Finns would not agree, but when the Red Army prepared to strike a major blow against them they accepted the British demands. They asked, however, that all Russian troops serving under Maynard's command be transferred to his left wing so that there should be no contact with their own troops. This settled the matter as far as Maynard was concerned, for agreement would effectively bar the Russians from sharing significantly in the proposed operation. "If the cat had been halfway out of the bag before, it was out completely now," he declared. "If Karelia was to come under Finnish sway, Russians must have no part in freeing her from Bolshevik domination." Armed hostilities seemed possible. Maynard arrested White Finns he found inside his lines and cabled London asking that Helsingfors be warned against occupying Repola on his exposed right flank.[7]

The critical situation on other civil war fronts prevented the Bolsheviks from reinforcing East Karelia, and Moscow sought to engage Helsingfors in negotiations. On 14 April Chicherin sent the Finns a severe note protesting their depradations along the Soviet frontier and their apparent intention, widely discussed in the Finnish press, of invading Karelia. Soviet Russia, he said, had no designs on Finnish territory and long ago had recognized the independence of Finland. In view of Soviet readiness to establish peaceful relations, he asked "whether it would not now be possible to begin an exchange of opinions concerning the manner in which this goal might be attained."[8] The answer came a week later when Mannerheim's volunteers crossed the border and seized Olonets. Even this invasion could not justify Soviet reinforcement of Karelia. The Soviet commander had to make do with what he had. Nor did Chicherin have any added weapons. He could only file another protest accusing the Finns of acting as the "tool of the Entente." "No doubt remained," he wrongly asserted, "that an organic connection exists between the military operations of the Finnish troops and the troops of the Entente powers, both of whom follow one and the same strategic plan."[9]

Given the appearance of military operations in Karelia, Chicherin can be forgiven his error. Its extent, however, can be measured by Maynard's reaction to the defeat suffered by the Finns at the end of June when, unsupported by his own force, they were driven back into Finland. "To my joy," he wrote, "the entire 'Volunteer Force' or 'Finnish National Army' or 9th Finn Army Corps, whatever may have been its correct title, faded away." Shortly after he had less cause for satisfaction, because once the Bolsheviks had finished with the Finns they were able to attend to him. When he launched his own offensive in July he met very stubborn resistance and was unable to capture Petrozavodsk. He had to withdraw, leaving East Karelia to the Bolsheviks.[10] Soviet victory was due to the inability of their enemies to cooperate. The French representative in northern Russia concluded it had been "naive to hope that it would be possible to put the Finnish army in motion without General Mannerheim ... putting too high a price on his co-operation."[11]

A SIMILAR DRAMA UNFOLDED on the southern approaches to Petrograd. There the prime actors were the Estonians and the White Russian Northwestern Army. The latter was built around a troop of some six thousand anti-Bolshevik Russian emigrés assembled by the Germans at Pskov the previous fall. They had joined the Estonians in opposing the Bolshevik advance in November and had remained at the front ever since. Like most White "armies," it was top-heavy with staff officers and did not perform well in the field. It was, however, the only *Russian* armed force available to the emigrés sheltered in Finland and Estonia, so they had to make the best possible use of it. General Nikolai N. Yudenich, its commander, was considered an able soldier, but was a poor politician. Although the cooperation of Estonia and Finland were essential to the existence, let alone success, of his army, he rudely dismissed their aspirations. "There is no Estonia," he is said to have declared, "It is a piece of Russian soil, a Russian province. The Estonia Government is a gang of criminals."[12] He thought no better of Finland and was reluctant to contemplate her independence. Between Finns and White Russians, wrote the French military attaché in Helsingfors, there was an "absolutely blind hatred."[13]

The political situation in Estonia was especially unstable. In the fall the Social Democrats had joined the government to aid in resisting the Soviet invasion. After the Bolsheviks had been beaten back, increasing differences with their bourgeois partners led the Social Democrats to resign their portfolios. The bourgeois parties favoured a less radical solution to the nation's social problems, in particular land reform, and wished to pursue a foreign policy closely aligned to that of Britain. Some bourgeois leaders even sought to have Britain establish a protectorate over Estonia. While rejecting the Bolshevik program, the Social Democrats sought a fundamental break with the past. They were, however, very vulnerable to political abuse from both the right and left. The bourgeois liberals demanded their continued support in defending Estonia against Soviet Russia while those groups who would normally support the outlawed Bolsheviks, especially the labourers of Reval, demanded that they seek a negotiated peace with Moscow.[14] In elections to the Constituent Assembly in April the Social Democrats won a plurality of seats. The government was reorganized, but the bourgeois parties were determined not to give way on the question of peace with Soviet Russia.[15] Konstantin Paets, the premier, while assuring the Social Democrats that he would urge the allied powers to approve Estonia's seeking peace with Moscow, privately informed London that he hoped the British government would emphatically reject such a move. He said peace "would be fatal as a whole to Estonia's future, as it would be no real peace and would give the Bolsheviks the opportunity they desire for spreading their influence in this country." He wanted London to make it clear that England "would scarcely be prepared to recognize [the independence of the] Estonia Republic in case of a separate peace." Paets added, however, that Estonia, whose own resources were exhausted, would require prompt financial assistance to continue the war against the Bolsheviks. The country also needed a firm guarantee of her independence, for many who favoured a separate peace with the Bolsheviks feared that "Estonia's continuing struggle might only conduce to re-establishment of a monarchist Russia in which she would ... be incorporated against wishes of whole population."[16]

Events in neighbouring Latvia increased the difficulty of maintaining popular support for the war. In mid-April, when the Germans upset the Latvian government and replaced them with one of their own choosing, Estonians feared something similar might happen to them. Rather than the Germans, they feared the White Russian Northwestern Army. "The real danger," reported the British minister in Copenhagen after meeting with his Estonian colleague, "appears to be that Estonian troops and workmen will lose courage if they gain impression that Germans and Baltic Germans may possibly be allowed to gain ascendency in their country. Rather than submit to this they are likely to come to terms with the Bolsheviks." The situation was made still worse on 27 April when Paets received a wireless message from Bela Kun, premier of the Soviet Hungarian government, offering to mediate between Estonia and Soviet Russia. As the message had been relayed by the transmitter at Tsarskoe Selo, there was little doubt that this was an authentic Bolshevik peace feeler. In bringing this message to the attention of the British representative, Paets said that the situation was grave as "no government could refuse the Hungarian offer, except with allied support." It was essential, he said, "for Estonia to know what was the allied attitude towards this question, and what help she had to expect."[17]

These telegrams created concern in London. Curzon wired the British delegation in Paris calling for the allied governments to reach an early decision about "their policy towards the Baltic Provinces" and the aid to be given Estonia. This was not possible. Lloyd George would do nothing, and Balfour found he could not get the other allies to reach a decision. With Kolchak apparently about to overturn the Bolsheviks, none of the allies wanted to back Estonia in what was likely to be a prompt confrontation with the new Russia authorities. All Balfour could do was to suggest that the Estonians be informed that the allies were earnestly considering the problem, and hoped to reach a decision soon.[18]

Events in the Baltic outstripped allied decision-making. In early May the White Russians of Estonia, excited by news of Kolchak's success, decided to advance on Petrograd. This embarrassed the Estonian government because it supplied the Russian army and, due to the organization of the front, would be virtually compelled to advance if the Russians did. Their front had been quiet since February, and with the rapid development of the German offensive in Latvia they did not want to mount an offensive against the Bolsheviks. Still less did they want to aid the Russian conservatives, but other considerations compelled them to do so. On 6 May Churchill had agreed to provide arms for Yudenich, and Britain's agents in the Baltic expected the Estonians to help in driving the Bolsheviks from Petrograd. As the Estonians attached great importance to pleasing the British, it would have been difficult not to cooperate. Moreover, if the Bolsheviks did collapse the Estonians wanted to be on the winning side. They thus agreed, however reluctantly, to cooperate with the Northwestern Army as it launched its attack on 13 May; the same day the Estonians, aided by a screen of British warships, landed troops thirty kilometres behind the Bolshevik lines at Luga Bay and pushed northeastward into Ingermanland.[19]

These operations met with unexpected success. The Northwestern Army was able to make surprising progress against a numerically superior Soviet force. Defections from Bolshevik ranks soon swelled the army to sixteen thousand men, and in a few days they had advanced fifty kilometres beyond Narva. Along the coast the Estonians advanced to within a short distance of the major fortresses guarding the southern approaches to Petrograd. Off shore the British squadron fought two engagements with units of the Soviet fleet based at Kronstadt. On 24 May the defection of additional Soviet troops forced the Red Army into a general withdrawal. Pskov fell two days later, and by the end of the month the Northwestern Army was approaching Gatchina only fifty kilometres from Petrograd. Flushed with success, the Whites decided to press on, but the Estonians called a halt to their own operations. They felt threatened by the German advance into northern Latvia. Thus they sent their army south to block von der Goltz the German commander, rather than east to bolster the Whites, fearing a possible Yudenich–von der Goltz conspiracy.[20]

The Bolsheviks were not prepared for a blow from this direction. In April they had focused their attention on the eastern front and drained Petrograd of its best troops. In May the Soviet Seventh Army numbered less than twenty-five thousand actual fighting men. Even so, it still outnumbered the White and Estonian forces and should have been sufficient to meet any challenge on the southern approaches to Petrograd. Still, as the White menace took shape the Bolsheviks ordered an increased state of readiness and even a certain reinforcement in men and material. Given the crisis on the eastern front, however, little in the way of help arrived before the onset of the White attack.[21]

Soviet military specialists dismissed the attack as an attempt to draw resources away from the critical fronts of the war. Some were even prepared to write off the city if necessary. Bolsheviks leaders looked upon Petrograd quite differently. Apart from its symbolic importance, it remained the home of the second greatest concentration of communists in all Soviet Russia. Its fall would diminish the proletarian base of the Soviet government and strengthen the conviction of the rival socialist-revolutionaries that Russia's future should be built on rural rather than urban foundations. Petrograd could not be surrendered without a fight, and the Politburo sent Joseph Stalin to take charge of its defence. On arriving, he immediately complained that few reinforcements had reached the city. He stressed, however, that what he needed was not quantity but quality, and asserted that "all we need to drive the whole pack beyond Narva is three infantry regiments – fit for action, of course – and at least one cavalry regiment." He described the situation in Karelia as tolerable, adding that "the Finns are maintaining a stubborn silence and, strangely enough, have not taken advantage of the opportunity."[22] He therefore did not realize the sharp clash of interest dividing the forces arrayed against him. It is also worth noting that in this first major report from Petrograd, as well as in shorter ones filed earlier, there is no mention of treachery as a threat to the security of the city.

This is significant, because Adam Ulam has attributed the course of subsequent events to Stalin, implying that they were indicative of his megalomania and obsession with treason even at this early date. "Predictably," Ulam writes, Stalin "discovered … a major plot of treason, found the directives of the commander-in-chief (Trotsky's protégé) harmful, and saved the day by his initiative – all of which developments he communicated without inhibition to Lenin."[23] The situation actually developed quite differently. To start, there was a significant and active resistance to the Bolsheviks in Petrograd, which was crowded with White sympathizers and probably harboured more individuals hostile to the Bolsheviks than any other Soviet city. As Kolchak advanced, the Whites of Petrograd began to prepare for battle. They were able to communicate with Yudenich, and, when the Northwestern Army attacked, the Whites in Petrograd also struck. "The Friends of Russia," as they styled themselves, advised Soviet forces that the Red Army was surrendering everywhere, and they should as well; the Whites, they said, were bringing not only liberation from Bolshevik tyranny but food for starving Petrograd. This message, spread widely by Whites and their sympathizers, accounts in part for the early victories of the Northwestern Army.[24]

As early as 1 April reports of counter-revolutionary activities in Petrograd had reached Lenin and caused him to order the Cheka to take "the most urgent measures" to oppose the counter-revolutionary intrigue. Moreover, Lenin, not Stalin, first raised the shrill cry of treachery, advising Stalin on 27 May:

The circumstances of the Whiteguard offensive against Petrograd, taken in their totality, compel one to assume the existence of organized treason behind our lines or, perhaps, even at the front. This is the only explanation for the attack with relatively small forces, the rapid advance and the frequent blowing-up of bridges on the main lines leading to Petrograd.

"Please pay greater attention to these circumstance, and take extraordinary measures to expose the plots."[25] By calling on him to pay "greater attention to organized treason" and take "extraordinary measures" against it Lenin seems to have implied that Stalin had not adequately evaluated the threat to Petrograd or the measures needed to combat it. Nor did Lenin confine his concern to ciphered telegrams. Instead, three days later, he issued a proclamation entitled "Beware of Spies."

Death to Spies! The Whiteguards' advance on Petrograd has made it perfectly clear that in the vicinity of the front line, in every large town, the Whites have a wide organisation for espionage, subversion, the blowing-up of bridges, the engineering of revolts in the rear and the murder of Communists and prominent members of workers' organisations ... Everywhere vigilance must be redoubled and a series of measures evolved and carried out with the greatest strictness to track down and capture spies and whiteguard conspirators ... [26]

With a proclamation of this sort ringing in his ears and the very real possibility of being held responsible for the loss of Petrograd, there is no need to have recourse to megalomania as an explanation of Stalin's conduct. Lenin had clearly made up his mind about the nature of the problem at Petrograd and was prodding

Stalin to take effective action. He always feared his agents would turn "soft" and not prove equal to the "hard" tasks they had to perform. Throughout the crisis Lenin peered fretfully over Stalin's shoulder prompting his every action in Petrograd.[27]

The continued White advance alarmed Lenin. The defection of Soviet troops increased, and the commander of the western front was forced to report on 10 June that a substantial part of the Seventh Army was no longer battleworthy and had lost contact with the army on its southern flank. A gap had been opened in the Soviet line through which the enemy could advance at will.[28] On learning of the new crisis, Lenin asked the Central Committee "to recognize the priority importance of the Petrograd front and to be guided by this in allocating troops." As the Soviet leaders had decided the day before to begin withdrawing divisions from the eastern front, reinforcement of Petrograd became possible. Two of every three divisions removed from the east were to be sent to the former capital.[29] The military situation, however, continued to deteriorate. On 12 June, as the Northwestern Army advanced on the fortress of Krasnaia Gorka on the southern approaches to Petrograd, its commandant led a mutiny within the garrison and surrendered the fortress to the Whites. Similar mutinies occurred at the nearby fortresses of Seraia Loshad and Obruchev, leaving the southern sea approaches to Kronstadt and Petrograd undefended. Stalin asked for and received immediate assistance; two armoured trains and five hundred communists were sent to help restore the situation. With Kronstadt laying down a heavy barrage, Stalin unleashed a land and sea attack which succeeded in recapturing the fortresses on 16 June.[30] Two days later he reported that having interrogated his prisoners he had "unearthed a big conspiracy in the Kronstadt area. The battery commanders of all the forts in the entire Kronstadt fortified area are implicated. The aim of the conspiracy was to seize possession of the fortress, take control of the fleet, open fire on the rear of our troops, and clear the road to Petrograd for [the Northwestern Army]." This explained, he said, why the Whites with their "relatively small forces, advanced so brazenly on Petrograd. The insolence of the Finns is now also understandable." Reinforcement of Petrograd, Stalin declared, was no longer necessary: "one division will be sufficient." Three days later the Red Army launched its counter-attack, and by the end of the month the Northwestern Army was in full retreat. Early in July, the crisis at an end, Stalin returned to Moscow where he reported that "the Red Army at Petrograd should win," but added, "Whether this is the calm before the storm, only the Finnish Government knows."[31]

STALIN WAS NOT ALONE in casting his gaze upon Finland. In the wake of the White débâcle everyone turned in that direction. Immediate aid was required, reported the French ambassador to Sweden, to save the Northwestern Army from a military catastrophe. The Bolsheviks, he continued, although badly shaken, would not fall by themselves "nor under the blow of poorly armed bands, feebly commanded and incapable of co-ordinating their efforts." Allied representatives in Helsingfors all agreed that only Finland could provide the aid needed to capture Petrograd.[32] Would the Finns drive the Bolsheviks from the city?

But, as in so many other aspects of the Russian question, the allies had no policy and leading figures within individual governments assumed diametrically opposite positions. The French foreign minister could ask a Finnish representative, "Why don't you just take this filthy city [Petrograd]?" while his chief deputy consistently opposed this action. In London the Foreign Office used strong language to discourage a Finnish initiative while Churchill, predictably, urged Mannerheim forward.[33] Far from being anyone's tool, the Finns remained passive while Yudenich advanced. They would aid the Whites, but only for a price. At the end of May Mannerheim told Yudenich that he would attack Petrograd with one hundred thousand men one week after Kolchak recognized Finnish independence and agreed to cede Pechenga, neutralize the Baltic Sea, allow the frontier between Russia and Finland to be determined by plebiscites, and aid him in securing allied military supplies and financial support for the campaign. As long as it remained possible that he might be able to snatch Petrograd from the failing Bolsheviks, Yudenich would not agree to Mannerheim's terms, but as soon as his army began to retreat he hastened to endorse the Finnish demands. Yudenich himself had no authority to accept the terms but he strongly recommended that Kolchak do so. The admiral, whose entire position in Siberia was beginning to collapse, wired a qualified acceptance.[34] This was not good enough for the Finns, who demanded that the allied powers guarantee any agreement with Kolchak and said they would not act without first receiving allied assistance "with money and munitions." As the allies were unprepared to offer either financial aid or a guarantee of a future settlement with Russia, the Finns had unwittingly laid the basis for that rarest of phenomena, an allied policy on some aspect of the Russian problem. On 7 July allied leaders decided that while they could neither recommend nor support aggressive Finnish action against Petrograd, they "would have no objection to that operation."[35] "A somewhat Platonic declaration," Mannerheim later observed, which produced no results.[36] Just how platonic can be seen in the way in which Churchill had foreseen the operation unfolding. He had wanted to include not only the Finns but, alone among his colleagues, the Germans as well. "No great harm would be done," he told his cabinet colleagues on 4 July, if the Finns and Germans liberated Petrograd. "We should have control of foodstuffs, and consequently could direct affairs. It would be for us to appoint a good Governor of the City, who would be acceptable to Admiral Kolchak, and then politely inform the Germans and the Finns that there was no longer any need for them to remain." The Finns foresaw something like this happening, so they politely informed the allies that they would have nothing to do with the operation against Petrograd.[37]

These developments came at a very inopportune time for Mannerheim. Under the new constitution adopted earlier in the year he was to be replaced as regent by a president elected by the Diet. Western refusal to support a march on

Petrograd combined with the failure of the East Karelia campaign to strike a shattering blow to his prestige. Mannerheim stood for the presidency but lost to K.J. Stahlberg. The new president and the Diet majority opposed the type of military adventure favoured by Mannerheim. The significance of the election was immediately understood in Soviet Russia. The Petrograd *Pravda* hailed it as a sign that the Finnish bourgeoisie had chosen the path of moderation in their relations with Soviet Russia. Trotsky attributed the outcome of the election to the hiding the Red Army had given the Finns at Olonets. The defeat had compromised Mannerheim and favoured the election of an opponent of intervention.[38] Trotsky proved a trifle optimistic; the next day British war planes, flying from Bjorko, bombed Kronstadt. The Soviet government, however, would not be provoked. Chicherin filed one more protest which reaffirmed that the Bolsheviks, while doing everything to protect Soviet soil from attack, would not waver in the pursuit of a peaceful settlement with Finland. Soviet armed forces would not cross the Finnish frontier.[39]

The Bolsheviks pursued the same policy with Estonia. By the end of July the Northwestern Army had again taken refuge behind the Estonian frontier, and many observers expected the Red Army to cross the border in pursuit of the enemy. The Bolsheviks, however, had no such intention, and when S.S. Kamenev, the newly appointed commander-in-chief, apparently issued ambiguous orders on this question, Stalin wrote to Lenin: "Please explain to the commander-in-chief that he does not have the right of declaring war." Kamenev defended himself by blaming the "bourgeois governments of Finland and Estonia" for spreading rumors that the Red Army was preparing to invade their territory. These were "total fabrications," he said, because not one unit of the Red Army had passed, nor would pass, the frontiers of Finland or Estonia. Every precaution would be taken to ensure that Soviet units would not violate the territory of either state.[40] The Bolsheviks did not want to do anything to diminish Estonian fear of the Whites or bring it to focus again on themselves.

THE EVENTS OF SPRING 1919 illustrate brilliantly the extreme divisiveness of the Bolsheviks' opponents on the front from Murmansk to Poland. National aspirations clashed sharply while conflicting Great Power interests provided added complications. The possible re-emergence of a conservative Great Russia projected one more dimension to the problem. Grotesque rivalry blotted out all possibility of cooperation, and abstinence from armed violence, where such forbearance was achieved, represented the crowning feat of statecraft. The result was to leave the Bolsheviks as masters of the region at a relatively small cost in military resources. Their enemies continued to hold the periphery and bases from which further assaults could be launched, but the Bolsheviks had not been dislodged from the strategic barriers to military penetration of their hinterland.

This success should not be viewed as being due wholly, or even primarily, to the failure of cooperation among Bolshevik enemies. The Bolsheviks were plagued by the same problems of national divisiveness and hesitant cooperation among theoretically allied forces. Their adherents were drawn from every quarter of the former Russian empire and were irrevocably influenced by all the national tensions characteristic of that "jail house of peoples." As part of their Marxist faith, however, they espoused a radical internationalism which should in theory have gone a long way to efface national prejudices. In practice some Bolsheviks did surmount national prejudice, but many others did not. Ideology was less important among the hundreds of thousands of members added to the party since 1917, and Russian nationalism, as Lenin was to testify time and again, remained a force to be reckoned with. Even some who sincerely professed proletarian internationalism were prepared to trample on non-Russian peoples in the name of a more rapid spread of revolution to the borderlands and beyond. Manifestations of such sentiments and realization in practice had given rise to widespread charges of Bolshevik imperialism and had laid the basis for that small degree of cooperation which the rival nationalities had been able to achieve during those months. Once established, the Soviet republics of Estonia, Latvia, Lithuania–White Russia, and Ukraine constituted a dual menace to the bourgeois regimes they confronted. In so far as they represented genuine grievances felt by the workers and peasants, they threatened the stability of the new social order; in so far as they were closely tied to the great power mounting in Soviet Russia, they threatened the national existence of each state. The new Soviet republics, however, did not always cooperate closely among themselves or with their great "fraternal" benefactor. As each Soviet republic began to take on a life of its own, conflict and tension, sometimes expressed in national terms, emerged. Although tension was greatest between Moscow and Kiev, it also existed between the Kremlin and the governments of the three Soviet Baltic republics. If left alone or mismanaged, it might easily have gotten out of hand and proved as destructive to the Bolsheviks as their adversaries. It did not, and the Bolshevik ability to cope with this problem contributed substantially to their success on the western front and ultimately to their victory in the civil war.

The national question had long concerned European Marxists, and they had turned to it with increasing frequency as the continent moved towards the Great War. Following the Russian revolution, the Bolsheviks became the first Marxists to have to deal with it on a practical basis. This had given rise to a wide spectrum of views which, in their theoretical manifestations at least, had been shoved into the background by the ceaseless emergency of the civil war.[41] Armed conflict, however, magnified the problem, and the complications of the western front lent it special urgency. When the Bolshevik Eighth Congress met in Moscow in March 1919, the problem was on the agenda.

The major task of the congress was the definition of a new party program. Events since the revolution had left the existing program in great need of revision. Clamorous necessity had rudely thrust such revision aside at the Sixth and Seventh congresses when first the revolution and then its survival had served to diminish the program's relative importance. It is a measure of the degree to which the

Bolshevik position had improved by March 1919 that the new party program could become the focal point of the Eighth Congress. Contained within the draft of this program was a definition of the party's attitude towards self-determination, the crux of the nationality problem. This definition had been hammered out in a commission chosen by Lenin. The program, with its sections relating to the nationality problem, largely reflected his thinking. Here he asserted that to achieve "real rapprochement and amalgamation of the workers and the peasants of all nations"

the colonial and other nations which are oppressed, or whose rights are restricted, must be completely liberated and granted the right to secede as a guarantee that the sentiments inherited from capitalism, the distrust of the working people of the various nations, will be fully dispelled and replaced by a conscious and voluntary alliance.

The workers of those nations which under capitalism were oppressor nations must take exceptional care not to hurt the national sentiments of the oppressed nations ... and must ... remove all traces of distrust and alienation inherited from the epoch of capitalism.[42]

Bukharin opposed this view. He and his supporters, who had earlier opposed the peace of Brest-Litovsk, again struck a pose of revolutionary purity. Whereas Lenin wanted the party to demand "self determination for all nationalities," Bukharin wished to limit the call to "self-determination for the working classes of every nationality." Self-determination by itself, he said, was a bourgeois slogan uniting all counter-revolutionary forces. The party of the proletariat should have a slogan which would not allow the bourgeoisie to hide behind such "fiction" as "popular will" or the "whole people." Where the proletariat did not yet form a class, where they did not understand the contradiction between their interests and those of the bourgeoisie, where society remained essentially undifferentiated – he cited the Hottentots, Bushmen, Negroes, and Hindus as examples – communists could call for unrestricted self-determination, for it would prove useful in the struggle against imperialism.

G.L. Piatakov, former leader of the Soviet Ukrainian government and an enemy of every form of Ukrainian nationalism, would not grant even as much as Bukharin. He opposed both proposals and spoke against all nationalist manifestations. The proletariat of all nations had to unite, not divide, and to pool their resources in an ever expanding economic and administrative unity. He called for a policy based on "strict proletarian centralization and proletarian unity." L.B. Sunitsa, speaking for the Bolsheviks of Orenburg and the First Army based on the borders of Turkestan, echoed this view, but the remaining speakers supported Lenin.[43]

Lenin responded very sharply. Bukharin, he said, asks "why do we need the right of nations to self-determination. I must repeat what I said opposing him in the summer of 1917 ... Don't halloo until you're out of the woods." Bukharin would cripple the Bolshevik party and Soviet government by refusing to recognize reality. "'I want to recognize only the right of the working classes to self-determination,' says Comrade Bukharin, that is to say, you want to recognize something that has not been achieved in a single country except Russia. That is ridiculous." The party program had to "speak of what actually exists" not what the party wanted to exist. "Since nations are at different stages on the road from medievalism to bourgeois democracy and from bourgeois democracy to prole-tarian democracy," the party had to accept these facts in determining its rela-tionship to each individual situation. Lenin was more abrasive with Piatakov, declaring that what he had said "was tantamount to asking what was the good of all this self-determination when we have a splendid Central Committee in Moscow. This is a childish point of view." Piatakov, like Bukharin, wanted to deny the differing pace of social-economic development experienced by each nation. Communists simply could not make the revolution in Russia the measure for revolutions elsewhere. "These are the kind of objections which induce me to say," said Lenin, coining the most famous words of the debate, "Scratch some communists and you will find Great Russian chauvinists." Lenin drove this point home forcefully. Russians, he told his comrades, were not loved throughout their former empire. In many areas, he said, "Great Russian" is synonymous with the terms oppressor and rogue. This had to be taken into account and opposed, but it could not be eliminated by decree. "We must be very cautious in this matter. Exceptional caution must be displayed by a nation like the Great Russians, who earned the bitter hatred of all the other nations; we have only just learned how to remedy the situation, and then not entirely."[44] The congress unanimously adopted the party program with its Leninist sections on the self-determination of nations.[45]

The significance of this document for the survival of Soviet Russia and the successful conduct of her foreign policy cannot be exaggerated. On one level it was an assault on Great Russian chauvinism; on another, it had far-reaching practical implications for non-Russian Bolsheviks exercising authority on the periphery of Soviet power. Brest-Litovsk had been the first Bolshevik break with proletarian internationalism; it had placed Russian interests above those of all other nationalities. This had developed, however, on a purely ad hoc basis, necessitated by German power and Bolshevik impotence. As soon as Germany collapsed and the relative power of Soviet Russia had increased, borderland Bolsheviks hastened to establish quasi-independent Soviet republics in their homelands. In the face of the inability of these Soviet republics to maintain their independence without substantial Soviet Russian assistance, and with the inability of Moscow to provide this assistance without seriously endangering its own security, Lenin again proposed a policy foreseeing the possible sacrifice of the borderlands. This time, however, he based his policy in the party program rather than the ever-shifting circumstances of political necessity. This would make it easier to enforce and less vulnerable to attack. Bukharin and Piatakov, chief opponents of the Brest-Litovsk policy and the subsequent reluctance to pursue too forceful a policy in the borderlands, recognized that Lenin's nationality policy was a further break with proletarian internationalism and opposed it energetically. While denouncing Great Russian chauvinism, the policy actually promoted it through the sacrifice of proletarian internationalism and the assignment of Russia to a special category within the family of nations. Theoretically all nations were equal and advancing steadily along the road to socialism, but clearly one, Soviet Russia, was more equal than the others, for she had already arrived, if not at the final destination, then at the threshold of that destination. With the adoption of the nationality policy, borderland Bolsheviks could no longer appeal to the Soviet Russian government solely on the basis of proletarian internationalism. Depending on how far their society had advanced on "the road from medievalism to bourgeois democracy and from bourgeois democracy to proletarian democracy," the Bolshevik Central Committee might decide that the bourgeoisie or, in the case of the Asian borderlands, even the medieval feudal lords, were more suitable guardians of the popular interest than the local Bolsheviks.

In short, adoption of the nationality policy freed Lenin from the necessity of having to enforce the claims of Soviet republics to any or all the territory they aspired to govern. It also provided him with a measure of the legitimacy of their right to rule, for, by implication, legitimacy could largely be determined by their ability to remain in power without too much assistance from Moscow. At a time when the borderland republics were under mounting pressure, this was of no small importance. They could be supported or sacrificed as circumstances required, and, with these articles embedded in the party program, Lenin would be beyond criticism. In March 1919, with the negotiations with Bullitt and the earlier response to the Prinkipo proposal, the possibility of sacrificing the western borderlands to promote the survival of Soviet Russia could not have been far from his mind. In practice, therefore, Lenin's assault on Great Russian chauvinism prepared the basis for its apotheosis, and his celebration of national self-determination provided a warrant for the abandonment of the western borderlands.

It also provided him with an incomparable advantage in dealing with the non-Russian peoples of eastern Europe and those of adjacent areas in Asia. In these cockpits of incandescent national hatreds Lenin could now appear, if he chose, with proposals rival national governments would find difficult to refuse. In particular, it allowed the Bolsheviks to sharpen the contrast between their image and that of the Whites. It identified them as disposing of something of great value to the non-Russian peoples of the former empire. It had an enormous appeal to those confronted with the demand of the White generals for a restoration of Russia, one and indivisible, and great propaganda value against any nationalist regime unwilling to negotiate with Moscow. It served as carrot and stick to urge the successor states of the tsarist empire into negotiations with Soviet Russia. Not that the policy required Lenin to initiate such negotiations or even respond favourably to any approach made to him. It was permissive and entirely open to interpretation. It was a classic of Lenin's statecraft, freeing him to pursue political profit wherever it offered itself.

MILITARY AFFAIRS FIRST offered Lenin an opportunity to profit from the new policy. The speed and forcefulness with which the challenge to the existing order emerged in the spring of 1919 suggests that military necessity, early perceived, provided the fundamental impetus for defining Soviet nationality policy at the Eighth Congress. Thus, the Red Army had undergone a fundamental change in late 1918 and early 1919 when it had expanded from an essentially Russian-based force to one encompassing many units raised in the western borderlands and organized into the armed forces of the new Soviet republics proclaimed there. These armies, of course, had originated in Russia, but had expanded when transferred to their native soil and taken on a very different character when placed under the authority of indigenous commissariats of military affairs. Although the Estonian, Latvian, and Lithuanian-Belorussian armies remained administratively subordinate to the commander of the Soviet western front and that of Ukraine to the Soviet Russian supreme commander, it was frequently difficult to ensure that orders of these Russian authorities would be executed in the borderlands. This was especially true as the borderland commissarists got their recruitment and procurement apparatuses working and could, at least to a certain degree, function independently of the Russian hinterland. On the one hand this encouraged insubordination, especially in Ukraine but generally everywhere in the borderlands, with local authorities proving unwilling to make sacrifices asked of them to support hard-pressed Red Army forces on the southern front and in Siberia. It also encouraged empire-building, again principally in Ukraine but also in Latvia and Lithuania. Podvoiskii had built an immense military commissariat in Ukraine employing more than three thousand officers in Kiev and twenty-two thousand specialists in the provinces. The small Lithuanian-Belorussian Soviet Socialist Republic boasted a central military apparatus of more than 550 specialists.[46] This was particularly serious in the spring of 1919 when available cadres largely determined the number of men who might be mobilized for the Red Army.

As early as 10 April, hardly more than a fortnight after the close of the Eighth Congress, V.S. Litovskii, a member of the Lithuanian-Belorussian Revolutionary Military Council, wrote to Lenin about the tendency he had observed at Vilna to isolate the republic's military commissariat from the Soviet system in general and to seek solutions to local problems at the expense of reinforcing the Red Army elsewhere.[47] Two weeks later Vatsetis reported on this problem as it related to the Red Army as a whole. In effect, he said, the Red Army was fighting two separate wars. In the west a series of Soviet republics enjoyed virtual autonomy and were not concerned about the war elsewhere. This was a serious threat to Soviet security, because half of the Soviet population resided in the west, while less than 40 per cent lived in those areas most threatened by enemy action. Thus, a minority of the Soviet population had to bear the burden of defeating Kolchak and Denikin. Population alone was not his prime concern; Vatsetis was much more interested in the cadre monopolized by the western republics. He estimated that, apart from their actual armies, they had more than twenty-four thousand men in the central and provincial organs of military administration. This represented an invaluable reserve capable of organizing, instructing, and leading full-strength military units. Borderland Bolsheviks had proved incapable of mobilizing major forces in their republics but would not release any of this cadre for more efficient work in the south and the east. This, he said, was a threat to the very existence of all Soviet republics and asked Lenin to place the armies of the western republics directly under his authority, to liquidate their separate supply and recruitment organs, and allow him to reinforce other fronts with cadre drawn from the west.[48]

This memorandum initiated a process which soon led to the complete unification of the armed forces of all the Soviet republics. It came at just the moment when events revealed the instability of the western Soviet republics and the questionable nature of investing large military resources in them. Thus, in addition to the inability of the Estonian and Latvian Soviet republics to make any headway against their bourgeois rivals, the Lithuanian-Belorussian Soviet Republic virtually collapsed on 21 April when Polish troops captured Vilna. The Soviet commissars scattered and were only able to reconstitute themselves as a government on reaching Russian territory.[49] Lenin was clearly shaken by this. Accordingly he embraced Vatsetis's proposal, telling Sklianskii that it was necessary to act upon it "*immediately*." Vatsetis would have left the western republics a quarter of their military staff and functionaries, but Lenin had no compunction about taking them all. "Calculate," he told Sklianskii, "a 24,000 command structure. If we assume a ratio of 1 [officer] to 10 [recruits] that means we could create an army of *240,000*."

With such figures dancing in his head and Kolchak advancing in Siberia, Lenin acted quickly. Four days later the Revolutionary Military Soviet of the Republic endorsed the proposal[50] and on 4 May the Bolshevik Central Committee resolved to end the separate existence of the armies of the lesser Soviet republics. To give practical effect to this decision the Central Committee ruled that henceforth the territory of each Soviet republic would form a single military district subordinate to the Revolutionary Military Soviet of the RSFSR, on an equal footing with Russian military districts. Military authorities in the non-Russian Soviet republics would have to execute "precisely and unconditionally" all orders issued by the Revolutionary Military Soviet.[51] Bound to the Central Committee of the Russian Communist Party by authority reaffirmed again at the Eighth Congress, and frightened by further reverses along the western front during May, the central

committees of the non-Russian communist parties accepted the decree and agreed
that Moscow should formulate the terms of a new order in Soviet military
affairs.[52]

On 1 June 1919 Lenin took advantage of this fear-inspired acquiescence to
go beyond strictly military unification into other areas of the political life of the
borderland republics: "While recognizing fully the principle of independence,
freedom and self-determination for the working masses" of all Soviet Republics,
read the decree, it was necessary to unify "the military organizations and military
headquarters, the Councils of National Economy, the railway administrations
and undertakings, the finances, and the Labour Commissariats" of the several
Soviet republics "in order that the management of national life may be concentrated in the hands of unified boards" to prosecute the civil war more efficiently.[53]

V.D. Bonch-Bruevich, secretary of the Sovnarkom, hailed this decree as "the
start of a new period in the course of the Great Russian Revolution," because,
as he said, "apart from command of the armed forces being unified, other spheres
of state activity ... also underwent unification."[54] He was not far off the mark,
for the decree had immediate force and transferred control over the most vital
aspects of the political and military life of the borderland republics to Moscow.
Lenin lost no time in exercising his new powers. On 5 June the government of
Soviet Estonia officially dissolved itself, together with the Communist Party of
Estonia. The latter became a section of the Russian Communist Party while the
remaining functions of the former were assumed by Soviet Russian state agencies.
The army of the former government was consolidated into a single division
directly subordinate to the commander of the Soviet Russian western front.[55]
To the south, the Bolshevik press in what remained of Soviet Latvia took up
Moscow's refrain. "No separatism, no partisan movement," the press intoned,
"A single Soviet Russian front, a single revolution against all counter-revolutionary fronts." At mid-month a conference of the Latvian Communist Party
resolved that "at the present moment the Latvian front is not as important as
other Soviet Russian fronts." Priority, they agreed, should be given to the struggle
against Denikin. The army of Soviet Latvia was renamed the Soviet fifteenth
Army and subordinated directly to the commander of the western front. Its units
were subsequently merged into one and renamed the Soviet 53rd division. The
army of Lithuania-Belorussia underwent a similar transformation, becoming the
Soviet Sixteenth Army early in June. Shortly after, most of these consolidated
Baltic forces were shifted to the southern front where they played an important
part in the defeat of Denikin.[56]

None of this could have been particularly pleasant for borderland Bolsheviks.
The very absence of any trace of protest suggests suppression of evidence on
the part of contemporary Bolshevik authorities and current Soviet historians.
The fact that Moscow could engineer this development, impose this sacrifice,
and transfer resources to the truly critical southern front was telling testimony
of its superior political and administrative organization in comparison with the

forces confronting it in the west. Had those opposing forces been able to achieve even a small degree of cooperation, Moscow would have been in deep trouble, but confronted with only mutually hostile states incapable of even the most elementary cooperation, Bolshevik common sense and political discipline provided Soviet Russia with an immense advantage in the civil war. Moscow could count on the support of its allies in the Baltic; the White Russians could only be certain of the enmity of the bourgeois regimes there. Although unnoticed at the time, the disappearance of Soviet Estonia in early June 1919 was soon to place another weapon in the Soviet political armoury – direct negotiations with the bourgeois regime of a border state of the former Russian empire.

CHAPTER EIGHT

The end of "spontaneous victories":
Ukraine, Hungary, and Bessarabia

Just as political and military events in the northwest swirled around the
Murmansk-Reval axis, so similar events in the south rotated around a line drawn
from Budapest to Novorossiisk. The fate of the revolution in Hungary was
inextricably bound to developments on the Soviet southern front, and events in
both areas depended heavily on circumstances in Ukraine. In April events seemed
to favour the Bolsheviks; a red tide was rising which appeared ready to sweep
away the last foundations of the old order in southeastern Europe.

Nowhere did this seem more likely than in southern Ukraine. The Bolsheviks
had forced Petliura to abandon the region entirely, the Volunteer Army had
retreated towards the Don, and the French had evacuated Odessa. The French
still held the Crimea, with a powerful fleet based at Sevastopol, but their hold
was precarious.[1] They had made no provision for the assault Moscow unleashed
in the spring, and had no way of stopping the Red Army before it reached
Sevastopol. Surveying the situation on 6 April, Colonel E.G. Trousson, commander of the French troops in the Crimea, dismissed his Russian allies as being
worse than useless. "The best," he said, "do nothing; the others live riotously."
They were universally hated and fled in panic at the first sound of a gun. Within
a few days he expected to have ten thousand Bolsheviks in front of him, and
he had no idea how to oppose them. "How much more tranquil it was in the
trenches opposite the *Boches*!" he lamented.[2]

Paris, nonetheless, called for the Crimea to be held. It was such an important
base, said Clemenceau on 8 April, that a serious effort had to be made to save
it.[3] Senior French officers knew this was impossible and showered Paris with
chilling telegrams. As with Odessa, they reported, it was not simply a case of
military defence. The civil population would have to be fed, and there were no
local supplies. They would have to be brought from the Mediterranean and
quickly. But food was not the major problem. The Russian population was hostile

and "rallying to Bolshevism." To hold Sevastopol it would be necessary "to expel the majority of the working population so that we will only have to defend ourselves from one direction." It would be better, they concluded, to abandon the Crimea voluntarily than wait to be driven into the sea.[4] Clemenceau reluctantly agreed,[5] but too late to permit a graceful departure. On 13 April the Red Army reached Simferopol and three days later appeared outside Sevastopol.

Neither the French not the Bolsheviks were spoiling for a fight. On 14 April Red Army commanders informed Admiral Amet of their desire to arrange "a *modus vivendi.*"[6] The admiral gratefully agreed and invited Soviet delegates aboard his flagship. The Bolsheviks told Amet "they had no desire to fight against the allies as their efforts were directed only against the Volunteer Army." The admiral replied that he had not allowed any of the Whites to take refuge in Sevastopol. He added that with the withdrawal of the last German troops from Kherson and the restoration of order in south Russia he believed the French mission in the Black Sea was over, and he was preparing to withdraw his squadron and the allied garrison from Sevastopol. The suspicious Bolsheviks asked how long the admiral thought it would take to complete the evacuation. Only days, replied Amet. This reassured the Soviet delegates, but they were less pleased when he refused to allow them to assume responsibility for public order in the city. This and outbursts of fighting between the opposing forces led to a temporary breakdown in negotiations.[7] Hostilities broke out again and the French squadron opened fire on the Bolshevik lines. Negotiations resumed and, late on 17 April, resulted in agreement to an eight-day cease-fire. The French would retain responsibility for public order in Sevastopol but would not prevent a revolutionary committee from taking control of the city administration.[8]

It should be noted that more than mere caution lay behind the Bolshevik desire to negotiate with Amet. It was not in the Soviet interest to fight pitched battles with western forces, still less to butcher them on a grand scale, since this would be grist for the mills of those favouring intervention in Russia. Far better to back western forces against the sea and then negotiate their safe withdrawal. The discipline demonstrated by this tactic impressed French officers who negotiated with Soviet representatives. Almost all remarked about the new willingness displayed by the Bolsheviks to seek common ground with the western powers. To them this seemed to indicate that the Soviet government was evolving "in the sense of order, security and national sentiment."[9] One French officer even went so far as to say that, on the basis of his own experience, the Soviet government might "soon prove to be an acceptable neighbour at the green table, making no worse an appearance than the French Directory in 1796 next to the Court of Austria." This view was never accepted in Paris; at the Quai d'Orsay it was branded as idiotic.[10] In spite of those events, Clemenceau still sought some way of holding Sevastopol; as late as 21 April he again instructed his military commander in the east to delay the evacuation of Sevastopol for as long as possible.[12]

Even as Clemenceau issued his instructions they had become meaningless. The morale of French forces sent to south Russia, never good, had already broken. French soldiers and sailors saw no reason to fight and die in Russia. They fell easy prey to Bolshevik propaganda. At the first sight of red flags surrounding Sevastopol the trouble began; on 16 April two Soviet sympathizers aboard the destroyer *Protet* were discovered to be planning to turn their ship over to the Bolsheviks. Three days later an anti-war demonstration erupted aboard the battleship *France* and spread the following day to the *Jean Bart*, flagship of the French squadron. Crews on both ships demanded an immediate return of the squadron to France. They struck the tricolor, ran up the red flag, and sent launches around the fleet to win the support of the other ships. Later that day five hundred angry sailors went ashore, joined ranks with local Bolsheviks, and paraded the streets shouting their support for the revolution. French soldiers and marines would not fire upon the sailors but a Greek contingent did. The French sailors withdrew to their ships where they would have opened fire on nearby Greek warships had their officers not removed the breech-blocks from the guns while their men were ashore. The Greeks did not improve matters by hoisting a dummy French sailor to the yardarm of their flagship.[13]

All this placed Admiral Amet and his officers in a terrible dilemma. If they attempted to restore discipline they might well focus the anger of their men on themselves, and naval officers in 1919 knew the terrible fate of their Russian and German counterparts who, in the previous two years, had attempted to stand in the way of mutinous seamen. Such a course did not recommend itself to prudent men who, even in their own minds, could not justify their presence in Russia. French military and naval authorities in south Russia had come to share a common contempt for the Whites and were not prepared to die for them.

The British viewed the situation differently. They still cherished illusions about the Volunteer Army and believed the French had treated the Whites badly. British naval officers, in particular, were horrified by the French unwillingness to take decisive action against the mutiny. They summoned supporting warships from Constantinople and let Amet know that they were ready to assist him if necessary. French officers did not find this comforting. It was bad enough that they had been forced to ask Greeks to fire on Frenchmen, but to men who had spent most of their professional lives viewing the Royal Navy as their chief adversary, the idea of using British guns to quell an uprising on French ships must have been almost nauseating.

For Amet, evacuation of Sevastopol offered the best way out of the problem, and, from the beginning of the crisis, he pressed it urgently upon Paris. Clemenceau, however, continued to grasp at straws. He hoped that the first reports of the mutiny had been exaggerated. When it became clear that "the first telegrams had exaggerated nothing," he finally agreed to an immediate evacuation. The British, however, intervened and urged the French to hold fast. As Clemenceau had not even told Pichon of the mutiny, the British were the first to inform the incredulous foreign minister of the situation at Sevastopol. He agreed that the port should be held and wired his high commissioner in Constantinople to this effect at the same time Clemenceau directed his officers to proceed with the evacuation. [14] The British had wanted Amet, if he could no longer control his men, to sail from Sevastopol with his squadron, leaving the French and Greek regiments behind to defend the port. The British said they would assume responsibility for the naval defence of Sevastopol and the Crimea. [15] For the French this was nearly as bad as asking the British to fire on the *France* and *Jean Bart*. To sail away, leaving a British admiral free to fight for Sevastopol to the last Frenchman, was unthinkable. Amet ordered the complete evacuation of Sevastopol. On 29 April the last allied ship cleared the port and the following day the Red Army entered the city. The Bolsheviks had captured the Crimea in less than two weeks and at virtually no cost in life or material.

IN A SIMILAR MANNER the Red Army moved effortlessly to the Bessarabian frontier. As the French withdrew to the Dniester they did not oppose the Red Army and indeed were grateful that the Bolsheviks did not pursue them too closely. French commanders reported that during the retreat many soldiers had declared they had "no more wish of fighting in Bessarabia than at Odessa." On 11 April General Berthelot informed Paris "that the combat value of French troops had almost entirely disappeared." This was not an exaggeration. In a private letter d'Anselme informed Berthelot that he was left "with an army of brigands like the bands of the middle ages." With this force he had to defend southern Bessarabia while four divisions of Romanian troops continued the defence north from Dubosary to Khotin. Communications with Bucharest were very poor, and the allied force had only forty locomotives to supply their needs. The Romanians were eager to see the French leave. They declared quite openly that they had no confidence in the French army. "It is necessary to call things by their real name," one Romanian told a French general, "your troops are Bolsheviks." On 3 May Berthelot informed Paris that the entire allied army had to be withdrawn, not merely from Bessarabia, but from all Romania. French power on the Black Sea and Pontic Steppe had collapsed completely. [16]

Moscow and Budapest welcomed the French débâcle. [17] The withdrawal of the single strongest foreign force from the region served to enhance the relative military strength of the two major Bolshevik centres. The need to establish a direct connection between them had been recognized immediately following the communist victory in Hungary. "In view of the fact that Ukrainian Soviet troops are at the present time approaching Galicia, where the situation is already revolutionary," Chicherin radioed Bela Kun on 23 March, "we are close to our Hungarian allies who stand in the back of our enemies." [18] The same day Lenin and his military high command instructed the Ukrainian military authorities of the need to establish direct overland contact with Soviet Hungary. [19] Soviet Ukrainian forces made steady progress towards Galicia, driving the remnants of

Petliura's forces north and west towards the Polish lines and reaching the river Zbruch, the prewar boundary with Austria-Hungary, in early April.[20]

Here they stopped and, despite the most compelling reasons to advance, did not stir for more than a month. Why? No documents speak to this question, but circumstantial evidence suggests that prudence governed the Soviet decision. Militarily, there was good reason for caution. The Bolsheviks had captured Kiev on 5 February, and, in the following two months, the Soviet Ukrainian First Army advanced more than 360 kilometres. It was exhausted, in need of reinforcement, and forced to cope with large numbers of Directory troops scattered in the Soviet rear. Moreover, the broad-gauge Russian railway track ended at the Zbruch; on the other shore began the standard European track of the former Austrian railways. Once into East Galicia, supply and communication would become more difficult, especially in April, with the spring thaw creating havoc with the roads.

Yet the desire to rush forward must have been very strong. Strij and Sambor, the gateways to the Carpathian passes south into Hungary, were nearly within reach. In 1914 the Russian Eighth Army under General A.A. Brusilov had seized these same passes in the teeth of ferocious Magyar resistance and driven to the southwestern slopes of the Carpathians in preparation for a descent onto the Hungarian plain. That descent never took place, but many Red Army officers must have served with Brusilov. In 1919, however, the Bolsheviks would not have had to fight their way through the passes; the Hungarian army would have come north to greet them. Nor was there a significant military force blocking the way to the Carpathians. In November 1918 when the Habsburg empire collapsed, Galician socialists had declared the independence of a West Ukrainian state with its capital at Lvov. This had provoked Poland which claimed Lvov, and in January the Poles had seized the city. Poland and West Ukraine had been at war ever since, with the Galicians able to count on the Directory in neighbouring Podolia not to disturb their eastern frontier.[21] In April, when the Bolsheviks reached the Zbruch, West Ukraine lost this shelter and, locked in their conflict with Poland, would not have been able to block a Bolshevik passage to the Carpathians. Militarily, therefore, the Bolsheviks could have pushed on to a junction with the Hungarians near Ungvar or Mukachevo in Ruthenia.

Good political reasons argued against such audacity. West Ukraine might be unable to stop a Soviet drive to the west, but the Bolsheviks had to anticipate that other armies might intervene. The Poles at Lvov and the Romanians at Khotin would threaten the northern and southern flanks of such a drive and, fearing a junction of revolutionary armies, would almost certainly try to stop it. Less distance separated the Poles and Romanians than that which divided the Bolsheviks and Hungarians. Although a Ukrainian army might make its way to the Hungarian plain, it would be in constant danger of being cut off and isolated. Other possible consequences were equally unattractive. In early April Lenin still hoped for a cessation of hostilities with the Poles in Belorussia and Lithuania;

the Bolsheviks would only provoke an enlargement of the conflict by a sudden thrust into Galicia. Given the urgent need to limit hostilities in the west while fighting Denikin and Kolchak in the south and east, it was far more advantageous for the Bolsheviks to allow the Poles and Galicians to slaughter each other than to unite them against the Red Army by a drive to the Carpathian passes. An equally negative reaction could be expected from the allies. At this time Lenin still hoped that something might come of the Bullitt proposals, and he would not have wanted an ill-considered move into Galicia to jeopardize the possibility of a negotiated settlement with the Entente. Moreover, far from assisting Soviet Hungary, a Bolshevik invasion of East Galicia might simply add to the peril of the Kun regime. Even a successful and sustained military connection between Ukraine and Hungary would not, by itself, guarantee the survival of the revolutionary Magyar republic. The military aid which Soviet Russia could send Bela Kun was definitely limited; Lenin did not even have sufficient military resources for his own armies. Soviet Hungary was surrounded by enemies and was much more susceptible to Entente coercion than Russia. The establishment of a direct link between Budapest and Moscow could provoke a military intervention in Hungary which otherwise might not materialize. In late March and early April, therefore, while making preparations for military cooperation, both Bela Kun and Lenin sought to draw their foreign antagonists into negotiations rather than challenging them to another round of armed conflict.

The magnitude of the Bolshevik victory in Ukraine nurtured a political ferment which also served to favour restraint in Galicia. The political spectrum shifted to the left and, for a brief while, Ukrainian nationalists attempted to take on a defensive socialist colouring. On 9 April, the Directory formed a new socialist government under Borys Matros. It proclaimed a policy of "self-reliance" and pledged not to seek the aid of "foreign armed forces from any country whatsoever." Internally the new government pledged democratic reform and measures "to combat all anti-social elements."[22] The proclamation reflected Soviet demands made several months before and suggested that the new Ukrainian government might be prepared to consider some form of cooperation. Even more promising was the re-emergence of Vladimir Vinnichenko from political retirement. In late 1918 he had unsuccessfully sought to arrange a compromise between the Directory and the Bolsheviks. His failure and the outbreak of full-scale civil war contributed to the rise of Petliura and his military party. Vinnichenko had left Ukraine for exile in Austria. In late March 1919 he believed the time had come for another effort to reach agreement with the Bolsheviks. He contacted Bela Kun, who brought him to Budapest where he outlined his ideas for transmission to Moscow. Vinnichenko proposed an alliance of Soviet Russia, Soviet Hungary, and an independent Ukraine. Each state would enjoy equal rights and aid each other against "imperialist aggression," especially against the Entente and their eastern European clients. This would allow Lenin to send immediate aid to Budapest and free all Bolshevik forces in Ukraine for deployment elsewhere. In exchange the Bolsheviks would recognize the sovereignty of Ukraine within its ethnographic frontiers, including East Galicia and Lvov. Existing Ukrainian regimes would be merged in a coalition government of communist and socialist parties. No member of the alliance would leave its troops on the territory of an ally any longer than requested to do so by that country.[23]

This extraordinary proposal requires some explanation. It is significant, for example, that it was made at a time when it seemed as if Bolshevism would sweep triumphantly into the heart of central Europe. It was eagerly embraced by the Soviet Hungarian government, itself a coalition of socialist and communist parties, who viewed it as a way of securing prompt aid from Soviet Russia. To Vinnichenko it seemed a way of saving something for the non-Bolshevik Ukrainian socialists from the wreckage created by Petliura. Moreover, on a purely abstract level, even Lenin might have found certain of its aspects – an open road to Hungary and the ability to draw freely on Soviet military resources in Ukraine – appealing. Unfortunately for its proponents, it was not based in the political realities of the moment; by spring 1919 the fighting of the previous winter had rendered it impossible. Although defeated, Petliura continued to command the loyalty of his troops and, not displaying the same hatred of the Poles as his West Ukrainian countrymen, was able to negotiate an armistice with Pilsudski and continue the war against Moscow. Nor were the Kievan Bolsheviks in any mood for compromise. Even Lenin would have found it difficult to impose such a bargain on his victory-flushed comrades. There is no evidence to suggest he even considered the possibility.[24] Thus, Kiev simply rejected the Vinnichenko proposal while Moscow did nothing to encourage a further effort at compromise. By the end of April aid for Hungary by way of Galicia either by invitation of the West Ukrainian government or in the teeth of its armed opposition had ceased to be viable options for Soviet policy.

This impasse developed at precisely the moment when Hungarian need for aid grew greater. On 16 April Romania, fearing Bolshevik encirclement and seeking to annex Transylvania, invaded the Magyar republic. Surrounded by other enemies and crippled by the allied blockade, Hungary could not mount an effective defence. In these circumstances Vatsetis told Lenin on 21 April that it was essential for him to receive "directions from the government" regarding military assistance to Hungary. Specifically he wished to know if a further advance in East Galicia was "admissible from the general political point of view," and if so "what final line is to be set for our troops to occupy." Lenin's reply, sent the following day, reflected his changed military priorities. Establishment of a direct rail link with Soviet Hungary, he told Vatsetis, was one of two main tasks for the Soviet Ukrainian army. "First in importance and necessity," however, was for the Soviet Ukrainian army to aid Soviet Russian forces in the Donbass, where Denikin was rapidly enlarging a military breakthrough achieved earlier in the month. Two days later Lenin confirmed this order in a telegram to Rakovsky at Kiev. "It is essential," he wrote, "to help us defeat the Cossacks and take Rostov at all costs, sparing no effort and as rapidly as possible, even at the cost of a temporary slackening off in the west of the Ukraine, for otherwise disaster threatens." This marked a break with earlier instructions in which an equal priority had been assigned to the two operations.[25] Now Lenin had settled the issue: the Russian southern front took precedence over Hungary.

What then was to be done for Bela Kun? The Hungarian leader had told Moscow on 27 April that "a junction with Soviet troops through Galicia is a vital question for us." Kun again suggested an accord with West Ukraine and announced he was sending an emissary to Moscow to deal with the question. In barely veiled language Chicherin responded *en clair* that the Soviet government agreed that Hungarian "mining specialists" should leave "as soon as possible for Russia," but warned that, "due to distortion in the last radio message from Budapest, Hungarian intentions concerning the shipment of coal from South Russia to Hungary ... are unclear to us." He asked for clarification.[26]

The "distortion" was, of course, political rather than atmospheric. Kun still thought in terms of aid coming by way of Galicia, whereas Moscow no longer thought this possible. Instead, Soviet attention had turned to Bessarabia, which seethed with unrest due to Romanian occupation and which had come alive with the appearance of the Red Army on the Dniester. Soviet Ukraine, with Rakovsky, a founder and organizer of the Romanian Communist Party, at its head had long been interested in fomenting revolution in the neighbouring kingdom and favoured military action against Bessarabia rather than Galicia.[27] The disposition of available armed forces and the difficulty of moving them north to Galicia similarly favoured a more southerly action. Soviet forces were also likely to secure the active support of dissident elements in Bessarabia and benefit from the moral collapse of the French army dug in along the southern course of the Dniester. It was unlikely that a junction with the Magyar army could soon be established by way of Bessarabia, but a Soviet invasion of the province might compel the Romanians to withdraw from Hungary. The Bessarabian gambit also appealed to Moscow and Kiev, because it would allow them to use the substantial force of the Ataman Grigorev, which had figured so largely in the liberation of Odessa. If Grigorev and his band could be convinced to fight in Bessarabia, they could form the spearhead of a potentially lethal blow against the French and Romanian armies while removing them from their native districts where they could only create trouble for the Soviet authorities.[28] Thus, Moscow and Kiev decided to go to the aid of Hungary through Bessarabia. On 1 May Chicherin and Rakovsky, citing the armed hostility of the Romanian regime to the Soviet governments of Russia, Ukraine, and Hungary, as well as the "illegal occupation" of Bessarabia, issued a joint ultimatum giving the Romanians forty-eight hours to withdraw from Bessarabia. The following day Rakovsky issued a further ultimatum demanding the withdrawal of Romanian forces from Bukovina.[29] Although no specific threats were made, it is clear that the ultimatums were intended as a prelude to the Soviet crossing of the Dniester.

It proved impossible for the Bolsheviks to launch a serious assault on Bessarabia. Kiev directed Antonov-Ovseenko to begin the invasion with whatever forces he had at his disposal, but they were inadequate for the task. The Bolsheviks could only mount a minimal operation against Romania. They organized a Bessarabian provisional government, issued a call for volunteers of Bessarabian origin, unleashed an artillery barrage across the Dniester, and even landed a small detachment on the western shore, but they were unable to cross the river in force. On the very day Rakovsky ordered the Soviet Ukrainian army into battle, Trotsky put his finger on why the operation was likely to fail. "The military victories in the Ukraine have not been so much victories of the army," he wrote, "as direct victories of the Revolution, i.e. phenomena of a more or less spontaneous nature." Initially, in both Russia and Ukraine, advancing revolutionary forces had appeared invincible, but the German army had brought an abrupt end to Russian illusions, he said, and submitted that "the first period, the period of spontaneous victories, had now come to an end for the Ukrainian revolution too."[30]

Trotsky did not go nearly far enough. Not only was the period of spontaneous victories at an end, the period of spontaneous defeats was at hand. The bulk of the Soviet Ukrainian army had been organized from independent partisan detachments, whose enlistment under the red banner had little to do with acceptance of Bolshevik principles. Now the Bolsheviks had formed their own government and were proving just as unpopular as previous regimes at Kiev. The Soviet Ukrainian army, therefore, began to disintegrate as peasant detachments began to react negatively to Bolshevik policies. First Grigorev and then Nestor Makhno, the two most important partisan commanders, rebelled against Kiev. The loyalty of Grigorev had been in question since 7 May when, rather than advancing on Bessarabia as ordered by Antonov-Ovseenko, he had arrested Bolshevik commissars, seized the railway network north of Odessa and advanced against Soviet strongholds in southwestern Ukraine. Loyal Soviet forces on the borders of Bessarabia, Bukhovina, and Galicia suddenly found an enemy in their rear and had to fight on two fronts. Any possibility of an armistice on the Zbruch or in Volynia evaporated, and plans for a campaign in Bessarabia became meaningless. Although Soviet commanders were able to bring the Grigorev rebellion under control by the end of May, it was impossible to resume the planned attack on Romania.[31] Circumstances in the east made such an operation appear as a dream out of a distant past.

EAST OF UKRAINE LAY the Soviet Russian southern front. Here four Soviet armies with many smaller formations held an irregular and imperfect perimeter around the southern course of the river Don and the adjacent region of the Kuban within which was contained the Volunteer Army of General Denikin and his Cossack allies. Since late 1918 fighting there had been more intense than on any other front of the civil war, but the necessity of reinforcing the Siberian front and the breathtaking perspectives of revolutionary opportunity offered in east-central Europe had distracted Soviet attention. Only Vatsetis appears to have had a clear understanding of the seriousness of the situation. Since October he had repeatedly insisted on crushing the Volunteer Army in the shortest possible time, but time and again he had been overruled and had seen badly needed resources transferred elsewhere. Thus, in March the southern front had still not crushed the Volunteer Army, and Denikin had begun to receive significant aid from the British. These supplies tipped the scale in Deniken's favour. First the Volunteer Army held the Bolsheviks and then took the offensive. Initially the issue remained in doubt, but by mid-April Denikin clearly began to gain the upper hand.[32]

Lenin was horrified. Like Vatsetis, he blamed the Ukrainian Bolsheviks for refusing to aid the southern front, but initially his position was ambiguous, for he refused to establish clear cut priorities for the use of available military resources. As long as Denikin did not appear to be gaining too great an advantage, Lenin was unwilling to force Kiev to reinforce the southern front. Not until 22 April did he decree that "the Ukraine must in duty bound recognize that the Donbass Front is unquestionably the most important Ukrainian front and carry out at all costs and without delay the task of supplying the Donbass-Mariupol sector with substantial reinforcements."[33]

The situation in the south grew even worse.[34] During the second week of May, while also seeking to counter the Grigorev rebellion, Lenin issued one order after another to reinforce the Red Army on the Don. That force could neither crush the peasant revolt which had exploded in its rear nor contain the Volunteer Army which had launched another, still larger, offensive. Worse was to come, for in the following week Denikin broke through the right wing of the southern front, shattering Makhno's detachments and turning the flank of the Soviet Thirteenth Army. Through this breach rode the cavalry corps of General A.G. Shkuro to harass the Soviet rear. Political shock followed military collapse, for in recoiling from the blow dealt him, Makhno withdrew entirely from the front and moved west towards the Dnieper rather than east to reengage Denikin. In a few days he too joined the rebellion against the Bolsheviks.[35]

The rapid suppression of the Grigorev insurrection was the only good news to reach Moscow from Ukraine in May 1919. In congratulating Rakovsky on crushing the rebellion, however, Lenin made it clear that there could be no change in established military priorities. "I insist," he wrote, "that the forces which are liberated [by the end of the insurrection] be sent to the Donbass." This allowed Vatsetis to achieve several of his own objectives. For months he had been trying to restrain the Soviet Ukrainian political and military authorities and compel them to contribute to the crushing of Denikin. Now he was able to act forcefully in this matter. "In view of the difficult situation on the southern front and the exhaustion of reserves," he ordered on 26 May that "the western portions of the Ukrainian front along the Dniester and in Galicia pass to the defensive" and that "the largest possible number of battle-worthy military units be separated from the structure of the Ukrainian front and be transferred to the southern front" Soviet Ukrainian authorities, of course, protested and sought to have the directive reversed. "Grigorev's bands," they argued, "had only been scattered, not annihilated," while a new conflict with Poland was already taking shape in the northwest. "The rapid dispatch of units to the southern front is now quite difficult."[36]

All true, but irrelevant. Faced with the collapse of the southern front, Lenin did not hesitate to sacrifice even the most vital interests of the Soviet periphery to reinforce the centre of Bolshevik power. Moreover, during the previous six weeks he had put in place the engine needed to suck military resources back from the borderlands to the heart of Soviet Russia. The unification of the armed forces of all the Soviet republics, including Soviet Ukraine, which became effective as from 1 June 1919, provided Bolshevik leaders with all the authority needed to enforce established military priorities. The reinforcement of the southern front now got under way in earnest, with Vatsetis abolishing the Ukrainian front as a whole and transferring all its forces to two entirely new RSFSR armies.[37] Although further defeats awaited the Bolsheviks before they could bring the Volunteer Army under control, by mid-year they had achieved the central control and organization necessary for eventual victory. As in the Baltic, a similar control and organization escaped their opponents. The sharply conflicting national aspirations of the non-Bolshevik regimes proved to be an impenetrable seal barring virtually all cooperation.

THE BOLSHEVIKS PAID a steep price for the reinforcement of the Russian centre. Soviet authorities lost most of their ability to influence events in Bessarabia, Bukhovina, and East Galicia. Due to the deep roots of local revolutionary organizations and the extreme unpopularity of the Romanian occupation, the Bolsheviks were able to continue an effective propaganda war in Bessarabia. The campaign was so extensive that the Romanians feared it would produce an insurrection. By June, however, they had ceased to fear a Soviet invasion. They realized that they had received "unexpected relief" from Grigorev and soon understood that as long as the Bolsheviks could not cope with Denikin, the Red Army would not invade Bessarabia. They could therefore leave the bulk of their army in Hungary and hold the Dniester with only a few divisions.[38] Consequently Bela Kun received little benefit from the confrontation on the Dniester, and Bucharest was free to devote itself almost unhindered to military operations aimed at crushing the revolutionary Magyar republic. Farther to the north, other events, equally uninfluenced by Bolshevik intervention, served to promote the eventual collapse of Soviet Hungary. From the very beginning of their revolution Hungarian communists had viewed control of the Carpathian passes as vital to their survival. For more than a month they were at least theoretically within the Bolshevik grasp. In late April this ceased to be true, as the Poles pushed south and east from Lvov to occupy the northern approaches to the passes. At the end of May, the Romanians moved forward to meet them and forced the West Ukrainian army to evacuate the remaining portions of Bukhovina still in their possession. Poland and Romania established a common frontier effectively blocking the Bolshevik path to the Carpathians.[39] The Red Army, wholly occupied on the Don, did not intervene.

The Poles, however, did not content themselves with blocking Bolshevik access to the west. They continued their advance to the Zbruch, liquidating the West Ukrainian republic and staking their claim to all East Galicia. The western powers refused to recognize the legality of this claim, but on 25 June authorized a temporary Polish occupation to protect the province from the Bolsheviks.[40] The Red Army was never to reach the Soviet Hungary of Bela Kun.[41]

Isolated in central Europe, the revolutionary regime in Budapest could not long survive. On 1 August they resigned and fled to Austria. Bela Kun, while sparing Lenin from his criticism, blamed other members of the Soviet Russian and Ukrainian governments for his fall. Rakovsky and Chicherin earned his special scorn for allegedly sabotaging efforts to aid Soviet Hungary. Lenin defended his lieutenants, telling Kun in late July that his charges were "absolutely without foundation." In his last message to Kun, Lenin reaffirmed his confidence in Chicherin and Rakovsky. "We are doing everything possible to help our Hungarian friends," he declared, "but our forces are small."[42]

Was Kun justified in his accusations? Did the Bolsheviks fail their Hungarian comrades? The charge cannot be substantiated. Chicherin and Rakovsky certainly did not undermine aid to Soviet Hungary. Rakovsky, in fact, continued to argue in its favour long after Lenin had abandoned any hope of effective assistance. Chicherin undoubtedly pointed out the international pitfalls of any serious effort to aid Bela Kun, but he did not formulate foreign policy in Moscow. Chicherin and Rakovsky both executed the will of the Bolshevik Central Committee and Politburo. Thus when Lenin informed Kun that Rakovsky and Chicherin "had been appointed by the full Central Committee" and that the committee was satisfied with their conduct, he meant that the policies adopted in Moscow were the policies of the entire party executive and not simply a few men.

But could it even be said that these policies were responsible for the fall of Soviet Hungary? No. Nothing indicates that even top priority for Soviet Hungary would have proved effective. To survive, Soviet Hungary required a more congenial international environment and the triumph of sympathetic revolutionary regimes in one or more neighbouring states. This did not happen. Instead, Soviet Hungary represented the revolutionary high-water mark of 1919. When the red tide receded Bela Kun was left stranded in Budapest and all the resources at Lenin's disposal were insufficient to establish and maintain a lifeline to Hungary. In the absence of such resources the Bolsheviks sought the next best means of aiding Soviet Hungary – to take Romanian pressure off the Hungarian army by creating a diversion in Bessarabia. The Grigorev insurrection put an end to this operation before it could be properly begun. Even though it did not take the Bolsheviks long to crush the insurrection, the very act of doing so destroyed the armed force intended for the spearhead of the Bessarabian invasion and totally disorganized their remaining forces in southwest Ukraine. They were also immediately confronted by the Makhno rebellion and the collapse of their southern front. "Our forces are small," Lenin told Kun, and he did not exaggerate. Lenin could either dissipate those forces and, in the context of the early summer of 1919, almost certainly lose everything, or concentrate them at the very centre of his own power and perhaps save the revolution in Russia. It is not surprising that he chose the latter.

CHAPTER NINE

The peace of Dorpat: "A dress rehearsal for an agreement with the Entente"

As 1919 passed its mid-way point Soviet leaders remained confident of the future. Denikin continued to advance in the south, but his troops did not form the vanguard of an allied army. "The bands of Denikin," said Trotsky, "are the totality of the army that the counter-revolution is today capable of launching against us. Denikin has nothing behind him, indeed his rear is hostile." Trotsky jeered at the western powers. "Anglo-French militarism," he proclaimed on 27 June, "is nothing more than an enormous cardboard stage set. It is internally empty. The revolution has exhausted it. It will soon collapse before the eyes of the entire world."[1] Lenin agreed. On 4 July he described the Entente as "nothing more than a giant with feet of clay."[2]

The collapse of Soviet Hungary undermined this optimism. Publicly Lenin put the best possible interpretation on that débâcle. Hungary, he said, had been too small to repulse her enemies, and Bela Kun had been unable to exchange space for time to obtain the experience needed to survive the imperialist onslaught. The fate of Soviet Hungary, he declared, would not dishearten Bolsheviks, because they knew that the triumph of the "Romanian Kolchaks" would be short-lived.[3] We do not know what Lenin said in private as he did not commit his thoughts to paper. Trotsky did, and thus we know what a profoundly depressing effect the events of July had upon his thinking. "The collapse of the Hungarian Republic, our reverses in the Ukraine and the possible loss to us of the Black Sea Coast," he wrote on 5 August, meant "that Anglo-French militarism will still retain a certain measure of vitality and strength, and our Red Army will, in the arena of the European paths of world politics, figure as a quantity of fairly modest proportions, not only for the purpose of attack but also for that of defence." Trotsky concluded that Soviet Russia should turn its attention to Asia. "The road to India may prove at the given moment to be more readily possible and shorter for us than the road to Soviet Hungary."[4]

Failure to contain Denikin also undermined Bolshevik confidence. The entire southern front simply went to pieces. On 25 June Denikin captured Kharkov, and five days later Wrangel's Cossacks entered Tsaritsyn. A *Te Deum* again rang out from the great cathedral on the Volga, and Denikin solemnly issued his Moscow Directive ordering a march on the very seat of Soviet power.[5] The fall of Tsaritsyn severed Moscow's link with Astrakhan and dealt a serious blow to the transport of the limited quantity of petroleum which the Bolsheviks were still able to smuggle from Baku. It again raised the spectre of Denikin and Kolchak joining forces somewhere near the western end of the Trans-Siberian railway. Kolchak was still on the run, but in the fluid military circumstances of the Russian civil war a reverse of the proportion just suffered by the Red Army could have nearly incalculable consequences.[6]

The Bolsheviks now fell to quarrelling among themselves. On 3 July Vatsetis was dismissed as supreme commander of the Red Army and was replaced by S.S. Kamenev, the victorious commander of the eastern front.[7] As Vatsetis was closely associated with Trotsky while Kamenev had quarrelled bitterly with him, many saw the action as a vote of no-confidence in the Commissar of War. Trotsky tendered his resignation, but Lenin would not accept it. Trotsky remained at his post, but immediately fell out with Kamenev on how to defeat Denikin. Prior to his dismissal, Vatsetis had planned to mass Soviet reserves on the right flank of the front and drive southeastward into the Donets Basin to force a wedge between Denikin and his Cossack allies.[8] Kamenev junked this plan and called for a concentration of forces on the left flank of the southern front where it would be easier to mass reinforcements drawn from Siberia. He wanted to recapture Tsaritsyn, thus re-opening the Volga to Soviet navigation, and drive directly to the heart of Denikin's power at Novocherkassk and Rostov. Trotsky said that this "approached the problem of the southern front as one of abstract strategy, ignoring its social base." In the Donets Basin the Red Army could count on the support of the indigenous proletariat. The Cossacks, on the other hand, would bitterly resist an attack on the Don. Relations between Denikin and the Cossacks were notoriously bad, and he had been unable to convince them to march north-ward with the Volunteer Army. Trotsky thought it political madness to attack them in their homes and force them to fight the Red Army. It was doing Denikin's work for him bringing into the war a force which otherwise would remain on the sidelines. Lenin, however, would not change his mind. Mistaking Trotsky's well-founded opposition to the proposal as merely a continuation of his quarrel with Kamenev, Lenin insisted that the offensive proceed as planned. On 23 July orders were cut "for the launching of the main thrust by the left flank of the [southern] front by mid-August."[9]

Western reaction to Denikin's successful offensive shows how important it was for the Bolsheviks to stop the advance of the Volunteer Army. The collapse of Kolchak, the political quagmire in the Baltic, and French flight from Ukraine had all contributed to a cooling of western interest in aiding the Whites. Denikin's sudden success rekindled interest in intervention. Churchill, always indefatigable in support of anti-Bolshevism, turned his attention to providing all supplies necessary for a march on Moscow. In the teeth of considerable opposition, he succeeded in obtaining approval for a continuation of aid to Denikin at the substantial level already being given. Henceforth the British decided to focus all their resources on Denikin's theatre of military operations.[10] The French also began to alter their policy. In the past they had nothing but contempt for the Volunteer Army; now they began to warm towards Denikin. Paris offered, and Denikin agreed to accept, French supplies for his army in Ukraine.[11] Even the Romanians, fearful they were witnessing the rebirth of Great Russia one and indivisible, sought to determine if they could gain the goodwill of Denikin without yielding Bessarabia.[12]

Denikin was not to be stopped. While the Red Army vainly tried to organize its August offensive Denikin unleashed the cavalry of General K.K. Mamontov, who broke through the junction of two Soviet armies and simply disappeared into the steppe. Riding in a wide arc behind Soviet lines he disrupted transportation, attacked supply centres, and temporarily occupied towns and cities in his path. Half the Soviet force assigned to carry out the August offensive could take no part in it, while the remaining armies, ordered by Lenin to begin their attack on schedule, proved ineffective.[13] Meeting stubborn Cossack resistance, the Bolsheviks were unable to draw off any of the Volunteer Army advancing north into the heart of central Russia and west to the major centres of Ukraine. By 13 August the fate of Soviet Ukraine was sealed. Denikin advanced at will, his "armoured trains reconnoitering far ahead of cavalry, meeting no opposition, and find[ing] no trace of enemy organization." Kherson fell on 18 August and Odessa a week later. The Bolsheviks abandoned Kiev without a struggle. Trotsky rightly observed that Denikin did not have a firm hold on Ukraine and his occupation would fall apart as soon as it was struck by a decisive blow,[14] but Lenin complained bitterly of the military incompetence which had allowed the enemy "to run amok." At the end of August nothing gave any hope that the military situation would improve before it deteriorated still further.[15]

The Soviet western front also came under extreme pressure. Since seizing Vilno in April the Poles, distracted by Germany and Galicia, had remained primarily on the defensive in Belorussia. While Kolchak and Yudenitch struck at the Bolsheviks, Pilsudski was content to consolidate his position in Lithuania and await developments. In July, with Kolchak and Yudenitch defeated and the serious threat posed by Denikin not fully apparent, Pilsudski elected to move forward in Belorussia. Here possession of the few railways was critical, and rival regimes fought bitterly for their control. In April the Poles had seized most of the important Vilno-Lida-Baranowicze-Luninets line. This left the Bolsheviks with the Molodechno-Minsk-Slutsk railway and in a position to threaten southern Lithuania and eastern Poland. Pilsudski wanted to drive them back to the next available parallel railway extending from Vitebsk through Orsha to Zhlobin. This would force the Bolsheviks to take up positions in marshy terrain which would impede any counter-attack they might contemplate. The Poles could then defend their new position with a minimum of troops.[16]

Even before the Polish summer offensive the Bolsheviks knew their western front was deplorably weak. Stalin asked for reinforcement, but in the developing southern emergency there was no way to send the west anything.[17] Thus, when the Poles launched a general offensive on 8 August they achieved complete success. Minsk fell on the second day of attack and the Poles easily pushed the Bolsheviks back to the Berezina river.[18] Stalin, on 11 August, described the situation as "ominous." Trotsky agreed. He told Lenin that "without reserves maintaining the western front will become impossible."[19]

There were no reserves. The western front could no longer be maintained militarily. How was it to be held? The experience of the previous year suggested a political shield. In August 1918 the Bolsheviks had faced a similar situation with too many enemies and not enough troops. They had survived by agreeing with the Germans to take "de-facto parallel action" against common foes.[20] The basis for a similar agreement with the Poles already existed. Pilsudski had no more reason to help Denikin than to aid Kolchak. Like the Germans a year before, he expected to clash with the armed forces opposing the Bolsheviks should they crush the Soviet government. From his point of view it was much better that Russian should slaughter Russian so that he could save his own army for a future clash with the victor. Marchlewski had already discussed mutual interest with representatives of Pilsudski in Warsaw and, on returning to Moscow on 18 June, informed his superiors of these discussions. Some Polish communist leaders in Moscow contended that it was useless to negotiate with a bourgeois government; others hoped it would soon be possible to bring communism to Poland on the bayonets of the Red Army. A majority, however, agreed to continue the negotiations, and, more importantly, Lenin did as well. On 10 July Marchlewski crossed the front to resume talks with Polish representatives.[21]

Marchlewski informed Alexander Wieckowski, who had earlier represented Poland in Moscow, that the Soviet government was prepared to make far-reaching concessions. Moscow would accept a Soviet-Polish frontier substantially to the east of the existing fighting front. Wieckowski indicated Polish interest in such an agreement, but with the western powers still at war with Bolshevism, Warsaw could not enter into official negotiations with Moscow. The Poles would only agree to informal talks aimed at a secret agreement. These would be conducted under the cover of negotiations for an exchange of hostages. A time and place was to be established later, but both governments would have to agree to the talks no later than 15 August.[22] By the time Marchlewski returned to Moscow and consulted his Polish colleagues, the military situation in the south had become so serious that no one objected even to the conclusion of peace with Pilsudski. Polish leaders met with Chicherin who, with Lenin's approval, agreed to form a Red Cross delegation led by Marchlewski to conduct the negotiations foreseen at Bialowieza. On 12 August, four days after Pilsudski had begun his offensive in Belorussia and less than forty-eight hours after Mamontov had broken through the southern front, Chicherin informed the Polish foreign ministry of this decision. All this was done on the basis of Lenin's personal authority. Chicherin did not inform the Politburo until four days later.[23]

The Poles did not respond until their troops had reached the Berezina. In effect, the operation was a test of Bolshevik goodwill. Marchlewski had said that the Soviet government was prepared to yield substantial territory to secure peace. The failure of the Red Army to put up a spirited defence in Belorussia confirmed the bargain and led to the implementation of the remainder of the agreement. On 26 August the Polish government, stressing the need to avoid any appearance of official negotiations, authorized the foreign minister to resume talks through the agency of the Polish Red Cross. A week later radio Warsaw informed Moscow that the talks could resume.[24] The Bolsheviks, however, received more than a simple resumption of negotiations. The Poles virtually ended military operations in Belorussia and refused to support a major anti-Bolshevik offensive in Latvia. More important, the Poles confirmed their hostility to Denikin. They openly paraded their sympathy for Petliura and secretly instructed their agents in Ukraine to suspend anti-Bolshevik activities.[25] The Bolsheviks were again able to benefit from de facto parallel action, cooperating with a confirmed enemy against a common foe.

The precariousness of this arrangement can be seen in Pilsudski's long-term objectives. Since July he had hinted that he wished to play an enlarged role in eastern Europe and had ignored criticism of his aggressive policies in Lithuania and Galicia. If he undertook a major role against the Bolsheviks he did not want to be subject to further criticism. But his resources were too limited to wage war against the Bolsheviks without substantial material and financial support. He was already in urgent need of supplies of all kinds, and if he did not receive prompt support from the allies, he told the French chargé d'affaires in early August, he would have to consider peace with the Bolsheviks.[26]

In mid-August and early September Pilsudski presented his views even more forcefully. He told French representatives that anarchy in Ukraine inspired Poles with the greatest concern. They believed that "only Polish intervention, political and even military, could re-establish order there." The Ukrainians, the Poles believed, were "unsuited to any perseverent effort and incapable of any spontaneous idea of order and organization." Nor could the Ukrainian problem be solved by Denikin, who was cordially hated throughout the Ukraine, nor by the Bolsheviks, who were equally detested, nor by the allies, who had already demonstrated their incapacity for constructive action there. Only the Poles, because of their numbers, geographic propinquity, and knowledge of Ukraine, could intervene successfully. Such intervention should not be seen as imperialism; it would simply be "an indispensable police measure."[27] With such ambitions, Pilsudski would clash with any Russian government. Lenin was prepared to make far-reaching concessions, but he would not surrender Ukraine.

FARTHER TO THE NORTH, circumstances more favourable to the Bolsheviks existed. In the Baltic provinces political authority was badly fragmented. German and White Russian armed forces threatened local governments and destabilized the region. The allied powers, uncertain of the outcome of the Russian civil war, were unable to formulate firm and consistent policies concerning the future of the new states. Fear, apprehension, and uncertainty characterized all political relationships. In the second half of 1919 the Bolsheviks were able to exploit these circumstances to enhance their security without committing significant military resources to the region.

Soviet policy came to be based on a well-coordinated effort to negotiate peace with the bourgeois governments of the region. The failure of indigenous communist parties to hold power and the pressing need to reduce the military pressure on Soviet Russia suggested this policy. So too did the popularity of peace within the new states. So attractive was it that in the late spring indigenous communists, defeated in their bid for power but still able to conduct underground political activity, made peace with Soviet Russia an integral part of their party programs.[28] The voluntary liquidation of the Estonian Labour Commune in early June was a signal that Moscow was ready to recognize the independence of the bourgeois republic of Estonia.[29] Estonian communists in Russia agreed fully with this measure. The newly formed Russian Bureau of the Estonian Communist Party Central Committee wrote on 12 June to the Central Committee of the Russian Communist Party that the restoration of the Estonian Soviet Republic should be sought only "by way of an internal revolution." It was desirable, they said, that Soviet Russia propose peace to the existing government in Reval and, provided the White Estonians ended their own military operations, to abstain from any attack on Estonian territory. At the end of the month Lenin endorsed these proposals and indicated that a new peace initiative should be undertaken when circumstances appeared favourable.[30]

The communists did their best to influence Estonian public opinion in favour of peace with Soviet Russia. In a manifesto of 2 July they pointed to the failure of the western powers to recognize Estonian independence. Instead they had recognized Kolchak as the Supreme Ruler of all Russia. Kolchak had announced that he recognized the independence of Poland, but not the Baltic states. He only promised autonomy to Estonia, and the allies had agreed that the Estonian question was to be settled as a domestic concern of a future Russian state. Even Nicholas II would have agreed to such terms. "There is no Estonian state, only a province or district with such administrative rights as the black-hundred 'national assembly' of Kolchak will be disposed to grant to it. There is no independence, only a counter-revolutionary war of the bourgeoisie against the proletarian revolution." The communists called for the overthrow of the Estonian government.[31]

A week later a mutiny did erupt among new conscripts of the Estonian army who objected to compulsory military service.[32] There is no evidence that the manifesto of 2 July played any role in igniting the mutiny, but the communists had accurately gauged the widespread nature of popular dissatisfaction with government policies. On 19 July they issued another manifesto. Here they charged that the bourgeoisie were waging class war under cover of alleged military necessity. The importance of this document, however, lay in the conclusion, where the Central Committee of the Estonian Communist Party declared that the eight-month civil war had shown that "the Estonian toilers must liberate themselves by way of direct internal struggle against the bourgeoisie." They then announced the liquidation of the Estonian communist government and called for peace with Soviet Russia as the first step in freeing Estonian workers for a decisive struggle against the bourgeoisie.[33] Although this remarkable document bristled with rhetoric and concluded with no less than six stirring revolutionary appeals, it was in fact nothing less than the unconditional surrender of the Estonian communists. For all the brave talk, it was clear that not only were they leaving the field of battle but so were their Russian friends. Estonia, declared the manifesto in heavy type, need no longer fear a Soviet attack, for henceforth "*not one red regiment of Russia will cross the Estonian frontier.*"[34] The inference was clear: Soviet Russia no longer threatened Estonian independence; the bourgeoisie need only fear the Whites.

The Bolsheviks had touched a sensitive nerve. The Estonian government was profoundly suspicious of the western attitude to Kolchak, and on 18 June joined seven other successor states of the former empire in a declaration denying that "the decisions of the organs of the Governmental Power of Russia, whatever they may be," could be of any concern to them. They had been created and continued to exist "by the free will" of their peoples and would regulate their affairs independently of any foreign authority.[35] Twelve days later the Estonian foreign ministry warned the British that allied willingness to leave the fate of Estonia in the hands of a future Russian national assembly could prove destructive of willingness to continue the struggle against Bolshevism.[36] By then fear of being left to the mercy of Kolchak or Denikin had become acute.

The events of August only added to this fear. The Estonians watched uneasily as Denikin's advance again energized local Whites and turned their gaze towards Petrograd. The arrival of British supplies for Yudenich had much the same effect. General Sir Hubert Gough, commander of the allied military mission to the Baltic states, wrote Yudenich on 4 August urging that he act promptly to seize the former Russian capital.[37] It was clear to both, however, that the Whites could not do this without the help of Estonia. On 8 August Gough personally asked the Estonians to cooperate in the assault on Petrograd. The Estonians told Gough that they would not aid the Northwestern Army until they received a guarantee of Estonian independence from the Russians. The British account of this meeting then records: "The Estonians refused to accept General Yudenich's guarantee and said that it must come from a regularly constituted Russian Government. In consequence of this, General Gough decided to form a Russian Government."[38]

So began one of the most bizarre episodes in the western effort to overthrow the Bolsheviks. What followed was later described by Lord Curzon as "the Ruritanian experiment of General Gough and his Merry Men." Gough left the problem in the hands of his deputy, Brigadier-General Frank Marsh, who on 10 August informed Russian leaders in Reval that they had forty minutes to organize a government prepared to issue the declaration demanded by the Estonians. Nothing could be done without Estonian help, he said, and threatened to cut off further British aid if they did not cooperate. The Russians protested bitterly but, with some further delay, did as they were told. On 14 August they announced the formation of a Northwestern Russian Government and issued a long and convoluted "preliminary declaration" purporting to meet the Estonian demands. When Yudenich shrank from endorsing this declaration, Marsh threatened to remove him from his command. "We have another Commander in Chief all ready," he told him. No wonder that Lord Balfour said these events "read rather like the prospectus of a bubble company."[39]

The British cabinet promptly repudiated the action of their agents in the Baltic. The key figures in the coup d'etat, as Balfour described it, were reprimanded and recalled to London. Yudenich then repudiated his pledge to the Estonians. This mattered little, for they had already found it wanting. Convinced that the Whites were not acting in good faith, the Estonians made aid to Yudenich contingent on western recognition of their independence. The western powers, who still feared alienation of a recrudescent Russia, would not agree.[40] As a result Estonia would not provide the aid for Yudenich which everyone agreed was necessary for his survival.

Still, the situation was volatile and could change with devastating swiftness. Talks at the general staff level continued and, on the initiative of General March, who remained behind after Gough's departure, a meeting of Estonian, Latvian, Lithuanian, and Russian representatives opened in Riga on 26 August to discuss a joint offensive against the Bolsheviks. A tentative plan was worked out and 15 September was chosen as the opening day of the offensive.[41] A major problem remained. How was the mixed Russian-German force at Mitau to be moved to the front line? Once commanded by General von der Goltz, it still contained many Germans and Baltic Germans who cordially hated the Latvians. It was now led by P.M. Bermondt-Avalov, a Caucasian adventurer who styled himself a colonel. According to one British source Bermondt-Avalov suffered from megalomania and fancied himself "as a possible future Tsar of Russia." The Latvians implored the British not to allow Bermondt's corps to pass through their territory. When told that this was essential for the operation, the Latvian prime minister and foreign minister warned that "if the Germans came towards Riga, the whole Lettish population, armed or unarmed, including the Cabinet, would go out to oppose them."[42]

The Bolsheviks observed these developments with growing unease. As early as 1 August Lenin warned Stalin that Petrograd was in extreme danger and inquired if the city's defences were ready for any blow.[43] In mid-month the British launched a combined air and sea attack against Kronstadt and succeeded in putting torpedoes into two battleships.[44] This and other British naval operations in the Gulf of Finland seemed to portend a new assault on Petrograd, and on 27 August the Council of Defence ordered a Bashkir division from the Turkestan front to reinforce the city.[45] The Soviet government concluded Petrograd could not be held merely by military means. A political defence was also necessary. The Soviet government decided to make its peace proposals explicit and unambiguous. On 8 August Lenin asked Bolshevik authorities in Petrograd their opinion of a suitable frontier with Estonia, and a week later the Politburo decided to proceed with peace proposals to all the Baltic states.[46] On 20 August preparations were sufficiently advanced to allow Lenin to tell William T. Goode, a correspondent for the *Manchester Guardian*, "that the Soviet Republic had decided to create a neutral strip or zone between their territory and Estonia, and would declare this publicly; that it was one of their principles to recognize the independence of all small nations."[47] Two days later, however, Chicherin told Goode that "Estonia must agree to it and negotiations must be opened." When he returned to Estonia Goode "could say that the Soviet Republic is ready to conclude its military operations and to open negotiations for this purpose."[48]

Despite such words, the Bolsheviks delayed issuing an official peace proposal. Fortuitous circumstances helped expedite its release. Thus, in the last week of August internal tensions within the Northwestern Army compromised its effectiveness as a fighting force. Relations between generals Rodzianko and Bulak Balakhovich, representing the extreme reactionary and the more moderate opinion within the army, had been strained for some time. Most Russian officers had little use for Balakhovich, but as he was popular among the troops and could get along with the Estonians, Yudenich felt he could not discharge him. Instead he was put in command of Russian troops at Pskov where cooperation with the Estonians was vital. Nevertheless, on 23 August Yudenich ordered the arrest of Balakhovich and his closest associates. When the Bolsheviks learned of this they mounted a sudden attack which caused the Estonians and both Russian factions to withdraw. On 26 August the Red Army entered Pskov.[49] These events provided additional evidence to the Estonians of the danger in cooperating with the Whites and a useful backdrop against which the Soviet peace proposal could be presented.

Reports of the British effort to construct a multinational anti-Bolshevik alliance also served as background to the peace proposals. Rumours of British intentions had filtered into Petrograd all summer, but on 28 August, Rosta, the Russian

Telegraph Agency, monitored a report originating with the British press concerning the effort being made by Churchill to organize a fourteen-state coalition against the Bolsheviks. The heavily marked copy of this report in Lenin's papers shows that he gave it careful attention, while Trotsky promptly prepared a short appreciation of the threat posed by the reported plan. He did not think that "Lord Churchill" would succeed in organizing the coalition but warned that if he did, it would have serious consequences for Soviet Russia. For most of the year it had been possible to relegate the western front to a third-class status; this had allowed the Red Army to concentrate its troops elsewhere. This could no longer be done if Churchill succeeded in organizing a multinational army.[50] It was all the more important therefore to lose no time in putting forward peace proposals to Estonia.

The success at Pskov and the news of a possible anti-Bolshevik coalition were both fortuitous. The convocation of the First Congress of Trade Unionists at Reval appears to have been carefully planned. Said to represent forty thousand Estonian workers, its 417 delegates included 379 communists and their sympathizers. The congress assembled just in time to hear the Soviet peace proposal broadcast by Radio Moscow on 31 August. Before being dispersed by the police, the congress passed resolutions demanding the government end its war against the Bolsheviks and open peace negotiations with Moscow.[51] "Small Estonia," Lenin subsequently wrote, "by way of its non-party conference of trade unionists gave a suitable response to mighty Britain – Britain which threatened us with an alliance of 14 states."[52]

How did this proposal differ from earlier Soviet initiatives to secure peace with Estonia? It was an official communication of the Soviet government, not a trial balloon or an unofficial offer conveyed by intermediaries of unclear authority. To be sure, it contained an element of propaganda in its assertion that the Reval government had acted contrary to the interests of the Estonian people in waging war against Soviet Russia, but Chicherin made it clear that the Bolsheviks would not allow the bourgeois nature of that government to stand in the way of peace between the two countries. Instead, he proposed negotiations based on Soviet recognition of Estonian independence. He asked the Estonians to set the time and place of these negotiations, warning that if they should continue their war against Soviet Russia, either alone or in company with other hostile elements, they would have to accept full responsibility for the consequences.[53]

The Soviet peace proposal exploded with devastating effect in Reval. The Estonian government immediately realized that the Soviet offer had to be accepted. William Goode reached Reval shortly after the peace proposal and testified publicly to the good faith of the Soviet government. Peace and sovereignty were aims of almost all Estonians and the Bolsheviks were prepared to concede both. White intransigence, absence of effective allied aid, war weariness, and mounting discontent in the army forced the Estonian government to inform Moscow on 4 September that they saw no obstacle to negotiations and suggested they begin at Pskov six days later. At the same time they sought to reassure the allies by telling them that they had agreed to negotiate "only to play for time in order to restore the morale of the army. There is, at present, no question of an armistice."[54]

Estonian motives did not interest their neighbours. Finland in particular informed Reval that it objected to unilateral negotiations with the Bolsheviks.[55] The Latvians were also worried by the Soviet initiative and invited their neighbours to send representatives to Riga to discuss it. Even before the conference met, Moscow surprised the Baltic states with still further peace proposals. On 11 September the Soviet government offered to negotiate peace with Latvia, Lithuania and Finland on terms analogous to those just offered to Estonia.[56]

Why were these proposals not made at the same time as the offer to Estonia? Solid evidence is wanting, but available documents suggest that Stalin was responsible. At the end of August the Lithuanians had just launched a surprise attack directed at Dvinsk, and Stalin was preparing a counter-attack. In these circumstances he said it was "unsuitable" to open negotiations. Nor could he understand why he had not been informed of the decision. Lenin submitted Stalin's telegram to the Politburo and presumably delayed publication of the peace proposal to Lithuania. At the same time he must also have decided to postpone the offer to Latvia and Finland to avoid the impression that Soviet Russia was intentionally excluding Lithuania from its peace program. Such an interpretation, with the implied threat to Lithuanian sovereignty, could have proved particularly damaging to the Soviet effort to woo Pilsudski. Preparations for launching the Soviet peace effort in Estonia, however, were too far advanced to allow postponement.

In less than two weeks the situation changed sufficiently to allow the other peace proposals to go forward. The Lithuanian offensive ground to a halt once the last sectors of Lithuanian territory had been cleared of the Red Army, Stalin's counter-offensive failed utterly, and the Poles, always suspicious of Lithuanian motives, launched a local offensive to enforce their claim to the disputed territory south of Dvinsk. And in early September the Poles successfully interposed themselves between the Lithuanians and the Bolsheviks, liquidating most of the Lithuanian sector of the anti-Bolshevik front and ending hostilities between the two.[57]

Initially the Baltic states had hoped to prevent Estonia from concluding a separate peace with Moscow; now they faced the same problem as Reval – how to cope with the explosive issue of peace. All feared to offend the western powers, but in the absence of a clearly stated allied policy, were at a loss to know how to please their distant protectors. On 16 September delegates of the three states cobbled together a number of resolutions designed to give the impression of a common front. In reality they were more a reflection of mutual anguish. "Peace with the Bolsheviks in the full sense of the word," they decided, was impossible; the best they could hope for was "a lasting cessation of hostilities."

To achieve this they decided to conduct negotiations together and formulate common peace terms at a further conference to meet at Dorpat. The Estonians would inform the Bolsheviks of this decision and seek a new date when negotiations could begin with all the Baltic states. The allies would be informed and their advice sought on all questions related to the negotiations.[58] None of the participants really wanted negotiations with the Bolsheviks. The Finns and Lithuanians were strongly opposed to talks, but felt compelled to participate in order to appease the war-weary in their own lands and place a brake on the Estonians, who would otherwise negotiate with Moscow separately. The Latvians remained uncertain, while the Estonians were sharply divided. The Reval government no longer trusted the army and hoped to still discontent in the ranks by agreeing to negotiate with Moscow, while the Estonian general staff feared that even the mention of peace would lead to a further deterioration of discipline and morale.[59]

The initial negotiations at Pskov did not last long. On 17 September the Estonian foreign minister, Jan Poska, met with Leonid Krasin and Maxim Litvinov to tell them of the decisions reached at Reval. Moscow, he said, would have to conduct simultaneous negotiations with all four states. The Soviet delegation, however, was only authorized to negotiate with the Estonians and broke off the talks the next day. At the same time Krasin affirmed Soviet readiness to resume negotiations either with Estonia alone or together with other states then at war with Moscow.[60] The talks had been conducted in a calm atmosphere in which the Bolsheviks had tried to put the Estonians at their ease. Poska left the conference with "the impression that the Bolsheviks sincerely desired to conclude peace."[61]

The Estonians turned again to the western powers. The British Foreign Office had warned Reval on 16 September to "take no action in the direction of peace." The British said they "would deplore individual action" and trusted that the Estonians would, "as heretofore, conduct their foreign policy only as part of a concerted plan with the Allied governments."[62] Poska responded irritably that "it was difficult for his government to conduct foreign policy as part of a concerted plan with the Allied Governments without knowing in what that plan consisted."[63] Consequently the Estonians decided to confront the allies directly with the urgent need to define their policy in the Baltic. "The Estonian Government," Poska informed London on 21 September, "would be pleased to know what role Estonia is expected to perform in the plan agreed upon by the Allied and Associated Governments, whether it would not be possible to inspirit our people and troops to undertake fresh sacrifices to bring about the overthrow of Bolshevik rule, by a formal acknowledgement of our independence, and finally what steps it is proposed to take to enable our troops to obtain supplies and equipment."[64] The British received nearly identical requests from Finland and Latvia, both stressing the need for allied recognition of their independence and substantial financial and military aid to allow them to continue hostilities against the Bolsheviks.[65]

These telegrams forced the allied powers to define their response to the Bolshevik peace offensive. The absence of a common accord on the Baltic, the unwillingness of any power to assume new financial burdens, and the need for prompt action combined to force London and Paris to respond separately to the urgent queries from the Baltic states. This led to a sharp divergence in British and French policy.

The French simply dug in their heels. They had neither men nor money to commit to the Baltic and considered the region to be primarily under British protection. They harboured a deep suspicion of all the Baltic nationalities, whom they considered to be potential clients of a recrudescent Germany. Nor did they want to anger a future non-Bolshevik Great Russia by recognizing the secessionist regimes in the Baltic. Thus, when the first appeals for a greater allied commitment reached Paris, the Quai d'Orsay retreated into negation. "We can neither threaten nor promise anything to the Estonians," one leading French official wrote, "and if the Finnish wish to act against Petrograd they will do it on their own account."[66] Further pressure from the Baltic states led to a hardening of this attitude. On 12 September the Estonian representative in Paris was told that "France would certainly not participate in any negotiations with the Bolsheviks ... Estonia would have to bear *alone and absolutely alone* the responsibility of its negotiations with the Bolsheviks."[67] The same day French representatives in Helsingfors were instructed not to promise the Finns anything but instead to allow them to develop their action in any way they wanted.[68] When confronted with the post-Pskov queries of the Baltic states, Paris responded that "nothing had changed in that which concerns French policy."[69]

The British response emerged quite differently. It was shaped by the earlier decision to liquidate all British commitments in Russia except to Denikin and the view that further involvement in the Baltic would be unwise. In early September Curzon had informed Lloyd George that the cabinet were in general agreement that no further aid should be given to Yudenich.[70] Similarly they agreed with the final recommendations of General Gough: "First – get rid of the German troops. Second – support the provinces and open trade with them. Third – drop the [white] Russians." The lone dissenter was Churchill who urged his colleagues to expand, rather than reduce, British involvement in the Baltic.[71] Officials at the Foreign Office were also alarmed by the apparent readiness of the Baltic states to consider some arrangement with the Bolsheviks and warned Curzon "there is little doubt that if nothing is done to stop them ... [they] will be quickly followed by Finland – and less quickly by Poland."[72]

On 24 September Lloyd George placed the question of British policy in the Baltic before the war cabinet. The minutes record only that "after a prolonged discussion" it was decided that the British government would not guarantee the independence of the Baltic states, furnish further military supplies, or provide them with a loan. "Responsibility for making peace with the Bolsheviks," they said, "must rest with the Baltic Provinces themselves." Churchill, however, continued to fight and submitted yet another memorandum explaining the great harm which such a decision would do to the White Russians.[73] Lloyd George, knowing that for the first time he possessed a real advantage in his struggle with Churchill for control of British policy in Russia, promptly increased the stakes. He asked the war cabinet if it was "in the interests of the British Empire to aim at a united Russia under any government." It was "inevitable that such a government would have a natural inclination to creep forward and ... result in a peril not only to the British Empire, but to the peace of the world." It was better he thought that Great Russia dissolve into its national components; "he personally did not view with equanimity the thought of a powerful united Russia of 130,000,000 inhabitants." Churchill could argue that in view of the service rendered by Russia to the allies during the Great War it was somewhat cold-blooded to suggest that Britain did not want a united Russia in the future, but only he disagreed with the prime minister.[74] Curzon informed his agents that while the British government continued to be interested in the welfare of the Baltic states and would insist on the withdrawal of German troops from their territory, they could not provide the aid and assistance recently requested by them. As a consequence, he said, the British government "feel that they are not entitled to exercise any pressure upon the free initiative of the Baltic states and that their Governments must be at liberty to decide upon such action as may be most conducive to the preservation of their own national existence. It is for them to determine with unfettered judgement whether they should make any arrangement, and if so of what nature, with the Soviet authorities."[75]

This response from the two allied powers served to strengthen the hand of those Baltic politicians who favoured an accommodation with the Bolsheviks.[76] The Finns were not so happy. Holsti, the French learned, had become very disillusioned with the British.[77] The French, too, were open to the charge of "uncertain and contradictory policy," for while Paris said it was leaving the question of negotiations to be decided locally, French agents continued to work actively against such talks. "I warned the Latvian government of the great danger of peace," reported the French military representative in Riga, "and counselled them to abstain from it."[78]

Consequently, when the ministers of the Baltic states reassembled at Dorpat at the end of September they were still unable to reach agreement. Estonia, Latvia, and Lithuania all wished to proceed with the negotiations but the Finns did not. Nor did the Estonian army. The latter two put forward preposterous demands to slow the pace of accommodation. The Bolsheviks, they said, should be forced to abandon Petrograd and Kronstadt before being granted an armistice. They should also be required to evacuate Karelia, Olonets, Ingermanland, and most of the Kola Peninsula. The decisions reached by the conference only served to paper over these differences. Estonia, Latvia, and Lithuania were empowered to propose the resumption of talks with Moscow while the Finns would subsequently inform the other three if they were prepared to participate. When the negotiations began they would demand "a neutral zone beyond state frontiers based on the ethnographic principal." The allies would be asked to administer this zone and "control the execution of the peace treaty." They also agreed that the Finnish population inhabiting the provinces of Olentz and Archangel and, in so far as possible, also the Finnish and Estonian inhabitants of Ingermanland "should receive self determination" with the right to secede from Russia.[79]

SIMPLE PRUDENCE COMPELLED the Baltic states to delay the resumption of peace talks with Moscow. In September the outcome of the Russian civil war, never clear, became still more confused as the Bolsheviks failed to regain control of the southern front. The Soviet government adhered stubbornly to the strategic plan adopted in July which concentrated the bulk of available reserves on the left flank of the front for use on the Don. This plan proved no more successful in September than in August, and its failure had the same consequences: the Cossacks tied down the bulk of the Red Army while Denikin advanced almost at will in Ukraine and the provinces south of Moscow. On 20 September Kursk fell to the Whites, followed ten days later by Voronezh. Further to the west the Volunteer Army occupied virtually all of Ukraine. Despite the most urgent appeals from Trotsky and other military leaders to shift the focus of the southern front from east to west, Lenin continued to insist that the Soviet offensive continue as planned.[80] The road to Moscow remained open, and on 14 October the Whites stormed into Orel only four hundred kilometres from the Kremlin. Baltic leaders hesitated to commit themselves to serious negotiations with the Bolsheviks.

Circumstances within the Baltic states engendered similar caution. Yudenich had protested every step taken in the direction of negotiations with the Bolsheviks and in early October prepared for independent action against Petrograd. His British military advisers urged him to attack as soon as possible. The Northwestern Army launched its attack on 12 October, aided by the British fleet in the Gulf of Finland and six tanks manned by British crews. Yudenich made rapid progress, first recapturing Pskov, then Jamburg and Krasnoe Selo. On 17 October Gatchina fell; Petrograd seemed within his grasp. Lenin saw the White offensive as a manoeuvre to distract Soviet attention from the south and was ready to abandon the city. Most of the Politburo agreed, but Trotsky insisted that Petrograd could be saved. His colleagues decided to give him a chance. They would provide no reinforcements, but Trotsky would be given full powers to defend the city. Preparations were also begun to evacuate those economic enterprises which could be moved and to destroy the rest. As Trotsky wished, the Council of Defence decreed that Petrograd was "to be defended to the very last drop of blood, not a single yard of ground yielded and fighting carried on in the streets."[81]

None of this proved necessary. As Trotsky suspected, the Northwestern Army was a phantom never numbering more than twenty-five thousand men. It was top heavy with officers and staff. Even the pitiful Soviet Seventh Army could field a larger force. Yet even after Trotsky arrived, Yudenich continued to advance and, on 18 October, reached the Pulkovo Heights from which he could see the spires of the old capital. Here, however, his advance ended. Insufficient manpower impeded supply of his army, and its whole right flank hung dangerously in the air. When Trotsky launched his counter-attack the Northwestern Army disintegrated. Within a week it was in full retreat.[82] A British admiral commented: "It would be difficult to recall any offensive ever conducted which has showed such an utter lack of intelligent leadership, or in which greater military mistakes have been made ... General Yudenich thought that the tanks on land, and our ships off the coast, would do everything for him and had no compensating plans of any sort."[83] At the height of White success, British naval intelligence had reported from Stockholm that the Bolsheviks had engaged "a fast motor boat ... to embark Lennin [*sic*], Trotsky, etc. should Petrograd fall." When this report reached London, together with the news of Yudenich's failure, a junior member of the Foreign Office minuted, "M.M. Lenin and Trotsky will not now require their motor boat."[84]

The disintegration of the Northwestern Army produced an immediate impact on Soviet relations with Estonia. Trotsky warned Lenin that Yudenich's right of asylum in Estonia would present a difficult problem and recommended an agreement to ensure that Estonia closed its frontier to the Whites. "Failing this," he said, "we must reserve the right to invade Estonia in pursuit of Yudenich." But Lenin indicated no interest in pursuing Yudenich into Estonia; he wanted to use all available forces in the south and east. Still Trotsky persisted, suggesting that if the Estonians did not disarm Yudenich and resume peace talks, Soviet troops should occupy Narva.[85]

This brought Chicherin into the debate. For over a year he had been seeking to engage hostile powers, virtually any belligerent state, in peace talks, and just when it seemed serious negotiations with Reval might actually get under way, he was not about to sit by quietly while the Red Army re-ignited the war with Estonia. "The present attitude there is favourable to us," he warned Trotsky on 22 October, "but any invasion by us of Estonian territory will at once alter this, rouse the peasantry and middle classes against us and again make an enemy for us." More importantly, he declared, "it will create the notion of supposed imperialism on our part, have a sharp impact on all the Baltic states ... disrupt the present line of concluding agreements along the entire front and, over and above that, again rouse the English Liberals and moderate Tories against us." He insisted that Estonia not be invaded. "The Estonian troops are not operating against Petrograd and Yudenich will not have to be pursued on Estonian territory if he does not withdraw to it."[86] This final observation was important, for it contained the substance of subsequent Soviet policy.

The Soviet leaders continued to argue. Lenin told Trotsky that he wanted to "switch *everything* against Denikin" and wanted no military side-shows in the

Baltic.[87] Trotsky denied that he wanted war declared on Estonia, only an official warning that "if Yudenich sets foot on the territory of Estonia without an attempt at repulse on her part the war will inevitably carry over onto the territory of Estonia."[88] At this point the total Soviet victory over Yudenich transformed the argument. The Estonians immediately informed Moscow of their desire to resume negotiations.[89] This did not satisfy Trotsky. Flushed with victory, he complained that he still had "not received an answer to the question of what is to be done if Yudenich crosses over on to the territory of Estonia." Lenin too became more belligerent, informing Trotsky on 27 October that the Red Army "must enter Estonia if they let in Yudenich." The same day Trotsky ordered the commander of the Soviet Seventh Army to make secret preparations to pursue Yudenich into Estonia.[90]

Estonia and Yudenich were only part of the threat to Soviet security in the Baltic. In mid-October the possibility of Finnish intervention also increased. Although the government rejected a plea from circles supporting Mannerheim for an immediate attack on Petrograd, they did order the first stages of a full military mobilization and directed the heavy artillery on the north shore of the Gulf of Finland to cooperate with the British squadron in naval operations against Kronstadt and other Bolshevik fortresses.[91] These measures caused Chicherin to warn Trotsky on 25 October that he was disturbed about Finland. Western radio transmissions had carried reports from Finland that Yudenich could not take Petrograd without outside aid. "Is this not an attempt by Finland," he asked, "to sell its aid more dearly? Yudenich's failure is such a scandal for the Entente that it will do everything to urge Finland on." It was not until the end of the month that it finally became clear that neither Estonia nor Finland would aid Yudenich, when the western governments declared publicly they would not provide the aid necessary for a renewed campaign against Petrograd. Soviet security was further enhanced when the Russo-German force commanded by Bermondt-Avalov turned on the Latvians and, rather than joining Yudenich, marched on Riga. It was clear by 30 October that no further attack could be mounted in northwestern Russia until the following spring.[92]

The surest guarantee of Soviet security, however, did not come from the Baltic, but from the southern front. There in mid-October, after five months of unbroken defeat, the Red Army decisively turned the tide against Denikin. At the end of September the rapid White advance had finally forced Lenin to abandon the fruitless assault on the left flank of the southern front and concentrate on reinforcing the centre. Reserves, including important Latvian and Estonian units drawn from the western front, were concentrated north of Orel. When that city fell to Denikin these reserves, named the Shock Group of the Southern Front launched a fierce assault on the Volunteer Army. On 20 October they entered Orel. Four days later Soviet cavalry commanded by S.M. Budenny occupied Voronezh. The Whites began a general retreat which soon turned into a rout. Far in Denikin's rear the anarchist bands of Nestor Makhno had also taken the offensive and rode at will across hundreds of kilometres of southern Ukraine sewing havoc and destruction in their path. They looted Volunteer Army supply bases, cut Denikin's communications, destroyed his transport, and forced him to divert troops from the north.[93] It was the beginning of the end for Denikin; the Volunteer Army would never recover.

MILITARY SUCCESS DID NOT alter Soviet political objectives. Moscow remained committed to the negotiation of peace with the Baltic states. The defeat of Denikin and Yudenich did, however, allow the Bolsheviks to speak more forcefully and contemplate, if necessary, the resumption of hostilities should the Baltic states prove uncooperative. Indeed, on 6 November the Politburo refused to rule out the possibility of invading Estonia should the Reval government give shelter to the remnants of the Northwestern Army. When the Estonians suggested that negotiations resume at Dorpat on 17 November, however, Chicherin promptly agreed.[94] The Politburo shelved consideration of further military operations pending the results of these negotiations.

The Estonians were well aware of their peril. Morale in their army had collapsed, and the government could not contemplate a continuation of hostilities through the winter. They also took a firm hand with Yudenich. Although it was politically impossible to intern those elements of the Northwestern Army which entered Estonia, they were confined to districts immediately adjacent to the small parcels of Russian territory Yudenich continued to occupy. The Estonians threatened to disarm any Russian soldiers found outside the border districts. Most of the Northwestern Army, therefore, remained on Russian soil, and Russian leaders who protested were ordered to leave Estonia. White newspapers which complained of this treatment were closed.[95]

Latvia too became interested in negotiating with Moscow. While the battle with Bermondt raged in the vicinity of Riga the Latvian government did not want to complicate their precarious existence with further hostilities against the Bolsheviks, and once they had defeated the Caucasian adventurer they had no wish to contribute to arrangements allowing his troops to remain anywhere within or near the borders of Latvia. The ferocious struggle against Bermondt had lasted more than a month. "The Letts take no prisoners at all," wrote one observer. "All the Germans and Russians that are wounded or otherwise are killed. The presumption is that the other side is doing the same thing. I have never seen such hate for one another as there is here." No wonder that the Latvians bluntly refused a British request to allow the remains of the Russo-German force to cross the country to fight the Bolsheviks. As Lithuania held only a small front against Soviet Russia and Finland would not act without western support,[96] fighting in the Baltic stopped. The time for serious negotiations had arrived.

Peace talks opened at Dorpat on 17 November. Soviet Russia was represented by Maxim Litvinov who arrived with power to negotiate virtually any agreement with the Baltic states. Ostensibly the talks were to deal only with the exchange of prisoners and hostages, but they immediately broadened to cover all issues in dispute between Soviet Russia and the Baltic states. The prisoner and hostage problem, Litvinov said, would be solved easily once an armistice had been signed. He underlined this point by concluding a prisoner exchange agreement with Lithuania, the one Baltic state, thanks to Poland, no longer in a de facto state of war with Soviet Russia. Similar pacts with the other Baltic states, he said, would have to wait the conclusion of armistice agreements. But Litvinov wanted essentially to talk of peace. He confirmed that Soviet Russia was prepared to recognize the sovereignty and independence of the Baltic states. The Red Army had already withdrawn from the territory claimed by Finland, Estonia, and Lithuania. It was prepared to evacuate Latgall, the last portion of Latvia still in its hands. In addition Moscow would consider payment of reparations for damage done by Soviet forces while in occupation of the Baltic states. The Soviet government, he stressed, sincerely wanted peace and was ready to give serious consideration to the legitimate concerns of the border nationalities.[97]

On 19 November the Estonians accepted the Soviet proposals. They said they wished to make a further effort to include the other Baltic states in the negotiations but agreed to proceed with separate talks if the others did not agree to participate by 1 December. They would not put this in writing. "For the moment, they propose a silent agreement," Litvinov informed Moscow, "to end military action by both sides on all parts of the front." The Latvians were less forthcoming. They told Litvinov that while wanting an armistice they feared an open agreement would cost them allied support in the struggle against Bermondt. They were prepared to conclude "a written, but secret, armistice," but not before the Bolsheviks reached an agreement with Estonia.[98] Before Litvinov left Dorpat, therefore, the basis for a cessation of hostilities with two of the four Baltic states had been reached.

Talks resumed on 4 December. Krasin and Ioffe replaced Litvinov who had departed for Copenhagen to begin prisoner exchange negotiations with the British. They faced an Estonian delegation headed by Foreign Minister Poska; the other Baltic states, while sending observers, would not join the negotiations. From the start the Estonians sought to narrow the scope of the negotiations; the Bolsheviks wanted to widen them. Poska said his government was only able to agree to an armistice; at the least the Bolsheviks wanted a preliminary peace. In any case, the Bolsheviks wanted an early agreement and complained of the delay which Estonia had already imposed on the negotiations. The Red Army, Krasin declared, had not stopped on the right bank of the Narva because it could advance no farther; it had stopped because the Soviet government had decided not to violate the Estonian frontier. Such forbearance, he suggested, would not last long if Estonia did not promptly reach an agreement with Moscow. Furthermore, Estonia would have to agree that its territory would no longer be used by Russian counter-revolutionaries as a base for new anti-Soviet intervention. This was a source of special difficulty, for Reval had just received an allied request not to take any measures against General Yudenich and his army.[99] Poska told Krasin of this and said Estonia would find it difficult to ignore allied wishes. The Estonians also feared that a formal armistice might cause the allies to impose the blockade on them as well as the Bolsheviks. They preferred a vague agreement without reference to Yudenich. The Bolsheviks would have no part of this, and negotiations reached an impasse. After a week of inconclusive bargaining Krasin left for Pskov to consult Moscow.[100]

The Estonian opponents of peace took advantage of this recess to spread alarm through the Baltic. The Estonian minister of war arrived suddenly at Helsingfors where he informed a badly shaken Holsti that Krasin had made peace dependent on three secret conditions. Moscow demanded, he said, that all foreign armies currently on Estonian soil be disbanded, that Estonia break off relations with all states still at war with Soviet Russia, and that Estonia close its territorial waters to foreign warships while placing its ports at the free disposal of Soviet Russian ships. This was pure fabrication, but Holsti believed it and immediately spread the alarm through the diplomatic community. He informed the British and French ministers of the menacing turn in the negotiations and implored them to ask their governments to assist the Estonians in rejecting Soviet demands.[101] It is worth noting that this appeal coincided with Clemenceau's well-publicized visit to London to discuss, among other matters, the Russian problem. It is not difficult to discern in the Estonian, and perhaps also the Finnish, action a keen desire to stampede the allied prime ministers in the direction of a more active policy in the Baltic. Nor did the effort fail for lack of energy, for day after day Holsti bombarded western governments with alarming reports and appeals for action.[102] But it was in vain. The Estonian Foreign Ministry, which favoured peace with the Bolsheviks, provided London with the genuine Soviet proposals, and when these were compared with the report from Finland, the striking divergence between the two was evident. Curzon, who on receiving the false report had asked the Admiralty to send ships to Reval, now ordered a reprimand for his minister in Helsingfors.[103] In the future the Foreign Office would treat reports from the Baltic with greater caution.

At Dorpat negotiations languished. Krasin, the real power in the Soviet delegation, had been summoned to Moscow to try to ameliorate the mounting crisis in Soviet rail transport. In his absence Ioffe could not settle even minor issues and, as a result, the talks drifted. The Estonians sought to take advantage of this to propose another adjournment, but Ioffe would not agree. Chicherin informed the Soviet delegation that the Estonians should be told that the "negotiations have reached their critical moment" and that they would have to guarantee that their territory would not be used to attack Soviet Russia.[104] In mid-month the Red Army began new operations. No effort was made to enter Estonia but those units of the Estonian army occupying positions in advance of the frontier were attacked and fighting soon spread to the entire front. Although this was a mere demonstration, it was clear that Moscow could alter its nature at any time. In such a case, one British agent reported, "the front will break, and if a retreat commences total disorganization of the [Estonian] army is inevitable."[105] Reval had to choose between an armistice or military defeat.

The Estonians quickly made up their mind. After a tour of the front in which he found the military situation discouraging, Prime Minister Tynisson urged his colleagues to sign the armistice as soon as possible.[106] Still, more than a week passed before actual agreement was reached and then it lacked the polished quality which the Bolsheviks had hoped to give it. Rather than being a preliminary peace treaty, the armistice passed over those areas in which agreement could not be reached. Nothing was said of future boundaries, withdrawal of armed forces, or the Russian Northwestern Army. Instead it was agreed that fighting would cease on 3 January 1920; the only neutral zone would be that small amount of territory already separating the two armies. The armistice would continue in force for seven days, after which it would be automatically renewed if mutually acceptable to the two parties. Twenty-four hours' notice had to be given prior to resumption of hostilities. Both agreed not to use the armistice to regroup their forces.[107] These conditions reveal the precarious nature of the agreement. The Estonians, peering fearfully at the victory of the Bolsheviks over the Whites, bent to the Soviet demand for a formal armistice but would not agree to the other terms demanded by Moscow. The Bolsheviks, wishing to conclude a formal agreement with at least one of their opponents, did not insist that their other demands be accepted immediately. Apparently believing that they had impressed Reval with their unwillingness to tolerate further military action by the North-western Army, the Bolsheviks were even willing to exclude all reference to this force from the armistice. But the price the Estonians paid for a bare-bones armistice was substantial. It offered them almost no protection against a re-sumption of the war. After seven days the Red Army could, with twenty-four hours' notice, strike at will, and it was doubtful if the Estonian army would be able to resist effectively. Thus the armistice provided great incentive to Reval to reach a final agreement with Moscow. The Bolsheviks, in short, had succeeded in fashioning a most useful weapon in their continuing struggle to compel the Estonians to make peace.

Despite intense Soviet pressure, the Estonian government could not proceed further until they were certain that the conclusion of peace with Moscow would not seriously damage relations with their Baltic neighbours and the allied powers. Reval was keenly aware of French hostility to even the slightest contact with Moscow, but the British view was far more important. British ships ruled the Baltic, and British policy protected Estonian independence. The Estonians would listen to London, not Paris, in deciding their future relations with Russia. Throughout January Reval sounded the British repeatedly and received the same reply. "There is no alteration in the attitude of [the British] government towards that of Estonia," Lord Hardinge told them on 26 January, "and that whether the Estonian Government makes peace or not with the Soviet Government must be

decided entirely in the interests of Estonia."[108] Actions, however, spoke louder
than words, and here the signal from Britain was unmistakably clear. Thus, on
16 January, acting at the behest of Lloyd George, the Supreme Council announced
that they had decided to lift the blockade of Russia.[109] Peace with Soviet Russia,
therefore, did not mean that Estonia would be locked behind the allied blockade.
There was also the problem of the Northwestern Army. In December the Supreme
Council had asked Estonia not to disarm this Russian force. The British now
sought to have the council allow the Estonians to deal with it as they saw fit.
The French objected, and, as a consequence, no representation could be made
by the council, but the Foreign Office recommended that the Estonians be allowed
to know informally that the British government did not object to the dissolution
of the remnants of Yudenich's force.[110] By the end of January the British attitude
was well known throughout the Baltic, with the result, as the American commissioner at Riga reported, "the French here are indignant."[111]

THERE REMAINED THE other Baltic states. The Estonian government had earlier
agreed to negotiate jointly with her neighbours, and, before signing a separate
peace with Soviet Russia, felt compelled to make one further effort to bring
them into the talks. This was done at a new Baltic conference which met in
Helsingfors from 15 to 22 January. The presence of a Polish delegation served
to exacerbate the divisiveness which had characterized earlier meetings. The
Poles, who were even then preparing to attack Soviet Russia, came to Helsingfors
to recruit allies for that war. The Lithuanians also came seeking allies, but against
Poland and not Soviet Russia. They asked Estonia and Latvia to join them in
an alliance against Warsaw. The conference, therefore, experienced several ugly
moments.[112] The Estonians and Latvians sought a defensive alliance against
Russia, monarchist or Bolshevik. The Finns, who did not wish to bind themselves
to allies who could not aid them in return, favoured only a form of military
consultation. Lithuania would do nothing in common with Poland, while the
Poles complained of the merely defensive aspirations of the others. Finland,
Latvia, and Poland all asked Estonia not to make peace with Moscow, but the
Estonians made it perfectly clear that they no longer felt bound to act in common
with their neighbours.[113] This angered the Poles, who later observed that the
Estonian attitude left the other delegations with "the very clear impression that
they were sustained by a Great Power – which could only be England."[114]

The Helsingfors conference did not cause a suspension of negotiations at
Dorpat. They continued and focused on economic questions. In their eagerness
for peace the Bolsheviks suggested that the economic articles of the treaty simply
provide a framework for additional agreements to be negotiated later. But the
Estonians wanted a detailed settlement included in the treaty itself. Primarily,
however, they wanted title to all former Russian property in Estonia and ex-
emption from responsibility for paying any of the debts and obligations of the
former Russian empire. The Bolsheviks would accept this if the Estonians would

agree that neither side owed reparations to the other. This created a problem, for in the settlement of claims the Estonians had hoped to secure a balance in their favour. They desperately needed money and saw the Bolshevik treasury as the place to get it. Moscow would not compromise the principle of mutual renunciation of claims but was quite prepared to pay the Estonians for signing the peace treaty. During 1918 the Soviet government had become quite proficient in the payment of extortionate bribes and did not balk at paying a small fee to Estonia. Provided that the Estonians were not simply trying to delay the conclusion of peace, Chicherin told Ioffe, the Soviet government was prepared to be quite generous. Thus, when the Estonians suggested that they receive a share of the Russian state gold reserve, Moscow readily agreed. On 13 January 1920 the Politburo authorized the Soviet delegation to offer the Estonians fifteen million gold rubles. Subsequently, timber concessions adjacent to the Estonian frontier were added to the agreement. On 2 February 1920 representatives of Soviet Russia and Estonia signed the treaty of peace at Dorpat.[115]

The settlement met the pressing needs of the two signatories. Given the type of peace treaties being concluded in Europe at this time, this was no small achievement. Estonia received the unqualified recognition of her independence and sovereignty within borders of her own choosing and with full title to all state property within those borders. This was obtained not from a shadow government but from the heirs and successors to Nicholas II who had successfully defended themselves against all Russian rivals. Soviet Russia, for her part, broke the front of capitalist states and obtained peace from a neighbouring bourgeois regime previously sworn to continue the war against Bolshevism. The significance of this will be examined below. Here it is sufficient to note that the Bolsheviks had pursued peace with Estonia so ardently, because they hoped it would be the first of many settlements ending the war with their western neighbours. To this end they were prepared to sacrifice not only the political freedom of borderland Bolsheviks and gold from the Soviet treasury but Russian territory as well.

The Bolsheviks allowed the Estonians a state frontier somewhat in advance of both the prewar provincial boundaries of Estonia and the area of unquestioned ethnographic Estonian settlement. In the north this included a slice of Russian territory east of the Narva river and in the south a wedge just west of Pskov. These accretions of territory are particularly significant when it is realized that these regions were exactly those then occupied by the Northwestern Army. The treaty specifically provided that neither state would in the future harbour any military force or political agency seeking to overthrow the government of the other and further called for disarming existing forces of this type no later than 1 October 1920. Clearly, Estonia in January did not feel ready to disband the Northwestern Army. The Estonians had stuck on this point since the beginning of negotiations and, at their end, they still would not budge. The Red Army, of course, could move at will into the territory occupied by the remnants of Yudenich's army, but unless the Estonians blocked their way with armed force, which they clearly refused to do, the White Russians would simply withdraw into ethnographic Estonia. But the last thing the Bolsheviks wanted was to invade Estonia in pursuit of Yudenich. What then was to be done? The Bolsheviks decided to make over the occupied territory to Estonia and let the Estonians deal with the problem at their leisure. By January 1920 the Northwestern Army was more an object of pity and scorn than a force to be feared. Demoralized, unpaid and unsupplied, abandoned by its better elements, it was almost entirely composed of invalids and non-combatants. The Estonians had sent control parties into its encampments to ensure that it would cause no mischief. The Bolsheviks clearly decided that the Estonians could be trusted to dispose of the problem themselves and the two parcels of territory, like the fifteen million in gold, was a small price to pay for an agreement which they confidently expected to open the way to many further peace treaties.[116]

WHILE NEGOTIATIONS PROCEEDED with Estonia, the Bolsheviks had also conducted secret talks for an armistice with Latvia. Throughout December and January war weariness and mounting unrest in the army increased pressure on the Latvian government to negotiate a settlement with Moscow. In addition, by mid-December the last German troops had left Latvian soil and the overriding need to please the allies diminished accordingly. By then the widening breach between French and British policy had also become apparent. Faced with division in allied councils, the Latvian government responded with dissimulation, telling representatives of Britain and France different stories according to what they seemed to want to hear. Nevertheless, as late as 9 December the Latvians tended to favour the stronger line taken by France. Before the end of the year, however, the Latvian position began to change as Riga contemplated the consequences of a Soviet-Estonian armistice. If the Estonians withdrew from the anti-Bolshevik front, Soviet troops could concentrate against Latvia. This was especially discomforting due to poor relations with Lithuania and Estonia. These bad relations arose from disputed boundaries and put pressure on Riga to settle with Moscow, for the continuing war with the Bolsheviks left Latvia vulnerable to pressure from her other neighbours. Estonia and Lithuania would be able to present unwelcome demands at those moments most awkward for Latvia.[117]

The Latvians responded in two ways. First, they opened negotiations with the Polish general staff. Relations between Poland and Lithuania were far worse than between Latvia and Lithuania, and the Poles were delighted to contemplate joint action against their common foe. They also wanted to establish a common frontier with Latvia by a joint attack on the Bolshevik position at Dvinsk. This would completely eliminate the Lithuanian portion of the anti-Bolshevik front and preclude any cooperation between the Bolsheviks and Lithuanians. At the same time, however, the Latvians also talked secretly with Moscow. As early as 8 December Krasin had discussed an armistice with the Latvian representatives at Tartu. After careful consideration, the Latvians responded on 19 December with counter-proposals calling for a secret, rather than an openly proclaimed, armistice. They also demanded the surrender of Latgall. It was agreed that if the Soviet government accepted these conditions they would signal their intention by inviting a delegation of the Latvian Red Cross to Moscow for the purpose of negotiating an exchange of prisoners and hostages. More was involved in this than the simple transfer of territory, for Latgall was the last territory actually held by the government of Soviet Latvia. If the Red Army abandoned it the Bolshevik government of Latvia would also cease to exist. Such a disappearance, of course, had been implicit in Soviet policy since August, but, unlike the Estonian Labour Commune, the government of Soviet Latvia had not yet been dissolved. When consulted by the Soviet Russian government, however, Latvian communists agreed that negotiations with bourgeois Latvia should continue on the terms set by Riga. On 24 December Moscow officially invited a Latvian Red Cross delegation to visit Moscow to negotiate an exchange of prisoners and hostages.[118]

The Latvians decided to pursue both policies simultaneously. On 30 December they agreed to a joint attack with Poland on Dvinsk and, at the same time, dispatched representatives to Moscow. While the latter crossed one part of the front the Latvian army launched its attack on Dvinsk from another. On 1 January the Poles attacked the city from the south. Two days later Dvinsk fell to the Poles who then turned it over to the Latvians while continuing their advance farther along the rail line to the north. The operation was a complete success. A common Latvian-Polish frontier, including direct rail link between Riga and Warsaw, was established, and Lithuania was effectively separated from Soviet Russia. The Bolsheviks put up only token resistance and withdrew into the Latgall countryside.[119] None of this stopped the Latvian Red Cross delegation from receiving a cordial reception in Moscow. The negotiations lasted two days, included an interview with Lenin, and were conducted in a "friendly atmosphere."[120]

When the delegation returned to Riga the Latvian government decided to continue with the talks in Moscow. The Estonian cease-fire placed them under great pressure and they knew they had to arrange their own affairs with Soviet Russia as quickly as possible. Nevertheless, Riga continued to play a double game. Just as they had concluded a military agreement with Poland before beginning talks in Moscow, so now the Latvians reached a second agreement to continue the military operation begun with the capture of Dvinsk. In mid-January the Poles and Latvians agreed to cooperate in military operations north and east of the city. It did not prove necessary to implement this second agreement, for the negotiations in Moscow indicated that the Bolsheviks were prepared to surrender Latgall. In two meetings on 11 and 13 January Chicherin agreed to a secret armistice, the prompt evacuation of Latgall, and the establishment of a demarcation line of Latvian choosing. In return the Latvians agreed to a two-month cease-fire.[121] As further evidence of Moscow's good faith the Latvian Soviet government declared themselves dissolved. In a proclamation to the Latvian workers they transferred their authority to the Communist Party of Latvia and declared they would no longer contend for state power in Latvia. Even then, however, Riga hesitated to sign a formal agreement with Soviet Russia. Instead, Latvia waited until it was clear that Estonia was proceeding to an actual peace treaty with Moscow and that Great Britain had no objection to this development. The lifting of the blockade also moved Latvia in this direction, for it became clear that trade with Soviet Russia would soon be resumed and, initially at least, was likely to be conducted through Baltic ports.

On 30 January a two-month armistice was signed in Moscow. It formalized the mid-month agreement and provided that neither government would support any organization or group aimed at the destruction of the other.[122] Unlike the Estonians, the Latvians did not officially consult Great Britain before reaching this agreement. Shortly after, however, the Latvian foreign minister did inquire if the British would object to an armistice and was told that London had no objection. Latvia, the British said, must have "full liberty to decide whether or not to conclude an armistice with Soviet Russia." Subsequently, the Latvians continued to mislead the French about the nature of the negotiations which had taken place in Moscow but informed Britain of the agreement concluded there.[123] Hostilities along a second portion of the Soviet western front had come to an end.

It was peace with Estonia, however, which the Bolsheviks celebrated. On 2 February Lenin told the All Russian Central Executive Committee that the treaty of Dorpat was of, "tremendous importance ... and epoch-making significance." It proved, he said, "that we were able to go forward as a proletarian and communist state." By winning peace with Estonia, "We have shown all the belligerent Entente powers who are opposed to peace that the sympathy we are able to evoke among our opponents and bourgeois governments, the sympathy of a small country, is more powerful than all that military oppression, all that financial aid and all those economic ties which link that small country to the powerful world states." Peace had been made possible, he said, by "our proving our ability to renounce in all sincerity, the use of force at the appropriate moment, in order to change to a peace policy and so win the sympathy of the bourgeois government of a small country, regardless of all the support given it by international capital." In displaying this ability the government had been able to "win the confidence of nations hostile to us."[124]

In a parallel statement Chicherin elaborated on these themes. Soviet Russia, he said, had no intention of attempting to spread communism by military means. Any attempt to do so could only compromise the revolutionary development of other lands, falsify the victory of the communist idea, and impede its development. Nor was it a question of seeking to conclude peace so as better to unleash a new war at a more advantageous moment. Soviet Russia sought a lasting peace with all states and was prepared to leave the task of revolutionary change to the proletariat of each nation.[125]

His report to the All-Russian Central Executive Committee stressed a different aspect of the peace negotiations. These talks, he declared, had begun primarily as a means of defending the western front at a time when the struggle against Kolchak and Denikin had diminished the Soviet ability to do this militarily. "With the course of time ... this initial goal of the negotiations with Estonia underwent a significant development and deepening. Our treaty with Estonia was converted, so to speak, into a dress rehearsal for an agreement with the Entente; it was changed into the first experience of breaking the blockade and into the first experiment of peaceful co-existence with a bourgeois state."

Such perspectives had not initially been envisaged, he continued, but when it became clear that Britain and France were badly divided and that certain powerful political circles in Britain had a special interest in securing the independence of the Baltic states, the basis for a compromise quickly emerged. Britain, he said, was "the cream of capitalist society, the supreme capitalist society, with the widest horizons and the most distant perspectives." France was "petit-bourgeois in mentality," unable to see far beyond her present difficulties, concerned primarily with regaining her lost investments in Russia and terrified of Germany. "Britain," Chicherin declared, "will compromise with any force which is strong: Denikin, Kolchak are defeating us – Britain stops talking about agreement with us. We grow stronger – Britain moves toward compromise with us." Britain wanted a special position in the Baltic; Soviet Russia was prepared to acknowledge that special position by recognizing the independence of the Baltic states and concluding peace with them. The Whites, on the other hand, could not accept British hegemony in the Baltic. Consequently, French capitalists, with their ties to old Russia, could not accept it either. But only Soviet Russia and Great Britain exercised real power in the Baltic, and thus the basis for a compromise came into existence. "Every word spoken at Dorpat," Chicherin declared, "reverberated on the banks of the Thames." The Soviet delegation had been careful to take every opportunity to speak of broader issues and the urgent desire of the Soviet government to conclude peace with its neighbours and the western powers. As a result, the price in gold, territory, and political compromise paid to the Estonians was minimal, given the results likely to be achieved by the conclusion of peace. Chicherin paid special tribute to Estonian communists who had made this policy possible by agreeing to abandon their armed struggle with the Estonian bourgeoisie. The class struggle would continue, nothing could stop it, but the victor in the world-wide duel between capitalism and communism would be the system which emerged victorious in constructive work. The concessions made to the Estonian and British bourgeois were necessary to obtain the opportunity to perform constructive work, and the Soviet government sincerely hoped that it would now be allowed to proceed with that labour.[126]

Two days later it fell to the Estonian communists, now in exile in Petrograd, to place the final communist seal on the peace of Dorpat. "The peace treaty," they said, "records the relation of forces not between pygmy Estonian state lords and gigantic Red Russia, but between Red Russia and world counter-revolution."[127]

While the Bolshevik leaders recorded their interpretations of the treaty of Dorpat, the Council of Ambassadors, meeting in Paris as the successor and surrogate of the former peace conference, discussed it also. The French denounced the treaty, but Britain did not find it objectionable. As no agreement on allied policy could be reached, the issue was referred to the heads of government who were to meet in London the following week.[128] The drama of the Soviet peace program, having achieved a stunning success in Estonia, was about to make its debut in London.

Soviet success did not arise from the terms which the Bolsheviks were offering. They were, in fact, substantially less attractive than those offered to Bullitt nearly a year before. Political success marched from the battlefields of the Russian civil war. In December 1919 and January 1920 the Red Army broke up the centres of White power in both Siberia and south Russia. There was no credible Russian regime other than that of the Bolsheviks. For the exposed Baltic states, clinging perilously to the shore of northern Europe, negotiation with Soviet Russia became a matter of life or death. Fortunately for them, the Bolsheviks clearly saw the need to display moderation in victory and, as Chicherin said, satisfy the British desire for a special position in the Baltic. The problem of the smaller states of eastern Europe was soon to become the problem of all Europe, for in the aftermath of the military settlement of the Russian civil war and in the absence of a concerted plan to reverse it, the rest of Europe was clearly going to have to come to terms with the masters of the new Russia.

CHAPTER TEN

"Co-existence of socialist and capitalist states": The Soviet initiation of peace negotiations with Great Britain

At the end of June 1919 Wilson and Lloyd George left Paris following the signing of peace with Germany. The peace conference continued but, with two of the major allied leaders gone, it lost much of its authority. Even before this loss, the peace conference had failed to act effectively in Russia. The allies could send money and munitions to Russian leaders but could not assume actual control of events. Russia was too large, remote, and tumultuous to be mastered by the resources available to the allies. The western powers needed a Russian ally to replace the tsar. Thus they had embraced Kolchak. But by July they no longer had a tsar-surrogate and their embarrassment was great and growing.

The disparity between words and deeds was revealed most clearly in the allied attempt to maintain the blockade of Russia following the conclusion of peace with Germany. As the western powers had never declared war on Soviet Russia they had no legal right to blockade her harbours. While the allies remained in a legal state of war with Germany they had overcome this deficiency by basing the blockade on their right as belligerents to obstruct German commerce. Products of Russian origin found outside of Russia were deemed to be bound for Germany and, hence, liable to seizure by the allies. But once hostilities were definitely at an end this argument would collapse. American and British views on the legality of blockades differed greatly, and the subject was certain to prove divisive. Allied leaders hoped that if Yudenich captured Petrograd they would not have to confront the issue. Yudenich, of course, did not capture Petrograd, and the problem did not go away. By mid-July the question had again come before the peace conference when the Swedes asked if the allies intended to impose any restrictions on their trade with Soviet Russia. The British and French simply wanted to declare the waters adjacent to Russia a war zone and inform the world that the alllies would not allow them to be used for the benefit of the Bolsheviks.[1] This amounted to a blockade in time of peace, and Wilson would not accept such a flagrant violation of century-old American policy. The best he could suggest was that his associates should try to convince the neutral powers to join in a tacit embargo. The American government was already denying clearance to American vessels bound for Soviet ports and "the same action by other government would accomplish the same purpose as a hostile blockade." The allies reluctantly agreed, and finally, on 2 October, they asked the neutral powers and Germany to deny their citizens clearance papers and passports necessary for travel to Soviet Russia and deprive them of banking and communications facilities needed for business with the Bolsheviks.[2]

The proposal was not well received in northern and central Europe. None of the governments to which it was directed were eager to accept decisions reached at a peace conference to which they had not even been invited. Resentment of the wartime blockade remained high, and to this was added the hostility of radical groups to any measures directed against Soviet Russia. In Stockholm the need for caution was underlined when several thousand demonstrators marched to the Foreign Ministry demanding that the government reject the allied proposal.[3] It was in Germany, however, that the greatest opposition emerged. Both government and public opinion were flabbergasted by the proposal, which came only days after Germany herself had been threatened with the reimposition of the blockade should she fail to heed the allied order to withdraw her troops from the Baltic.[4] Even so, the government reacted cautiously. Only when German ministers reported a lack of enthusiasm for the proposal in Scandinavia and Switzerland, did they act.[5] On 22 October the German cabinet rejected the proposal, and a week later the Auswärtiges Amt informed the allies that Germany would not act as requested. The neutral powers quickly followed suit.[6] The German decision was decisive. "It is clear that restriction[s] on maritime trade with Soviet Russia would have no practical value if they did not apply to German ships," Sir Eyre Crowe wrote from Paris, "and as soon as the Treaty of Peace comes into force there will be no weapon by which we could entail Germany's co-operation if she is not prepared to give it voluntarily."[7]

Allied policy soon suffered an even more devastating blow. President Wilson had no intention of abandoning his effort to promote liberal democracy in Russia, but in his mind American acceptance of the League of Nations came before everything else, and he put aside plans for further aid to the anti-Bolsheviks until he could persuade the Senate to give their formal approval to the treaty of Versailles.[8] In early September Wilson undertook a tour of the United States to build popular support for the League. The effort proved too great, and on 2 October he suffered a stroke from which he never fully recovered. This ended American involvement in Russian affairs. Wilson could not act and others were unable to act without his approval. Decisions ceased to be made, and American representatives were left without instructions.[9] The president's authority was further undermined in mid-November when the Senate adopted a series of reservations to the League Covenant which Wilson was sure to reject. Statesmen in Europe drew the logical conclusions. On the same day the Senate repudiated Wilson, Philip Kerr warned Lloyd George that the British government could no longer count on the participation of the United States in the regulation of world affairs. [10] The Russian problem effectively became one to be settled by the British and French alone.

None of this was lost on Lloyd George. By early December he had already concluded that the United States would cease to play a major role in European affairs. [11] He saw this as an opportunity to settle the Russian problem in his own manner. With Washington in chaos and France left friendless on the continent British power and prestige would increase rapidly. [12] Whitehall could only benefit from the weakness of others and the very impermanence of the British position required that the advantage be grasped at once. Lloyd George believed that British prosperity depended on a rapid pacification of the continent with a quick return to normal (in other words, prewar) economic life. The restoration of civil peace in Russia was an integral part of this larger design. With the collapse of allied cooperation, Lloyd George believed it necessary to move quickly to protect Britain's vital political and economic interests.

Changes in the British political world in late 1919 greatly aided the prime minister. The transition from war to peace was marked by the demise of the war cabinet and the restoration of regular cabinet government. This greatly reduced the influence of the Tories and, because of the size of the new cabinet and relative inexperience of the new ministers, increased that of the prime minister. Similarly, Balfour left the Foreign Office and was replaced by Curzon, who lacked the political authority of his predecessor. The new ministers were less influenced by international considerations than the war cabinet and more attuned to the desiderata of internal politics. They wanted to reduce government spending (particularly military), balance the budget, reduce taxes, and promote commerce abroad. A perceived failure in all these areas had contributed to a sharp fall in government popularity which was reflected in the loss of one parliamentary by-election after another throughout the previous nine months. Such considerations would prove decisive in allowing Lloyd George to pursue a much different policy with regard to Russia than in the past.

CIRCUMSTANCES IN EASTERN Europe clearly demanded a new policy. By late 1919 all anti-Bolshevik armies were in full retreat, and the battlefield appeared finally to have rendered its verdict. The time had come for a political settlement, and the Bolsheviks were eager to open negotiations. They therefore renewed their long-standing effort to engage the western powers in peace talks. On 20 August Lenin spoke to William T. Goode of the *Manchester Guardian* concerning the Soviet peace proposals Bullitt had carried to Paris in the spring. "They still held good," he said, "with such modification as the changing military situation might indicate." Similarly, he reaffirmed Soviet recognition of the independence of Finland and the Baltic states. [13] The following month Lenin emphasized this point when he told a correspondent of the *Christian Science Monitor* that those "who expect from us, after peace is concluded, not only resumption of trade relations, but also the possibility of receiving concessions in Russia" were absolutely right. "A durable peace," he concluded, "would be such a relief to the working people of Russia that they would undoubtedly agree to certain concessions being granted. The granting of concessions under reasonable terms is desirable also for us, as one of the means of attracting to Russia, during the period of the co-existence side by side of socialist and capitalist states, the technical help of the countries which are more advanced in this respect."[14]

This is noteworthy not only because it represents Lenin's first recorded reference to the co-existence of socialist and capitalist states but also because it reworked an old theme in Soviet peace propaganda – economic gain from the conclusion of peace. For most of 1919 (but not 1918) this had been presented in a derisory, sometimes insulting, manner – that of helpless Russia offering economic exploitation in exchange for peace. Now postwar economic cooperation was projected as a mutually beneficial enterprise, a real possibility rather than mere propaganda. Less than two weeks later Lenin reaffirmed this new approach. On 5 October he was asked by a Chicago *Daily News* correspondent, "What is the position of the Soviet Government in respect of an economic understanding with America?" and responded, "We are decidedly for an economic understanding with America – with all countries, but especially with America."[15] Although Lenin specifically mentioned economic relations with the United States, he did not exclude other possibilities. This was not overlooked by Lloyd George.

Even before these Soviet signals reached western Europe, he had begun to bring his opposition to intervention further into the open. He did so indirectly, leaving substantial room for manoeuvre. Following a meeting of the Supreme Council in Paris on 15 September, he provided reporters with a statement from "an official British source" that the allied leaders intended "to allow the Russia revolutionists to settle their own affairs and work out their own salvation in any way they please with the sole limitation that the New Russia respects the rights of its neighbours." In fact, the council had done no such thing, but the statement created a sensation in London. Utter confusion followed when allied spokesmen denied the report. "What is the Russian policy of the Prime Minister?" asked *The Times* on 18 September, "Is it also the Russian policy of the Allies and Associates? Was it, or was it not, discussed by the Paris Conference on Monday?" The next day Reuters reported that it has been "officially informed that there is no ... change of policy regarding Russia."[16] Lloyd George again withdrew into silence to await developments.

One of these was the opening of negotiations for an exchange of prisoners with Soviet Russia. In the spring the Foreign Office had bowed to public opinion and contacted Moscow in an effort to secure the release of several hundred British civilians and servicemen held prisoner by the Bolsheviks. Unofficial negotiations had followed, and on 11 October Curzon invited Chicherin to send a representative of the Soviet Red Cross to Denmark. Chicherin agreed.[17] He lost no time in beating the peace drum. On 29 September he told an American reporter that if the allies would cease military operations in Russia and raise the blockade Soviet Russia was prepared to establish economic relations, assume the debts of the former imperial regime and end its propaganda against western government. When Maxim Litvinov was sent by Moscow to Copenhagen, therefore, he received credentials empowering him to negotiate peace and the restoration of commercial relations as well as an exchange of prisoners.[18]

Lloyd George used the prisoner-exchange negotiations to secure a steady stream of information concerning Soviet readiness to settle outstanding differences with Great Britain. James O'Grady, the British representative, served as the ears of the prime minister, who heard every word spoken by Litvinov at Copenhagen.[19] By the end of the year, as a result of these talks, Lloyd George had obtained the entire Soviet brief. In exchange for peace Moscow would accept the loss of Poland, Finland and the Baltic states. Asian frontiers still had to be settled, but in fixing them, vital Soviet interests would have to be respected. The Soviet form of government was not negotiable. Russia and its allied Soviet republics would not assume the trappings of bourgeios democracy; they would remain single party "dictatorships of the proletariat." All financial and economic questions were negotiable, but Moscow would not be content with the mere lifting of the blockade. Soviet Russia had to have actual peace and normal political relations. Mutually advantageous economic relations would follow.[20]

While waiting for the full Soviet brief Lloyd George had to deal with yet another attempt by Churchill to revive intervention. Bereft of a surrogate tsar, Churchill now settled on Boris Savinkov to act as spokesman for a new "democratic" anti-Bolshevism. Savinkov, who had already played an important role in the Provisional government of 1917 and the abortive Socialist Revolutionary attempt to unseat the Bolsheviks in 1918, had long maintained that Kolchak and Denikin lacked sufficient popular support to prevail against the Bolsheviks. He now asked for allied support in mobilizing the peasants and non-Russian peoples of the former empire to drive the Bolsheviks from power. Churchill endorsed this scheme and recommended its adoption by the allied prime ministers when they met in London in mid-December.[21]

Lloyd George had other ideas. Soviet victory in Russia and political chaos in Washington provided the prime minister with the leverage he needed to convince Clemenceau to withdraw French support from the Whites. The French premier emerged from his first meeting with Lloyd George describing the Russians as "orientals" and saying that he never liked the Whites and had no further use for them. He abandoned them entirely in exchange for a pledge of strong British support against Germany and a somewhat weaker commitment to Poland.[22] Lloyd George, however, remained highly suspicious of Polish aspirations, and at the December conference every time the subject arose he and Clemenceau clashed. Clemenceau argued that the allies needed Poland to help keep Germany in order. Lloyd George reminded Clemenceau of Pilsudski's plan for a Polish march on Moscow and warned that "if the Polish army were re-equipped it must not be for an attack on Russia."[23] Here then the great crisis of 1920 loomed out of the dying days of 1919.

For the moment Lloyd George had his hands free to deal with the Russian question. Yet he still could not contemplate dealing directly with the Bolsheviks. The French and Americans remained steadfastly opposed to such a step,[24] and his Conservative supporters in Britain would not tolerate too open a move toward Moscow. In shaping a policy which his political associates could accept, he did not draw his inspiration from the Foreign Office or even his own secretariat, but instead from long-time associates in the Ministry of Food. On 6 January 1920 E.F. Wise, who had worked closely with Lloyd George at the Exchequer before moving to the Ministry of Food and becoming chief British representative on the Supreme Economic Council, sent him a proposal for a new allied economic policy in Russia. The Wise memorandum became the basis for Lloyd George's Russian policy. It carefully marshalled the facts regarding prewar trade with Russia and revealed the serious economic consequences resulting from its suspension. The blockade had failed, he said, and should be lifted. Britain should take the lead in this, for she stood to benefit most from renewed commerce with Russia. He also provided Lloyd George with a means of avoiding the stigma of bargaining with the Bolsheviks, for he suggested that it was not necessary to deal with the Soviet government to reopen trade with Russia. This could be done through the Russian agricultural cooperative organizations. These, he claimed, were free of Bolshevik control and could be dealt with through their western representatives. The Bolsheviks would be so pleased to see the end of the blockade that they would probably agree to "any reasonable economic or other conditions that we are likely to impose."[25]

This was the scheme which Lloyd George presented to the Supreme Council in Paris on 14 January. To be sure, he neglected to mention the advantage foreseen for Great Britain, and he took special care to add an anti-Bolshevik touch to the proposal. His plan, he said, would destroy Bolshevism, for "the moment trade was established with Russia, Communism would go." Wise rather than Curzon accompanied him to the council; the problem, he said, did not concern the Foreign Office. At the meeting two well-coached representatives of the Russian cooperatives testified to the independence of their organization from the Bolsheviks. The Russian cooperative societies, they said, had an abundance of raw materials to exchange for western manufactured goods. They did not believe the Bolsheviks would attempt to prevent the cooperatives from engaging in trade with the west. Neither Clemenceau nor the Italian premier objected to what they described, quite accurately, as this "very remarkable proposal." Two days later the Supreme Council resolved "to permit the exchange of goods on the basis of reciprocity between the Russian people and Allied and neutral countries." This was to be done through the Russian cooperatives. Lloyd George carefully edited the statement released at the end of the meeting to remove every mention of the Bolsheviks. The allied powers, he said, were only entering into commercial relations with the Russian people. The Supreme Council solemnly declared that "these arrangements imply no change in the policy of the Allied governments toward the Soviet Government."[26]

Lloyd George had scored a remarkable victory. By unveiling his policy in the Supreme Council and translating it into the policy of the allied powers before discussing it with his own colleagues he had completely outmanoeuvred those who would otherwise have attempted to block its acceptance. This was all the more remarkable, for while doing so he also aborted one final effort by Churchill to rekindle the war against Soviet Russia. Churchill had taken advantage of Lloyd George's absence from London to create alarm among the remaining ministers concerning the safety of British forces in the Caucasus and the possibility of armed insurrection in Britain itself. When Lloyd George learned of these fears, "red revolution and blood and war at home and abroad" as Maurice Hankey described them, he summoned his leading ministers to Paris. Once there they were left to cool their heels while he secured allied approval of his Russian policy. The London newspapers had learned of much of this and had speculated furiously about the possibility of war against the Bolsheviks. When the Supreme Council announced their decision to lift the blockade, therefore, there was great surprise in London. "The first results of the deliberations [in Paris]," commented *The Times*, "is somewhat unexpected."[27]

Even Churchill had to express his professional respect for the political skill of his chief. "Your strategy is masterly," he told Lloyd George. You saw me going in one direction and you blocked the way. I tried another and found it blocked too ... I fought you, and you have beaten me, yet I cannot help admiring you for it."[28] Back in London the prime minister had no difficulty in having his policy ratified by the cabinet. When his opponents should have been questioning him rather closely about his actions in Paris, he focused their attention on the possibility of armed insurrection in Great Britain and heatedly debated with them the best way of countering this threat. "Throughout the discussion," wrote Tom Jones, "the PM did a lot of unsuspected legpulling as he does not believe in the imminence of revolution."[29]

How did the Soviet government respond to the allied initiative? Moscow had not been left without prior warning. In late December Litvinov had alerted them to the possibility of a dramatic change in policy. "From private conversations with O'Grady," he wrote on 22 December, "I have gained the impression that the British government is not opposed to radically altering its relations with Soviet Russia."[30] When O'Grady returned to Copenhagen after Christmas he confirmed that Lloyd George would seek to have the Supreme Council agree to the restoration of trade with Russia.[31] Still, nothing had prepared Moscow for the exact form this would take. The idea of conducting trade through the Russian cooperatives took the Narkomindel as much by surprise as the Quai d'Orsay.

The initial Soviet response, therefore, simply took note of the allied decision and compared it with armed intervention. Within a day, however, the Bolsheviks had realized the significance of the allied announcement, and Radio Moscow broadcast two triumphal declarations entitled "End of the Blockade" and "Victory!" The Red Army, both said, had forced the allied powers to acknowledge the failure of their policy in Russia. All the same, this official Soviet statement urged continued caution and vigilance. "The Entente continued their hypocrisy," failing to contact the Soviet government directly and saying they were prepared only to resume commercial relations with "the Russian people." Clearly they still wished to ignore the Soviet government, and this, said Radio Moscow, "cannot help but give us pause for thought." The foreign commerce of Russia, it reminded everyone, had been nationalized, and "all commercial relations between foreign states and Russia are impossible without prior agreement with the Russian government."[32]

Nevertheless, the Soviet government responded enthusiastically to the allied initiative. Contrary to the fable told to the Supreme Council, the Russian co-operative societies had already come firmly under Bolshevik control.[33] The Soviet government, as a result, could easily accept the western proposal. This officially reached Moscow on 20 January in a radio message from the Paris representatives of the Russian cooperative societies asking if the Soviet government would authorize the cooperative central office (Tsentrosoiuz) to export grain and raw materials, receive western imports, and guarantee the safety of all goods to be shipped to Russia. They further asked for Soviet safe conduct to allow them to visit Moscow in order to arrange the details of the proposed commercial exchange. Three days later they received an affirmative reply to all their questions. The following week Moscow proposed that a delegation from Tsentrosoiuz be sent to western Europe to hasten the renewal of commercial relations.[34] The long process of negotiating a resumption of economic ties with the West had begun.

The Soviet government was eager to accelerate that process and, to do so, acted promptly to bring the prisoner exchange negotiations at Copenhagen to a successful conclusion. On 18 January Litvinov presented O'Grady with a draft agreement on the exchange of prisoners. This draft, which provided for the return of most, but not all, British prisoners proved unacceptable to the Foreign Office which substituted a draft of its own. London instructed O'Grady that Litvinov would have to accept the British draft without change. If he did not, O'Grady was to break off negotiations and return home.[35] The Bolsheviks, however, were not to be bullied. They viewed the prisoner exchange negotiations as part of the much larger problem of regularizing relations with the West and were not about to part with all British prisoners until they were certain that the scheme adopted by the Supreme Council would eventually lead to peace. They would return sufficient prisoners to justify the negotiations but retain enough to ensure their bargaining position in future talks. Contrary to his instructions, but well within the spirit of the negotiations, O'Grady accepted the Soviet compromise. On 12 February the agreement was signed.[36]

Lloyd George now sought to hasten the start of trade talks. On 6 February he told the American ambassador that he thought the Soviet government was "changing colour," and a stable regime would be "brought about by opening the country to trade."[37] Washington did not share these views but, given the continuing paralysis of American government, the State Department could do nothing to prevent Lloyd George from pushing ahead with his policy. The French also were incapacitated by political crisis. On 17 January the French parliament had turned on Clemenceau and refused him election as president of the Republic. Instead they had chosen Paul Deschanel, a political mediocrity. Clemenceau resigned immediately and was succeeded by Alexandre Millerand. The new premier was without experience in foreign affairs but refused all advice offered by his predecessor.[38] Despite mounting concern regarding Lloyd George's Russian policy[39] the French were unable to formulate their objections until 6 February, when they informed their allies that they felt the question of commercial relations with Russia was being dealt with contrary to the January decision of the Supreme Council. The British agreed to deal with the question at the next conference of allied leaders, but meanwhile Lloyd George was free to act as he wished. "As we have now embarked on a policy of restricted commerce with Soviet Russia," minuted Lord Hardinge, "it is desirable that there should be no further change of policy except in the direction of expansion."[40]

The manner in which both British and Soviet representatives had begun to describe the future development of commercial relations between Russia and the West had alarmed the French. They knew that the well-informed British minister to Denmark had said that the peace, just concluded between Estonia and Soviet Russia "would not be long in being generalized."[41] In addition, Jean Fabre, who kept a close watch on Soviet internal affairs from Helsingfors, reported in early February that "the decision of the Supreme Council is, in general, considered as constituting, for the Bolsheviks, a capital success while the official [Soviet] world affects to see in it the premises of an impending peace which will consecrate the Maximalist regime." The conclusion of the Anglo-Soviet prisoner exchange agreement simply added to French alarm, especially as it included a provision allowing Litvinov to remain almost indefinitely in western Europe. In the previous year Whitehall had refused to receive Litvinov in Britain and had found it difficult to persuade Denmark to allow its capital to be used for negotiating with the Bolsheviks. Now, however, when the French chargé in Copenhagen opined that "no one could force a western European country to extend its hospitality to Litvinov," the British minister responded coolly "that if necessary Litvinov would be received in a Scottish city, Aberdeen for example."[42]

All of this was simply too much for the Quai d'Orsay. The Foreign Ministry advised forthright opposition, and this was the line adopted by Millerand in his first official meeting with the other allied prime ministers in London between 19 and 24 February. The Bolshevik decision to Sovietize all the cooperative societies in Russia and appoint Litvinov as their western European representative, he said, "constituted a negation of the principles involved in the exchange of goods between individuals." Millerand also pointed to the devastated Soviet economy and argued that, from a purely practical point of view, the western powers could gain nothing from commerce with Russia. He urged an end to further contacts with the Russian cooperatives. The best policy was to do nothing. He believed Soviet Russia would soon collapse, because "the Bolshevik system ... would never be capable of organizing anything."

The British and Italians greeted these views with incredulity. Francesco Nitti, the Italian premier, replied that he did not know if western Europe could obtain any economic resources from Soviet Russia, but it was necessary to try, for otherwise they would remain dependent on the United States for many raw materials.[43] Nor could he accept the concept of benign neglect. The allies had to pacify the continent, and they could not do so with Russia still at war. He did not believe the Bolsheviks would disappear by themselves, especially in the absence of military force. Millerand, he concluded "had expressed the view that the Bolshevik Government could not last; whereas he, Signor Nitti, doubted whether it would ever end." Clearly Lloyd George had primed the Italian premier carefully and was now able to step forward in his favourite role of peacemaker. He expressed the desire to resume commercial relations if possible and to determine the true state of the Russian economy. Thus he proposed that the allied premiers ask the League of Nations to despatch a commission of inquiry to Soviet Russia to determine the actual political and economic situation there. When the Supreme Council had received the League report they would be better able to resolve the question of whether to pursue the restoration of economic relations.

The French liked none of this, but in exchange for an explicit rejection of establishing diplomatic relations with Moscow they agreed to re-endorse the establishment of commercial relations with Russia. They also agreed to sending a commission of investigation to Russia, on the explicit but publicly unstated pledge of Nitti and Lloyd George not to act independently until the League report would allow the allies to frame a common policy.[44] It was significant that the United States was not even represented at this conference and had not influenced its decisions in any way. Lloyd George retained the initiative and was free to continue reshaping British policy towards Soviet Russia.

WHILE THE ALLIES DEBATED, the Bolsheviks impatiently awaited some concrete action. Only when commerce again began to flow would it be possible to pass from a state of war to peaceful reconstruction. This was the message which Lenin and Chicherin issued repeatedly during February 1920. They missed no opportunity to speak with foreign reporters on the subject. Lenin in particular conveyed a growing sense of impatience to see allied words translated into deeds. He pointed to the disparity between the two as well as the preparations for war under way in Poland. By the end of the month he had begun to portray the verbal lifting of the blockade as only one further move in the allied chess game against the Russian revolution. Lenin expressed the hope that these manoeuvres would soon end and real negotiations begin. Russia, he stressed, intended to attack no one and wanted only peace. To start the wheels of commerce going Russia would pay for what it needed in gold but hoped soon to cover its foreign purchases with the sale of grain, flax, and other raw materials.[45] Nor did the Bolsheviks ignore the United States. Noting the American absence from European councils, Chicherin turned directly to Washington at the end of February, declaring that "the United States can play a gigantic role in the realization of [the reconstruction of Russian economic life]." He also renewed the long-standing Soviet bid for peace negotiations with the United States.[46]

The allied announcement of 24 February reaffirming their intention of restoring trade with Russia received a warm welcome in Moscow. Lenin ridiculed the proposed League of Nations inquiry but moved quickly to send his own delegation to western Europe. On 25 February the Tsentrosoiuz announced they were sending Leonid Krasin, Victor Nogin, Solomon Rozovkii, and L'ev Khinchuk to join Maxim Litvinov.[47] Krasin was known and respected in western Europe, and his presence at the head of the delegation indicated the seriousness which Moscow attached to the negotiations. For all his public bravado regarding the defeat of the allied powers, Lenin privately insisted on the need to reach agreement with them. In an essay entitled "On Compromises," written in March 1920 but not published until sixteen years later, he asked, "May an advocate of proletarian revolution conclude compromises with capitalists or with the capitalist class?" He answered: "Of course," provided that it is "an agreement that is legitimate from the angle of the proletarian revolution."[48]

Krasin's instructions have not yet been published, but evidence regarding their origin does exist and suggests a careful, meticulous process of preparation.[49] In addition, portions have appeared in Soviet publications. In one Chicherin is quoted as telling Krasin: "We must not appear in the role of the pitiful suppliant. Once the Russian foreign minister Gorchakov said: 'Great powers do not need recognition, they declare their own existence.' In 1917 we declared our own existence, year by year we grow stronger and the day is not far off when we will be recognized. History itself will force the imperialists to do this."[50]

At the end of March Chicherin wrote further, this time to Litvinov, saying: "Let England look on the trip of Krasin as a serious trip for the foundation of commercial relations, and not as a preliminary contact without final and precise decisions. It is especially important to us that we obtain concrete commercial results and not merely declarative statements. The very fact of the delegation being composed of such experts is a sign that concrete business decisions are expected."[51]

Krasin was welcome in western Europe; Litvinov was not. John Duncan Gregory, head of the Russian division in the Foreign Office, described the commissar of foreign trade as "primarily a business man interested in setting

Russia on her legs and is not properly a Bolshevik politician," while everyone in Britain remembered Litvinov as a meddling troublemaker. The Foreign Office felt he had taken unfair advantage of O'Grady in the prisoner exchange negotiations. Gregory had described him as "a slippery Russian Jew" wholly alien to "recognized Anglo-Saxon methods," while Lord Curzon wrote that Litvinov had "walked around [O'Grady] while he clung too closely to the bottle." Nevertheless, on 3 March, Gregory warned Curzon that the envoy was one of the Soviet government's chief propagandists and "they will be obviously put out by our refusal to receive him. We don't want a row at the outset, as it is of the first importance to have Krasin over here and get to work seriously." He suggested that Litvinov could be kept at Copenhagen "to see through the execution of the Prisoner Agreement." This was adopted.[52] Moscow was informed that Litvinov was not welcome in Britain, but the Foreign Office would facilitate his continued presence in Copenhagen. After an initial objection, Litvinov was reported as being prepared to remain in Scandinavia.[53]

The American government would not negotiate directly or indirectly with Moscow. The State Department feared, however, that the British were seeking an unfair commercial advantage in Russia and felt compelled to inform London confidentially that it no longer could justify continuing the existing restrictions on American businessmen wishing to trade with Russia. Washington, in fact, was in no hurry to abolish trade restrictions and was only seeking to avoid the charge of leaving American merchants at a disadvantage to their European competitors. Therefore, when the British and French asked Washington to delay the abolition of existing regulations, the State Department was pleased to leave American restrictions in place.[54] In reality, American policy remained in chaos. In an informal conversation the American commissioner for the Baltic truthfully informed his Soviet counterpart that "for the past six months the United States has not had a foreign policy."[55]

The French, like the Americans, had no genuine alternative to the British policy but were in a far better position to block it. This remained French policy throughout the spring of 1920. Moscow responded by seeking to reconcile France to the existence of the Soviet government. This had been Bolshevik policy since October 1918 but now became a central feature of Soviet tactics. Moscow knew that the French were primarily concerned about the fate of their investments and the impact of the Russian revolution on the European balance of power. They tried to reassure Paris that they would honour the obligations of former Russian governments. In early March Victor Kopp, speaking to the French representative in Berlin, went so far as to say that Moscow was prepared to guarantee the payment of Russian debts through the deposit of a large quantity of gold in French banks.[56] When a representative of French commercial interests arrived in Copenhagen, Litvinov repeatedly declared "we wish to pay our debts, but we can not do it until the [civil] war is over on the different fronts created against us by France." But Litvinov went far beyond the promise of simple financial restitution. He knew France was alarmed by its weakened position in the postwar world and especially by its relationship with Germany. Thus, he expressed Soviet sympathy for France and suspicion of the Reich. He said that Germany could not provide the economic assistance needed to rebuild Russia. Only the western powers possessed the resources needed for reconstruction, but they, or at least France, insisted on pushing the Poles into a war which Warsaw could not win. The French were promoting chaos. Nor did Litvinov fail to play on Anglo-French antagonism. Moscow understood, he said, that Britain "wants to weaken Russia and to do so, supports all the small states ... But a weak Russia is not in the interests of France and, as a consequence, [we ask] why this ... double game? Why should France push Poland into war, sending airplanes, thousands of officers, munitions, money?" The French were working against themselves and playing the British game. British policy, he said, was aimed at reducing both Russia and France to slavery.[57] All this reached Paris, was duly noted, and made no impression at all. The reports were branded as tendentious and ignored. The Millerand government continued the policies established at the beginning of the year.[58] The allies, therefore, remained as divided as ever.

The Krasin mission arrived in the midst of this controversy. They reached Copenhagen by way of Sweden, stopping for several days in Stockholm. In early April Krasin met the Swedish press in an effort to dispel the many rumours which had begun to circulate about his mission. In the previous month he had been depicted in the west as being not really a communist, but instead a crypto-capitalist, a reluctant revolutionary, and a lonely businessman among fanatics. Some western newspapers even reported that he was prepared to lead a counter-revolution. He was widely expected to place large orders for every kind of merchandise, and, as a consequence, he attracted countless speculators. His press conference shattered these illusions. He was a long-time member of the Bolshevik Party, he told the reporters, a commissar in good standing, and a foe of counter-revolution in any guise. Moreover, he was interested in purchasing only a very few items, primarily locomotives and agricultural machinery. The Russian economy could not be restored until the transport system was repaired and the peasants would part with their surpluses. Western aid was vital to achieve both objectives, first through the sale of locomotives and farm machinery, for which he was prepared to pay gold, and second, by the conclusion of peace which was the only condition in which commerce could be restored. In Russia all commerce had been nationalized and could not be conducted independently of the Soviet government. The French minister in Stockholm described Krasin as displaying "a near arrogant frankness," while British observers said he had "thrown off the mask of co-operation." "Actual trade," they concluded, "will most likely be almost ignored by the present delegates whose role will be to ascertain on what terms Russia can obtain peace and help in reconstruction."[59]

The negotiations, which began at Copenhagen on 7 April, fully justified this evaluation. Opposite Krasin sat a committee representing the Supreme Economic

Council. It was chaired by E.F. Wise and included Owen O'Malley of the British Foreign Office and J. de Halgouet representing the French government. The Soviet delegation first sought clarification of the allied position regarding Russia. Had the western powers completely abandoned the blockade? Could Russia trade freely with the neutrals? What was the allied attitude towards countries still at war with Russia? How could trade be resumed so long as war continued and the Soviet government remained unrecognized? Wise, of course, could say nothing regarding the conclusion of peace, but he assured Krasin that "the public statement of policy of the Supreme Council must be understood to imply that all necessary steps would be taken to facilitate trade." All obstruction would cease, he said, "so soon as it was a question of the execution of contracts agreed in principle between Russia and Allied or neutral firms." The best way to remove those obstacles was for the Russian delegation to proceed to London and enter into direct negotiations with business houses interested in the resumption of trade with Russia. This raised the question of who would go to London. Seemingly this issue had been settled in mid-March when Litvinov had agreed to remain in Copenhagen. Krasin now reopened the question, saying he could not believe the allies were serious in wanting talks if they would not give way on such a trivial point; Wise responded that, if the Soviets felt the issue so unimportant, it was they who were not seriously interested in negotiation. Litvinov, said Krasin, was the most experienced member of the Soviet delegation, and they needed him in London. In his absence the delegation would have to send every important question to him for consideration. Wise, who knew he could not compromise on this issue, simply replied that Litvinov was persona non grata.[60]

Much more was involved in this issue than either side would admit. The British truly loathed Litvinov and did not want to deal with him, but they also believed it would be easier to reach an agreement with Krasin if Litvinov did not accompany him to London. On a more sinister level, they wished to divide the Soviet delegation physically in order to compel it to engage in extensive telegraphic communication, which the British secret service were able to monitor.[61] The Soviets also had unstated reasons for their position. Chicherin's instructions to Krasin clearly indicated that he was seeking to take the first step in the restoration of Russia as a great power, and he did not wish the Soviet delegation to appear as political mendicants. Above all, he wished to avoid any implication that Soviet Russia was prepared to accept a dictated peace. It was demeaning, he felt, to have the British vet the Soviet delegation.

Each side now sought to impress the other. When Wise again refused to accept Litvinov, Krasin suggested the talks be held elsewhere. Wise said this would be impractical as most of the companies with which the Russians wished to negotiate were located in Great Britain. Progress elsewhere, said Wise, "would be painfully slow, if possible at all." Progress without Litvinov, responded Krasin, would be equally slow. Then, said Wise, the initial negotiations were at end. The Foreign Office approved this decision, for they believed the Soviets were bluffing and would give way as soon as they were convinced that the British position was firm.[62] The Soviet delegation, however, were not bluffing and informed Moscow that the allies did "not desire to conclude peace and instead wished to continue the present indefinite situation."[63] They also suspended commercial negotiations with the representatives of British firms in Copenhagen and approached the Italians, asking that the talks be transferred to Rome. Nitti was sufficiently interested to ask the opinion of the British government. The Foreign Office responded negatively, Curzon saying the Soviet request "must be absolutely turned down."[64] The following day Moscow sent Krasin new instructions. He was told that the negotiations required Litvinov, and Krasin communicated this decision to the British. The deadlock was complete.

EVENTS IN THE RUSSIAN civil war now overtook these negotiations. In the north General Miller had managed to survive the winter, but in February further mutinies ripped through his army. On 17 February he asked the British to intercede with Moscow to obtain favourable terms for the surrender of his government. The Foreign Office did as requested, Chicherin responded favourably, but it was far too late.[65] Miller was forced to flee on 19 February; three days later the Red Army entered Archangel. Within days Murmansk also fell, and Soviet authority was established over all northern Russia.

The favourable Soviet response suggested a more timely British initiative might avoid further bloodshed in south Russia.[66] As a negotiated end of the civil war corresponded with the British desire for peace in eastern Europe, the Foreign Office turned its attention to this possibility. On 16 March Denikin had been forced to evacuate Novorossiisk. Only the Crimea remained to him, and, given the state of his army, he was unlikely to hold the peninsula for long.[67] In these circumstances the British cabinet decided on 31 March, as H.A.L. Fisher confided to his diary, "to tell Denikin to wind up affairs and come to terms with [the] Soviet Government." Curzon wired Denikin that London felt he should abandon his struggle and was prepared to ask Moscow for an amnesty for his followers. He was entirely frank in specifying the reason for this action, saying that continued resistance in south Russia "would be likely seriously to compromise the present Allied policy of resuming trade with Russia and could only prolong distress in that country and retard the eventual establishment of normal economic conditions."[68]

The Whites responded disingenuously. When the British ultimatum arrived Denikin had just resigned and been replaced by Baron Wrangel. As a condition of accepting command Wrangel had insisted the other generals agree to accept British mediation of the end of hostilities with the Bolsheviks. In reality he did not intend to capitulate and accepted the British proposal only because he had no alternative. Even in accepting it he suggested a two-month delay before the Red Army be allowed into the Crimea. During this time he hoped to rebuild his army and apply to France for the aid necessary to continue the struggle. The

French were hesitant, but given their determination not to recognize Bolshevik power in Russia and the imminence of Pilsudski's attack on the Red Army, they did not reject the proposal out of hand.[69]

Unaware of this intrigue, the British proceeded to seek a negotiated end of the civil war. On 11 April Curzon informed Chicherin of Wrangel's acceptance of British mediation and asked that Moscow agree to a general amnesty and inform London of the terms on which the Soviet government would accept the surrender of the Volunteer Army. It was in the Soviet interest, he said, to bring the war to an end. "We are expecting the arrival here in a few days' time of your delegates to discuss the ways and means by which trade between our two countries may be resumed. Such intercourse is vital for the economic recovery of Russia; as long, however, as civil war is proceeding in Russia it cannot be undertaken with any reasonable prospect of success." He warned that if "the commencement of these negotiations were to synchronise with military carnage in South Russia ... [they] could not be prosecuted in the face of a public opinion that would result from any such proceedings and they would accordingly be doomed to failure from the start."[70]

This message contained three elements of great importance to the Soviet government. First, it fully embraced the oft-repeated Soviet thesis that a restoration of commercial relations between Russia and the West first required an end to the civil war. Second, it clearly linked the trade talks with broader issues arising from the war. Finally, it acknowledged officially, for the first time, that the Russian trade delegation soon to arrive in Britain represented the government of Soviet Russia and not merely Tsentrosoiuz. Chicherin fell gleefully on all these points, informing Litvinov on 12 April: "In [Curzon's] telegram the delegation is referred to as our delegation and not the delegation of the Tsentrosoiuz and with our acceptance of the offer to mediate is coupled the possibility of Krasin's success. We propose to link up to this also the question of Poland, Japan and your visit [to London]."

The Foreign Office did not find this amusing at all. Chicherin, of course, had not sent them a copy of his telegram, but they received one from the British secret service who were reading all traffic exchanged with Litvinov. "This is preposterous," minuted one official, while the head of the Russian Department wrote: "I don't think we ought to tolerate for a moment being outmanoeuvred by the Soviet government. It is undignified and we gain nothing." The director of naval intelligence thought the Soviet object was to repeat the northern Russian scenario, making no commitments to Wrangel while the Red Army stormed the Crimea. He suggested that Chicherin be told that should the Red Army attempt to advance into the Crimea "they will be prevented from doing so by our war vessels." This was scotched by Sir Eyre Crowe, who indicated that cabinet had not authorized such action and, in any case, doubted that British warships alone could bar the roads into the peninsula.[71]

The real problem for the Foreign Office was the Soviet linkage of the British initiative with other large issues and the question of Litvinov. Both appeared in Chicherin's response of 14 April. While welcoming the British proposal for ending hostilities in south Russia, the foreign commissar tied it not merely to the trade talks but to all questions at issue between Great Britain and Soviet Russia. Chicherin had been waiting for eighteen months to raise these issues and, in one great sweep, he poured them all on the table. "The whole complex of questions touching our relations is linked up, in your note," he told Curzon, "with the settlement of this one particular matter raised by you. *We for our part declare that the many questions outstanding between our two Governments are likewise interdependent, and their discussion should now be approached on the basis of your declaration.*"

Moreover, as Curzon had given "humanitarianism" in explanation of British interest in the fate of the Volunteer Army, so too did Chicherin in raising still another matter, "the fate of the ex-members of the Hungarian Soviet Government, our former ally, now held in prison in Austria." He asked Curzon to use his influence in securing the release and free passage of these men to Soviet Russia. He concluded by declaring: "The Russian Government considers that the solution of this and other questions outstanding between our two Governments may best be reached by direct negotiations between our representative in London, Litvinov, and the British Government."[72] At one stroke, therefore, Chicherin attempted to promote Litvinov from a simple member of the Tsentrosoiuz delegation, still cooling its heels in Copenhagen, to plenipotentiary Soviet representative in London with whom the British government were invited to negotiate the settlement of all questions outstanding between the two governments.

In the best of circumstances this would not have gone down well in London, but the manifold weaknesses of contemporary wireless communication now intervened to render a difficult situation nearly critical. Chicherin had prepared his response to Curzon on 12 April and marked it for wireless transmission to London. For four days, however, the British station at Carnarvon refused to receive it. By 14 April he had grown concerned about this delay and sent his response by telegraph to the British representative at Reval. The latter received the message on 15 April and relayed it in code to the Foreign Office where it arrived the following day. Unfortunately only a single individual was then decoding incoming telegrams, and the Soviet message did not reach the Russian desk until late on 17 April. By then, alerted by the intercepted telegram from Chicherin to Litvinov of 12 April, British officials had grown alarmed by the apparent silence of the Soviet government. Fearing the worst, they decided to send a second telegram expressing disappointment at not having received a reply to Curzon's proposed mediation. Further confusion arose from the imminent departure of Curzon for San Remo where the Supreme Council was about to meet. He appears to have been shown a draft of this second telegram but clearly did not have time to ponder its meaning, for here his officials had him say that if mediation were not accepted the Royal Navy would be ordered to defend the Crimea from Soviet invasion. As Crowe had noted only days before, this was not the policy of the British government and probably beyond the ability of the Royal Navy. Nevertheless, it was sent on the evening of 17 April over the signature of Lord Curzon, an action which caused the foreign secretary, subsequently stung by Chicherin's caustic remarks sent in response, to demand a full inquiry. His reaction to the intricate answer given him, reflected in the sequence of events noted above and below, caused him to comment acidly: "I think that the Order of Jesuits would derive much pleasure from our explanations."[73]

Only after the threatening telegram of 17 April had been sent to Moscow did Chicherin's message of three days before emerge from the code room. Even then the Foreign Office made no effort to respond to it until two days later, when a second message arrived from Chicherin reporting that British vessels in the Black Sea were bombarding Bolshevik forces. Not surprisingly, he related this to the British threat of 17 April and concluded that his message of 14 April had not reached London. When a repetition of Chicherin's original telegram reached the Foreign Office in the afternoon of 19 April, Lord Hardinge finally acknowledged receiving the first message. Noting Lord Curzon's absence at San Remo, he said that "a few days' delay in replying may unavoidably occur." In the meantime, "to avoid any misunderstanding," he reaffirmed the warning contained in the minatory telegram of 17 April.[74] Chicherin responded at once that he could not conceal his "astonishment" that the British government had "found it possible to base a diplomatic step of great importance upon what ... would be perhaps described as inadequate ascertaining of facts." He deplored this recourse to threats and the adoption of an aggressive attitude, which he warned would only endanger the establishment of trade relations with Soviet Russia. Nevertheless, while denying any submission to British threats, the Soviet government reaffirmed the conciliatory proposals contained in their message of 14 April.[75]

As if this situation was not sufficiently confused, it now transpired that the Bolshevik forces being shelled by British warships were marching down the eastern shore of the Black Sea, and were not bent on invading the Crimea. The British naval commander in the Black Sea with the approval of the Admiralty, had undertaken to defend nearly thirty thousand Cossacks who were being driven south towards the Georgian frontier by the Red Army.[76] By this time the questions involved in relations with the Bolsheviks had become so complex that the Foreign Office referred them all to the British delegation at San Remo.[77] There they did not seem so great. The allied prime ministers had fallen into acrimonious dispute over issues related to Germany, and nearly a week passed before Lloyd George drew the attention of his colleagues to eastern Europe. Even then, despite the alarming telegrams from London, he turned only to the question of trade with Russia.[78]

Lloyd George had to deal with Soviet wilfulness. Litvinov had mounted a major effort to promote Rome as an alternative to London as a site for further talks, and the Italians had not immediately rejected the possibility. But Nitti had no intention of acting independently. When Lloyd George, having first obtained the support of Millerand, asked him to join in rejecting the Soviet initiative, the Italian premier agreed.[79] In a telegram of 25 April, Nitti told Krasin that the allied powers would neither negotiate with Litvinov nor admit him to their countries. "Subject to this," he concluded, "the Allied representatives will be prepared to meet the Russian delegates *in London* at the earliest date convenient to them."[80] Lloyd George, in short, had received everything he wanted.

This left the retreating Cossacks and terms for the Volunteer Army in suspense. Neither were discussed at San Remo, and Lord Curzon dealt with them on behalf of the British government, not the Supreme Council. This was in accord with British policy, as Whitehall knew that its continental allies could not contribute anything to the solution of these problems and would only complicate them further. Thus, on 24 April, Curzon instructed the Foreign Office to tell Chicherin that British ships had attacked Bolshevik forces on the Black Sea coast because they were advancing on Batum, a town occupied by a British garrison. The British government regarded this movement as an act of war which British forces were bound to resist. He flatly refused to receive Litvinov in London or link negotiations for an end to hostilities in the Crimea with the release of Soviet prisoners in Austria, but continued to insist on his own connection between the trade talks and the fate of the Volunteer Army.[81]

The problem of the retreating Cossacks was quickly solved. The small number who wished to continue the war against the Bolsheviks were evacuated by British warships to the Crimea. Others dispersed into the mountains while the remaining twenty thousand surrendered on 2 May to the Red Army at Sochi.[82] The larger issue of Wrangel's army remained. Chicherin has originally described Curzon's telegram as insolent,[83] but events elsewhere soon diverted Moscow from the hard line developed in the previous month. The Polish invasion of Ukraine, to be dealt with in subsequent chapters, served to moderate Soviet policy in relation to the British government. Chicherin allowed four days to elapse before responding to the foreign secretary. On 29 April he declared that Curzon's telegram had been "carefully considered by the Russian Government" and although Moscow deeply regretted the refusal to aid the Austrian prisoners, it was "loath to impede the suggested agreement." The Soviet government would accept the surrender of Wrangel's army "under the same conditions as suggested in my radio of February 21st with reference to the White Guards of the North." Chicherin signalled the new flexibility in Soviet policy by adding that "if further conditions are to be suggested by the British Government they can be best

discussed in direct negotiations with our representative who is now in Copenhagen." This, of course, was Litvinov, but here too he sounded the retreat by
concluding "if another method is preferred by the British Government to come
to an agreement the Russian Government is ready to consider the corresponding
proposals in a most friendly spirit."[84]

When Chicherin's message reached London in early May, the Poles were well
launched into their offensive and officials at the Foreign Office advised Curzon
to delay a positive response in order to see how events developed. They also
noted that the Volunteer Army no longer feared imminent annihilation. Instead,
Wrangel had just entered into an agreement with the atamans of the Don, Terek,
and Astrakhan Cossacks whereby they acknowledged him as commander-in-
chief while retaining autonomy in internal affairs. They had empowered him to
conduct their foreign relations and in this capacity he had conveyed appeals from
them to the British government, asking that Whitehall recognize their autonomy
and aid them in achieving peace with Soviet Russia. They wanted Moscow to
refrain from interference in the internal affairs of the Cossack states, evacuate
their territory, and agree to an allied guarantee of the special accord to regulate
their future relations with Soviet Russia.[85] This was equivalent to demanding
the Soviet evacuation of most of south Russia as the Red Army was then in
nearly complete occupation of the three Cossack districts – something quite
different from that upon which the British government had originally embarked.
Nevertheless, in the circumstances of early May, Curzon decided to respond
evasively to Chicherin. He insisted on "a cessation of all hostilities both in the
Crimea and on the borders of the Caucasian states where [Soviet] forces are
engaged in conflict whether with British forces or with those who are friends of
Great Britain." On the Crimean front he suggested that Moscow "communicate
directly with General Wrangel with a view to the initiation of definite negotiations." He proposed, "if all parties agree, to despatch a British officer to take
part in the deliberations." He again reiterated the necessity of the Soviet government ordering a cease-fire. "Negotiations," he said, "are doomed to failure
whether in Europe or in Asia as long as Soviet forces are engaged in open
hostilities with those whom we are actually defending with our arms or in whose
political independence we are closely concerned. The only method by which
peace can be successfully re-established is by an assurance to desist from these
attacks."[86] At a time when Wrangel was regrouping and Pilsudski's legions
were halfway to Kiev, Moscow could only suspect that the British had taken a
long step backward from their earlier interest in hastening an end to hostilities.

IN THE SPRING OF 1920, therefore, the international position of Soviet Russia
remained extremely anomalous. On 1 March 1920 Lenin had announced that
"never has the international position of the Soviet Republic been as favourable
and as triumphant as it is now," but by the end of the month he had to adopt a
more subdued evaluation. "The States of the Entente are neither at peace with

the Bolsheviks nor at war with them: they have recognized us and they have not recognized us."[87] The Bolsheviks had triumphed in the civil war, yet Wrangel still held the Crimea. The allies had lifted the blockade, but commerce had not resumed. Negotiations had begun with the western powers, but only at Copenhagen. And in the midst of this uncertainty the Poles exploded into Ukraine. The issue of war and peace was again entrusted to the generals, and no further progress in the settlement of outstanding issues could be made until the battlefields rendered their verdict. In May 1920, however, there was more than one battlefield, and if Polish troops were marching on Kiev, Soviet troops had already arrived in Baku, opening an entirely new chapter in Soviet relations with the western powers. The military verdict in the Caucasus, as well as Ukraine, would have to be rendered before a definitive settlement of Soviet relations with the western powers would be possible.

CHAPTER ELEVEN

"We should take Baku":
Soviet policy in the Caucasus, 1919–1920

In the chaos of 1918 the Bolsheviks had lost control of the Caucasus. Germany had established a protectorate in Georgia while Ottoman Turkey overran Armenia and Azerbaidzhan. For a brief while the Bolsheviks had been able to hold Baku, but in September they lost it to the British who, in turn, were driven out by the Turks. Ottoman occupation of Baku, however, was contrary to the bargain which Moscow had struck with imperial Germany. In the supplementary agreements to the treaty of Brest-Litovsk, Berlin had allotted the city and its oilfields to Soviet Russia. Consequently, the Narkomindel complained bitterly to Berlin while the Soviet Eleventh Army, based in Dagestan, prepared to invade Azerbaidzhan. When Germany, failing fast in the last days of the Great War, proved unable to dislodge the Turks, Moscow delivered a virtual declaration of war to Constantinople. But the kaleidoscopic events of November 1918 outran even the Bolsheviks, for before the Red Army could strike, Great Britain, having just forced the Ottomans to sign the armistice of Mudros, reoccupied Baku. From Baku the British pushed north into Dagestan, where they were joined by elements of the Volunteer Army. The Bolsheviks were forced to withdraw quickly and, in a catastrophic retreat across the Kalmyk steppe, suffered terrible losses. Only one-third of an original one hundred thousand men arrived safely at Astrakhan on the northern shore of the Caspian Sea. Soviet power in the Caucasus and North Caucasus had been dealt a devastating blow.[1]

Devastating but not fatal, for the British struck quickly but not decisively. They had sent only a small force into the Caucasus and that with only a very limited mission: "Our policy in the Caucasus at present is to ensure that the terms of the armistice are complied with in full by the Turks, to re-open the railway and pipe line between the Black Sea and the Caspian, and to that end to occupy Baku and Batoum, and probably Tiflis, and so much as may be necessary of the railway." The British government hoped to see the emergence of strong independent states in Georgia, Dagestan, Azerbaidzhan, and Armenia, but did not intend to establish a protectorate or maintain a permanent force in the region.[2] When this was realized in the Caucasus, British prestige declined rapidly, further destablizing an already shaky political situation.

In these circumstances the Bolsheviks sprang back quickly. Although the Caspian front received no reinforcement, available manpower was sufficient to keep the Volunteer Army at a safe distance from Astrakhan. Politically, the party began to recover almost at once. In November 1918 they established a provisional buro of Baku party organizations and two months later reactivated party cells in Tiflis, Batum, and Poti. Late in January 1919 they held a congress at Vladikavkaz which elected a Caucasus Regional Committee. Shortly after A.I. Mikoian arrived in Baku to take charge of party work there. The Bolsheviks used Astrakhan as a base for supporting their political activity in the Caucasus, creating a "sea expedition" to maintain contact with Baku. Initially the connection was very tenuous as the British patrolled the Caspian, but when the Royal Navy withdrew and turned over their flotilla to Denikin the situation improved. But the Caspian connection was not the only problem, for in July the Whites occupied Tsaritsyn and severed central Russia's direct link with Astrakhan.[3] Only when the Tsaritsyn block was broken could effective communication between Moscow and the Caucasus be restored. Then, the sea expedition was able to carry not only money, men, and revolutionary literature south to Baku but return with petroleum urgently needed for the fuel-starved engines of Soviet Russia.[4]

The economic circumstances of 1919 greatly favoured the recrudescence of Bolshevism in the Caucasus. Prior to 1917 the area's trade links had been almost entirely with Russia; with those links severed all sectors of the economy (agriculture as well as industry) were ruined. The oil industry – the largest single employer in the Caucasus – was hardest hit. Drilling for new wells ceased, production fell off sharply, oil refineries closed, but still a huge surplus accumulated. By mid-1919 petroleum was being poured into the sea. Yet there was a world market for every barrel of oil produced, the problem was transportation. The pipeline was too small and railway tank cars too few to carry any but a trickle of Baku's oil production to the Black Sea. Marketing and transportation facilities were directed to the north, not to the west. The Bolsheviks had no difficulty in attracting large audiences ready to listen to their message, to go on strike and to participate in political demonstrations.[5] In May 1919 General W.M. Thomson, commanding the British army in the Caucasus, wrote: "Our occupation has brought no material benefits, on the contrary, prices continue to rise, the purchasing power of the rouble is 1/20 of what it used to be, we support Denikin who, in the eyes of the young Republics, is a far worse enemy than Bolshevism."[6]

Everyone noted the extreme hatred and suspicion existing between White Russians and the emergent republics in the Caucasus. Denikin did not merely refuse to recognize the independence of these republics, he wanted to destroy them. No sooner had the British reoccupied Baku than representatives of no less than three separate White Russian authorities descended on the city and "vigorously demanded the deposition of Tatar Government."[7] Denikin, like Yudenich in the Baltic, viewed the successor states of the empire as destined to be reabsorbed into "Russia one and united" and refused to deal with them on a basis of equality.

The Bolsheviks too had their share of difficulties. Time would vividly illustrate that their ranks were filled with Great Russian chauvinists, but in 1919 they succeeded in projecting an image immensely more sympathetic to the local peoples than any other Russian party. This had been the aim of the Ninth Party Congress, which had proclaimed the right of all peoples to national self-determination.[8] This bore special meaning for the Caucasus, because in the past the Bolsheviks had opposed the emergence of independent nation states and insisted that self-determination be achieved in the framework of continued close association with Soviet Russia. The Bolsheviks never abandoned the latter but in the summer of 1919 reshaped it to allow for a greater expression of nationalist aspirations. This feeling was especially intense in Azerbaidzhan, and Baku Bolsheviks were the first to respond to it. Already in the spring of 1919 they had wished to proclaim as their goal an "independent Soviet Azerbaidzhan." This, however, was not acceptable to Bolsheviks elsewhere in the Caucasus, and in early May a party conference held in Baku rejected it.[9] However, in Moscow, the Politburo in mid-July decided to accept in principle the future independence of a Soviet Azerbaidzhan. The following month the Central Committee confirmed this decision.[10] Although the ruling spoke only of Azerbaidzhan, it possessed great importance for the remainder of the Caucasus, for it would have been difficult, if not impossible, to recognize the independence of a Soviet Azerbaidzhan without doing the same for Georgia and Armenia. The decision, therefore, served to shape not only the future power struggle in the Caucasus but the future relationship of the region to Soviet Russia.

The oilfields of Azerbaidzhan and Dagestan served as a powerful magnet attracting Soviet attention to the region. Even as Kolchak advanced on Moscow, Lenin found time to turn his attention to the Caspian. He urged his commander at Astrakhan to attack Dagestan in order to secure the oil at Petrovsk and Grozny, but the operation, undertaken in late April, proved to be a total failure. The Mountain Government of Dagestan arrested many leading Bolsheviks and the British Caspian flotilla scattered the Soviet ships sent to support the insurrection.[11] Soviet hopes for prompt restoration of access to Caspian oil suffered a severe blow.

Ironically, the political consequences of this failure proved to be favourable to the Bolsheviks. Denikin, with his hostility to all national minorities, responded to the Bolshevik coup by reinforcing his own garrisons in Dagestan. Having first seized Petrovsk and Derbent he then occupied Temir-Khan-Shura, dispersing the Mountain Government and forcing its leaders into exile. This sent a shock wave through the Caucasus, focusing fear of Russian reconquest on the Whites, a fear which was accentuated as the Volunteer Army advanced south towards the still undefined frontiers of the Caucasian states. The British attempted to establish a demarcation line between the Volunteer Army and its Caucasian adversaries but with little effect. Denikin had the military advantage and occupied all of Dagestan and the North Caucasus. In reaction Azerbaidzhan and Georgia concluded a military alliance against him. They asked Armenia to join, but Erevan was more fearful of Turkey than the Whites. The two allies might have taken more energetic action against Denikin, but the British War Office pressed them to abstain from further action. Denikin, for his part, played on British anti-Bolshevism by alleging that the Caucasian republics were in league with the Bolsheviks. Restrained by Britain, the governments of Azerbaidzhan and Georgia were seen to hesitate in the defence of their own independence and consequently suffered acute political embarrassment. The Bolsheviks appeared to be the only resolute foe of Denikin and therefore secured substantial political advantage in Azerbaidzhan and Georgia.[12]

In the summer of 1919 the Russian civil war came to focus increasingly on the struggle between Denikin and the Bolsheviks. Both sides directed virtually all their resources to this front leaving the others to get by as best they could. Thus Denikin reinforced his army from units earlier sent to the North Caucasus while Lenin ruthlessly stripped all other fronts to strengthen his armies south of Moscow. Despite the high priority attached to obtaining an assured supply of petroleum, Moscow had no choice but to turn its back on the Caucasus. During the autumn of 1919 Denikin continued his pressure on Azerbaidzhan and Georgia, even increasing it when he felt himself near victory over the Bolsheviks. In October he launched a trade war against Georgia and coolly informed Azer-baidzhan that, basing himself on the treaty of Turkmanchai, he would not tolerate Azeri ships on the Caspian Sea. All trade on the Caspian would have to be carried in Russian vessels. Nor did defeat cause any relaxation of tension. As the Volunteer Army began to retreat, it was feared at first that Denikin would conclude an armistice with the Bolsheviks, allowing him to crush the Caucasian republics.[13]

Fear of Denikin soon gave way to an even greater concern about the magnitude of Soviet success. As early as mid-November a worried Persian government began to peer north of the Caspian and view the situation as "extremely grave." Subsequent reports conveyed mounting alarm, until by Christmas one major observer warned London that "recent Bolshevik successes are likely to give an impetus to ... one of the most important of Bolshevik aims, namely, to turn the Moslem world against the British Empire."[14]

This was a correct evaluation of Bolshevik policy. Since the first days of the revolution Soviet leaders had been eager to inflame the peoples of the East against their colonial, primarily British, masters, but the unrelenting pressure of events in Europe had served to rivet the attention of Moscow on Europe. The pace of European events did not diminish in the summer of 1919, but their substance – no longer favourable to the early development of proletarian revolution – forced Soviet leaders to turn their gaze towards Asia. Trotsky, always sensitive to the changing revolutionary tides, was the first to herald this turn. In early August the fall of Soviet Hungary led him to conclude "that the incubatory, preparatory period of the revolution in the West [might] last for indeed a considerable time yet." He believed, however, as he told his Central Committee colleagues in a secret memorandum, that the situation was quite different in the East. There the defeat of Kolchak had opened the gateways to Asia and the Red Army constituted "an incomparably more powerful force ... than in the European terrain." The Red Army, he asserted, could "upset the unstable balance of Asian relationships of colonial dependence, give a direct push to an uprising on the part of the oppressed masses and assure the triumph of such a rising in Asia." Operations in the east, he continued, presupposed a strong base in the Urals, and he proposed that "the idea we had in the spring of last year under the influence of the German attack – that of concentrating industry in and around the Urals – should be revived." [15]

Although couched in highly optimistic terms, Trotsky's analysis betrays considerable pessimism regarding revolutionary development as foreseen by the Bolsheviks in previous years. His reference to "the idea we had in the spring of last year" is especially revealing as the "Ural-Kuznetsk redoubt," as it was called, had been conceived as a base for a final stand of the revolution against German militarism. The circumstances of August 1919 were clearly not as bad as those of March 1918, but were sufficiently discouraging to prompt Trotsky to call for a fundamental reorientation of Soviet military and political strategy.

There is no direct evidence to indicate how the Central Committee reacted to this proposal, but in the following weeks the Narkomindel took up a line which suggests that Trotsky's memorandum had been endorsed, at least in part, at some very high level of party and state. The Foreign Commissariat, which had devoted most of its attention to the West for nearly a year, now developed a much enhanced interest in the East. Chicherin himself announced this interest in the 13 August 1919 issue of his commissariat's Vestnik. Here he expressed many of the same views as Trotsky but placed them in the context of the historical development of Russian foreign policy during the previous century. As a youth Chicherin had studied tsarist foreign policy in detail, and he drew freely on this knowledge to illustrate his argument for an eastern orientation to Soviet policy. At the end of the Crimean War, he said, Prince Gorchakov had advised Alexander II that no major task stood before Russia in Europe. On the other hand, Gorchakov had advised that the East offered Russia a "huge field of activity," and had concluded that "the future of Russia lies in Asia." Alexander had endorsed this view and thus established one of the primary policies of his reign. Chicherin believed the policy of 1856 was relevant to Russia in 1919. In both cases Russia had fought a great war, suffered military defeat, and stood on the brink of economic collapse. In each case the country had faced a Europe nearly united in its opposition and had been forced to contemplate a long period of political isolation from the affairs of the continent. And in each case the leaders had the option of turning to Asia to redress the imbalance in Europe. Gorchakov and Alexander had chosen this option and Chicherin argued that Soviet Russia should do so as well. The foreign commissar asserted that Russia, because of its geographical location and peculiar social-economic development, had a special role to play in Asia. Prior to 1917 Russia, while seeking to exploit less developed neighbours, had itself been ruthlessly exploited by the more advanced capitalist states of the world. The Russian proletariat, therefore, could relate more easily to the oppressed nations of the East than western workers with their substantially different historical experience. In particular, the Russian proletariat, having successfully taken power, could show the way to socialist revolution in Asia. Asians and Russians, he proclaimed, opposed a common enemy, "western European and American super-imperialism," which sought to maintain its oppressive hold on Asia and restore it in Russia.[16]

These views were soon endorsed by the Central Committee; on 20 August Elena Stasova, their secretary, wrote to the Caucasus Regional Committee: "We consider that the present moment is extremely important in the sense of influence upon the Moslem East, which, with its desire for liberation from the imperialists' yoke, can provide immense support for the revolutionary cause."[17] As noted above, it had already been decided "at an appropriate moment, to declare Azerbaidzhan an independent Soviet Republic." and Chicherin was given new latitude to amplify Soviet propaganda in the east. On 22 August he issued a declaration to the workers of Azerbaidzhan, Dagestan, and Georgia warning them that Denikin intended to restore Russian rule over their lands. They could expect no help from the British who were already preparing to leave the Caucasus. Only Soviet Russia eschewed foreign conquest. Communism stood for the self-determination of all peoples and sought only to defend the revolution in Russia. "And if you, Moslems and Georgians of the Caucasus, are satisfied with the form of government of your republics," Chicherin concluded, "then live in peace, constitute yourselves as you wish and restore good neighbourly relations with us."[18]

It is difficult to determine the impact of Chicherin's declaration in the Caucasus, but the British thought it considerable. "This sort of propaganda in the Caucasus," wrote one Foreign Office official, "has a very subtle effect, as those in authority hold that the majority of the people would rather try their independence as promised by Lenin than again fall under any form of the old Russian regime."[19] Chicherin soon widened the range of his propaganda assault. At the end of August he directed an appeal to the workers and peasants of Persia, and in mid-September he launched another broadside in the direction of the same groups in Turkey. In both he identified Britain as the oppressor of all eastern peoples and held up Soviet Russia as a model of how liberation could be achieved.

In the first of these messages he declared that the Soviet government did not recognize the treaty recently concluded between the Shah and Great Britain which effectively converted Persia into a British protectorate, and in the second he warned the Turks that the Sultan was about to surrender the Straits and Constantinople to the British. To both he said, "the Russian working masses extend ... their brotherly hand," a not entirely rhetorical phrase given the changing fortunes of war. "Very soon," proclaimed Chicherin, "our valiant revolutionary Red Army will be crossing Red Turkestan and will be approaching the boundaries of oppressed Persia."[20]

This was no idle boast, for on 13 September, the Soviet First Army broke through the remnants of Kolchak's southern front and joined hands with Bolshevik regiments in Turkestan. The road to Tashkent, sealed since the previous year, lay open. Coming as it did when the Bolsheviks were in full retreat in central Russia, this victory seemed to suggest a fundamental shift in Soviet strategy not dissimilar to that suggested by Trotsky. "The Red Army," wrote the French high commissioner at Constantinople, "appears to offer only weak resistance to Denikin, Petliura and Poland in order to give full attention to the South-east; their aim appears to be to reach the Caspian Sea, to occupy its shores, Baku in particular, once and for all to separate Denikin from Kolchak and to penetrate, either effectively or through active propaganda, the Caucasus (now evacuated by the British), Persia and the eastern vilayets of Turkey."[21] This was only partly correct. It identified Soviet objectives in the Near East but greatly overestimated the priority assigned them. But as important as the East had become in Soviet calculations, the West nevertheless remained paramount. In September 1919 Moscow was not abandoning the West, much less Ukraine. Indeed, the Bolsheviks were only beginning to fight in the west and had not yet managed to mobilize the full force needed for victory. Thus they were unable to mount a major military operation in the southern borderlands and would remain incapacitated until they had achieved victory in central Russia. As late as mid-October the Red Army continued to draw on the southeastern and Turkestan fronts to reinforce the defences of Moscow.[22]

Denikin's defeat changed all this. Within a month Bolshevik minds were fixed firmly on expanding their operations into the southern borderlands. In late November a congress of Moslem communists gathered in Moscow to hear Soviet leaders outline their emerging policy regarding the peoples of the East. Lenin told them that the victory of the Red Army in the civil war was of "colossal, epochal significance" for their peoples. It would show them, weak as they were, that emancipation was "now quite practicable, from the standpoint not only of the prospects of the international revolution but also of the direct military experience acquired in Asia." Despite the importance of this victory, Lenin stressed that the prospects in Asia were still greater. It was clear, he said, that the socialist revolution would include "a struggle of all the imperialist-oppressed colonies and countries, of all dependent countries, against international imperialism."

This struggle, he predicted, would then merge with that in Russia and the two together would promote socialist revolution in the most highly developed areas of the world.

It is self-evident that final victory can be won only by the proletariat of all the advanced countries of the world, and we, the Russians, are beginning the work which the British, French or German proletariat will consolidate. But we can see that they will not be victorious without the aid of the working people of all the oppressed colonial nations, first and foremost, of Eastern nations.

Lenin confined himself to theory. He left it to the leader of the Azeri communists to draw practical conclusions from the emerging doctrine. "We must proceed to unification," said Nariman Narimanov, "Without fail the northern Caucasus, Dagestan and Azerbaidzhan must unite with Soviet Russia."[23]

By late 1919 political circumstances in the Caucasus had begun to tilt in favour of the Bolsheviks. The withdrawal of the British army seriously destabilized the region and, as one allied observer reported in mid-November, "the three republics ... were at daggers drawn with each other on almost all points."[24] Economic activity had declined still further with more than thirty thousand workers unemployed in the petroleum industry alone. Social conflict increased accordingly and, in late September, Narimanov could report with satisfaction that in Azerbaidzhan the workers' frame of mind was "to a high degree revolutionary and purely Bolshevik." The Mussavat regime, he said, had lost popular support and survived only by police repression. He dismissed the Azeri army as being of low fighting ability. The Bolsheviks had not yet challenged it, but to the north in Dagestan armed opposition to the Whites had become widespread. The Communist Party there sought to assume leadership but lacked the necessary means. In mid-October they petitioned the Caucasus Regional Committee to supply them with arms and ammunition for an insurrection.[29] S.M. Kirov conveyed their appeal to Moscow which, given the magnitude of the emerging Soviet victory over Denikin, received it sympathetically. In November the Central Committee instructed the Soviet Eleventh Army to supply the insurgents with arms and ammunition while directing the Caucasus Regional Committee to provide them with money and technical assistance. In subsequent weeks Petrovsk, Derbent and Temir-Khan-Shura fell to anti-Denikin insurgents, and on 30 December the Soviet Eleventh Army was ordered into the north Caucasus. Mikoian reported to the Central Committee: "the course of events is bringing us inevitably in the coming months to a general Caucasus wide uprising against the existing governments of the Transcaucasian republics. Even local revolutionary forces can achieve this and hold out for some time until relieved by the arrival of the Red Army."[25]

As the Red Army approached the Caucasus, the Soviet government launched a diplomatic offensive designed to aggravate relations among their enemies and

further reduce the prestige of the existing indigenous regimes. On 2 January
1920 Chicherin sent radio messages to the governments of Azerbaidzhan and
Georgia proposing military cooperation against White Russian forces remaining
in the region.[26] This had the desired effect of worsening relations between
Denikin and the Caucasian republics. All three looked for support to Britain,
but Denikin sought protection for his armed forces while the two republics asked
London to urge the White Russians to leave the region as quickly as possible.
The Whites, they said, were only attracting the Red Army and could play no
constructive role in the defence of the Caucasus. At the same time both Georgia
and Azerbaidzhan urgently called for British assistance against the Bolsheviks.
They wished recognition of their sovereignty, substantial financial aid, and military supplies for their armed forces. Their immediate response to Chicherin's
proposal, however, was to declare neutrality in the Russian civil war and proclaim
their readiness to defend their "liberty and sovereignty against any foreign attack."[27] This response, though certainly not unexpected, caused the Soviet
Politburo to direct the Narkomindel "to conduct a policy of greatest restraint
and distrust" in relation to the two republics. Chicherin promptly complied,
broadcasting bitter denunciations of the two governments and branding them as
accomplices of Denikin acting in the service of the allied powers against the
best interests of their own peoples.[28] Lenin emphasized this point when speaking
before the Central Executive Committee on 2 February. Noting the refusal of
the two governments to join Soviet Russia against Denikin, he declared ominously: "We shall see how the workers and peasants of Georgia and Azerbaidzhan
look upon all this."[29]

The allied governments also focused on the Caucasus. The events of late 1919
had caused them to give up on Denikin. In December he had demanded that the
allies send two army corps to retrieve his shattered fortunes, but this was impossible. French reports described his position as catastrophic, and even the
sanguine Churchill had given up hope.[30] When the allied heads of government
met in Paris in mid-January, therefore, they had no difficulty in agreeing to
suspend further aid to the Volunteer Army. The petitions from Azerbaidzhan
and Georgia, however, were received quite differently. Tiflis and Baku did not
ask for allied troops. No one was prepared to provide financial aid, but recognition
would cost nothing, and the allies still had large quantities of military supplies
at their disposal. The allies were all the more sympathetic for, unlike Denikin,
the Caucasian regimes seemed ready and able to defend themselves. Lloyd
George compared them to the Baltic states and warmly supported the proposed
measures. Nor was their cause injured by the substantial French interest in the
oilfields of Azerbaidzhan. As a result the Supreme Council reached easy agreement to grant de facto recognition to the two republics and provide them with
arms for defence against the Bolsheviks.[31]

As in so much regarding allied policy in Russia, this was too little and too
late. The Bolsheviks, on the other hand, moved swiftly to complete their prep-

arations for the conquest of the Caucasus. In late 1919 they created the Azerbaidzhan Communist Party, in theory independent of the Russian party but in
truth Moscow's chosen instrument for waging political war against the bourgeois
government at Baku. It was directly controlled by the Caucasus Regional Committee of the Russian Communist Party based at Astrakhan. That committee,
led by Kirov, funnelled millions of rubles to the Azerbaidzhan communists and
other party organizations active in the region.[32] In addition, Kirov sent party
activists to organize and discipline the frequently unruly guerrilla bands in the
North Caucasus. In early 1920 these groups were subordinated to the Soviet
Eleventh Army also based at Astrakhan. Most important, however, was the
formation on 18 January of an independent Caucasian front commanded by M.N.
Tukhachevskii and including G.K. Ordzhonikidze on its military council. In a
parallel political action taken at the same time the Bolsheviks established a Buro
for the Restoration of Soviet Power in the North Caucasus with Ordzhonikidze
as its chairman and Kirov as his deputy.[33] The new front had at its disposal
over one hundred thousand men, with a further thirty-five thousand reinforcements on the way. Lenin carefully specified its mission. On 28 February he
informed Ordzhonikidze: "We are in desperate need of oil. Work out a manifesto
to the population saying that we will slaughter all of them if they set fire to and
sabotage the oil fields and the oil wells and, conversely, that we will spare
everyone their lives if Maikop and particularly Groznii are handed over intact."[34]
The March offensive drove the Whites from the Kuban and the north Caucasus.
In the west Novorossissk fell on 28 March, while to the east the Bolsheviks
captured Groznii on 24 March and Derbent the following day. Temir-Khan-
Shura, capital of Dagestan, and Petrovsk followed shortly after. On 31 March
Ordzhonikidze announced the formation of a North Caucasus Revolutionary
Committee with himself as chairman and Kirov his deputy. Lenin rejoiced that
Groznii had been captured with its petroleum installations intact and 270,000
tons of benzine still safely stored in its tanks.[35]

Bolshevik victory reverberated through the Caucasus. As early as 4 March
the Azeri minister for foreign affairs predicted that Petrovsk would fall and the
Volga be open within five weeks. His Georgian counterpart told allied representatives in Tiflis that the Georgian government was seeking all means "to
defend its frontiers against the peril of an enemy invasion."[36] Although Georgia
and Azerbaidzhan still refused to cooperate with the Bolsheviks against Denikin,
both began to ponder opening political and commercial negotiations with Moscow. On 1 March the prime minister of Azerbaidzhan, while visiting London,
informed Lord Hardinge that "his country desired commercial relations with
Russia in the same manner as the countries of the Allies" and asked how his
government should respond if approached by Moscow with proposals of peace.
Hardinge responded that if his government thought fit to make terms with the
Soviet government on equitable conditions, no objections would be raised in
London.[37] Five days later in a joint letter the London delegations of Azerbaidzhan

and Georgia informed the Foreign Office that their two countries desired "normal and good neighbourly relations [with Soviet Russia] and economic intercourse based on the formal recognition by Russia of the independence of the Trans-Caucasian Republics" and they sought the good offices of the British government in achieving this objective.

This was quite out of the question. The two republics were told they would have to fend for themselves in negotiating with Moscow.[38] A similar attitude informed British thinking regarding the provision of military supplies promised in January but still undelivered two months later. Both Tiflis and Baku complained bitterly[39] but without effect. When British agents, spurred by the complaints of local governments, raised a clamour in London they received a very cold reception. "These men at a distance, even the best, are apt to lose all perspective," Curzon sniffed on 21 March. Two days later he added: "I look with great suspicion upon the Azerbaidzhan Government which seems always to have one leg in the Turkish, the other in the Bolshevik camp, its body being poised in unstable equilibrium in Entente territory between." Curzon, in fact, doubted the alarming reports reaching him from the Caucasus. He felt that direct negotiations with Moscow were far better than armed resistance and thought "it would be better to divert arms [from Georgia and Azerbaidzhan] to enable the Armenians to defend themselves against the Turks."[40]

Even as Curzon wrote, the Soviet government prepared for the invasion of Azerbaidzhan. Singly and collectively, Bolsheviks throughout the Caucasus clamoured for Soviet military intervention in all three states. On 15 March the Caucasus Regional Committee of the Russian Communist Party petitioned Moscow for authority to send the Soviet Eleventh Army across the Caucasus into Georgia and Azerbaidzhan.[41] Its authors must have doubted if their petition would be granted. Six months before they had witnessed the sacrifice of the Baltic Bolsheviks on the altar of political and military expediency, and there could have been little doubt in the minds of men such as Ordzhonikidze and Kirov that if necessary Lenin would sacrifice their interests as well. The two situations bore many similarities. In each instance the Red Army had driven the Whites onto the territories of recently founded non-Russian successor states of the former empire. In both cases these states were either not engaged in war against Soviet Russia or involved only to a minimal degree. Furthermore, they had the political backing of the allies, and Moscow understood clearly that the negotiation of peace would enhance the possibility of a more general settlement with the western powers. Finally, in September 1919 and March 1920 Soviet Russia faced a major military challenge (Denikin in the fall, Pilsudski's Poland in the spring) requiring the immediate concentration of the greatest number of battle-tested troops as possible. Ordzhonikidze and Kirov had to fear that Lenin would again sacrifice the parochial interests of the Bolshevik periphery for the more basic concerns of the centre. Thus they pressed Lenin to expand, rather than halt, military operations in the Caucasus. This pressure was quite successful, for on 17 March Lenin telegraphed to Ordzhonikidze: "It is extremely essential that we should take Baku. Every effort is to be directed toward this." The fact that he specified Baku, rather than the Caucasus as a whole, makes it clear that he realized the pitfalls of such an operation and sought to avoid the Red Army becoming bogged down in a protracted conflict.[42]

Why did Lenin agree to the invasion of Azerbaidzhan? No documents at present available speak to this question, but several good reasons may be offered. First was the need for oil. Groznii was a major source of petroleum but insufficient for Soviet needs; only Baku could satisfy the Soviet internal demand and leave sufficient for export. Second was the ease with which the oil could be taken. Azerbaidzhan simply could not defend itself. Not only was its army weak; it was outflanked by the Caspian Sea on which Soviet flotillas could operate with impunity. Finally there was the need to act quickly before assistance, whether from Georgia, Persia, or the allies could arrive. For these reasons and perhaps others not immediately apparent, Lenin instructed the Red Army to seize Baku. On 20 March S. Kamenev had written him indicating that by the end of the month all tasks originally set the Caucasus front would be completed and asking for new instructions from the government. The supreme commander stressed the need to transfer as many troops as possible to the southwest front, where a Polish attack was expected by the end of April. He clearly favoured a suspension of hostilities in the Caucasus but noted that revolutionary developments there might demand a different policy, but only if it did not involve a lengthy campaign. Two days later Kamenev had received his answer (although the Soviet authorities have not yet seen fit to publish it) and issued his own directive: "Military action against the Georgian army will not be opened and troops of the [Caucasian] Front will not cross the frontier of Georgia." On the other hand, once the Eleventh Army had occupied the Terek region "they [were to] continue their offensive ... with the task of seizing the entire region of the former province of Baku."

The overwhelmingly Russian composition of the army about to descend upon Muslim Azerbaidzhan clearly worried Lenin. He discussed this problem with Nariman Narimanov, already designated as head of the Soviet government to be installed at Baku, and sent him to see Chicherin and Stalin. Narimanov satisfied both commissars. Stalin appointed him commissar for Muslim affairs in the Caucasus while Chicherin assured Lenin that "no one knew Baku and the Baku Muslims better than Narimanov." Still Lenin worried, and as the date of the Soviet invasion approached he wired Ordzhonikidze, telling him "to display the maximum of good will towards the Muslims ... , demonstrate in every way, and, moreover, with all possible solemnity, sympathy for the Muslims, their autonomy, their independence and so on."[43]

In the field, neither the Central Committee of the Azerbaidzhan Communist Party nor the staff of the Soviet Eleventh Army were much interested in Muslim susceptibilities. Both had received authority to proceed with the invasion of Azerbaidzhan and were acting vigorously to this end. Preparations were simplified by the fact that the Mussavat government had recently become involved in a war against Armenia and the bulk of its army was bogged down along the western frontier in the region of Karabakh. Only three thousand troops were stationed along the critical Ialama-Baku railway leading south from Derbent, with a further two thousand men providing the garrison of Baku. Some of the latter were of doubtful loyalty, and the Bolsheviks expected little resistance to their coup. On 21 April Tukhachevskii and Ordzhonikidze ordered the attack to begin six days later; they expected a five-day campaign. On 23 April they were so certain of victory that they amended their original order (for the Eleventh Army to occupy Baku province) to encompass all of Azerbaidzhan.[44]

At first the concentration of Soviet troops north of the frontier did not alarm either Baku or Constantinople. On 9 April, in an interview given to Commander Luke, the British representative in Baku, the Minister President Usseybbekov stated "he did not fear Bolshevik attack." He believed he could make peace with Moscow on the basis of an advantageous trade treaty by which Azerbaidzhan would supply Soviet petroleum needs.[45] Within days this false confidence evaporated. On 22 April, the minister for foreign affairs said an "organized attack by the Soviet on ... Azerbaidzhan" was imminent. To ward it off, he said, Baku "had given the Soviet plainly to understand that [the vast stocks of oil vital to Soviet Russia] will be destroyed in the event of an attack or unsuitable peace terms." This was no deterrent at all, exactly the opposite. If Lenin had any doubts about the occupation of Baku before receiving this threat, he now abandoned them, ordering instead that special steps be taken to protect the oil at Baku.[46]

The Bolshevik invasion of Azerbaidzhan began early on the morning of 27 April. Four armoured trains crossed the Samur River and proceeded unhindered directly to Baku. At midday a delegation of local communists demanded the government's resignation. Bolshevik insurgents began to occupy key positions throughout Baku, seizing arsenals, disarming the police, releasing political prisoners, occupying the radio station and, in particular, taking control of the petroleum industry. As expected, two regiments of the garrison passed to the Bolshevik side, and little actual fighting occurred. Resistance proved impossible. At 2 a.m. two Soviet gun-boats took control of the port and two hours later the first of the Bolshevik armoured trains arrived at the railway station. Under this pressure the Mussavat government yielded, transferring power to a three-man Bolshevik committee who promptly proclaimed Azerbaidzhan a Soviet Socialist Republic. The revolutionary committee appointed a council of people's commissars with Nariman Narimanov as chairman and foreign commissar. Within two days the Soviet Eleventh Army had occupied most of Azerbaidzhan, while the Caucasus Revolutionary Committee headed by Ordzhonikidze established itself in Baku. At one leap the Bolsheviks had vaulted the Caucasus and established themselves on the threshold to south Asia and the east.[47]

But what now? Lenin exulted at the conquest, saying in a speech of 29 April that the revolutionary triumph in Azerbaidzhan meant "that we now have an economic base that may put life into our whole industry."[48] Chicherin viewed the seizure of Baku as opening a door to Asia and an event of "first class significance in the development of ... international politics."[49] Soviet leaders in the Caucasus especially viewed the fall of Baku in this light. No sooner was the Bolshevik hold on Baku secure than the Red Army pushed out towards the frontiers of Armenia and Georgia. Communists there had been informed of the impending invasion of Azerbaidzhan and now waited impatiently for the arrival of the Red Army on the territory of their own states. As in Azerbaidzhan, local uprisings had been prepared to greet the Red Army and, in the first days of May, communist insurrections erupted in both Georgia and Armenia. Appeals for help were received in both Moscow and Baku, and Ordzhonikidze petitioned Moscow for authority to send the Eleventh Army west to Erevan and Tiflis. On 3 May he told Lenin he expected to be in Tiflis no later than the fifteenth, while the following day he was even more optimistic, predicting the fall of the Georgian capital by the twelfth.[50]

Lenin was not nearly as militant. From the sun-bathed shores of the Caspian revolutionary prospects never looked better, and the whole region appeared ripe for the picking. From the Kremlin the political world looked vastly different. Even as Ordzhonikidze wrote, the Poles plunged deeper into Ukraine. The divisions Ordzhonikidze wanted to send to Tiflis were needed at Kiev, and the Red Army high command clamoured for their return. Furthermore, the British had chosen this moment to open negotiations for the surrender of the Volunteer Army. The Soviet government was not particularly eager to accept British mediation, but Curzon, in his telegram of 3 May, had linked the conclusion of an Anglo-Soviet trade agreement with an end of hostilities in both the Crimea and the Caucasus.[51] Moscow placed a very high value on the trade negotiations with Great Britain, seeing them quite correctly as the most efficient vehicle for bringing an end to foreign intervention and an indispensable step to the regularization of the international position of Soviet Russia. Their importance can be seen in a letter Chicherin wrote to Litvinov on 4 May. In it he speculated at some length about the possibility of better relations with Britain and then, referring to the issues raised in Curzon's telegram of 3 May as "lesser matters," indicated that he felt the Soviet government could comply with the British demands. "We have already taken all valuable [positions]," in the Caucasus, he said, and felt that "more than one sincere whiteguardist" would be shocked by the proposal for a negotiated amnesty. Therefore the Soviet government decided to restrain Ordzhonikidze. The foreign commissar recommended, and Lenin approved, a cessation of hostilities in the south. "In my opinion Chicherin is right," Lenin wrote to Trotsky on 4 May, "concerning the suspension of military activity in the Crimea and in the Caucasus."[52]

On May 4 the Politburo approved this cautious approach to the political-military situation and new orders began to flow from Moscow to the south. The Kremlin had not yet responded officially to the revolutionary triumph in the Caucasus, and now Lenin, as chairman of the Russian Sovnarkom, issued a government statement on the subject. It was an anemic greeting, welcoming the birth of "the independent Soviet Republic of Azerbaidzhan," but it said *not a single word* about the revolution elsewhere in the East or even in the Caucasus.[53] Urgent directives issued to the new Soviet authorities at Baku spelled out the significance of this omission. "The Central Committee," Lenin instructed Ordzhonikidze, "orders you to withdraw [your military] units from the precincts of Georgia to the frontier and abstain from attacking Georgia." This did not go down well in Baku. Ordzhonikidze responded on 7 May that the directive would "be carried out precisely," but then went on to indicate the widespread nature of the insurrection already under way in Georgia and assert that "with our movement to the frontier the rising in [these] regions is inevitable. What do you order us to do – support it or not?" In a further message of the same day Ordzhonikidze assured Lenin that negotiations would be undertaken with the Mensheviks in Tiflis but asked that "the proclamation of Soviet power" in Georgia be made a primary condition of peace. This brought an immediate rejoinder from Lenin declaring that Ordzhonikidze's effort to support the revolution in Georgia was "in fundamental contradiction to the Central Committee decision. It may have pernicious consequences. In no event will the Central Committee allow it. We categorically demand an end of this action's [execution] and the erasure of the decision."[54]

Lenin had good reason to lecture his subordinates in the Caucasus. At the very moment he received Ordzhonikidze's telegram of 7 May, Chicherin was signing a peace treaty with Georgia. In the previous month the foreign commissar had twice offered to respect the independence of Georgia in exchange for absolute neutrality in relation to the remnants of the Volunteer Army and a promise not to serve as a base for action hostile to the government of Moscow.[55] The Georgian Mensheviks had originally ignored this offer, but with the sweeping Soviet victory in the North Caucasus and a total want of support from the western powers, they opened secret negotiations with Moscow.[56] Noe Zhordania, president of Georgia, sent Grigol Uratadze to determine what terms the Soviet government would offer. Uratadze made the trip with great difficulty, being held virtual prisoner at Rostov for several days, but finally arrived at the end of the month. Ordzhonikidze pleaded with Lenin not to negotiate, but the Soviet leader ordered the talks to proceed. "After negotiations with Tiflis," Lenin wired Ordzhonikidze on 5 May, "it is clear there is no reason to rule out peace with Georgia."[57] And indeed there wasn't. Given the Soviet political desiderata of the moment – a cessation of hostilities everywhere except the Polish front and satisfaction of Curzon's conditions for the continuation of trade talks with Britain – the treaty was of inestimable value. In it Moscow acknowledged the independence of Georgia and recognized, for the most part, the boundaries claimed by Tiflis. This included the port and province of Batum but not the strategic mountain passes leading from Russia into the heart of Georgia. Tiflis agreed to prevent its territory from being used to attack any Soviet republic. Moscow undertook similar responsibilities with regard to Georgia, but required Tiflis to liberate all individuals arrested for acts performed on behalf of Soviet Russia. The Communist Party of Georgia was legalized, and imprisoned members were to be released at once. The treaty came into force immediately upon signature and did not require special ratification.[58]

It would have been difficult to draft a treaty better suited to Soviet needs. While granting the cessation of hostilities demanded by Curzon and required by the Polish crisis, it left the strategic mountain passes in Soviet hands. Moscow could send the Red Army into Georgia whenever it wished. In the meanwhile the Georgians would have to expel or intern the remnants of the Volunteer Army who had crossed into their territory. Moreover, the treaty was so ambiguously worded that Moscow could interpret it to mean that Georgia would have to expel all allied military personnel from its territory. This was of special importance, for Batum was garrisoned by an allied force, and the treaty recognized the province and port as belonging to Georgia. Moscow, therefore, was free to use this lever any time it wished to bring pressure on Tiflis and could use the continued presence of allied troops at Batum to invalidate the entire agreement. Finally, by writing freedom of action for the Georgian Communist Party into the treaty, Moscow had provided itself with the means to bring down the Menshevik government whenever it wished. Under Soviet protection the Communist Party of Georgia was sure to prosper, and any effort by the Mensheviks to hinder its activities could be said to violate the treaty and justify "fraternal assistance" by the Red Army for their "brothers" in Georgia. With this treaty Moscow could stay its hand and wait for a more propitious moment to strike.

Similar, yet different, circumstances temporarily preserved the independence of Armenia.[59] With fewer people and resources than Azerbaidzhan or Georgia, it also had the smallest indigenous communist party in the Caucasus. Thus Armenia attracted less attention than its richer neighbours and lacked influential party leaders to promote its accelerated Bolshevization. But Armenia was strategically important because its territory impinged directly upon that controlled by the Turkish nationalists of Kemal Ataturk. Moscow and Baku wished to breach the Armenian barrier erected by the allies to bar cooperation among the states seeking to exclude western influence from the region. Hence Ordzhonikidze, on taking power, had immediately called for the Armenians to withdraw from the disputed Karabakh region.[60] Non-compliance would serve as the pretext for the Soviet invasion of Armenia, which was to have been preceded by communist insurrections throughout the country. But just as in the case of Georgia, this scenario was reversed at the last moment by Moscow. The insurrections, in fact, occurred,[61] but the Red Army did not ride to the rescue. Instead, Uratadze, the Georgian representative in Moscow, conveyed Soviet peace proposals to the government at Erevan. The Armenians lost no time in sending representatives to Moscow but were unable to reach agreement with the Soviet government. The Soviets insisted on access to Kemalist Turkey, a condition the Armenians would not grant. Fighting, therefore, continued in the disputed region throughout the summer, with Soviet troops supporting communist insurgents. But, due to the broader requirements of Soviet policy, it did not expand into a full-scale invasion of Armenia. The Soviet authorities at Baku could have overthrown the Dashnak regime but, as with Georgia, were held in check by Moscow. The Caucasus, having burst into sudden flame, subsided during the summer of 1920.[62]

THE SOVIET GOVERNMENT had deliberately chosen to abstain from using decisive military force in Georgia and Armenia. It showed no such restraint in dealing with the remnants of Denikin's Caspian flotilla which, with the fall of Petrovsk, had fled to Enzeli seeking the protection of its British garrison. Consisting of ten gun-boats, seven transports, and four smaller vessels, when commanded by the British in 1919 it had exercised effective control over much of the Caspian Sea, and even under White Russian officers was able to threaten the transport of petroleum to central Russia. By May, however, the local Persian authorities had interned the ships, and the British commander at Enzeli had ordered the removal of the breech-blocks of their guns to make it impossible for the flotilla to take further part in operations against the Bolsheviks. This, however, was not known to the Soviet government who, in any case, considered the vessels to be their own property. In mid-April F.F. Raskol'nikov, commander of the Soviet naval forces on the Caspian, inquired of Trotsky how he was to deal with the flotilla at Enzeli and, with Lenin's approval, was told:

The Caspian must be cleared of the White fleet at all costs. If a landing on Persian territory is required, it must be carried out, and the nearest Persian authorities notified of it and told that the landing is being undertaken by the officer in command with the exclusive object of carrying out a military assignment, which arose only because it was beyond the power of Persia to disarm the ships of the White Guards in her harbour, and that Persian territory remains inviolable for us and will be evacuated immediately after the completion of the military assignment.[63]

Accordingly, the Volga-Caspian flotilla began to prepare for a surprise assault on Enzeli. Coordinated with a cavalry raid across the border into Persia, Raskol'nikov's gun-boats arrived at dawn on 18 May, shelling the port and landing two thousand marines.[64] They found a British garrison of five hundred men. After a brief skirmish Raskol'nikov succeeded in cutting the British line of retreat. An armistice was concluded, and the Bolsheviks agreed to allow the British to withdraw along the road to Resht and Teheran.[65]

The Bolsheviks had struck yet another blow at the collapsing structure of the ill-considered peace settlement. British prestige in Persia suffered a blow from which it was never to recover. Having established a de facto protectorate over Persia the previous year the British stood revealed as being unable even to defend themselves. Worse still was the blow to British self-confidence, for the arrival of Raskol'nikov at Enzeli threw the British government into near panic. They did not debate how to defend their position but only the line to which they should retreat. Even the truculent Churchill was prepared to fall back as far as Mesopotamia if necessary. The British, unable to respond to the Bolshevik challenge militarily, decided to seek a political solution. "The Cabinet generally felt," their secretary recorded on 21 May, "that advantage should be taken of the forthcoming conversations with M. Krasin, if possible as a condition of entering into trade relations, to effect an all-round settlement which would include the East." The garrison at Enzeli was withdrawn to Kasvin north of Teheran. A week later the cabinet decided that even if the Bolsheviks withdrew from Enzeli British forces would not reoccupy the port.[66] The British were on their way out of Persia and had no intention of suffering further humiliation in the north.

The Bolsheviks, or the Soviet Russian armed forces at any rate, also prepared to leave. Chicherin explained the Soviet occupation in a friendly tone, ascribing it to the need to remove the threat to secure navigation of the Caspian Sea, and denying that Russian forces would remain in Enzeli any longer than necessary to remove Denikin's flotilla and military supplies. Trotsky, in fact, in congratulating Raskol'nikov on having "brilliantly discharged" his assignment, ordered him to withdraw from Enzeli and in the future "apply all the manpower and resources at [his] disposal to transporting petroleum from Baku" to Astrakhan.[67] Moreover, the Narkomindel, clearly worried about the aggressive initiative consistently shown by Soviet plenipotentiaries in the Caucasus, telegraphed to Ordzhonikidze and Raskol'nikov on 24 May: "Our military units must not advance beyond the environs of Enzeli for any reason. You must announce at once that notwithstanding the presence of Russian military units, Persia retains its authority in Enzeli." Two days later Raskol'nikov received formal orders to withdraw all Soviet Russian armed forces from northern Persia, an operation which was completed on 6 June 1920.[68]

The Red Army and Volga-Caspian flotilla left Enzeli, but did not return it to the representatives of the government of Persia. In attacking Enzeli the Bolsheviks had made good use of local revolutionaries – progressive nationalists known locally as Jangalis under the leadership of Mirza Kuchuk Khan – and two days before Raskol'nikov withdrew from northern Persia these forces united to proclaim a Soviet Socialist Republic of Gilan with its capital at Resht.[69] Kuchuk Khan and the Jangalis had been helped to power by the Bolshevik invasion but were in no way controlled by Baku, much less Moscow. The insurgents in Gilan took on all the trappings of the Russian revolution, calling their government the

Council of Peoples Commissars, their armed forces, the Red Army, and mouthing revolutionary slogans. But from the Soviet point of view they were clearly "bourgeois-nationalists." Their program called for abolition of the monarchy, establishment of a republic, protection of life and property, liquidation of all existing treaties with foreign powers, and protection of Islam. Ordzhonikidze advised Lenin: "There is not and cannot be any talk of a Soviet government in Iran. Kuchuk Khan will not even agree to pose the land question. Only one single slogan is put forward: 'Down with the British and the collaborationist Teheran Government.'"[70]

These Bolshevik military triumphs were sufficient to alter the Persian attitude towards Soviet Russia.[71] For more than two years Soviet influence in Persia had been minimal, largely due to the collapse of Russian power which had accompanied the revolution. Even Soviet willingness to renounce the accumulated rights and privileges of the Russian empire in Persia made little impact as the British, fearing the loss of their own privileged position refused to allow Teheran to accept the offer. In fact, the Anglo-Persian treaty of August 1919 had reduced Persia to little more than a British protectorate.[72]

The Soviet government sought to oppose British influence in Persia by reaffirming the renunciation of earlier-acquired Russian privileges and properties. Chicherin also launched a bitter attack on the treaty of 9 August 1919, describing it as a shameful and absolutely illegal agreement. At the same time the Narkomindel extended its first feelers to Kuchuk Khan. The latter had been in rebellion against the central government since 1917 and had been at war with the British since their arrival in the Enzeli region in late 1918. Chicherin now addressed a greeting to Kuchuk Khan congratulating him on his struggle for independence.[73] Despite serious ideological differences he and the Bolsheviks soon established a close relationship based on mutual hostility to Britain and the British supported regime in Teheran.

Soviet influence, however, did not become significant until the defeat of Denikin brought the Red Army into striking distance of the Persian frontier. This created alarm in Teheran, where the prime minister asked in early January 1920 how the British intended to defend Persia against the Bolsheviks. All inquiries were either ignored by the British or answered evasively.[74] Equivocation generated Persian fear that the British might abandon them. By mid-March, therefore, the Persian authorities began to think of initiating their own negotiations with the Bolsheviks. On 14 March the Persian foreign minister informed the British he was "considering [the] selection of a suitable person for [a] mission to Moscow." This did not please Curzon who said he was startled by the suggestion and lectured the Persian foreign minister on his country's obligations to Britain.[75]

The fall of Azerbaidzhan caused the Persian government to inform Moscow of its desire to establish mutually acceptable relations with Soviet Russia and the wish to send a plenipotentiary, Captain Nazym-Khan, to negotiate an agreement. Moscow responded that it was prepared to open negotiations at once.[76] The Soviet landing in northern Persia, however, delayed the opening of these talks. On 31 May the Persians demanded Soviet withdrawal before negotiations began. Nor was Teheran satisfied when Chicherin announced early in June that the withdrawal of Soviet *Russian* forces was complete, for the Bolsheviks had left Kuchuk Khan in control when they left. Subsequent protests brought a response that the Soviet government could not be held responsible for the dispute between Kuchuk Khan and Teheran and it would have to be settled by the Persians themselves. Non-interference, in fact, became the official Soviet policy in the conflict between Gilan and Teheran. In reality, Soviet authorities in Azerbaidzhan provided Kuchuk Khan with a wide variety of assistance but, held in check by Moscow, would not support him militarily. This was not good enough for Teheran who not only refused to open negotiations with Moscow but carried their complaint to the newly founded League of Nations. The League, however, was hardly the agent to restore the shah's authority in northern Persia; nor were the British, who continued to withdraw despite pleas from Teheran for military assistance. British failure to protect their Persian clients led in late June to the collapse of the government, and with them went much of British influence in Persia. In August the new government of Mushir-ed-Dowleh proposed the resumption of negotiations with Moscow.[77]

Thus, in Persia, as in the Caucasus, the arrival of the Red Army on the frontiers of states possessing few means of self-defence and little prospect of foreign assistance brought an immediate demand for negotiations with Moscow. The rapid end of the Russian civil war brought an often meteoric rise in the influence of the victor and a ready willingness on the part of Moscow to exercise it. Russian influence was again a major factor in the politics of southwest Asia and a potent force which no one could ignore.

NATIONALIST TURKEY WAS ALSO drawn into the orbit of Soviet Russia. Turkish nationalists and Russian Bolsheviks had little in common, but their hostility towards Britain provided sufficient attraction to bring them together. Moscow could not cooperate with the supine government of the sultan but was prepared to enter into relations with the hardy Anatolian insurgents led by Mustafa Kemal. Kemal had begun his rebellion in May 1919 when it became clear that the victorious powers intended to dismember not merely the Ottoman empire but its ethnically Turkish core as well. Withdrawing to central Anatolia, he had gathered around him all who were prepared to fight to defend Turkish unity. His movement gathered strength with every passing month but failed to influence the western powers who, led by Britain, sought to create a large Armenian state in the east and sanction Greek annexation of Smyrna in the west. Kemal needed the financial and political support of some outside power. It was not surprising then that with the arrival of the Red Army in the Caucasus he should turn to Moscow for aid. Overwhelming Soviet victory in the Russian civil war was not an unmixed blessing, for many Turkish nationalists were actively seeking to extend their influence over both Azerbaidzhan and Dagestan, but the shift in the regional balance of power was too favourable to ignore. On 26 April 1920 Kemal asked Soviet Russia to recognize his new government and assist him in expelling the western powers from Turkish territory. Specifically, he sought weapons, supplies, and money as well as assistance in breaching the Georgian and Armenian barrier erected by the Entente to separate Russia and Turkey.[78]

Kemal's letter did not reach Moscow until 1 June. Chicherin, after consulting Lenin, responded two days later, warmly greeting the new Turkish state, calling for the establishment of diplomatic relations, agreeing in principle to cooperation, but carefully ignoring the specific requests contained in the Turkish petition. Kemal had suggested coordinated military operations against Georgia and Armenia; the foreign commissar in reply proposed Soviet mediation to "determine by justice and right of national self-determination, clearly defined frontiers" between Turkey and the states of the Caucasus. This was not really what Kemal had in mind, but in a second letter of 20 June he agreed to give Chicherin an opportunity to negotiate with Erevan. He readily accepted the Soviet proposal to establish diplomatic relations, saying that a Turkish delegation headed by Bekir Sami, the foreign minister, had already left for Moscow. Russia, newly confirmed in its Soviet constitution, again stepped forward as a major power in the complex politics of southwest Asia.[79]

The Straits question had always been an integral part of these politics and, with the Red Army having reclaimed the Russian shore of the Black Sea, on 16 May 1920 Chicherin issued an official statement outlining the Soviet position on this issue.

Soviet Russia considers that the Bosporus and Dardanelles are the interest solely of the Black Sea states; ... Russia does not recognize any other international status of the Straits. The Supreme Council has not conducted negotiations with Russia regarding the Straits. Great Britain has refused to conduct negotiations on questions such as this, and, therefore, Russia enjoys full freedom of action in relation to the Straits.[80]

The events of early 1920 ensured that Soviet Russia would never again be ignored in the East. The stunning four-month sweep of the Red Army from Rostov and Astrakhan to Vladikavkaz, Baku, and Enzeli struck fear in the hearts of even the coolest adversaries. In a confidential minute prepared for Curzon on 20 May 1920, two days after the humiliation suffered at Enzeli, the normally imperturbable Lord Hardinge wrote:

Once the evacuation of Tabriz and Kasvin has been effected the fall of Teheran is inevitable ... the Europeans of Teheran will be obliged to fly towards the south, and anarchy and destruction will prevail. If and when a large Bolshevik force is concentrated at Kasvin and Teheran, the flanks of both India and Mesopotamia will be exposed and the Bolsheviks will be in a position to choose whether to attack in the east or in the west.

He then sketched two horrific scenarios, one ending in "an Afghan-Bolshevik alliance ... accompanied by war on India by Afghanistan," and a second in which "the whole of Persia will, for all practical purposes, have become Bolshevik." Some, he allowed, might consider such a possibility exaggerated but concluded "there is absolutely no reason why it should be so and we have seen the manner in which the Bolshevik armies overcome opposition and are able to conduct operations at immense distances from their bases."[81]

The Soviet government had not the slightest intention of undertaking this type of military operation. The Red Army was, in fact, regrouping to fight the Poles and Wrangel. Even if such defensive measures had not been necessary, it was unlikely that Moscow would have ordered military adventures of the variety described by Hardinge. Trotsky who, as Soviet commissar of war, was in a better position to judge the capacity of the Red Army and the Bolshevik party to mount major military-political campaigns, wrote to Lenin on 4 June 1920:

All the information about the situation in Chiva, Persia, Buchara and Afghanistan testifies to the fact that a Soviet revolution in these countries would at the present moment cause us the greatest possible difficulties. Even in Azerbaidzhan the Soviet Republic is not capable of standing on its own feet, in spite of the oil industry and its old connection with Russia. Until the situation in the west has been stabilised and that of our industry and transport improved a Soviet expedition in the east may prove to be no less dangerous than war in the west.

"It follows from this," he continued, "that a potential Soviet revolution in the east is now advantageous for us chiefly as a major item of diplomatic barter with England." He concluded by stressing that Moscow had to "continue in every way to emphasize through all available channels our readiness to come to an understanding with England with regard to the east." This, in fact, was already the policy of the Soviet government as indicated in the Politburo decision of 4 May to suspend military activity in the Crimea and Caucasus in the interest of promoting trade talks with Britain. Krasin had arrived in London where, as Lenin noted on the above telegram, he was already doing exactly as Trotsky suggested.[82] Moreover, the Narkomindel was using every available channel to convey the Soviet message to Britain. Thus, in speaking to a British correspondent sent by the *Daily Chronicle*, Chicherin declared flatly: "Please tell [Lord Curzon] from me that the best way to end our action in influencing peoples to the south-east is for Great Britain to make peace with us." He promised that "on peaceful relations being established with Britain, we should at once cease our propaganda in that direction." Here then was one of the basic themes which would run through Soviet negotiations with Britain – an end of anti-British activities in the East in exchange for peaceful relations with Soviet Russia. And already in May 1920 Chicherin specified the limits of such a compromise. He promised an end to Soviet efforts to influence the peoples of the east "in favour of communal ideas," but immediately added smiling, "any appreciation of these ideas which would automatically result from the existence of a Communist state near at hand, would be something we could not prevent."[83] Curzon never saw this report, for his officials did not take it seriously. They and the rest of the world would soon discover that this was, in fact, the basis of Soviet policy. In the spring of 1920 the Russian revolution, its aims and ideals had only taken their first step into Asia through the door at Baku.

CHAPTER TWELVE

"Astoundingly attractive offers":
Attempted peace negotiations
with Poland

Throughout most of 1919 Poland did not constitute a major focus of Soviet foreign policy. Surrounded by more threatening enemies, the Bolsheviks had been content to reduce military activity on Russia's western frontier to a minimum. In the summer Moscow had even concluded a tacit bargain agreeing to a continuation of hostilities at a level advantageous to Poland but not threatening Soviet security. As Pilsudski dreaded the prospect of a restored "Russia, one and indivisible" much more than the perpetuation of Bolshevism, he was delighted to contribute in this way to the defeat of the White generals. In the fall of 1919, however, Pilsudski began to reshape his policy. Anticipating Soviet victory, he intended to put Poland forward as the successor to the White Russians in the struggle against Bolshevism. He wanted a mandate from the western powers to overthrow Bolshevism and restore order in Russia. This would allow him to restructure eastern Europe around a powerful Poland, federated with the western borderlands of the former tsarist empire, and confine Russia to its ethnographic frontiers. Warsaw, rather than Moscow, would dominate Ukraine and become the greatest power in the east. [1]

Pilsudski did not lack imagination; he was, however, short of cash. The new Polish state had entered the world bankrupt and its army was ragged, underfed, and poorly armed. A campaign such as imagined by Pilsudski was simply beyond Polish resources. He said if the allies wished Poland to advance on Moscow with an army of five hundred thousand men it would cost £600,000 a day. None of the allied leaders were interested. They still expected the Whites to win and did not take the Polish offer seriously. [2]

The sweeping victories won by Denikin in the fall reinforced the allied preoccupation with the Whites. The Poles also watched Denikin but with apprehension and fear. As his armies took Kiev and advanced rapidly westward towards the lines held by Polish troops in East Galicia, Warsaw was forced to contemplate what might happen when the two armies met. The French feared hostilities would erupt spontaneously and warned Warsaw to avoid the slightest clash. Pilsudski, in fact, instructed his troops to exercise the greatest caution when they encountered the Volunteer Army, but the White Russian attitude alarmed Poles of all political persuasions.[3] It was clear that although Denikin acknowledged Poland's sovereignty he saw it as extending only to the Privilinsk region (essentially Congress Poland of 1815) and not to the borderlands. Significantly, the Supreme Council, pondering the fate of East Galicia, postponed their decision to allow the Russian situation to clarify. The Poles knew, however, that if Denikin did reach Moscow they had little chance of having their territorial claims in the east recognized by the allies.[4]

Denikin's triumphal march also threatened the Ukrainian nationalist movement. Petliura's troops, in fact, had been the first to enter Kiev after the Soviet withdrawal, but they, in turn, were forced from the city when the Volunteer Army arrived the following day. Denikin had grudgingly acknowledged Polish sovereignty, but he refused to recognize a similar claim for Ukraine. Thus the Whites continued military operations against Petliura, driving the remnants of his army back towards the Polish lines in East Galicia. Pilsudski and Petliura recognized Denikin as a common enemy and, from early September, began to cooperate. The Poles ceased hostilities against the Ukrainians while Petliura went to Warsaw to negotiate further with Pilsudski.[5]

Denikin's ascent had a similar impact on Soviet-Polish relations. In early September Pilduski agreed to resume the negotiations begun that summer at Bialowieza. The new talks commenced at Mikaszewicze on 9 October. Marchlewski again represented Moscow; M.S. Kossakovski initially represented Warsaw, but he was subsequently joined by M. Birnbaum and I. Boerner, the latter a confidant of Pilsudski.[6] The importance of the talks for Soviet Russia can be seen in a 15 October Politburo resolution declaring that until further notice "questions about the northern and western front were to be considered only from the point of view of the security of ... the Moscow-Tula region and ... Petrograd." The next day the high command transferred the entire Soviet Twelfth Army from the western to the southern front.[7] Only a thin screen of Soviet troops remained to face the Poles in Ukraine, but Pilsudski did not engage them in combat. Instead, in late October, he crossed the Zbruch, the prewar boundary separating East Galicia from Ukraine, and at Petliura's request advance to Kamenets-Podolski where he met the left wing of the Volunteer Army as it advanced into the virtual military vacuum of western Ukraine.[8] In contrast, the main body of the Volunteer Army was brought to a stop at Orel where the Bolsheviks broke the momentum of the White offensive. Denikin was never to regain the initiative, and by the end of October his troops were streaming south in full retreat.

In the following month the talks at Mikaszewicze achieved substantial success. On 2 and 9 November agreements were reached for an exchange of hostages, followed shortly after by one for a cessation of hostilities. On 14 November the

Politburo approved this truce except for a clause terminating Soviet military operations against Petliura. Marchlewski was instructed to inform the Poles that Moscow would conduct its own negotiations with Petliura and could not make its relations with him contingent on a third party. The Polish demand that the negotiations be kept entirely secret, however, was accepted.[9] Boerner did not object to the deletion of the clause regarding Petliura. He left for Warsaw on 24 November and returned at the end of the month with the final response of the Polish government. Pilsudski declined to conclude a formal armistice, suggesting instead that the two sides exchange verbal promises not to cross the line specified in the draft agreement. This was not what Moscow wanted, but it accepted it. On 6 December 1919 Chicherin told Marchlewski to assure Boerner that the Red Army would respect the agreement. Boerner repeatedly emphasized how hatred of Denikin and *raison d'état* compelled Pilsudski to deny aid to the Volunteer Army.[10] Moscow accepted this testimony and the verbal promise of a truce as well. Both corresponded to the facts and necessities of November 1919; these facts and necessities were about to undergo a total reversal.

Without doubt Pilsudski hated Denikin, but once the Whites were defeated he had to take the next step in promoting Polish primacy in eastern Europe. In negotiating with the Bolsheviks he had insisted on absolute secrecy, so as to avoid, he said, the displeasure of the Entente. This was moonshine. He required secrecy for quite different reasons. On the one hand he did not want to feed the already blazing fires of the Polish peace movement. Nor did he wish to test the morale of his army. If it became known that Moscow had offered favourable terms, both the Sejm and army might refuse to fight any longer. Primarily, however, he did not wish to bring hostilities to an end. Once the Bolsheviks disposed of Denikin he intended to attack them, and he did not want any written agreement getting in his way. Far from wishing to conceal the negotiations from the allies, Pilsudski made sure they learned about them. As early as 1 November the Polish foreign minister informed a member of the British embassy that "the Polish Bolshevist [i.e. Marchlewski] who formed part of the Red Cross Commission which was negotiating with the Poles at the present time had certainly made astoundingly attractive offers," while six days later Pilsudski told Sir Horace Rumbold, the British minister, that Poland might come to an arrangement with the Bolsheviks. He wished to know what was British policy with regard to Russia.[11] The French were not informed in this manner, but when they got wind of the talks they received a lengthy, but incomplete, description of the meetings at Mikaszevicze.[12] Thus Pilsudski, having solicited and received favourable Soviet peace proposals, promptly leaked them to the western allies as a way of pressuring them to reconsider their earlier refusal to back him in a war against Moscow.

None of this made any impact in London, where Rumbold's telegram elicited no response. In Paris it was another matter. While the Quai d'Orsay resolutely refused to endorse Pilsudski's Ukrainian ambitions, they did have the question of East Galicia reconsidered by the Supreme Council. In addition, Paris placed continuous pressure on London to adopt a more favourable attitude towards Poland. The British prime minister, however, continued to see Poland in a negative light, saying that the Poles "had always been a very troublesome people in Europe." [13] Allied decision-making was thus paralysed and a common policy impossible. Britain would not aid Poland, and France, though favourably disposed to Warsaw, would not commit itself to Pilsudski publicly for fear of alienating Britain. Frustration in Warsaw mounted, where the prescient French minister noted the impatience felt in "official Polish circles to profit from the [White] debacle." [14]

AS EASTERN EUROPE UNDERWENT kaleidoscopic change, so too did the Polish political world. In late November a protracted ministerial crisis led to the fall of the Paderewski government and, in mid-December, to the formation of a new cabinet headed by Leopold Skulski, a founder of the National Peasant Union. Stanislaw Patek, a personal friend of Pilsudski who shared his eastern aspirations, was given the Ministry of Foreign Affairs. Leading National Democrats were appointed undersecretaries in the Foreign Ministry. Although opposed to Pilsudski on most issues, they shared his wish of extending Polish boundaries and influence far to the east. "We would no more return Lvov, than agree to yield Cracow or Warsaw," proclaimed one National Democratic leader in December. [15] The ministerial crisis set off alarm bells in Moscow. Chicherin thought, incorrectly, that the agreement just concluded with Pilsudski had lost much of its significance. He feared the new government would be inclined to reach agreement with Denikin and attributed this, again wrongly, to the Entente which he said was "making a new attempt to unite the borderlands against us." [16] This was to be the central theme of Moscow's interpretation of the Soviet-Polish conflict. Already on 22 December Trotsky joined the chorus. "The interventionists are now constructing their policy on an alliance of the border states and attach vast importance to a link-up between Denikin's troops and the Poles." The conclusion he drew from this was "the need to strengthen the Twelfth Army by all possible means." [17]

This line won rapid acceptance in Moscow, where on the same day Chicherin addressed a new note to the Polish government. During the previous nine months the most significant portion of Soviet relations with Poland had been conducted in the clandestine manner so loved by Pilsudski. Now the Bolsheviks, fearing allied-inspired Polish aggression, broadcast their peace appeal for all to hear. They did so all the more readily, for on 28 November a Polish government spokesman had declared that Soviet Russia had never proposed peace to Poland. Chicherin denied the veracity of this declaration, reminded Warsaw of the proposals presented to Wiechowski in April, reaffirmed Moscow's "steadfast desire to put an end to all conflicts with Poland," and again asked the Polish government "to enter immediately into negotiations with a view to concluding a stable and enduring peace." This, said Chicherin, was being prevented by "foreign sources ... in conflict with the real interests of the Polish people."[18] Three elements of this message are significant. First, despite references to earlier proposals, Chicherin did not mention the more recent and significant talks at Bialowieza and Mikaszewicze. Clearly Moscow remained ignorant of Pilsudski's true intentions. The extent of this error can be seen in a memorandum Marchlewski sent the Central Committee on 24 December in which he polarized the views of Pilsudski and the National Democrats. While correctly noting their divergent views on Denikin, Marchlewski failed to appreciate how deeply Pilsudski was committed to expansion in Ukraine.[19] A second significant feature is the heavy emphasis placed on alleged foreign, meaning allied, influence in blocking the conclusion of peace. This led to a final characteristic, the assumption that agreement between Russia and Poland would come easily in the absence of western interference. These would remain constant themes until the outbreak of hostilities in April.

Pilsudski made good use of the Soviet peace proposal. The foreign ministry passed it to allied representatives with the comment that it would increase the pressure on the government to make peace. This too was the line taken by Patek when he arrived in Paris to promote Polish ambitions in the east. On 31 December 1919 he called on Berthelot and read him the Soviet message. He said he wished to know the views of the allies and France in particular regarding peace with Moscow. The French response could only warm his heart, for Berthelot replied that "France would never treat with the Soviets: she considered the Bolsheviks as a band of brigands who have seized power by violence, imposed their domination by terror, committed crimes of every order, and disorganized the social and economic life of Russia for a very long time. There must not be any negotiations with them for this would recognize indirectly the legitimacy of their crimes and the regularity of their government."

Berthelot could not and did not counsel a continuation of war, but a more definitive rejection of peace could not be imagined.[20] From Warsaw, Pralon, the French minister to Poland, astutely informed Paris: "The menace of the Bolsheviks, victors over Yudenich and Denikin, will provide a ready pretext to General Pilsudski to take so-called precautionary measures thanks to which he will ably push to the East the front held by his troops."[21] Reporting from Copenhagen, Litvinov wrote in much the same vein. Early in January he wired Moscow: "Pilsudski has gone to the Eastern Front where the Polish press predicts major events."[22]

Polish policy clearly carried with it the threat of expanded military operations, and from late December the Soviet government began to look to its defences. The western front had been stripped to reinforce the south at the height of Denikin's drive on Moscow. Now a dangerous wind began to blow from the west. Marchlewski had no hesitation in writing on 24 December: "*I consider an offensive by Polish army in the near future to be entirely possible.*" Early in January 1920 the Soviet high command created a new front, the southwestern, to bolster defences in the region. Three armies (the twelfth, thirteenth, and fourteenth) were assigned, among other tasks, "to defend the Kievan region from possible Polish attack."[23] Available resources were meagre indeed. It was all very well to form a new front, but in truth this was a mere regrouping of existing forces. Nor would reinforcement be available soon, because Denikin still had to be driven from the Kuban and North Caucasus, operations which were certain to consume valuable time and resources. Still, the Polish threat loomed larger with every day. The Polish government did not even respond officially to the Soviet proposal of 22 December. Instead, the Foreign Ministry authorized Polish newspapers to declare that the Bolshevik radio message "lacked precision, contained no proposition relative to the Polish frontiers and did not even speak of the cessation of Bolshevik propaganda in the interior of Poland." No definite answer to Moscow's proposals would be made, it was said, until the allied powers had been consulted.[24] Still more threatening was a report received from Litvinov that rumours circulating in Berlin indicated that Poland was about to proclaim general mobilization and Marshal Foch as well as several major anti-Bolshevik leaders were expected soon in Warsaw where they would organize a new White Army to attack Moscow. From information such as this Soviet leaders drew increasingly pessimistic conclusions.

Aware of their military weakness, the Soviet government sought to fend off attack by taking the political offensive. On 28 January the Sovnarkom issued a solemn declaration reaffirming "the inviolable principle of national self-deter-mination" and that they "unconditionally recognized ... without any reservation the independence and sovereignty of the Polish Republic." They promised that the Red Army would not conduct military operations west of the existing line separating them from the Polish armed forces and asserted that "insofar as the essential interests of Poland and Russia are concerned there is not a single question, territorial, economic or other that might not be settled peacefully, by negotiation, mutual concessions and agreement." Significantly, the Sovnarkom also declared that it had "not entered into any agreements or pacts, with Germany or with any other country, aimed directly or indirectly against Poland."[26] This, of course, was true but differed in spirit from the rest of the declaration. Most of the document promised peace. The mention of Germany suggested punishment should Poland refuse it. Here, publicly for the first time, emerged another theme which would run through Soviet-Polish relations for the next two decades.

On the same day Chicherin opened political hostilities on yet another front. Soviet policy contended that Poland was being pushed into war by the western powers and, therefore, it was "to the workers of the allied countries" that the foreign commissar addressed himself. He warned that "the dark forces in Europe, the Clemenceaus, the Churchills, the Northcliffes, are zealously preparing a fresh attack on Soviet Russia." Their aim was "to fling Poland against Soviet Russia and force the Poles to go to the assistance of Denikin." Soviet Russia, he said, was no threat to Poland; it wanted to conclude peace. Only "the reactionary imperialist policy of the allied governments" stood in the way.[25]

Throughout this initial phase of the Soviet-Polish crisis the Bolsheviks believed that the western powers were seeking to use Poland to save Denikin from defeat and that the pressure for war came from the West rather than from within Poland itself. There was a certain element of truth in this. From the moment Denikin realized that the defeat of his army at Orel was not merely a temporary reversal but the beginning of a general rout he urgently sought Polish aid to relieve the pressure on his hard-pressed divisions. By the end of December the Whites were clamorously demanding an immediate Polish offensive against the exposed right flank of the Red Army and blaming their own failure entirely on the "anti-Russian policy" conducted by Pilsudski.[26] This call was received sympathetically by Churchill in Britain and by Franchet d'Esperey, the commander of allied armies in the east, but was rejected by both the French and British governments. At a meeting of the heads of delegations of the five great powers in Paris on 5 January 1920 the question of Polish aid for Denikin was examined and set aside. No one believed anyone could save Denikin from disaster, least of all the Poles.[27] The Soviets were wrong, therefore, in laying blame on the allies. At this time (prior to the installation of the Millerand government in France) only a limited number of allied leaders sought to have Poland aid the Whites, and their counsel was rejected by governments which had lost all faith in the Volunteer Army. The pressure for a Polish campaign against Moscow came from Warsaw, and specifically the Belvedere Palace, Pilsudski's residence; it was a policy designed to enthrone a Great Poland as master of eastern Europe, not save Great Russia for Denikin.

Pilsudski would not help Denikin, but he did not hesitate to take advantage of the White débâcle to improve his own military position in Podolia. In late December 1919 and early January 1920 the Polish army moved forward into the vacuum left by the retreating Whites to establish a new front based on the Uszyca River, Proskourov, Starokonstantinov, and the Slucz River. Behind this line Pilsudski improved communications, opened a direct rail line from Warsaw to Kamenets-Podolski, and reinforced his army. Only in mid-January did the Red Army approach this new position when they occupied Vinnitsa further east and marched on towards Zmerinka.[28] As the Polish army enlarged its zone of occupation Pilsudski intended to place newly occupied territories under Ukrainian administration. He hoped it would soon be possible to move Petliura and his government from Kamenets-Podolski to Vinnitsa. Pralon saw through this policy. For Pilsudski, he said, "Russia, in whatever form reconstituted poses above all a grave threat to Poland; it is important to reduce its strength as far as possible and then interpose between it and the Polish Republic a series of buffer states which will be led by the necessity of a common defence and nationalism to ally themselves militarily and economically with Warsaw against Moscow."[29]

During December and January Pilsudski continued to seek western support for this policy. In addition to sending Patek to promote his campaign, he also enlisted General Henrys, chief of the French Military Mission in Poland, who returned to France at the same time and filed a warm endorsement of the Polish proposals.[30] When Patek arrived Clemenceau still governed France, but in mid-January he was replaced by a new cabinet headed by Alexander Millerand. The Millerand cabinet, with the presidency of the Council shifted from the War Ministry to the Quai d'Orsay, inclined towards a greater militancy; Maurice Paléologue, the newly created secretary general at the Foreign Ministry and former ambassador to the court of Nicholas II, wished to pursue a much more active policy than the former team of Clemenceau and Berthelot. The latter, at least since mid-1919, had been inclined to surround the Bolsheviks in barbed wire. Millerand and Paléologue wanted the neighbours of Soviet Russia to scale the wire and wage war against Moscow.[31]

The new leadership still had to cast its policies in terms acceptable to the British. But just as Lloyd George had begun covertly to pursue a Russian policy at variance with that proclaimed by the Supreme Council, so now did Millerand and Paléologue. While not departing publicly from the decision to abstain from counselling Poland to make war on Soviet Russia, the French government now decided to provide Warsaw with the military supplies needed to attack Moscow. No advice was given on how best to use these materials, but from the Polish proposals advanced repeatedly since September, it was clear that Pilsudski, suitably armed, would need no encouragement to attack the Bolsheviks. In his interviews with the Polish foreign minister, Millerand emphasized that peace with the Soviet government offered no security; it would only provide the Bolsheviks with an opportunity "to await the most favourable occasion to attack Poland." The French premier did not advise the Polish government to adopt an aggressive attitude but only sought to warn Patek "against the consequences which would follow for Poland, and for the rest of Europe, from an unreflective confidence [in Soviet promises]." The significance of this declaration is enhanced still further by noting that Millerand had originally concluded with the words "the acceptance of Bolshevik peace offers." These certainly were the words used in his talks with Patek. Only subsequently did he replace this with the more diffuse "an unreflective confidence."[32]

French acquiescence still left Pilsudski without British support. Lloyd George clearly did not want Pilsudski to disrupt the general pacification of the continent for which he hoped. When meeting Patek for the first time on 15 January in Paris, and hearing what he considered "extravagant claims for Polish boundaries," the prime minister warned him "as to the consequences of provocative action of the kind." Lloyd George was so concerned about Poland's intentions that when Patek crossed the channel the following week he took the opportunity to issue yet another, far sterner, warning. In an interview held on 26 January the prime minister noted the departure of almost every other anti-Bolshevik army from the field and warned Patek there was a "grave risk that Poland might be left to face a Bolshevik concentration by itself." He wished "to make it perfectly clear that the British government did not wish to give Poland the slightest encouragement to pursue the policy of war." On 29 January the cabinet approved the language he had used in speaking with Patek.[33] The following day Curzon instructed Rumbold to inform the Polish government in detail of what Lloyd George had told Patek. Rumbold sent a four-page letter to the Polish Foreign Ministry recapitulating all the objections raised in London to any policy favouring a continuation of armed hostilities against Soviet Russia.[34]

Patek understood, but did not appreciate, British policy. In a letter to his cousin written in late January he praised the French and censured the British. "What an admirable Minister of Foreign Affairs," he said of Millerand. "He is so French ... and consequently just as Polish as your great Marshal Foch!! These two men will not allow themselves to be outwitted by the merchants on the other side of the English Channel." He was returning to Poland, he concluded, "to report ... the words of comfort from our dear brothers of France! Their promises will be kept, I am sure ... while in a short while the result of the Copenhagen talks will be as nebulous as the Prinkipo projects proved to be formerly."[35]

This report was not well received in Warsaw. Pilsudski had sought the open support of the entente, not merely the covert backing of France. His problem was rendered even more difficult by the insistent demand from Moscow, renewed on 4 February, for the immediate opening of peace negotiations. Despite the best efforts of Polish censorship, this proposal became known immediately in Warsaw and placed the government under further pressure to examine the possibility of a negotiated peace with Moscow. Confronted with Polish public opinion and British policy, Pilsudski had to accept the distasteful necessity of at least appearing to negotiate. The prospect was abhorrent because open negotiations had no part in his plans. In his view the situation in Soviet Russia in early 1920 was comparable to that in Germany prior to its collapse in 1918, and one more sharp blow would bring down the Bolshevik regime. He believed that the Red Army was on its last legs and would likely soon melt away to nothing when its peasant soldiers went home for spring planting. He insisted that the Bolsheviks could not be trusted to honour any treaty they might sign, and even after the conclusion of peace he would have to keep a large army ready to defend Poland from renewed Soviet aggression. He accepted the necessity of responding to the Soviet proposals, therefore, as a basis for war rather than peace, with the intention of proceeding slowly, hoping that circumstances might still allow him to escape actual peace talks.[36] While continuing his military preparations, he gave orders to draft peace proposals consistent with his design for Polish hegemony in eastern Europe, and consequently unacceptable even to the Soviet government.

The justification for these proposals had already been prepared. The Poles were very sensitive to the charge of imperialism levelled against them and sought to cloak their designs in political idealism. They did not see how they could hand back territory already wrested from the Bolsheviks, as this would subject the population of these areas "to a barbarous regime."[37] To humanitarianism the Poles added self-determination and rectification of historical injustice. Both

were advanced to justify what became the central feature of the Polish peace
proposals – the demand for Russian "de-annexation" of all territories obtained
as a result of the three partitions of Poland in the eighteenth century. What was
meant by de-annexation? It was a term used to avoid the more accurate, but
unpalatable, expression "Polish annexation." Warsaw demanded that the Russians withdraw to the frontier of 1772 in order, theoretically, to allow the peoples
west of this line to determine their political future free from coercion. Soviet
Russia was to recognize the independence of all successor states formed on this
territory and undertake to leave them at liberty to order their own affairs. In
addition, Moscow was to return all property taken from territories within the
frontiers of 1772, share the assets of the Russian state bank, and indemnify Poles
for all destruction, requisition, and confiscation of property committed on their
territory since the outbreak of the Great War. Finally, the peace treaty, when
completed, was to be submitted for ratification to "the Supreme Organ representing the will of the Russian people." In defence of the first and most contentious proposal, the Poles declared that the three partitions in the eighteenth
century represented an historical crime which could only be set right by the de-
annexation they demanded.[38]

   In mid-February the substance of these terms was leaked intentionally to
Rumbold and Pralon. Surprisingly, given the policies of their two governments,
the British minister was more tolerant than the French. "These conditions," he
wrote on 13 February, "are bound to be so framed as to contain the maximum
guarantee, which it is possible to obtain from the Soviet government that it will
keep its engagements." Pralon, on the other hand, attributed the extreme nature
of the peace proposals to the megalomania of Polish politicians. Far from seeking
peace with Moscow, he said, "the Polish army awaited the order to march against
Bolshevism to seize their long coveted objectives: Kiev ... the Dnepr to Mogilev
and, on the left, the approaches to Vitebsk." Pralon thus rendered a clear account
of Pilsudski's intentions while Rumbold was far too willing to take the Polish
leader at his word. In mid-March, however, when the Polish government released
the official version of their peace proposals, the British minister warned Patek
that even if the Bolsheviks would agree to these terms, which he doubted, "and
then violated their agreement and attacked [the] Poles, [the] latter could count
on no help whatever from Great Britain."[39] This made no impression on the
Polish government because they understood perfectly that they would receive
no aid from Great Britain; they therefore chose to ignore all warnings from
Westminster and proceeded with the preparation of their spring campaign against
the Red Army.

   This required the military supplies promised by France in January. Patek had
been given unofficial assurance of this support but nothing concrete in the form
of promised deliveries. When Henrys returned to Warsaw, therefore, he was
summoned to the Belvedere where Pilsudski and Patek told him impatiently that
they needed "to know exactly and as soon as possible what material and financial

aid Poland could expect from its allies." They would have seven hundred thousand men in the field by the end of April but were largely unable to arm the new recruits.[40] The same day Patek addressed a note to Millerand, enclosing a comprehensive list of the war material and equipment Warsaw needed to put the Polish army on a wartime footing. The Poles asked for everything: rifles, machine-guns, artillery, ammunition, hand-grenades, uniforms, airplanes, locomotives, freight cars, trucks, tents, and horses. The cost would be substantial. The French obviously did not wish to assume this burden alone, so, far from trying to conceal the Polish request from the British, they forwarded a copy to London. London received the Polish request with incredulity. "The Polish government has lost its head!" exclaimed one member of the Foreign Office, while another asked pointedly, "Who can have encouraged the Poles to make these preposterous demands?" Lloyd George made it amply clear that the British would not support the Polish army. The two allies were unable to agree: the British advised the Poles not to make war; the French told them not to make peace. More importantly, Millerand now proceeded to provide the supplies promised in January. In late February he "approved the dispatch of 80 million francs worth of powder, and rifle and artillery ammunition for the Polish army – urgently needed 'because of operations in the coming spring.'"[41]

The Bolsheviks received a steady stream of newspaper and wireless reports concerning the intentions of the Polish and allied governments. In early February, when intent had not yet crystallized into actual preparation, Soviet leaders remained hopeful of a peaceful settlement with Poland. Time and again Lenin spoke out about the seriousness of the Polish situation but continued to express confidence that agreement could be reached with Warsaw.[42] Moreover, he continued to insist that the western states, and not the Poles, constituted the primary obstacle to peace. The split in allied ranks was sufficiently apparent, however, that from mid-February Lenin began to shift his fire from the allies in general to the French in particular. By the end of February Moscow had become aware of both the Polish demand for the frontiers of 1772 and French efforts to arm Pilsudski's army. Lenin responded by sharpening both the focus and tone of his rhetoric. "We know that France is inciting Poland," he said on 1 March, "flinging millions into that country, because France is bankrupt anyhow and is now putting her last stake on Poland." The Polish ruling classes, he said, were foolishly doing the French bidding. "Since Poland responds to our peace proposal by silence, since she continues to give a free hand to French imperialism, which is inciting her to a war against Russia, since fresh trainloads of munitions are arriving in Poland every day and the Polish imperialists threaten to start a war on Russia," he warned, "we say, 'Just try it! You'll get a lesson you'll never forget.'"[43]

In March the Bolsheviks redoubled their effort to conclude peace with Poland. At this time a representative of French interests wishing to resume commercial relations with Russia on the basis of the January Supreme Council resolution had reached Copenhagen and opened talks with Litvinov. Although the agent did not represent the French government, he communicated with his principals through the Quai d'Orsay, and anything said to him was certain to reach official circles. Litvinov took this opportunity to inform Paris that once France abandoned its effort to destroy the revolution in Russia, Moscow was prepared to establish cordial relations. The Soviet government was quite prepared to pay its debts, he said, but could not do so until peace was restored in eastern Europe. Chicherin also instructed Litvinov to suggest to the Poles and the French that, if they refused to make peace Moscow could ally herself with a resurgent Germany. "Reports have reached us," he wrote, "that the Ludendorff circle wishes to join us against Poland." Chicherin said the Soviet government would not adopt such a policy but added that "those who are spreading slander about [Soviet] intentions against Poland" should be made aware of this overture. Should the Poles march on Moscow the German militarists might attack them in the rear. In such an event Warsaw could expect little aid from the French whose army, according to Ludendorff, had lost much of its military effectiveness.[44]

NEITHER THE THREAT OF German involvement nor the direct appeal to France represented the main line of Soviet policy. In the future Moscow would pursue variants of both, sometimes simultaneously, but in early 1920 the Soviet position was too tenuous to essay *die Grossepolitik*. Poland, therefore, had to remain the focus of Soviet policy and in early March Chicherin turned again to Warsaw with a further peace proposal. In it he expressed regret at the failure of the Polish government to respond substantively to earlier Soviet initiatives, but reaffirmed the absence of any aggressive intent against Poland. Despite the Polish resumption of hostilities he promised the Red Army would not retaliate by undertaking major military operations of its own. He concluded with the hope that the Polish government would no longer delay the opening of negotiations.[45] Not all Soviet leaders approved this initiative. Litvinov warned that in Copenhagen it was seen as a sign of weakness, and Trotsky agreed. The views of other Soviet leaders are not known, but no further initiative was taken prior to Poland's agreement at the end of March to open the long-delayed negotiations. In mid-month, when Poland's peace conditions became generally known, another argument broke out among Soviet leaders. Chicherin did not wish to address these conditions until they were officially communicated to the Soviet government, Trotsky considered it a mistake to ignore them. To do so, he said, would mislead the Poles and induce them "to think that we shall accede to their terms and [would] make the Poles go further along a path which will inevitably end in war." Again the opinion of other Soviet leaders is unknown, but the Bolsheviks took no official position on the Polish terms at this time. Lenin defended this policy when addressing the Ninth Congress of the Russian Communist Party on 29 March. War preparations, he said, were then under way in states bordering Russia. "That is why we must manoeuvre so flexibly in our international policy and adhere so

firmly to the course we have taken, that is why we must be prepared for anything."
He was satisfied with the way "the war for peace" had been conducted – "with
extreme vigour ... yielding splendid results." Yet the measures taken for peace,
he warned, had to "be accompanied by intensified preparedness for defence."[46]

These preparations had been accelerated in the previous two months. Soviet
leaders devoted increasing time to the needs of the western and southwestern
fronts, but given operations elsewhere, they could not send significant reinforcements.[47] By the end of February, Lenin considered the situation so serious that
he wired Trotsky, then at Ekaterinburg, that it was "essential to take emergency
measure for the rapid delivery to the Western Front of everything that can be
got from Siberia and the Urals." But there was not much to be had from these
areas: both had already been drained to reinforce other fronts of the civil war.
By early March Lenin even began to consider drawing on the strategically
important Caucasus front for reinforcements.[48] The situation soon grew more
threatening, for at this time, Pilsudski undertook a limited offensive to improve
the position of his army. The Poles advanced beyond Borisov and Mozyr, ac-
centuating the separation between the Soviet western and southwestern fronts
and virtually severing direct contact between them. The depleted ranks of the
Soviet armies could not hold the Poles who moved up easily to take the positions
they wanted.[49] On 11 March Lenin wired Smilga and Ordzhonikidze, saying
that as the Poles appeared determined to wage war, the main focus of Soviet
defence was no longer the Caucasus but "preparation for the most rapid rede-
ployment of a maximum of troops to the Western Front." This position was
subsequently formulated as a government directive to the high command, who
then began the reinforcement of the western and southwestern fronts, including
an order for Budenny's entire First Horse Army to be redeployed to the southwest.
While awaiting these reinforcements, Soviet troops in Ukraine were ordered to
stand on the defensive.[50]

Pilsudski's preparations for this forthcoming campaign included a vigorous
diplomatic offensive among most of Poland's neighbours, seeking to enlist them
in the military operations about to begin. Pilsudski had little difficulty in per-
suading Petliura to ally himself with Poland, but the other governments proved
more difficult. Ideally, he would have liked to lead a coalition of the entire
borderland stretching from Finland to Romania, but this was impossible because
Poland was at war with Lithuania and Estonia had just concluded peace with
Moscow. Pilsudski was left with a possible alliance with Finland, Latvia, and
Romania. To promote this design he summoned a conference of borderland states
to assemble in early March at Warsaw. He wanted them, under Polish direction,
to agree not to make peace until the Soviet government had accepted all their
demands. In short, Pilsudski was asking his neighbours to underwrite his demand
for the frontiers of 1772. They were not impressed. In exchange he offered to
underwrite their territorial claims on Soviet Russia, but this did not amount to
much. Many Finns dreamed of a Greater Finland extending to the White Sea

and beyond, but the incumbent regime in Helsingfors sought more modest frontiers which, with the exception of portions of East Karelia, they already possessed. The same was true of Romania, which already held Bessarabia and did not aim at further conquests.[51] In the case of Latvia, Moscow held no territory claimed by Riga. The Poles in fact occupied much of Latgall themselves and told Riga that they would not yield this province unless the Latvians agreed to join the campaign against Soviet Russia. Neither this nor the assertion that Lithuania was an "internal" problem of Poland endeared Warsaw to Riga.[52] As a result, the conference broke up at the end of March having served only to expose the issues dividing Poland and her neighbours.

The Soviet government did not remain idle in the face of this Polish diplomatic offensive. It launched a political counter-attack designed to promote Moscow's preferred solution of eastern European problems. Essentially this was the acknowledgment, within generous frontiers, of the sovereignty and independence of the borderland states in exchange for the conclusion of peace and regularization of relations with Soviet Russia. The successful execution of this policy became increasingly important, for failure threatened not only to magnify Soviet security problems in eastern Europe but also undercut the Soviet effort to make peace with the allies. Although France and Poland did their best to prevent peace between Soviet Russia and its neighbours, Moscow was aided by a general fear felt throughout the region of becoming too closely linked with what many saw as Polish adventurism and megalomania. The demand for the frontiers of 1772 heightened this fear. The British viewed it with derision and sought an end to hostilities in eastern Europe. British permissiveness, therefore, licensed those who wished peace with Moscow and now moved to end hostilities with the Bolsheviks.

PEACE WITH FINLAND WAS of special importance to Moscow. No other border state, except Poland, posed a greater threat to Soviet security, for Finnish armed forces held the fate of Petrograd in their hands. Moscow, therefore, had good reason for satisfaction when at the end of February, following the fall of Murmansk, the Finns urgently asked that the Red Army not pursue the Whites into the Karelian parishes of Porajarvi and Repola. In exchange they promised to disarm and intern the anti-Bolsheviks and, at a later time, regulate the international status of the two parishes.[53] Two days later Chicherin replied affirmatively. He said the Red Army would not enter the parishes. But this could only be a temporary arrangement and was entirely contingent upon the Finns actually interning the White troops. This and other questions, he said, could only be fully regulated at a peace conference which should be convened as quickly as possible. Chicherin's message created a sensation at Helsingfors. To avoid the loss of Porajarvi and Repola it was felt the government would have to open negotiations with Moscow. "The procedure is classic," reported the French minister to Finland. "One must recognize that Chicherin has executed it ably."[54]

A cabinet crisis followed. On 4 March 1920 three ministers resigned, bringing down the government of Juko Vennola. The mutual recrimination which followed was heavily laced with the rhetoric of Finnish nationalism. This caused Chicherin to warn Lenin on 21 March that there has been "an outburst of chauvinism in Finland" and Soviet Russia should "be ready on the military side for anything."[55] The same day he addressed a telegram to Helsingfors calling attention to the failure of the Finnish government to address the question of peace. Helsingfors, he said, had before it "the choice of either very favourable results for Finland if it decides on immediate negotiations with Russia or the renunciation of such results if it engages itself in coalitions hostile to the Russian Republic."[56]

The Soviet peace bid struck a sympathetic note in Helsingfors. On 14 March, in what the French minister saw as an editorial intended by the Finnish Foreign Ministry to prepare public opinion for a change in policy, the *Helsingin Sanomat* noted the lifting of the allied blockade of Russia and Moscow's desire for peace. "It goes without saying," it concluded, "that we are obliged to take these facts into consideration." The following day R. Erich succeeded in forming a new government. Holsti remained as foreign minister and the careful examination of Soviet peace overtures continued.[57] For the moment, however, under joint Franco-Polish pressure, Holsti continued to temporize. Thus on 18 March he wired Moscow, complaining that the Red Army had occupied villages within Porajarvi.[58] The following week he proposed the establishment of a neutral zone between Repola and Pechenga. Chicherin responded that this was tantamount to an armistice and suggested that negotiations begin at Petrograd in four days. This was not what Holsti had in mind; he wanted some unilateral Soviet concession before agreeing to talks. He, therefore, responded on 28 March asking Moscow to evacuate Pechenga before the beginning of negotiations. Chicherin would have none of this and replied that questions of substance could only be discussed when actual negotiations began. Holsti finally agreed to open negotiations but suggested they be held in Rajajoki, a small town on the Finnish side of the border with Russia.[59]

The failure of the Warsaw conference was also the signal for the other border states to seek improved relations with the Bolsheviks. Thus, on 31 March Estonia concluded a trade treaty with Soviet Russia. This was important, because Estonia remained Moscow's only link with the outside world and the pact served to protect Soviet commerce in the event of a war with Poland.[60] The Soviet government also placed a high value on improved relations with Latvia. Although an armistice had already been concluded, it had not worked well and required improvement. The front line of the two armies were too close and spontaneous hostilities erupted continually. This had not led to serious fighting, but in the tenuous circumstances of early 1920, with both Poland and France urging Latvia to attack Moscow, the army clearly possessed considerable scope for mischief. Chicherin proposed to enlarge the neutral zone between the two armies. The Red Army, he told Riga, would unilaterally withdraw farther east. He asked the

Latvians to withdraw westward for the same distance. Unofficially he said they could have peace on the advantageous terms already accepted by Estonia. Like its neighbours, however, Latvia did not act until the Warsaw conference had ended in failure. Then, still smarting from the Polish threat to retain Latgall, Riga proposed, on 26 March, that peace talks begin immediately. The Soviet government suggested talks begin in Moscow on 5 April 1920.[61]

Similar, yet sharper, circumstances led Lithuania to move towards Moscow. Relations with Poland remained bad, and Kovno was determined to take advantage of the impending Soviet-Polish crisis to strengthen its own position. Lithuania had not even been invited to the Warsaw conference and therefore felt even less constrained than the other Baltic states in making overtures to Soviet Russia. In particular, Kovno was outraged that the Poles had recently advanced still farther into Lithuanian territory south of Dvinsk. Fully aware they would receive no help from either the allies or Germany, the Lithuanians resolved to seek advantageous terms from Moscow. On 31 March Kovno informed the Soviet government of its readiness to conclude peace provided the Bolsheviks would recognize the independence of Lithuania within its ethnographic boundaries. These were specified as including, broadly speaking, the former provinces of Vilno and Grodno.[62] As they were the prime bone of contention between Warsaw and Kovno, this was an invitation to Moscow to involve itself in the Polish-Lithuanian dispute. Moscow declined to take sides. Although prospects for peace with Poland appeared dim, the Soviets did not want to provoke Pilsudski prior to the opening of negotiations. So Moscow responded diplomatically, saying that "the question of assignment of this or that town will also be left to the conference." The two states shortly agreed to open negotiations in early May.[63]

The addition of Latvia and Lithuania to the states either negotiating or actually at peace with Soviet Russia was of great importance, for it freed the right wing of the Soviet western front from the threat of attack. The Bolsheviks could now breathe more easily and devote their full attention to Poland.

IN SEEKING TO ISOLATE Poland, Moscow also sought to engage the governments of Romania and Czechoslovakia in negotiations aimed at regularization of relations. The opening of relations with Romania was of special importance, for with the collapse of Denikin the Red Army quickly moved westward to the Dniester. Across the river lay Bessarabia. Bucharest avidly sought international recognition of its annexation while Moscow refused to acknowledge its loss. Seemingly, therefore, a community of interest should have existed between Romania and Poland. It did not, or at least was insufficient to overcome political forces driving the two apart. The Romanians feared being involved in an endless war in pursuit of unattainable Polish objectives. Thus, the Poles, while refusing even to discuss the location of their future frontier, absurdly insisted that the Romanians bind themselves absolutely to its military defence.[64] Bucharest was not even certain that it was in its best interest to see Ukraine fall under Polish domination. Still, Romania was painfully aware that it had taken Bessarabia from Russia and the triumphant Bolsheviks might seek to retrieve it. In that event Polish aid would be most welcome. They could not, therefore, reject the Polish proposals out of hand.

Bucharest fretted, in the presence of so many other peace overtures, at the failure of Moscow to address a similar bid to themselves.[65] It was with substantial relief, then, that they received a message from Chicherin on 24 February proposing that Romania open negotiations for a regularization of relations. The note had been carefully drafted to leave no doubt about the Soviet desire for peace while simultaneously conveying a slight hint of menace should the proposal be rejected. "The *successful military operations* of the armies of both the Russian and Ukrainian Soviet Republics have created the *urgent necessity* for Russia and Romania to begin negotiations to regulate through mutual agreement the relations of their two peoples," wrote Chicherin. Moscow, he said, believed that "all contentious issues, including all territorial questions [read: Bessarabia], could be settled by way of negotiation."[66]

This placed the Romanians on the same footing as the Poles, and like their northern neighbours, they turned to the allied powers for advice. There they confronted the same schizophrenia as Warsaw. France would not suggest peace; Britain would not counsel war. Bucharest, however, had already made up its mind to open negotiations, and on 3 March accepted the Soviet proposal. Chicherin lost no time in suggesting that the talks be held in Kharkov, but this was unacceptable to Bucharest. Instead, the Romanians proposed Warsaw, a choice they must have known would prove unpalatable to Soviet Russia.[67]

Poland and Romania were also divided by their aspirations in central Europe. Romania had aggrandized itself not only at the expense of Russia in Bessarabia but also of Hungary in Transylvania. Hungarian-Romanian relations remained very strained, therefore, and were unlikely to improve in the future. Poland, on the other hand, was on excellent terms with Budapest and wished to cooperate with Hungary against Czechoslovakia. The latter, like Romania, had benefited at Hungary's expense, receiving Slovakia from the failing Magyars in 1918. Czechoslovakia had also quarrelled with Poland over the important coal-mining and transportation centre of Teschen while aspiring to a leadership role in central and eastern European affairs which Poland found unpalatable and offensive. Poland would have liked to see the collapse of Czechoslovakia with Ruthenia passing to itself and Slovakia reverting to Budapest, thus creating a common Polish-Hungarian frontier. Revisionism of this sort appalled the Romanians and caused them to fear for the safety of Transylvania. It also drew them more closely to Czechoslovakia in defence of their respective acquisitions from Hungary. Czechoslovakia opposed Polish aggrandizement and was certain to counter it by every available means. As the crisis with Poland began to mount, therefore, Moscow, on 25 February, turned to Prague with the same peace proposals conveyed to other east European capitals.[68]

Eduard Benes, the Czechoslovakian foreign minister, greeted this initiative with quiet satisfaction. He had no love for Bolshevism but he wanted an end to foreign intervention in the Russian civil war. Peace with Moscow would lay the basis for what he hoped would be a large and expanding role for Czechoslovakia in the new Russia. Needless to say, he opposed Pilsudski's apparent intention of continuing the war against Soviet Russia. Successful Polish aggrandizement would greatly weaken Czechoslovakian political influence; failure would per- petuate east European instability which Benes saw as threatening the very ex- istence of the new Czech state. After receiving contradictory allied advice on how to respond to the Soviet initiative, he signalled Chicherin on 10 April that Prague was ready to open negotiations.[69] He proposed to send a commission to Moscow to "enter into contact with Russian authorities and study, on the one hand, the question of [Czech] nationals and prisoners of war in Russia, and, on the other hand, the question of our future economic relations. The commission could also determine what other problems needed to be examined." On 22 April Chicherin greeted this proposal with satisfaction, agreeing that Benes could send a Czech commission of inquiry to Moscow, while announcing that he would send a similar body to Prague.[70] The political isolation of Poland was complete. Warsaw would have to face Soviet Russia alone.

PILSUDSKI DID NOT MIND. He would have enjoyed leading the other eastern European states into battle, but he did not think their absence impaired his military advantage. If they did not recognize Polish hegemony now, they would when he had smashed Soviet Russia. His preparations were nearly complete, and he was eager to proceed with his plan. This included a much-belated positive response to the persistent Soviet demand for peace talks. Pilsudski, of course, had no intention of negotiating anything. Count Skrzynski, the Polish minister in Romania, informed his French colleague in late March: "Our response is so firm, our demands so extensive that the Bolsheviks will be unable to accept them. Then it is war. It will take place."[71] The Polish note of 27 March informed Chicherin that Poland was prepared to open negotiations at Borisov, on the Smolensk-Minsk road, beginning on 10 April. On being informed of the dispatch of Soviet representatives, the Poles promised to suspend hostilities for twenty- four hours in the vicinity of that city.[72]

This tardy response was not well received in Moscow. The Soviet government had wanted a general armistice and the Polish offer of a limited cessation of hostilities was unacceptable. Nor did the Soviets like the idea of sending their plenipotentiaries into the Polish lines as if they were abjectly suing for peace. On 28 March Chicherin rejected the "merely local and temporary cessation of hostilities" as well as Borisov as a suitable site for negotiations. Instead he suggested a general armistice with talks to take place in some neutral country, perhaps Estonia. Warsaw refused.[73] Chicherin immediately saw the significance of this rejection. The Poles, he wrote Lenin on 2 April, were seeking "the most advantageous way for them to let things blow up in the eyes of public opinion." He received authority to reject Borisov again, and in his reply placed the entire responsibility for the continuation of the war on the Poles, questioning the sincerity of their professed desire for peace. He could not agree to hold peace talks at a site in the midst of a war zone and wholly unequipped for a major conference. While the Soviet government still favoured an Estonian city, they would also agree to Moscow, Petrograd, or even Warsaw.[74]

The Soviet position proved embarrassing to Warsaw. Both foreign and domestic critics began to ask why Pilsudski, created Marshal of Poland on 3 April, refused a general armistice and any site other than Borisov. The Poles replied that the nature of warfare in eastern Europe made a cessation of hostilities along a front of more than a thousand kilometres "difficult to arrange." They also expressed fear of the effect of Bolshevik propaganda on their war-weary troops and said they wished to avoid fraternization among soldiers of the opposing armies. Bolshevik propaganda was also given as the reason for insisting on Borisov. Communication facilities there were sufficient to link the two delegations with their capitals but would not permit the distribution of Soviet propaganda. They had to reject any major city, even Warsaw, as offering too good a stage for the expression of Bolshevik propaganda.[75]

This was casuistry. Pilsudski gave his real reasons to French representatives in Warsaw. He rejected a general armistice, he told Henrys, because he enjoyed a substantial military advantage and wanted to make the most of it. He wanted to be able to attack at the time and place of his choosing and did not wish to impede his freedom of action. Borisov was essential to his plan. He had chosen it for the same reason the Bolsheviks rejected it: it was located in the very midst of the war zone. Heavily armed Polish soldiers were everywhere, and he hoped their presence would intimidate his enemies. Most important, however, he controlled access to the town. He could not only stop the Bolsheviks from using the conference for propaganda purposes but prevent anyone else from influencing either the Soviet or Polish delegations. He told the French that he feared British influence should the conference meet anywhere other than his armed camp, but there is no reason to suppose that he wanted any other influence – foreign or domestic – to intrude upon what he clearly viewed as *his* negotiations.[76] The Soviet refusal to meet at Borisov surprised many at Warsaw, who had expected that their proposals would be accepted without discussion. Pilsudski was not among them; he was quite content to have the conference fail. In his reply to Chicherin on 7 April, therefore, he struck a lordly pose and rejected the Soviet position entirely. His note was a virtual ultimatum saying that the Polish government considered a further exchange of notes about the character and place of negotiations to be pointless.[77]

The Polish note created alarm in Moscow. Chicherin wrote to Gukovskii and Litvinov, his only two representatives abroad, that Warsaw was playing a double game. While preparing for war they were trying to convince their own people and foreign governments of their readiness to make peace. The foreign commissar devised a new strategy to cope with this double game. Instead of merely continuing the fruitless argument with Warsaw, he now turned to the western powers. On 8 April, in identical notes he advised the British, French, Italian, and American governments of the impasse in negotiations and sought assistance in identifying a conference site acceptable to both Poland and Russia. It was in their interest to do so, because Poland's continuing belligerency hindered the restoration of commercial relations and threatened the economic recovery of all Europe. It was simply intolerable and "unprecedented in diplomatic history that peace negotiations should fail to materialize because no agreement could be reached as to the place of negotiations." As the western powers were clearly able to influence Poland, he asked them to urge Warsaw to accept some site other than Borisov. Moscow would accept "any town in a neutral country, or of the Entente, even London or Paris," but would not meet in a military zone or near it.[78]

Chicherin's proposal had the desired effect of throwing the onus of failure to negotiate squarely on Poland. Neither the British nor the French were prepared to host a Soviet-Polish peace conference, but the Foreign Office told the Polish chargé d'affaires on 19 April that Whitehall thought the Polish government should "modify their uncompromising attitude with regard to the place of meeting." The French, of course, took no official position on this issue, but were delighted by anything which caused trouble for Moscow. All the same, Hector de Panafieu, the new French minister in Poland, viewed the emerging crisis with less equilibrium. He thought Pilsudski's ambitions vastly exceeded Poland's resources and military confrontation with Soviet Russia might lead to wholly unanticipated consequences. Paris, too, feared Pilsudski's megalomania but not to the extent that it was prepared to prevent him from attacking Moscow.[79]

The Soviet appeal took the Polish government by surprise. They blamed the British. The Polish minister in Rome told his French colleague that Warsaw "had serious reason to believe that London had inspired the tactics and pretensions of the Soviet government." Patek in particular was startled. Panafieu described him as "assez désemparé." It was decided to send Patek to Paris for discussions on how to counter the Bolshevik propaganda victory. Pilsudski, however, had no doubts and simply continued to prepare for war.[80]

One preparation was to conclude negotiations with Petliura. The failure to reach agreement with the other border states lent special importance to an accord with the Ukrainian National Republic. If Pilsudski had to abandon his dream of marching into battle at the head of a grand alliance of border states, he still did not wish to undertake the campaign alone. Although the Ukrainian National Republic was unable to contribute real strength to the Polish offensive, it could offer a certain camouflage for the naked aggression involved. Warsaw had no difficulty in convincing the powerless Petliura to sign a treaty of alliance. In it he abandoned his claim to all territories (East Galicia, western Volynia, Polesia, and Kholm) demanded by Pilsudski. In exchange the Poles recognized the sovereignty of the Ukrainian National Republic on all other territories which it claimed, including those within the Polish frontiers of 1772 – in other words, much of the area which Poland demanded from Soviet Russia. Petliura also pledged not to conclude any international agreements directed against Poland and guaranteed full cultural rights to Polish residents of Ukraine. Supplementary military and economic agreements subordinated the Ukrainian army and economy to the control of Warsaw. All agreements were signed on 21 April.[81]

The realization of a second objective – the reversal of Finland's refusal to bind itself to Warsaw – proved more difficult. The Poles had expected greater success in securing the cooperation of Finland. The Finnish delegates at the Warsaw conference had proved quite sympathetic and, despite strict orders from Helsingfors, had signed political, military, and economic conventions binding their country to Poland in its confrontation with Moscow. Their work had promptly been disavowed when they returned home. Nevertheless, the Polonophiles of Finnish politics did obtain their government's agreement that neither country would conclude peace with Soviet Russia without the consent of the other. The Poles acccepted in advance that "grave circumstances, foreign or domestic" might compel Finland to treat separately with Moscow. If so, Helsingfors promised to give Poland suitable warning.[82]

While negotiating with Poland the Finns had also begun to talk with the Russians. "The Finns are running with the hare and hunting with the hounds," one member of the Foreign Office commented.[83] Negotiations for an armistice began at Rajajoki on 12 April. Although inconclusive, they were important as the first face-to-face meeting of the two since 1918. The Soviets offered Helsingfors the frontier of 1914 and the neutralization of Repola and Porajarvi. They asked that Finnish armed forces be withdrawn from the two parishes while promising that the Red Army would not occupy them. The Finns for their part asked the Soviets to evacuate the western portion of the Kola peninsula, East Karelia west of the Murmansk railway, and the northern portion of the Olonetz region to the river Svir. Neither would budge from its initial position, and when the Finns demanded a more acceptable Soviet proposal, the Bolsheviks broke off negotiations on 24 April. The rupture would be only temporary, they said, to allow them to consult Moscow, but they left at once for Petrograd. The breach did not imply a resumption of hostilities. Neither side wished renewed fighting,[84] but both realized their future relations would be greatly influenced by the armed conflict about to erupt in the south.

Pilsudski now made his final preparations. On 16 April he discussed his invasion plans with General Henrys, who reported that Pilsudski intended to strike his major blow at Soviet forces in Ukraine. He hoped to destroy the armies of the Soviet southwestern front and advance to the Dnieper, install Petliura at Kiev, and detach Ukraine from Moscow. The following day Poland went on a full wartime footing. The borders were closed, and railway, telegraph, and radio traffic came under military control. On 23 April Pilsudski, accompanied by General Henrys, left Warsaw for Rovno from where he intended to direct his invasion of Ukraine.[85]

The Red Army was not ready for this challenge. Soviet resources were simply stretched too thinly to allow the timely reinforcement of the western and south-western fronts. Still, even as the Polish army attacked, the Red Army high command was sending troop trains into Ukraine and White Russia. Far to the east, Budenny's First Horse Army, having just driven Denikin from the Kuban, had begun to ride northwest towards Kiev. It could not reach the Ukraine before Pilsudski had a virtually free run on the Dnieper, but it would arrive in force by early summer.[86] Then the real test of arms would begin. Henrys, a sympathetic supporter of Pilsudski, had written: "Given the present situation of the two armies the possibilities envisaged by the Chief of State do not appear exaggerated. But if active operations are prolonged it might prove difficult to assure the maintenance of the Polish army." Despite French support, the Polish army still lacked essential equipment, and the strain which combat would place on the primitive supply service would not improve matters.[85] Pilsudski was well aware of his army's deficiencies; he was counting on the Red Army being in even worse shape. That this army had defeated Yudenich, Kolchak, and Denikin impressed him not at all. They were all Russian officers and had organized their armies on the old tsarist pattern. Pilsudski held both the Russian officer corps and their creations in sovereign contempt. He had little more respect for the Red Army, which was still commanded almost entirely by Russians. It had not yet met a worthy opponent; Pilsudski intended to make good this deficiency.

CHAPTER THIRTEEN

"A frantic acceleration of the offensive against Poland" : Soviet policy in eastern Europe, April-August 1920

Pilsudski launched his offensive with a proclamation saying that Polish troops came as liberators and would remain in Ukraine only until its people were able to defend themselves from Russia. Petliura, in a proclamation of his own, warmly thanked Poland for its fraternal assistance and called for the support of all Ukrainians in the task of national reconstruction.[1] Initially Pilsudski achieved striking success. His cavalry advanced eighty kilometres in two days, seizing the important centres of Berdichev and Zhitomir. Soon afterwards they severed communications between the Soviet Twelfth and Fourteenth Armies. It was an unequal struggle and the shattered Soviet divisions poured back towards the Dnieper. There they had to meet another Polish force advancing from Belorussia to meet Pilsudski's main forces in Ukraine. The junction of Polish forces at the confluence of the Pripet and Dnieper rivers established a continuous front from Lithuania to the Romanian frontier. They then advanced to Kiev, which fell on 7 May.[2]

This apparent disaster did not alarm the Soviet high command. Although momentarily unable to repel the Polish offensive, they had longer-term plans well in hand. In particular they kept close tabs on the First Horse Army as it rode west across southern Ukraine to its assembly point on the right bank of the Dnieper south east of Kiev. "The present advance of the Polish front to the east, to Kiev, is advantageous for us," wrote S.S. Kamenev, the Soviet supreme commander, "because inevitably it will lead to the extension of the Polish right flank which will be left hanging in air."[3] The Soviet government reflected the confidence of their generals. Men who had lived through the great military emergencies of 1918 and 1919 did not find that of 1920 especially daunting. Lenin said he had no "doubt that this new attempt by the Entente imperialists to strangle Soviet Russia [would] fall through just as the Denikin and the Kolchak ventures [had]." This highlighted the Soviet belief that Pilsudski had been unleashed by the Entente, or at least by France. Poland was dismissed disparagingly. "On the part of Poland itself," Trotsky wrote, "the war bears a plainly Bonapartist character, even if this is only third-rate Bonapartism, caricatural, low-powered, literary, combining romanticism with petty knavery: ... in a word ... Pilsudski."[4]

In the days immediately following the Polish invasion, another element emerged in the Bolshevik analysis. Soviet leaders had not abandoned their belief in the ultimate success of the world workers' revolution, but recently they had concluded that their need for peace was so great as to compel discretion in the pursuit of their revolutionary aspirations. Discretion, however, was distasteful to the Bolsheviks and only grudgingly accepted. Real progress towards peace was needed to justify it, and, given the Polish invasion and their own stunning success in the Caucasus, its value seemed less apparent than before. Bolshevik minds again turned to thought of revolutionary foreign policy. War and revolution were closely entwined in their ideology, and experience had taught them that the former served to promote the latter. Lenin ascribed the tenacity of the western bourgeoisie in seeking to destroy Bolshevism to the awareness that they were fighting "to retain power at home, and that it is not the Russian or the Polish question that is being decided, but the question of their own survival."[5]

It was in Poland, however, that Bolshevik leaders expected the war to have its most immediate effect. They saw Poland as being ripe for revolution. The sharpening class struggle, they believed, had driven the Polish bourgeoisie to support such an arch adventurer as Pilsudski and seek their salvation in war against Soviet Russia. Trotsky asserted that "the Polish bourgeoisie have themselves placed their fate on the table ... They have backed themselves into a corner, for there can be no doubt about the outcome of this war. The *szlakhta* and bourgeoisie of Poland will be destroyed. The Polish proletariat will transform their land into a socialist republic." One further revolutionary possibility interested Lenin. In his view the Entente had driven Poland to attack Soviet Russia "in order to widen the barrier and deepen the gulf separating the proletariat of Germany from us."[6] Lenin had never abandoned the importance he attached to revolution in Germany. Revolution there, he believed, was likely to spread to all of Europe. Thus Lenin hoped to shatter the barrier erected to keep Germany and Soviet Russia apart.

Soviet leaders, therefore, viewed this unwanted war with considerable optimism. Initially their major concern was the British. Whitehall had just opened negotiations for the surrender of the Volunteer Army, but in the days following the Polish attack London fell silent. This led to a review of the entire basis of Soviet foreign policy, which until then had been aimed at consolidating Soviet Russia's international position through a negotiated settlement with Britain. If the British government had decided to back Pilsudski, then the Bolsheviks had to find another fulcrum on which to base their foreign policy. Bolshevik thought turned almost instinctively to Germany, and for a moment the Soviet government considered sending Krasin to Berlin. Such a mission, Chicherin advised Litvinov, "would exert pressure on Britain, because she has always feared a Russian economic agreement with Germany, but it is permissible only if the British have already turned against us, and our hostile step serves as punishment for their own hostility." A final decision, therefore, could not be made until British intentions were clear. Fortunately this did not take long. That same day Curzon responded he was ready to continue negotiations for the surrender of Denikin's army.[7] This was interpreted in Moscow as meaning that the basic line of British policy remained unchanged. On 5 May Chicherin informed Litvinov that the Soviet government had decided Krasin would go to London as planned. The same day Lenin took Curzon's note as sufficient warrant to gloat publicly that "the imperialist powers cannot take a single serious step in political matters without disagreeing ... no matter how the representatives of the imperialist powers ... try to reassure us that there is full unanimity among the Allies, we know that this is not the case."[8]

These were comforting words, but somewhat misleading. Lloyd George continued to seek a settlement with Moscow, but his policy enjoyed little support. He said the Poles had "gone rather mad," predicted that they would be defeated, and branded them "a menace to the peace of Europe."[9] This was not the Foreign Office view. Sir Horace Rumbold and his staff favoured the Poles and shaped their reports accordingly. In London the Northern Department of the Foreign Office always put the best interpretation on Polish motives while blackening those of the Bolsheviks. Lord Curzon had no sympathy for the Poles but was an ardent Russophobe who loathed the Soviet government. Gregory said the Poles were not guilty of aggression. "They have all along been conducting active operations; the fact they are now making a successful offensive seems hardly a reason for a protest which was not previously forthcoming ... Poland's action may or may not have been wise: but she has done nothing to which we can take exception. Mr. Lloyd George told M. Patek on January 26th that 'Poland must take the full responsibility for deciding as between war and peace.' She has done so and chosen war." This view was adopted by the Foreign Office which blandly denied that the Polish offensive in Ukraine constituted an outbreak of war.[10]

These views became the basis for replies given in the House of Commons to questions concerning British policy in the Soviet-Polish war. They originated as a result of certain awkward coincidences. On 3 May King George V sent a message of congratulation and "sincere good wishes" to Marshal Pilsudski on the occasion of Poland's chief national holiday, the anniversary of the ratification of the Polish constitution of 1791. The telegram and Pilsudski's response were unrelated to the war, but when published on 10 May they created an outcry from all elements in Britain sympathetic to Soviet Russia. The discovery that the War Office was shipping rifles, artillery, and airplanes to Poland elicted an uproar. Investigation revealed that these were the final delivery of weapons assigned to Poland in the previous year, but this made little difference to those who suspected the British government of inciting Polish aggression. British dockers refused to load these weapons and called for the labour movement to join them in opposing support for continued intervention in Russia. Official explanations satisfied few domestic critics of the government and did nothing to relieve Soviet anxiety. Litvinov warned Moscow not to "succumb to the sweet tones" of the messages Curzon sent seeking the negotiated surrender of the Volunteer Army in the Crimea.[11]

While the Soviet international situation remained unclear, their military position improved steadily. By mid-May the Poles had achieved their maximum success, slowly expanding their hold on the left bank of the Dnieper in the direction of Cherkassy. Some optimists even spoke of the impending fall of Odessa.[12] The results, in fact, proved to be ephemeral. By the second week in May Soviet reinforcement had reached a level sufficient to unleash a counter-attack. The bulk of the Polish army was concentrated in Ukraine, so when the Red Army passed to the offensive in Belorussia Pilsudski could not stem the advance. The Poles were taken by surprise and forced to retreat fifty to eighty kilometres in less than two weeks. The Soviet aim was to advance on Vilna, thus separating the Polish and Latvian armies while opening direct communication with Lithuania. By the end of May this objective was nearly achieved.[13]

The primary Soviet counter-attack was being prepared in Ukraine. Throughout the final weeks of May reinforcements, the First Horse Army in the van, arrived in the vicinity of Kremenchug and Ekaterinoslav ready to attack the exposed left flank of the Polish army. Originally the Soviet plan called for a vast encirclement of Pilsudski's forces south of Kiev, with Budenny advancing in his first leap as far west as Berdichev. An undertaking of this type, however, required that virtually all reinforcements be concentrated on the southwestern front. With the western front engaged in its own offensive and the Crimean front coming to life, the Soviet high command could not focus single-mindedly on Ukraine. By early June the scope of the counter-attack had to be reduced. Although the destruction of the Polish army at Kiev remained the Soviet aim, the initial objective was redefined as the region around Fastov rather than the more spectacular leap originally planned. On the morning of 5 June Budenny led his army into the gap between the two Polish forces operating against Cherkassy and Odessa.[14]

Military success, therefore, provided the backdrop for the next round of Anglo-Soviet negotiations. Previously these had been conducted at long distance; now, in late May, Krasin arrived in London to open face-to-face talks with the British government. These concerned much more than the Soviet-Polish war, but throughout much of the summer the eastern European crisis was the focus of negotiation. As before, the Soviet government wanted to know the extent of British support for Poland. In his first meeting with British ministers on 31 May Krasin posed his "first and most important question ... were the two governments to be at war or peace?" He said Moscow believed "the Polish attack would have been quite impossible unless one or more Entente powers had rendered them assistance." Lloyd George denied this, but Krasin replied that the Poles did not have a single munition works and "without such factories they would never have dared to attack Russia unless they had been granted or promised warlike supplies from the Great Powers." Krasin had wanted a clear statement of British policy and he received it. Lloyd George said that he "considered it necessary to emphasize most strongly that Britain had not and was not rendering assistance to Poland." Aid had been promised only if Poland was attacked "in the precincts of her lawful territory" by Soviet Russia. "If, on the other hand, Poland attacks the Soviet Government she does so at her own risk and responsibility and she must herself reckon with the consequences of a step like this." When Krasin asked whether this response was made in the name of all the allies or only that of Britain, Lloyd George replied that this was only Britain's answer. For his part the prime minister also had some concerns. He wanted assurances that the Bolsheviks would cease all anti-British activities in the east and promise not to spread revolutionary propaganda abroad. Throughout the meeting, however, he repeatedly stressed his desire to conclude a trade pact with Moscow.[15]

This satisfied Krasin. He wrote to Chicherin and Litvinov that peace with Great Britain was possible. Lloyd George had spoken in a very friendly and convincing manner. Once it was clear that the negotiations in London were making progress, France and Italy would have to participate and Poland would be forced to make peace. The assurances Lloyd George wanted were not unreasonable. They could be given to obtain a trade treaty. Such a pact was essential, for it would greatly influence other governments.[16]

Other Soviet leaders disagreed. Litvinov believed the amiability of Lloyd George was merely a façade meant to confuse the Soviet government and lead them to make needless concessions in Poland and Persia.[17] Chicherin concurred, seeing Lloyd George's cordiality as chicanery designed "to fleece us of everything we have" while giving nothing in return. In particular he was incensed by the British effort to avoid recognition of the Soviet government and treat political problems within the context of trade talks rather than through formal peace negotiations. Nor was he impressed by the seeming split in the Entente. "France," he wrote, "is only playing that role in international relations that certain elements of the British government themselves support and desire."[18] Most important, Lenin believed his plenipotentiary was being deceived. He believed Britain was aiding both Poland and Wrangel.[19] Chicherin's response of 6 June echoed these thoughts. He told Krasin that Lloyd George was trying to hypnotize him and was seeking to discover Soviet intentions while not revealing his own. This, said Chicherin, was "the purest of swindling" and required great care in negotiations. Lenin simply would not accept British good faith. The same day he instructed Chicherin to admonish Krasin: "That swine Lloyd George has no scruples or shame in the way he deceives; don't believe a word he says and gull him three times as much."[20]

A similar truculence now came to inform Lenin's view of the Polish war, and he began to speak with contempt for his adversaries. Pilsudski and his associates, he said, were characterized by "revolutionary talk, boastfulness, patriotism, chauvinism and sheer claptrap." The next time Soviet Russia talked peace, he said, it would "not [be] with ... the Polish landowners and bourgeoisie, but with the Polish workers and peasants."[21] Reports from the front reinforced this mounting revolutionary militancy. The offensive launched by the First Horse Army in early June achieved immediate success, smashing one Polish army and threatening to isolate another. On 7 June Zhitomir fell; four days later the Red Army entered Kiev. By mid-month the Poles had been thrown back beyond the start line of their April offensive. Worse still, they had no reserves; so when Budenny launched a new offensive at the end of June, he was able to advance almost without opposition. In Warsaw ebullient overconfidence gave way to sullen silence. The American chargé d'affaires, with rare understatement, reported on 12 June that the Poles were "experiencing a feeling of depression."[22]

The military débâcle led to the fall of the Skulski cabinet. On 23 June Ladislas Grabski formed a new government with Prince Sapieha, then Polish minister in London, as foreign minister. The first task of the new government was to seek the aid of all political parties in the organization of national defence. Wincenty Witos, soon to become prime minister in an all-party coalition, wrote of this meeting: "The mood was funereal. After a short pause all eyes turned towards Pilsudski. He sat silent, head lowered, eyes trained on the floor ... Each of us remembered well the recent boasts, his stubbornness, his dislike of peace talks, his disregard of the enemy, and considered him rightly to be the maker of this catastrophe and grief."[23] Nevertheless Pilsudski remained as chief of state; a week later the Sejm appointed him chairman of a new State Defence Council. One of their first acts was to appeal for greatly increased military assistance. In conveying it to the allies, Prince Sapieha warned that the very existence of Poland was at stake as "the Bolsheviks might reach Warsaw in about three weeks' time if not checked."[24]

THE POLISH CRISIS EMERGED in the context of the abrupt termination of the first phase of Anglo-Soviet trade talks and a meeting of allied leaders in Belgium. At the end of June Lloyd George had issued an ultimatum to Krasin, demanding to know if the Soviet government was prepared to accept certain British conditions for the continuation of negotiations. Krasin had been sent to Moscow to obtain the Soviet answer. At the same time Lloyd George had crossed the channel to meet his allied colleagues. The conference had originally been summoned to deal with German problems, but, on arrival, the allied leaders were confronted with the news that the Polish front had collapsed and the Red Army was marching on Warsaw. On 3 July Marshal Foch and Sir Henry Wilson told Millerand and Lloyd George that the Poles were in great danger and something should be done to help them. The British prime minister, who only the day before had described the Poles as lunatics, was not easily moved. There is no precise record of the talk, but Lloyd George is said to have exclaimed that he would do nothing "until Patek came to him cap in hand." Warsaw would have to seek peace with Russia and come to terms with all her other neighbours.[25] Clearly these were conditions the Polish government did not want to accept, but military disaster compelled them to do so. On 6 July Patek, cap symbolically in hand, called on Lloyd George. He was given a stern lecture and asked what Poland wanted. Peace replied Patek, but said the moment was "inopportune" as the Polish army was in flight and to propose peace would give the appearance of weakness. Poland, therefore, wanted war material, "not to make war, but because strength was as necessary to the making of peace as it was to the prosecution of war." Lloyd George inquired if Poland had recently proposed peace, and when given a negative reply made it clear that such a proposal was an absolute prerequisite for any aid the allies might offer. In addition he told Patek that Poland would have to abandon her imperialist policy with regard to Czechoslovakia and Lithuania. "Let Poland accept true nationalism and not imperialism as the basis of its policy," said the prime minister, "and she would find that Great Britain would stick by her loyally."[26]

What aid could the allies offer? Neither Britain nor France could send troops. The best they could do was to rearm the Polish army and send staff officers to improve its efficiency and organization. They could also offer political support, but only if "Poland abandoned in deed, as well as in words, its imperialist and annexationist policy." Grabski, who had just arrived to represent Poland, said that "Poland understood that it was her own fault that she was in this condition, and that she had to change her policy both towards her neighbours and the Allies." This was exactly what Lloyd George wanted to hear and he responded that "if Poland was ready to give assurances to this effect then Great Britain was prepared to consider what steps it could take to press Russia to make peace, and if Russia refused, what help she could give Poland to preserve her independence." Millerand endorsed the British position, pledging that the allied powers "would make every possible effort to give effective help to Poland."[27]

How were the allies to provide that effective help? Soviet acceptance of the British terms Krasin had carried to Moscow provided a possible answer. Lloyd George suggested to Millerand that they accept the Soviet note as a basis for discussion while "tacking on to [it] a proposal for peace with Poland." As it was unlikely that the Soviet-Polish conflict could be settled without reference to many other hotly contested issues, he further suggested that the allies propose a conference be held in London at which representatives of Soviet Russia and its neighbours could negotiate a general peace. France could then "come in as one of the protectors of Poland's independence."[28] This was an audacious proposal, for if accepted it would swing the French government away from their long-standing refusal to negotiate openly with Moscow. He clearly hoped to harness not only Poland and Russia to his eastern European policy but France as well.

Millerand tentatively accepted the plan but then refused to participate in the proposed conference unless Moscow first recognized that it was bound by "the engagements of previous Russian governments towards foreign countries." He insisted that it was politically impossible for him to do otherwise. Lloyd George then announced that if Millerand would not join him the British government would send the memorandum on their own responsibility. The French premier did not object.[29] As a result, when the allied premiers met with Grabski, Lloyd George spoke only for Great Britain. He asked the Poles to seek an immediate armistice from Soviet Russia and to participate in the London conference of east European states. The Polish army was to withdraw to the provisional eastern frontier established by the peace conference in December 1919, except in East Galicia where the two armies would stand on the line held at the time of the armistice. Vilna was to be handed over to Lithuania and the Poles had to accept in advance the frontiers which the Supreme Council would assign them. Grabski found all this very distasteful. He sought to avoid binding agreements but was told that if he "thought that Poland could not only preserve its own independence, but also the rights of Polish peoples beyond the frontier, they had no objective in appealing to the Powers." In the end Grabski had to sign, with certain modifications, the agreement Lloyd George presented him. In exchange the Poles obtained a pledge that if the Russians did not agree to an armistice, the allies would "give Poland all the assistance, especially in war material, which is possible, consistent with their own exhaustion and the heavy liabilities they are carrying elsewhere, to enable the Polish people to defend their independence and national existence."[30]

When Lloyd George informed Moscow of these decisions he added his own sugggestions that the Bolsheviks also sign an armistice with Wrangel, the Whites retire to the Crimea, and Wrangel be invited to London at the time of the conference of east European states. Britain, said the prime minister, was bound "under the Treaty of Peace to defend the integrity and independence of Poland within its legitimate ethnographic frontiers," and asked for "a definite reply within a week as to whether Soviet Russia accepts the aforesaid proposal for putting an end to the war in Eastern Europe."[31]

The British note arrived in Moscow on 12 July and compelled the Soviet government to define their intentions regarding Poland. Soviet leaders had to decide if they were prepared to defy the allied powers. Lenin, who had grown more confident with every passing week that the Red Army could continue its victorious march, took a clear cut stand against accepting the British proposals. "I think that all this is a piece of knavery aimed at the annexation of the Crimea," he wrote Stalin on 12 July. "The idea is to snatch victory out of our hands with the aid of false promises." Trotsky, on the other hand, while rejecting British interference in the Crimea, wanted it "stipulated in one form or another, that we do accept British mediation ... [and] that we agree to negotiations in London." Neither gave a detailed argument in explanation of his position. Trotsky subsequently cited lack of confidence in the Polish revolutionary movement and fear of military disaster as the main reasons for his desire to accept the British offer.[32] By implication Lenin had greater confidence in the Polish Communist

Party and the Red Army. In combination he believed they would succeed in establishing the workers' and peasants' Poland about which he had spoken so frequently since late April.

In any case Lenin was not prepared to slow the advance of the Red Army. On 12 July, after receiving the British proposals, he wrote Sklianskii: "The international situation, especially [the British] proposal (annexation of the Crimea in return for a truce with Poland, the Grodno-Belostok line) demands a frantic acceleration of the offensive against Poland. Can you manage it? All of it? Resolutely?" Even the sober advice of the high command could not shake Lenin's buoyant optimism. Kamenev, in a memorandum of 15 July, warned that the Red Army only had equipment and supplies for a further two months of heavy fighting. This was sufficient, he thought, to capture Warsaw and advance to the German frontier of 1914, but both might prove beyond reach if the other border states, perhaps as a result of western instigation, should come to Poland's assistance. Even complete victory would create serious military problems, he said, for the destruction of Poland would mean a vast enlargement of the front without any appreciable increase in the number of men needed to hold it. The Red Army would be left without reserves and vulnerable to a concentrated attack at any point. This was exactly what had happened to Denikin the previous fall and by implication Kamenev warned the same could happen to a seemingly victorious Soviet Russia in the autumn of 1920.[34]

Similarly Marchlewski and other Polish communists poured cold water on the revolutionary potential of their countrymen. Karl Radek, in particular, argued forcefully against the conceit that *Polish* workers would rise in support of a *Russian*, even Bolshevik, army. Lenin would not listen.[35] He sought out the more congenial advice of I. S. Unshlikht, one of the most militant Polish communists, who assured him that the arrival of the Red Army would trigger a revolution in Poland.[36] Having witnessed the success of combining proletarian internationalism with armed force in other parts of the former Russian empire, Lenin was quite ready to put it to the test in Poland. When the Central Committee met on 16 July only Rykov supported Trotsky's demand for "an immediate conclusion of peace, before the army should grow too exhausted."[37]

The war with Poland would continue, but the decision had to be concealed. Moscow had placed too much emphasis on the pacific nature of its foreign policy suddenly to abandon it. A frank declaration of Soviet policy might well galvanize the Entente to extend effective assistance to Poland. As a consequence, the response to the British telegram was drafted in a highly deceptive manner. Dripping with sarcasm, the note of 17 July nevertheless continued the long-standing Soviet emphasis on seeking peace while projecting an image of reason, generosity, and magnanimity. Chicherin denied that Soviet Russia needed the good offices of Great Britain to conclude peace with Poland. Moscow, he said, had already concluded peace with three of its neighbours, had negotiations under way with two others, and was able to complete the process without outside

Survival and Consolidation

interference. There was no need for a conference of eastern European states. Soviet Russia would not reject a Polish proposal to open peace talks. Generous settlements had been negotiated with Estonia, Georgia, and Lithuania and the Soviet government was prepared to show equal generosity to Poland. Moscow, was even ready "to agree to a territorial frontier more favourable to the Polish nation" than that proposed in the British note of 11 July. Only once did Chicherin even hint at the actual policy of the Soviet government. At the very end of that part of the message dealing with Poland he declared truthfully but opaquely:

Soviet Russia is the more ready to meet the interests and wishes of the Polish people in regard to the terms of peace the farther the Polish people go in their internal life along the road which will create a firm foundation for truly fraternal relations between the working masses of Poland, Russia, the Ukraine, White Russia and Lithuania and will provide a guarantee that Poland will cease to serve as an instrument of aggression and intrigue against the workers and peasants of Soviet Russia and other nations.[38]

The foreign commissar displayed greater candour in regard to the Crimea. He refused to negotiate with Wrangel but again offered an amnesty if his army surrendered. He concluded on a positive note, indicating that the Soviet government wished "to eliminate every conflict between Russia and Great Britain" and placed their hopes for peace in a resumption of the talks suspended at the end of June. Moscow, he said, was sending an "enlarged delegation ... to London with the object of conducting negotiations ... on the basis of the British memorandum of 1 July and the Soviet reply of 7 July."[39]

WHILE THE POLITICIANS sparred at long range the soldiers fought on a battlefield which moved steadily westward. In July the Red Army skilfully exploited their great victories of the previous month. In the south they advanced toward Brest-Litovsk, Lublin, and Lvov. In the north they captured Vilna, Grodno, and Bialystok. Every directive spoke of the need for ever greater efforts to accelerate the offensive and keep the Poles running. By the end of the month Soviet strategists were drafting orders to take Warsaw within three weeks and advance as far west as the German frontier of 1914.[40]

Military success led to a quickening of negotiations with Lithuania. Talks under way since spring became critical as the Red Army approached Vilna. The issue could not be deferred, because the Petrograd-Warsaw railway ran through Vilna, and its possession was vital to Soviet military operations. Initially the Lithuanians demanded territory extending to Minsk and beyond, while Moscow demanded joint military operations against Poland. Allied pressure caused the Lithuanians to choose neutrality and reduce their territorial pretensions to the provinces of Kovno, Vilna, and southern Suwalki. In early May a Lithuanian attack on Poland would have been very helpful to the Red Army; by July it was redundant. Moscow, therefore, was prepared to exchange the disputed provinces for Lithuanian neutrality. A simple expedient was devised to give the territory to Lithuania without impeding Soviet military operations. In the treaty of Moscow, signed on 12 July, the Soviet government recognized Lithuanian sovereignty in the three provinces while a secret annex specified that for the duration of the war with Poland, the Red Army retained the right to use the territory in question. This simply placed a legal gloss upon faits accomplis. The Red Army pushed on towards Warsaw.[41]

Word of the continued advance of the Red Army reached London at the same time as the Soviet note of 17 July. The British cabinet reviewed the crisis at their meeting of 20 July and approved three further measures to deal with it. They agreed to propose to Millerand the sending of an Anglo-French mission to consult the Polish government regarding the proposed armistice, inform the Soviet delegation then at Reval that they could not proceed to London until an armistice had been concluded with Poland, and send a new note to Moscow stressing the great importance the British government attached to the end of hostilities between Poland and Soviet Russia.[42] Curzon sent these messages the same day.

Lenin reacted with scorn and sarcasm. He instructed Chicherin to answer Curzon in an "arch-polite fashion." Chicherin was to wait two days before sending his response – "there is no reason to spoil them."[43] Chicherin's reply of 24 July said that Soviet military authorities had been ordered to open armistice negotiations with the Poles, announced Soviet readiness to send delegates to London to meet the representatives of the "leading powers of the entente" once the surrender of Wrangel and his army had been completed, and expressed his "astonishment" that the British government would suspend trade talks after Moscow had accepted all the conditions for the opening of these negotiations. "Durable, peaceful and friendly relations," he warned, "will be extremely difficult if agreements once adopted are violated on the following day ... or if conditions already accepted are, after the adoptions of agreement, supplemented by new and unexpected conditions not stipulated before."[44]

In different circumstances the British government might have reacted negatively to a lecture of this type, but with the fate of Poland and perhaps central Europe hanging in the balance, Lloyd George was pleased to accept the Soviet reply as sufficient warrant to allow the delegation at Reval to proceed to London. The Foreign Office tried to suggest that it was "perhaps a little early to allow Krassin [sic] back," but Lloyd George and Curzon thought that if Moscow proposed unreasonable terms "we shall be in a better position to modify these with [the Soviet delegation] under our thumb than if they are at a distance." As a consequence Curzon signalled Moscow that the Soviet delegation could proceed to London and suggested that they be authorized not merely to conclude a trade agreement but also "to discuss preliminary arrangements for the proposed peace conference." The Soviet delegation, now led by Lev Kamenev, with Krasin as his deputy, left almost at once for London.[45]

The British also found it difficult to enlist the Poles in their scheme for the pacification of eastern Europe. Pilsudski did not want to accept the conditions imposed upon Grabski, and at first they were not even released to the public. The French minister reported that the Polish government felt humiliated by the necessity of seeking an armistice. The Poles wanted to fight, not negotiate, and continued to ask for military assistance, including allied troops, to throw back the Bolshevik invader. When the British called upon Warsaw to ask for an armistice, the Poles proved refractory.[46] Rumbold was forced to call on Prince Sapieha three times before the Polish government finally asked for an armistice on 22 July. Negotiations did not begin promptly. The Polish proposal, signed by General Tadeuz Rozwadowski, chief of the Polish general staff, asked for talks to begin on 25 July. Radio Moscow, however, said that the text it had received specified talks beginning on 30 July.[47] Either by accident or design the Polish message was mutilated in transmission. Simple operator error or atmospheric disturbance cannot be ruled out. In 1920 radio telegraphy was primitive and atmospheric disturbance, especially in the summer, frequently played havoc with reception. Still it is odd that only one word, and that the most important, was received incorrectly. The fact that neither Pilsudski nor the Bolsheviks were in any hurry to open negotiations and both had agreed to an armistice only to satisfy the British makes design appear a more likely explanation than accident.

But whose design? Both were capable of tampering with the message to delay a cessation of hostilities. The Bolsheviks were determined to capture Warsaw and reach the German frontier of 1914. Pilsudski was already preparing a major counter-attack and did not want anything to stand in its way. Two British documents suggest Polish responsibility for the "error." The first is Rumbold's detailed despatch concerning the difficulties encountered in convincing the Polish government to seek an armistice. In recounting his third interview with Sapieha he reported that the foreign minister had said "that one reason for the delay in the despatch of the radio which he had already prepared, was that, at the last minute the Chief of State had telephoned to say that he wish[ed] to see the text of the message before it was sent out." This referred to the Foreign Ministry note to Chicherin regarding the armistice and not that of Rozwadovski to the Soviet high command. Why did Pilsudski hold this message back? Did he wish to remove any reference to 25 July, the date set for the meeting by the Council of State Defence? In any event, it contained no such reference and only went forward the following afternoon. It was also this message, framed in very general terms, not the highly specific Rozwadovski text, which Sapieha sent Rumbold. The British minister relayed it to London, where it was accepted as proof that Poland had asked for an armistice.[48] Was this bad faith on the part of Pilsudski or were the Bolsheviks responsible? Unfortunately no other documents speak to this question but, given the selective nature of available Soviet records, this silence need not point to Polish responsibility. For the moment the issue must

remain unresolved. It is sufficient to note that while both sides denied responsibility, both believed they would benefit from the delay.[49]

At the end of July the Bolsheviks began to prepare for the destruction of the
existing Polish state. The approach of the Red Army quickened the pace of
Communist Party activity within Poland and facilitated direct communication
with Moscow. Polish communists appealed for Soviet help, and the Politburo
agreed to give it. Since the beginning of the war the Bolsheviks had summoned
an increasing number of Polish communists, active elsewhere in Soviet service,
to Moscow in order to form a cadre of party and state officials to move into
ethnographic Poland with the Red Army. Julian Marchlewski, Felix Dzerzhinskii,
Felix Kon, Edward Próchnik, and Josef Unshilikht were chosen to organize the
future Poland.[50] In late July they moved to Bialystok, where they proclaimed
themselves the Provisional Revolutionary Committee of Poland and announced
their intention, on reaching Warsaw, of creating a Polish Socialist Republic of
Soviets.[51] This followed the classic formula of backing proletarian internationalism with armed force and demonstrated the seriousness of the Bolshevik intention of destroying, not merely defeating, the Pilsudski regime. The political
struggle for the fate of Poland had begun.

Western governments were not certain of the outcome of that struggle. This
had led them to send a mission to report on the political and military situation
in Poland. Its composition reflected allied discord. Lloyd George chose
Sir Maurice Hankey, secretary to the cabinet, and Lord D'Abernon, ambassador
in Berlin. Hankey confided to his diary: "[Lloyd George] knows that I have both
a dislike and contempt for the Poles, and that I don't believe, in the long run,
anything can be done to save them, and finally I am doubtful if they are worth
saving." D'Abernon shared this contempt. Although he wanted to help the Poles,
he did not have much hope of success. To a substantial degree he agreed with
Hankey that it was "inevitable sooner or later that Russia gets a coterminous
frontier with Germany, and that ... we ought to orient our policy so as to make
Germany and not Poland the barrier between eastern and western civilization."[52]
Millerand sent Jules Jusserand, ambassador to the United States, and General
Maxime Weygand, chief of staff to Marshal Foch. Both were militantly anti-
Bolshevik and committed to saving Poland from Soviet Russia. They doubted
the ability of the Poles to defeat the Red Army by themselves, but neither saw
Germany as an alternative barrier to Bolshevism. To them Poland was a bulwark
against both Germany and Russia. They were deeply suspicious of Pilsudski and
certain Polish factions (army officers and bureaucrats who had served Austria-
Hungary before and during the Great War) but were deeply committed to the
preservation of a sovereign anti-Bolshevik Polish state. Polish military and political incompetence was about the only thing the mission could agree upon.
Well before reaching Warsaw they had already decided what needed to be done.
"The impression that one gathers is that Pilsudski has been the evil genius of

Poland," Hankey wrote to Sir Henry Wilson on 23 July; "everyone agreed that the first thing to do was to get rid of him or at the least provide him with a French Chief of Staff to take actual command of the Polish army."[53]

This proved impossible. Although direct contact only heightened their suspicion of Pilsudski, they were unable to remove him from command. The marshal was not even interested in the hundreds of French officers Weygand was able to put at his disposal. "His attitude was clearly inspired by jealousy of any interference with his military arrangements and functions and it was this jealousy," Rumbold reported on 31 July, "which led the Mission not to insist on the appointment of General Weygand as titular Chief of Staff." Instead Weygand agreed "to place his services unreservedly at the disposal of the Polish Chief of Staff."[54] Pilsudski also continued to dominate Polish politics. The State Council of National Defence would not oppose him, and the newly formed all-party government enjoyed no authority. "To-day the peasant Prime Minister [Witos] has gone off to get his harvest in," the scandalized D'Abernon wrote on 27 July, "notwithstanding the grave menace at the gates of the capital!" The tenacity with which Pilsudski clung to power excited ever greater suspicion. First Panafieu then his colleagues voiced the fear that Pilsudski would come to terms with Moscow on the basis of himself heading a Soviet government of Poland.[55] Although absurd, the accusation illustrates the absence of trust between Pilsudski and allied representatives.

THESE DEVELOPMENTS STRONGLY influenced Moscow's attempt to negotiate peace with its other western neighbours. The Soviet-Polish war both enhanced the Soviet desire for peace and encouraged the border states to take advantage of it. Initially Moscow wished to prevent them from allying with Warsaw, but as the tide turned the hope of creating a Soviet government in Poland provided a new rationale for reaching negotiated settlements with the remaining border states.

Peace with Finland was of special importance. Although the Finns were not actually planning to resume hostilities, Moscow could not afford to be taken by surprise.[56] If an armistice could not be negotiated, the Red Army would have to retain troops which were badly needed elsewhere on the Finnish front. The government of Finland did not favour peace. They were not prepared to follow Pilsudski's example, but neither were they ready to accept the terms offered by Moscow. They hoped through further delay to secure additional territories east of the existing frontier and thus satisfy Finnish expansionists. This position was challenged by the Social Democrats who favoured peace and threatened to bring a motion of no-confidence if the government did not change their policy. Dr Erich, the prime minister, had little hope his government would survive such a motion and, therefore, was forced to advise allied representatives that, at the least, he would have to give the appearance of satisfying the socialist demand.[57]

Moscow sought to exploit the problems of the Finnish government. On 11 May, Chicherin addressed another note to Helsingfors in which he proposed convening a formal peace conference. This was not a welcome proposal, but given the political circumstances, the Finnish government was forced to accept it.[58] They were, however, only stalling for time and turned at once to Warsaw proposing that the two act in concert in negotiating with Moscow. Here they encountered difficulty, because Pilsudski was not yet ready to negotiate. He first wanted to reconquer the Polish frontiers of 1772, but the Finns could not wait. On 22 May the Finnish foreign minister proposed that peace negotiations begin at Tartu on 10 June; Chicherin promptly agreed. The fundamental position of the Finnish government, however, remained unchanged. They had again disarmed their socialist opponents and retained a free hand to return to cooperation with Poland. They had promised to meet the Russians but were not bound to conclude any kind of agreement.[59]

From the first day of the peace conference the Finns demanded the cession of Petchenga and East Karelia. Nor would they agree to either an armistice or the clearing of minefields in the Gulf of Finland. At first, they pinned their hopes on Pilsudski regaining the initiative, but as the Poles fell back, Helsingfors again sought western assistance. Holsti asked (unsuccessfully) for a British naval squadron to be sent to the Baltic and when Lloyd George proposed that an eastern European peace conference assemble at London, the Finnish government eagerly agreed.[60] Soviet rejection of this proposal left the Finns at the end of July with little hope for external support of their demands.

The Bolsheviks responded to Finnish intransigence in two ways. At Tartu they offered Helsingfors the frontiers of 1914 and, provided agreement was reached promptly, those portions of East Karelia in which Finland was most interested.[61] In East Karelia they approved the formation of a Karelian Labour Commune which, in best Soviet style, promptly summoned a Congress of representatives of "Karelian toilers." The Congress asked Soviet Russia to liberate Repola and Porajarvi.[62] This put the Finns on notice that if they hoped to annex these districts, they would have to agree, at the very least, to a formal armistice with Soviet Russia. When the Finns ignored this warning, Moscow allowed the commune to continue their own military operations against Repola and Porajarvi. This was sufficient to drive the Finnish Freikorps from them. It began to appear that far from crystallizing in Finland's favour, the new political circumstances of eastern Europe might become frozen in a decidedly hostile configuration. In mid-July when the Bolshevik delegation at Tartu ominously asked for a two-week delay in negotiations to return to Moscow for new instructions, it appeared as if the Finns might face a substantial increase in Soviet demands.[63]

The negotiations resumed at the beginning of August, and Helsingfors soon noted a greater, rather than lesser, Russian willingness to make concessions. The Soviet delegation proposed to postpone negotiation of a definitive peace and concentrate instead on the conclusion of an armistice. They no longer demanded the suppression of paramilitary organizations, the clearing of minefields, or the closing of Finnish ports to warships of states hostile to Soviet Russia. They even agreed to an armistice line which left Porajarvi and Repola under Finnish control. They would not, however, surrender Pechenga. The scope of the concessions caused Helsingfors to give serious consideration to the proposals. The socialists continued to demand peace, and if the government waited any longer Moscow might withdraw these unexpectedly favourable terms. Helsingfors gave its assent and on 13 August the armistice was signed. It did little more than ratify the status quo, for actual hostilities had largely ceased the previous year. The agreement settled no outstanding issues and even provided for a possible resumption of hostilities at the end of a month.[64] Nevertheless, it was of great importance to Soviet Russia. It was very unlikely that Finland, having once concluded an armistice would be able to resume hostilities. Public opinion in general and the socialists in particular were strongly opposed to war. The armistice offered none of the benefits of belligerency or peace, and as a resumption of the former appeared unlikely, the attractions of the latter were likely to increase. Britain was clearly leading the way to the resumption of trade with Russia, and Finnish merchants were just as interested in the Russian market as businessmen elsewhere. The armistice of 13 August 1920, therefore, was a major step in extracting one more state from the quasi-alliance which had confronted Soviet Russia since late 1918. This extraction was significant, for Finland, with the prowess of its army and propinquity to Petrograd, was an important element in any anti-Bolshevik front. Its cessation of hostilities clearly unhinged the entire northern flank of such a front and greatly reduced pressure which could be applied to Soviet Russia from the west.

The armistice also greatly weakened Poland. Finnish participation in the war, never likely, was now rendered even more improbable. Soviet Russia, therefore, enjoyed a freer hand in settling with Poland. The armistice demonstrated once again that Soviet Russia possessed both the will and ability to reach agreement, unassisted, with even such a hostile neighbour as Finland. At a time when Britain was trying to assume the role of peacemaker, and thus potentially arbiter, in eastern Europe, it was important for Moscow to establish its unquestioned ability to conduct an independent policy unfettered by extraneous influence. It was all the more important that this be done, because precisely at the same time Moscow was preparing to liquidate the bourgeois Polish state and create a soviet republic in its place. The outside world, and Britain in particular, would find this far easier to accept if Moscow concluded generous peace settlements with its other, more reasonable, neighbours. Finland, therefore, was to testify to the good character of the Bolsheviks.

The Latvians were assigned a similar role. Negotiations with Riga followed much the same path as with Helsingfors. Begun in mid-April, the talks initially made little progress. The Latvians wished to await the verdict of battle and were under strong Polish pressure to avoid a quick settlement. Pilsudski warned that if the Latvians uncovered his left flank in Belorussia he would seize any territory, including Dvinsk, considered necessary for his military operations. In the negotiations at Moscow, therefore, the Latvians put forward unacceptable territorial demands. They held to these until the Red Army had driven Pilsudski away from their frontiers and then accepted the favourable boundary offered by Moscow. With Lithuania and Finland about to sign agreements with the Bolsheviks and the Red Army approaching Warsaw, the Latvians decided nothing further could be gained from delay.[65] On 11 August negotiations ended in the signing of a formal peace treaty. Moscow recognized the independence of Latvia absolving the new state of responsibility for all debts and other obligations to Russia. Both promised not to allow their territory to be used to attack the other and renounced all claims to compensation for expenses incurred in the period of hostilities. Like Estonia, Latvia received a substantial timber concession in Soviet territory adjacent to the new frontier. Both promised the prompt conclusion of a commercial treaty to be based on the most-favoured-nation principle and to exempt goods in transit from all duties and imports.[66] Moscow, therefore, demonstrated further proof of its willingness to conclude generous settlements with previously bitter enemies.

By mid-August Soviet Russia had regained the political momentum lost to Poland in the spring. For a few months Pilsudski had slowed Moscow's progress towards the conclusion of peace with its east European neighbours. The war which he had unleashed, however, served to hasten the conclusion of peace with the other states in the region. By mid-August, in fact, Soviet Russia had succeeded in negotiating treaties pacifying its entire frontier from the Arctic Ocean to the Baltic. Peace with Latvia was especially important as it opened yet another port, Riga, for the conduct of Soviet foreign trade. Valuable in themselves, the treaties also allowed Moscow to focus its attention on the far greater problem of Poland.

DURING THESE MONTHS THE way in which Moscow envisaged the solution of the Polish problem underwent radical change. Initially it had differed little from that foreseen for the other east European states. Moscow had repeatedly and sincerely offered Warsaw peace on "astoundingly attractive" terms. Pilsudski's rejection of peace and unleashing of war led Moscow to a severe reassessment of its former position. Unfortunately this reassessment is poorly documented in Soviet sources and can only be glimpsed in its broadest outlines. It had been based on many considerations: exasperation with the failure to engage Pilsudski in meaningful negotiations; reluctance to allow the Poles to regroup for a second assault; over-confidence engendered by victory in the civil war; the apparent impotence of the allied powers in east Europe; a broadly based desire, felt even at the highest levels of the Bolshevik party, to punish the Poles for their attempt to disrupt Soviet power, and the wish to eliminate the challenge which a bourgeois

Poland posed to Moscow in the borderlands of the former Russian empire. In addition there was the very real desire to spread the revolution westward, disrupt the Versailles settlement, and establish a common frontier with Germany. The stakes were high and Lenin and his colleagues chose to gamble rather than pursue a safer policy of seeking to consolidate power east of ethnographic Poland.

Once made, the decision had to be concealed, for the adoption of an overtly aggressive foreign policy could have undermined the entire international position of the Soviet state, built up with so much hard work and sacrifice. Moscow was gambling but not staking everything on the Polish card. Soviet diplomacy did its work well. Poland was virtually isolated. The generous terms and reasonable approach taken with the other east European states and the Entente were probably sufficient to secure their assent in the destruction of bourgeois Poland. France, of course, remained violently opposed but was largely impotent. Everything depended on the success of the Red Army at Warsaw.

CHAPTER FOURTEEN

"The policy of the bayonet, as usual, has broken down": The end of the Polish ephemeron

In the summer of 1920 Europe moved towards its first major international crisis since the end of the Great War. For the moment only Poland and Soviet Russia were actually at war, but if the Red Army defeated Pilsudski, its victory would undermine the Versailles settlement. The allies sought to end the conflict but received little cooperation from the belligerents, who silently agreed to continue their struggle. Britain might wink at this effrontery, but France, with far more invested in the postwar settlement, grew angrier with each day. Accusations and threats, admonitions and warnings again filled the political vocabulary of Europe.

The first contact between Soviet and Polish negotiators took place in this poisoned atmosphere. On 1 August they met at Baranowicze, where the Poles were told their credentials were not in order. They were only authorized to negotiate an armistice while the Soviet government now demanded that they obtain authority to sign the preliminary conditions of peace. The Soviet representatives suggested that once the Poles obtained the necessary credentials, peace talks should begin on 4 August in Minsk. The Poles refused and returned to Warsaw.[1] This development was not entirely unexpected. As early as 20 July Panafieu had warned Paris that Moscow might follow Patek's example and refuse an armistice until the conclusion of peace. He might also have added the example set by the allies in November 1918 when they refused an armistice until Berlin had agreed to terms which guaranteed that the German army would be unable to resume the war. This policy was adopted sometime before Kamenev and Krasin left Moscow for Great Britain. In Stockholm on 31 July Krasin told reporters that no armistice would be granted until Moscow was certain the Polish army would be unable to resume hostilities.[2] Moreover, on 1 August, Stalin told the commander of the Twelfth Army, "We have succeeded in arranging things in such a way that we will not present the armistice conditions to the Poles until 4 August and not 30 July, that is to say that you still have four days at your disposal." Until ordered otherwise he was to "continue operations against the Poles without any consideration of date."[3] In other words, Moscow was urging the Red Army to occupy as much Polish territory as possible before the end of hostilities.

The Poles made the most of the new Soviet proposal. On the one hand it allowed them to attack Soviet credibility. They told D'Abernon that "[the] Bolsheviks were humbugging and laughing at everybody, both Poland and [the] Western Powers."[4] It also gave them new scope for delaying negotiations. They waited until London pressed them to meet the Bolsheviks at Minsk before informing Moscow that they were prepared for peace talks provided the Soviet government informed them in advance of the principles which would serve as the basis of negotiation. Allegedly the uncertainty of early radio transmission again intervened. Although the Polish message was broadcast on 5 August, it was not received in Moscow until two days later and then, according to the Soviet account, in a badly mutilated form which did not include the demand for the principles governing the negotiations.[5] All this might be true, but it stretches coincidence to the breaking point. Political, rather than atmospheric, interference appears a more likely explanation. Both accused the other of bad faith, and both were probably right. Moscow did not wish to reveal its negotiating principles until the talks had begun, and it appears too convenient that exactly this part of the Polish message should have been lost in transmission. It is difficult not to see a Soviet editor, probably Chicherin, coolly deciding which portion of the Polish message would be officially acknowledged in Moscow.

None of this amused Lloyd George, who had the Foreign Office file a strong protest with Chicherin warning that if the Soviet invasion of Poland did not cease, the British government would be forced to consider the aid which could be given Warsaw.[6] He also took advantage of the arrival of Kamenev and Krasin in London to read them a stern lecture. The Soviet government had broken their word, he said, and were refusing to conclude an armistice. Kamenev denied his government had been insincere. Moscow only wanted guarantees that Pilsudski would not use an armistice to prepare for a resumption of hostilities. When Lloyd George inquired what guarantees Moscow wanted, Kamenev referred vaguely to partial demobilization and a stoppage of military supply of the front. Lloyd George insisted, however, that the British fleet would sail in three days unless he received assurances that the Soviets intended to halt their offensive. He also wanted a response to the proposed London peace conference. Kamenev asked if the Poles would not delay negotiations still further if they knew of the British intention. That was "exactly why he was not announcing it," replied the prime minister. He would wait three days before doing so. That evening Lloyd George instructed D'Abernon to inform the Poles that they should give the guarantees sought by Moscow. It was essential, he concluded, that the Polish government "should give no legitimate grounds for the case that they have contributed to delay, or that they are unreasonable in regard to the terms of the armistice."[7]

Few were impressed by these measures. The French chargé d'affaires reported that Curzon had no confidence in them. Sir Henry Wilson wrote scathingly: "So the poor little fool is thinking of declaring war on the Bolsheviks having thrown away every card in the pack."[8]

The Bolsheviks were certainly not swayed. Kamenev did not feel the warning required any change in policy, while Litvinov viewed it as "the last pressure" Lloyd George could bring to bear. Both agreed, however, that open support for a Soviet government in Poland would injure the Russian position in Britain. They also took note of the naval preparations ordered by Lloyd George. On 5 August Litvinov observed the arrival of six British warships in Copenhagen and signalled Kamenev, "perhaps they are for the renewal of the blockade in case of rupture." The next morning Kamenev wired Chicherin that the British fleet had been ordered to sail. This did not overly concern him, but he urged Chicherin to inform him of the terms to be offered the Poles "and also the guarantees from the entente upon which we should consent to an immediate [armistice]." He believed that Britian was seeking a way out and would support "the most rigorous guarantees within reason, even in spite of France."[9]

Chicherin had sent Kamenev the Soviet terms on 5 August. They included the demobilization of the Polish army, its future limitation to one conscript class of fifty thousand men, demobilization of war industries, the barring of foreign troops and war materials from Poland, an armistice along the existing battle front at the time of agreement, withdrawal of the Polish army some fifty kilometres to the west of this line to form a buffer zone, and an eventual state frontier based on the Curzon line modified in Poland's favour. Most controversial, however, were further stipulations requiring the "arming of the [Polish] workers under the control of representatives of the trades unions of Russia, Poland and Norway" and the surrender to the Red Army of all arms "except those necessary for the above mentioned army and for the workmen."[10] The effect of these terms would be to leave a theoretically independent Poland unable to defend itself from external attack or internal insurrection. Warsaw would either fall into the hands of the Red Army or be included in the buffer zone which the Poles would have to evacuate. In either instance, with the arming of the proletariat the Polish Revolutionary Committee would be free to establish themselves there. Seven years later, in reviewing these events Litvinov did not hesitate to characterize the Soviet proposals as "demands of a revolutionary character."[11]

These conditions did not reach London until 7 August. On the sixth, therefore, when Lloyd George demanded to know the Soviet terms, Kamenev had to submit a list based on what he knew of earlier Soviet deliberations and his own understanding of the British political world. In these circumstances, he included the partial demobilization and disarmament of the Polish army, the stoppage of supplies from abroad and the departure of foreign officers, but omitted all reference to any conditions inferring the sovietization of Poland. Lloyd George even balked at these conditions. The two men then produced a document which called for a ten-day truce from 10 August along the line on which the two armies stood at that time. Neither army was to use the cessation of hostilities for reinforcement, while the allies would promise to send no troops or supplies to Poland. Soviet representatives would be allowed to monitor Polish points of entry to ensure that no war materials entered Poland. Negotiation would begin at once to draft the conditions of an armistice and preliminaries of peace. Moscow was asked to reply no later than the morning of 8 August.[12]

Kamenev and Krasin endorsed this proposal. Litvinov did as well but warned it would "not prevent the Poles from re-organizing their army, and stopping panic and disintegration among their troops." Nevertheless he advised acceptance. He feared that the British workers, whose unions were opposing any British involvement in the war, might not persist "till the bitter end … and if they lost a general engagement in England, a situation would be produced analogous to that which exists in France, and Churchill's hands would finally be left free." He suggested, however, that the "shortest possible time be given for negotiating the armistice and peace."[13]

Moscow did not agree. The Red Army continued to advance and the Soviet government showed no inclination to stop. Lloyd George's ultimatum, however, did seem to improve the ability of Radio Moscow to receive transmissions from Warsaw, and Chicherin lost no further time in responding to the several-day-old Polish offer to enter into simultaneous negotiations for an armistice and preliminaries of peace. On 8 August he radioed Warsaw suggesting negotiations open at Minsk on the eleventh.[14]

The French would not accept this proposal. They believed it threatened Polish independence and with it the Versailles treaty. When Millerand met Lloyd George at Lympne on 8 August he wanted the two western powers to issue a proclamation declaring their intentions. Lloyd George replied that he did not see the value of the proposed proclamation as neither Britain nor France were able to send troops to Poland. Millerand agreed that allied troops could not be sent to eastern Europe, but Germany had to be warned not to expand in the east. If France could not act in Poland she could on the Rhine, and Germany should know this. Moreover, pressure could be placed on Moscow by organizing the border states, reimposing the blockade, aiding General Wrangel, and expelling Kamenev and Krasin from Britain. Lloyd George wanted none of these measures, for each was contrary to his general policy of maintaining the peace in central Europe and restoring it in the east. He temporized, therefore, insisting that the Poles and Soviets might reach an acceptable agreement at Minsk, and there should be no breach with Russia until the results of that conference were known. He did agree, if direct negotiations failed and the Bolsheviks continued their advance, that he would accept some of the French measures, including the restoration of the blockade, aid to Wrangel, and the expulsion of Kamenev and Krasin from Britain. Before taking any action, however, he wanted to be certain that the Poles were ready to help themselves. He wanted them to make a public declaration that they intended to fight to the end for their independence, dismiss Pilsudski, and act upon the military advice tendered them by the allies. Millerand agreed, and the two formulated a joint declaration specifying the conditions under which they would offer further aid. The touchy question of Pilsudski was dealt with by demanding that the Poles "appoint a Commander-in-Chief who shall have no other functions and will accept the effective assistance of Allied officers."[15]

The agreement was bogus, the two governments moving in different directions: the French towards increased aid to Poland, the British towards a Soviet-Polish accommodation. The facade of Anglo-French unity collapsed the following day. Both governments acting independently reached decisions unacceptable to the other. Millerand returned to Paris and promptly recognized the regime of General Wrangel as the de facto government of Russia. Before this decision became known in London, Lloyd George had also broken step with Millerand. Thus, on 10 August, the prime minister had to face both a delegation from the Council of Action, organized to block British intervention in the Soviet-Polish war, and the House of Commons. Both were stormy sessions, and in both instances the prime minister said that if Poland refused fair conditions, Britain would not support her. If, however, Russia submitted conditions inconsistent with Polish independence and Poland continued to fight, the allies were bound by the League Covenant to offer assistance.[16]

Kamenev now decided to use his knowledge of the terms his government intended to offer the Poles. Lloyd George had been demanding these terms for nearly a week, and immediately following the prime minister's statement in Commons Kamenev sent him a note outlining the Soviet conditions. These repeated the terms transmitted to him by Chicherin on 5 August in all but one very important point, the arming of the Polish proletariat. As late as the previous day he had warned Moscow "that the artificial establishment of a Soviet regime in Poland may cause [the support of British labour for Soviet Russia] to cool."[17] On his own initiative, therefore, he decided to disguise the Soviet intention of arming the Polish workers. Instead of submitting the actual Soviet condition, he wrote that the Poles would be required to hand over to the Red Army all weapons and arms not required for the needs of their reduced army and "civic militia." Behind this anodyne term, obviously chosen so as not to alarm the British, stood the reality of a revolutionary Red Guard intended as the armed force of the nascent Soviet Republic of Poland.

The deception worked perfectly. Lloyd George told a hastily assembled conference of ministers early in the evening of 10 August that "the [Soviet] terms were not nearly as severe as had been imposed by the Allies upon Germany and Austria, and he did not think that Great Britain could make war in order to secure better conditions than these." His colleagues agreed and decided to assume that Moscow was acting in good faith. They did not assume this of France. Fearing an attempt to block the armistice, the British decided to recommend that Poland accept the Soviet terms without referring them to Paris. The French would merely be informed and asked to give similar advice. Rumbold was to inform the Poles that London was "of the opinion that provided these terms are *bona fide* offered at Minsk, and that no substantial addition is made to them they would appear to leave the independence of Poland within her ethnographic frontiers unimpaired." Poland was free to secure better terms if possible but was told that Britain "could not assume the responsibility of taking hostile action against Russia if the conditions now offered ... were refused."[18]

D'Abernon reported this telegram "fell like a bombshell" in Warsaw. Rumbold said that Sapieha "was so agitated that it was impossible for me to discuss the matter calmly with him." He exclaimed that even if Poland were to be deprived of all allied support she would not accept the terms. He declared that any Polish government which accepted the conditions approved by London would be over-thrown in twenty-four hours with a Bolshevik regime taking its place.[19] The French were appalled. Paléologue told Henderson, the first secretary of the British embassy, that he "much regretted" that instructions had been sent to Rumbold without previous consultation with the French government. He said the British action was "absolutely contrary to the policy agreed upon at Lympne" and under no circumstances would France join Britain in advising Poland to accept the Soviet terms. Paléologue instructed Jusserand to tell Sapieha "that Poland could count on the complete support of France." The Anglo-French split was complete.[20]

It was also public, and Moscow rejoiced. "Our victory is a great one," Lenin informed Stalin on 11 August, "and will be complete if we smash Wrangel ... You, for your part, should make every effort to take the whole of the Crimea without fail." On the same day he ordered Karl Danishevskii, head of the Soviet delegation at the Minsk conference, to stiffen the terms to be presented the Poles. Yet talks had still not begun, and only on 14 August did Polish representatives cross into Soviet-held territory. This did not bother Moscow. "The Poles are temporizing, and have not arrived in time," Lenin told Stalin. "This is of tremendous advantage to us."[21]

This great victory, however, was flawed. It had been won, in part, by con-cealment of the intention to sovietize Poland. Viewed from Moscow, sovieti-zation appeared as a natural development flowing from the failure of Pilsudski's adventure and the apparent collapse of bourgeois Poland. War had again brought revolutionary consequences, and Moscow was simply attending the birth of one more Soviet republic. Kamenev and Litvinov saw the situation quite differently. Both understood at once that western observers, even those sympathetic to the Bolsheviks, would view sovietization as the loss of Poland's independence. They tried to convince Moscow either to modify or conceal its objectives. Neither Lenin nor Chicherin understood this. They had intended that Kamenev publish the Soviet demand for arming the Polish workers; they had not wanted him to transform an obvious Red Guard into an innocuous "civic militia." Chicherin, at first, did not grasp the significance of Kamenev's actions. Thus on 11 August he sent him an *en clair* telegram saying that while the Soviet government "acknowledges that the clause demanding the arming of workers is unprecedented in history, it felt such action was necessary to guarantee the rights of the Polish proletariat and the safety of Russia at the same time providing an adequate national defence which is impossible to use for imperialistic ends."[22]

Kamenev was not at all amused and the following day again urged that "the point about the arming of trade unions should be presented at Minsk as the creation of a citizen's militia." Before Chicherin received this advice he returned to the theme of his earlier message. "Have you explained in the press," he asked on 12 August, "the idea of arming the workmen as a new type of guarantee of peace? To the imperialist land proprietors we oppose the class which does not want war. Is it not possible to boom this point by agitators so as to bring it home to a wide public?" Kamenev must have nearly died! Chicherin wanted him to boom the very issue he most wanted to conceal. "To boom the arming of the workmen at the present moment here is absolutely disadvantageous," he replied on 13 August, "and only likely to spoil the situation."[23] Chicherin now realized what Kamenev had done. He replied with alarm that he could "not understand why, in the laying down of your conditions, no mention is made of the arming of the workmen." This, he said, had placed the Soviet government "in a very awkward position as the later publication of this very radical condition will give an impression of perfidy." Before receiving this rebuke, perhaps expecting it, Kamenev wrote on 14 August: "[Our recent success has] been achieved in a measure both unexpected and wide by means of calculated manoeuvres. It would be a colossal mistake to destroy that which has been achieved by obstinately insisting on the wording of one point which was put forward by me under quite different conditions and calculated to produce a different effect and which, to judge from your telegram, has now assumed the form of some sort of new doctrine."[24]

More separated Kamenev and the Soviet government than the issue of the civic militia. They differed fundamentally on the tactics to be pursued at Minsk. Kamenev's view, as on the question of arming the Polish workers, was deeply influenced by the political climate in Britain. He did not wish to endanger liberal and socialist support of Soviet Russia. He was especially impressed by the Council of Action and their militant stand against British assistance to Poland. On 12 August he reported that the Council of Action had summoned a special congress of two thousand delegates to meet the following day and said almost wistfully that "it would be fine to receive for tomorrow's congress news that the Minsk Conference has met, and that the terms presented by us strictly correspond with the published terms." Litvinov concurred completely, wiring urgently to Chicherin that he considered "it would be extremely important to conclude peace or at least an agreement regarding the preliminary conditions with the present Polish government before occupying Warsaw and sovietizing Poland."[25]

Neither Kamenev nor Litvinov objected to the ultimate sovietization of Poland, which had been adopted as party policy the previous month, but only with the tempo and manner with which this was accomplished. But on the same day Kamenev launched his final appeal for moderation, Lenin communicated his contrary, and decisive, view. "The whole matter in my opinion bases itself on the fact that France and [the Polish government] by breaking off the meeting itself at Minsk, will break off the probable armistice. I hope that England will not be able to fight and without her everything falls to the ground. There is hardly any news from Poland and the little that we have confirms our decisions in the plenary session of the Central Executive Committee. Increasing watchfulness and we should win these campaigns."[26] Lenin continued to aim at the main chance and, unlike his representatives abroad, was prepared to accept whatever negative consequences occurred as a result in western Europe.

ALL THESE CALCULATIONS paid scant attention to the Poles. Since their military collapse in late June they had come to be treated with diminishing respect by both their allies and enemies. Lloyd George virtually ignored them and subordinated even their most vital interests to his own political desiderata. Millerand displayed greater concern for Polish security and independence but only because this was in the immediate interest of France. The French continued to hope, and work for, the recrudescence of a powerful, anti-Bolshevik Russia and would have gladly sacrificed Poland on that altar. The Quai d'Orsay harboured a deep suspicion of Polish motives and feared betrayal at every instant. Like Lloyd George, the French sought to manipulate Poland rather than genuinely cooperating with its government. Moscow did the same. Poland offered a stage for yet another revolutionary drama, and the Bolsheviks sought to set it in the same manner as everywhere else in the borderlands. The existing government was cast as the villain; local revolutionaries, suitably led by a cadre of major Soviet officials, appeared as the hero. The Red Army acted as protagonist, securing a constantly expanding territorial base for the Muscovite cadres who styled themselves first as a revolutionary committee, then as a provisional regime, and ultimately aspired to present themselves as a fully fledged Soviet government.

Pilsudski had other ideas. His army had been defeated but not scattered. He carefully conserved his resources, choosing to reinforce the southern front while appearing to neglect the eastern approaches to Warsaw. As a result Budenny's advance had been slowed dramatically, and in mid-August the Soviet southwestern front had still not captured Lvov or Lublin. In the north, however, Tukachevskii had advanced at will, out-flanking Warsaw to the north, reaching East Prussia, advancing into the Polish corridor and threatening to sever the vital rail line between Danzig and central Poland. The allied mission, fearing total collapse was imminent, attributed the impending disaster to Polish recklessness and incompetence.[27] The use of manpower mystified allied observers, who attributed it either to the parochialism of Galician-born generals or part of Pilsudski's alleged plan to strike a bargain with the Bolsheviks. It was neither. By reinforcing the south Pilsudski kept Budenny from joining Tukachevskii in front of Warsaw. Meanwhile to the north the Red Army advanced into a military vacuum drawn ever westward by almost no Polish resistance. In early August a gap began to open between the two Soviet fronts. This gave Pilsudski the opportunity for which he had been waiting. In the previous month he had quietly begun to concentrate a striking force north of Lublin between the Vistula and Wieprz. His plan was to await the maximum separation of the two Soviet fronts and then drive his divisions into the gap between them. Weygand gave the plan his full support. On 13 August he cabled Paris: "The battle on the Vistula is imminent. It must be decisive." Privately he wrote Foch saying he did not believe the Bolsheviks would take Warsaw. He described Pilsudski as calm and confident. Nor had the marshal's flair for the dramatic failed him. "Alea jacta est" were his last words before leaving for the Wieprz. "He is right," observed Weygand, "and it is not only the fate of Poland which is at stake."[28]

The Bolsheviks contributed substantially to Pilsudski's success. Their triumphant sweep into Poland brought with it problems of logistics, reinforcement, and communication which could not be solved. The number of actual combatants dwindled, and the Red Army was forced to live off the land. Most messages had to be sent by primitive radio transmitters which frequently malfunctioned, and Moscow, therefore, had to make decisions on the basis of chronically insufficient information. Worse still was the Soviet failure to coordinate the military operations of their western and southwestern fronts.[29] Each had different priorities and the latter was distracted by the necessity of containing Wrangel and guarding against the possibility of Romania entering the war. This situation demanded correction, and on 2 August the Politburo decided to merge all Soviet forces fighting Poland into Tukachevskii's western front, leaving the southwestern front to concentrate exclusively on Wrangel. This proved difficult to execute. High command directives for the Twelfth, Fourteenth, and First Horse armies to prepare for transfer to the command of the western front were sharply criticized by the southwestern front military council. Both Egorov, the commander, and Stalin, his commissar, protested that without these armies they would be unable to stop Wrangel, who was then advancing north from the Crimea. In particular they sought to retain Budenny's cavalry army.[30] This caused Lenin and S. Kamenev to hesitate. Delay followed delay, and Kamenev did not order the transfer of the Twelfth and First Horse armies until 13 August.[31] Tukachevskii then ordered the latter to support his attack on Warsaw but could not contact Budenny. On 12 August Stalin had directed Budenny to capture Lvov, and when Tukachevskii's command reached the First Horse army, they were heavily engaged in this operation. Budenny replied on 16 August that after taking Lvov he would proceed toward Warsaw. Tukachevskii had to issue two further orders before Budenny, on 20 August, actually broke off his attack. By then it was far too late to help the western front. Pilsudski had already launched his counter-attack.[32]

The Polish offensive began on 16 August. Pilsudski paraded five divisions into a gap 112 kilometres wide held by one small Bolshevik formation. Success was immediate. On the first day the Poles could not even find the Red Army and advanced nearly sixty kilometres to the northwest. The following day they marched thirty kilometres farther, wreaking havoc in the Soviet rear. On 18 August Tukachevskii ordered a general retreat which soon turned into a rout. One Soviet army was forced to flee into East Prussia, where it was disarmed and interned. Four other armies fought their way through the Polish encirclement but lost most of their equipment and more than sixty thousand men taken prisoner. At the end of the month the Poles held Bialostok and Brest-Litovsk. "The battle of the Vistula," Henrys reported triumphantly, "has been definitely won."[33]

The Polish offensive took the Bolsheviks by surprise. Tukachevskii had expected to encounter the mass of the Polish army defending Warsaw; early on the morning of 17 August he was still unaware of Pilsudski's attack.[34] Later in the day, as the first reports of the Polish offensive reached Moscow, the Soviet government reacted with stunned incredulity. We have only notes, probably written by Lenin in a meeting called for some other purpose, to gauge this reaction, but they make it clear that initially he did not understand the seriousness of the situation. Someone appears to have advised him to seek a quick armistice with the Poles. This caused him to scribble furiously: "The Commander-in-Chief has no right to dither. If the *War* Department or the Commander-in-Chief *does not turn down* the capture of Warsaw, it *must be taken.* (What special measures for this are being taken, tell me?) To talk of *speeding up* the truce when the enemy is advancing is idiocy." And somewhat later in the meeting: "Now that the Poles have gone over to the attack along the *whole* line we must not snivel (like Danishevskii) for that is ridiculous. We must devise a *counter-move*: military movement, holding up all negotiations, etc."

Lenin demanded to know what S. Kamenev intended to do, and received the rather weak recommendation that two divisions, originally intended for use against Wrangel, be moved to Brest-Litovsk. Lenin approved, saying it was "ultra-important to finish off Poland." Sklianski, with whom Lenin was exchanging these notes, obviously concluded that his chief still did not understand the military situation. "I think [S. Kamenev] wants to [redirect the two divisions]," he wrote, "not so much to finish off the Poles as to stop them exploiting their success and pushing us back." Lenin, however, persisted and demanded "at whatever cost Warsaw must be taken in 3-5 days."[35]

Tukachevskii's order for a general retreat permitted no further illusions. The Politburo met on 19 August and took the full measure of the disaster. They reversed the priorities previously assigned the western and southern fronts, the latter now being recognized as having precedence.[36] This reflected an assumption that victory in Poland was no longer possible and it had become essential to eliminate Wrangel. Numerous directives followed from this decision. Moscow informed its main committees in Siberia and the Caucasus that they were to provide additional men and material for the Wrangel front. The Communist Party of Ukraine received the same order.[37] Lenin told the western front they were unlikely to receive further reinforcement. The Lithuanian communists were ordered to pull in their horns; they had just sought permission to organize an insurrection and were refused. "The present moment, while we are pulling back from our advance on Warsaw," Lenin wrote, "is quite unsuitable."[38] As the Bolsheviks withdrew from Poland, however, Lenin hoped to leave as much trouble as possible for Pilsudski. On 19 August he ordered the Eastern Galician Revolutionary Committee to provoke a rising of the local peasantry and on the following day he instructed the Polish Revolutionary Committee to promote the peasant seizure of large estates. Neither was intended as the beginning of a Russian-style peasant revolution but were ordered with the hope of setting the Polish countryside afire behind the retreating Red Army. "It is unlikely," Lenin informed Kamenev laconically on 20 August, "that we will soon take Warsaw."[39]

The sudden turn in military fortunes had sobered the previously giddy Bolsheviks. Predictably, it had the opposite effect on the Poles. As early as 18 August Weygand warned Paris that they were again talking of frontiers far in advance of the Curzon line. Jusserand followed with a similar warning, and on 22 August Paris, which now had one eye firmly fixed on the Crimea, admonished Pilsudski not to seek boundaries far in advance of the ethnographic frontier. London tendered similar advice.[40] The allied call for prudence fell on deaf ears. The Poles, Panafieu reported on 30 August, "had already passed from the extreme discouragement which had transformed them into suppliants with regard to the Great Powers, to ambitious pride which, after victory, drives them to return to their megalomaniacal ideas and to pursue an independent policy."[41]

THE BATTLE OF WARSAW served to obscure the opening of negotiations at Minsk. The Poles had sent a large delegation headed by the deputy foreign minister, Jan Dabski, who met the Soviets, led by Karl Danishevskii, for the first time on 17 August. Moscow was confident that Warsaw would fall on the sixteenth[42] and had prepared far more onerous terms than those submitted to Lloyd George. In these, Poland was required to restore the damage done in Soviet territory, pass legislation for the free division of the land (with priority given to the families of Polish citizens killed or incapacitated in the war), grant Soviet Russia and the Ukraine free transit through Polish territory for passengers and freight, leave the Volkovysk-Belostok-Graevo railway in Soviet hands, proclaim a political amnesty, and publish all materials and documents relating to the war.[43] The core of the Soviet demands – disarmament of the Polish army and arming of the proletariat – remained the same, but following Kamenev's advice the putative Red Guard was described as a civic militia. These were, despite the sugar coating of sovereignty and ethnographic frontiers, very harsh terms, well calculated to leave Poland at the mercy of her Soviet neighbour. The inclusion of mandatory land reform suggests the conscious emplacement of a legal mechanism by which the Bolsheviks could legitimately intervene in Polish internal affairs should the reform not be conducted according to their wishes. It does not require much imagination to see Chicherin (with his profound knowledge of half a millennium of Russian foreign policy and certain memory of the use Catherine II had made of the Polish dissidents) as the author of this audacious clause. At the last moment, perhaps after being informed of Pilsudski's counter-attack, Danishevskii appears to have had second thoughts as to whether the new terms should be presented to the Poles. Lenin lectured him: "Remain cold-blooded and maintain an arch-firm posture, not conceding one iota so long as the Poles fail to show that they seriously wish peace."[44]

Negotiations proceeded slowly and fruitlessly. The Soviets, knowing that the fall of Warsaw was no longer imminent, were prepared to let the talks drift. The Poles were ignorant of Pilsudski's success and therefore uninterested in proceeding to substantive negotiations. The report, received on 21 August, of the Polish victory completely altered the situation, and when the conference resumed on 23 August the Poles took a very hard line. Eleven of the fifteen Soviet conditions, said Dabski, were wholly unacceptable. They were nothing less than an elaborate assault on the independence and sovereignty of Poland. Poland would not agree to unilateral disarmament nor Soviet intervention in its internal affairs. Least of all would they agree to arm a revolutionary Red Guard disguised as a civic militia.[45] The Minsk conference was nearly at an end. Already on 20 August Prince Sapieha had told the allied mission that the original instructions given the Polish delegation would have to be "re-examined," and five days later he ordered them back to Warsaw. The Poles accused the Bolsheviks of "superlative bad faith," a charge readily endorsed by the allied mission. Lord D'Abernon, drawing on his long experience and richly developed preju-dices, provided the gloss. "With an intimate acquaintance with Armenians, Syrians and Greeks, some experience of jockeys and racing touts," he wrote, "I am prepared to back the Soviets to give any of them, in trickery and chicane, any amount of start and a good beating."[46]

Moscow levelled similar charges at its enemies. With great bitterness Lenin informed Kamenev on 20 August: "It is quite clear that Lloyd George and Churchill have apportioned the roles and that Lloyd George, under cover of pacifist phrases, supports the actual policy of the French and of Churchill and makes fools of idiots like Henderson and company." He instructed Kamenev: "Use all your forces to explain this to the British workers. Write articles for them yourself and develop this idea, teaching them the theories of Marx." As the military situation in Poland deteriorated, so did Chicherin's grasp of what was possible in Great Britain. "The hour has struck when it is time to pass from defensive pacifist watchwords to offensive ones," he wrote on 22 August. "It would be well if the workers were to demand now no longer merely peace with Russia, but assistance for Soviet Russia against Poland and Wrangel. The workers themselves could form volunteer detachments for fighting on the Polish front." Kamenev had a much clearer view of the situation. As he had consistently warned against naked military aggression, he was able to place himself at a distance from the consequences. On 24 August he wrote: "The policy of the bayonet, as usual, has broken down 'owing to unforeseen circumstances'." He urged Moscow to emphasize negotiation. The demand for arming a workers' militia, he said, could easily be dropped in exchange for a British pledge "to oblige the Poles to renew the negotiations broken off by them on the basis of the remaining points."[47] This grossly overestimated the strength of the Soviet position but pointed the way to the only realistic line of retreat.

Lloyd George was conducting his own retreat. The break with France and Tory criticism had left him dangerously isolated. At mid-month, therefore, as he prepared to take his summer holiday, he sought sympathetic political associates. Italy had usually played an unobtrusive role in allied councils but now Lloyd George turned eagerly to Rome. There the weak government of Giovanni Giolitti stood in equal need of external validation and, *mirabile dictu*, shared similar views on eastern and central Europe. Both Downing Street and the Quirinal, in stark contrast to the Quai d'Orsay, favoured measures to hasten general pacification rather than strict enforcement of punitive treaties; rapid continent-wide economic recovery, by necessity including Germany; an end to military adventures in eastern Europe; and a settlement with the Bolsheviks which would integrate Soviet Russia in the political and economic life of Europe. Over the previous six months this community of vision had only gained Giolitti a highly circumscribed and under-publicized supporting role in allied councils, but with the collapse of the entente cordiale Lloyd George invited the Italian premier to share centre stage in a hastily organized meeting at Lucerne. Lloyd George had planned a holiday in the Alps but the meeting in Switzerland brutally emphasized French isolation while providing a broadly European, rather than narrowly allied, stage for the pronouncements to issue from the meeting. As a consequence, Lloyd George made a great display of travelling through France without leaving his train or seeing a single French leader. Only a terse communiqué noted his passing. On 22 August he met with Giolitti.[48]

The eastern European situation remained unclear. Pilsudski had plainly won a major victory but the full extent of Soviet defeat was still unknown. Lloyd George had already grown uneasy about his acceptance of a Soviet-sponsored "civic militia" but had not yet measured its possible impact on Polish independence. Neither had Giolitti and, as a consequence, both men remained more suspicious of Poland than Soviet Russia. Both agreed that "the Poles were rather a light-headed people and might be disinclined at this moment to agree to reasonable terms." This posed a threat to the peace of Europe, said Lloyd George, because "until peace could be secured with Russia, [the continent] would continue in a state of unrest." Giolitti willingly affirmed "that peace must be achieved everywhere at any cost." The two leaders produced a draft communiqué which emphasized the urgent need of peace, the economic fruits which would follow, and the pointlessness of further intervention in Russia. At the same time they warned: "[a]ny attempt to dictate to another country what form of government it shall enjoy or from what classes of the people it shall draw its army would both constitute an unwarranted infringement of its liberties and independence." In conclusion, they expressed their gratification "that such conditions are not included in the Soviet's official terms of peace ... as communicated to the British Government."[49]

Such terms, of course, had been presented the Poles at Minsk, and this became known in Lucerne the following day. As the two premiers had not yet issued their communiqué they were able to revise it. Lloyd George had been informed of the sharp reaction in Great Britain to the attempted deception and instinctively trimmed his sails. He spoke of Soviet bad faith and said that Moscow should be warned that Great Britain and Italy would not allow a "Red Force" disguised as a civic militia to overthrow the Polish government. Giolitti agreed, but when Lloyd George produced a draft communiqué including a vague passage promising "assistance to Poland in certain eventualities," the Italian premier demurred. Italy, he said, "could give nothing," while Lloyd George promptly added that "Great Britain could not give very much." The two therefore agreed to delete this innocuous reference, thereby establishing that whatever prohibition they placed on Moscow would have to be enforced by the Poles. As they had just learned "that the Red Army would be almost entirely destroyed," they were free to cut as dashing a figure in defence of Polish independence as they wished.[50] The resulting document was sheer rhetoric. Its final clause declaring that "negotiations of any kind with a government which so lightly treats its word becomes difficult if not impossible," was the linchpin of the document. Rephrased, it said that further negotiations would be difficult *but not impossible*. The communiqué was, as its authors intended, a call for further negotiations. Both the introduction and conclusion repeatedly stressed the blessings of peace and the horrors of war. The document, in short, summoned Moscow to abandon its adventure in Poland and return to the bargaining table.[51]

The Lucerne communiqué was sent to the Soviet delegation in London for transmission to Moscow. Kamenev told Chicherin on 24 August that "the whole note [was] calculated to produce a split in the [British] labour movement," an interpretation which received reinforcement the following day when the Council of Action asked the Soviet government "to give up the clause referring to the militia." Kamenev again advised Moscow to yield on this point. He described the communiqué as equivalent to a declaration of war and ominously informed Chicherin that the Soviet delegation was preparing to leave London.[52] Intentionally or otherwise, Kamenev had overreacted. This was underlined by the

Manchester Guardian which advised him to read between the lines of the Lucerne communiqué. Moscow, said the newspaper, should ignore the rude language and note that Lloyd George continued to adhere strictly to his pacifist policy. The "thunder of the communiqué" was only "the noise of a sledge hammer striking an open door." The two premiers had taken aim only at the militia clause of the Soviet proposals, and Moscow could easily agree to let this condition drop.[53]

This was precisely the position adopted by the Soviet government. Kamenev was ordered not to leave Britain except under duress, and Chicherin filed a lengthy reply to the Lucerne communiqué. Although branding it a piece of propaganda, he declared the Soviet "desire ... for peace is ... so paramount" that Moscow had decided "fully to meet the wishes of the British and Italian governments." He withdrew the demand for a Polish civic militia and, following Kamenev's advice, pretended that this was the only peace condition to which the British and Italian governments could take exception. He concluded with the bald and wholly unwarranted declaration that the removal of this condition "restores the full agreement with the [British and Italian] Governments which existed before this divergence arose."[54]

This was an ingenious interpretation carefully calculated to emphasize the isolation of France and restore unity in the ranks of Soviet supporters in Britain. Kamenev sarcastically wired his "sincere congratulations to the authors" of this "excellent" note. "In the circumstances prevailing here," he said, "it takes the place of a big military victory."[55] And indeed, developments in Britain and Poland had already outdistanced the facile assumptions on which the note was based. The aggregate of the remaining conditions which Soviet Russia had presented at Minsk constituted almost as great a threat to Polish independence as the militia clause and would have been accepted, if at all, only in the event of total military collapse. In late August the Polish army was advancing rapidly and neither Lenin nor Lloyd George was in any position to dictate to Pilsudski. In Great Britain the political tide was running with equal force against the Bolsheviks. Lloyd George had not intended the Lucerne communiqué to serve as the prelude to a rupture of relations with Soviet Russia, but many of his Conservative allies began to move in that direction in the final days of August. Galvanized by Soviet defeat in Poland, mounting labour unrest in Britain and what they considered Bolshevik subversion, leading Conservatives mounted a campaign to expel the entire Soviet delegation. Only with great difficulty did Lloyd George succeed in breaking the momentum favouring a rupture of relations with Moscow. Although Kamenev was only partly aware of the extent of the campaign being mounted against him, he had no difficulty in measuring its impact on British relations with Soviet Russia. On 30 August he asked for permission to return home; in early September it was granted.[56]

The Soviet government decided it was time to place negotiations with Poland on a new footing. On 27 August Chicherin conceded it had been a mistake to hold negotiations at Minsk. He proposed that talks be resumed in a neutral country, preferably Estonia. The Poles had never intended to break off negotiations entirely and therefore responded positively. They suggested that the talks be held at Riga. Chicherin agreed on 1 September.[57] If Riga could not be considered entirely neutral, it was far better than other alternatives. The gruelling experience of the previous six months had finally placed the governments of Poland and Soviet Russia in a frame of mind conducive to a negotiated settlement.

The Polish Revolutionary Committee had failed as miserably as the Red Army. They were a hastily organized body with little influence. Unlike similar Bolshevik committees, they lacked a widespread, well-entrenched, illegal party organization to do their bidding. The repressive apparatus of the Polish state functioned with reasonable efficiency and Dzerzhinski, of all people, complained of the terror conducted by Pilsudski's police.[58] In the final analysis, both Lenin and Dzerzhinskii relied on the Red Army to achieve victory in Poland. In earlier campaigns Soviet legions benefited enormously from waging war in territories where they were received as liberators or at least not with hostility. This was true not only in Great Russia but in Ukraine and even Azerbaidzhan. This was not the case in Poland, where it proved impossible to overcome the centuries-old Polish hatred of the Russians. Nor was Polish hostility informed by mere secular nationalism. The Roman Catholic church also rallied the faithful against Bolshevism. This side of the conflict was highlighted in mid-August when the Polish Revkom, preparatory to entering Warsaw itself, moved to Wyszkow, about fifty kilometres northeast of the capital. There they made themselves at home in the local church, evicting its old priest from his residence. Short days later, in the midst of their hasty departure, they scornfully exclaimed "now, call in your cardinals to exorcise the house."[59]

Lenin pronounced the official verdict on the Soviet failure in Poland. A few months after the disaster he told Klara Zetkin:

What happened in Poland was perhaps bound to happen. Our intrepid victorious vanguard could not receive any reinforcements from the infantry nor any weapons or even stale bread in sufficient quantity, and therefore had to requisition grain and other prime necessities from the Polish peasants and petty bourgeoisie. This made the latter look upon the Red Army men as enemies, and not as liberating brothers ... The peasants and workers, gulled by the followers of Pilsudski and Daszynski, defended their class enemies, allowed our gallant Red Army men to starve to death, enticed them into ambuscades and killed them.[60]

This, of course, is far too fatalistic and stems in part from Lenin's substantial role in the decision to proceed with the invasion of ethnographic Poland. In the chill wind of the Russian fall he had no desire to probe too deeply into the reasons which had impelled him in the heat of summer to order his army to march on Warsaw. Neither did his colleagues who had joined him in that decision.

It had been officially ratified by the Central Committee on 16 July. Radek, Rykov and Trotsky had dissented, but none chose to remind the party of their opposition. Neither advocates nor opponents wanted to conduct a genuine post-mortem, perhaps because all feared selection as scapegoat to bear the sins of failure. It was far better to nod agreement when Lenin blamed the gullible Polish peasants and workers. By 19 August, however, the Soviet government clearly understood how risky their policy had become, for once Pilsudski launched his counter-attack, exhibiting the power still at his disposal, they lost no time in writing off the Polish ephemeron and deciding to turn at once to the liquidation of Wrangel.

CHAPTER FIFTEEN

Seeking a "substitute" for peace: Anglo-Soviet negotiations, May-November 1920

In early May 1920 the Soviet government decided to give priority in its foreign policy to the conclusion of a trade agreement with Great Britain. In pursuit of this aim it postponed a final assault on Wrangel's army and suspended military operations against Armenia and Georgia. Lord Curzon had insisted on both measures, and Moscow had complied.[1] The questions remained, however, as to whether these concessions would actually promote the desired agreement.

Before the talks could begin, the Soviet government had to make certain preparations. In February the allied premiers had agreed to ask the League of Nations to send a commission of inquiry to study economic and political conditions in Russia. Their findings were to provide a basis for further discussion of the resumption of trade, and Lloyd George had promised Millerand not to act independently until the report allowed the allied powers to frame a common policy on Russia.[2] In March the League Council had asked if Moscow was willing to receive the delegation. The Bolsheviks did not like the proposal but did not wish to issue a flat refusal. They allowed seven weeks to elapse before responding on 7 May, that while agreeing in principle to the visit, for military reasons they could not receive the delegation until the end of hostilities with Poland. This served as a test of the British interest in proceeding with negotiations. Although the League objected London did not, silently signalling that the talks should begin.[3]

Moscow also sought to improve its bargaining position. Great Britain had to be shown that Soviet Russia could enter into commercial relations with other states. Italy had been approached in April, but had proved unreceptive. Moscow had then briefly considered sending Krasin to Berlin, but this was considered too provocative. Instead, the Soviets turned to Sweden. For more than a month Soviet representatives had dangled fat contracts before the eyes of Swedish industrialists, who were told that they would be signed when the Swedish government concluded a trade agreement with Moscow. At first the government resisted, but yielded when Krasin threatened to break off his commercial negotiations in Sweden. A series of agreements followed quickly. On 14 May the Swedish government agreed to the establishment of commercial relations, the exchange of permanent trade representations, the right of these representations to unhindered courier and cypher communication, and protection from confiscation of all goods and gold involved in commercial exchange between the two countries. The following day Krasin concluded an agreement with a consortium of Swedish companies worth one hundred million gold crowns. In a separate agreement signed the same day Krasin placed an order with the firm of Nydquist and Holm for one thousand locomotives to be delivered over a period of six years.[4] This could not begin to slack the Soviet thirst for western manufactured goods and was largely designed for its political impact on the impending negotiations in London. "We doubt that Scandinavian industry is able to participate significantly in the restoration of our transport system," Lenin cabled Krasin on 8 May. "We attach significance to the conclusion of the agreement primarily because of the influence it will have on the major locomotive construction plants of Europe and America."[5]

Before leaving for London, Krasin wanted assurances that he would be allowed to negotiate personally with Lloyd George. Earlier in the month he had sought these assurances through a Norwegian intermediary, but on 4 May he put these questions directly to his British counterpart in Copenhagen. He also sought assurances that Litvinov would be allowed to remain in Denmark. Four days later he received a positive response to all his inquiries. A week later he sailed for Britain.[6]

In London the British government had also been preparing for the negotiations. Opinion there was badly divided. E.F. Wise struck the most positive note. "If we refuse to trade," he concluded, "the result will merely be that the gold and platinum will go elsewhere."[7] The Board of Trade took a more forceful position. Their memorandum, submitted to cabinet on 26 May, stressed the desirability of securing recognition from the Soviet government of their responsibility to satisfy the financial claims of private British subjects arising from the nationalization or confiscation of their property in Russia.[8] The Board of Trade, like Wise, however, was quite prepared to dispense with "the positive obstacles to trade" even before negotiations began. They did not believe that any significant volume of trade was possible until the Soviet government established their financial reliability through recognition of Russian pre-revolutionary obligations, but pending a settlement of this issue they did not want to continue restrictions on British subjects wishing to trade with Russia at their own risk. On 14 May they had asked cabinet for authority to issue a press release announcing that no legal obstacles prevented British subjects from trading with Russia. This was merely a statement of fact as the legal obstacles to trade had expired with the conclusion of peace with Germany, but this was not widely known, and throughout the first months of 1920 Whitehall had deliberately declined to publicize it. Curzon still objected, and cabinet decided to defer publication of the press release.[9]

Curzon was determined to obtain the greatest possible political benefit from the commercial negotiations with Krasin. On 27 May he sent the cabinet a memorandum asserting that the Bolsheviks were prepared to pay almost any price for the assistance which Britain was in a position to give. He wanted that price paid "in a cessation of Bolshevik hostility in parts of the world important to us, [rather] than in the ostensible interchange of commodities, the existence of which on any considerable scale in Russia there is grave reason to doubt." In addition to the return of remaining British prisoners, he wanted an end to anti-British Soviet action in Afghanistan and Persia, a guarantee of the independence of Armenia and Georgia, and an amnesty for Wrangel's army.[10]

These and other views were put before a conference of ministers the following day. After lengthy discussion it was agreed that "before opening negotiations in regard to trade ... the British government should insist on the negotiation of a comprehensive political agreement with the Soviet government, on the lines suggested" by Curzon. The conference also confronted the problem of allied representation at the meetings with Krasin. It was decided that Curzon should invite the French ambassador to attend the first meeting. If he refused the British would then consider whether the Italian chargé d'affaires should be approached.[11]

The final decision represented one more instalment of the protracted political struggle with France over how to deal with the Russian problem. Until now Lloyd George had pursued his policy under the cover of Supreme Council resolutions drafted in deliberately vague terms to secure French assent. With Krasin in London and the mandate of his colleagues to seek a political settlement with the Bolsheviks, he no longer needed this cover. This was fortunate as he knew it was unlikely that the French would agree to open political negotiations with Moscow. It was essential, however, that they be invited to the meeting with Krasin. For six months Lloyd George had been solemnly promising the French to abstain from such negotiations, thus securing their reluctant assent to his vague Supreme Council resolutions, and now that he was about to break decisively with them he was determined to shift responsibility for the rupture onto their shoulders. In this he had the enthusiastic cooperation of Curzon, who had just experienced the exhilaration of apparently having his own Russian policy adopted by his colleagues. In time, Curzon would learn how little Lloyd George felt bound by this policy, but on the afternoon of 28 May he summoned the French ambassador to hear the decision of the British government. As expected, Cambon refused to meet Krasin and again rehearsed all the French objections to direct political negotiations. The British then used the French decision to exclude the Italians, who were told that the inter-allied character of the discussions had to be abandoned due to the refusal of the French government to participate.[12] With the moment of truth at hand and their own vital interests in the balance, the British wished to talk privately with Krasin.

The Bolsheviks were of the same mind. They had come to London ostensibly to negotiate with representatives of the allied Supreme Council, but in fact they wanted to talk directly with the British government and in particular the prime minister. In early May Krasin had let it be known that "It was no good negotiating with Mr. Wise or Mr. Grant Watson because they appeared to have no powers. All they could say was that they would refer any point at issue to London. What they wanted was someone who had full powers to say 'yes' or 'no' to any given proposition." The Soviets disliked multilateral negotiations and believed they were more likely to achieve their objectives through a series of individual agreements reached with their adversaries. They further believed that once they had concluded an acceptable agreement with Great Britain, the strongest of the imperial powers, the others would have little choice but to follow the British example. Thus Krasin gladly accepted the British invitation to meet separately with Lloyd George and his ministers.[13]

The talks which began on 31 May were to continue, with interruptions, for over eight months. The basic areas of disagreement – restitution or compensation for British property nationalized or confiscated in Russia, security for Soviet gold deposited to guarantee commercial transactions in Britain, termination of Soviet anti-British activities in Asia, and Bolshevik propaganda in Britain – even in the best of circumstances would have required some time to negotiate.[14] The summer of 1920 was not a good time to negotiate these or any other issues dividing Britain and Soviet Russia. The talks immediately became snarled in the Polish question, and until that issue was resolved the settlement of most bilateral issues was deferred.

THE CRIMEA WAS NOT AMONG these. Curzon continued to seek a negotiated end of hostilities there and, when Chicherin agreed, announced on 17 May that he would endeavour to arrange for talks "in which General Wrangel and British military and political representatives [would] participate." Although fearing British bad faith, the Soviet government ordered the Red Army to abstain from offensive operations in the Crimea and responded on 20 May that they would consider "in the most amicable spirit" amnesty proposals for the remnants of the Russian White Guards "that the British representatives [would] put forward during the impending armistice negotiations."[15] None of this went down well with Wrangel. He had begun to reorganize his army and, with the Polish invasion of Ukraine, believed he could continue the struggle against the Bolsheviks. He now began to portray the Crimea as "a healthy nucleus round which could be centred all movements which declare themselves against Bolshevik tyranny" and the base from which the remainder of Russia could some day be saved from "permanent anarchy." Curzon rejected these pretensions and responded that it should be made clear to General Wrangel "that he must not expect any change in [British] policy as the result of the Polish offensive."[16]

It is doubtful whether Wrangel expected a different response. Since November the Whites had grown progressively disillusioned with the British, and they now turned to France. Initially they received only moral support, but on 8 May they were informed that the French government would supply the general with the rations and military equipment needed to defend the Crimea. In addition, the French fleet would protect its shores and, if need be, "contribute in every way possible to effect the evacuation of the peninsula." The French, of course, did not inform the British of this pledge, but its substance could not long be concealed. "I cannot speak with certainty," Admiral de Robeck cabled from Constantinople on 20 May, "but there is something on foot between the French and Wrangel." [17]

Wrangel now freed himself from British tutelage and prepared to take the offensive. He decided to strike along the only rail line leading out of the peninsula, towards Melitopol, in the region between the Dnieper and Sea of Azov. Here he hoped to find badly needed foodstuffs while avoiding the right bank of the Dnieper and a possible confrontation with Pilsudski and Petliura. Wrangel was no more prepared than Denikin to acknowledge the independence of Ukraine but was not strong enough to take a firm stand on the issue in the summer of 1920. Negotiations were begun in Warsaw for a tripartite anti-Bolshevik pact, but in the meanwhile he gathered his forces to strike at the Soviet Thirteenth Army guarding the Taurida province against an attack from the south. [18]

These preparations could not long be concealed, and on 1 June Curzon informed Admiral de Robeck that General Wrangel should be warned that if he took the offensive against the Red Army, the plan for negotiating an amnesty would inevitably fall through and the British government would be "unable to concern themselves any further with the fate of his army." [19] Wrangel admitted he was about to attack the Bolsheviks, but said that he could no longer feed the population of the Crimea, and had to obtain additional food supplies. On 6 June his forces took the offensive against the Red Army. The British cabinet decided this absolved them of all further responsibility for the safety of Wrangel's army and directed that the British military mission be withdrawn from the Crimea as soon as possible and the Royal Navy "abstain from assistance of any kind to [the White forces]." [20]

Moscow was taken by surprise. Although Wrangel's intentions had been perfectly clear, Lenin had chosen to ignore the almost daily warnings sent by Stalin concerning the seriousness of the situation. [21] On 30 May, while instructing Chicherin to consult with Stalin to obtain from him "*all* material about British aid to Wrangel," he told him to wait two weeks before sending Curzon "an even-tempered (unabusive) note of protest proving that Britain is deviating from the truth." [22] This instruction is indicative of the importance which Lenin attached to the effort to secure improved relations with Britain, for he seldom issued directives specifying moderation of language and euphemism. The importance of Britain can also be seen in his response to Stalin's increasing insistence that prompt steps be taken to deal with Wrangel. When Stalin asked for reinforcement on 2 June, Lenin refused, adding that he should keep in mind the Politburo decision of early May to suspend military operations there. Stalin replied impudently: "Have it your way. I recall the decision of the Politburo; but since Wrangel is disregarding that decision and, on the contrary, is preparing to attack, and since it is quite possible, moreover, that he will break through our front, I considered it my duty to take precautionary military measures."[23] Stalin did not back down; the next day he wired that it was essential to smash Wrangel at once. Lenin would not hear of it, describing the proposal as "manifest utopia" and insisting that no action be taken without approval from Moscow. "It is understood," Stalin replied on 5 June, "that nothing will be done without the sanction of the Central Committee."[24] The Crimean front, therefore, remained stationary. On the following day Wrangel launched his offensive, achieving the easy breakthrough which Stalin had predicted.

Lloyd George realized that Wrangel's offensive could damage his effort to reach a settlement with Soviet Russia. He could not negotiate with Krasin while helping Wrangel make war against the Soviets. Yet this was the appearance given by Wrangel's offensive, and one which the prime minister had to dispel promptly for the sake of British public opinion, if not for the more callous sensibilities of Moscow. Accordingly, on 10 June he sent Wise to inform Krasin of the decision to withdraw British protection from Wrangel. Krasin asked if this would be made public, and Wise replied that Lloyd George would announce it in Parliament.[25] Soviet leaders sought to extract the greatest possible political advantage from the British embarrassment. As early as 5 June, Trotsky suggested to Lenin that the British officially notified that their insistence on a suspension of hostilities had only allowed Wrangel to regroup his forces and resume the offensive. In particular, British public opinion should be reminded of Curzon's threat "to bombard Russian ports in the event of the continuation of our own offensive."[26]

This became the basis of the Soviet response. Lenin immediately branded Wise's statement "a lie and a swindle." "They have provided weapons, coal and a *Fleet* – and they then make this statement *through* 'Wise' (= Bullitt?)," he wrote. This referred to the Bullitt mission of the previous year which Lenin had subsequently come to consider as a hallmark of western duplicity. He therefore instructed Chicherin to inform Krasin that "the scoundrel Lloyd George is swindling you scandalously and brazenly; don't believe one word and swindle him in return." He also told him to address a telegram to Curzon, no longer couched in the unabusive language suggested two weeks before but instead in the form of derision. "Of course, after you have *already* supplied the arms, then *he* [Wrangel] has taken the offensive, and not *you*, and after you supplied the *coal*, then *he* commanded the ships, and not you, etc.," wrote Lenin.[27]

Chicherin instructed Krasin as directed and then sat down to compose his telegram to Curzon. In doing so he dipped his pen deeply in the poisonous ink he reserved for such occasions. After commenting at length on the British responsibility for Wrangel's offensive, he went on to say that the Soviet government considered it "more important to ascertain what actual effect will be given by the British Government to their present opposition to Wrangel's aggressive move." Recalling that Curzon had only recently threatened Moscow with new military operations if the Soviet government attempted to drive the Whites from the Crimea, Chicherin declared: "We claim the right to expect that the same measure will be applied to Wrangel now that he is the obstacle to the accomplishment of the will of the British government, and we would find it expedient to be timely informed thereof in order to enable us to co-ordinate our measures in this respect with those of the British government directed to the attainment of the same end." Having maliciously twisted the lion's tail, Chicherin concluded by focusing on the genuine concern of the Soviet government. As Wrangel had apparently been removed as an impediment to an understanding with Great Britain he asked "what obstacle still stands in the way of general negotiations between our governments aimed at a full agreement on all pending questions."[28]

Chicherin would have been delighted to know that his impertinence had raised the hackles of the Foreign Office. "It is absurd," exclaimed Lord Hardinge. "No answer," decreed Curzon.[29] But Lloyd George also read the telegram and, in his meeting with Krasin on 16 June, attempted to answer the question contained in its final sentence. He conducted a review of the negotiations, noting where general agreement had been reached and where problems remained. In the first category he placed the willingness of the two governments to abstain from supporting the enemies of the other. Both were also prepared to provide reasonable facilities, including free communication, for the commercial representation of the other. Britain for its part was prepared to abandon the blockade and aid in the sweeping of mines. The British government would not object to the deposit of Soviet gold in British banks for commercial purposes, but the problem of private lawsuits remained. Lloyd George thought it might be better for the moment that the gold be deposited in a neutral country as the basis of credits involved in commercial exchange. All British prisoners in Russia were to be repatriated and Moscow was to respect the independence of Georgia. Lloyd George thought there were only two points outstanding. The first was that "the Soviet government must undertake not to conduct propaganda or to interfere in any way in Turkey, Persia, Afghanistan, etc., in return for a similar undertaking by Great Britain not to support General Wrangel or the enemies of Russia"; secondly, "that the Russian government, if and when peace has been established, will accept liability to pay its debts to private traders."

Krasin had already indicated a willingness to exchange mutual pledges of non-interference in the countries specified by Britain, but in the context of mid-June with Pilsudski and Wrangel, supported by France, waging war against Soviet Russia, he had to broaden the scope of this question. "Even if Great Britain agreed to cease supporting Poland and Wrangel," he asked, "what security was there that the other Allies would not support them, thus leaving Soviet Russia in just as bad a position as ever?" Lloyd George said he would "do his best to persuade the French government to come into the arrangement too."

The second problem was just as difficult because it involved the contradictory assumptions on which the policies of the two governments were based. Lloyd George said the commercial community would have no confidence in the Soviet government until it recognized its pre-revolutionary debts to private traders which was essential to the resumption of trade relations. Krasin explained the manifold difficulties which this presented to the Soviet government, but said that, in exchange for British recognition of liability for damages caused in Russia by intervention in the civil war, some agreement might be possible. The prime minister replied that this was a question of state debts which was an entirely different matter and should not be confused with debts owed to private individuals. Krasin responded that Russians found it "very difficult to understand why a private person in Russia who was damaged was not to be compensated while the private trader whose property had been confiscated was to be paid." This might appear reasonable to bourgeois governments but the Bolsheviks could not accept it as a principle. Could this question not be postponed until the negotiation of a final peace settlement in which all claims could be treated globally?[30] At the end of this meeting, therefore, Krasin had received a clear answer to the question posed by Chicherin in his telegram of 11 June.

Unfortunately we do not have Krasin's account of this meeting. It is clear from Chicherin's subsequent response to Krasin, however, that following his meeting with the prime minister, he recommended some form of Soviet recognition in principle of pre-revolutionary debts owed to British traders. This emerges from two lengthy telegrams sent Krasin on 25 and 26 June in which the foreign commissar asked pointedly what advantage Soviet Russia would obtain from such recognition. Provided the British were prepared to pay a high enough price, not merely paper promises, but genuine removal of all barriers to trade, then, and only then, would it be possible to make this "colossal concession." There was also another side to this question. It had been raised at the Labour Party conference at Scarborough, which had passed a resolution against allowing private interests to stand in the way of a resumption of trade with Russia. "Our relations to labour organizations" and "the value we place on agitation," wrote Chicherin, "is so great that it changes the situation profoundly." Other issues also had to be clarified. Despite the British disavowal of Wrangel, they still seemed to be providing him with aid. Britain, he said, was "playing a perfidious and base double-faced game," not only in the Crimea, but in the Far East as well, where Japan was pursuing an expansionist policy in Siberia. Japan, asserted Chicherin, was "a country which is closely bound in alliance to England and for the policy of which the whole Entente is responsible." Krasin should make a point of stressing "the seriousness of the Japanese question and its influence on our relations with England."

THESE POLITICAL COMPLICATIONS, however, appear secondary in comparison with those arising from the Polish war. Chicherin told Krasin that Warsaw would soon seek western aid in obtaining peace from Soviet Russia. Such overtures would not be received sympathetically. Moscow, in fact, wanted to create a political atmosphere that "would put difficulties in the way of [their] applying to us in the interests of peace with Poland." This would inevitably lead to increased tension, but Chicherin emphasized that "a cooling of relations between us and the Entente would just now be advantageous." Here was the impact of the mounting optimism that Poland could be sovietized by the Red Army and the initial subordination of a policy of rapprochement with Britain to that of pursuing more ambitious political objectives in central Europe. This should not be seen as a reversal of policy. It was a tactical measure designed to reduce western influence on Soviet policy. It was part of a larger plan to give the Red Army time to complete the conquest of Poland. Whatever developed, Moscow intended to return to negotiations not only with Britain but France as well. In the event of negotiations breaking down, Chicherin told Krasin, "we consider that [the] rupture would be temporary and that England herself would soon begin to curry favour with us." Although Chicherin did not say so specifically, it is clear that at this time he anticipated the eventual trade agreement could include the recognition in principle of private debts demanded by the British. This concession would teach the French a lesson. "May all the French rentiers tear their hair," he said, "because their ministers are Clemenceau and Millerand, and not Lloyd George, and because the idiotic policy of the French government has deprived them of what their English confreres have received! You must drum that into every Frenchman."[31] At the end of June, therefore, the Bolsheviks were prepared to accept a temporary interruption of negotiations with Britain to facilitate the conquest of Poland, but expected shortly after to be able to conclude a satisfactory trade agreement and thus bring pressure on France to abandon its unrelenting hostility to Soviet Russia.

Lloyd George was also prepared for a temporary suspension of the trade talks. After a month of negotiation he had failed to secure the concessions he wanted from Krasin, and in reading the intercepted telegrams from Chicherin he could see that the Soviets were hardening their position. When one further meeting revealed that Krasin was inflexible, Lloyd George decided to force the issue by presenting a virtual ultimatum. In a letter of 30 June he demanded categorical replies on whether the Soviet government was prepared to accept the British position on the mutual cessation of hostile acts, return of prisoners, debt recognition, and the exclusion of personae non grata. The final point referred specifically to Litvinov but was also designed to protect Whitehall from the charge that the trade agreement would open Britain to a flood of Bolshevik agitators. As Moscow had already assented to the first two conditions, it was debt recognition which Lloyd George wished to test. He gave Krasin one week to obtain a reply and warned that in the absence of an affirmative response "the British Government [would] regard the negotiations at an end, and in view of the declared unwillingness of the Soviet Government to cease its attacks upon the British Empire [would] take counsel with its allies as to the measures required to deal with the situation."[32] He did not object when Krasin said he would have to return to Moscow to consult with his government. The decision would have to be taken in Moscow, and Lloyd George believed, quite rightly, that Krasin was the firmest advocate of an agreement with Great Britain.

In Moscow Krasin found a government intoxicated by military success and inclined to view the future with considerable optimism. "There is no need to make a pessimistic evaluation of the current situation," Chicherin told him, "indeed, to the contrary, we do not have to deprive ourselves, as we did in making earlier concessions, of that which we have won over the course of some time." This did not mean rejection of the British conditions; exactly the opposite. "Speaking among ourselves," Chicherin wrote to his representative in Estonia, "The British note represents a great diplomatic victory."[33] And it did, because it offered the opportunity of stringing the British along while the Red Army got on with its work in Poland. In these circumstances the Politburo accepted the principles laid down in the British note while Chicherin, in communicating this decision to Curzon, announced that the Soviet government viewed the proposals as being "equivalent to an armistice between the two countries." He said Soviet Russia only wanted peace and "this had been prevented solely by the absence of a similar desire on the part of Great Britain."[34] This was true as far as it went, but Chicherin was clearly seeking to position the Soviet government favourably in terms of British public opinion for the Polish crisis which was virtually certain to develop later in the summer. He wanted as many references to "peace," "armistice," and "cessation of hostilities" on the record as possible to impede, if not halt entirely, any British effort to aid Poland.

This tactic originated with Lenin who advanced it even more forcefully than Chicherin. The foreign commissar, in fact, was inclined to take a harder line with Britain than his chief, but Lenin carefully kept him in check. When Soviet leaders discussed the manner in which talks with Britain should be conducted, L.B. Kamenev, who had been suggested as leader of the Soviet delegation, proposed that the negotiations be conducted "in the broadest agitational sense" with the delegates speaking "widely and publicly to everyone of the history of intervention ... and touch upon and raise every question of eastern politics from Turkey to China." Chicherin endorsed this view; Lenin did not. He would not allow the self-indulgence of polemicizing with British leaders in their own capital. "The plan of comrade Kamenev is fundamentally wrong," he wrote on 10 July, "with Britain it is *only* a question of trade. Chicherin is not right. We must only send 'merchants' to Britain: they will sell for 2 1/4 kopeks and buy for 1 3/4 kopeks. Exposures there are harmful. This is not 1918. That is for the Comintern. All of Kamenev's arguments are arguments *against* his going [to London]."[35] As it turned out Kamenev did lead the Soviet delegation, but not with the mandate he sought. The Bolsheviks would attempt to shape British public opinion but not in a "broad agitational" manner. They would seek to aid the Red Army in Poland while not endangering the trade treaty with Great Britain.

Should the two conflict, however, Lenin had already established his priorities: the Soviet delegation was instructed "to hold firm and do not fear a temporary rupture of the negotiations."[36]

This position hardened as the Polish crisis deepened. In mid-July the Soviet government rejected both the proposal for British mediation of the conflict and the call for a London peace conference of east European states. Curzon's proposal to invite Wrangel to London at the same time but not as a member of the conference was greeted with derision. "We could permit the intervention of England in questions of the Crimea only on the basis of reciprocity," said Trotsky, "that is on the basis of our putting forward demands in relation to Ireland." Lenin thought the proposal was "a piece of knavery aimed at the annexation of the Crimea ... The idea is to snatch victory out of our hands with the aid of false promises."[37] All the same, the Soviets reacted differently to the British proposals concerning Wrangel. The White general had advanced beyond the boundaries of the Taurida province, and there was little prospect of the Red Army, deeply committed to the Polish venture, being able to deal effectively with him in the near future. Chicherin responded, therefore, that Moscow was still prepared to guarantee "the personal security" of Wrangel and his army if they surrendered immediately.[38] This, of course, was unlikely, but it was useful to offer further proof of Soviet willingness to end the civil war in a manner acceptable to Great Britain. When the Red Army did crush Wrangel, the British would be in no position to protest.

The Bolsheviks now felt the real power provided by the arrival of the Red Army in Poland. When Lloyd George sought to apply pressure by postponing a resumption of trade negotiations until hostilities had ended in Poland, they coolly reaffirmed their willingness to negotiate directly with Warsaw and, reversing their former position, agreed to participate in a general east European peace conference. They attached two conditions: Wrangel first had to capitulate, and the conference was to be limited to the representatives of Soviet Russia and "the leading powers of the Entente."[39] This was a bid to be recognized henceforth as a great power nearly on a par with the allied powers, with whom Moscow was alone prepared to negotiate the fate of eastern Europe independent of the petty states of the region. The western powers, France included, were invited to tell "the mutinous ex-general Wrangel" to surrender while he still could save his life and advise the Poles to accept whatever terms Moscow would offer them.

Such indeed was the future, but not in the summer of 1920. The balance of power had definitely shifted in favour of Soviet Russia but not nearly to the degree suggested in Chicherin's telegram of 23 July. Although defeated, the Polish army remained intact and a force to be dealt with before the Bolsheviks could send a proconsul to Warsaw. Important elements within the British government remained opposed to the negotiation of a trade treaty with Moscow, let alone a general settlement of east European affairs. And in Paris the French government would not engage in any negotiations with Soviet Russia. Although

Lloyd George was prepared to accept the Soviet telegram of 23 July as sufficient warrant to resume negotiations, in order to secure his colleagues' approval he had to persuade them to join him in closing their eyes to the real meaning of the message. He claimed to believe that it meant that "the [Soviet-Polish] armistice was on" when neither party had even broached the subject. When Curzon pointed to the part of the Soviet response which said they were only prepared to meet with the leading powers of the Entente, Lloyd George described it as ambiguous. What mattered, he said, was to get the Soviet representatives to Britain as quickly as possible. He then revealed his profound ignorance of Soviet politics. "Trotsky [he said] had been over-ruled by Lenin. Trotsky wanted to dictate peace at Warsaw. Lenin did not want it and has had his way. Unfortunately Trotsky would be at the Armistice. But Kamenev was Lenin's man and it would be useful to have him here."[40] As a consequence Curzon telegraphed Chicherin suggesting that the Soviet representatives proceeding to London for the negotiation of the trade treaty also be authorized "to discuss preliminary arrangements for the proposed peace conference." Moscow needed no further encouragement; Kamenev and his mission left the same day for London.[41]

Lloyd George could not get the French to endorse his proposal to enlarged negotiations with the Bolsheviks. Millerand found "the frankness ... with which Chicherin said that he expected the Allies to treat with the Soviet Government" to be remarkable. They intended, he said, "that no one in the world should mix up in their affairs," and, as a result, "even if he had no other objection to meeting the Soviet representative," he would not sanction French participation in the proposed conference. Lloyd George insisted that a clarification of the Soviet position be sought from Moscow, but two attempts in five days elicited no reply.[42] The Soviets were only interested in a conference held on their own terms and had given their highly qualified acceptance primarily to ensure that Kamenev would be allowed to proceed to Britain. With the delegation already in London, Chicherin was under no pressure to clarify Moscow's view of the proposed conference.

For the first two weeks of his stay in Britain, Kamenev had little time to devote to any question other than Poland. His meetings with Lloyd George, however, were free-wheeling affairs, and the prime minister repeatedly returned to the question of the peace conference he had hoped to convene in London. Kamenev concluded that in the interest of securing British assent to direct Soviet negotiation with Poland it would be best to put an end to the proposed conference. He wrote Lloyd George saying that Moscow saw no point in convening a general conference of east European states. Only a meeting of the representatives of Soviet Russia and the directing powers of the Entente, as suggested by Chicherin in his note of 23 July, "might genuinely guarantee the general peace of Europe," because "without the aid of those directing powers, the other states could not fight against [Soviet Russia]." He said the aim of the proposed conference "would be to regulate the international position of Russia and decide all questions between it and the allies in the name of general peace and prosperity." Lloyd George replied there could be no conference unless the Polish question was on the agenda. France would not attend a conference which did not deal with that question, and he would not summon a conference in which France did not participate.[43] The problem, in fact, extended far beyond the issue of Poland, for as Millerand had made clear two weeks before, he would not participate in any conference in which the Soviet Union was represented. On August 10 Kamenev was able to inform Chicherin that "the question of the transfer of the Russo-Polish negoti- ations to the London Conference does not exist any longer."[44] The conference was dead.

ALL THESE DEVELOPMENTS show the hostility with which France reacted to Moscow's effort to secure a negotiated regulation of its international position. Wherever the Bolsheviks turned – Poland, the Crimea, the Baltic, Great Britain – they found the French government seeking to promote war against them. Time and again they had tried and failed to open a dialogue with Paris. French policy was determined by many factors, political and economic; the Bolsheviks attrib- uted it primarily to the latter. Krasin exclaimed to one journalist: "You French are of a cupidity which is beyond imagination. Gold, our gold, fascinates you. For you the Russian problem is merely a question of your purse ... 'My money!' [you shout] 'and to hell with everyone else!'"[45] This was a view widely shared in Moscow. Moreover, the tactic of seeking political allies among the economic elites of western states was well established in Soviet diplomatic practice and had usually proved effective in softening the policies of even the most hostile governments. A similar approach to France, using the same golden tools, there- fore, emerged quite naturally from the past experience of the Soviet government in dealing with western countries.

There were, however, real problems in adopting this method to France. Else- where the Soviets had been able to work through entrepreneurial elites seeking enrichment either through the exploitation of Russian resources or international trade. While such individuals were not absent in France, they did not possess the same influence as elsewhere and were overshadowed by the multitude of smallholders who had invested heavily in Russian state bonds prior to the rev- olution. These securities had been repudiated by the Soviet government in 1918 and, given the popularity of this action within Russia, it could not easily be reversed. Nevertheless, the Soviet government fully realized the impediment which this created for the normalization of relations with France and had signalled repeatedly, but in the most confidential manner, that they were prepared to negotiate a settlement of this emotionally charged issue. Moscow had hoped that, once Britain had opened negotiations, Paris would follow suit and that the problem could be dealt with in the context of a general settlement with France. These hopes had not been realized, and in early August, with the entire inter- national position of Soviet Russia hanging in the balance, Moscow decided to take the initiative in an effort to break French opposition to the regularization of its position in international affairs. It required France to accept that in the future Soviet Russia would occupy much the same position in European affairs as tsarist Russia prior to the Great War.

The origin of the Soviet initiative cannot yet be established. With the exception of two documents, Soviet sources do not refer to the subject. One of these, however, is a telegram intercepted by the British which indicates that Chicherin approved of the step but only after it had been taken. On 14 August he wired Kamenev: "Krasin's journey to France would certainly be acceptable were it not for the recognition of Wrangel by France."[46] Thus, the approach to France appears to have been initiated by the Soviet mission in London. It probably had a dual origin, the first arising from the general effort to interest western businessmen in the restoration of economic relations with Russia, the second emerging from the international crisis generated by the approach of the Red Army to Warsaw. Kamenev, on his arrival in London, probably provided the necessary political sanction to proceed forcefully with the undertaking.

In any case, French documents reveal that near the end of July Robert Henri Muller, a businessman of unidentified provenance, visited the French embassy in London and presented a plan for the resumption by the Soviet government of payments due on the pre-revolutionary Russian state debt. He was interviewed by J. du Halgouet, the delegate of the French Ministry of Commerce who represented his government in the strictly commercial negotiations which Krasin was in theory conducting in London with the committee struck by the Supreme Council in the spring. Muller, however, could produce no proof of Soviet intentions nor any power authorizing him to treat in the name of that government, and in the absence of such authorization was told that further discussion was pointless. A week later, after Kamenev's arrival in London it should be noted, Muller again called at the embassy and asked du Halgouet to meet him that evening at the British Empire Club, where he promised to bring the proof of Soviet intentions demanded by the French delegate. Muller, in fact, did much more. He brought Krasin, who told the surprised du Halgonet that he and Kamenev were empowered to negotiate with the French government practical means of regulating the problem of Russian debts. He also listened while Muller presented a plan by which Moscow would assume the prewar debts of the tsarist government and convert them into new Soviet securities. The Soviet government would receive a new loan of £100 million to help finance the economic recovery of Russia. Together the two would form a single issue of new Soviet bonds valued at £1,000 million with interest at 5 per cent and a sinking fund of 1/2 per cent to redeem the securities at maturity. Interest and principle were to be guaranteed by the British and French governments. Halgouet received a memorandum of this plan which Krasin described as a "suitable base of discussion." The following day he sent a formal note to du Halgouet confirming their conversation of the previous evening and the readiness of the Soviet government to negotiate the question of Russian state debts. He was prepared to go to Paris at the convenience of the French government to begin these negotiations and, together with Kamenev, was fully empowered to conclude every type of agreement, "including treaties restoring peaceful relations." The same day Muller motored to Lympne in the hope of presenting these same documents to Millerand, who was there conferring with Lloyd George. Warned in advance, the French premier refused to see his enterprising countryman.[47]

The French were embarrassed and angered by the Soviet initiative, but not impressed in the slightest. During the conversation at the British Empire Club, Krasin had expressed his belief that the French government could not refuse to negotiate with Moscow on a question such as the regulation of the Russian debt. Halgouet, who was far better informed on this subject, hastened to disagree, declaring a bit too grandly that the French government would not abandon Poland "for a few billion [francs]." Much more was at stake for the French than Poland; the entire Versailles settlement was in the balance and they were not about to abandon that at any price. Moreover, the terms did not appear either favourable or realistic in Paris. They were, said the Quai d'Orsay, in the interest of Soviet Russia but not France. It was very unlikely that the additional £100 million demanded by Krasin could be raised on the tight money market of 1920. Even if it could, it would greatly complicate the issue of loans more important to the French government. "Credit is not infinitely elastic," warned this report, "and Soviet Russia does not appear to have merited the sacrifices which would accompany the raising of a foreign loan in its favour." Furthermore, the British and French governments could hardly consider guaranteeing such a loan as, in the event of default brought about either by the bad faith of the Soviet government or its fall, they would be left holding the bag. The French government gave the Soviet proposal no serious consideration. Millerand directed his ambassador in London to instruct du Halgouet "to avoid all contact with the Russians. He is to extricate himself as best he can from a very embarrassing situation."[48]

French embarrassment, however, had only begun. August 1920 was a month of red faces for everyone involved in the hate-filled and poisonous affairs of eastern Europe; within two days of the meeting of Lloyd George and Millerand at Lympne both the French and British governments would come close to collective apoplexy as a result of the unexpected action of the other. Lloyd George returned to London and without reference to Millerand accepted the peace terms which Kamenev said would be offered to the Poles at Minsk. Millerand produced an equally disturbing surprise for Lloyd George: his government recognized the regime of General Wrangel as the de facto government of south Russia.

The two actions were not directly related. French recognition had been in preparation since mid-July. If Wrangel fulfilled certain conditions – in particular acknowledgment of responsibility for the international obligations of previous Russian governments – Millerand announced on 20 July that France was prepared to recognize his regime as the de facto government of south Russia. Wrangel fulfilled these conditions, and in the context of the developing Polish crisis, Millerand felt compelled to act quickly. A substantial increase in aid to Wrangel constituted an important part of the French plan to assist Poland, but French law required that such expenditure could only be made on behalf of officially recognized governments. Recognition required the sanction of the Council of Ministers, and as the French government planned to disperse for the summer holiday after their session of 10 August, Millerand brought his decree to that meeting, where it was approved and signed. Only afterward did he learn of Lloyd George's action.

The French ambassador had informed the Foreign Office of the policy Millerand had announced on 20 July, but in the flood of information engendered by the Polish crisis its significance did not register in Whitehall.[49] Lloyd George had not been informed of it as he listened to Millerand expound at Lympne on French plans for increased material aid to Wrangel in the event the Bolsheviks did not grant the Poles an acceptable armistice. Thus news of the French decision took London completely by surprise on the afternoon of 11 August.

A second surprise quickly followed. That same day London learned that the American government had issued their own statement on the east European crisis. Appearing above the signature of Secretary of State Bainbridge Colby, it theoretically responded to an Italian request for information regarding Washington's position on the rapidly changing Russian problem. In reality the State Department, largely for reasons of domestic politics, had been waiting for an opportunity to express its views on the east European situation, and hurriedly released the statement which has since become known as the Colby note.[50] In it, the secretary of state denounced the Bolsheviks and reaffirmed the refusal of the United States to recognize Soviet Russia. While not opposed to an armistice in the Soviet-Polish war, Colby rejected outright any attempt to expand the armistice negotiations into a general European conference which, he said, "would in all probability involve two results, from both of which [the United States] strongly recoils, viz., the recognition of the Bolshevist [sic] regime and a settlement of the Russian problems almost invariably on the basis of a dismemberment of Russia."[51] Although seemingly aimed at Moscow, Colby in fact had fired over open sights directly at Downing Street, as it was Lloyd George who was seeking the objectives denounced by the secretary of state. Predictably, Paris was delighted while London, smelling collusion in the coincidence of the dual attack on British policy, reacted negatively. Rome, the theoretical recipient, was simply confused.

British surprise swiftly changed to anger and focused sharply on Paris. Curzon sent one heated telegram after another while summoning the French ambassador for an explanation. Fleuriau wired the Quai d'Orsay that the situation was "grave." The recognition of Wrangel, he said, had "shaken the confidence of British public opinion in the Anglo-French entente and handed the Bolsheviks a weapon in their propaganda against us." Curzon summoned Lord Derby, the

British ambassador in France, from his vacation to speak with Paléologue. "The whole thing as I see it," wrote the foreign secretary, "was the French reply not to Warsaw (because they did not know what we had done there), but to Lympne. Millerand had tried to get us to repudiate Kameneff and all his work at Lympne; and having failed, went back to Paris and sought to queer our pitch there." This was intolerable. It was, he said, "the second splash of the French in 4–5 months. Could the Alliance survive a third? This is the point of view that the French seem to have ignored."[52] Derby dutifully returned to Paris where he held several meetings with Paléologue in an attempt to sort out Anglo-French differences. This was not possible, as Curzon wanted a French declaration that they "would ... use their great influence with [the] Poles to induce the latter to accept reasonable terms of peace and assurance that if such terms are offered by the Soviets, [they] will not give any material assistance to Wrangel." The French would do neither and all their assurances that they had not acted in connivance with the Americans and were prepared to negotiate the wording of a joint statement acceptable to both governments did not satisfy either Lloyd George or Curzon. The foreign secretary dismissed the latter as "a form of words that would bridge over a gap that has real existence." Lloyd George decided he no longer wanted to paper over the dispute with France.

All this was grist for the Bolshevik mill, and they looked on with sheer delight as the entente collapsed. "France, it seems, has finally decided to help us," Kamenev wrote on 12 August. "Even if the whole Wrangel story was thought out by Lloyd George and Millerand as blackmail," he wrote the next day, "then the matter went far beyond its authors' intended scope. A real conflict has been created and a very deep cleft made." Chicherin instructed Kamenev: "We must at once make up to England, simultaneously carrying on with all our resources a furious campaign against the dishonourable and shameless policy of France."[53] Kamenev did not have to do much other than watch as the Council of Action voiced disapproval of any further British involvement with Wrangel. His contribution was a note to Lloyd George specifying everything Britain had done to help Wrangel and asking what attitude the British government would take following his recognition by France. The lesser bureaucrats at the Foreign Office were not impressed. "The object of this note, apart from propaganda," wrote J.D. Gregory, "is probably to drive a wedge in between us and the French. So in any reply we may give, we must clearly avoid repudiating the latter to the Bolsheviks." Lord Curzon, who was better informed, reacted more cautiously. He told his subordinates that Churchill had managed to continue certain aid to Wrangel even after the cabinet had washed their hands of the general and warned that "we must be careful on these points." The British reply, issued on 16 August, made no reference to France.[54] Insofar as circumstances allowed, it defused domestic criticism without further alienating Paris.

UNTIL MID-AUGUST the Bolsheviks held the initiative in the rapidly changing political struggle to determine the shape of Russia's postwar relationship with the western powers. With the defeat at Warsaw this initiative was lost. In a matter of days they found themselves on the defensive seeking to prevent a complete collapse of their painfully won political foothold in Britain. Their enemies, exhilarated by the Bolshevik failure in Poland, sought to organize the rupture of British relations with Moscow.

Well before the defeat at Warsaw, the Soviet government had unwittingly begun to provide their British enemies with weapons to use against them. The flow of candid telegrams exchanged between Moscow and the Bolshevik mission in London passed regularly into the hands of those British leaders most opposed to any settlement with Soviet Russia. When this correspondence revealed Kamenev's attempt to conceal Soviet objectives in Poland and active encouragement of the Council of Action, they saw their chance to force a change of policy on the prime minister. The added discovery of Soviet financial support for the *Daily Herald* allowed them to take the first step in this direction.[55] The *Herald* was the most influential of all Labour publications and, because of its constant criticism of the government, was felt to be a thorn in the side of the cabinet. It had come under the close scrutiny of the Home Office, which had uncovered its tie to the Soviet government. On 17 August this information was presented to the cabinet, who were told that the Soviet mission had "indulged in propaganda and generally been guilty of conduct which was not compatible with the conditions under which [they] had been permitted to proceed to England." Lloyd George succeeded in obtaining a postponement of the issue but had to agree that Curzon should prepare a note of protest to be sent to the Soviet delegation "requiring an explanation of the breaches of the conditions on which they [had been] received in [Britain]." After the meeting, Lloyd George convinced Bonar Law, the leader of the Conservative party, and Curzon that "the actual presentation of the communication to M. Kameneff should be delayed for the present," but no sooner had he left for his holiday in Switzerland than the Admiralty released a selection of documents relating to Soviet financing of the *Daily Herald*. These documents were published on the morning of 19 August with *The Times* even identifying them as "wireless messages ... intercepted by the British Government." There followed a torrent of abuse in which much of the press called for the immediate expulsion of Kamenev and Krasin.

Kamenev was obviously shaken by this sudden turn of events. He warned Chicherin not to make matters worse by taking any action in reply, and advised caution in the sending of messages to London. "Do not telegraph even in cipher unnecessary or superfluous matters."[56] At the same time, however, he used the same ciphers to submit a lengthy report detailing his financial support for the *Herald*. To be sure he instructed the recipient that "this telegram is to be destroyed on being read," but it is difficult to imagine what danger he thought might await it in Moscow. In committing it to the British post office he provided the worst enemies of Bolshevism with further evidence to use against Krasin and himself. Their position was already precarious, and Kamenev warned Chicherin on 24 August that the Soviet mission had already begun preparations to leave Britain.

Chicherin responded that Kamenev was "exaggerating the turn in Britain's policy ... this is not the first time Lloyd George has been guilty of similar vacillations. You should not regard them too tragically; tomorrow he may adopt quite an opposite attitude. Do not get alarmed at the shrieks of the press and do not take them in earnest; they are done by order of the Government; all this can be changed quickly."[57]

This was excellent advice. The two Soviet delegates had to stand their ground and determine the strength of those opposing them. Chicherin understood how quickly the political wind could change in Britain. In the circumstances of late August 1920, however, the crisis had been precipitated not by the vacillation of Lloyd George but the attempt by a small group of ministers to force a change in policy towards Russia. The prime minister, however, refused to give way. When Bonar Law sought his concurrence in a decision to expel the Russian delegates, he warned of the dangers, foreign and domestic, inherent in such a step. If not done properly it could shake the peace of Europe and the political tranquillity of Britain. He asked that a final decision be postponed until his return to London.[58]

Once back in Downing Street, Lloyd George had no difficulty in regaining control of government policy. In the interval Kamenev had secured Moscow's permission for a brief return to Russia and on 9 September asked Lloyd George for an interview before leaving Britain. This allowed the prime minister to deal with the question of expulsion in a manner favourable to continuing negotiations with Soviet Russia. Thus he returned to his tactic, used so successfully in the spring, of dividing Soviet envoys into acceptable and unacceptable categories. Six months before, he had gladly accepted the judgment of his political opponents that Litvinov was a dangerous revolutionary who should not be allowed to return to Britain; now he cast Kamenev in the same role. As before, he insisted that Krasin was a reasonable man with whom the British government could do business. Although his colleagues did not necessarily share his view of Krasin, they were prepared to suspend judgment while authorizing the prime minister to tell Kamenev that he would not be allowed to return to Britain. Lloyd George received Kamenev on the next day and charged him with attempted concealment of Russian intentions in Poland, financing of the *Daily Herald*, and collaboration with the Council of Action. Lloyd George focused his attack on Kamenev, carefully excluding Krasin from criticism and even singling him out as having behaved, as far as the British government knew, in a quite satisfactory manner.[59] By the end of the interview it appeared as if the trade negotiations themselves could continue.

It remained for the two governments to decide the issue. On 15 September Krasin, who remained behind with the remainder of the delegation following the departure of Kamenev, asked for new instructions. "It is possible," he told Moscow, "either to present an ultimatum and leave Britain in the event of its rejection or to wait for an unspecified length of time while seeking to excite, by way of individual transactions, the greed of the City for our gold and by way of the indirect pressure of the City to influence the government." While awaiting a decision, Krasin decided to test the interest of British commercial circles in obtaining orders from the Soviet government. He concluded contracts worth more than £1,700,000 with five Yorkshire firms and waited to see what reaction would follow. It was highly gratifying. "The publication of our deal," he wired Moscow on 18 September, "has produced a sensation in the City. Inquiries are pouring in, attempting to determine if we intend to do any further business." Two days later the Central Committee, at the request of the Foreign Commissariat, agreed that Krasin should continue negotiations for the conclusion of a trade treaty.[60] On 25 September Chicherin issued a carefully worded note protesting the treatment of Soviet representatives in London but neither summoning Krasin home nor suspending negotiations. He did, however, state "that the agreement reached between the two Governments by the exchange of notes at the beginning of July must now be considered lapsed," indicating that if the British wished to continue the negotiations they would have to do so without the benefit of the assurances given earlier by the Soviet government.[61]

Churchill and the other opponents of an agreement with Soviet Russia were not long satisfied by Kamenev's expulsion. Within a week they sought to expel the rest of the Soviet delegation. Curzon, who had no interest in a trade treaty per se, now joined those who wanted to expel Krasin, arguing that the remaining Soviet representatives were as culpable as Kamenev and should suffer the same fate. Churchill's language was far more colourful: "As long as any portion of this nest of vipers is left intact it will continue to breed and swarm." Lloyd George did not find it difficult to block this move, but could not obtain cabinet sanction for a resumption of the negotiations. His opponents argued that the Soviet government had only released a small number of the British prisoners and negotiations should cease until the remainder had been liberated. A decision regarding the resumption of negotiations, therefore, was postponed and Curzon was instructed to demand the release of the prisoners and warn Moscow that until they were freed no resumption of trade was possible.[62] The foreign secretary dispatched this telegram the following day. He warned that, "unless by October 10th we have definite evidence that the conditions laid down as to the release of British prisoners are being complied with, we shall take whatever action we consider necessary to secure their release."[63]

The day after receiving Curzon's ultimatum Chicherin filed an interim response in which he informed the foreign secretary that the time had come to "terminate [the prisoner] affair, settle dates, places, technicalities."[64] He also wrote Krasin, approving his proposed attempt to bring indirect pressure on the British government through expanded contacts in the business world while warning him to avoid further involvement in British politics. On 5 October Chicherin provided Krasin with the official Soviet response to the British ultimatum. It was a lengthy document in which the foreign commissar declared that "the Russian government

[was] *prepared* to return without exception all British war and civil prisoners who are still in Soviet Russia" and was also "*prepared* to render assistance in the matter of Englishmen detained at Baku." Similarly he asserted that the Russian government was "*ready,* as previously, to accept in full the agreement outlined" in the notes exchanged in early July.[65] This was very clever wording, for while expressing Soviet preparedness to meet the British demands, it did not actually commit Moscow to anything. It was clearly designed to elicit a response detailing British desiderata for a resumption of trade talks. Chicherin applied added pressure by instructing Krasin to publish the British note and his own response immediately.

This had the desired effect. Curzon wrote to Lloyd George on 8 October fulminating about the reply he had received from Chicherin. "The Russians ... have got ahead of us ... by publishing it together with my note." The following day the Foreign Office, with Lloyd George's approval, responded to Moscow in a long message bristling with invective but focused on the specific details of prisoner exchange. In addition it required that the Soviet government give as-surances that they would desist from "hostile propaganda, direct or indirect, and more particularly from military action or propaganda aimed at British interests or the British Empire in Asia." When these *desiderata* had been met, the British government would be prepared to renew the trade negotiations. Critics had no difficulty interpreting the message. "Despite the energy of the terms employed," wrote du Halgouet on 11 October, "the British Secretary of State hardly insists on more than the liberation of the prisoners."[66]

Moscow viewed the British message in the same light and on 13 October informed Curzon that it accepted his plan for the exchange of prisoners. Chicherin did not even mention the trade agreement or propaganda. This delighted the Foreign Office which had been trying to secure the release of some of the prisoners for over two years. The exchange proceeded smoothly and was completed in the following month.

While this barrier to negotiations was being removed, the Soviet government took other steps to enhance their bargaining position. The trade agreement with Sweden had helped initiate the negotiations in London and with the virtual rupture of relations with Britain, the Bolsheviks sought to expand their commercial contacts on the continent. Operations in Copenhagen increased, and Litvinov opened negotiations for a trade agreement with Norway. Moscow also sought the full-scale resumption of trade with Germany. All of these ventures were expected to have a salutary effect in Britain. Despite the hiatus in negotiations, therefore, Krasin did not leave London. Instead, he signed still further contracts with British companies for the sale of goods to Soviet Russia. Each contract included a clause specifying that it became final only upon the conclusion of an Anglo-Soviet trade treaty.[67] As the fall of 1920 witnessed a serious decline in the British economy, an increasing number of companies were prepared to enter into such contracts, thus enlisting them in the ranks of those who favoured the earliest possible signing of an Anglo-Soviet commercial accord. October also witnessed the conclusion of peace with Finland and an armistice with Poland. In early November the fate of Wrangel was sealed, and with it the last hope in the foreseeable future of a non-Bolshevik Russia. The end of the civil war created a favourable political climate for those who wanted an Anglo-Soviet agreement.

First among these was the prime minister who was, as Hankey wrote to Curzon on 28 October, "very anxious to press on towards the re-opening of the Russian trade negotiations." Another letter from Hankey, this time to the British ambassador in Berlin, indicates the reason for this anxiety. Lloyd George, said Hankey, was "very anxious that trade with Russia should not fall entirely into the hands of Germany ... it is of political importance, at a time of considerable unemployment here, that the government should be able to show that they have left no stone unturned in order to obtain orders."[68]

In this favourable context the Soviet government chose to launch their most determined effort since August to bring about a resumption of the long-stalled trade talks. On 9 November Chicherin dispatched two notes to London. In the first he drew the attention of the British government to the unsatisfactory state which the commercial negotiations had reached and complained of the "obstructionist character" of British policy. His second note addressed the contentious issue of hostile actions and propaganda which he had intentionally ignored while waiting for the exchange of prisoners to be completed. The Soviet government, he said, had already declared their willingness to enter into a reciprocal obligation with the British government to abstain from all hostile acts and propaganda directed against each other. That obligation, however, was not yet in force. It was, instead, "inseparable from and dependent upon the conclusion of a trade agreement between the Russian and the British Governments." Until the conclusion of that agreement, therefore, the Soviet government was under no obligation to abstain from actions deemed hostile by the British, and Britain had no right to protest that such actions were in violation of an existing accord. In both notes Chicherin urged the British to resume negotiations.[69]

These notes provided the basis of discussion in a meeting of Krasin with Wise on 11 November. Krasin clearly did not like the tone of the first note, saying that it "left something to be desired" and "was not in any way to be regarded as an ultimatum." He stressed, however, that if they were unable to reach agreement quickly "he would have to return to Moscow and it would be impossible to resist the argument of those who opposed him that the policy of moderation had failed and that only by recourse to other means could Russia force recognition from the Powers."

Wise asked Krasin, who agreed, not to publish the notes until they had been properly considered by the British government.[70] Curzon was not in London, and the problem could not be considered in his absence. Lloyd George asked Hankey to write the foreign secretary telling him of "the urgency of discussing the question of trade with Russia at the earliest possible moment." "It may be true [wrote Hankey] that Russia is not in a position to give orders for which she can pay, but unless the right to trade is sanctioned almost at once, it will, in the Prime Minister's view, unquestionably be alleged and widely believed that one cause of unemployment is the refusal of the government to complete the trade agreement."[71]

The stage was thus set for a confrontation within the British government on the issue of trade with Russia. Lloyd George sensed correctly that he held a psychological advantage over his opponents and was determined to exploit it. The collapse of Wrangel and mounting unemployment had cut the ground from under the feet of Churchill and Curzon. He knew he could bully the foreign secretary and did. Curzon had no popular following, and when unsupported by the Conservative leadership, he had to back down. Churchill was more difficult but still manageable. Lloyd George let him know that his threat of resignation was not credible.[72] Rarely has the importance of timing in politics been more clearly shown. Lloyd George and his war secretary had been engaged in a protracted struggle over this issue since early 1919 and at no time prior to this could the prime minister have taken such a stand. In the circumstances of late 1920, however, Churchill's extreme anti-Bolshevism appeared increasingly quixotic, and the prime minister was able to ignore him.

In two brutal meetings held on 17 and 18 November, the British cabinet grappled with the question. The ministers tacitly accepted Chicherin's contention that Soviet Russia was under no obligation to abstain from hostile acts and propaganda against the British empire until the proposed trade agreement between the two states was actually signed. "A chivalrous sensitiveness might easily have led a country governed by ordinary diplomatic conventions, to cease from propaganda at once,"[73] observed the Lord Chancellor, but everyone was well aware that such sentiments were foreign to Moscow. No one was prepared to say that any form of words would guarantee the future good conduct of the Soviet government; The majority held that the Bolsheviks were more likely to cause trouble for the British empire in the absence of an agreement than if restrained by a voluntary undertaking. Similarly, no one believed that a resumption of trade with Russia would make any significant contribution to the British economy; the majority shared the view of Lloyd George that it was politically unwise for the government to be seen as a barrier to that trade which might develop. Eventually only four ministers opposed a resumption of negotiations with Moscow. Churchill insisted that the minutes show that the decision "would not be assumed to hamper the discretion of Ministers in public statements regarding the Bolshevist system of government." 'It seems to me," he said, "you are on the high road to embrace Bolshevism. I am going to keep off that and denounce them on all possible occasions."[74]

The British government, of course, were not about to embrace Bolshevism. Lloyd George revealed the truth at the meeting of 18 November. "We would not want this [trade] agreement, if we were at peace with Russia. *It is a substitute for that.*"[75] The protracted struggle within the British cabinet simply to secure authority for the negotiation of such a limited agreement was indicative of how far the two states still stood from peace. And the British, it should not be forgotten, were the most flexible of all western governments. Within three days of the British decision the French government formally renewed their opposition to the talks. On the same day, in Washington, the French ambassador listened approvingly as the American secretary of state condemned the British for "pursuing the dangerous chimera of the establishment of commercial relations with the Soviets ... The only certain result would be to prolong the existence of an atrocious regime."[76]

The hostility and hatred which stood as barriers to peace did not emanate solely from western sources. Krasin was not indulging in mere rhetoric when he had warned Lloyd George that in the absence of an Anglo-Soviet trade agreement opponents of moderation were likely to get the upper hand in Russia. Just as no British minister wanted to embrace the Bolsheviks, Soviet commissars had no desire to throw their arms around British imperialists. Paradoxically, the chief attraction of an agreement for both sides was its anticipated negative benefits – the prospect of being freed from the unwanted attention of the other. This was clear from the debate within the British government, and it is equally clear from Lenin's reaction to the British decision to proceed with the talks. He received this news on 19 November and with obvious satisfaction passed it to Chicherin, but also called the attention of the foreign commissar to a more disturbing report which had just reached him indicating that the British were concurrently considering the military occupation of Batum. The report proved unfounded but the incident illustrates the conditioned response to expected hostility which three years of undeclared war had developed in Moscow and from which Soviet leaders, no less than their British counterparts, wished relief.

On the question of Russian debts, however, the two governments did not share even negative aspirations. Lloyd George still insisted that the Soviet government acknowledge their responsibility to pay pre-revolutionary obligations to British subjects, and other British ministers demanded much more. Lenin had also addressed this problem in his note of 19 November to Chicherin. "As to the debts question," he wrote, "[any agreement] must clarify, in an absolutely precise way, that we are not obligated to pay."[77] In short, the two governments had agreed to conduct further negotiations, but they were still a long way from the limited agreement which even the most flexible leaders in Moscow and London were prepared to sign.

CHAPTER SIXTEEN

Final French failure:
The preliminary peace of Riga
and the destruction of Wrangel

The three months following the battle of Warsaw proved decisive in determining whether peace would be restored in eastern Europe. As the Red Army began to retreat from Poland, however, there was little indication that a cessation of hostilities was near. The issues which had prolonged hostilities in eastern Europe for nearly two years beyond the end of fighting in the West had not been resolved, and the rival armies remained locked in inconclusive combat. Generalized war, it seemed, could continue indefinitely.

The French government were the primary partisans of battle. They hoped the Bolsheviks would finally collapse under the strain of endless warfare. Initially this was a negative policy counselling clients to reject peace, the "barbed wire" unrolled by Clemenceau when France itself could no longer wage war against Soviet Russia. Millerand had continued this policy to avoid an open break with Britain. In late August, intoxicated by Pilsudski's victory, the Quai d'Orsay abandoned negation and urged its clients to vault the barbed wire and frontally assault the Bolsheviks.

Michael Carley has shown that this turn in French policy was directed by Maurice Paléologue, the powerful secretary general of the Quai d'Orsay.[1] Paléologue had served as ambassador in Petrograd prior to the revolution and had close political ties to the most conservative elements of Russian society. He had not enjoyed the confidence of Clemenceau, but when Millerand became premier in early 1920, Paléologue assumed virtual control of French foreign policy and gave it an ultra anti-Bolshevik configuration. With Pilsudski again victorious, Paléologue set out to organize a single anti-Bolshevik front extending from the Baltic to the Black Sea. In a telegram of 28 August to all major capitals he declared: "The European states and especially the Powers of the Entente have the greatest interest in profiting from the Polish victories to destroy once and for all the Bolshevik government." Soviet enemies, however, would have to act quickly to prevent Moscow from taking advantage of approaching winter to rebuild the shattered Red Army. They would also have to act in concert, because a decisive blow could be dealt the Soviets only by the combined armed forces of Poland, Romania, and General Wrangel. Paléologue asked French representatives to present his plan to the governments concerned and seek agreement to pool their military resources for a final assault against the Bolsheviks. The secretary general was well aware of the reluctance of the Romanian government to test the loyalty and offensive capacity of their army by ordering an invasion of Ukraine, but said that Bucharest need only agree "to fix on their front a part of the Bolshevik forces, leaving to the Poles and especially to the Russians of General Wrangel the task of more active operations."[2]

It should be noted that this initiative occurred at exactly the moment that British opponents of the policy of Lloyd George were attempting to force a rupture of relations with Moscow. The Quai d'Orsay watched this drama with great interest, hoping for the success of the insurgents and a radical reversal of British policy toward Russia.[3] If political discretion prevented the French from calling openly for the expulsion of Kamenev and Krasin from London, nothing inhibited them from seeking the ejection of Litvinov from Denmark. Litvinov had been a thorn in their side for nearly a year and his presence in Copenhagen, with the opportunity which it offered for the collection and dissemination of information, was considered undesirable. On the same day as Paléologue opened his campaign to form a single anti-Bolshevik front in eastern Europe, therefore, he asked the Danish government to drive "the Russian agitator" from their country.[4]

Paris did not limit itself to asking other governments to initiate or continue hostilities against Soviet Russia. The French, like the British, had found it difficult to secure the release of their citizens held prisoner in Soviet Russia. They had made repeated attempts to do so since 1918, but had achieved only limited success. Moscow, therefore, still held several hundred French prisoners, and their arrest provided Paris with a ready pretext for the resumption of armed hostilities. To be sure, given the reduced size of the French armed forces, such hostilities could not be undertaken on any significant scale, but in urging their clients to attack Soviet Russia the French had to be prepared to make some armed contribution to the proposed crusade. On 25 August Millerand broadcast an ultimatum demanding that Moscow release all French prisoners by the end of September. "If, by 1 October, a single Frenchman is still held in Russia against his will," he concluded, "I will be forced to order the French fleet to take whatever guarantees are deemed necessary in southern Russia."[5] The date on which the ultimatum was to expire is significant, because the French could not hope to organize the single anti-Bolshevik front in much less than a month. If successful, however, they would need to be in a position to assist their clients in launching the joint offensive against the Red Army. The expiration of the ultimatum was to serve as the warrant for this assistance.

Every part of the French plan failed. France had broken free of British tutelage in Russian affairs but simply lacked the means and the will to carry out such a scheme. Nor did French clients share a common view of this Parisian vision. Mutual suspicion and territorial rivalries divided them as surely as in the past. Soviet Russia was able to take advantage of all these shortcomings, and, being far stronger than the Quai d'Orsay imagined, emerge from the contest with a greatly improved political and military position.

General Wrangel proved to be the only enthusiastic recipient of the French proposals. His dependence on France was so great that he endorsed the plan immediately, suggesting that military operations be placed under French command and initially aim at forming a continuous front of anti-Bolshevik forces. He proposed that Pilsudski direct his legions to the southeast while the Army of South Russia advanced to meet him.[6] On 6 September Millerand submitted this proposal to Foch, saying France had to do everything possible to bring an end to the Soviet government and asking, "to what degree [Wrangel's plan] appeared realisable." Foch responded three days later that the proposal appeared to merit study. Its success, he said, depended on political cooperation, and asked that the issue be raised in Warsaw. The following day Foch reported that Wrangel had just offered to come to Paris "to co-operate in the elaboration of an aggregate plan of action" and urged Millerand to agree. He suggested that the Poles also be invited to participate.[7] On 15 September the Quai d'Orsay tendered this invitation, stressing that Foch believed that "the Polish army and the Army of South Russia must, *without delay*, co-ordinate their efforts to struggle against the Soviet armies."[8]

This represented the high point of French success. The tide, in fact, had already turned against them, as can be seen in the Romanian response to the proposal. The Romanians were not interested in a resumption of hostilities and for two weeks managed to avoid even discussing the plan. In the meanwhile they sought the attitude of the British government. Lloyd George, of course, counselled peace and warned against helping Wrangel, saying that if the general was successful, "he was not likely to be more accommodating than Soviet Russia about Bessarabia." The allies had earlier agreed in principle to the transfer of Bessarabia to Romania, but the actual treaty embodying this decision had not yet been signed. This was due to the objection of the United States and the reluctance of France to defy Washington. Lloyd George was pleased, therefore, to inform the Romanians that the British ambassador in Paris had been given full powers to sign the Bessarabian treaty and "there were no difficulties as regards the British government."[9]

This information allowed the Romanian government to reject the French proposals. On 15 September General Averesco told the French minister that neither public opinion nor Romania's finances would permit a new war. Wrangel, he noted, was unwilling to recognize Romanian sovereignty in Bessarabia, and the Army of South Russia did not inspire his confidence. The Romanian government, he said, would not abandon their wait-and-see attitude. The same day Take Jonesco, the foreign minister, said much the same thing to Millerand at Aix-les-Bains. He stressed Romanian impatience over the delay in signing the Bessarabian treaty. The French premier promised to recommend that General Wrangel accept Romanian sovereignty over Bessarabia but did not receive anything in return. Romania would contribute nothing to the French attempt to organize a single front against Soviet Russia.[10]

But it was Polish refusal to cooperate that proved lethal to the French proposal. Pilsudski should have been a willing recruit in the French scheme, but he was not. He hated Russians even more than Bolsheviks, and the French plan aimed at the restoration of a great and conservative Russia. The French dream was Pilsudski's nightmare as it was incompatible with Polish hegemony in eastern Europe. The marshal must have been particularly offended by the French assumption that Poland should play the leading role in the destruction of its own political future. He, not Wrangel, commanded an army able to pose a serious threat to the Bolsheviks, but he was being invited to place it in the service of Great Russia, not Poland. Small wonder, then, that Pilsudski did not respond enthusiastically to the French proposal.

Polish disinterest was heightened by the French attempt to halt the eastward advance of the Polish army at the German trench line of 1916. Paléologue feared that an advance beyond this point would, as in the spring, mobilize Russian national sentiment behind the Soviet government and, in the absence of a prior political agreement concerning the future Polish frontier, alienate even the profoundly nationalist politicians grouped around Wrangel in the Crimea. In early September, when he learned that the Poles intended to advance into Lithuania, White Russia, and Ukraine, he filed an immediate protest in Warsaw. Nothing, he said, could justify such a military operation and warned that "if Poland persisted in its erring ways, it risked obliging [France] to absolve itself publicly of all responsibility" for this action. This telegram, dispatched to Warsaw less than a week after Paléologue had summoned Poland to join a single anti-Bolshevik front, confused both the Polish government and the French minister. Panafieu responded that it appeared difficult to pursue both policies simultaneously and asked for clarification. Paléologue explained that France was only trying to restrain Poland from seeking frontiers "which would be a cause of weakness by diminishing its homogeneity while preparing a [future] conflict with reconstituted Russia."[11] The Poles were clearly not impressed. On 3 September Pilsudski had warned Henrys that a suspension of military operations would force him to make peace at once. Once his forward movement stopped, the Bolsheviks could concentrate their forces and break through whatever defensive line he might establish. He therefore continued his advance, while Sapieha warned Paris that if Poland ceased hostilities Moscow would be free to concentrate all its forces against Wrangel.[12]

Pilsudski, it was clear, would not enlist in the French scheme on the terms offered by Paléologue. The French request of 15 September to send Polish representatives to meet with Wrangel in Paris provided him with an opportunity to put forward his own terms. He did so with characteristic bluntness, telling Henrys on 16 September that Poland could not continue the war unless he could obtain from Wrangel "some firm engagements ... assuring Poland territorial advantages more favourable than those foreseen by the allied powers." In the absence of such an agreement the Polish government would have to negotiate peace with Soviet Russia. That would be the end of Wrangel, because the Bolsheviks could then send a force three times the size of the Army of South Russia to the Crimea. He would not negotiate with Wrangel in Paris, but if the Russian general would send "qualified representatives" to Warsaw who were prepared to reach an agreement "leaving more latitude than the Entente in the determination of frontiers," he believed that it would be possible to convince the Polish people to continue the war. [13]

Pilsudski, for all his bluntness, had not specified the precise latitude he wished in fixing the Polish frontier. This was left to General Rozwadowski, chief of the general staff, who told Panafieu that Poland wanted "concessions of a political and economic order ... in the Ukraine and in White Russia." In fact, Wrangel should abandon both areas and confine his own attention to South Russia, the Urals and Siberia. [14] Such terms were hardly acceptable even to Wrangel. More to the point, they were equally unacceptable to France as they violated every interest which Paris sought to promote in Russia. The French sought the overthrow of the Soviet government not merely to destroy Bolshevism but also to create a new basis for the close military, political, and economic cooperation which had characterized their relations with Russia prior to the revolution. Pilsudski's terms sought to perpetuate, even institutionalize, the chaos of eastern Europe and thus deprive France of the surrogate tsar it had sought since 1917. The French plan for a single anti-Bolshevik front had collapsed completely.

THE OTHER HOSTILE MEASURES also misfired. September witnessed the failure to drive Soviet diplomatic representatives from western Europe. Paris dared not intervene as Lloyd George again wrested the initiative in Russia affairs from his British opponents and blocked the expulsion of Krasin. Kamenev was barred from returning to London, but the French realized this actually strengthened the hand of those who wished a trade treaty with Soviet Russia. Similarly, the French had nothing to celebrate when Litvinov departed from Copenhagen. They had sought his expulsion but instead he left voluntarily for Christiania, where he opened negotiations with Norway. When the Quai d'Orsay asked Norway to abandon these talks, the French minister was told that public opinion, expressed in a unanimous vote of the Storting, favoured a resumption of commercial relations with Russia. The negotiations, therefore, would continue. [15]

The ultimatum demanding the release of all French prisoners produced equally negative, yet quite surprising, results. The French government, of course, quite sincerely wanted these unfortunate men and women released, but it is difficult to view the ultimatum as an instrument designed primarily to achieve this goal. Such threats had proved useless in the past; Moscow was far more likely to respond defiantly. Moscow had no difficulty grasping the intent behind the French ultimatum. "This is an evident threat to bombard or take Odessa or some other towns," Chicherin wired Kamenev on 26 August.[16] This did not frighten the Bolsheviks; they had defeated earlier French attempts to establish an armed presence on the north shore of the Black Sea. But in September 1920 Moscow was intent on ending intervention as quickly as possible. This required the subordination of all emotional satisfaction to the single goal of peace and the international recognition of Soviet authority within acceptable frontiers. A further trial of arms with France, no matter how successful, would not promote these desiderata. It would complicate the already difficult negotiations in London and possibly incite the French to even further hostility. Thus, Moscow had to forego the pleasure of defying the French. Chicherin in responding to Paris on 26 September concluded with the unexpected declaration that: "Nevertheless, the Russian government are animated by such a desire to avoid any further blood-letting that they have resolved to yield in the face of brutal force." The French were hoist with their own petard. They received exactly what they had demanded but had lost the pretext for a resumption of hostilities. The Soviet government promptly published their declaration in France, forcing the embarrassed Quai d'Orsay to deny that their ultimatum had been an "act of violence" and asserting that it had been motivated solely by "the will to save French citizens threatened by certain death if forced to suffer the rigours of a further winter in Russia."[17] In the circumstances Moscow could not have asked for more.

Soviet agreement to release the remaining French prisoners marked the end of the aggressively hostile anti-Bolshevik policy adopted by the Quai d'Orsay at the end of August. It had failed utterly and had to be abandoned. Even before this failure was evident, the French government had begun to have second thoughts. The naval authorities in the eastern Mediterranean warned that, given their many other obligations and insufficient manpower, they would find it difficult to undertake significant operations in the Black Sea, while Paléologue himself believed it unwise for a French officer to take command of the anti-Bolshevik front he sought to build in eastern Europe. Nevertheless, had Paléologue been left in charge of the Quai d'Orsay, he would probably have attempted to continue the aggressively anti-Bolshevik policy pursued throughout August and September. At the end of September, however, the resignation of Paul Deschanel as president of France brought Millerand to the Elysée and his replacement as prime minister and minister of foreign affairs by Georges Leygues. This, in turn, led to a significant change at the Quai d'Orsay, where the post of secretary general was abolished and Philippe Berthelot regained the influence he had lost at the beginning of the year. Leygues and Berthelot were profoundly anti-Bolshevik, but the archly aggressive quality which Paléologue had lent French policy towards Russia departed the Quai d'Orsay with him. The acute problem, experienced at this time, of financing France's international debt certainly contributed to the rethinking of foreign policy aims.[18]

Soviet policy flowed directly from the decisions taken in the week following the failure to take Warsaw. Within a matter of days Moscow revised its entire approach to negotiations with Poland from a rather crude attempt at coercive

diplomacy to a genuine effort to conclude peace. To underscore this change
Lenin sent Karl Radek to Minsk to tell the Poles that, provided they were not
acting as agents of France and sincerely wanted peace, "it would be easy" to
reach agreement. In confidence he said that the Soviet government was prepared
to grant Poland very favourable frontiers. Territorially they were only interested
in Ukraine and were prepared to make substantial concessions in other areas if
Poland would abandon Petliura and recognize the government of Rakovskii. The
Poles were clearly impressed, and Sapieha told Rumbold on 2 September that
he "did not see how the allies could object to the Poles accepting any ... territory
which the Bolsheviks are prepared to give them."[19]

The allies could and did object, but, of course, for vastly different reasons.
Britain still favoured the Curzon line as Poland's eastern frontier, while France
opposed any negotiations with Moscow. The Poles rejected both remonstrances.
While seeking an even better offer from Wrangel, they decided to see what they
could get from Moscow. Peace negotiations were set to resume at Riga in mid-
month and on 11 September the Polish Council of State Defence drafted new
instructions for their delegation. Radek's declaration, while encouraging, had
also been vague, and there was a wide variety of opinion concerning the eastern
frontier to be sought at Riga. Everyone agreed the Polish delegation should
demand all of East Galicia, but unanimity dissolved as the council debated the
frontier north of the Zbruch. The military representatives wanted to anchor the
line on the Dnieper and Dvina, but they were in the minority. The council
eventually agreed on the German trench line, suitably altered in Poland's favour.
This left the northern extremity of the proposed frontier undefined, presumably
because the outcome of military operations then under way could not be foreseen.
The Poles, however, clearly hoped to minimize Soviet influence in Lithuania
and maximize their own in Latvia. This would require a common frontier with
Latvia while physically separating Russia and Lithuania. This would allow Poland to dominate Lithuania, and, by implication, contained the unwritten principle of the position now adopted by the Polish government. That principle was
the tentative division of the lands in dispute between Poland and Russia. The
Polish instructions allowed their delegation to recognize and sign agreements
with the Ukrainian Soviet Socialist Republic, thus accepting the Soviet position
advanced by Radek at Minsk, but the unstated quid pro quo was to be Soviet
acquiescence in Polish domination of Lithuania. As the German trench line neatly
divided Belorussia, the proposed apportionment of the western borderlands was
complete. The Polish delegation was composed primarily of Pilsudski supporters
and led by Jan Dabski, a friend of the marshal. They could be expected to pursue
his objectives.[20]

The Soviet delegation, now led by A.A. Ioffe, reached Riga ahead of the
Poles. They brought Moscow's ratification of the Soviet-Latvian peace treaty
but little else. The Soviet government had not yet prepared final instructions for
their delegation and delayed doing so until Ioffe had the opportunity to determine

Polish intentions. The choice of such an experienced diplomat and his conveyance of the ratification of the peace treaty with Latvia, however, were clear signals that Moscow wished a prompt end to hostilities. His first statement on arriving in Riga was intended to reinforce this image. Russia, he said, "has not changed her peace conditions; she does not, however, consider them as categorical." He was prepared to receive counter proposals. More importantly, he announced that "Russia was not concerned in the settlement of boundaries between Poland and Lithuania."[21] In "a frank and private conversation" with the Latvian foreign minister held three days later, however, he stressed that the Poles would have to recognize him as representing Ukraine as well as Russia. Thus he reaffirmed both Moscow's commitment to peace and its resolve to remain master of Ukraine.[22]

The Soviet government, however, still had no indication of what position the Poles would take at the conference. On 16 September, Lenin wired Ioffe that "the Plenum of the Central Committee will meet on the twentieth. By the evening of 19 September send your conclusions regarding the Polish frame of mind, whether peace is possible, if it can be hastened and on what conditions, and in particular how stand the questions of Lithuania, Bielorussia and Eastern Galicia."[23]

As soon as the Polish delegation reach Riga, Ioffe conferred with Dabski and, as far as can be determined from subsequent events, concluded that there was a basis for agreement. When the first plenary session of the conference met on 21 September the Poles silently, but effectively, made their position clear by failing to object to the credentials submitted by the Soviet delegation. These were signed by both Lenin and Rakovski, and prior to the meeting, considerable doubt had been expressed as to whether Dabski would agree to negotiate with Ioffe in his dual capacity for to do so would recognize the sovereignty of Soviet Ukraine. Therefore there was, as the British observer reported, "some surprise at today's meeting when the Poles accepted the Russians' credentials without discussion. It had been thought that the struggle for the Ukraine would begin at this point."[24]

Lenin now had to specify his own peace proposals. Until then the Poles had only been told that, apart from Ukraine, other territorial questions could be easily negotiated. This had been dictated by the need to liquidate Wrangel's army before the end of the year. Militarily this made good sense. Soviet Russia would derive much more benefit from eliminating Wrangel than continuing the war against Poland. Politically, however, this was a difficult position to take, even among the leaders of the Russian Communist Party. The war against Poland had been popular and many felt that it should be continued until the fortunes of war again favoured Russia. "Do you happen to know," Lenin told Klara Zetkin some time shortly after mid-October, "that the conclusion of peace with Poland encountered great resistance here at first, just as had been the case with the Brest-Litovsk Treaty? I had to wage a most desperate struggle, as I stood for accepting the terms of peace, which undoubtedly favoured the Poles and were very harsh for us."[25] This was an exaggeration, for the opposition to peace with Poland was not nearly as strong as that which had tried to bar capitulation at Brest-Litovsk.

It is difficult, in fact, to compare the two, for much of the earlier battle had been fought in public while this one was conducted behind locked doors. Lenin consulted the Soviet high command, who advised him on 23 September not to concede a frontier north of the Zbruch beyond a line extending south from the river Shara to the Stir. East of this line ran the tactically important Baranovich-Rovno railway needed to supply whatever defences would be built along the new frontier. Lenin accepted this as the maximum permissible concession and instructed Chicherin to adhere to it strictly. The foreign commissar took this proposal and a draft declaration for the use of Ioffe before a meeting of the Central Executive Committee. A reporter from the *Manchester Guardian* was present and subsequently informed the British representative in Riga that the proposed concessions were strongly opposed by Bukharin, who argued that they "would not be effective and by creating temporary hopes of peace would weaken the Russian effort." The peace proposal was approved by a two-thirds majority, but "Bukharin and others demanded that their names should be recorded as voting against it." Lenin promptly authorized Ioffe to offer Poland these concessions. "For us," he said, "everything consists of, first, having an armistice in a short time, and, second, and more important, in having a real guarantee of a genuine peace within ten days." If this was not possible, Ioffe was to expose the procrastination of the Poles and certify "the inevitability of a winter campaign."[26] Peace was at hand, therefore, only if the Poles agreed to it promptly and tacitly sanctioned the destruction of Wrangel's army.

The Poles were well aware of the importance of time. On 11 September Sapieha had discussed this issue with Panafieu, promising him that the Polish delegation would "play for time ... to reduce the danger which would threaten General Wrangel after the conclusion of peace."[27] This was before the collapse of the French effort to form a single anti-Bolshevik front and the failure of Wrangel to offer the Poles more favourable terms than those suggested by Moscow. Two weeks later the Poles could be reasonably certain that they would receive nothing further from either France or Wrangel. Therefore, on 24 September, when Ioffe tabled the Soviet declaration just received from Moscow, they felt free to examine it solely from the perspective of their own self-interest. It asserted Soviet readiness "to sign immediately an armistice and the preliminary conditions of peace on the basis of ... a [frontier] running considerably more to the East than the boundary fixed by the Supreme Allied Council on December 3rd 1919." It was only valid, however, for ten days after which Moscow was free "to alter the proposed conditions."[28] It focused, therefore, on the element of time, which was crucial from the Soviet perspective, while leaving the territorial issue intentionally vague. In the secret negotiations which followed, of which we unfortunately do not have a record, Ioffe undoubtedly continued to emphasize that agreement had to be reached by 5 October. At some point he would also have had to reveal the "maximum" concession which he had been authorized to make. Given the great benefit which Moscow clearly expected to obtain from the end of hostilities, the Poles had every reason to ask if the Shara-Stir line was the best frontier they could get. They were well aware of the importance of the Baranowicze-Rovno railway, and the Polish army, in particular, wanted a frontier to the east of it. There was also the question of the frontier north of Belorussia. Would Moscow accept a common Polish frontier with Latvia? The Poles decided to find out how badly the Bolsheviks wanted peace within the time limit which had been set.

They did so in two ways. Pilsudski sent the Polish army across the Shara-Stir line and advanced towards the Baranowicze-Rovno railway. In the north they captured Grodno and marched onwards in the direction of the Latvian frontier. The out-numbered Red Army put up a stiff resistance, but having no strategic reserve, was forced to give ground everywhere. [29] Pilsudski, as Ludendorff had done two and a half years before, simply took what he wanted. Polish diplomacy modelled itself on that of Germany at Brest-Litovsk; Dabski drew out the negotiations until the marshal had done his work.

The Bolshevik reaction to these events is somewhat unclear. The Soviets have not yet published the messages exchanged between Ioffe and Moscow during this ten-day period so it is necessary to draw what inferences are possible from peripheral evidence. British and French documents indicate that in the days following 24 September Ioffe "spoke pessimistically of peace prospects." The Poles, on the other hand, were reported to believe that Russia was prepared to accept a substantial expansion of their influence in the Baltic states, particularly in Lithuania. Considerable substance was added to this belief when Chicherin announced on 25 September that, in exchange for a similar pledge from Warsaw, Moscow was willing to recognize the neutrality of Lithuania in the Soviet-Polish War. [30] Until then the Lithuanians had fought together with the Red Army to oppose the Polish advance north of Grodno. In the following days the Red Army withdrew from Lithuania in the direction of Minsk while Pilsudski opened a wide breach between his adversaries. By the end of the month the jubilant Poles were reporting that Ioffe had accepted all their demands and appeared ready to accept a frontier even more favourable than the Polish government had originally sought. [31] In Moscow Lenin spoke bitterly about the delay in concluding peace. "It appears," he said, "that Poland is too closely bound up with the whole system of international imperialism." If this were the case, it followed from a Bolshevik perspective that they would be unable to secure peace at any price. As a result, the Soviet high command took the first steps to prepare for a winter campaign against Poland. On 4 October S. Kamenev ordered the creation of a reserve army to take shape behind the crumbling western front and, on the following day, turned his attention to strengthening the defence of Minsk. [32]

These measures proved unnecessary, for on 5 October Ioffe and Dabski signed
a protocol pledging themselves to conclude an armistice and preliminary peace
no later than 8 October.[33] This was preceded by a verbal agreement which settled
most issues, including the future Polish-Soviet frontier. Despite this protocol,
the actual treaty was not signed until 12 October. This was due to Pilsudski's
determination to ensure Soviet acceptance of one further annexation. Vilna was
still held by Lithuania, a situation which Pilsudski found intolerable.[34] Worse
still, the Polish government, under extreme allied pressure, had agreed to a
cessation of Lithuanian-Polish hostilities and the establishment of a demarcation
line which the Polish army was not to cross. Pilsudski had not agreed to this
arrangement and did not intend to respect it. As he could not simply seize Vilna,
he decided to stage a mock mutiny of the division immobilized by the imposition
of the demarcation line. On 11 October the division commanded by General
Zeligowski, theoretically in defiance of but actually under orders from Pilsudski,
occupied Vilna.[35] This *coup de théâtre* would poison east European affairs for
a generation. Its timing was linked directly to the signing of the Soviet-Polish
treaty. Moscow's signature would give tacit approval to the seizure of Vilna.
Pilsudski calculated that Moscow's need for peace was so great that the Bolsheviks would not refuse to sign the completed document. The day after Zeligowski marched into Vilna, the Soviet and Polish delegations, led by Ioffe and
Dabski, affixed their signatures to the treaty of Riga.

The treaty of 12 October, except for the conclusion of an armistice, was
essentially an outline of a future peace treaty. Thus the two sides pledged to
include in a future treaty provisions for free choice of citizenship; protection of
minority nationalities; exchange of prisoners; amnesty; economic agreements;
conventions for commerce, navigation, and communication; rights of transit;
and the establishment of diplomatic relations. In this initial treaty they mutually
renounced claims for war expenses and indemnities. The frontier was fixed in
the manner sought by the Poles, running from the Zbruch north to a line east
of the Baranowicze-Rovno railway and then north-eastward to the Latvian frontier,
thus creating a corridor between Soviet Russia and Lithuania. The two also
agreed to abstain "from any kind of interference in the internal affairs of the
other" and include in the future treaty an obligation "neither to create nor support
organizations" seeking "to conduct armed struggle against the other ... [or
having] as their aim the overthrow of the State or the social order of the other
side."[36]

Superficially, the Poles appeared triumphant. They virtually dictated the placement of their frontier and could probably have obtained a line still farther to the
east if they had wanted. Contemporaries focused sharply on this aspect of the
treaty. Boris Bakhmetev, the leading anti-Bolshevik Russian representative in
the United States, described it as "the brilliant triumph of Polish imperialism,"
while Panafieu denounced the treaty as a manifestation of "Polish megalomania."[37] In London the Foreign Office was very critical. "The corridor to

Latvia," wrote one official, "is an amazing suggestion, [and] bound to lead to trouble. The Poles already have one corridor, that to Danzig which should surely have sufficed." The Poles, of course, rejected this criticism. Sapieha told his representatives abroad that in extending its frontier eastward Poland was merely gathering the fruits of victory.[38] In strictly military and territorial terms the Poles were victorious. As the vanquished party, however, the Soviet government was oddly pleased with the bargain they had struck. Ioffe, reported the British representative in Riga, was "well satisfied with his achievement,"[39] and although Bolshevik commentators described the terms as onerous, the treaty was considered to be a triumph for Soviet diplomacy. This was due primarily to the free hand which it gave the Bolsheviks to deal decisively with Wrangel.

Moscow also derived other benefits from the treaty. Even viewed in the simple territorial terms, the Soviets had not done badly. Lenin placed this aspect of the question in perspective when he reminded a Moscow meeting on 15 October that in the spring, the Soviet government had sought peace with Poland on the basis of a frontier established along the front line as it then existed. That line was fifty to one-hundred and fifty kilometres to the east of the frontier just established at Riga. "Thus," he said, "though we signed a peace at a time favourable only to the enemy, when our troops were on the retreat and Wrangel was building up his offensive, we signed a peace treaty on more favourable terms."[40] This highlighted a very important aspect of the Riga accord. The Soviet government, despite military weakness, had been able to bring their chief east European adversary to the bargaining table and emerge in short order with an armistice and a preliminary peace. The loss of territory possessing little economic or strategic value was of minor importance in comparison to the political significance of this achievement. Nor had Moscow been forced to accept foreign mediation, as mooted by Lloyd George. Soviet Russia had clearly failed to climb into the ranks of the great powers, but the Bolsheviks had firmly established that those who had to do business with Russia would have to conduct it with them. They had also provided striking evidence that they could conduct negotiations in an efficient and practical manner, dispelling many of the myths which had been spun by their adversaries to discredit Soviet envoys and their behaviour abroad. Indeed, the French representative in Riga reported with "regret" that "all foreign journalists ... [had] been astonished to observe that [the Soviet] delegates to the [Peace] Conference had a humane, and even bourgeois, countenance." The journalists had been favourably impressed, he said, by "the good behavior, dedication to work, serious private life and abstinence from orgies of the [Soviet] delegates as well as by the modesty of the dresses worn by the women of the delegation."[41] With the conclusion of the preliminary peace of Riga, Soviet Russia regained the momentum, lost for two months, towards the pacification of its frontiers and the regularization of relations with other European states.

The impact on Finland was almost immediate. Helsingfors had concluded an armistice with Soviet Russia on 14 August, but following the battle of Warsaw lost interest in a prompt conclusion of peace. Resumed hostilities were unlikely, but the Polish victory served to relieve the pressure felt by the Finnish government in the course of the previous two months to sign a formal peace treaty with Moscow. As the military advantage passed to Pilsudski, the Finnish opponents of peace grew stronger. Already on 20 August the British minister in Helsingfors reported that the Finnish foreign minister had instructed his delegation at Dorpat "to do their utmost to spin out [the negotiations with the Bolsheviks]."[42] The opening of Soviet-Polish negotiations at Riga promptly altered this outlook. The delegation at Dorpat had already concluded that no further concessions could be expected from the Russians, and on 27 September asked for permission to begin final negotiations on the basis of the best terms they could obtain from the Bolsheviks. Helsingfors urged further delay but authorized the delegates to proceed as requested. By early October a draft treaty had been prepared which was sent to the two governments for final approval.[43] The Finns then waited to see how the negotiations at Riga would end. "From the moment Poland makes peace," Erich told the French minister, "Finland can only follow its example."[44] On 14 October it did so, concluding peace with Soviet Russia two days after the Poles signed the treaty of Riga.

The two documents were quite similar. Although the Dorpat accord took the form of a definitive peace treaty, it was nearly as tentative as the Riga agreement. Only territorial and navigation issues were given final form. Finland received Pechenga and a corridor to the Arctic Ocean; Soviet Russia obtained the districts of Repola and Porajarvi. This amounted to a confirmation of the *status quo*, because Finland already held Pechenga while having only a small garrison in the disputed districts. This force was to be withdrawn within forty-five days following the ratification of the treaty. The Soviet government promised to incorporate the two districts into a larger autonomous region whose people were to enjoy cultural freedom and certain unspecified national rights. Other clauses regulated navigation in the Gulf of Finland. Almost all other issues were reserved for subsequent settlement by the special commissions that were to be formed following ratification of the treaty. The two agreed, however, to establish diplomatic relations, an undertaking not included in the preliminary peace of Riga.[45] The treaty represented a considerable success for Soviet diplomacy. Moscow was primarily interested in pacifying its western frontier, and peace with Finland represented a long step in this direction. With the signing of the treaty of Dorpat the Soviet government had concluded peace with all its Baltic neighbours. This, coupled with the preliminary peace of Riga, argued forcefully for the Soviet right to speak in the name of Russia in international affairs. As long as a rival Russian government remained in existence, however, that right would be contested and Moscow was unlikely to obtain even de facto recognition from the Great Powers. Before the Soviet position could be further consolidated, therefore, the Bolsheviks had to destroy the government of south Russia.

THE DECISION TO GIVE PRIORITY to operations against Wrangel meant that in the future the Soviet high command would direct reinforcements, as they became available, towards the Crimea rather than the western front.[46] This could not be accomplished immediately, however, because time was required to redirect men and supplies towards the bases chosen for military operations against the Crimea. Nevertheless, by the end of August Soviet resistance in the south had stiffened. The Bolsheviks concentrated on driving Wrangel from the Kuban, and in mid-September the general was forced to shift the focus of his operations to the northern shore of the Sea of Azov. There he sought to capture Rostov and break into the Donets Basin but found his path blocked. On 28 September the Army of South Russia reached the farthest point of advance, well short of their objective.[47] Until then Soviet measures had been primarily defensive. As soon as Ioffe reported that peace with Poland was probable, however, the Bolsheviks began to build the military machine which was to crush Wrangel. They entrusted this task to M.V. Frunze, who on 21 September was named commander of a new southern front originally composed of three armies and based at Poltava. Three days later the First Horse Army was subordinated to the new front and ordered to the Dnieper to face Wrangel's left wing.[48]

Frunze did not have an easy task. Wrangel still held the initiative and was trying to destroy the Soviet Thirteenth Army. For the moment, Frunze said, he had "to hold out at all costs" on the left bank of the Dnieper and also cover the Donets Basin "without committing [the Soviet] right bank group, which [was] not yet ready." The morale of his troops was also low, and he complained bitterly that Budenny's cavalry were slow in taking up their assigned position on the Dnieper.[49]

Moscow already knew the situation was serious. Everything available was rushed south, together with numerous political workers led by senior members of the Central Committee. Lenin ordered Budenny to do everything necessary to hasten his arrival on the Dnieper, while the Soviet high command raided the Caucasus for more troops to send to Frunze.[50] Even before the armistice with Poland, Lenin began to eye the remaining units of the southwestern front facing Pilsudski east of the Zbruch. He proposed "to take a certain risk and withdraw some units from the South-Western Front for the quickest and surest possible annihilation of Wrangel." Trotsky, however, feared that this might "provoke Pilsudski to attempt the seizure of Kiev."[51] The issue went before the Politburo on 13 October, where it was decided, on the recommendation of S. Kamenev, to draw reinforcements for Frunze from the western front rather than the badly depleted Soviet divisions in the southwest. The latter would be left in place until it was certain that the Poles would not violate the armistice.[52]

In the following two weeks Frunze completed his preparations. As new divisions and necessary supplies arrived, his confidence increased substantially. On 15 October he reported a general advance would begin in a week and he had "no doubt of its victorious outcome." Lenin immediately warned against excessive optimism and stressed that the simple defeat of Wrangel north of Perekop was insufficient. "You must at all costs enter the Crimea right on the heels of the enemy." Frunze remained buoyant. The result of the recent fighting, he told Lenin on 18 October, "signifies also the beginning of the strategic collapse of Wrangel." He voiced two concerns: the onset of bad weather, and the continued failure of Budenny to bring his First Horse Army into position.[53] Lenin could do nothing about the weather, but he again wired Budenny ordering him to "take the most heroic measures" to reach the Dnieper as soon as possible. Wrangel, he said, was possibly "attempting to take cover in the Crimea. It would be the greatest crime to let him slip out of our grasp." Wrangel, in fact, had begun a general withdrawal on 23 October, with the intention of retiring to the Crimea for winter.[54] He had received ample warning of the impending Soviet offensive and had no desire to give battle on the exposed steppe north of Perekop. With the assistance of the French fleet, however, he hoped to defend the isthmus until spring. Over the winter he expected Soviet rule to be shaken by numerous peasant rebellions which would allow him to resume the offensive at a moment of his choosing. The stage was thus set for a decisive engagement at Perekop. On 26 October Frunze issued his final orders and assured Lenin that Wrangel could not withdraw into the Crimea before it began. Ominously, however, he added that there was "only one chance in a hundred of immediately capturing the isthmus." This was too much for Lenin, who angrily replied that he was outraged by the optimistic tone of this message, when Frunze clearly did not expect to succeed in the important task set him "long ago."[55] Long ago was only five weeks, but to the impatient Lenin it must have seemed closer to five years.

There was, in fact, no contradiction. Frunze had merely promised to begin his attack before Wrangel could withdraw into the Crimea; he knew, and properly reported to Lenin, that his main force had little chance of reaching the isthmus before the Whites. And so it happened. On 28 October, when Frunze launched his attack, all of Wrangel's mobile forces were still north of Perekop. The Red cavalry reached the isthmus in one day but not in sufficient force to capture it. The next day a second Soviet column reached the isthmus of Chongar, the only other entry to the Crimea, but was unable to dislodge the strong force defending it. There followed a five-day battle in which Wrangel succeeded in withdrawing his entire force into the Crimea. Frunze then brought up his infantry and artillery to force the two isthmuses. The bombardment which followed was very heavy, comparable to one on the Western Front in 1916 according to one British observer, and broke the morale of the White troops. On 10 November the Red Army entered the Crimea.[56]

The end came quickly. Wrangel had made no preparations to defend the Crimea south of Perekop and chose instead to evacuate the peninsula. He had first broached this subject with the French on 5 November and four days later asked for aid in embarking all his wounded and the families of his officers and officials.

When Frunze broke into the Crimea, Wrangel appealed for French assistance in evacuating as many of his army who wished to escape the Bolsheviks and offered his entire navy and merchant marine as compensation.[57] He also asked for British help. The British cabinet considered his appeal and rejected it, reminding him that in the spring they had offered their assistance in seeking an amnesty but he had declined their help. They were, thus, unable to "undertake any further responsibilities whatsoever" towards his army or government.[58] The French accepted Wrangel's offer and sent their fleet to Sevastapol to rescue the remnants of the Army of South Russia.[59] This was unnecessary, because on 11 November Frunze broadcast an offer of amnesty in exchange for the surrender of the White forces and their equipment. He promised a "full pardon for acts committed during the civil war" and "unimpeded departure" for those not wishing to remain in Russia, provided they swore a solemn oath to abstain from participation in further struggle against the Soviet government. Lenin criticized "the excessive lenience" of the terms but was prepared to accept them, provided Wrangel did not attempt, as in fact he did, to make off with the remaining warships of the Russian Black Sea Fleet. If Wrangel did not acccept the terms, he said, "we ... must deal with him mercilessly."[60] There was no response to the Soviet proposal, for as Wrangel prepared to leave Sevastapol he was not thinking in terms of abandoning the struggle but of renewing it in the spring. He had placed his surviving forces under the protection of France not to be carried safely into exile but to begin their reorganization for a new campaign.[61] In three days Wrangel embarked the best of his troops and an equal number of civilian refugees, some forty thousand in all, and steamed for Constantinople under the French flag. On the afternoon of 14 November the evacuation was complete; the following morning the Red Army entered the city unopposed.[62]

The Red Army occupied Sevastapol almost three years to the day on which the Russian civil war had begun atop the Pulkovo heights in November 1917. At that time the newly created Soviet government disposed only of a makeshift militia; in 1920 Frunze commanded a professional army which included considerable cavalry and artillery in addition to disciplined infantry. This army received the usual compliment paid by the Whites defeated in battle by the Bolsheviks. The military prowess displayed by the Red Army in the Crimean campaign, said one of Wrangel's close associates, "indicated an excellent command, certainly foreign."[63] By this the Whites attempted to convey the impression that they had been vanquished by German (which was meant by "foreign" in this context) rather than Russian officers and were, therefore, less responsible for defeat. This, of course, was nonsense; the Red Army did not achieve victory as a result of German, or any other foreign, leadership. Instead the Bolsheviks had painfully put together an army which had driven all their Russian opponents from the field. In November 1920, however, it was far from clear that the Russian civil war was at an end. Wrangel still hoped for a return engagement and other smaller forces, supported for the most part by Pilsudski, remained active in

Ukraine. Quite reasonably, therefore, the immediate response of the Soviet high command to the victory in the Crimea was to redeploy the armies of the southern front to ensure the defence of the Black Sea coast.[64]

In the three months since the battle of Warsaw the Soviet government had achieved a remarkable consolidation of power. By abandoning the attempt to create a Soviet Poland and instead seeking peace with Pilsudski and Finland, they had secured the opportunity to crush Wrangel. Having done so they remained as the only government exercising de facto power in Russia and most portions of its borderlands. This served to clear away one of the last barriers to serious negotiations for the conclusion of a trade treaty with Great Britain. Even the French recognized the significance of the destruction of the government of south Russia. With Soviet Russia in control of the Black Sea coast all the commercial transactions proposed by Krasin could be realized. Soviet commerce in raw materials alone could soon be expected to reach a yearly value of five hundred million francs.[65] Commerce of this magnitude would attract many entrepreneurs who had previously been uninterested in trading with Soviet Russia and greatly facilitate the regularization of relations with other states. It was none too soon, however, because in late 1920 the primary focus of Soviet foreign policy remained a satisfactory settlement with Great Britain and the negotiation of a trade treaty with Germany.

CHAPTER SEVENTEEN

"Getting Poland away from the Entente": Soviet-German relations

In the seventeen months which followed Versailles the Bolsheviks pursued a consistent policy of seeking improved relations with Germany. During this period they brought the civil war to a victorious conclusion, forced the remaining allied armed forces to withdraw from European Russia, and tentatively stabilized their previously undefined western frontier. They realized, however, that even this precarious stability had been obtained in a partial power vacuum brought about by the enforced withdrawal of Germany from eastern Europe. Germany had been hobbled, not crushed, by Versailles and it continued to possess the latent attributes of a great power. Bolshevik policy, therefore, sought peace, trade, and political cooperation with the Reich.

Initially Berlin sought the opposite, aiming to align Germany with the western powers against Soviet Russia. Only when it became brutally clear that this policy had failed did Brockdorff-Rantzau give serious consideration to exploring the possibility of cooperation with Moscow. Rantzau, however, did not remain in office long enough to bring about change in policy. He resigned rather than be associated with the acceptance of Versailles, and the new government of Gustav Bauer, with Hermann Müller as foreign minister, continued to pursue an accommodation with the western powers. This was the policy recommended by the permanent officials of the Auswärtiges Amt, who believed Germany should direct its gaze on "the Russia of the near future" and do nothing to endanger good relations with the government which the Whites would establish when they reached Moscow. "Bolshevism is doomed ... to fall," wrote Franz Zitelmann, the resident Russian expert at the Auswärtiges Amt, on 7 July 1919.[1] A week later Haniel von Haimhausen, the under state secretary, advised the new government "to continue the struggle against Bolshevism" and aid the Whites in the Baltic.[2]

Other German leaders did not share this confidence in the Whites. Müller informed the National Assembly: "It is pointless to prophesy future developments in Russia. The early fall of the Soviet government has been predicted for a long time. But today we must accept the fact that in the center of Russian life, especially in Moscow, Lenin still rules."[3] Nevertheless, he still opposed opening negotiations with the Soviet government, which he feared would complicate Germany's relations with the western powers.

The new economics minister, Robert Schmidt, felt differently. Prior to the change of government the economics ministry had advocated a restoration of trade with Soviet Russia, and under Schmidt's direction continued to do so. The difficult transition to peace had created chaos in the German economy and manufacturers were desperate for markets and raw materials. Russia, even when torn by civil war and ruled by the Bolsheviks, attracted German attention. The allies had no influence in Russia, and German merchants reported the readiness of the Soviet government to resume commercial relations. This was given official form in late July 1919 when Victor Kopp, an agent of the Soviet government, arrived in Berlin. Just prior to leaving office Brockdorff-Rantzau had authorized his admission, and the new government had not revoked it.[4]

Kopp appears to have reached Germany by way of Lithuania, where unsettled political conditions delayed him for several weeks. Once in Berlin he consulted with sympathetic German socialists who advised him to ignore the Auswärtiges Amt and approach the German government by way of the better disposed Economics Ministry. On 2 August he sent Oskar Cohn, an Independent Social Democrat and long-time Soviet supporter, to consult with Schmidt. Cohn told the minister that "the Russian delegate" possessed credentials signed by Chicherin giving him full powers to begin negotiations for a resumption of Soviet trade with Germany. As a start Russia wanted to exchange flax, leather, wood, copper, and other raw materials worth three hundred million marks for an equal value of German agricultural machines, pharmaceutical goods, and locomotives. Trade could be conducted through Lithuania, which was in desperate need of capital and the same manufactured goods as Russia. Lithuania wanted financial assistance and German banks could make cooperation in facilitating Russian-German trade a condition of any loan. Lithuania would receive a share of the products to be delivered to Russia. In this way Berlin and Moscow could begin to separate Lithuania from the Entente.

There was much more. Chicherin had given Kopp a full brief, and Cohn proceeded to put it before Schmidt. For example, he called attention to the article in the Versailles treaty which reserved for Russia and the border states the right to claim reparations from Germany. In the event it was exercised, Germany, already crushed by Entente demands, could only offer compensation in territory, "and that meant the loss of East Prussia." Germany, Cohn said, "had every interest in getting Poland away from the Entente. Soviet Russia is already prepared for negotiations regarding the renunciation on its part of the reparations promised in the Peace Treaty." Here in outline was almost the entire program for Soviet-German cooperation which Moscow would develop in the following three years. No wonder Schmidt found it attractive; in reporting the conversation to Bauer, the minister said he wanted to meet with Kopp the following week and asked that the Soviet proposals be discussed at the next meeting of the cabinet.[5]

The Foreign Ministry were not impressed and met with officials of the Economics Ministry on 6 August to convince them of the impracticality of trade with Soviet Russia. Economic conditions in the areas controlled by the Bolsheviks, they said, had deteriorated to the point where trade had collapsed completely. Fuel was no longer available for the railways, and it was impossible to move through the countryside without a strong military escort.[6] Schmidt did not accept these arguments and insisted that the issue be discussed in cabinet the following day. There, Schmidt was instructed to be discreet in talking with Kopp.[7] We do not know if he heeded this injunction, because there does not appear to be any record of the meeting. At some time during August, however, Müller joined these talks and reported to the cabinet on 1 September that Kopp's credentials were authentic and vested him with "vast full powers." He and Schmidt had conducted "wide-ranging conversations" with the Soviet representative in which they had emphasized that the Bolsheviks had to avoid any attempt to influence political developments in Germany; at no time had "a tie" with Moscow been discussed. The cabinet then considered the possible restoration of relations with Soviet Russia but decided "for the present to await developments."[8]

These developments were under way on the steppes of south Russia. Denikin had begun his march on Moscow, and Berlin continued to believe that the Whites would win the civil war. This view was reaffirmed in late August when a change in personnel brought new men to power in the Eastern Department of the ministry. Gustav Behrendt was appointed head with Ago von Maltzan as his deputy. It was the latter appointment which was important, because Behrendt was little known outside the ministry, while Maltzan soon took charge of Germany's eastern policy and guided it with a forcefulness which had been lacking since the November revolution.[9] Initially this involved no change of direction, because Maltzan too believed the Whites would win the civil war and carefully cultivated their representatives in Berlin.[10] Nor was his confidence in the Whites easily shaken, holding to this line after all hope for either Denikin or Yudenich was gone. At the end of the year he even canvassed allied military representatives in Berlin to determine if, in the wake of the White disaster, the western governments might allow Germany to undertake the military overthrow of the Bolsheviks. Maltzan was clutching at straws; neither Britain nor France would agree. By early January 1920 Maltzan had to concede that the Soviet government was likely to survive "for at least three to four years."[11]

Meanwhile the Soviet government began to apply pressure for Berlin to recognize the verdict of the battlefield. As early as November Kopp began to suggest ways of surmounting allied barriers to the resumption of Russian-German trade

and asked Müller to designate an official of the Auswärtiges Amt with whom
he could deal with this question in confidence. The foreign minister was not at
all helpful, deflecting the Soviet protest and saying that Kopp should deal with
the Economics Ministry on questions of trade.[12] Moscow gave the Germans a
further month. Then Chicherin broadcast two protests concerning White recruitment in Berlin, while Kopp again appeared at the Auswärtiges Amt to solicit a
more positive German attitude towards the resumption of trade. Both initiatives
received evasive answers.[13] Moscow, nevertheless, persisted, and on 27 December, when Kopp again called on Müller, he spoke much more forcefully,
observing that early in January the Versailles treaty would become fully oper-
ational and Germany would regain much of its freedom in international affairs.
He asked if the German government then intended to resume relations with
Soviet Russia. Müller continued to temporize[14] but realized that a resolution of
the issue could not long be delayed. If the Germans hoped to obtain any international leverage in Russia they would have to deal with the Bolsheviks. If they
did not enter into some form of relationship they might well find Soviet Russia
aligned against them. Maltzan concluded that it was in the German political and
economic interest to place no further impediments in the path of a restoration
of private trade with Soviet Russia. "The danger already exists," he said, "that
England has the jump on us."[15]

Karl Radek was doing his best to put the fear of Britain in German hearts.
Still a prisoner at the end of 1919, he had been moved to a private home where
he was allowed to receive visitors from the German political and economic elite.
Soviet victory had transformed him into a virtual ambassador with whom everyone interested in Russia wished to speak.[16] Steps were also taken to arrange his
repatriation, and on 10 January he prepared to leave Berlin. He was in an
expansive mood and told his visitors that the Whites were defeated on all fronts.
Moscow would make peace with Britain in the spring; negotiations were already
under way at Copenhagen. The Soviet government, however, also wanted talks
with Germany. He claimed Russia had a vast store of raw materials worth more
than four billion marks ready for export, but the Germans would have to decide
quickly to resume economic relations with Soviet Russia, because otherwise
Moscow might reach a prior agreement with Great Britain.[17] In an article written
just shortly before this interview Radek took an even harder line, warning the
Germans not to expect "for a moment ... the same concessions ... which we
offer Entente capitalism." The West had greater power and far more capital than
Germany and would be treated accordingly.[18] A week later he left Germany in
far grander style than he had arrived a year before.

Even before Radek left German soil Kopp had presented himself at the
Auswärtiges Amt. Meeting with Maltzan on 17 January, he said Moscow had
instructed him "to offer [Germany] the immediate opening of official relations."
Maltzan said this might be possible if limited to "a resumption of economic
relations and the establishment of official trade agencies." He had just learned

of the Supreme Council decision to permit private trade with Russia and warned his superiors that a prompt response to the Soviet proposals would be necessary. Kopp had promised to submit these in writing the following day and telegraph Litvinov at Copenhagen "to await a decision of the German government before reaching agreement with Britain." [19] In retrospect this can be seen as a transparent attempt to rush the German government into agreement. In reality, Litvinov was not conducting economic negotiations, but Maltzan had no way of knowing this. The next day Kopp appeared at the foreign ministry with the written proposals of the Soviet government. In the six-point document Moscow called for both governments to declare their readiness for the prompt restoration of "full official relations," to pledge non-intervention in the internal affairs of the other, to resume trade promptly on a state regulated basis, to seek secure trade and postal routes on sea and land and if possible by air, to exchange commissions for the care and repatriation of prisoners of war, and to agree to the establishment of a Russian trade agency in Berlin and a similar German office in Moscow. [20] Although extensive, the proposals were also flexible. Essentially, Moscow wanted some form of recognition from the German government, a firmer footing in Berlin, and the prospect of further negotiations.

German reaction was mixed. Haniel, now state secretary, who remained staunchly anti-Bolshevik, favoured outright rejection; Maltzan thought otherwise. The political tie foreseen in the Soviet declaration was not in Berlin's interest, he said, because it might elicit a negative allied reaction, but the possibility of a rapid resumption of trade should be left open. The proposal to begin the exchange of remaining prisoners of war, he suggested, offered a starting point for opening relations. The Versailles treaty, now fully in force, had made Germany responsible for the repatriation of all its prisoners of war. This process had already begun, and it was only logical that it be extended to Russia, where the Bolsheviks still held twenty thousand German prisoners. The British were already negotiating for the release of a far smaller number of prisoners, and Germany could cite these talks as a precedent. Haniel, however, remained unimpressed, and Müller kept Maltzan's recommendation under advisement. [21]

The conclusion of the Anglo-Soviet prisoner exchange agreement ended this indecision. When the cabinet met on 13 February the economics minister proposed that Kopp be recognized as a "semi-official plenipotentiary for the resumption of economic relations" and that Germany send a similar representative to Russia. Müller agreed, but stressed the need for continued caution. Germany, he thought, should "follow a path similar to that taken by Britain at Copenhagen." He proposed, therefore, that Kopp be recognized as the "semi-authorized agent for prisoner of war and economic questions." The cabinet approved, deciding to "make the attempt to resume economic relations with Russia." [22]

This decision did not go down well with the officials of the Auswärtiges Amt, who urged still further caution on their minister. Müller, therefore, altered it significantly in practice. Thus, in direct imitation of the British, as Maltzen had suggested, he limited the initial round of negotiations to the prisoner of war question. On 16 February Kopp was summoned to the Foreign Ministry, where he was told by Müller and Maltzan that the German government had decided to seek a prisoner exchange agreement and was asked if he had authority to conduct these negotiations. Kopp replied that he did and was prepared to open these talks immediately. He presented his credentials the same day and the next afternoon received a letter from Müller recognizing him as "the plenipotentiary of the Soviet Russian government for the regulation of Prisoner of War Affairs."[23] The first official step towards the restoration of Soviet-German relations had been taken.

Negotiation proceeded rapidly. Moritz Schlesinger, who headed the prisoner of war department of the War Ministry, completed talks with Kopp by the end of February. They prepared a draft treaty which Kopp was to take to Litvinov for approval. The cabinet were to consider it at their meeting of 12 March.[24]

This was cut short by the attempt of disgruntled army officers and reactionary politicians to overthrow the government. The Kapp-Lüttwitz putsch, as it is known, began on the morning of 13 March, when a Freikorps brigade, scheduled to be disbanded in compliance with allied demands, marched into Berlin and installed a government headed by Wolfgang Kapp, a Prussian civil servant and founding member of the ultra-right Fatherland Party. The Ebert-Bauer government, informed that they could not depend upon the Reichswehr to defend the capital, fled to Dresden and then Stuttgart. From there they organized a general strike which soon forced Kapp to resign. The putsch had come to an inglorious end, but its political consequences had just begun to be felt. The government found it difficult to end the strike, particularly in the Ruhr, where considerable fighting had taken place and executive committees composed of local majority socialists, independent socialists, and communists had assumed power.

The putsch forced the government to postpone all other business while attempting to cope with the crisis. The prisoner exchange agreement, therefore, did not receive their approval and remained in abeyance.[25] Once the government had fled, Kopp found it advisable to go underground as he had no diplomatic immunity. Nor did the return of the government improve matters, because Bauer resigned and a new cabinet had to be formed. Only on 27 March did Müller succeed in forming a government, and he found, it impossible to proceed with the agreement completed nearly a month before.

The Soviet reaction to the putsch and its aftermath made continued progress toward improved relations with Germany very difficult. The Bolsheviks persisted in viewing events in Germany through the prism of their own revolutionary experience and were not surprised, therefore, that the more extreme elements among the erstwhile military allies of the German Social Democrats would attempt to overthrow the republic. Thus Lenin initially saw Kapp as a German Kornilov and the putsch as a further step towards the long-anticipated German November revolution. The Bolsheviks had no stake in either the German Social

Democrats or the Weimar Republic and would not mourn their passing. They were, in fact, considered to be the chief impediments to a deepening of the German revolution and had to be swept away before the German communists could take power. Political realism demanded that Moscow try to deal with them as long as they held power, but Lenin had little expectation of significant success. As late as 18 February, when asked by a German correspondent as to the possibilities of an economic alliance between Russia and Germany, he replied: "Unfortunately, they are not great. The Scheidemanns are bad allies. We stand for an alliance with all countries without exception."[26] Indeed, a reactionary militarist regime, such as that which Kapp sought to establish, would be far more favourable to Soviet interests than the Weimar Republic. With their thirst for revenge, the former were likely to provoke the Entente, especially France, and perhaps ignite a resumption of hostilities from which Soviet Russia could only benefit. Karl Radek took this line on 16 March, when he observed that a seizure of power by the German right could significantly improve the international situation of Soviet Russia by compelling France and Poland to turn their attention to Germany rather than continue the preparation of war against Moscow. To this could be added the impact which a new war would have on German society, enhancing, in the Bolshevik view, the opportunity for successful revolution. Perhaps considerations such as these led the Central Committee of the German Communist Party to refuse for several days to join the general strike called by the Social Democrats to resist the putsch.[27]

All this would have been sufficient to halt the movement of the German government toward some arrangement with Moscow, but events following the collapse of the putsch gave them still more reason for pause. On 25 March the Executive Committee of the Communist International issued a manifesto referring to the German government as "the murderers of Karl Liebknecht and Rosa Luxemburg" and calling them a cowardly gang who had "fled from Berlin in fear of their own generals." They called upon the German workers to arm themselves and press onward to victory.[28] These were empty words. Karl Radek revealed the ignorance and uncertainty which gripped Moscow when he radioed Germany on 29 March, asking bluntly if there were any communists at the three stations to which he had directed his message who could provide him with a "clear report regarding the situation in Germany." In particular he wanted to know "which government was in power, which regions and cities were in the hands of the Communists and Independents, which tactics the Independents were following and what forces were at the disposal of the Red Army."[29]

As the German government pulled themselves together and read the file containing these messages they too wanted answers to questions of their own. When Kopp called again at the Auswärtiges Amt he was asked to account for the Soviet communications. He attempted to deny their significance, saying that the language was extravagant but it should not be taken too seriously.[30] He sent the German complaint to Chicherin, who simply denied the charges, indicating that none of the messages had originated with the Soviet government. "If the German government would allow us a better link with our representative Victor Kopp," he said "such misunderstandings will be made impossible."[31] By a better link Chicherin meant communication by diplomatic courier and cipher, privileges denied the Soviet government by Berlin. He implied that if Moscow could communicate freely with Kopp they would not have to solicit vital information from any source ready to provide it.

Other events placed the issue of Soviet propaganda in a different perspective. Soviet broadcasts were offensive, but they did not pose any real threat to German internal stability or vital interests. Moscow sympathized openly with the German communists, but no evidence could be found linking the Soviet government with the Ruhr insurrection. When Berlin sent the Reichswehr to restore order in the Ruhr no protest came from Moscow. The French, however, said it violated the Versailles treaty and sent their own army to occupy Darmstadt, Frankfort, and Hanau until the Reichswehr withdrew from the Ruhr. Here was a real threat to the territorial integrity of the Reich and further evidence that France still hoped to destroy German unity. Both London and Washington had approved the use of the Reichswehr to crush the revolutionary movement in the Ruhr but had been unable to prevent Paris from seizing further German territory.[32] French intransigence and Anglo-American inability to temper it caused grave anxiety in Berlin. The Germans needed external support, and quite naturally turned again to the east. This further entrenched a political pattern, observable since 1918: when threatened in the west, the Germans would seek better relations with Moscow.

THIS WAS THE MANNER IN which the situation developed in April 1920. Not only had the French enlarged their zone of occupation, but the allies as a whole began to demand that Berlin fulfill all aspects of the peace treaty, especially those calling for disarmament, payment of reparations, and extradition of war criminals. Thus in spite of hostile Bolshevik propaganda and even refusal to admit the proposed German commission of inquiry, Berlin still went ahead with the original plan to seek improved relations with Moscow.[33] At the moment it is not possible to say when and by whom this decision was made. There is no reference to it in the published documents of the Müller cabinet, the remaining papers of the Auswärtiges Amt, or relevant memoirs. The decision must have been made very shortly after the French occupation of Darmstadt, Frankfort, and Hanau, however, because a week later Grant Watson reported that Kopp had arrived in Copenhagen on 10 April, bringing the draft prisoner exchange agreement for Litvinov's approval. Kopp then returned to Berlin where, on 15 April, a Thursday, he requested a meeting with Adolf Köster, the new German foreign minister. Köster was not immediately available, but Maltzan said he could see him on Monday.[34] Watson believed that Litvinov had given final approval to the agreement, but from the one available Soviet document on the subject it appears that he referred the question to Moscow, because on 17 April

Chicherin wired Kopp that a counter-proposal was being sent by courier. A footnote indicates that this document had not been found in the Soviet archives.[35] Instead, the draft which Kopp had taken to Copenhagen was signed in Berlin on 19 April.

What had happened? Did Kopp fail to receive Chicherin's telegram, or did he ignore it? Either is possible. Chicherin's telegram was sent on Saturday and may not have been delivered before Kopp went to the Auswärtiges Amt on Monday. Conversely, Kopp, who was vested with "vast full powers," may have decided that he had best sign while the Germans were willing. In any case, the treaty was not disavowed by the Soviet government, and it is easy to see why. Whatever modifications Chicherin wanted could be left for subsequent negotiation. The significance of the treaty lay in the fact that it was the first contractual agreement concluded between Soviet Russia and Germany since the end of the Great War, a seventeen-month period in which successive German governments had tried and failed to align themselves with the allied powers against Bolshevism. Of equal importance, Berlin agreed to define Russian prisoners as "all Russians or former Russian subjects who have come into German hands, whether fighting for the former Russian Empire, or for the Russian Soviet Republic, or against the Russian Soviet Republic." As Robert Williams has so aptly pointed out, "[t]he treaty thus challenged the legitimacy of any non-Soviet émigré organization in Berlin ... and ... came close to extending de jure recognition to the Soviet government."[36] Less satisfactory was the specification that prisoners were to be repatriated though "welfare centres" to be established by each government on the territory of the other. Although this provided a legal mechanism for Kopp's continued presence in Germany and the sending of a German representative to Russia, its vagueness was presumably the cause of Chicherin's last-minute attempt to alter the treaty. As it stood, the article only promised that "the scope and duties of such welfare centres will be regulated by a special agreement." More than two months would elapse, in fact, before final agreement was reached on this point. Only on 7 July would a supplement define the scope and duties of the centres and provide Moscow with the contractual right to maintain contact with its representative in Berlin using ciphered messages and sealed courier bags.[37] The agreement was reciprocal, but in mid-April the Germans were not yet ready to send their own representative to Russia and would not have wanted to grant a de facto unilateral advantage to the Bolsheviks. If Kopp wanted the agreement signed promptly, therefore, he had to accept the article as written.

Germany's worsening relations with Poland also contributed to the decision to seek further ties with Moscow. The Reich had already lost Posen and West Prussia to Poland, and plebiscites would soon be held to determine the fate of Upper Sileisa, Marienwerder, and Allenstein. If the vote proved unfavourable to Poland, Berlin feared that Pilsudski would try to take the disputed territories by force.[38] With its reduced army and exposed western frontier Berlin realized it could not respond militarily to the Polish challenge. Unaided they could not escape the bonds imposed at Versailles. Soviet Russia was not only entirely outside the Versailles system, it was still at war with France and Poland. Moreover, in early 1920 all signs pointed to a new campaign in the spring.[39] The Germans watched these developments with fascination. They believed that the Bolsheviks would seek to crush Poland. Projecting their own hatred of Poland onto the Soviet government, they assumed quite wrongly that Moscow, rather than Warsaw, would be the aggressor. How, they asked, should Germany respond? Hans von Seeckt, soon to head the Reichswehr, had already formulated his answer. Having branded Poland as "the mortal enemy of Germany, the creature and ally of France, the thief of German soil, [and] the destroyer of German culture," he concluded: "Let no German hand be raised to save Poland from Bolshevism, and if the devil wants to take Poland we should help him."[40]

These views were shared by the Auswärtiges Amt. Müller told his colleagues on 13 February that they should expect an intensification of Soviet-Polish hostilities. Germany, he thought, should not intervene but "ride the Russian horse in order to prevent the loss of Upper Silesia to Poland." He did not fear a Soviet invasion of Germany; "they would digest Poland and be satisfied." The primary danger arising from a Soviet victory over Poland, Miller thought, was political subversion. Great care would have to be taken to prevent the Bolsheviks from extending support to German communists, but he clearly did not consider this insuperable. Like Seeckt, he preferred to confront any problem at the German frontier rather than seeking to preserve Poland as a buffer. "A Russian victory over Poland," he observed with satisfaction, "could influence favorably our position in Upper Silesia and Danzig."[41]

Soviet frustration in the attempt to negotiate peace with Pilsudski led Moscow to consider ways in which Germany might be induced to cooperate in a joint effort to render Poland more tractable. This was part of the brief with which Kopp had arrived in Germany and that which was meant by "getting Poland away from the Entente." No doubt it must have been raised repeatedly by Radek in conversations with German leaders prior to his return to Russia. At the time it led nowhere, because the German government were not even prepared to acknowledge the presence of a Soviet representative in Berlin, much less cooperate against Poland. Other Germans were not nearly as reticent and extended feelers to Moscow concerning possible cooperation. Thus, on 14 February Chicherin informed Litvinov that reports had reached Moscow "that the Ludendorff circle wishes to join us against Poland." Presumably this was part of the preparation for the putsch unleashed the following month, and not too much should be made of it, as the generals involved were simultaneously extending feelers to the British, offering them assistance in crushing Bolshevism![42] Chicherin, in any case, denied Soviet interest in such a combination and instructed Litvinov to warn the Poles of their peril should they insist on continuing the war against Russia.[43] The report should not be ignored, however, as it reflected both the political logic arising from Poland's simultaneous pursuit of expansionist objectives at the expense of its two great neighbours and the advantage which Moscow hoped to draw from it. In February the Soviet government still hoped to negotiate peace with Warsaw and, among other tactics used for this purpose, sought to put the fear of Germany in Polish hearts.

It is unlikely, therefore, that the proposal for a Soviet-German alliance submitted by two alleged Soviet agents to an unidentified member of the Auswärtiges Amt on 9 and 11 February, actually originated in Moscow. Robert Himmer has accepted the authenticity of the proposal and argued that it was a part of an effort by Trotsky to prepare Russia for the anticipated Polish offensive.[44] A close reading of the documents suggests, however, that the proposal probably originated with the "agents" themselves, possibly to collect information which they might find useful in working their passage with the Soviet government. The first agent was identified only as "a political personage of the Ukraine but who is in closer touch with Soviet Russia." The second man was unknown to the German official but introduced as "a friend of Litvinov" and as just having arrived from Moscow. No mention is made of either man possessing credentials authorizing him to speak on behalf of the Soviet government or any other party. It should also be noted that the proposed alliance was not limited to Germany but was also intended to extend to a third power, coyly identified only as a state "which sits in the Far East." Clearly this was Japan (not Turkey as Himmer suggests), a power which no one in Moscow could possibly imagine as an ally of Soviet Russia. Moreover the information submitted by the two men about conditions then existing in Russia was vague and frequently in error. It was, however, together with the scheme of a Japanese-Russian-German triple alliance (originally formulated when it was expected that the Whites would win the Russian civil war), the type of information which well-informed émigré circles in Berlin might be expected to possess in the late winter of 1920.[45] These men, therefore, were more likely to have been opportunists, possibly agents provocateurs, than agents of the Soviet government or any political circle in Moscow. Despite the willingness of the German official to meet them again there is no record of their having returned to the Auswärtiges Amt.

In time, however, the mounting threat to the Soviet western frontier did bring the Bolsheviks to make genuine proposals for joint action against Poland to the German government. In fact, for a short while in April and early May 1920 the Soviet government debated the possibility of a radical reorientation of their entire foreign policy from the objective of seeking to consolidate their international position through agreement with Britain to one of alignment with Germany to build the best possible defence against a perceived attempt on the part of the Entente, including Britain, to renew intervention in Russia. Agreement with Britain was clearly the preferred policy, but only if it resulted in peace. As long as the British position remained in doubt the Bolsheviks had to retain the option of turning to Germany. Thus, in mid-April, as the Polish menace grew daily,

Kopp made a direct political approach seeking dramatically greater cooperation with Germany. He sought to ascertain the possibility of organizing "a combination between the German and Red armies with a view to proceeding against Poland together." This thoroughly nonplussed Maltzan, who replied that Soviet propaganda, which included calling the German head of state a hired thug, made such a combination very unlikely. The conclusion of this bizarre conversation casts in high relief the grotesque political environment of Berlin in April 1920 and its negative impact on Soviet-German relations. Kopp, who suffered constant harassment from German right-wing extremists, asked for police protection, and, when Maltzan agreed, gratefully assured him that, "in the not too distant future" when a Soviet government was established in Berlin he would return the favour by placing Maltzan "under his personal protection."[46]

BOLSHEVIK PROPAGANDA AND German fear of revolution were not, however, the primary impediment to Soviet-German cooperation. German authorities were sufficiently confident of their hold on power to overlook these considerations when it suited their purpose. Nothing came of the Soviet April overtures because they ran counter to established German policy. Berlin still intended to allow the British to set the pace in economic negotiations with Soviet Russia and, while refusing to aid Pilsudski, did not intend to inflame the French by attacking Poland. In these circumstances it was fortunate for Moscow that the British were not, in fact, backing Poland or seeking to continue intervention. Had this been the case the Germans would probably have adopted an even more negative attitude towards Soviet Russia. As it was, Moscow soon established that there was reason to believe that Lloyd George was serious in wishing to negotiate a settlement. On 5 May Chicherin instructed Krasin to proceed to London, and for the moment economic and political negotiations with Germany were postponed.

There was no postponement of the Soviet-Polish war. Pisudski's impressive victories in late April surprised the Germans but did not cause them to change their view of the war. In June the tide turned and the Red Army began the long march which would, in time, bring them to the German frontier. Berlin remained unconcerned. On 21 June, State Secretary Haniel told the foreign affairs committee of the Reichrat (the upper house of the German parliament), that the Soviet advance posed no immediate threat to Germany. Major von Böttischer, representing the Reichswehr, explained that the Red Army was still nearly four hundred kilometres from the German frontier and correctly estimated that the Russians would not reach it until August. He did not believe the Red Army would seek to cross the frontier. This estimate of Soviet intentions, was based on information conveyed to the Reichswehr by one or more Red Army officers sent to Germany in the early summer of 1920. They brought an accurate account of the Soviet counter offensive unleashed against Pilsudski in June and the military results expected to follow from it.[47]

As the Red Army offensive gathered momentum, Moscow provided Berlin with further assurances of Soviet goodwill. When Gustav Hilger, the newly appointed head of the German prisoner exchange commission, arrived in Moscow on 22 June, he was cordially received by Chicherin. The war against Poland, he said, was purely defensive and in no way influenced the foundations of Russian foreign policy, which was one of peace with all peoples. Soviet Russia only wished "to enter into close economic, political and cultural relations with the German people as soon as possible."[48] Maltzan officially thanked Kopp for the Soviet statement but must also have explained verbally that the German government was less concerned by military aggression than political subversion. In any case, a wire from Chicherin on 2 July declared that Soviet government representatives abroad had been expressly forbidden to interfere in the internal affairs of the states to which they were accredited.[49] These pledges were received cautiously in Berlin. Haniel referred approvingly to Chicherin's telegram of 2 July when testifying before the foreign affairs committee, where he said there was no evidence to prove that Kopp was interfering in the internal affairs of Germany.[50] He did not, however, change anyone's mind. This did not prevent the Germans from signing the supplementary accord to the prisoner exchange agreement which established the reciprocal privilege of both governments to communicate with their representatives by courier and cypher.[51] With Hilger now in Russia and the Red Army approaching the German frontier, Berlin no doubt felt the need for an assured communication link with Moscow.

In the midst of these developments the German political world underwent a significant change. Elections for the Reichstag in June resulted in a substantial loss of votes for the Social Democrats and the Democratic Party, while parties to the political left and right of the former Weimar coalition increased their number of deputies. It proved difficult to form a new government as neither the old coalition, nor any one party could command a majority in the Reischstag. A prolonged crisis ensued which was only resolved by the Social Democrats acquiescing in the formation of a bourgeois minority government composed of the Centre Party, Democratic Party, and People's Party. This was a significant shift to the right, with the sixty-eight-year-old Konstantin Fehrenbach of the Centre Party becoming chancellor. Walter Simons, a non-party "specialist," was named foreign minister. Simons was a distinguished jurist, but he lacked political influence and a practical knowledge of the Auswärtiges Amt.[52] As a result the authority of the permanent officials increased and Maltzan assumed even greater importance than previously. Together with the decline of the Social Democrats, this produced a more favourable political environment for improved Soviet-German relations. Realpolitik, at which Soviet Russia excelled, came to assume greater importance at the Wilhelmstrasse.

Initially, however, the new German government had to deal with the allies who had summoned them to Spa to account for the failure of Germany to fulfill the obligations assumed at Versailles. Heading the agenda were disarmament and reparations. For eleven days (5–16 July) the German delegation, including Fehrenbach, Simons, and Seeckt, were subjected to unrelenting pressure to accept the allied demands. On several occasions the conference nearly collapsed but struggled on to a series of paper compromises which the French considered inadequate and the Germans felt to be grossly unfair.[53] Fehrenbach and Simons returned to Berlin with a heightened awareness of French hostility and how little the British could contain it.

During their absence the eastern crisis had deepened. At the end of the first week in July, Haniel had informed Simons that Poland would be "thrashed soundly." The government, he added, would have to deal with the consequences of this development in a month if not sooner.[54] The Germans also had to deal with the consequences of the parallel Bolshevik decision to attempt to install a Soviet government in Poland. Kopp appears to have learned of this sometime in early July, but it is not clear what use, if any, Moscow intended him to make of it in Berlin. In any case, he soon became clamorous in his demand to discuss the consequences of Polish defeat with Simons.

Kopp had attempted to see the foreign minister before he left for Spa but had been politely rebuffed. On 14 July he was back again, saying he had to see Simons as soon as he returned. Events in the Soviet-Polish war and at Spa made a "prompt clarification of German-Russian relations desirable and necessary." He alleged that the Entente was seeking peace on the basis of Soviet acceptance of the Versailles treaty and, while denying that Moscow would accept this offer, insisted it was necessary to define a different basis for the relations of the two countries.[55] This, it should be noted, was an argument drawn from the original brief with which Kopp had arrived in Germany. It had been refashioned to fit the changed circumstances of July 1920 but was purely abstract and reflected neither any negotiations then being conducted by Moscow nor the intent of the Soviet government. Kopp, however, was careful, both in this and a second meeting with Maltzan five days later, to stress that he spoke only with the knowledge of his government and not at their bidding. He said he had been recalled for consultations and did not want to leave Berlin without learning how the German government viewed the future development of relations with Soviet Russia. He then revealed that Moscow did not intend to make peace with Poland "under the aegis of the Entente" but hoped instead to install a socialist government in Warsaw. "He knew that Germany was bound by the Versailles peace and could take no initiative in this question. Russia on the other hand was free to demand far reaching concessions from Poland." To promote "good-neighbourly" and future economic relations, he implied that Moscow would urge a socialist government in Warsaw to yield the Polish corridor and Upper Silesia to Germany and agree that Germany and Russia should have a common frontier south of Lithuania in the vicinity of Bialystok.[56]

Kopp met Simons the next day, suggesting in a "tentative and non-binding" manner that Germany and Russia renounce the treaty of Brest-Litovsk and its supplements, proclaim that a state of peace existed between them, convene a conference to work out the concrete conditions of that peace, and exchange political representatives on a "provisional basis." This had to be done promptly,

before Soviet Russia made peace in order to present the entente with a fait
accompli. Kopp reported that Simons had accepted all his proposals but had
added that he also considered it necessary for the Soviet government to issue "a
formal declaration that the murderers [of Count Wilhelm von Mirbach] had
received due punishment." This referred to the July 1918 assassination of the
German minister in Moscow[57] and had not previously arisen in the discussions.
It was soon to assume considerable importance, but here it appears to have been
dealt with quickly, the Soviet envoy saying that, in so far as he could remember,
"a number of very heavy sentences had been handed down in punishment" and
the foreign minister responding that the German government would be satisfied
by a Soviet statement concerning the sentences. Simons said he would address
a personal letter to Chicherin on the subject.[58]

The letter, in fact, was already being prepared, but first Simons had to deal
with a more pressing matter. The advance of the Red Army made it essential
that Germany insulate itself from the Soviet-Polish war and forestall, in so far
as possible, any western pressure to assist Poland. On 20 July the cabinet officially proclaimed German neutrality, equipping themselves with all the rights
provided by the Hague convention and laying the legal basis for measures to
bar German territory to the belligerents.[59] This provided a welcome justification
for the reinforcement of the Polish frontier. It also allowed Berlin to seek allied
permission to raise a local defence force in East Prussia and send the Reichswehr
to the southern boundaries of Allenstein and Marienwerder. Plebiscites had
already confirmed the desire of the local population to remain with Germany,
but the allied powers had not yet recognized the results of the balloting and
small contingents of their armed forces, sent to oversee the elections, had still
not been withdrawn. Berlin now asserted that the maintenance of Germany's
neutrality and the protection of its frontiers made it "indispensable" for the allies
to authorize the sending of German troops into Allenstein and Marienwerder.
None of the allies would agree to the raising of an East Prussian militia, but
only France objected to German occupation of the plebiscite areas.[60]

Neutrality allowed the Germans to strike at Poland. On 23 July Berlin banned
the transit and export of weapons destined for the belligerents. Although this
appeared to treat the two sides equally it was, in fact, aimed at Warsaw. Soviet
Russia had no need to seek arms; Poland did. Indeed, France was seeking to
arm Poland, and the most direct route was through Germany. Moreover, Germany
would soon have to deliver a substantial quantity of arms to the allied powers,
and France had already suggested that a portion of them be diverted to Poland.
By invoking neutrality the Germans hoped to avoid rendering assistance to
Poland. A measure taken the next day was designed to place the Reichswehr in
direct contact with the Red Army. Citing the need "to regulate any incidents
which might arise from the present military situation," the Auswärtiges Amt
asked the belligerents to send liaison officers to German army headquarters in
East Prussia. This again appeared to treat both equally but favoured the Russians

who, unlike the Poles, had much to discuss with the Germans other than the
regulation of border incidents. The Poles immediately protested that the German
action was tantamount to the recognition of the Soviet government. Simons's
response was chilling. Germany, he said, had recognized Soviet Russia in March
1918, and the suspension of diplomatic relations was due solely to the Soviet
failure to satisfy German demands arising from the assassination of Count Mirbach. Regulation of this question, he declared, was "the only major issue which
prevented the exchange of representatives by the two governments."[61]

This, of course, was patently untrue, but it was a precise statement of the
position adopted by Simons two days before in preparing a letter for Chicherin.
He attributed the rupture of relations solely to the Soviet failure to provide
Germany with "necessary satisfaction" for the murder of Count Mirbach. "I do
not fail to appreciate," he continued, "that because of the political turmoil in
Russia, the punishment of the murderer and his accomplices, which we had to
demand, was at the time arduously difficult for your government and is now
almost impossible." Nevertheless German "national honour" required public
satisfaction prior to the resumption of neighbourly relations. This could be provided by a brief ceremony in front of the former German embassy. He specified
that the German flag should be raised while a company of Soviet troops, commanded by an officer, gave a military salute and solemnly paraded in front of
the building. Then discussions concerning the economic and political relations
of the two countries could begin.[62]

There are several interpretations of this extraordinary proposal. Wipert von
Blücher suggests it originated with the precedent-conscious specialists of the
Auswärtiges Amt legal department. Gunter Rosenfeld sees it in a more sinister
light as intended to thwart the resumption of Soviet-German relations, while
Herbert Helbig believes it was designed to delay the resumption of relations until
the reaction of the allies could be determined. Gerhard Wagner dismisses these
interpretations and concludes that it is more probable that in presenting this
demand "Simons gave vent to his juridic heart," which moved him to seek
removal of the Mirbach question as an impediment to the improvement of relations with Moscow.[63]

This does not explain why the politically astute officials of the Auswärtiges
Amt did not object to such a narrow-minded approach to this important question.
Simons did not simply pluck this issue from thin air and make it the core of his
letter to Chicherin. It had been under careful examination since early in July,
and Maltzan was clearly delighted to discover that no record could be found of
Moscow providing "necessary satisfaction" for the Mirbach murder. This points
to a political explanation. Its purpose was to obfuscate the reasons for the rupture
of relations in November 1918 and draw a veil over the conduct of German
policy towards Russia in the period which followed. The rupture and continued
severance of relations had not been caused by the Mirbach murder or the alleged
failure of the Soviet government to provide Germany with "necessary satisfac-

tion." They occurred as part of a fifteen-month German effort to find a basis for cooperation with the allies and make good some of their losses in the Great War. Berlin had tried to conjure a great Bolshevik menace to western civilization and convince the allies of their need for Germany's service in destroying it. The allies, however, had repeatedly spurned this offer, and now circumstances had arisen in which a certain degree of cooperation with the Bolsheviks, particularly in regard to Poland, was seen to be very much in the German interest. Part of the price which Moscow demanded was the restoration of political relations with Berlin, and although the Germans were prepared to pay it, they were in the awkward position of having to explain this decision in terms of past policy. They clearly did not believe that it was acceptable either in terms of domestic or international politics simply to acknowledge that Moscow had made them an offer which they could not refuse. Thus they clutched at the Mirbach issue, dead as the count himself, to redefine the past in politically useful terms. By attributing the hiatus in Soviet-German relations solely to this cause, Simons was able to put in place a seemingly simple mechanism for its elimination. Had he touched upon any other aspect of the Soviet-German past, daunting complications would have risen to delay a restoration of relations far beyond the anticipated arrival of the Red Army on the German frontier. Instead he summoned Mirbach's ghost and provided a simple ceremony to banish it forever. Even as Kopp departed for Moscow bearing Simons's letter, Maltzan drafted the scenario for events which would follow Soviet acceptance.[64] Voltaire would have understood perfectly.

Moscow also understood but did not like the Russian role in this German scenario; it invited the Bolsheviks to accept responsibility for the hiatus in Soviet-German relations and play an inferior, even subservient, part in their resumption. In the summer of 1920 the Soviet government believed that Russia was well on its way to restoration as a major power in Europe. Such a power could not act in the way Simons demanded, nor did there appear to be any good reason why it should.

The Soviet government, therefore, reacted negatively to the German proposal. Lenin had already instructed Chicherin on 22 July to tell Kopp that he should confine himself to commercial negotiations. The same day the foreign commissar informed his envoy in Berlin that the Soviet government refused even to mention Mirbach in any agreement they might reach with Germany. Moscow greatly desired friendly relations, he said, but not on a one-sided basis.[65] This attitude hardened by the time Kopp reached Moscow. On 2 August, in his official reply to Simons, Chicherin firmly rejected the German proposal. He proposed that discussions for a resumption of "economic and also, as far as possible, political relations" begin at once in Berlin.[66] Two days later Kopp left Moscow with the letter for Simons. With him went a German courier bearing a report from Hilger (who had been in Moscow in the summer of 1918) confirming Chicherin's account of the Mirbach murder. Hilger added that it would be very difficult for the Soviet government to comply with Simons's wishes as the building which had served as the German embassy in 1918 was now the office of the Third International.[67]

While this exchange of views took place, the Red Army reached the German frontier in East Prussia. In the next two weeks the Bolsheviks advanced westward, south of the German border and into the Polish corridor.[68] This gave the Germans ample opportunity to observe the Red Army. The Soviet troops appeared ragged and worn after their three-month campaign but were a tough, disciplined fighting force commanded by experienced officers. They were fewer in number than the Germans had expected and were only lightly armed. Soviet commanders freely admitted that they were marching on Danzig and hoped to cut the Polish link with the sea. They did not stop at the boundary of 1914, as Berlin had hoped, but nowhere violated the existing frontier. Soviet commanders repeatedly stated that they had strict orders to respect the German frontier and abstain from violence against the German population. That population, in fact, greeted them as liberators, and the Russians responded by replacing the Polish administration with one drawn solely from the German community. This, however, raised the question of which Germans were to be given power. Local German revolutionaries asked for the establishment of soviets in the occupied territory, while the German liaison officer demanded the restoration of the pre-Versailles German municipal administration. The Red Army did not establish Russian-style soviets, but the more broadly based municipal assemblies they did create were quite sufficient to disturb the Auswärtiges Amt. The questions soon became moot as the Red Army was forced to abandon the region, and the Polish administration was restored.[69]

The German government had good reason to be satisfied. The Red Army appeared able to defeat the Poles without posing a serious threat to the Reichswehr. More importantly, no internal disturbances accompanied the Russian arrival. The prospect for restoration of the 1914 frontier appeared good. It was important, however, that events not move too quickly. Berlin did not want its hand forced by a premature effort of the German population to seek reunion with the Reich, and the Auswärtiges Amt repeatedly instructed its agents in East Prussia to stifle agitation for this purpose. Such agitation could lead to allied occupation of the Ruhr. Patience was necessary because only Russia, in the context of its negotiations with a new Polish government, could raise this issue, and even then, the revision of Germany's eastern frontier would require at least tacit allied consent.[70]

The Germans, therefore, were disappointed on 12 August when they read Chicherin's letter. The absence of any counter-proposals particularly disturbed Maltzan until Kopp said that, while the Soviet government would not agree to Simons's ceremony, they were prepared to issue an official statement of regret for the death of Mirbach, provide a full account of the measures taken to punish those responsible, and guarantee the future safety of German representatives in Russia. Once this question was settled, Moscow would send a "suitable diplomatic representative" to Berlin to open economic and political talks with the German government. Kopp also conveyed a verbal assurance that the military operations which the Red Army had been forced to conduct in the Polish corridor would not prejudice the return of this territory to Germany. A Soviet government in Warsaw would agree to a new frontier based on ethographic principles. Kopp was confident of Soviet victory, asserting that France was isolated and Britain had "irrevocably sold" Poland to the Bolsheviks. He left Maltzen with the impression that Moscow was very sure of its arrangement with Britain but still preferred to reach an understanding with Germany before concluding a binding agreement in London.[71]

Events of the previous two days seemed to justify Kopp's optimism. Lloyd George had called for Poland to accept the Soviet peace terms, Britain and France had broken openly, and the Red Army was at the gates of Warsaw. Maltzan did not hesitate to recommend acceptance of Kopp's proposal for a settlement of the Mirbach issue. Simons and Kopp, he suggested, should then conclude "a private, written agreement" specifying "the territorial settlement in the east." Diplomatic relations between Soviet Russia and Germany would be resumed, with Kopp recognized as Soviet chargé d'affaires and a German mission sent to Moscow. The mission would receive the official Soviet statement of regret for the Mirbach murder and open political and economic negotiations. Maltzan recommended that these talks be held in Moscow to insure that the Entente had no opportunity to interfere. This recommendation had to be sent to Switzerland where Simons had gone for his summer vacation. The foreign minister had originally intended to return to Berlin to conduct the talks himself, but changed his mind when he learned that his own proposal had been rejected by Chicherin. Simons was clearly unhappy, but accepted Maltzan's recommendations and allowed him to work out an agreement with Kopp. This was embodied in a memorandum of 20 August which retained the tripartite disposition of the Mirbach question, the German mission to Moscow, and the opening of negotiations there, but no longer mentioned a territorial agreement or specified Kopp as the presumptive Soviet chargé d'affaires. Economic negotiations, although beginning in Moscow, were to be completed in Berlin.[72]

The proposed agreement was overtaken by the Soviet defeat in Poland. The deletion of the critical question of Germany's eastern frontier pointed starkly to the erosion of its political base and the remainder of the accord quickly collapsed. The Mirbach issue disgusted the Bolsheviks,[73] and although they had apparently been ready to accept the Kopp compromise as long as they believed Polish collapse was near and agreement with Germany vital, they now rejected it. On 19 August the Politburo reversed Soviet military priorities, giving first place to the struggle against Wrangel. The impact on Soviet policy concerning Germany followed immediately. Chicherin icily advised Kopp: "My explanation in the letter to Simons about Mirbach settles the affair. To apologize in any form whatever is still unconditionally inadmissible for us."[74] It was inadmissible

because in the altered circumstance Soviet Russia had nothing to gain in humouring Simons. The retreat from Poland quickly destroyed the economic, as
well as the political, foundations of the agreement. When it appeared as if the
Polish barrier to Soviet-German trade would be smashed Moscow had rushed a
commission to Berlin to buy a thousand locomotives. An agreement was quickly
reached and still further purchases were made to relieve other shortages, but
rapidly advancing Polish troops quickly severed the only railways by which these
commodities could be sent to Russia.[75]

The Germans also drew logical conclusions from the Soviet débâcle and
returned quickly to their prior policy of allowing Britain to set the pace in
restoration of economic relations with Soviet Russia. Simons assured Lord Kilmarnock that "there was not a word of truth" in rumours concerning a German
agreement with Moscow, and Maltzan prevaricated equally in saying to a lesser
British representative that he had always felt that German policy towards Russia
"must coincide with that of England."[76] The Germans, however, carefully calculated the degree to which Soviet Russia had been damaged by defeat in Poland
and the resurgence of Wrangel. Both were considered serious setbacks but unlikely to topple the Bolsheviks, who would survive, it was thought, because of
the absence of any organized opposition.[77] Moscow and Berlin, each for its own
reasons, desired a temporary halt in progress towards a restoration of official
relations. It was necessary to await the verdict of battle and its impact upon the
political structure of Europe. Both therefore adopted an intransigent position on
the Mirbach issue. On 2 September Chicherin informed Kopp that the Politburo
categorically refused to return in any way to the Mirbach affair. "Our *rapprochement* with Germany [he declared] must not depend on this absurdity, but
on a comprehensive understanding of the political and economic interests which
cause the two states to support each other in certain relations. The moment can
soon come in which our diplomatic support in well-known questions can be very
valuable for Germany." The armistice with Poland reinforced this stand. On the
same day it was signed, Chicherin wrote to Kopp: "We will not go to Canosa
and humble ourselves on account of Mirbach. We believe, however, that the
German government will recognize their own advantage, and not persist in this
absurdity."[78]

The Germans did persist, and there was no progress towards restoration of
official relations. Prospects even dimmed somewhat when Moscow sent Grigorii
Zinoviev to urge the congress of the German Independent Socialist Party to seek
affiliation with the Communist International. Despite his promise not to deliver
political speeches, the head of the Comintern delivered an impassioned four-
hour address summoning the Independent Socialists to revolutionary action.[79]
The German government deported Zinoviev, and Maltzan warned Kopp against
further Bolshevik interference in the internal affairs of Germany. It was not a
major incident but one which reminded German politicians of the ambiguous
nature of their relationship to the Bolsheviks and did nothing to promote its

further development. Berlin, however, made no move towards Wrangel or other anti-Bolshevik leaders. In September and October the Auswärtiges Amt was repeatedly urged to do so but did no more than listen to a variety of proposals made on behalf of the Whites. These were hardly attractive, because they called for immediate aid in return for the promise of an uncertain cooperation in the future and were made by men already in the pay of Poland and France.[80] The Germans could not realistically hope that in the foreseeable future any of these groups could aid them in a protracted struggle with the allies. The best they could offer was to prolong the chaos in Russia at a time when the German government wished the opposite.

Politically, the Germans had returned to their earlier "wait and see" attitude in regard to Russia, but even during this stalemate the Bolsheviks made some progress towards expanded economic relations. They had gold to spend and they used it to stimulate German interest in renewed access to the Russian market. The Auswärtiges Amt no longer wished to prevent private trade with Russia, and Kopp was able to enlist their support in arranging payment for the locomotives ordered earlier from German factories. He also obtained their aid in establishing his legal right to enter into commercial transactions in the name of the Soviet government and block any attempt of private individuals having claims against Moscow to seek confiscation of Russian state funds brought into Germany to finance German-Russian trade.[81]

This did not amount to much. After seventeen months Moscow had little to show for its almost ceaseless effort to improve relations with Germany. Much had been discussed but very little accomplished. The two governments had concluded a prisoner exchange agreement, exchanged low-level representatives, and established a communication link. In addition, a trickle of trade had begun to flow. Past antagonism, mutual suspicion, and contradictory aspirations served to inhibit further improvement in relations. Both knew from bitter experience that neither viewed the other as a permanent fixture in the politics of Europe. Given the opportunity, each would seek to destroy the other. In this lethal atmosphere it is not surprising that rapprochement made little progress. That which was made may be attributed to the mutual hatred of Versailles.

While drawing Germany and Soviet Russia together, however, Versailles also inhibited rapprochement. Allied, and especially French, restraint on Berlin was far more effective than on Moscow. A vengeful France sat menacingly on the demilitarized border of a partly disarmed Germany. Soviet Russia, on the other hand, had driven the allied expeditionary forces from its territory and had little fear that they would return. Victory bred confidence and, having been attacked by Poland, Moscow resolved to shatter the Versailles eastern bastion. Berlin was delighted, and this reaction provides a measure of the real degree to which past antagonisms and fear of Bolshevism restrained German willingness to cooperate. While ensuring the internal security of the Reich, the Germans prepared to reap the benefits of Soviet victory. Clearly they far preferred the Bolsheviks to Pilsudski. Berlin, however, was unable to play an active role in the destruction of Poland. They remained outwardly loyal to the obligations imposed by the peace treaty and adopted neutrality, not belligerency, in the conflict. Berlin insisted that Moscow initiate the reconstruction of eastern Europe. Only if the Bolsheviks succeeded in establishing a client regime in Warsaw were the Germans prepared to participate in this reconstruction. They would then have willingly acceded to a request to renegotiate the Polish frontier. When the Bolsheviks proved unable to stage this elaborate production, the Germans simply maintained their outward pose of neutrality. The need to restore full political and economic relations with Moscow decreased with every kilometre the Red Army retreated; the necessity of not antagonizing the allies increased accordingly, and Berlin postponed a further development of its Russian policy.

Even in defeat Soviet Russia was able to ransom itself by drawing on its immense territory to slack the thirst of expansionist neighbours. Defeat, however, also imposed a greater degree of caution. Faced with German timidity and having decided that peace with Britain was essential to the consolidation of Soviet power, the Bolsheviks had to subordinate their relations with Berlin to the primary objective of a treaty with Britain. As a result, in late 1920 Moscow was no more prepared than Berlin to move to a full restoration of relations. That question, therefore, remained in suspense, with a slight movement in the direction of restoration but with no certainty of its ultimate realization.

CHAPTER EIGHTEEN

"The right to an independent existence": The treaties with Britain, Poland, and Germany

In mid-November 1920 the Bolsheviks celebrated their victory in the Russian civil war. The defeat of Wrangel and the conclusion of an armistice with Poland marked the end of hostilities. Lenin saw the latter as being especially important. Poland had aspired to replace Russia as the single greatest power in eastern Europe and had failed. Due to the role which Poland played in the western political system, however, Soviet victory had far more than regional significance. "The Red Army proved that the Treaty of Versailles is not so very stable," Lenin proclaimed, "The world saw that a force exists to which the Treaty of Versailles holds no terror."[1] Elation, however, was tempered by an awareness of the limitations of victory. Soviet successes, Lenin said, had been tremendous, but in 1917 the party had "stated emphatically that victory could not be permanent unless it was followed by a proletarian revolution in the West." That revolution had not occurred; the bourgeois states had emerged from the aftermath of the world war with their social orders intact but had been unable to destroy the revolution in Russia. "Without having gained an international victory, which we consider the only sure victory, we are in a position of having won conditions enabling us to exist side by side with capitalist powers, who are now compelled to enter into trade relations with us. In the course of this struggle we have won the right to an independent existence."[2]

Lenin did not believe this right had been won primarily by military means. Victory would not have been possible without the Red Army, which had sealed the fate of every adversary, but there could be no question of comparing its strength with that of the capitalist powers. Soviet Russia had succeeded, he said, "not because we have proved militarily stronger and the Entente weaker, but because throughout this period the disintegration in the Entente countries had intensified, whereas our inner strength has grown." Capitalist competition and class struggle had prevented all of the great imperialist powers from sending

large armies to Russia, and intense rivalries among them obstructed cooperation
in defence of even their most basic common interests. For the previous two and
a half years Lenin had based his foreign policy on exploiting division within
and among the capitalist powers and, in the aftermath of Bolshevik victory in
the civil war, intended to continue in the same manner. "Whenever thieves fall
out," he was fond of saying, "honest men come into their own."[3]

Lenin identified three radical antagonisms within the capitalist world. All had
been generated by the world war which had enriched the United States (and, to
a far lesser degree, Japan) while impoverishing Europe. The first was between
Japan and the United States, both of which hoped to exploit the Pacific basin.
Although the United States was many times richer, Japan had taken advantage
of the war to seize China. The United States, said Lenin, would not allow Japan
to keep "this plum." "It is absurd to think that a stronger capitalism will not
deprive a weaker capitalism of the latter's spoils." The Americans would seek
"to grab everything they can" from the Japanese, and war would result. This
would allow Soviet Russia to improve its own position in Siberia. The second
antagonism, between the United States and the rest of the capitalist world, could
be used similarly. "America is strong," wrote Lenin, "she is everybody's creditor
and everything depends on her; she is being more and more detested; she is
robbing all and sundry and doing so in a unique fashion." Rather than accu-
mulating colonies like Britain and France, she was seeking to use her great
economic strength to force her way into all the markets of the world. The third
antagonism was between the Entente and Germany. Here the victors in the Great
War were seeking to take by force the economic resources necessary for German
existence. Lenin identified Germany as "the world's second country in economic
development" and was deeply impressed by its technological sophistication. "It
is on such a country that the Treaty of Versailles has been imposed, a treaty she
cannot possibly live under. Germany is one of the most powerful and advanced
of the capitalist countries. She cannot put up with the Treaty of Versailles."
Soviet Russia could benefit enormously from these circumstances. The German
ruling classes, although hating communism, had realized their "only means of
salvation lies in an alliance with Soviet Russia." A careful management of these
and other, lesser, antagonisms, Lenin believed, would promote Soviet security
in the post-civil-war world.[4]

Soviet experience in combating foreign intervention provided the inspiration
for this policy. It suggested that economic levers were the most efficient tools
to widen the cracks in the capitalist world. This had been the basis of Lenin's
policy towards Germany in 1918 and western Europe the previous year. Soviet
peace proposals had been put forward together with commercial prospectuses
and drafts of trade treaties. Commercial agreements provided manufactured goods
to rebuild Russian industry, recruited a widening circle of influential individuals
personally interested in the promotion of peaceful relations, and excited the
interest of still more merchants in the expansion of profitable trade. Trade required

peace, which thus became the common interest of the Soviet government and those with whom they did business abroad.[5] But Lenin did not intend to rely merely on trade treaties to recruit allies in the capitalist business world. Instead, in the fall of 1920 he began to elaborate an approach based on the granting of concessions to foreign capitalists interested in the direct exploitation of Soviet natural resources. Commercial exchange was a satisfactory method of enlisting the support of middle-range merchants but did not promise sufficient profit to interest the largest entrepreneurs. They could only be attracted by large-scale undertakings which promised equally large profits. Thus, on 23 November the Soviet government issued a decree establishing the conditions on which large-scale concessions for the direct exploitation of Soviet raw materials could be granted to foreign capitalists.[6]

In theory this was designed to obtain foreign technical and material support of the development of Soviet raw materials, but its primary purpose was political. Although the policy had many antecedents, the decision to promulgate the concessions decree appears to have been triggered by the visit of Washington Vanderlip to Moscow in late October 1920. Vanderlip was a free-wheeling American entrepreneur who appears to have traded on having the same family name as the famous, but unrelated, American banker. Vanderlip had made a good impression on Krasin the previous summer, and the commissar had provided him with an introduction to Lenin. Lenin thought Vanderlip was "a capitalist shark" but was impressed by his reputed influence within the Republican party and delighted to hear his conviction that Japan and the United States would soon go to war. Japan, he had said, needed oil and hoped to obtain it in the Kamchatka peninsula over which it had exercised control since 1918. To forestall this possibility, Vanderlip had proposed that Soviet Russia sell Kamchatka to the United States. Lenin had countered with a proposed sixty-year lease, with the right for Vanderlip to develop the oil, coal, and fishing resources there as a concession to be granted by the Soviet government.[7] An agreement had been concluded on this basis, contingent, however, on the support of the American government and their diplomatic recognition of Soviet Russia. Lenin explained the agreement in this way: "The Far East is dominated by Japan, who can do anything she pleases there. If we lease America Kamchatka, which legally belongs to us but has actually been seized by Japan we shall clearly be the gainers." In this way Lenin hoped to use concessions to divide his enemies. He doubted that much economic benefit would result from such agreements but believed that they would contribute to the security of the Soviet state. In addition, he stressed the "tremendous propaganda value" of the policy. It would advertise Soviet willingness to contribute raw materials to the postwar reconstruction of the world economy. It proved this could be done peacefully, through negotiation, which would make it "more difficult for the Imperialist countries to attack us." Even if no concessions were granted, which Lenin thought possible, Soviet Russia would benefit from the publicity.[8]

Lenin had no illusions regarding the end of armed hostilities. "While capitalism and socialism exist side by side," he said, "they cannot live in peace: one or the other will ultimately triumph – the last obsequies will be observed either for the Soviet Republic or for world capitalism." He saw the Soviet republic as being surrounded by imperialist countries far stronger than itself and ready to use any means to destroy it. Soviet Russia, therefore, had to defend itself with every available weapon. When asked if this included a possible alliance with one capitalist state against another, he answered "of course." The end of hostilities simply meant that the struggle would continue using different means. "Concessions," he warned on 26 November, "do not mean peace; they too are a kind of warfare, only in another form, one that is to our advantage ... The war will now be conducted on the economic front."9

THIS WAS THE CONTEXT in which the Soviet government viewed their negotiations with Britain. These talks had been delayed by the Soviet-Polish war, and only in mid-November did the British government authorize detailed negotiation of the proposed trade treaty. This decision was a major determinant in shaping Lenin's larger policy. "New times are setting in," he observed. "[British] war schemes have miscarried and they now have to fight in the economic field ... [this] is a tremendous step forward."10 The British decision, in fact, had recast the Anglo-Soviet conflict. Lloyd George had long before accepted that the Bolsheviks could not be defeated militarily and that their conduct could be modified only through the skilful use of economic incentives. Now this view had been adopted by the cabinet as a whole. Curzon and Churchill, however, continued the struggle on the new field of battle. They brought forward a long list of grievances regarding Soviet policy in Asia and demanded the treaty prohibit the dissemination of Bolshevik propaganda anywhere in the British empire.11 Advocates of the treaty also hastened to include clauses they believed would increase British leverage in the future development of relations with Moscow. They were alarmed by the mounting evidence "that a bad period of trade [had to] be anticipated [that] winter" and by information "published in the press of a gigantic order obtained by Mr. Vanderlip." A conference of these ministers chaired by Lloyd George on 25 November concluded: "Whatever might be the truth as to the alleged orders said to have been obtained by Mr. Vanderlip ... it was estimated that from a political point of view it was desirable to remove all governmental obstacles to trade."12 On the following day the full cabinet examined the trade agreement drafted by the Board of Trade. The most important clauses were those allowing either party to terminate the agreement at three months' notice and specifying the Soviet obligation to pay debts due British subjects as a consequence of the revolution.13 The cabinet approved this draft, but also included the prohibition of propaganda demanded by opponents of the treaty. Even so, the minority (Curzon, Churchill, Milner, Chamberlain, and Long) insisted on recording their objection to the treaty as a whole.14

The trade treaty question also generated tension in Moscow. Soviet leaders continued to emphasize the importance of a settlement but were determined not to allow the British to dictate its terms. In 1919 they would have agreed to virtually any terms London might have offered. In late 1920 the situation was different. They were now far stronger and the international situation was less fluid. They had to assume that agreements reached in this context might bind them for an indefinite period. They were also influenced by their perception of western governments as executive committees of the bourgeoisie. If they were to deal with businessmen, they had to act like them. "We have to bargain," said Lenin, "as no businessman will respect us if we do not."[15] But how hard should they bargain? Chicherin wanted only minimum concessions. Krasin was more flexible. He did not wish to delay the resumption of trade for the sake of arguing highly contentious political issues. Lenin stood in the middle. He shared Chicherin's reluctance to compromise Soviet political interests but also recognized the urgent necessity of reaching agreement with Britain. Thus he allowed the foreign commissar to criticize Krasin's handling of the negotiations while carefully preventing the erection of any insuperable barrier to an ultimate accord.

Chicherin launched his attack even before London presented Krasin with a draft treaty. He had been outraged by the British refusal to receive Soviet envoys whom they considered undesirable; first Litvinov, then Kamenev, had been declared persona non grata. The British would negotiate only with Krasin, whom they found acceptable because of his low-key approach to politics. For this reason Chicherin considered him inadequate. He wanted to send his own representative to conduct the political side of the negotiations. He therefore instructed Krasin to inform the British of his intention to enlarge the Soviet delegation and equip them with a powerful radio receiver with which they could remain in contact with Moscow. Krasin was also told to adopt a very narrow interpretation of the obligation to pay private British citizens for goods or services supplied to Russia. Only those who had acted on the explicit order of the Soviet government should be compensated. Krasin heaped derision on all three proposals. Only Persia and Turkey, he said, were denied the right of excluding unwanted foreign envoys. To insist on its renunciation was "to demand that England be reduced in matters of international etiquette to the status of Turkey ... Sevastopol in any case is not sufficient for this and Berlin is not yet ours." The British government were likely to allow the Soviet mission to operate a radio receiver but would demand reciprocity. This seemed dangerous, as "a wireless receiving station is really of no use to us whereas the British General Staff and the Admiralty will probably be glad to have a receiving station in Russia." He considered the proposed limitation on debt recognition equally impractical. The Central Committee had already accepted compensation "without any reservation; now it is too late to reject it."

Chicherin responded with equal venom. The Soviet government continued to recognize the British note of 30 June as the basis for a commercial agreement, but he could see no reason for allowing the British to "insert innovations and make [their original] conditions worse." Nor could he understand "why an obscure text should be interpreted in a sense unfavourable to us." In conclusion, he referred to the Groman Commission, a Soviet agency established in the spring to assess the liability of foreign powers for damages caused Russia through intervention in the civil war. This body, said the foreign commissar, was being reorganized, but "conflicts continue. We hope to set up the commission soon." As its findings were intended to provide the basis for a countervailing Soviet claim to western demands for the payment of Russian debts, Chicherin's meaning was clear. He implied that the conclusion of the trade treaty would be delayed indefinitely if the British insisted on Soviet recognition of pre-revolutionary Russian debts. The meaning, in fact, was too clear, at least for Lenin. He had been following this exchange, and upon reading Chicherin's telegram exploded in anger. He covered his copy with exclamations marks, returning it to Chicherin with a note accusing him of creating chaos and disorganization. The Groman Commission was not being reorganized, he said; it had been liquidated and would not be restored. He told Krasin the same but warned him to cease quarrelling with Chicherin. Lenin had no intention of allowing negotiations to drag on while the Soviet bureaucracy conducted a detailed study of the damage done by allied intervention. Nor did he intend to pay Russia's pre-revolutionary debts. To be sure, the two issues were inseparable, but Lenin had decided to reverse the order in which they were addressed. "Communicate how many billion gold rubles we need as counter-claims to [those] of Britain," he instructed Krasin. [16]

Lenin's admonition did nothing to restore peace between Chicherin and Krasin. On 29 November Chicherin proposed that Krasin be recalled to convince the British to accept more favourable terms. The Politburo postponed a decision while seeking Krasin's opinion. [17] Well before receiving this inquiry the Soviet envoy had taken a position opposed to Chicherin. Krasin had received the British draft treaty on 29 November and concluded that an agreement could be reached in a short while, perhaps a week. His major concern was the absence of a clause protecting Soviet gold from attachment by British courts. He was confident, however, that the British would agree to this protection. He concluded that "the maximum acceleration of negotiations is ... essential since the critical nature of the Irish question may lead to the fall of the Cabinet which in its turn would delay the [trade] agreement for some time." The following day he urgently requested final instructions, but promised he would not sign the treaty without final approval from Moscow. [18]

Chicherin was horrified. On 2 December he informed Krasin that the British draft was absolutely unacceptable. Krasin was not to make counter proposals of any kind. He submitted his views to the Politburo who, on 4 December, agreed to reject the draft treaty and insist upon "the text and letter of the British note of 30 June on the questions of propaganda and debts." All details were to be worked out during the subsequent negotiation of a peace treaty. [19] This was an effort to thwart what the Bolsheviks saw as a brazen attempt to trap them in a disadvantageous framework of political and economic obligations prior to any negotiation of the issues involved. The next day Chicherin told Krasin: "We refuse to add even a single letter to the July agreement. Without a political conference we cannot limit our activity in the East, since only at such a conference will the concrete obligations that bind us be compensated by concrete obligations binding England."[20] Chicherin was authorized to present these views directly to the British government. In a long telegram addressed to Curzon immediately after the meeting of the Politburo, he said there could be no modification of the original agreement without the fullest discussion of the many political differences still separating the two governments. Krasin had to accept the Politburo decision, but he warned that agreement might not be possible on these terms.[21]

The Politburo decision put an end to any possibility of a rapid conclusion of the trade treaty. The Foreign Office even hoped that it might lead to a rupture of relations. They were to be disappointed, because in December the political current driving the government towards agreement with Moscow grew stronger. In Yorkshire the only textile mills working full time were those with which Krasin had concluded contracts.[22] The press soon reflected these circumstances. Newspapers in the Midlands first took up the theme and were soon followed by major London journals. On 12 December the *Sunday Times* attacked Curzon for obstructing the trade treaty and shortly after the *Financial Times* joined the chorus, urging that trade relations with Russia be resumed. A small volume of trade had already begun, but due to the absence of a trade treaty, its financing had to be conducted through Sweden. The charges for this were considerable and represented a total loss to the British economy. The only remedy, reported the British commercial attaché in Stockholm, was an agreement which would allow the Soviet government to pay for its purchases through the direct shipment of gold to London.[23]

These were the very arguments made by Krasin in his negotiations with the Board of Trade. The pace of these talks increased in December as both sides sought a new basis of agreement. Krasin warned Sir Robert Horne, the president of the Board of Trade and principal British negotiator, that should the talks fail, no further Soviet contracts would be placed in Britain and existing ones would be void. He asked for a guarantee of the security of Soviet gold from legal attachment and the right to re-export any gold sent to Britain. British law set the price of gold below its value on the world market, and as a consequence the Soviets did not intend to sell it in Britain. Instead, they wished to use it as security and re-export it when they had established their credit. Horne thought a re-export licence could be issued but declined to give special legal protection to Soviet gold. He believed that the trade treaty itself would provide adequate protection and suggested that Krasin bring a small amount of "gold to England on a trading transaction and have a test case in the British courts." The issues of Russian debts and Soviet propaganda were canvassed without success. Horne wanted to examine the relationship between the Soviet government and the Comintern, but Krasin would not discuss the issue. The lack of progress discouraged Krasin; on 17 December he wired Moscow that he did not believe agreement was possible on the basis specified by the Politburo. He asked to be recalled for consultation and a final resolution of Soviet policy.[24]

Before Moscow could reply, Lloyd George summoned Krasin to a meeting on 21 December. The prime minister had grown impatient with the delay in reaching an agreement and had decided, as Hankey informed Curzon, to bring matters to a head. On learning of this, the foreign secretary wrote Lloyd George reminding him of the points to which he attached great importance. He would not agree to delete the references to specific countries in which the Soviet government were to abandon propaganda and hostile activity against the British empire nor to call a political conference to discuss the questions raised by Chicherin. Curzon did, however, make one major concession; all mention of the Caucasus could be removed from the treaty.[25]

With this in hand, Lloyd George hoped to find a basis of agreement. At the meeting he asked Krasin to "state what were the main ... differences of opinion between the two governments." The Soviet envoy replied: propaganda, gold, debts, and a conference to settle political differences. Lloyd George adhered to Curzon's brief, repeatedly refusing to accept the necessity of a political conference prior to the conclusion of the trade treaty and insisting that the treaty preamble specify those Asian countries in which Soviet Russia would desist from propaganda and hostile activity against the British empire. He said that Krasin had to understand that "it would be almost impossible for him to get an agreement of this kind through unless those who were specifically interested in those particular countries [named in the British preamble] were satisfied that hostile propaganda would cease." He quickly added, however, that "if there was any special objection to the inclusion of the Caucasus on the ground that it was part of the old Russian Empire, then he did not press that." Lloyd George also gave ground on the British reformulation of the Soviet requirement to pay past Russian debts, promising to discuss the matter with his colleagues. He held firm, however, on the question of security for Soviet gold, but assuring Krasin that "if an unfavourable decision were given in the Courts which would make trading impossible the British Government would reconsider" the whole question. The prime minister urged Krasin to accept these terms. He said he had "promised not to sign the Trade Agreement until its terms had been made known in the House," and added, "[it] was rising on Thursday and would not meet again until February 15th. Unless the House, therefore, could be informed on the following day, no Trade Agreement could be completed until it re-assembled." This could not move Krasin, because he lacked authority to accept these terms. He could only promise to convey them to his government. Having done so, he was summoned to Moscow for consultation.[26]

Last-minute negotiations delayed Krasin's departure. Lloyd George had warned his colleagues that the negotiations might fail, and they decided that if the talks did break down "it was desirable that they should fail on an issue like hostile propaganda, which could be popularly understood, rather than on more technical questions affecting the payment of debts and the sale of gold." Sir Robert Horne took this line on the afternoon of 22 December when he informed the House of Commons that negotiations had reached an impasse because of the failure of the Soviet government to provide evidence of its willingness to suspend hostile propaganda against the British empire.[27] As part of this plan but also to promote the treaty itself, the British made further concessions regarding gold and Russian debts. Horne abandoned the attempt to get a more precise definition of Soviet obligation to pay Russian debts and gave Krasin written authorization for the re-export of Soviet gold sent to Britain. Title to the gold would first have to be established in the British courts, but Krasin was assured that the trade treaty, by extending de facto recognition to Soviet Russia, would be sufficient to establish this title. On 11 January 1921 Krasin received this statement and a new draft of the treaty embodying the changes negotiated during the previous six weeks. He left immediately for Moscow.[28]

Krasin had achieved considerable success. He had persuaded the British to alter substantially their position on all questions except propaganda and the summoning of an Anglo-Soviet political conference. Even here the new draft made the promise to abstain from hostile propaganda reciprocal and foresaw a bilateral political conference *after* the conclusion of the trade treaty. Krasin endorsed the agreement and was ready to present his case in Moscow. He argued that once the treaty was signed "it will not be so easy for the Curzons and Churchills to break it off; neither the Labour Party nor the City will allow them to do so." Instead, it could be used as a lever to secure agreements with other western powers and by means of them "free ourselves from the English political and economical cabal." Soviet Russia could then threaten Britain with a rupture of relations, "and this threat will then be more real than dozens of the most curt notes."[29]

Chicherin was not impressed. Krasin had failed to get concessions in precisely those areas the foreign commissar considered most important. The proposed treaty *did* place limits on Soviet freedom of action in Asia prior to any thorough discussion of the issues involved. Chicherin feared, as he told Litvinov, that the proposed agreement gave Great Britain "such political advantages that it would not be necessary to grant any further recognition to the Soviet government for a prolonged period."[30] He therefore launched a new polemic against the British refusal to undertake political negotiations. His note of 31 December was worded sharply enough to provoke an equally abrasive reply from Curzon. Chicherin then used this response to issue an even harsher indictment of the British government. Lower ranking members of the Foreign Office prepared a further rebuttal, but Curzon cut them short. On 12 January, knowing that Krasin was on his way to Moscow where a final decision would be taken, the foreign secretary minuted: "This discussion is purely academic, and I don't propose to add to it."[31]

WHILE ANGLO-SOVIET HOSTILITIES had moved to the economic front, Soviet-Polish relations had not. In mid-October, when the preliminary peace of Riga had been signed, Polish troops stood to the east of the agreed frontier, and despite the obligation to do so, Pilsudski did not order his army to pull back. Instead, he allowed his Russian and Ukrainian allies to reinforce their detachments in this area. In late October and early November three armed groups took shape. In the north on the River Pripet near Minsk, General Stanislav Bulak-Balakhovich commanded fifteen thousand Russians. To the south, near Rovno, General B.S. Peremykin led another Russian force of similar size. Further south, beyond the Zbruch, General Wiktor Pavlenko stood at the head of more than twenty thousand Ukrainians. None were in direct contact with the others, and all depended on the Poles for liaison and communication. Pilsudski denied any responsibility for these units, but in reality he and the French military mission in Poland provided them with technical assistance and material support. They also directed the three towards a common military and political program aimed at carving out an enlarged territorial base in Belorussia and Ukraine while waiting for spring to undertake a more ambitious campaign against the Bolsheviks.[32]

The Soviet government viewed these developments with apprehension. At this time Wrangel had not yet been defeated, and the Red Army was deploying all available reserves north of Perekop. Strict orders had been given to the two Soviet fronts facing Poland not to violate the armistice or attack hostile formations east of the newly established frontier. Indeed, in Podolia the Bolsheviks went further, negotiating a two-week armistice with the Ukrainian forces there.[33] This was necessary as Pavlenko commanded the largest of the three groups and, with calvary poised at Zherminka, was in a position to strike at the rear of Frunze's army. The armistice neutralized this threat. The Bolsheviks, however, were livid. Initially they could only file toothless protests, but by the end of October they were able to insert a note of menace in a warning delivered to the Polish peace delegation in Riga. Here they referred not only to the Russian and Ukrainian detachments operating east of the new frontier but also to the Polish forces of General Zelegowski which had occupied Vilna. "Some detachments of Zeligowski's troops," said the Soviet protest, "have penetrated into the territory ceded to Poland, and known as the Polish corridor, and these detachments were accompanied by some units belonging to Balakhovich and Savinkov." Both were described as "a factor unquestionably calculated to endanger the continuance of the armistice."[34] Here was a triple threat, for the note clearly implied that failure to comply with Soviet wishes would place at risk not only the provinces ceded at Riga but also Vilna. All the same, the Bolsheviks waited patiently until Pilsudski announced he was ready to withdraw from the territory east of the Polish frontier, and only then did they prepare to attack his Russian and Ukrainian clients.[35] The three White commanders did not wait. Following the plan prepared by Pilsudski and the French military mission, they launched a coordinated attack against the Red Army on 10 November.

The attack had been timed to coincide with the resumption of peace negotiations at Riga. Pilsudski, who hoped to postpone the internal consolidation of Russia for as long as possible, sought to create circumstances which would delay the conclusion of peace. In this, as in the Vilna adventure, he acted independently of the Polish government who, as long as the marshal retained the confidence of his army, were powerless to stop him. This was very awkward. The Polish delegation could never be certain how Pilsudski would react to any agreement concluded with the Bolsheviks, while the latter, in negotiating with Dabski, had to present arguments which the marshal would find compelling. With the campaign against Wrangel coming to an end, Moscow possessed an ample store of such arguments, but their forceful presentation soon threatened the fragile peace of eastern Europe and with it the fundamental Soviet aim of negotiated settlements with their western neighbours.

Ioffe opened the new phase of negotiations at Riga by meeting privately with Dabski on 13 November. He charged the Poles with violating the armistice, and said Pilsudski had to withdraw his army to the new frontier and end his support of Balakhovich, Peremykin, and Pavlenko. Otherwise Soviet Russia would have to consider the resumption of hostilities. The Poles could not negotiate peace and then allow their protégés to continue hostilities against Soviet Russia. In a matter of days Wrangel would be finished. If the Poles wished to resume the war they would have to accept the consequences. Dabski replied weakly that "technical" problems had prevented the withdrawal of the Polish army. More truthfully, he described Balakhovich, Peremykin, and Pavlenko as the "former allies" of Poland. Moscow should not expect Poland to turn against them and act as its gendarme. The Polish army would leave Soviet territory, he promised, but it could take time, perhaps months. Ioffe said this was not satisfactory, and demanded that a precise date be established. Dabski yielded, and the next day the two agreed that the withdrawal should begin on 19 November.[36] As this would allow the Red Army to liquidate the remaining White forces, Ioffe gave his assent to the official opening of the peace conference.

Complications arose immediately. Pilsudski refused to honour the agreement, and on 20 November Ioffe informed Grabski that it was "not possible to proceed with any of the work of the Peace Conference" until he did. Subsequently, British and French representatives in Riga reported that Ioffe had acted at the behest of Dabski who wished to apply pressure to Pilsudski.[37] Whatever the case, Dabski promptly wired Witos, the prime minister, asking that the army observe the treaty obligations assumed by Poland, warning that failure to do so might lead to a resumption of the war and threatening to resign if the army continued to obstruct the peace negotiations. This brought no immediate response as Witos, for some unexplained reason, did not receive it until five days later.[38] Meanwhile the Red Army began to apply their own pressure, attacking all White forces in Belorussia and Ukraine. The Soviet offensive soon drove Balakhovich, Peremykin, and Pavlenko back into Poland. Pilsudski also withdrew, and only on the Zbruch did a brief engagement take place between Soviet and Polish forces. The Russian and Ukrainian detachments were disarmed as they entered Poland and, although not interned, were taken to camps some distance from the frontier.[39] In Warsaw the minister of foreign affairs was openly critical of Pilsudski. Prince Sapieha told the British chargé d'affaires that "his policy [was] to ensure scrupulous observance of all Poland's undertakings in order to obviate any possible pretext for a Bolshevik attack." He considered Pavlenko and Balakhovich as finished and frankly admitted that he was greatly concerned by the suspicion with which Polish policy was viewed abroad. He attributed this to Pilsudski but believed that the government was "strong enough to hold on the line which it has marked out for itself."[40]

He was nearly as critical of Dabski, whom he clearly saw as a rival. Sapieha told Panafieu that Ioffe had terrorized the chief Polish delegate.[41] He, therefore, attempted to take the lead in bringing about a resumption of the stalled negotiations. On 26 November he radioed Chicherin rejecting the accusation that Poland had violated the armistice, suggesting that Moscow was merely trying to delay serious negotiations and proposing that a date be fixed for the signing of the final peace treaty.[42] His note was read in Moscow as a rather barefaced attempt to evade responsibility for continued hostilities and diminish Dabski's role in the negotiations. Chicherin responded in a lengthy message which one British observer described as "all bombast." In substance, however, Moscow agreed to the resumption of negotiations but insisted that they be left to the delegations at Riga. In this manner Chicherin blunted Sapieha's attempt to play a larger role in the peace talks. On 6 December Radio Moscow announced that the negotiations had resumed in the Latvian capital.[43]

The crisis in Soviet-Polish relations had not passed. Instead, it grew deeper and expanded to include the Baltic states as well. All three republics sheltered large numbers of Russian emigrés, and, throughout the fall, Moscow had grown increasingly concerned about their activities. Not only had the Whites begun to recruit among the emigrés, but once again, as in 1919, had begun to view Latvia as a base from which to attack Soviet Russia. In October documents came to light indicating that associates of Savinkov had been planning to overthrow the Latvian government and march Balakhovich's army into the republic. In each case Moscow issued a strongly worded protest, but the Latvian government did nothing to hinder recruitment or propaganda. The police discovered that the Whites had in fact planned a coup, but it had been badly bungled.[44]

The Bolsheviks were determined to prevent Balakhovich from establishing an armed base anywhere near the Soviet frontier. In particular they did not want him to find refuge with Zeligowski in Vilna. The Soviet government would not tolerate the creation of a substantial base from which they could be attacked in the future. Indeed, that base might be enlarged by first attacking Latvia which, unlike Lithuania, had a common frontier with Russia. The Latvians were sufficiently alarmed by Zeligowski's campaign to warn Warsaw not to allow the general to threaten Lithuanian independence.[45] The Lithuanians knew they required more substantial assistance. They had sought aid from Britain and France, but the allies had chosen to submit the Vilna question to the League of Nations. Kovno, therefore, turned secretly to Moscow, requesting Soviet aid if Zeligowski should attempt to crush Lithuania.[46] There is no record of the Soviet response, but in mid-November both Ioffe and A. Aksel'rod, the Bolshevik plenipotentiary in Kovno, were reported to have told Lithuanian representatives that it would not be long before the Red Army drove Zeligowski from Vilna. The Red Army provided the best warning of possible Soviet action as it continued to build up its forces along the Baltic and Polish frontiers.[47]

The decision of the council of the League of Nations to hold a plebiscite in Vilna and send a military force to police it made the situation appear still worse. Zeligowski and Balakhovich were bad enough, but an allied military force of any size based for any reason near the Soviet frontier immediately sparked fear of renewed intervention. Ioffe and Aksel'rod issued warnings that the Red Army would advance on Vilna if an allied military force was sent there.[48] When these had no effect Moscow decided to issue an official statement. This took the form of a note which Ioffe addressed to Dabski on 11 December, rejecting the contention that Zeligowski was a rebel. He remained a Polish general, his troops were a regular part of the Polish army, and "he could not carry out war operations without active support from Poland." Zeligowski, the note continued, had given refuge to the "rebel band" of Balakhovich and provided a gathering place for "White Guard elements from the Baltic Republics." Ioffe warned that as Poland was responsible for Zeligowski, "all hostile actions against the Soviet Republic issuing from the territory of Zeligowski will therefore be regarded as actions undertaken by the Polish Government against the Russian Soviet Federative Socialist Republic."[49] Askel'rod submitted a copy of this note to the Lithuanian foreign minister, adding that he hoped it would prove "that the Russian Soviet Federative Socialist Republic will always be a faithful ally in fighting against the military adventurer, Zeligowski, as well as against any encroachment upon the independence of minor peoples."[50] It is unclear on whose authority, if any, Aksel'rod issued this statement. Soviet sources make no reference to it, and in 1920 it is difficult to imagine Lenin and Chicherin using the term "faithful ally" to describe Soviet Russia's relationship to any bourgeois government. The note itself, however, was quite sufficient to reverse any Lithuanian inclination to have a League of Nations military force sent to Vilna. Kovno preferred not to provoke a Bolshevik attack on the city.[51]

The Poles were not so cooperative. On 14 December Dabski replied to the Soviet note, citing paragraph one of the preliminary peace treaty excluding Soviet Russia from any involvement in fixing the Polish-Lithuanian frontier. At the same time he denied that Soviet Russia was threatened by Poland. The area held by Zeligowski did not adjoin Soviet territory, the Polish army controlled the entire border region, and the anti-Bolshevik military formations which had recently withdrawn into Poland had been "immediately disarmed and interned." In his second note to Dabski on 16 December Ioffe reiterated these concerns, denying any desire to interfere in the fixing of the Polish-Lithuanian frontier but asserting that Moscow could "not be indifferent" to the events taking place in the district occupied by Zeligowski.[52]

Ioffe did not limit himself to the exchange of notes. He also bandied words with Dabski, "smilingly" asking in one conversation: "Why should we not have a Zeligowski?"[53] Given the large number of men from the Baltic republics serving in the Red Army, this threat was taken quite seriously. Rumours spread rapidly, as Sir Percy Loraine reported from Warsaw on 20 December, that the Bolsheviks were forming "two or more divisions to attack Zeligowski; that these troops will use the same pretexts as Zeligowski when he made his *coup* and that [the] Soviet government will disavow their action."[54] A war scare swept through the Baltic. French and American representatives in Riga asked their governments to send warships to evacuate foreign citizens if necessary.[55]

Professional soldiers knew better. Although a few French officers contributed to the panic through alarmist reports, military opinion in general discounted an imminent Bolshevik attack. Neither Pilsudski nor the Polish general staff believed that Moscow was planning to resume the war.[56] The British and French general staffs reached similar conclusions. As early as 13 December the British staff concluded that the Red Army had been redeployed in an essentially defensive configuration. The French staff decided the Bolsheviks were "proceeding to a rational regrouping of their forces along the entire western front" and concluded there was no danger of an immediate Soviet attack.[57]

Moscow had no intention of attacking the Baltic states. It would not tolerate the presence of foreign armies on their territory but, for the moment, it wished to preserve their independence. Lenin saw them as bones of contention stuck in imperialist throats. It was in the French interest for them to be reabsorbed into a Whiteguard Russia while Britain wanted them to remain in her sphere of influence. Lenin would let Britain have them (much in the same way as he was ready to let the United States have Kamchatka) so long as this enhanced Soviet security. The independence of the Baltic states was important in another way. It was best expressed by Ioffe: "If we wished we could wipe countries like Estonia and Latvia from the map. But we will not do it in order to prove to Europe that it is possible to conclude peace with Soviet Russia and count on the agreement being kept."[58] The sudden eruption of allegations of intended Soviet aggression, therefore, were not merely without substance but potentially dangerous to fundamental Soviet interests. When Chicherin learned of these reports he issued an immediate denial.[59] Other measures soon followed, including assurances of improved relations with Latvia, a press conference in which Ioffe denied Soviet Russia was preparing to attack any of its western neighbours, and delivery of a similar statement to all foreign representatives in Reval.[60] These had the desired effect, and the war scare began to recede. At Riga, however, no progress towards peace had been achieved, and in mid-January 1921 Soviet-Polish negotiations, like those under way in London, had reached a dead point.

A third set of negotiations had not even reached the bargaining table. Since early in the year Moscow had sought and failed to engage Romania in peace talks. The Romanians feared the spread of revolutionary propaganda, especially in Bessarabia, and continued to doubt that the Bolsheviks would be the ultimate victors in the Russian civil war. Bucharest also had to contend with the divided counsel of the allied powers. In reality the Romanians were not unhappy with this situation. The authoritarian regime of King Ferdinand was not subject to public opinion, and no significant commercial interests clamoured for the opening of economic relations. They were content to observe, rather than participate in, the final phases of the Russian civil and Soviet-Polish wars. With the Red Army fully engaged against Pilsudski and Wrangel, the Romanians were free to respond evasively to Moscow's many proposals for the opening of peace talks.

Romania looked to the west and north for help in holding the territories acquired at the end of the Great War. The allies had failed to recognize Romanian sovereignty in Bessarabia, and in the fall of 1920 Bucharest appealed repeatedly for this recognition. Simultaneously, Romania joined with Czechoslovakia and Yugoslavia in forming the Little Entente, an alignment aimed at any Hungarian attempt to regain the territories lost to the three in the previous year. France not only endorsed the Little Entente but also favoured its enlargement to include Poland. At French urging, Romania agreed to seek this enlargement. In return France withdrew its objection to allied recognition of Romanian sovereignty in Bessarabia. The Bessarabia treaty was finally signed on 28 October 1920. When Take Jonesco, the Romanian foreign minister, went to Warsaw to ask Poland to join the Little Entente, however, he received a cool welcome. Prince Sapieha said Poland rejected any combination including Czechoslovakia or directed against Hungary. The latter was the only central European state which had been willing to help Poland during the recent Soviet war, while Czechoslovakia had been openly hostile. Sapieha proposed instead that Poland and Romania conclude a bilateral defensive alliance to guarantee their frontiers with Soviet Russia. Jonesco showed little interest in this proposal.[61]

Subsequent events soon caused the Romanians to reconsider. On 1 November, having learned of the Bessarabia treaty, the Soviet governments of Russia and Ukraine issued a joint declaration saying they were not bound by it in any way.[62] Shortly after the Red Army disposed of Wrangel, the communications from Moscow, formerly phrased in cordial terms, took on a different tone, calling on Romania not to allow its territory to be used as a base for attacking Soviet Ukraine.[63] Chicherin also took a firmer line on the long-discussed bilateral negotiations, saying they should examine "all questions of interest to Romania and Russia" and asking whether Bucharest was ready "to fix immediately the time and place" for these talks.[64]

The initial Romanian response was quite volatile. Apparently incited by the Polish minister, Count Skrzynski, the Romanian prime minister, General Averesco, sketched a bold plan for a spring offensive. Thirty divisions (ten each from Poland, Romania and the "western powers") would advance on Kiev, "temporarily reconstitute" Ukraine, and feed Europe from its reserve of cereals. The credibility of this plan, which the French minister accurately described as a fantasy, was not enhanced by Averesco's assumption that Britain would contribute five divisions or that his putative allies would agree that the Romanian army be assigned "the most difficult" role in the offensive, that of guarding the rear![65] Cooler heads soon prevailed. As soon as it became clear that neither Warsaw nor Paris, let alone London, would consider this enormity, the Romanians decided to re-examine the Polish proposal for a bilateral defensive alignment. In early December Jonesco informed Sapieha that he was ready "to envisage an entente of an exclusively defensive character" guaranteeing the eastern frontiers of the two countries. Sapieha responded favourably, and the two governments decided to work out the military details of the agreement. The French, who had been appalled by the initial Romanian proposal, lent their enthusiastic support.[66]

Discussion had only begun when reports reached Bucharest that the Red Army had begun to mass on the Romanian frontier. A large force was concentrated along the upper reaches of the Dniester where it seemed poised to attack northern Bessarabia, thus driving a wedge between the Polish and Romanian armies. As the river was frozen and the local population unhappy with Romanian rule, the situation appeared ominous. The Romanian army began to reinforce the threatened region but lacked confidence in their ability to repel an immediate invasion.[67] The Romanians decided to play for time, postponing the meeting with the Bolsheviks for as long as possible.[68] Thus there followed a further exchange of radio messages which elicited a Soviet denial of aggressive intent but did not contribute to an actual meeting of Soviet and Romanian representatives.[69]

Was Romania in any danger of Bolshevik attack? There was little substance to the fear of invasion which gripped the Baltic states in December, but the Romanians may have had better reason for concern. The two situations were quite different; no agreement of any kind had been reached with Romania. More importantly, the Bolsheviks had a genuine interest, at least in the short run, in maintaining the emergent status quo in the Baltic, but they had no such interest in regard to Romania. From the Bolshevik perspective Romania had not only stolen Bessarabia but had also become a key element in the French security system which Moscow would have been glad to destabilize. Moreover, a campaign in Bessarabia against the Romanians was more likely to succeed than one in the Baltic against Pilsudski. On balance, Moscow must have been very tempted to try its luck in a swift campaign to move the Soviet frontier from the Dniester to the Danube. There is evidence that the Soviet government gave serious consideration to such a campaign, for on 4 January 1921 Chicherin asked Lenin: "If our foreign security is involved is it permissible in principle to conduct political negotiations with the [Hungarian] government?" Such negotiations would have been an essential part of any decision to invade Bessarabia, because a Soviet attack on Romania was likely to trigger a Hungarian attempt to regain Transylvania. Lenin replied that such talks were "of course permissible in principle" but of no practical value at the moment. Chicherin was not to open political negotiations with Budapest. Still, the question must have come before the Politburo, because five years later, in vastly different circumstances, Chicherin himself confided to Briand and Berthelot that in 1921 the Red Army high command had wished to attack Romania, but the Soviet government had rejected the proposal.[70]

If this subsequent statement of Chicherin is true, the Soviet decision must have been taken early in the new year, because on 8 January Ioffe was careful, in his press conference concerning the war scare, to include Romania among the countries which he said were in no danger of Soviet attack. One week later, in yet another call for negotiations, Chicherin went much further. Here he explicitly abandoned the earlier Soviet insistence on discussing "all the controversial questions which concern Romania, the Ukraine and Russia" and declared: "We are ready, in the higher interests of peace, to limit the agenda of the future conference to those practical questions whose solution is the most urgent such as *the re-establishment of commercial relations and the regulation of navigation on the Dniester.*"[71] This implied that the two countries were not at war and that Moscow was prepared to accept the loss of Bessarabia and recognize the Dniester as the Soviet frontier.

The relief felt in Bucharest was immediate and palpable. Jonesco described the Soviet message as being of an ultra-friendly nature and boasted that "he intended to continue this procrastination as indefinitely as he was able." The revival of Romanian confidence was also felt in their negotiations with Poland. Previously they had been eager to conclude a military convention, but when General Haller arrived to negotiate this agreement in mid-January the talks dragged on for three weeks without agreement. The Romanians asked pointed questions about Polish relations with Czechoslovakia and Lithuania, noted the still undefined nature of the Soviet-Polish frontier, and rejected a Polish proposal that the two countries pledge, in the event of a Soviet threat to either, to mobilize their armies on the same day. The Romanians refused to enter into any binding military agreement until a political convention was concluded between the two governments.[72] They were now in the happy position of not having to make concessions either to Poland or Soviet Russia. From Warsaw they wished a guarantee of their Dniester frontier without risk of being dragged into some future Polish adventure in Russia. From Moscow they wanted peace without formal agreement or regular diplomatic relations. They got both.

The Poles had forced the Bolsheviks to accept a state boundary well to the east of their ethnographic frontier, but the allied powers had not recognized it in treaty form and, given Britain's attitude, were unlikely to do so in the future. Poland needed whatever international recognition of this frontier it could muster and, more importantly, the promise of assistance should this prove necessary.

Romania was the only possible source of aid, and Poland had to accept the terms Bucharest offered. Jonesco drove a hard bargain. The defensive alliance concluded on 3 March 1921 became operative only if either Poland or Romania was "attacked without provocation on its part along its present eastern frontier." The Romanians would not promise to mobilize their army prior to an actual Soviet invasion of Polish territory. Nor would they allow the treaty to come into force prior to ratification of the final Soviet-Polish peace treaty specifying the exact eastern frontier of Poland. It is not surprising that Sapieha confessed to the French minister "that he had hoped for better."[73]

Chicherin may well have used the same words. On 31 January Jonesco agreed to a meeting of Soviet and Romanian representatives but only to establish the agenda for a subsequent bilateral conference. He later agreed that this first meeting be held in Reval. But then he did not name his representative until 20 March, and at mid-year no meeting had taken place. Soviet-Romanian relations remained in exactly the state which Jonesco wished.[74] With the end of hostilities in eastern Europe, Moscow had lost the leverage needed to compel Romania to restore diplomatic relations. Only by threatening war could Moscow move Bucharest in this direction, and this was too high a price to pay. Soviet-Romanian relations would remain severed for more than a decade.

IN MID-JANUARY 1921 WHEN Krasin had left London, the future course of Soviet foreign policy continued to hang in the balance. That policy was definitely inclined towards finalizing the agreements then being negotiated with Britain and Poland, but there was no certainty that unforeseen developments would not interrupt or reverse further movement in this direction. Krasin was worried, and his concern was apparent to those with whom he spoke on his way back to Russia. In public he spoke about the British opponents of the treaty; in private he attacked its Soviet adversaries. In Stockholm he told Swedish friends (who promptly passed along the information to French intelligence) that there was "a very strong current of opinion in the Soviet government opposed to the Anglo-Russian agreement,"[75] and he carefully prepared for the possibility that the treaty might fail. While in Stockholm he met with both the Swedish foreign minister and Ago von Maltzan, who was on a tour of German diplomatic missions in Scandinavia. Little is known of what passed between them, but they certainly discussed the implications for Soviet-German relations of the possible failure of the Russian negotiations with Britain.[76] In his conversation with the foreign minister Krasin stressed the importance which Moscow attached to commercial relations with Sweden and suggested that Swedish business interests were in a position to profit from any delay in the signing of an Anglo-Soviet accord.[77]

Krasin arrived in the Soviet capital on 26 January and went directly to a ten-hour meeting of the Central Committee. Little time appears to have been devoted to discussion of the treaty with Britain which suggests that the Central Committee merely endorsed a decision taken earlier by the Politburo. The opposing view, presumably presented by Chicherin, was rejected. The foreign commissar later recorded that Lenin had "categorically insisted" on its conclusion, and this undoubtedly proved decisive.[78]

Why was this decision taken? No primary documents speak directly to this question. Indirect evidence suggests, however, that the Politburo and Central Committee must have been deeply impressed by mounting evidence pointing to the rapid disintegration of the Soviet economy. As Lenin admitted six weeks later at the Tenth Party Congress, the Soviet government had badly managed the food and fuel supplies of the republic. For want of coal the railways were unable to deliver grain and raw materials to the cities. Even apart from the fuel shortage, the railways were in chaos as old equipment was falling apart and could no longer be repaired or replaced. Meanwhile in the countryside the peasants had begun to offer armed resistance to government requisition of their crops. The growth of peasant insurgence (which the government called banditry) and poor administration of Red Army demobilization had created circumstances in which trains could not operate along even the most important rail lines without armed escorts. These conditions would soon lead to the promulgation of the New Economic Policy, but well before then they had begun to influence Soviet foreign policy. One week after the Central Committee resolved to proceed with the British trade treaty the Sovnarkom approved the immediate purchase abroad of more than 330,000 tons of coal, which could no longer be delivered in Petrograd from the many coal basins in the south. With conditions such as these, the Soviet government could hardly contemplate too forceful a foreign policy. Early in the new year any thought of retaking Bessarabia from Romania was put aside and late in January the Central Committee decided to settle with Britain on the best terms which Krasin could obtain.[79]

A decision to conclude a treaty and its actual conclusion are two different things, and Chicherin was still able to pursue his own objectives. His primary concern was modification of the treaty's preamble, which he feared would unduly limit Soviet freedom of action in Asia, without London accepting (or even discussing) similar restraints on British action. This must have been the basis of his presentation to the Central Committee, and although the Plenum accepted Krasin's report they did not bar Chicherin from seeking an improved preamble. Chicherin, in fact, seems to have been given a free hand to prepare the amendments which Lloyd George had invited Krasin to submit. The result was a very odd message sent on 4 February informing Curzon of Soviet acceptance in principle of the trade agreement. The introduction expressed "satisfaction that, in so far as the terms of the trade agreement itself are concerned, there are no such profound differences ... as might prevent agreement being reached" between the two governments. The remainder, however, heaped invective and recrimination on British policy in Asia. The key paragraph presented the wording which Moscow wished to add to the preamble. Here the British were invited to give an undertaking to "desist and refrain" from "any hostile action or propaganda in any form against the interests or the security of Soviet Russia" not only in the countries already specified in the British draft but also in those newly independent countries which had once been a part of the Russian empire. The British were also asked to refrain from encouraging hostile action against Soviet Russia on the part of Japan, Germany, Poland, Romania, Hungary, Czechoslovakia, Bulgaria, Greece, and Yugoslavia and to promise they would "not interfere in Soviet Russia's relations with other countries nor hamper these relations." In conclusion, Moscow proposed that both countries promise "to respect the independence and integrity of Persia, Afghanistan and of the territory of the Turkish National Assembly."[80] This was especially provocative as the British has sought continuously to limit the independence of Persia and Afghanistan and in 1921 continued to seek partition of the territories claimed by the Turkish National Assembly. In short, the bulk of the document had been written by Chicherin, and it was hardly designed to facilitate agreement with London.

Chicherin continued to attack the treaty. In the telegram of 4 February he had been as provocative as possible, but he had been forced to work within the limits established by the Central Committee. On 7 February, however, he went further, calling in a Norwegian journalist and provided him with an interview which was then addressed to the *Daily Herald* in London. Here he cast doubt on the economic value of the trade agreement and sought to incite Curzon by threatening British interests in the Middle East. He denied that Soviet Russia had pursued an aggressive policy. "On the contrary," he said, "trouble-making elements have been consistently discouraged by us, as for instance, in Persia, where we persuaded the Azerbaijan Government to suppress irresponsible elements which were making a Communist revolution." This restraint, he warned, would end if the trade agreement was not signed. The situation would then become more critical as "it is due to our caution that the Middle and Near Eastern powder magazines have not already blown up." When asked if the signing of the trade agreement did not mean Soviet "desertion of oppressed peoples," Chicherin responded that the purpose of the Soviet amendments to the preamble was to provide for "the formal recognition of oppressed peoples like Persia. We cannot desert Eastern peoples."[81] In effect Chicherin was telling Curzon that trade agreement or no trade agreement, Soviet Russia would continue a vigorous policy in the Near and Middle East.

Curzon was enraged by Chicherin's telegram of 4 February, but he did not give public vent to this anger. He confided it to a confidential memorandum circulated to the cabinet. Here he exclaimed: "With so colossal and finished a liar it is useless to cope. Nor, after my last reply, which I said would be the last of the series, would I propose to do so. The fusilade might go on till the dark-haired among us become grey, the grey-haired white, and the white bald."

There still remained the problem of the amended preamble. Curzon described the amendments as ludicrous in their absurdity and said they were "a prize illustration of Soviet humour. The brightest touch of the latter is when we are required to respect the independence and integrity of the 'territory of the Turkish National Assembly,' i.e., Mustapha Kemal!" Chicherin had obviously struck a very sensitive nerve. Curzon, however, intended to get his own back. He proposed replacing the lengthy Soviet amendment with "a simple sentence to the effect that we accept a similar obligation [to that required of the Soviet government] 'in the new independent States which formed a part of the former Russian Empire' – and leave it at that." He reminded his colleagues that they had earlier agreed that when the treaty was signed a letter would be handed Krasin indicating in greater detail British knowledge of Soviet activities in the East. That letter had been brought up to date, he concluded triumphantly, "and will, I think, have a damping effect even upon the humour of M. Chicherin." This became British policy. When Chicherin inquired on 21 February why he had not received a reply to his note of 4 February, Curzon responded that the issues involved would be dealt with when Krasin returned to Britain.[82]

Krasin did not reach London until 4 March. He had been delayed by urgent negotiations in Riga and Berlin. In the German capital he had informed the Auswärtiges Amt that he possessed full powers to sign the trade treaty with Britain and expected a rapid and successful conclusion of the negotiations.[83] The Germans thought he was over-confident, and events of the following days seemed to justify their pessimism. Reports of the insurrection at Kronstadt preceded Krasin and galvanized opponents of the treaty.[84] He had to wait a week before resuming negotiations. He then used every means to hasten the talks to completion. In this he had the eager assistance of the Board of Trade. They and the prime minister were more interested in British unemployment than Russian unrest. Once Krasin learned that the Board of Trade were ready to proceed with the treaty he must have realized that the Kronstadt insurrection had actually strengthened his hand. Given the instability of the Soviet regime, Moscow would be grateful for virtually any agreement. Until then, he could justify almost any concession as a small price to pay for restoring the international prestige of Soviet Russia. Chicherin, of course, would pay the price, as his amendments to the draft preamble were the major obstacle to agreement, but in the circumstances of mid-March, Krasin was free to deal with the question as he chose.

The final negotiations proceeded very rapidly. On the morning of 11 March Krasin presented Chicherin's amendments. This was for the record. That same afternoon he sent Nikolai Klishko, his deputy, to tell E.F. Wise that he was prepared to abandon Chicherin's amendments and accept a formula by which the British would promise to refrain from anti-Soviet action or propaganda in the successor states of the former tsarist empire. Klishko stressed that Krasin was anxious to conclude these negotiations: "Krasin could sign anything which he himself approved within the next week. After that time it would be much more difficult to sign without first referring to Moscow. This involved the possibility of mischievous intervention by Chicherin. If nothing happened for a fortnight he would certainly have to refer to Moscow with some explanation of the delay."[85]

Lloyd George now staged his own political theatre. On 14 March he placed the official Soviet proposals before cabinet without informing them of the signal he had received from Krasin. The ministers rejected Chicherin's amendments but, over Curzon's protest, decided to make a counter-offer which corresponded precisely to the terms Krasin had said he would accept. At the last moment it was decided to exclude both Asia Minor (meaning Turkey) and Persia from the list of countries marked for specific reference in the original preamble. The cabinet decided that the guiding principle of the treaty "should be the safeguarding of our Empire in the East." The Board of Trade were given full powers to conclude the agreement on this basis. Two days later, on 16 March, the Anglo-Soviet treaty was signed. At the same time Krasin was handed Curzon's letter identifying Soviet activities in the regions of India and Afghanistan which the British said had to end "if the good faith of the agreement [was] to be observed."[86]

Krasin had signed the treaty without further reference to Moscow. The day before its signature, Lenin had no idea that the treaty was about to be concluded.[87] Nor did Chicherin, who on 20 March telegraphed Krasin: "We had not expected that your negotiations would end so quickly." Clearly this was the way Krasin wanted it. He only broke his silence when the treaty was signed. He then described it in the best possible terms, reporting the exclusion of Persia and Turkey from the preamble and the British pledge to abstain from anti-Soviet activities in the former Russian borderland. Certain words were held up as trophies, Krasin calling special attention to British acceptance of "independent state" to describe Afghanistan and "peace treaty" to characterize the political agreement to be concluded subsequently between Soviet Russia and Great Britain. Significantly he did not even mention Curzon's letter. Chicherin seems to have learned of it from the British press.[88]

The foreign commissar had no other choice than to welcome the trade treaty. "A new era is now opening in the history of Anglo-Russian relations," he said on 22 March. His next words, however, indicated that little had changed. "We will strictly abide by our obligations, and we have every right to expect that Britain will honourably execute her obligation to abstain from hostile activities."[89] The gulf separating Great Britain and Soviet Russia can be measured by comparing these words with those of Curzon uttered a month before: "We shall keep our undertaking and the Soviets will not keep theirs; but the conviction has now been forced upon us that this is an inseparable feature of dealing with such people."[90] Subsequent events would confirm the structural hostility embedded in Anglo-Soviet relations. For the moment, however, Chicherin's most eloquent response to the Anglo-Soviet trade agreement was his own treaties with

Persia, Afghanistan, and Turkey. The first two had been signed in late February, the last two days after the British treaty. Chicherin knew that this last treaty in particular would find little favour in Britain but obviously took delight in telling Krasin: "Britain cannot demand from us that we take back Kars and Ardahan from Turkey or that we go to war against Turkey. A territorial delimitation is necessary for the avoidance of war."[91]

Understandably, Krasin took a more positive view of the treaty. He readily acknowledged its defects, in particular that it was only a trade agreement and did not provide de jure recognition, but he believed these were outweighed by its commercial advantages. It had broken the gold embargo and opened British markets to Soviet commerce. For Krasin, however, the importance of the treaty extended beyond Britain, because he felt other trading nations would soon be compelled to follow London's example.[92] Lenin shared this view. It was "correct for us to compromise in order to achieve a trade agreement with Britain," he told the Tenth Party Congress. He immediately added, however, that he did not expect the treaty to bring either substantial trade or much improved relations with Britain. Economically, Britain was not as advanced as Germany or America, and the tenuousness of Anglo-Soviet relations arose "from such an objective tangle of causes that no amount of skill on the part of the Soviet diplomatists will help." Thus, he concluded, "we need a trade treaty with Britain owing to the possibility opening up for a treaty with America, where industrial capacity is so much greater."[93] Here, Lenin was less than frank. He would have liked a treaty with the United States and, in mid-March 1921, still cherished the hope that the new Harding administration might move in that direction, but this was not the basis for the treaty with Britain. As will be shown below, the Anglo-Soviet treaty was more closely linked with the Soviet desire to expand political and economic relations with Germany, and here "America" was actually a code-word for the Reich.

The protracted negotiations, therefore, ended on a very indecisive note with almost all major issues left for later resolution. The treaty did, however, confirm the suspension of armed hostilities. These had sputtered out the year before but seemed ready to resume at almost any moment. The trade agreement was only a "substitute for peace," but it contributed to the general pacification of Europe. It brought two further advantages to the Bolsheviks. As Lenin and Krasin expected, other governments soon followed the British example and concluded trade agreements with Soviet Russia. France did not but, given French intransigence, the very existence of the Anglo-Soviet agreement served Moscow by further dividing the two allies. The treaty, however, did little to improve Anglo-Soviet relations. Even the framework which it provided for the further development of these relations was incomplete. Given the motives, attitudes, and reservations of the two governments, it is hardly surprising that their relations would prove far from cordial.

THE FIRST SIX WEEKS OF 1921 yielded no further progress in the talks at
Riga.[94] Four issues blocked agreement. Three were debated at length, but the
fourth, which hovered over every meeting, was rarely mentioned. Repatriation
of prisoners, extension of the period for renouncing the armistice, and gold were
inscribed on the open agenda. The first concerned Warsaw deeply, because the
Bolsheviks held more than five hundred thousand Polish prisoners. Agreement
in principle had been reached in late December, but the Bolsheviks would not
agree to begin repatriation immediately. They linked this issue with an extension
of the period allowed for renouncing the armistice. In October this had been set
at two weeks; Ioffe now demanded that it be extended to six. The Bolsheviks
had good reason to make this demand. Except for the prisoners and a share of
the Russian gold reserve, Poland already had almost everything she could hope
to obtain from a formal peace treaty. If Soviet Russia released the prisoners and
did not satisfy the Polish appetite for gold, Warsaw would have little incentive
to sign a final treaty. The Bolsheviks feared that the Poles might base their future
relations with Russia on the preliminary treaty of October.[95] This would be very
disadvantageous to Soviet Russia; under the agreement either side could resume
the war with only a two-week warning. As a consequence the Red Army would
have to be kept at a high state of readiness. A six-week warning would do much
to avoid this and, in fact, was so ample as to give the Poles little reason for not
signing a final peace treaty. Warsaw, therefore, rejected the Soviet demand,
which in turn hardened Moscow's determination not to release the Polish prisoners.

Gold was at the root of this impasse. The Poles wanted as much as they could
get, while the Bolsheviks wanted to give them none at all. Warsaw sought
compensation for 150 years of Russian exploitation and claimed 1.6 billion gold
rubles. Most claims were impossible of settlement within the context of the peace
conference and, together with Russian counter-claims, were ultimately referred
to mixed commissions created to settle accounts between the two states. In the
preliminary treaty, however, the Bolsheviks had promised Warsaw an unspecified
share of the Russian gold reserve, and the Poles were determined to obtain it as
part of the final peace settlement. This followed the precedent established by
Moscow in concluding peace with the Baltic states. There the Soviet government
had agreed to pay Estonia fifteen million gold rubles, Lithuania three million,
and Latvia four million. In December Dabski demanded three hundred million
gold rubles as Poland's share of the imperial Russian treasury.[96] This did not
sit well with Moscow. The Soviet gold reserve, though large, was not inex-
haustible and was needed for the resumption of trade. The Bolsheviks were
prepared to make a substantial payment to Poland, but not in the form of gold.
In line with his general aim of attracting foreign entrepreneurs, Lenin wanted
to make the payment to Poland in the form of concessions to exploit under-
utilized Soviet economic resources. This would contribute to Soviet economic
growth while recruiting political allies with a vested interest in the maintenance

of peace. Even when Chicherin reported on 3 January 1921 that the Poles would probably settle for a tenth of their official claim, Lenin refused. And so it stood for seven weeks. Although the Poles said they would settle for one hundred million gold rubles and suggested they might agree to a still further reduction, Warsaw would not abandon the claim entirely. This reinforced the Bolshevik fear that Warsaw might refuse to sign a final treaty, and this strengthened their own resolve not to part with the Polish prisoners.

Upper Silesia was the issue which hovered above the final stages of the conference.[97] At Versailles the allies had decided that the fate of this province should be settled by plebiscite, but continued disorder there had forced postponement of the consultation. In early 1921 allied leaders still had not set a date for the election, but it was unlikely to be later than March. Both Berlin and Warsaw believed the Soviet invasion of Poland had influenced the East Prussian plebiscites. Poland had appeared so close to collapse that even Polish voters had cast their ballots for Germany. The Polish government wanted no disturbance along its eastern frontier prior to the Upper Silesian plebiscite and, if possible, wanted to conclude peace with Soviet Russia before that date. The Germans naturally preferred the opposite and, at the very least, hoped that Moscow would delay a final peace treaty with Poland until after the plebiscite. This conflict allowed Moscow to negotiate with both Poland and Germany. As will be shown below, early in March Krasin discussed the issue in Berlin, but this was certainly not the first time it had been raised. Ioffe must also have discussed it with Dabski. In any case, after mid-January Prince Sapieha began to hint darkly to allied representatives that the Bolsheviks appeared to be intentionally delaying negotiations at Riga, perhaps with the object of influencing the Upper Silesian plebiscite in favour of Germany.[98] By mid-February this pressure appears to have produced some result as Sapieha, when visiting London, affirmed his belief that the delay in concluding the peace treaty "was due largely to German intrigue," and said he was now prepared to consider Soviet economic concessions instead of gold. At about the same time the Poles decided to send their minister of finance to Riga to meet with Krasin who had joined Ioffe in the negotiations.[99]

Krasin arrived in Riga on 19 February; five days later he and the Polish finance minister struck the bargain which was the basis of the second treaty of Riga. Krasin had been authorized to pay the Poles thirty million gold rubles, but no more. The Poles accepted, and the rest followed easily. On 24 February agreements were signed to begin repatriation of prisoners and to extend the period in which the armistice could be renounced from two to six weeks. It is probably no coincidence that three days before, the allied prime ministers announced that the Silesian plebiscite would be held on 20 March.[100]

The compromise, however, did not lead to the immediate conclusion of the treaty. Although Lenin told the Moscow Soviet on 28 February that it would be signed in the near future, many details remained unsettled. Even the timing had not been resolved. Krasin made this clear when he reached Berlin. There on

2 March he asked the Auswärtiges Amt if they were interested "in accepting the offer of the Soviet government to delay the conclusion of the Russo-Polish peace treaty until after the Upper Silesian plebiscite, and, if so, were [they] ready to provide in return that which Kopp had demanded." They were very interested, but because whatever Kopp had demanded (it is not specified in the memorandum) had a "financial character" the Auswärtiges Amt could not give a definite answer until "the internal departments of the German government had given their approval."[101] The same day, however, the issue became academic as Moscow, under pressure of the Kronstadt insurrection, settled the issue in Poland's favour. Chicherin wired Kopp that the Soviet government had decided to conclude the peace treaty as quickly as possible. This meant further concessions. The Poles had demanded a redrawing of the frontier, and Moscow agreed to give Poland a further three thousand square kilometres of territory.[102] In the circumstances of early March this was a small price to pay for Polish cooperation, and events of the next two weeks proved Moscow had received value for this territory. As the Kronstadt crisis deepened, Poland adopted a sympathetic attitude towards Moscow. The Polish government decided to sign the peace treaty in spite of the internal disturbances in Russia. Prince Sapieha expressed the fear that the "overthrow of the Soviet government would mean a period of anarchy" in Russia and spoke of the "results of six months hard work being lost at the last moment." Poland, he said, wanted to stabilize its eastern frontier "which could only be secured by the signature of the peace treaty."[103] This attitude was naturally appreciated in Moscow where it was compared favourably with the somewhat equivocal stance of the German government. For a brief moment, Polish and Soviet interests marched together.

The treaty signed on 18 March was a lengthy document which, with necessary modifications, confirmed the preliminary agreement of October 1920 and created an elaborate framework for a general settlement of accounts.[104] It was a peace of necessity. Both Poland and Soviet Russia were exhausted. Their economies were near collapse, with finances in ruin and transport in chaos. Neither could afford to maintain large armies, and both had been forced to begin demobilization prior to the conclusion of peace. Each badly needed whatever international legitimacy the other could give by signing a formal peace treaty. For Poland it meant the fixing, at least temporarily, of its long eastern frontier. For over two years Pilsudski and other Polish leaders had preferred a front line to a state frontier not of their choosing. An open fontier seemed to offer the opportunity of yet further expansion, perhaps even the restoration of the great Rzeczpospolita (Commonwealth) of the eighteenth century. By March 1921 they had changed their minds. Chaos rather than opportunity appeared to beckon from the East, and they sought to stabilize that which they had won from two and a half years of bitter fighting. For Soviet Russia the treaty meant peace with the last of the new states which had arisen in the western borderlands of the former tsarist empire. It was the culmination and most difficult part of a two-year struggle to achieve this objective. The Bolsheviks, like the Poles, had once perceived opportunity in the existence of an open frontier. The borderlands might link them directly with Germany. Frustrated in 1919, this desire had been reborn during the march on Warsaw. Lenin had not wanted war with Poland in 1920, but when Pilsudski forced it on him he sought to maximize the political consequences of apparent military victory. Apparent victory gave way to actual defeat, and Lenin was again disabused of the idea of carrying Soviet influence to central Europe on the bayonets of the Red Army. By the spring of 1921 a fixed frontier looked just as good to the Bolsheviks as it did to Poland. The line drawn at Riga was an accurate reflection of the balance of power as it then existed.

This was both the strength and the weakness of the Riga settlement. It was acceptable to both sides because it did reflect so faithfully the realities of the time. These had been tested in battle, and few wished to repeat the exercise. But the realities of 1921 were unlikely to remain for long. Exhaustion, chaos, and ruin would pass with time. Then other realities would assert themselves. Russian numbers and resources, Bolshevik dynamism and will, would one day be thrown into the balance. The Soviet government viewed the provisions of the Riga accord as illegitimate and transitory. Moscow had already deployed political structures (the Ukrainian and Belorussian Soviet Socialist republics) which by their very existence openly challenged Polish sovereignty in the conquered eastern provinces. And the Bolsheviks, with their well-established tradition of accepting political realities, were the least hostile of any Russian government which might conceivably replace them. The monarchists or Socialist Revolutionaries were even less likely than the Bolsheviks to accept for long the verdict of Riga. No wonder that the closest friends of Poland shook their heads. The Quai d'Orsay, which had sought so long to restrain Polish expansionism, issued a blunt warning. In February Berthelot told Pilsudski and Sapieha that Poland would excite Russian nationalism by pushing its frontiers too far to the east. Sooner or later Russia would again be a great power, and Poland would then be crushed if it had not previously obtained the acceptance of its existence within legitimate ethnographic frontiers. The French subsequently recognized the line fixed at Riga as the de facto frontier but refused to assume any responsibility for its maintenance. The British were even more critical. Ronald Lindsay gave the verdict of the Foreign Office, which in this instance was general throughout Whitehall: "The western boundary of Russia will one day be confirmed or refined after another clash of arms. As it has recently been changed drastically after 130 years of stability we need not speculate as to finality."[105] The terrible events of a generation hence loom from the silent pages of the archives.

IN THE FALL OF 1920 no further progress was made towards the improvement of Soviet-German relations.[106] Moscow was eager to resume negotiations but Berlin refused. The international situation was filled with too many uncertainties. The Germans did not know if the Soviet armistice with Poland would harden into peace, if the Soviet government would defeat Wrangel or, in the event they did, if the Bolsheviks would subsequently be able to keep their grip on Russia. It was equally unclear if Krasin's negotiations in London would eventually prove fruitful. Nor were the Germans certain of their own prospects. They still hoped for a favourable revision of Versailles and feared a premature agreement with Moscow would jeopardize it. Their only certainty was the continued support which Soviet Russia gave the German Communist Party, and this hardly recommended an agreement with Moscow.

In November some of this uncertainty began to fade. The Red Army crushed Wrangel, peace talks resumed at Riga, and the British presented Krasin with a draft trade agreement. Viktor Kopp again became a frequent caller at the Auswärtiges Amt. As soon as the Red Army had broken into the Crimea, he sought to interest the Germans in expanded economic relations. On 12 November he told Simons that he could not manage Soviet commercial affairs in Germany alone and that by refusing entry visas to Soviet specialists, the German government were effectively blocking the further development of trade. Simons replied that the ban had been imposed due to the misconduct of Zinoviev, but he was prepared to consider the admission of "genuine experts," provided the Soviet government allowed a German economic expert to join Hilger in Moscow.[107] A week later Kopp returned with a counter proposal. He told Maltzan that Moscow had received the German suggestion "quite sympathetically," but believed it was time to resume the economic negotiations that had been suspended in September.[108] Maltzan offered no encouragement that the talks could be resumed in the near future. Six days later Simons agreed that three Soviet specialists could join Kopp. He assumed that in return Moscow would allow a German economic expert to join Hilger.[109]

This was unacceptable to Chicherin. On 7 December he again instructed Kopp to seek the resumption of negotiations with Germany. Chicherin wanted some visible sign of the evolution of German policy in a manner favourable to Soviet Russia. Preferably this should include political negotiations, but Chicherin refused to discuss the one issue which the Germans insisted on including in such talks. "Unconditionally decline any reminiscences about Mirbach," he ordered. This left Kopp with a very difficult brief. The Germans continued to insist that they were unprepared to resume either political or economic negotiations. They had also named Paul Stähler as the economic expert they wished to send to Russia and demanded that he be given the necessary visa for the trip. Kopp could not give this visa because the Soviet government feared Berlin would be satisfied with merely sending Stähler. Worse yet, Moscow submitted a list of twenty Soviet experts for whom it wanted visas. Maltzan took a hard line and refused further action until Kopp had issued the promised visa. Kopp did so, but on 19 December suggested that instead of a single expert Berlin send a large official delegation to negotiate a trade treaty. He was told this was out of the question and only Stähler would be sent.[110]

Stähler got no further than Riga. On 3 January 1921 Chicherin informed Kopp that Stähler would not be allowed to enter Soviet Russia until other issues were settled. He wanted Kopp recognized as the official trade representative of the Soviet government and joined by a deputy who would take charge of economic and commercial affairs. Other specialists would also have to receive visas, because otherwise further Soviet orders could not be placed. The Germans protested bitterly, threatening to reduce, rather than increase, the number of Soviet specialists allowed in Germany and refusing to consider any improvement in Kopp's status so long as Moscow persisted in barring Stähler. Soviet-German relations had reached an impasse. Simons angrily told Kopp on 14 January that if the Bolsheviks thought they could treat an official German representative in this way, "then we will have to draw the consequences from it."[111]

The impasse appears to have been broken by Maltzan and Krasin on either 14 or 15 January. Maltzan had expected to meet Krasin in Stockholm during the second week of January to conclude the sale by a consortium of Swedish and German industrialists of a substantial quantity of railway equipment to Soviet Russia, but the commissar had been delayed by last-minute negotiations in London. Having determined that the Stockholm negotiations were proceeding satisfactorily, Maltzan returned to Berlin on 14 January. Krasin reached the German capital on the same day.[112] There is no record of their meeting, but it is difficult to imagine who else could have negotiated the agreement. Kopp did not have the authority or, after the Stähler affair, the confidence of the German government. Simons could have conferred with Krasin, but probably left the meeting to Maltzan in order to avoid unwanted publicity. A compromise was quickly arranged. In return for Stähler being allowed to proceed immediately to Moscow, the German government would officially recognize the Soviet trade office in Berlin and allow its expansion as Moscow wished. A conference would be held in Riga to hasten the repatriation of German prisoners of war still in Russia. At the end of the conference the German delegate Moritz Schlesinger would proceed to Moscow where, together with Hilger and Stähler, he would open trade talks.

On 15 January Stähler receiving permission to proceed to Moscow. Two days later Kopp himself departed for Moscow, announcing in an official note to the Auswärtiges Amt that while he was away two deputies would exercise his authority. One was specifically entitled "Leader of the Trade Agency." The Auswärtiges Amt took no exception to this unilateral assumption of enhanced status.[113] More importantly, Simons sent for Moritz Schlesinger and informed him that in addition to conducting the prisoner-of-war negotiations in Riga he was also to go to Moscow to resume the stalled commercial negotiations. For the Riga conference he received a full set of official credentials, but for the Moscow talks he received only verbal instructions. "See what you can do!" Simons told him. In this manner the foreign minister did not commit himself to anything and could, if necessary, deny that negotiations were even under way.

This also allowed him to determine if an agreement with Soviet Russia was possible and have it available should political circumstances warrant its conclusion. It was the opposite of the negotiating procedure desired by Moscow, and Krasin would have had to approve it before leaving Berlin. The remainder of the compromise unfolded quickly. Schlesinger left immediately for Riga where on 22 January he concluded an agreement with the Soviet representative in Latvia permitting the rapid repatriation of German prisoners of war still in Russia. Four days later the Stockholm negotiations on the sale of railway equipment to Russia were crowned with equal success.[114] The path was open for trade talks with Moscow.

These negotiations did not proceed smoothly. Schlesinger was not favourably impressed by the economic chaos or lack of personal security which he found in Russia. He was even less impressed by the lack of concern shown by Soviet officials for the problems of German citizens awaiting repatriation. Only after he dealt with the latter issue did he turn to questions of trade. Here his task was to construct the legal framework for future economic relations, but Soviet officials did not really want to discuss this question. They preferred a more general agreement, with legal questions to be settled at a later date. When convinced that Schlesinger had no authority to discuss larger issues, they tabled proposals which would have given them a free hand to develop their commercial operations in Germany while restricting those of Germany in Russia. In a letter to Maltzan Schlesinger exclaimed that in Moscow "parity is an entirely unknown concept."[115] A lengthy meeting with Chicherin and Radek did not improve the situation. Radek remarked sarcastically: "We want to discuss *grosse Politik* while you only want to talk about old pants." Schlesinger feared he would have to return to Berlin empty-handed, but on 14 February Krasin agreed to reciprocity in the legal status of the trade representations to be established in a future treaty. This was recorded in a lengthy protocol and, together with a further agreement on repatriation of prisoners of war, signed on 18 February.[116]

Berlin was pleased with Schlesinger's work but unready to embody the protocol in a formal trade agreement. Maltzan observed that the British had not yet reached agreement with Moscow, and, thus it was "not opportune" for Germany to conclude a treaty with Soviet Russia. He suggested, however, that parts of the protocol could be implemented informally.[117] This was begun in early March when Krasin reached Berlin and installed Boris Stomoniakov as head of the Soviet trade delegation. Stomoniakov, he insisted, would do business in the name of the Soviet government and not in his own, as Kopp had done. Krasin also stressed the importance of concluding the treaty as soon as possible.[118]

Even as Krasin spoke, the western powers were taking decisions which would drive Germany into Soviet arms.[119] A month before, the allies had decided that Germany should pay 226 billion gold marks in reparations. On 1 March Simons replied that Germany could not pay that amount; he offered thirty billion instead. This caused the allies to occupy Duisburg, Düsseldorf, and Ruhrort on the right bank of the Rhine, separating them and the left bank of the Rhine from the rest of Germany by a tariff barrier and threatening to confiscate 50 per cent of the value of German exports to their countries. Simons was acclaimed throughout Germany, but western sanctions threatened serious disruption of the German economy. Trade with countries not subject to allied influence, Soviet Russia in particular, assumed a new importance. When Krasin signed the trade agreement with Britain the way was clear for Germany to conclude a similar treaty. On 18 March Maltzan informed the British ambassador of this intention, reminding him that under the terms of the Versailles treaty Germany was bound to recognize any treaty an allied power concluded with Russia. Germany, he said, was "anxious to follow the lead of England." The following day Simons submitted the Moscow protocols for cabinet approval.[120]

Allied intransigence had driven Germany towards agreement with Moscow; disorder within the Reich now arrested this movement. In mid-March the German Communist Party launched another bid for power. The März Aktion, as this attempted coup was known, had many causes, but the Executive Committee of the Communist International clearly had a hand in its origin. In early March they sent three emissaries to Germany, including Bela Kun, for the express purpose of promoting an uprising. No evidence is available to indicate precisely who in Moscow knew of this mission or exactly what it was expected to accomplish, but it is unlikely that it was sanctioned by more than a small number of Comintern leaders.[121] It was contrary to every other aspect of Soviet policy and produced predictably negative consequences in Germany, where otherwise Soviet aims were well on the way to being realized. With a communist insurrection under way, it is understandable that the ministries responsible for public order would not look favourably upon a treaty with Soviet Russia. On 26 March the cabinet postponed approval of the treaty.[122]

The Auswärtiges Amt had been blocked but not defeated. Simons immediately reaffirmed his commitment to the Moscow protocols, and in early April Maltzan and Kopp reworked them in the form of a draft treaty. In defending the Foreign Ministry position, Haniel told the Reichsrat foreign affairs committee on 4 April that the allied threat made it essential for Germany to seek a way out of its difficulties through an agreement with Soviet Russia.[123] The broad political support for this position was reinforced by secret negotiations then reaching fruition for Soviet collaboration in the clandestine rearming of Germany. On 7 April Kopp reported initial success and sought approval for sending of a German officer to Moscow "for further examination of the matter on the spot." Lenin approved immediately.[124]

Germany had possessed special importance for the Bolsheviks since their seizure of power in 1917. Initially and spasmodically thereafter, this had been viewed in terms of the revolutionary potential of German society. After Brest-Litovsk and throughout most of the civil war, this revolutionary potential had been discounted in favour of more immediate benefits which cooperation with the existing regime in Germany could bring. On 11 April Lenin had reaffirmed this pragmatic approach: "For Russia an alliance with Germany opens gigantic economic perspectives independent of how soon the German revolution will triumph. We are able to reach agreement with the bourgeois government of Germany because the Versailles treaty condemns Germany to an impossible position while an alliance with Russia opens vastly different possibilities."[125] Four days later Chicherin presented the Politburo with the draft treaty prepared by Kopp and Maltzan. They decided certain changes were necessary. In particular they wanted the German government to sever relations with anti-Bolshevik Russian groups active in Germany and recognize "the representation of the R.S.F.S.R. in Germany as the only Russian representation in Germany." Moscow asked the German government for permission to send a special envoy, Aron Scheinmann, with its counter-proposals.[126]

By the time Scheinmann reached Berlin the German political world was in turmoil. The allies had declared Germany in violation of the Versailles treaty. The United States, to which Simons had appealed for mediation, refused to intervene. The French army had begun to mobilize and, in Upper Silesia, Polish insurgents sought to void the verdict of the plebiscite which had gone in Germany's favour. On 5 May the allies threatened to occupy the entire Ruhr if Germany did not agree in six days to fulfill their demands.[127] The Fehrenbach government resigned.

At the time of their resignation the cabinet had still not approved the Soviet treaty. Seemingly further action had to await the formation of a new government. Such was not the case. Instead Maltzan summoned Scheinmann to the Auswärtiges Amt and concluded the treaty. He would not agree to the Soviet formula for describing the Russian Soviet Federative Socialist Republic representation in Berlin, as he feared that it would compel the German government to place anti-Bolshevik Russians at the mercy of the Soviet government. A compromise, however, was quickly reached; the German government recognized the Soviet representation as "the only representation of the Russian state in Germany." What followed next was truly extraordinary. On 6 May Maltzan himself signed the treaty, inserting a clause which put it in force from the moment of signature! This highly unorthodox procedure brought a sharp remonstrance from President Ebert,[128] but nobody sought to invalidate the agreement. With the Reich in danger, Berlin had to seek whatever help might be available from Soviet Russia.

De facto recognition had never been an issue in the negotiations, because Berlin had already recognized Soviet Russia de jure at Brest-Litovsk. Diplomatic relations had been severed in November 1918, and in 1921 had still not been officially restored. The treaty carefully avoided any reference to this subject but was in fact an elaborate agreement for the restoration of political and economic relations. *Izvestiia* hailed it as such on 14 May, adding correctly that it marked the recognition by Germany of Bolshevik victory in the civil war. *Izvestiia* also spoke glowingly of prospects for German-Soviet economic relations and the breach with the allies that Germany allegedly made by concluding the treaty.[129] Both observations were far from the mark. The Germans concluded the agreement despite a pessimistic evaluation of the devastated Russian economy, and neither Britain nor France was greatly disturbed by the agreement.[130] The treaty, in fact, did little more than acknowledge and regulate an arrangement that had evolved slowly over the course of the previous two years. The very manner in which it was finally concluded pointed to past and future difficulties in Soviet-German relations. As in June 1919 and April 1920, allied sanctions had driven a reluctant German government towards improved relations with Moscow. In all instances the movement was minimal, virtually the least which could be done in the circumstances. Further movement was restrained by the deep suspicion with which the Germans viewed the Bolsheviks. The latter, for all their talk of wanting to develop far-reaching cooperation, still hoped for revolution in Germany. It remained to be seen if a common fear of the western powers would provide a sufficient base on which the two could fashion a workable relationship.

CHAPTER NINETEEN

Federation and alliance: Soviet policy in Southwest Asia, 1920–1921

By the summer of 1920 Soviet nationality policy had begun to take final shape. It was, in fact, two policies, one relating to the non-Russian nationalities of the former tasarist empire, the other to the peoples beyond the old imperial frontier, especially in Asia. The first aimed at the reconquest of much of the former empire and its restructuring along national lines as a federation of socialist soviet republics. Although theoretically sovereign, the new states would actually be controlled by the Russian Communist Party. Beyond the frontier Soviet aims were different. There they sought to foster nationalism, attack imperialism, and acquire political influence. These aims served Soviet interests in both Asia and Europe. Great Britain was the principle power in South Asia, and Soviet security would increase as British influence diminished. The Bolsheviks also believed that British vulnerability in Asia would make Whitehall more tractable in Europe. Krasin had been sent to explore this hypothesis, and his findings reinforced an already existing reluctance to become engaged in military adventures in Asia. In the borderlands there was a solid base for the establishment of Soviet power, but beyond them was only political quicksand into which the Red Army could easily sink. The military demands of the Polish war and the final assault on Wrangel only added to Soviet caution. At the same time, however, the Bolsheviks could not be too cautious, for then no one would take them seriously. The policy which emerged, therefore, was politically dynamic and verbally inflammatory, emphasizing promises and propaganda, but was also tactically flexible and committed a minimum of resources beyond the borders of the old empire.

The Second Comintern Congress and First Congress of the Peoples of the East provided the Bolsheviks with platforms from which to proclaim their nationality policy. It was based on a set of "theses on national and colonial questions" drafted by Lenin in early June, the underlying idea of wich was "the distinction between oppressed and oppressing nations." The latter, though few in number, possessed "colossal wealth and powerful armed forces"; the former, while more than 70 per cent of the world's population, were "either in a state of direct colonial dependence" or "semi-colonies" such as Persia, Turkey, and China. Soviet Russia naturally sympathized with the oppressed nationalities. Lenin therefore concluded that communists should support national liberation movements against imperialism. He emphasized that this included communists of oppressed nations who might not be inclined to support what he readily recognized as bourgeois-democrats. This did not go down well with many communists who objected strongly to supporting bourgeois-democrats of any kind, but Lenin stood his ground.[1] When the Congress debated the issue, he allowed M.N. Roy, an Indian communist, to put forward supplementary theses far more critical than his own of bourgeois nationalism in the colonies. The Congress unanimously adopted both sets of theses, but those of Roy were subsequently ignored. Lenin's remained in force.[2]

The theses inscribed the motto "federation and alliance" on the banners of the Red Army as they advanced south. They served to legitimize the subsequent development of Soviet policy in the borderlands and Asia. Thus, the seventh thesis formally endorsed the Soviet style of federation as "a transitional form to the complete unity of the working people of different nations." The fifth and sixth theses explained the nature of the alliance which Soviet Russia hoped to fashion with the peoples beyond whatever frontier was established in the south. In all instances, "the struggle of the world bourgeoisie against the Russian Soviet Republic" was to be considered "the central point of world politics." As a result, there could be no salvation for oppressed people "except in the victory of Soviet power over world imperialism." All oppressed peoples, therefore, had to ally themselves with Soviet Russia. The precise form of this alliance would "be determined by the stage of development reached by the communist movement among the proletriat of each country or by the revolutionary liberation movement in the undeveloped countries and among the backward nationalities."[3] Soviet needs and interests would be the measure by which every issue would be judged; all others would be subordinate to them. This was a clear policy, but one which would be difficult to implement. Lenin's authority had served to quiet most objections in Moscow. Soviet prestige served the same purpose a month later when the First Congress of the Peoples of the East assembled in Baku. The two thousand Asian revolutionaries drawn from twenty-nine nationalities who answered the call of the Communist International posed few difficult questions regarding Soviet intentions. Instead, they celebrated their mutual hatred of British imperialism and returned home to announce the imminence of revolution from the north.[4] "Bourgeois nationalists" would prove far more critical.

Afghanistan illustrates the problems Soviet Russia faced in the attempt to regain the tsarist frontiers in Asia and establish satisfactory relations with the peoples to the south. Distance and the fortunes of war complicated this process. Central Asia was linked to Russia by only a single railway extending sixteen

hundred kilometres from Orenburg to Tashkent. The Bolsheviks held most of
Turkestan throughout the civil war but could not keep a firm grip on Orenburg.
For much of 1918 and 1919 either the city or its southern approaches were in
enemy hands, effectively separating Turkestan from Russia. The revolution in
central Asia, therefore, developed in isolation and in a manner unsatisfactory to
Moscow. The Soviet government in Tashkent possessed all the trappings of its
Russian parent but functioned as a settler regime primarily intent on keeping the
indigenous population in subjection. Attempts to alter the political climate in
Tashkent by Central Committee resolutions proved futile, and not until the fall
of 1919, when the Red Army reopened the rail link to central Asia, could effective
measures by taken. In November a five-man special commission arrived to
enforce the will of the Soviet Russian government in Turkestan.[5]

These circumstances contributed to the slow pace of establishing political
relations with Afghanistan. The policies of the Tashkent Soviet were repugnant
to the government of Afghanistan who, in any case, was bound by treaty to have
foreign relations only with Britain. Those relations were bad, however, and in
April 1919, following the accession of Emir Amanullah to the Afghan throne,
war ensued.[6] As Soviet Russia was also at war with the British, Amanullah
addressed a message to "His Mightiness the President of the Great Russian
State" proposing the two countries establish friendly and direct relations. The
difficulties involved can be seen from the time it took to complete one exchange
of messages. Amanullah had written on 7 April; his greeting did not reach
Moscow until 21 May. Five days later Lenin accepted the Afghan proposal; his
response did not reach Amanullah until July. In the interval Amanullah had
decided to send Muhammad Wali Khan to Europe to announce the end of British
control over the foreign relations of Afghanistan. He was unable to proceed
beyond Tashkent, however, as the rail line to the north was blocked. His arrival
prompted the government of Soviet Turkestan to send N.Z. Bravin to Afghanistan. Moscow also named him as its agent to the emir. Bravin reached Kabul
in late July but his presence, like that of Wali Khan in Tashkent, was largely
symbolic as he had no way of receiving instructions from either Tashkent or
Moscow.[7]

The reopening of the Orenburg-Tashkent railway permitted Moscow to establish closer, if still somewhat distant, contact with Afghanistan. Wali Khan was
at last able to go on to Moscow, where he arrived on 10 October. He was given
a warm welcome by Chicherin and Lenin, but time had overtaken his mission.
When he left Kabul the Anglo-Afghan war was just beginning; by the time he
reached Moscow it had been over for four months. Wali Khan, in fact, was soon
recalled to Kabul, but he did not return empty-handed. With him went a letter
from Lenin to Amanullah hailing Afghanistan as "the world's only independent
Moslem state." It was the Soviet wish, he said, to negotiate a series of agreements
with Afghanistan designed not only to strengthen their bilateral relations but also
to allow both countries "to continue the joint struggle against the most predatory

imperialist government on earth – Great Britain." At the same time Yakov Z. Surits was sent to represent Soviet Russia in Kabul.[8]

Early 1920 was hardly the time to conclude ambitious agreements. Central Asian politics remained fluid, indeed potentially volatile, and neither government was ready to cast its future relationship in treaty form. Amanullah dreamed of a greater Afghanistan with influence extending far beyond its borders. The Bolsheviks were determined to restore the frontiers of 1917 with their influence paramount in Afghanistan but that of the emir excluded from Soviet territory. Expectations of improved relations with their common enemy, Great Britain, also served to divide them. Afghanistan had already begun negotiations for a treaty of friendship with Great Britain, and in January Soviet Russia initiated its own talks with London. Progress in both served to cool the ardour in Kabul and Moscow for an alliance against Britain. Soviet leaders in particular grew cautious and were determined not to be drawn into an Asian adventure. British military intelligence regularly intercepted and deciphered radio messages exchanged between Moscow and Tashkent, and on the basis of this traffic reported on 30 March: "The Central Government ... is clearly determined to keep a firm hold on the conduct of affairs, and ... not to be entangled in an alliance with Afghanistan which, even if it were restricted to a defensive alliance, might, by involving the Bolsheviks in military operations against Great Britain, turn out to conflict with the development of their aims for recognition by the Powers of Western Europe."[9] Soviet caution compelled Afghanistan to explore improved relations with Britain, and in April an Anglo-Afghan conference opened in India.

Soviet and Afghan ambitions clashed in much of the region. In the northwest, Amanullah sought to assert his sovereignty over the districts of Kushk, Panjdeh, and Merv. Prior to the late nineteenth century, Afghanistan had exercised a distant suzerainty over the Turkoman tribes of these districts, and following the revolution the emir sought to restore his influence there by establishing consular posts supported by strong military escorts. Afghan officials fostered Turkoman separatism, and in the fall of 1919 Kabul asked for Soviet approval of Afghan annexation of the districts.[10] Further to the east lay the former Russian protectorates of Khiva and Bukhara. Since 1917 the two khanates had regained their independence and successfully defended it against attempts to impose Soviet rule from Tashkent. Bukhara was of strategic importance, because it lay between Turkestan and northern Afghanistan. Amanullah wanted Bukhara as a buffer and had sent troops to aid its khan against the Tashkent Soviet. In 1919 he sought assurances that Soviet Russia would respect the independence of both khanates. Moscow was unwilling to yield either the khanates or the Turkoman districts, but military weakness and the desire to avoid provoking Afghanistan prompted a cautious response. Khiva and Bukhara, Moscow said, had already exercised their right of self-determination, and Soviet Russia recognized their independence; sovereignty in the Turkoman districts could be determined by popular vote. These were hardly the answers Amanullah wanted, but without alienating

Moscow and thus forfeiting future Soviet aid against Britain, he could not press his claims any further.[11]

The first half of 1920 witnessed a steady improvement of Soviet fortunes in central Asia. The reforms of the Turkestan Commission converted Tashkent from a beleaguered fortress into a major centre of Soviet power. In particular, the elimination of privileges previously enjoyed by the Russian minority enhanced Soviet prestige in central Asia. The commission was also able to draw in a limited, but significant, manner on the military resources of Soviet Russia and build an army far larger than any other in central Asia. Political prestige and armed force proved to be an unbeatable combination. A build-up of Red Army strength in Transcaspia convinced the Afghans to withdraw their troops from the Turkoman districts. The Turkestan Commission then turned to Khiva, where it gave its support to the Young Khivans, a group of dissident intellectuals and merchants who had assumed the leadership of Uzbek opposition to Turkoman rule. In January 1920 the Red Army invaded the khanate, easily overcame Turkoman resistance, and installed the Young Khivans in power. Five months later Khiva was proclaimed the Khorezmian People's Soviet Republic.[12]

Bukhara took longer. Its emir was stronger and commanded greater support. Amanullah sent him both men and weapons. The Turkestan Commission, however, were not without resources. As in Khiva, they made use of dissident merchants and intellectuals whom they organized as the Young Bukharan Party. The latter, however, were not as unified as their Khivan counterparts, and it took them longer to organize a revolution. Tashkent could not simply invade Bukhara, because on 10 August it had been ordered by the Politburo "not to initiate an attack on Bukharan territory or military units." Such action could be taken "only if a more-or-less popular Bukharan revolutionary centre (even on our territory) requests such support." Not surprisingly, this happened. In late August Bukharan revolutionaries seized the border town of Chardzhui, organized a congress of the Young Bukharan Party, and appealed for the help of Soviet Turkestan. The Red Army promptly entered the khanate and, after several days of battle, captured the fortress of Old Bukhara. The emir fled, and a Soviet-backed government replaced him. A month later Bukhara was proclaimed a Soviet republic.[13]

The elimination of independent Bukhara restored the former imperial frontier in central Asia. This was a major Soviet aim, but the caution with which it was achieved suggests larger issues were involved. Given that the Baku Congress of the Peoples of the East opened at precisely the moment the revolution began to unfold in Bukhara, it is reasonable to conclude that Moscow was eager to impress the delegates with yet another revolutionary victory in the east. The Soviet government presumably also wanted to impress the British. The events in Bukhara occurred at the same time as the crisis in the Soviet-Polish war. Moscow may well have calculated that the rise of a revolutionary tide apparently running strongly in the direction of India would cause London to accept a Soviet Poland and the trade treaty with Russia.

By itself, the fall of Bukhara would not make much of an impression in London. To alarm Britain it would have to be linked to some substantial improvement in Soviet-Afghan relations, suggesting an imminent assault on India. But how could this be done without actually becoming entangled in such a risky venture? Soviet caution in early 1920 had already disillusioned Amanullah and contributed to his decision to resume negotiations with the British. These talks had not led to an agreement,[14] and their failure provided a new opening for Soviet diplomacy. By early summer Suritz, the Soviet envoy, was again negotiating with Amanullah. Here, too, was a reason for caution in Bukhara. Too blatant a move there could send Amanullah recoiling towards the British. A revolutionary veil would make it easier for the emir to accept the harsh reality of Soviet Bukhara, especially as the Bolsheviks could say quite truthfully that the new regime would facilitate the delivery of Soviet aid to him. The latter was an important consideration, as Amanullah had demanded a large Soviet contribution to any joint effort undertaken against the British. As the Bolsheviks prepared to crush Bukhara, therefore, they instructed Suritz to promise the Afghans "one million gold rubles, a wireless station, anti-aircraft guns, 80 aeroplanes, the installation of a telegraph from Kabul to Kushk via Kandahar, technical and military experts, 5,000 rifles, and the erection and installation of a smokeless powder factory."[15] The operative word here was "promise"; Moscow was prepared to deliver very little. For example, on 29 May the foreign commissariat informed the Afghan representative in Tashkent that Soviet Russia was ready to deliver a radio station to Kabul. Three months later it arrived, but there is no evidence to indicate that Afghanistan received anything further from Soviet Russia during the summer of 1920.[16]

These negotiations, which were carefully monitored by British military intelligence, produced exactly the effect which Moscow wanted on the government of India. Soviet leaders would have been shocked to learn the extent of British knowledge of their negotiations with Afghanistan, but they could not object to the conclusion which the viceroy drew from this information. On 8 June Lord Chelmsford wired London: "We are entirely opposed to attempting any *entente* with Afghanistan against the Bolsheviks ... Our policy should be to detach the Bolsheviks from the Afghans, *vide* our proposals of agreement with the Soviet Government."[17] Thereafter, the viceroy and the India Office supported Lloyd George's policy of reaching agreement with Moscow. In September, when Soviet-Afghan relations briefly deteriorated, Lord Chelmsford considered aiding Amanullah if he asked for assistance, but such a request never arrived and the viceroy soon returned to his former position.[18] The voice of India was just one of many heard in the British cabinet, but it contributed to the ultimate decision to extend de facto recognition to the Soviet government.

The invasion of Bukhara strained Moscow's relations with Afghanistan. Afghan troops helped defend the emir, and both they and the Afghan ambassador were taken prisoner. V.V. Kuibyshev, Moscow's chief lieutenant in central Asia, later reported the Afghans had been the "only military unit to offer serious resistance." The ambassador was thoroughly interrogated and revealed the full extent of Afghan activities in the khanate. On 10 September, however, the Turkestan Commission resolved that "diplomatic relations between Afghanistan and Bukhara must be preserved." Kuibyshev insisted that the new government view the activities of the Afghan ambassador as having been taken without the approval of his government. He also insisted that they officially inform Kabul of their wish for friendly relations with Afghanistan. Kuibyshev thoughtfully provided them with a text which they dutifully signed and sent to Kabul.[19]

Soviet sources are nearly mute on the initial Afghan response to events in Bukhara. Chicherin in his year-end report for 1921 only records that Kabul learned of the "revolution" in Bukhara on 10 September, and three days later Suritz signed a friendship treaty with Afghanistan, which the Soviet government subsequently repudiated.[20] This suggests that Suritz sought to soothe Afghan ire by making concessions that Moscow thought unnecessary. Tensions increased still further when the Soviet government instructed Suritz to inform the emir of the charges brought against his representatives in Bukhara. Moscow was careful to ascribe these delinquencies to "insufficient contact between the Afghan central authorities and their local representatives," but also gave its full support to the new government of Soviet Bukhara.[21]

At this point Amanullah decided to invite the British to resume negotiations. The latter, however, soon learned of the Suritz treaty and did not respond promptly. Thus the emir had to proceed cautiously, recognizing Soviet Bukhara in early November and pressing Moscow to accept the Suritz treaty.[22] By then, however, Moscow was in no hurry to conclude any treaty with Afghanistan. Negotiations with Britain had just entered what was hoped to be their final stage, and the Bolsheviks did not want to put them at risk by concluding a treaty with Kabul. Only in late February, when Krasin was confident he could bring his talks to a successful conclusion, did the Soviet government reopen negotiations with Afghanistan. The emir was more than ready. In January a British mission had arrived in Kabul, but after a month of talks no agreement was near. Amanullah was well aware of the Anglo-Soviet negotiations and seems to have feared that the two might include some agreement contrary to his interests in the treaty nearing completion in London. Did the Soviet government incite this fear? Probably, but no substantiating evidence is currently available. Soviet sources are again mute concerning the final phase of negotiations. For whatever reasons, the Afghans agreed to accept Soviet revisions of the September draft treaty.[23] The final document was signed by Chicherin and Wali Khan in Moscow on 28 February 1921.[24]

The treaty was quite different from the one envisaged at the opening of negotiations. Rather than some kind of alliance against Great Britain, the treaty was carefully crafted to avoid offending Whitehall. On the contrary, it was designed to protect the parties from the danger of either one concluding an agreement with Great Britain directed against the other. Thus, article two bound both "not to enter into any military or political agreement with a third state which might prejudice one' of them. Subsequent events would show the need for this article, as while the treaty remained unratified Afghanistan secretly sought an offensive-defensive alliance with Britain against Soviet Russia![25] Amanullah was clearly impressed by the return of Russia to central Asia.

The entire document celebrated this return, enshrining Soviet policy and interests in treaty form. The two parties embraced the principle of "the freedom of Eastern nations on the basis of independence and in accordance with the general wish of each nation" and proclaimed their acceptance of "the independence and freedom of Bukhara and Khiva, whatever may be the form of their government, in accordance with the wishes or their peoples." Although Moscow agreed "to hand over to Afghanistan the frontier districts which belonged to the latter in the last century," "self-determination of the population inhabiting [them]" was to be observed, with its expression to be "settled by a special treaty between the two states." Soviet sovereignty was therefore assured on the entire territory of the former Russian empire in central Asia. Recognition of the independence of Khiva and Bukhara also allowed Moscow to exclude Afghan influence from them, because in agreeing to allow Afghanistan to open five consulates "within the boundaries of Russian Central Asia," the Bolsheviks did not have to include the newly proclaimed Soviet republics. In return for these five establishments, the Afghans had to allow Soviet Russia to open an equal number of consulates in their territory. Three were in the north, but two (Ghazni and Kandahar) were in the south near the frontier with India. This was virtually the last vestige of the initial anti-British focus of the treaty. Originally intended as centres from which propaganda could be projected into India, they were now designed to gather information concerning conditions along the northwest frontier of India.

The treaty was not without benefit to Kabul. Since August 1919, when the British had officially recognized Afghanistan as "free and independent," no other state had acknowledged that independence. Soviet Russia now did so. In addition, Moscow agreed "to the free and untaxed transit through her territory of all kinds of goods purchased by Afghanistan either in Russia herself, through State organizations, or from abroad." This broke the British ability to control Afghan imports. Soviet Russia also promised "to give Afghanistan financial and other assistance." This assistance was spelled out in a separate protocol in which Soviet Russia promised a yearly subsidy of one million gold or silver rubles, the construction of a telegraph line from Kushk to Kabul, and readiness "to place at the disposal of the Afghan Government technical and other specialists." All reference to military aid was eliminated.[26]

The treaty benefited both countries but Soviet Russia the most. It secured Soviet objectives in central Asia, conformed to Soviet needs in negotiations with Britain, and gave Afghanistan only limited scope to pursue foreign policy aims inconsistent with Soviet interests. Despite these self-serving features, it also added lustre to the image of Soviet Russia as the great friend of the peoples of the East. Moscow may not have given Afghanistan any more than was necessary to achieve its objectives, but it did not invade its territory or attempt to reduce it to a dependency. When compared with British policy in South Asia or that of Russia before the revolution, Soviet policy towards Afghanistan appeared benign.

THERE WAS NOTHING BENIGN about Soviet policy towards Armenia. It closely resembled that conducted in Bukhara. Both had formed parts of the tsarist empire, and in 1920 Armenia separated Soviet Russia from an independent Asian power with which Moscow felt it essential to establish a common frontier. It stood between the Bolsheviks and Kemalist Turkey and would probably have been overrun in May had the war with Poland and negotiations with Britain not taken priority over Soviet objectives in the Caucasus.

Hostilities in the Caucasus, however, did not end. Anti-Soviet rebellions in Azerbaidzhan punctuated the summer, and Moscow, which had hoped to reinforce the western front with units drawn from the Caucasus, had to leave most of the Eleventh Army to defend Baku.[27] As the summer wore on, insurgency spread to the North Caucasus and the Kuban, threatening to disrupt Soviet rule in this vast and strategically important area. The scope of insurgency was sufficient to attract the attention of Soviet enemies. General Wrangel laid plans to link up with the Kuban insurgents and then drive south to Baku. Georgia sent what aid it could to the North Caucasus, and the allies, when considering measures to stop the Soviet march on Warsaw, contemplated similar assistance.[28] Soviet success in ending the Polish war and crushing Wrangel prevented the further development of these plans, but not before Moscow had been given a very serious fright.[29]

Fighting also continued between Soviet Azerbaidzhan and Armenia and the peace negotiations held in Moscow during May and June proved fruitless. Armenia demanded the evacuation of Karabakh and Zangezur; Azerbaidzhan refused. Chief of the Bolshevik Kavburo, Ordzhonikidze, feared surrender of the disputed districts would discredit the Soviet government in Azerbaidzhan. Unable to draw on the military resources of Soviet Russia, he raised irregular troops from the local population and continued the struggle. The Armenians, who had finally begun to receive the arms promised them by the allies in January, also elected to fight. The entire border burst into flames, and in July the Armenians had to abandon much of Nakhichevan, thus opening a direct overland route to the Kemalists in northeastern Anatolia.

Moscow sought to end the fighting. The primary strategic prize to be won in Armenia was the railway leading to the Turkish frontier, and this was beyond the grasp of Soviet forces. On 2 August Trotsky wrote that "in view of Wrangel's success and of the alarm in the Kuban," hostilities with Armenia had to be postponed.[30] By this time Armenia was also ready to end the fighting. The military threat to her southern frontier grew more serious with every day, and the Armenians wished to have their hands free to fight the Turks. On 10 August an armistice was concluded in Tiflis. Military operations were to cease at once, with Soviet troops remaining in occupation of the disputed districts. This was not to prejudice their ultimate disposition, and Armenia was left in control of the single railway linking them to Erevan.[31] Although not mentioned in the treaty, it was understood that B.V. Legran would proceed at once to Erevan as Soviet plenipotentiary representative in Armenia. The British were stunned. Commander Luke, their representative in the Caucasus, informed the Armenians that it "amounted to an act of revolt against Great Britain."[32]

Far worse was to come, because the balance of power in the Caucasus had shifted irrevocably against Britain. The emerging contest was between Soviet Russia and Kemalist Turkey, with Armenia and Georgia as the chief bones of contention. When Bekir Sami, the Turkish foreign minister, travelled to Moscow to seek Soviet aid against the allied powers but acceptance of Turkish control of Armenia, his reception was less than cordial. He asked for an offensive-defensive alliance; Chicherin said this was out of the question. Soviet Russia was prepared to grant Turkey limited forms of political, financial, and material assistance but would not assume the broad commitment implied by an alliance. Nor would Moscow sanction Turkish aggrandizement in Armenia. Chicherin, in fact, told Bekir Sami that Armenia was a Soviet preserve and the Turks should keep out. Bekir Sami replied that Armenia was an obstacle to the delivery of Soviet aid to Turkey. Chicherin promised the Bolsheviks would remove this obstacle as soon as possible, but for the moment their hands were tied by the war in Poland and negotiations with Britain. Bekir Sami expressed suspicion of these negotiations, suggesting Soviet Russia was prepared to sacrifice Turkey to obtain a favourable agreement with Britain. Chicherin responded by making similar allegations concerning Turkish negotiations with France. The Moscow talks, therefore, were heated and inconclusive. At the end of a month the two finally reached agreement on several major issues: mutual recognition; the abrogation of obsolete treaties; non-recognition of international instruments imposed on either by force; Soviet non-recognition of international agreements relating to Turkey but not recognized by the nationalist regime; Soviet acceptance of Turkish boundaries as defined in the National Pact; regulation of the Straits, consistent with Turkish security, by a future conference of the Black Sea powers; and an exchange of information regarding secret negotiations with other powers. These were put in the form of a draft treaty and initialled on 24 August.

The question of Armenia, however, remained unsettled, and Chicherin would not sign the treaty until it was resolved. He even demanded that Turkey recognize the Armenian right to self-determination not only within the prewar Russian boundaries but also in the eastern provinces of the former Ottoman empire. Chicherin said that this would result in Turkey losing only a small amount of territory, but Armenia as a whole was to become a Soviet republic. Bekir Sami branded this a violation of the National Pact and would not even discuss the proposal.[33] It is difficult not to see this as a convenient means to avoid signing the treaty at a time when this would have compromised Krasin's negotiations in Britain. It also allowed Moscow to postpone aiding Turkey at a time when all available Soviet resources were needed to fight Poland and Wrangel. The Bolsheviks could barely meet their own military requirements in the Caucasus; they had no reason to supply Ataturk. Bekir Sami went home empty-handed.

For the moment Moscow wanted peace in the Caucasus. Ankara did not and neither did Erevan. Soviet weakness encouraged both nationalist Turkey and Armenia to pursue their conflicting objectives by force. In August the sultan's government at Constantinople had been forced to sign the treaty of Sèvres which divided most of the Ottoman empire among the allied powers and their clients. It provided for a large Armenia but did not define its frontier with Turkey, which was to be drawn subsequently by President Wilson of the United States. The Dashnak government in Erevan chose not to wait and in September invaded the eastern provinces of Turkey. The nationalists welcomed this attack. Faced with the threat of Greece in western Anatolia, they had long wished to smash Armenia to avoid a two-front war. Western and Soviet support for Armenia had induced caution, but in late September this changed. Sèvres proved that moderation made no impression on the allies: Soviet Russia was unable to intervene, and Armenia had taken the initiative. The Turks counter-attacked and soon drove the Armenians from the eastern provinces. The Armenians sent appeals for help in all directions. The League of Nations, the United States, the allied powers, and Georgia were all asked to intervene.[34] Soviet Russia was not approached.

Moscow was watching these developments carefully. It wanted to protect Soviet interests in the Caucasus without becoming involved in hostilities with Turkey. The Bolsheviks remained ready to aid Kemal against the allies, but only at a time and to an extent of their own choosing. They feared the allies had instigated the Armenian crisis to provoke a rupture in Soviet-Turkish relations. Moscow, therefore, offered to mediate. Ankara tepidly agreed, but the Armenians equivocated. The resumption of Turkish-Armenian hostilities in late September marked the failure of Soviet mediation and illuminated Bolshevik weakness in the Caucasus. On 29 September the Bolshevik Central Committee recognized the necessity of reinforcing the Soviet Eleventh Army.[35] Recognizing necessity and actually sending reinforcements were two different things. At the end of September no troops could be sent to the Caucasus. Lenin warned that Soviet policy "had to show maximum caution,"[36] and in early October Chicherin told Ordzhonikidze that military intervention was out of the question unless Turkey advanced farther into Armenia. Ordzhonikidze was "to conduct a systematic peace policy in order to avoid a serious crisis in the Caucasus." Soviet Russia, said Chicherin, "remained ready to mediate between Armenia and the Kemalists."[37]

Ordzhonikidze favoured a more forceful policy and succeeded in stiffening the new proposal presented the Armenians on 12 October. This took the form of a draft peace treaty in which Moscow agreed to recognize the independence of Armenia with boundaries based on the principle of national self-determination, and Erevan was to renounce the treaty of Sèvres and accept Soviet mediation in its dispute with Turkey. Armenia was to place its railways under Soviet control and allow the Red Army to advance to its southern frontier. In short, the Bolsheviks were asking the Armenians to place themselves under Soviet protection. As the Turkish advance had halted, the Armenian government did not feel compelled to accept the Soviet proposal. Instead they asked Moscow to use its influence to secure Azerbaidzhan's evacuation of Karabakh, Zangezur, and Nakhichevan and Turkish withdrawal from the Anatolian districts west of Erzerum. These were not serious counter-proposals: the Armenians were playing for time, still hoping for allied assistance.[38]

Well before the Armenian response reached Moscow the Soviet government again reviewed their policy in the Caucasus. On 12 October the preliminary peace of Riga had been signed with Poland. Wrangel still had to be crushed, but Moscow could anticipate a time in the near future when substantial reinforcements could be sent to the Caucasus. In these circumstance Chicherin presented three proposals to the Politburo. They called for the establishment of Soviet power in Armenia, support of this new Soviet government, and "political aid for them in stopping the further advance of the Turks." Lenin endorsed these proposals, and on 14 October they were adopted by the Politburo. Stalin was sent to Baku to take charge of Soviet policy in the Caucasus.[39]

The Turks did not wait patiently while the Bolsheviks assembled their forces. On 24 October they resumed their offensive and a week later captured Kars. They then pushed on to the rail centre of Alexandropol' which surrendered on 7 November. These developments brought only expressions of sympathy from the western powers and forced Erevan to seek Soviet assistance. On 28 October the Armenian government signed a protocol accepting Soviet mediation. Moscow was to seek the withdrawal of nationalist troops to the Russian-Turkish frontier of 1914 and Turkish recognition of Armenian independence and sovereignty within borders to be drawn in a future Soviet Russian–Armenian peace treaty. The same day Radio Moscow broadcast a statement disassociating the Soviet government from Turkish action against Armenia.[40]

In the following month the Soviet government discovered how little influence they could exercise in the Caucasus with the depleted military force at their disposal. In early November Chicherin sent two confidential appeals to the Turkish government to cease their military operations against Armenia. Neither received a response, and the Turks continued to advance towards Erevan. There was no way of knowing whether Kemal even received the Soviet appeal, but on 11 November Chicherin repeated his earlier request by radio and had it published in Latvia and Lithuania where it would receive the immediate notice of the foreign press. Ankara promptly praised the proposal but did not explicitly accept it. Meanwhile the Turkish army advanced to within a few miles of Erevan. Hostilities did not cease until 18 November when Kazim Karabekir, the Turkish commander, concluded an armistice which provided for a Turkish-Armenian peace conference to meet in Alexandropol' a week later.[41] Soviet Russia was not invited.

Soviet leaders viewed these developments with alarm. In mid-November Stalin sent two appeals for reinforcement of the Red Army in the Caucasus. Even Krasin expressed his concern. On 16 November, he forwarded a report "from sources in close touch with the Foreign Office" concerning possible collusion "between the British government and Kemal Pasha on the basis of the occupation of Baku by the Turks." "Have we not perhaps allowed the Turks to proceed too far into Armenia?" he inquired.[42] Lenin too began to ponder this question. With Wrangel crushed, he was clearly ready to face this challenge. The only question was how many divisions would be sent. Stalin apparently wanted eighteen; Lenin would only agree to half this number, six being sent south as fast as the hard-pressed Soviet railways could carry them. Lenin pointedly asked Stalin why he wanted so many divisions, almost certainly suspecting his lieutenant had developed ambitions exceeding the aims of the Soviet government. Lenin was prepared for war but did not want it. In fact, when the Politburo reviewed the situation on 17 November they resolved "to adopt in relation to Georgia, Armenia, Turkey and Persia a maximally conciliatory policy, i.e. directed above all to the avoidance of war."[43]

The Soviet government wanted peace but would not give up Armenia. In Turkish hands Armenia would threaten Soviet Azerbaidzhan, where a large part of the population was susceptible to Turkish influence. Azerbaidzhan and the northern Caucasus already seethed with unrest, and a Turkish army based in Armenia could easily ignite a widespread revolt. The oil of Baku was at stake, and the Bolsheviks would not allow it to be put at risk. Turkish occupation of southern Armenia was bad enough, but in late November the situation grew worse. When Karabekir met Alexandre Khatisian, the head of the Armenian delegation at Alexandropol', he said that Turkey desired a strong Armenia as a buffer against Russia. The Turks actually wanted a protectorate over Armenia but were prepared to leave the Dashnaks in control of the districts around Erevan and Lake Sevan. As their only other option was to turn to the Bolsheviks, whom they believed would leave them nothing, many Armenian leaders were prepared to accept the Turkish offer.[44] When Moscow learned of the offer, it sent Budu Mdivani, Soviet representative in Turkey, to renew its offer to mediate the Armenian-Turkish conflict. When he arrived on 18 November, Karabekir told him his services were not needed, as the Armenians had accepted the Turkish conditions.[45]

Since mid-October the Bolsheviks had been preparing an insurrection in Armenia; Ordzhonikidze now orchestrated a classic Bolshevik borderlands revolution. At Baku he raised a special regiment of Armenian troops who, together with leading members of the Armenian Communist Party, were sent to a base in western Azerbaidzhan. In Erevan he contacted dissident members of the Dashnak government prepared to support a Soviet regime in Armenia. The most important of these was General Dro, the minister of war, who remained opposed to cooperation with the Turks. On 29 November the Armenian regiment crossed the frontier and seized the border city of Dilijan. The communist leadership proclaimed themselves the Revolutionary Committee of Armenia, broadcast an appeal for a national uprising, and asked the Soviet Eleventh Army for assistance. Ordzhanikidze, of course, sent the Red Army into Armenia. On 2 December Dro took power in Erevan, proclaiming Armenia a Soviet republic and concluding a treaty with Legran in which Soviet Russia recognized the frontiers of Armenia existing prior to 23 October, and promised "to defend the independence of the Soviet Republic of Armenia." Ordzhonikidze announced that Azerbaidzhan had "voluntarily renounced" its claim to Karabakh, Zangezur, and Nakhichevan and ceded them to Soviet Armenia. On 4 December the Red Army marched into Erevan.[46]

This stopped the further erosion of the Bolshevik position in Armenia, but left the Turks in control of all the territory they had won in the recent war. Worse still, as the Bolshevik action unfolded, Karabekir concluded the treaty of Alexandropol' with the Dashnaks. It confirmed the earlier agreement, in which the Armenians surrendered everything wanted by Turkey, and allowed the Dashnaks, if attacked, to ask for Turkish military assistance.[47] In many ways it resembled the Treaty of Brest-Litovsk which the Central Powers had concluded with Ukraine on 9 February 1918. The Dashnaks had already fallen from power when they signed the treaty, and for it to have any validity they would first have to be restored by foreign bayonets. Karabekir, however, was not General Hoffmann, the Turkish army did not face a revolutionary militia, and the balance of power in the Caucasus did not resemble that in eastern Europe two years before. The Red Army now stood opposite the Turkish lines and blocked their farther advance into Armenia. On the other hand the Bolsheviks would not use force to expel the Turks from the disputed territory. To do so would undercut their entire eastern policy and play into the hands of their western enemies. The events of early December, therefore, led to a stalemate. Moscow asked the Turks to withdraw from Alexandropol' and negotiate a new peace treaty with Soviet Armenia. Turkey refused. Nevertheless, broader political considerations soon led the Bolsheviks to resume the assistance to Turkey that had been suspended at the height of the Armenian crisis.[48] Events in neighbouring Georgia, however, soon led to renewed tension in Soviet-Turkish relations.

THE SUMMER OF 1920 HAD passed quietly in Georgia. The Menshevik republic encouraged dissidence in the north Caucasus and considered intervention in Armenia but kept the peace with Soviet Russia. Moscow, fully engaged elsewhere, was content to do the same, but there was no relaxation of tension. Local Bolsheviks had expected the arrival of the Red Army in May and were bitterly disappointed when Soviet troops had stopped at the frontier. Nor were they satisfied with the limited political freedom granted them in the peace treaty. They wanted to destroy the Menshevik government, not coexist with it. As a consequence they did not initially alter either their rhetoric or their tactics and, as a consequence, continued to be subject to police repression. They complained to Kirov, the Soviet representative in Tiflis, who filed repeated remonstrances warning the Mensheviks that their action against the Communist Party of Georgia violated the peace treaty. At the same time he told the local Bolsheviks they would have to wait until Moscow was ready to support an insurrection in Georgia.[49]

In the fall Soviet-Georgian tension came to focus on the strategically important port of Batum. It was the Black Sea terminus of both the Baku railway and pipeline and, thus, the export point for the mineral and petroleum wealth of the Caucasus. In Bolshevik hands it would facilitate the economic recovery of Soviet Russia, while its possession by any other power would seriously compromise that recovery. Britain had occupied the port from the end of the Great War until July 1920.[50] Soviet Russia did not want the British to return or another power to take their place. This was precisely the threat which emerged in late 1920. The Bolsheviks had benefited greatly from the many divisions among their adversaries, and any sign of rapprochement directed against them created alarm in Moscow. In October such a movement appeared to take shape around Turkey. Impressed by the strength of the Ankara regime, France began to urge revision of the treaty of Sèvres. In exchange for concessions in western Anatolia, the French believed Kemal could be won away from Moscow and encouraged to build a barrier against Bolshevism in the Caucasus. Some British officials agreed, and although London continued to insist on the maintenance of Sèvres, there was much talk of its revision.[51] The role of Georgia in such a revision formed a necessary part of these discussions.

The Mensheviks wanted a voice in any revision of Sèvres. In October they opened negotiations with both the Turkish nationalists and the western allies. They had sought assurance that the Turks would not attack Georgia and would respect its frontiers, which they defined as including Batum and Ardahan province. This brought a response from Ankara declaring that the nationalists "considered the existence of an independent, strong and friendly Georgia as essential" to their own interests and asking where their delegates could meet those of Georgia.[52] In the meanwhile the Mensheviks had sent their foreign minister to western Europe seeking de jure recognition of Georgia, admission to the League of Nations, and material assistance for its army. The Mensheviks, he said, were prepared to cooperate commercially and politically with the western powers. This included a willingness, as Britain desired, to make Batum a free port and provide freedom of transit on Georgian railways for the commerce of Armenia and Azerbaidzhan.[53]

Rumours of these negotiations soon reached the Bolsheviks and on 21 October Radio Moscow broadcast a report that the Soviet government had learned that Great Britain had asked Georgia for a long-term lease on the port of Batum. This brought an immediate denial from the Foreign Office, which was received with disbelief in Moscow.[54] At the end of October Turkey had begun its assault on Armenia, and Moscow feared that this might develop into a concerted attack on Baku. On 29 October Lenin warned Stalin: "I consider it beyond doubt that Georgia will hand Batum over to the Entente, probably secretly, and that the Entente will march on Baku. Study the matter and take urgent steps to fortify the land and sea approaches to Baku."[55] Here the word "Entente" takes on a new meaning, for it was clearly meant to include nationalist Turkey as well as Britain and France. The only army that could possibly march on Baku was that of the nationalists and in the following month Moscow based its policy on the assumption that Ankara either had or was about to become an ally of the western powers. Such a development would not only threaten Soviet interests in the Caucasus but undermine their policy everywhere in South Asia. Until the na-tionalists actually jointed their enemies, the Bolsheviks did not even want to make a public reference to such a possibility. Instead they sought to preserve the image of continuing Soviet-Turkish cooperation. In the following month, therefore, Moscow directed its accusations against the "Entente" but clearly meant Ankara. The Bolsheviks sought to tell Kemal to keep out of Batum without accusing him publically of wanting to take it.

The first Soviet warning was triggered by the rapid advance of Turkish troops into Armenia. Uncertain of Turkey's intentions, Moscow wanted to clarify its own position. In a note of 31 October addressed to the government of Georgia Aron Sheimann, who had replaced Kirov as Soviet representative in Tiflis, referred to the "continued rumours of the forthcoming occupation of Batum by the English" and warned that "the occupation of Batum by the English, *inde-pendent of the form such occupation may take*, would be considered a grave and indisputable breach of the [Soviet-Georgian peace treaty]." On 4 November the Georgian government responded by denying the rumours and affirming their resolve to safeguard Georgian sovereignty and territorial integrity.[56] Two weeks later Moscow issued an even more explicit warning. Here the cause appears to have been the defeat of the Venizelos government in Greek elections held on 14 November. Venizelos had been the architect of Greek expansionism in An-atolia, and it was generally believed that his defeat would modify Greek policy and facilitate allied rapprochement with the Turkish nationalists. Moscow lost no time in telling Britain to keep out of the Caucasus. On 16 November Chicherin wired Curzon declaring that the Soviet government would consider British oc-cupation of Batum "a direct menace to the security of our ally, the Azerbaidzhan Soviet Republic, and of Russia herself." Two days later a similar warning was delivered to Tiflis; both documents were given wide publicity. The British were puzzled by the warning and promptly denied any intent to occupy Batum. The Georgians answered with a restatement of their response to the first Soviet warning.[57] Neither satisfied the Bolsheviks, because they still had not received any indication of Turkish reaction to the oblique warning to keep out of Batum.

The Turkish response finally arrived at the end of November, and was sufficiently positive to produce substantial relief in Moscow. Nationalist hopes for a rapprochement with the western powers had been dashed in the days following the Greek elections, when both London and the new regime in Athens reaffirmed their support for Sèvres.[58] Kemal still needed Soviet aid and on 29 November he addressed a glowing telegram to Chicherin expressing "admiration" for Soviet Russia, denouncing the "criminality" of western imperialism, and calling for a "close alliance" between Soviet Russia and nationalist Turkey. This was followed three days later by a telegram from the Turkish foreign minister denying that the nationalists had negotiated with the British for the creation of an anti-Soviet front in the Caucasus and calling for the resumption of negotiations for a Soviet-Turkish friendship treaty. Chicherin agreed the next day and asked the Turks to indicate where they wanted to meet and what they wished to discuss.[59] On 8 December the Turkish foreign minister indicated the nationalists wanted to settle "all affairs in the Caucasus," the question of a military alliance, and the preparation of joint plans against the Entente. This document has not been published and Soviet sources do not mention that the Turkish foreign minister indicated a preference for a place of meeting, but on the following day Chicherin responded that the Soviet government was pleased to accept the Turkish proposal for a conference to be held in Moscow. Given the later uncertainty over the conference site, Chicherin may have attempted to force his own preference on the Turks. He certainly altered the remainder of the Turkish proposal, first by calling for the participation of Soviet Azerbaidzhan and Soviet Armenia and then ignoring the final two agenda items submitted by Ankara. With Krasin's negotiations in London again moving forward, the Bolsheviks were not eager to commit themselves to joint action against the Entente. Primarily they wanted to obtain Turkish assent to Soviet rule in the Caucasus. By the same token they did not want to inhibit Turkish military operations against the western powers; therefore the following day Chicherin signalled Ordzhonikidze to resume material and financial aid to the nationalists. The Turks were to be told this was a sign of trust, but this was manifestly untrue. Chicherin told Sheimann on 10 December that although the Kemalists had returned to a Soviet orientation, they might again pose a serious danger to Russia. "In particular," he added, "the passage of Batum into Turkish hands is unacceptable." The Bolsheviks, in fact, decided to keep the Turks on short rations. Ordzhonikidze was told to provide them with gold, but only in small amounts.[60]

Following the revolution in Armenia, Soviet-Georgian relations deteriorated rapidly. Georgian Bolsheviks clamoured for permission to organize their own insurrection. The Kavburo clearly sympathized, but were bound by the Politburo decision of 27 November from using the Red Army against the Menshevik republic. Moscow remained too unsure of success in the negotiations with Britain and Turkey to approve an insurrection in Georgia. Britain's position remained unclear, but Moscow knew a Soviet invasion of Georgia would immediately precipitate a crisis with Turkey over Batum. The Kavburo, however, were not prepared to wait. They seem to have feared that Moscow might allow Georgia to assume a role in the Caucasus analogous to Latvia and Estonia in the Baltic. In 1919 Lenin had sacrificed the communist parties of Latvia and Estonia for the sake of negotiations with Britain, and for all the Kavburo knew he might do the same in Georgia. Ordzhonikidze and Stalin were tied too closely to the Communist Party of Georgia to allow this without a struggle.[61] After December the Kavburo commanded the resources of two Soviet republics and a rapidly expanding army and did not hesitate in using them to exacerbate Soviet Russian relations with Georgia. Azerbaidzhan stopped the sale of petroleum to Tiflis, Armenia occupied part of the disputed province of Borchalo, and Georgian communists were licensed to organize resistance to increasingly unpopular Menshevik policies. This agitation provoked many arrests, allowing the Georgian Communist party to portray the police repression as a violation of the Soviet-Georgian peace treaty and call upon Moscow for help. Ironically the Mensheviks also appealed to Soviet Russia, but for relief from the confrontationist policies of Baku. Well aware of the greater militancy of the Kavburo, they repeatedly asked Moscow to restrain Ordzhonikidze.[62] The Central Committee did so. In mid-January they rejected a further proposal that the Red Army be used to support an insurrection in Georgia. They decided that neither the internal nor external circumstances of Soviet Russia warranted such a step and instructed the Kavburo to enforce the policy already given them: the Red Army was not to enter Georgia and peace was to be maintained with the Mensheviks.[63]

The Central Committee reviewed their policy at the end of the month. Stalin had prepared a new evaluation of the situation which said a revolutionary situation existed in Georgia and asked that Ordzhonikidze be allowed to organize an insurrection, to be supported by the Red Army if necessary.[64] Lenin was still not prepared to authorize an invasion of Georgia, but circumstances had changed. On 26 January, the day on which the Central Committee met, Krasin reached Moscow bringing the first complete report of his meeting with Lloyd George in which the British prime minister had categorically expressed official British disinterest in the fate of Georgia. Krasin also conveyed his belief that the trade agreement with Britain could be concluded quickly on terms acceptable to Soviet Russia. This must have suggested to many Soviet leaders that it would be desirable to solve the Georgian question before unforeseen circumstances led to a change in British policy. Such a move was still likely to trigger a confrontation with Turkey, but here too time favoured a prompt solution of the Georgian question. It was clearly desirable to face the problem while the nationalists still needed good relations with Moscow. None of this completely persuaded Lenin. Others must have been convinced, because the Central Committee passed a series of resolutions that clearly sought to bridge the gap between two conflicting positions on the Georgian question. The first emphasized a political approach, directing the Narkomindel to apply further pressure on the Mensheviks "but to delay a rupture with Georgia." In addition the Kavburo was instructed to examine what "real guarantees (control commissions, etc.) [could be] demanded by diplomatic means from the Georgian government" to prevent the Mensheviks from aiding dissident groups in the Caucasus. The second position foresaw an eventual resort to force, asking the Kavburo to report on the readiness of their military forces for war with Georgia and directing the Red Army high command to prepare for such an eventuality. Nothing was said about the preparation of an insurrection in Georgia.[65]

Available Soviet documents on events in the following two weeks reveal a politically chaotic landscape strewn with the collapsing structures of the Soviet government. Thus the Kavburo took more than a week to prepare its report on possible military action in Georgia, and Ordzhonikidze did not respond at all. On 5 February Lenin anxiously wired him to "answer immediately," and on 8 February he demanded further information from Ordzhonikidze and its verification by I.T. Smilga, a member of the Revolutionary Military Council of the Caucasus Front.[66] No answer came from Baku, and on 12 February Lenin learned that telegraphic communication with the Caucasus had collapsed completely. He demanded that the military authorities "appoint a *responsible person*" to restore communications and threatened: "If this is not done, I will have those responsible here *committed for* trial."[67]

It was too late. On 11 February Ordzhonikidze had taken matters in his own hands and had authorized an armed uprising in the neutral zone separating Soviet Armenia and Georgia. The insurrection took place on the following day and received the support of elements of the Eleventh Army.[68] Only after the Red Army had seized a position from which they could advance easily on Tiflis was telegraphic communication restored between Moscow and Baku. Was the breakdown in communications accidental or political? Lenin's explosive response suggests that he suspected the latter. He had little choice but to endorse the action after the fact, but demanded that Ordzhonikidze "guarantee success." He also warned that "we are having to go without bread for want of transport and that we shall therefore not let you have a single locomotive or railway truck."[69]

Ordzhonikidze did not think his task difficult; he was wrong. The sovietization of Georgia proved to be far more arduous than the earlier operation in Armenia. This was due, in part, to inadequate Soviet preparation. No part of the Bolshevik rear was secure. The Eleventh Army lay at the end of a long line of communication and supply extending from a thoroughly exhausted central Russian base through rebellious districts tenuously held. This would not have been so serious if the Red Army had to fight a poorly armed or demoralized enemy. Georgia was neither. It had and was continuing to receive allied arms and only recently had been granted de jure recognition by the western powers. The Mensheviks had held power in Georgia nearly as long as the Bolsheviks in Russia. They were experienced and effective, enjoying a broad (although far from universal) base of popular support. The Bolsheviks also had to contend with the near certainty of foreign intervention. The Turkish army stood ready to enforce nationalist claims, and a clash with Turkey could lead to a general war in the Caucasus with the allies, or at least France, supporting Ankara. No wonder Lenin feared the outcome of the Soviet invasion of Georgia.

It did not go well from the start. No sooner had the Eleventh Army entered Georgia than the Dashnaks rose in rebellion behind them. Soon most of Armenia was in their hands, including Erevan which fell on 18 February. Worse still, the Turks were reported to be helping the Dashnaks.[71] Ordzhanikidze, realizing he could not fight a two-front war, took up a defensive position in Armenia and pushed on to Tiflis. Erevan remained in Dashnak hands until April, and summer came before Soviet authority was restored throughout Armenia.[72] Meanwhile the campaign in Georgia continued. It took two weeks of hard fighting for the Bolsheviks to reach Tiflis, where they triumphantly proclaimed Georgia a Soviet republic. The triumph was tarnished, however, as the Mensheviks withdrew into the mountains and continued the war. On 2 March Lenin sent his "warm greetings to Soviet Georgia" but clearly revealed his desire to bring hostilities to an end as quickly as possible. He emphasized the "tremendous importance to devise an acceptable compromise for a bloc with Jordania or similar Georgian Mensheviks." The Georgian Revolutionary Committee (Revkom) did propose a coalition government, but the Mensheviks refused.[73] Throughout February the Georgian government continued to hope for French intervention, asking in particular for the occupation of Batum. Since the opening of hostilities the French had assisted in defending the Black Sea coast, but Paris never considered sending an expeditionary force. The British had already ordered their fleet not to intervene. The Mensheviks nevertheless continued to fight, offering stiff resistance to the Bolsheviks but having to fall back first to Kutais and then to Batum.[73]

The Soviet invasion of Georgia spurred the crisis with Turkey which Moscow had feared. Ten days after the Red Army began its march on Tiflis the nationalists demanded that the Georgians evacuate the districts of Ardahan and Artvin. The Mensheviks had to accede.[74] This brought the Turkish army within a short distance of Batum and as the Bolsheviks themselves approached the city, created the circumstances for a possible armed clash. The Mensheviks, whose army was disintegrating, hoped to use these circumstances to prolong their existence as a de facto government. The Turks wanted to occupy Batum in the hope this occupation could be made permanent. The Mensheviks could offer no resistance but did not wish to surrender the city. On 7 March, therefore, they reached a verbal agreement with Colonel Kiazim Bey, the nationalist military representative in Batum, permitting the Turkish army to enter the city while leaving the government of Georgia in control of its civil administration. The following day nationalist troops took up defensive positions surrounding the city and assumed responsibility for its "internal order" (read: prevention of a Bolshevik insurrection).[75] This was a highly unstable situation; the Mensheviks were seeking Turkish protection while awaiting French intervention, whereas the Turks were attempting to impose something similar to the Alexandropol' 'solution' on Batum.

Within days the unstable agreement collapsed. The Mensheviks grew increasingly suspicious of the Turks and asked the French to approach Ankara seeking Turkish de jure recognition of Georgia. They wanted an agreement concluded "under the auspices of France to preserve Georgian sovereignty in the provinces occupied militarily by the Turks and to guarantee the interests of both Georgia and the Entente while permitting the continuation of resistance to the Bolsheviks." Even had time allowed, which it didn't, France could not have acted in this way. The French were negotiating secretly with the nationalists but were not yet ready to act independently of Britain and certainly did not have the resources to support such a policy. The French realized Georgian resistance was near an end and were quite ready, rather than have the Bolsheviks take the city, to see it occupied by the Turks.[76] When the Mensheviks realized this and that continued resistance might lead to Georgia's permanent loss of Batum, they opened negotiations with the Bolsheviks. First an armistice was arranged and then, on 16 March, an agreement which allowed the Red Army to advance in force into the city. The following day Kiazim Bey declared himself military governor of Batum, but he commanded only two thousand troops. The Bolsheviks did not want to fight but were ready to do so rather than leave Batum in Turkish hands. The armistice with the Mensheviks, however, allowed the Bolsheviks to erect a political screen from behind which to attack the Turks indirectly. They organized a supposedly autonomous revolutionary committee which received the support of more than ten thousand Georgian troops who had sought refuge in Batum. On 17 March these troops engaged the Turkish garrison. Russian troops were also sent into the city but were not used in the fighting. While the battle raged, the Menshevik government boarded an Italian vessel and sailed into exile escorted by French warships. Fighting ended the next day with the port and most of the city in Bolshevik hands.[77]

These sanguinary events served as the backdrop for the final stage of Soviet-Turkish negotiations.[78] As a result of hardening positions on the future organization of the Caucasus, the talks took longer to begin than originally expected. Both governments viewed their relationship in a broader context, but regional authorities continued to focus on this divisive issue. Neither the Kavburo nor the Turkish Eastern Army were willing to concede either Armenia or Georgia to the other. The Kavburo and the government of Soviet Armenia wanted Soviet Russia to demand Turkish evacuation of Kars and Alexandropol', but Lenin refused. At his request, however, Chicherin addressed several messages to Ankara indicating Soviet displeasure with the treatment of Armenians in Turkey. These were not well received by the Turks, who had their own complaints to file concerning Bolshevik treatment of the Islamic population in Soviet republics.

The nationalists attempted to display their sympathy with this population, especially in Azerbaidzhan, by proposing that the Soviet-Turkish conference meet in Baku rather than Moscow. Chicherin responded that the Soviet government considered the conference so important that they had designated the entire collegium of the Foreign Commissariat, including himself, as their representatives, and therefore it would not be possible to meet in Baku. In mid-January the Turks finally agreed.[79]

Turkish agreement to meet in Moscow was closely linked to revived nationalist hope for western assent to the revision of the treaty of Sèvres. Throughout December revisionist sentiment among allied leaders continued to grow, and on 10 January further pressure was added when the Turks defeated the Greeks at the first battle of Inönü. Following this battle the British cabinet decided it would be necessary to open direct talks with the nationalists. On 23 January the allied powers invited Turkish authorities, including the nationalists, to attend a conference at London to discuss revision of Sèvres. The nationalists were eager to talk directly to the allied powers, but realized that the ability to conclude an agreement with Moscow constituted an important part of their bargaining position. Kemal, therefore, decided that a Turkish delegation should proceed to Moscow before the opening of the London conference.[80]

The Moscow conference was stormy. The Turkish delegation was headed by Yussef Kemal Bey, the economics minister, and Ali Fuad Pasha, who had recently been appointed ambassador in Moscow. They refused to meet with the representatives of Soviet Armenia and Soviet Azerbaidzhan and would negotiate only with Soviet Russia. After some delay Chicherin agreed, but then took an equally hard line in rejecting the nationalists' substantive demands. They wanted the Bolsheviks to yield Batum and recognize the validity of the Treaty of Alexandropol'. They also wanted the Soviet government to commit themselves publicly to a military alliance with Turkey. Moscow could not accept these demands. The first two threatened Soviet control of the Caucasus and the flow of Baku oil to world markets. The third, while enhancing the Turkish position in London, could well have killed any hope of concluding the Soviet trade agreement with Britain. All three were rejected, but the Turks were told that as long as they opposed the western powers they would receive unofficial Soviet aid.

In the midst of the talks Moscow learned that the Turkish Eastern Army had begun to move towards Batum. When this was called to the attention of the Turkish delegation, Ali Fuad replied that the Soviet government should consider the occupation of Ardahan, Artvin, and Batum as "merely the natural fulfillment" of the Turkish National Pact.[81] Lenin concluded that the Turks were playing for time while their troops marched on Batum. On 9 March he decided to have Stalin "speak frankly with the Turkish delegation in order to clarify the situation" and conclude negotiations that day. A lengthy argument followed, but agreement was reached to partition Armenia and Georgia. Turkey would receive Kars,

Ardahan, and Artvin; Alexandropol' would revert to Armenia, and Batum would remain with Georgia. The Bolsheviks obtained what they believed essential to the security of the Caucasus, and the nationalists retained the three provinces with the highest percentage of Turkish population. This, however, was only a verbal agreement and over a week passed before the final treaty was signed, while the Turks waited for the outcome of negotiations in London. There Bekir Sami tried, but failed, to secure the agreement of Lloyd George to a revision of Sèvres acceptable to Ankara. On 16 March these negotiations collapsed with the prime minister warning Bekir Sami that the Greeks were free to resume the war against Turkey.[82] Two days later the Turks signed the treaty of Moscow. Both governments agreed to date the treaty 16 March, the anniversary of the allied occupation of Constantinople.

The treaty contained the provisions agreed upon in August and the territorial settlement just reached in Moscow. The text carefully avoided reference to cooperation against other powers but spoke glowingly of "the right of [Eastern] peoples to freedom and independence and ... to choose a form of government in accordance with their wishes." It was a model of the type of treaty that Ankara wished to negotiate with the western powers, as Moscow recognized Turkish sovereignty within the boundaries set by the National Pact (except Batum), abrogated earlier Ottoman-Russian treaties, declared a regime of capitulations incompatible with Turkish sovereignty, and freed Turkey of all financial obligations to Russia. Looking to the future, both governments agreed "to entrust the final elaboration of an international statute for the Black Sea and the Straits to a special conference of delegates of the littoral countries on condition that any decision they arrive at shall not involve any derogation of Turkey's complete sovereignty or of the security of Turkey and its capital Constantinople." Also looking to the future, but framed with reference to the immediate past, Moscow and Ankara promised "not to allow the formation or the existence on their territory of organizations or groups claiming to be the Government of the other party, or of parts of its territory, nor the existence of groups whose object is to engage in struggle against the other State." This obligation was extended to include "the Caucasian Soviet Republics," and Soviet Russia also promised to secure the recognition by these republics "of the articles of the present treaty of direct concern to them."[83]

The treaty was a major achievement for both nationalist Turkey and Soviet Russia. The alternative was armed hostility or continued uncertainty which could deteriorate into open warfare at any time. The nationalists had to stabilize eastern Anatolia in order to drive the Greeks and British from their western provinces. Even in the absence of this necessity, they would still have lacked the resources to pursue an expansionist policy in the Caucasus. Such a policy, which Moscow would bitterly resist, required the material support of at least one western power and would have involved them in an international adventure the end of which could not be foreseen. Soviet Russia, for its part, required peace in the Caucasus even more badly than in eastern Europe. In March 1921 Georgia remained unsubdued, Armenia had slipped from Soviet hands, and insurgency raged in many other areas. Peace allowed Moscow to consolidate its power behind the frontier established with Turkey. Furthermore, the treaty served to inhibit Turkish aspirations in the Caucasus and, to the extent to which the Bolsheviks were able to tighten their grip on the region, limit the damage which Turkey might inflict in the future if, as was entirely possible, Ankara were to alter its foreign policy orientation. Kars, Ardahan, and Artvin were a small price to pay for these benefits.

Both states also drew positive benefits from the treaty. It was for Ankara the first great success of nationalist foreign policy, a ringing affirmation of Turkish self-determation and national sovereignty at a time when neither had received international recognition. This was no small achievement and provided a model for future agreements with the allies. In March 1921 Turkish sovereignty was far from secure, and as long as Lloyd George insisted on making the Turks fight for their independence, Kemal would need Soviet aid. Small wonder that he ordered the treaty signed. For Moscow the treaty provided protection for fundamental Soviet economic needs. Once the Bolsheviks had pacified the Caucasus they would be able to exploit its abundant mineral and petroleum resources. Possession of Batum ensured that these resources could be sold on the world market. The article concerning the future navigation of the Straits provided them with a voice in the regulation of a question vital to their military and economic security. The treaty, however, promoted Soviet interests far beyond the Caucasus. It was carefully drafted to avoid unnecessary provocation of Great Britain and thus contributed to the broader Soviet aim of restoring political and economic relations with the western powers. This was done without sacrificing the image of Soviet Russia as the great friend of the peoples of the East. In fact, the Turks and their "great friend" had nearly gone to war and had even fought a pitched battle (by proxy on the Soviet side) in the streets of Batum, but this had to be measured against the much larger conflict then in progress in western Anatolia. As in Afghanistan, Soviet policy appeared benign in comparison with that of the other European powers.

SOVIET RELATIONS WITH PERSIA developed in a far different manner than those with Turkey. They were influenced by many of the same circumstances which governed the latter but lacked their range of contradictory expectation and dread. In part this was due to the different nature of the regimes in Turkey and Persia. Kemal led a strong nationalist movement enjoying popular support, prestige extending far beyond the borders of Turkey, and the loyalty of a battle-tested army. Persia was the opposite. It was a feudal monarchy with which it was difficult to deal because of its government's lack of authority and continued dependence on Great Britain. The stakes involved in the two relationships also influenced their differing development. The Caucasus were a rich prize vital to subsequent Soviet economic development. The Bolshevik party had deep roots there, and many influential leaders were closely tied to the region. Soviet leaders had few ties with Persia and little interest in its economy. The primary object of Moscow was to reduce British influence to a level compatible with Soviet security. Soviet concern focused primarily on the Persian approaches to Baku. The British had twice entered Baku from that direction in 1918, and the Bolsheviks wished to make certain that they did not do so again.

In May 1920 the Red Army had driven British troops from the southern shore of the Caspian. Soviet occupation of Enzeli enhanced the security of Baku but in turn posed a direct threat to Teheran. This alarmed the British and jeopardized the opening of Anglo-Soviet trade talks. Shortly Russian troops were withdrawn, but the Bolsheviks did not leave Enzeli. Instead the region became a responsibility of the new government of Soviet Azerbaidzhan, who sent their own troops into northern Persia and supported local revolutionaries when they established the Soviet Republic of Gilan.[84] Gilan was a political façade behind which the Bolsheviks concealed their military occupation of northern Persia. It is significant that neither Soviet Russia nor Soviet Azerbaidzhan officially recognized the Gilan Soviet Republic. Had circumstances developed differently, it might have become the base from which Soviet power was established in Persia, but this contingency did not arise. Instead, the very limited role allowed it quickly led to disillusionment. Kuchik Khan and his Jangalis followers broke with the Bolsheviks in July and took up arms against them.[85] The small Soviet garrison had to fight both the Jangalis insurgents and Persian Cossacks sent by Teheran to drive them from northern Persia. This nearly led to disaster. In late August the Cossacks recaptured Resht and advanced nearly to Enzeli before being stopped. A month later the situation had not improved, and on 24 September Ordzhonikidze wired Lenin: "The Persian problem must be resolved in one way or the other: either strike at them, or make peace with the Shah's Government and quit Enzeli."[86]

The Soviet government had already reached a similar conclusion. They had noted that the new government of Mushir ed-Dowleh refused to ratify the Anglo-Persian treaty of August 1919 and had asked to send a special envoy to Moscow to discuss the restoration of diplomatic relations. These developments appeared promising, whereas the situation at Enzeli did not. On 27 August Chicherin agreed to receive the Persian envoy in Moscow.[87] Negotiations, however, did not proceed immediately. Mushaver-ul-Mamalek, the Persian ambassador in Constantinople, had been named as Teheran's special envoy and it took him more than a month to reach Baku. Soviet authorities questioned him closely before allowing him to proceed to Moscow. He told them that "if the Azerbaijan army evacuated Enzeli, the Persian Government would engage not to allow the British Army or British officers to pass Kasvin in the direction of Resht and Enzeli." This proved satisfactory, and on 25 October he departed for Moscow. The Bolsheviks, however, had not yet established a firm policy. As late as 11 November Baku instructed its military commander at Enzeli to fortify his position and "await result of negotiations at Moscow with the Shah's government. It is not impossible that policy will be altered in favour of further determined action in connection with a general plan of activity in the east."[88] Word that the British were prepared to begin final negotiation of the trade treaty ended Bolshevik indecision. Within a week they informed Mamalek of their readiness to reach agreement on the previous basis of abandoning all Russian rights and privileges acquired in Persia over the previous century. They would evacuate Enzeli when they were certain that Britain would withdraw from the remainder of Persia. On 7 December Chicherin presented an outline of this agreement to a plenum of the Central Committee and received their approval for final negotiation.[89]

In mid-December the Soviet proposals were presented to Mushaver-ul-Mamalek in the form of two draft treaties. The first dealt with the liquidation of former Russian properties and the restoration of diplomatic relations. It also abrogated all former treaties between Persia and Russia, promised mutual non-interference in domestic affairs, cancelled debts, granted Persia equal right to navigation of the Caspian Sea, and made a few border rectifications in Persia's favour. Moscow proposed that the second treaty be kept secret. Here the Bolsheviks asked for special rights they clearly found embarrassing. They asked Persia to agree that "should any hostile army try to attack Russia through Persia and the latter be unable to prevent it, Russia will have the right to send an army into Persia." They also wanted an amnesty for those who had taken part in the revolution in Gilan and permission for "the extension of socialism and guild organizations in Persia if not directed against the government." Subsequently Moscow also asked to occupy Enzeli for as long as the Caucasus were threatened by invasion.[90] Prior to learning of the final secret article, the Persian government was quite pleased with the Soviet proposals. Even the final secret article did not substantially alter this evaluation, as the British reaffirmed their earlier decision to withdraw their army entirely from Persia.[91] This allowed the Prime Minister Sipahdar-i-Azam to say that the secret article could be deleted, as there was no further reason for Moscow to fear an invasion of the Caucasus. He also insisted on the deletion of the proposal to allow the extension of socialism and guild organizations but agreed to amnesty for the revolutionaries provided they surrendered their arms. Azam also agreed that Russia could send its army into Persia in the circumstances specified by Moscow but insisted that this and the lesser secret articles be included in a single public treaty.[92]

The British were not nearly as pleased. Lord Curzon even believed the negotiations were a sham designed to conceal the actual intention of an "immediate Bolshevik advance on Teheran." Lord Chelmsford, the viceroy of India, did not share this view. He believed the Soviet proposals were genuine and that Persia's best chance was to gamble on their sincerity. He viewed the situation far more realistically than Curzon. "The Bolshevik proposals," he wrote on 5 January, "appear particularly shrewd, devised to undermine our position, and to further their main end in Persia, viz., internal rupture under the influence of Bolshevik propaganda. Ostentatious abnegnation of Czarist gains and ambitions in Persia is meant to throw Great Britain's general attitude and demands under the Anglo-Persian Agreement into high relief." Curzon, however, continued to interfere in the negotiations, seeking to press his views on Azam and delaying the process of reaching agreement. In mid-January this brought a protest from Moscow. The Soviet government warned Teheran that "if Persia [were] entirely subservient to Great Britain she [could] hope for nothing from Russia."[93]

Shortly afterwards Azam sent his counter-proposals to Moscow where they were well received. On 22 January Lev Karakhan, deputy commissar of foreign affairs, in an official note, set forth the Soviet position on the evacuation of northern Persia. Moscow shared the view of Teheran "that all foreign troops, both Azerbaidzhani and British, must leave Persian territory." Azerbaidzhan, he said, also accepted this position and was prepared to withdraw its troops at the same time as Britain. Karakhan proposed the formation of a commission composed of a British and Azerbaidzhani member with a Persian chairman to work out the details of joint withdrawal from Persian territory. Azam accepted this proposal and wanted it included in the final treaty, but when he approached the British they refused.[94] While awaiting resolution of this issue the remainder of the treaty was put in final form. Karakhan agreed to the transfer of the acceptable secret articles to the public treaty. He also agreed that the treaty should not mention the Soviet interest in fostering socialism and guilds in Persia. Instead, the two governments would present their views on this subject in an exchange of notes. Karakhan and Mamalek also produced the final wording for article six which gave the Soviet government the right to send their army into Persia if a third power should turn that country into a base for military operations against Russia.[95] By early February the treaty was complete except for the article to govern the withdrawal of Azerbaidzhani troops from Enzeli.

It did not prove possible to resolve this issue in the treaty. The procedure devised by Persia and Soviet Russia depended on British cooperation, and Curzon refused. A further attempt might have been made to secure British cooperation if events in Persia had not overtaken the negotiations. On the night of 21 February, however, Colonel Reza Khan seized power in Teheran. The new government, although politically and socially conservative, were determined to limit British influence in Persia. They based their foreign policy on the rejection of the Anglo-Persian agreement and completion of the treaty with Soviet Russia. While profoundly anti-Bolshevik, they sought to restore Persian independence. They did not ask Curzon to cooperate. Instead they instructed Mamalek to sign the treaty without the article governing the withdrawal of foreign troops. As this reinforced the independence of the new Persian regime without impairing the Soviet position at Enzeli, Moscow was pleased to agree. The Soviet-Persian treaty was signed on 26 February 1921.[96]

The treaty was advantageous to both governments. It granted Persia title to properties of substantial value and legally ended the privileged position Russia had possessed prior to 1917. As such, it served as a model for Persian nationalists who wished to eliminate the privileged position enjoyed by other European powers. In particular it was a blow directed against Britain. The new government was able to take credit for the treaty. The price it paid was the deletion of any reference to the withdrawal of the Azeris from Enzeli. It was convinced, however, that these troops would be withdrawn once the British army left Persia. As the British had decided to leave in the spring, Teheran had good reason to believe that, even without a written agreement, the Azeris would depart shortly after. In addition, the Persians had to agree that the Red Army could return if Persia became a military base for a third power. It is significant, however, that neither Azam nor Reza Khan objected to this. It was more of a warning to a third power (in other words, Britain) than an invitation for the Soviets to send their army into Persia. Indeed, it was the Bolsheviks who found this article embarrassing; the Persians insisted that it be included in the public treaty and not be hidden in a secret annex. They wanted no foreign troops on their soil and, for the moment at least, this appeared to promote that objective.

The treaty was equally advantageous for the Bolsheviks. They gave up nothing they wanted, reaffirmed (with only minor changes) the frontier of 1917, and promoted the type of political development they desired in Persia. Moscow had wanted to reduce British influence and succeeded. In particular the Bolsheviks had wanted to ensure that Persia would not be used as a base to attack the Caucasus. With the British army about to leave, this seemed assured. In any case, the Red Army would remain at Enzeli until the British left. In the meantime, Soviet prestige in Persia and throughout Asia benefited from the surrender of Russia's former privileges and properties. The treaty, therefore, secured basic Soviet aims at a minimal price.

BOLSHEVIK POLICY TOWARDS the peoples of the East did not develop in an Asian vacuum; it was an integral part of the broader foreign policy of Soviet Russia. It was deeply influenced and largely determined by the fortunes of the Russian civil war, the resources available to the Soviet government, and the desiderata of more general policy. By the time Pilsudski was stopped and Wrangel defeated, the Bolsheviks were left with barely sufficient strength to settle affairs in the south. In the end it was enough, but it was a close call. A war with Turkey could have proved disastrous. This development of Bolshevik policy was not accidental. Soviet resources were limited and shrinking; the Politburo had to establish rigid priorities and did so, choosing to eliminate their major Russian rivals and protect the European centre of Soviet power before turning to the borderlands. The drive on Baku was the one major exception to this rule, but its petroleum was essential to the Soviet economy.

The Politburo also established priorities in foreign policy. The first was to promote the division of their opponents, in particular to separate Britain from France. A negotiated settlement with Britain was the key to both this objective and that of assisting Germany to obtain greater freedom in foreign affairs. Soviet policy in the East played a supporting role to these objectives. Agreement with Britain carried with it the necessity of modifying Soviet policy in Asia. When London moved towards agreement with them the Bolsheviks reduced their pressure on the British empire. In the fall of 1920 when the British trade talks resumed, the Bolsheviks began to give final shape to the policies which would lead to their treaties with Afghanistan, Persia, and Turkey. It is significant that Lenin did not approve the invasion of Georgia until Britain had signalled its political disinterest in that country. It is also significant that both Afghanistan and Turkey sought military alliances with Moscow and that these were rejected in part to avoid the possibility of clashing with Britain.

Other influences also shaped Soviet policy. Bolshevik interest in the problems of the East had grown steadily after the revolution and with it the desire to promote an acceleration of the social, economic, and political processes which would move "backward" areas towards eventual revolutions of the Russian style. Greater familiarity with these countries convinced Soviet leaders of the profound difficulties inherent in such a process and did not encourage them to seek revolutionary solutions in the East. Marxist doctrine was not allowed to stand in the way of policies calculated to draw maximum benefit from existing social configurations. The interests of local party organizations also influenced the shaping of Soviet foreign policy. Borderland Bolsheviks had a strong moral claim on the central leadership to ensure that their localities were not left outside the boundaries of a Soviet republic when hostilities came to an end. This was clearly one of the impelling reasons for seeking to return to the boundaries of 1914. Similarly, local Bolsheviks received a hearing when they sought Moscow's support for the neutralization or elimination of hostile centres of power adjacent to existing Soviet frontiers. If prewar boundaries or enhanced security could be obtained at little cost (Khiva and Bukhara) or were related to vital state concerns (Enzeli and Batum), they received support. When the political cost was too great (Kars, Ardahan, and Artvin), local interests were sacrificed. Georgia as a whole might have been sacrificed had Ordzhonikidze and Stalin not intervened. Although successful, the Soviet invasion of Georgia unleashed rebellion in Armenia and nearly led to war with Turkey. Most fortunately for Soviet Russia, British intransigence forced the Turks to continue their war with Greece and left the Bolsheviks free to pacify the Caucasus.

At the end of the Russian civil war the Bolsheviks had largely restored the prewar boundaries of the former tsarist empire in southwest Asia. In addition, they had completed satisfactory political agreements with their southern neighbours recognizing these boundaries, regularizing relations, and contributing to a sharp decline in British influence. In all three countries they had given their encouragement and support to nationalist regimes attempting to free themselves from various forms of western, primarily British, control. This support did not preclude clashes with all three and the harsh enforcement of what Moscow considered its own rights. Nevertheless, this was done without seriously injuring its carefully crafted image of great friend of the peoples of the East, because in comparison British policy appeared so much worse. It was also achieved without impairing the broader aim of negotiating a modus vivendi with Britain, because London realized that, if unrestrained by some form of agreement, the Bolsheviks were capable of wreaking still further havoc in their empire in the East.

Although substantial, the Soviet achievement was not as great as it might first appear. Except for Turkey, which the Bolsheviks treated very carefully, no power in the area commanded a substantial army. The British were determined to withdraw their last troops from the region while continuing to pursue policies offensive to the local governments. It is little wonder that their influence collapsed so quickly. Essentially the Bolsheviks retraced the steps of their tsarist predecessors, moving into a near political and military vacuum until they reached the boundaries of the established states of southwest Asia. The Cossacks had ridden on horseback; the Red Army travelled by train and returned to lands still bearing the deep imprint of fifty or more years of association with Russia.

CHAPTER TWENTY

"Not a step further towards the East" : The creation of the Far Eastern Republic

In the summer of 1919 the defeat of Kolchak opened the gates of Asia for the Bolsheviks. Soviet leaders were briefly tempted to shift the focus of their military operations from Europe to the East. The civil war was nearing its climax and the Red Army was in retreat everywhere except Siberia. Should the opportunity offered by Kolchak's defeat be grasped immediately or should Soviet resources be reserved to finish off Denikin and Yudenich? An Asian strategy was attractive to many, and had the Bolsheviks been driven from Petrograd and Moscow they might have adopted it. In March 1918 they had briefly considered a retreat into a Ural-Kuznetsk redoubt, and defeat in central Russia might well have driven them there in 1919. This, however, would have been a strategy of despair and not a triumphal march. The civil war would be won in central Russia, not in the heart of Asia. The Bolsheviks marshalled their forces against Denikin and won.

Siberia and the Far East, however, could not be ignored. Kolchak had been defeated but not destroyed and, in October 1919, still held Siberia east of Omsk. This was a vast territory from which the Whites and their foreign backers could mount a new campaign if not cleared from the region. In addition, it was rich in natural resources and held a population which, because of Kolchak's brutal policies, was ready to welcome the Red Army. The Soviet government, therefore, decided to gather the spoils of victory while preparing to claim the entire far eastern legacy of the tsarist empire. This had to be done, however, at a minimum of cost and without provoking further foreign intervention.

The Far East at this time was essentially a self-contained political system. China, its largest component, was badly divided and rendered impotent by war-lordism and regional rivalry. A central government sat in Peking but was little more than a façade for a galaxy of warring generals. In Sinkiang and Mongolia weak local governments exercised limited power over vast territories without reference to Peking. Japan was the single indigenous great power. There was no part of the Far East in which the Japanese were not interested, but their authority was greatest in Manchuria and north China. They had taken advantage of the Russian civil war to send their army into the Maritime and Amur provinces of the former tsarist empire, and had extended their influence still further by supporting Cossack atamen in Transbaikal and elsewhere. Chief among these was G.M. Semenov, whose band controlled Chita and the eastern approaches to Irkutsk. The United States was the chief foreign rival of Japan in Siberia. President Wilson had sent American troops there in July 1918, and fifteen months later they still remained, more of a hindrance to the Japanese than the Bolsheviks. Britain and France had also sent small contingents to Siberia, but they were of little political importance. The Czechs, on the other hand, who had provided a convenient pretext for foreign intervention in 1918 by seizing the Trans-Siberian Railway, were a major factor. For over a year they had refused to fight the Bolsheviks, but they still controlled much of the railway. They used it to promote their own interests and, to a lesser extent, those of the Socialist Revolutionaries, the only Russian political party with whom they sympathized. The Czechs and Socialist Revolutionaries cordially hated Kolchak, Semenov, and the Japanese. Both wished to put a moderate socialist regime in the place of the discredited admiral. The tensions and rivalries rampant among these hostile groups would provide the Bolsheviks with ample scope to practise the political skills already acquired at the opposite end of Eurasia. But great care had to be exercised, because the Japanese were a formidable foe with a large, well-equipped, and highly disciplined army.

Bolshevik success developed with unexpected swiftness. In early November their armies reached the Irtysh and prepared to assault Omsk, the capital of Kolchak's Russia. In the ensuing battle they shattered the morale of the White army, which either surrendered or fled in panic to the east. The latter had to march along the *trakt*, the two footpaths paralleling the Trans-Siberian Railway, because the Czechs would not let them use the railway itself. Nor would the Czechs give priority to the admiral's own train, which also carried the gold reserve of the Omsk government, and it took him a month to reach Nizhne Udinsk. There he was held virtual prisoner until all Czech trains had passed. A single Soviet division followed in pursuit while partisans attacked the railway at many points. The Whites attempted to make a stand at Novonikolaevsk but were overwhelmed. On 20 December the Red Army entered Tomsk.[1] Socialist Revolutionaries and Mensheviks joined in Irkutsk to form a Political Centre with the aim of transforming the Russian Far East into a democratic republic independent of Soviet Russia. Such a republic, they thought, might be acceptable to both Tokyo and the Bolsheviks as a means of avoiding a military confrontation. Initially, they sought to negotiate with a group of Kolchak's ministers who had reached Irkutsk in November. These talks collapsed when Kolchak, on reaching Nizhne Udinsk, appointed Semenov as commander-in-chief of the remaining

White forces in eastern Siberia. The Political Centre feared the ataman would send his troops into Irkutsk and, on 24 December, with the aid of the Czechs, attempted to seize power. The coup was only partly successful, and allied representatives intervened to halt fighting and reopen negotiations. The admiral, however, would not agree to the proposed democratic republic and on 5 January 1920 transferred his remaining authority to Denikin in European Russia and Semenov in the Far East. Fighting again erupted, and the Political Centre took power throughout the remainder of Irkutsk.[2]

Even before securing their hold in Irkutsk, the Political Centre had opened negotiations with local Bolsheviks for support in forming an independent Far Eastern Republic. These talks took place in an unstable political environment. Semenov was reported to have ordered his Cossacks to recapture the city. It was also known that the remnants of Kolchak's army were approaching Lake Baikal and behind them came the Red Army. The Bolsheviks could not contact Moscow and, therefore, decided in the threatening circumstances to attempt cooperation with the Socialist Revolutionaries and Mensheviks. On 8 January, they agreed to send delegates to Tomsk, together with those of the Political Centre, to contact the Siberian Buro of the Communist Party. The Czechs agreed to keep Semenov out of Irkutsk and provide safe conduct for the two delegations to the Red Army frontline. This was not stationary, because Soviet troops were advancing rapidly and, by early January, had engaged the rear guard of the Czech Legion. Neither wanted to fight, however, and talks began for a cessation of hostilities. The Irkutsk delegations were allowed to pass through the frontline and on 18 January arrived in Tomsk.[3]

The Irkutsk Bolsheviks were not agreed on the object of the negotiations. Some wanted only a temporary arrangement until the Red Army reached Irkutsk. Others, including A.M. Krasnoshchekov, the chairman of the Bolshevik Irkutsk Provincial Committee, sought an equally temporary, but longer-lasting, agreement to create the type of buffer state proposed by the Political Centre. Was Irkutsk to be included? Bolshevik strength there was substantial, and Krasnoshchekov apparently wanted the city to offset the greater influence of the Socialist Revolutionaries in the countryside. Other Bolsheviks, traumatized by more than a year of White rule, wanted Irkutsk safely within the frontiers of Soviet Russia. Moscow quickly settled the dispute. It was seeking to end the civil war as quickly as possible and avoid a clash with Japan. Already on 9 January the Fifth Army had been warned of the possibility of encountering elements of the Japanese army west of Irkutsk and instructed not to initiate hosttilities.[4] When Krasnoshchekov reached Tomsk and informed Moscow of the plan for a buffer state, Lenin replied enthusiastically. Only one or two Bolsheviks had to join its government. An agreement was reached specifying that the frontier between Soviet Russia and the buffer state was to be established along the Oka and Angara rivers, west of Irkutsk. The Political Centre agreed that the Trans-Siberian Railway was to be cleared of foreign troops and that Kolchak and his gold were to be handed over to Soviet Russia.[5]

Events at Irkutsk quickly overtook this agreement. Although the Czechs surrendered Kolchak and the gold to the Political Centre on 15 January, they refused to fight the remainder of the admiral's army, now under the command of General V.O. Kappel, which threatened Irkutsk from the west. Nor could the White garrison be trusted with its defence. The weakness of the Political Centre was clearly evident, and they had to turn to the Bolsheviks for military assistance. In return the local Bolsheviks demanded that power be transferred to their own Revolutionary Committee. The Political Centre resigned on 21 January, and four days later the Bolsheviks proclaimed Soviet power throughout the entire Irkutsk region. The Bolsheviks also received custody of Kolchak and his gold reserve. They were able to mobilize sufficient partisans to defend the city, but for several weeks the issue remained in doubt. On 7 February they executed Kolchak to foreclose any possibility of his liberation. Shortly after, the military balance tipped decisively in their favour. The Kappelites were forced to by-pass Irkutsk on their march to the east, and the Bolsheviks succeeded in negotiating an armistice with the Czechs. The latter agreed to evacuate Siberia east of Baikal.[6]

These events forced a re-evaluation of the agreement with the Political Centre. Some members of the Siberian Revolutionary Committee wanted to scrap it entirely and proceed to the sovietization of the entire Russian Far East.[7] The central authorities disagreed profoundly. They knew of the Polish plan to attack Ukraine and did not want any distraction in the Far East. On 17 February the Politburo adopted a resolution "unconditionally in favour of the policy of supporting a buffer state." Trotsky, who was then at Ekaterinburg, told the chairman of the Siberian Revkom: "The creation of a buffer state must be expedited so that military operations and diplomatic negotiations to the east of Lake Baikal can proceed under the aegis of the buffer state. Beware of the snares of the Japanese interventionists."[8] Two days later Lenin decreed:

We must furiously abuse the opponents of a buffer state ..., threaten them with trial before a Party court and demand that all in Siberia shall give effect to the slogan: "Not a step further towards the East; every effort to be exerted to speed up the movement of troops and locomotives to the west of Russia." We shall be idiots if we let ourselves be carried away into a stupid sally into the depths of Siberia while at the same time Denikin comes to life again and we are attacked by the Poles. This would be a crime.[9]

Nevertheless, there could be no question of abandoning Irkutsk: Soviet power was firmly established there, nothing stood between it and the Red Army, it was an ideal base for Bolshevik action in the Far East, and Central Siberia could be far better defended if the Red Army held the railway tunnels immediately to the east of the city. In early March Soviet troops entered Irkutsk.[10]

The collapse of Kolchak wrecked havoc with the policies of the interventionist powers and threatened their continued presence in the Russian Far East. Already on 8 December 1919 the Japanese had asked Washington how the United States thought the allied and associated powers should deal with the crisis in Siberia.

Without indicating a preference, the Japanese proposed three alternatives: the sending of military reinforcements, maintenance of the status quo, or withdrawal of the forces already there. The Japanese had hoped for a prompt response but did not get it because of the political chaos created in Washington by the illness of President Wilson. A month later, when they did get an answer, it fell like a bombshell in Tokyo. Instead of recommending a joint policy, the Americans said they would unilaterally withdraw their troops from Siberia as soon as the evacuation of the Czech Legion was completed. To add insult to injury, the American decision was known in Vladivostok before the State Department officially informed Tokyo. Although Lansing said the United States would not object to a decision of Japan "to continue single-handed the stationing of her troops in Siberia, or, to send a reinforcement in case of need," he added in writing that he assumed any measures taken would be aimed at achieving "the announced purposes which induced the co-operation of the American and Japanese governments in Siberia."[11] As these had been defined by Wilson and were the antithesis of Japanese ambitions, Lansing was inviting the Japanese either to defend American interests or get out of the Russian Far East.

This was an ideal situation for the development of Soviet policy, and on 24 February Chicherin addressed new peace proposals to the American and Japanese governments. He told Washington that following the conclusion of peace, American commerce and industry could "participate to the widest degree in the great business of restoring the economic life of Russia," adding that the United States could play a "gigantic role in the accomplishment of this task." He extended a far more explicit offer to Tokyo. The Soviet government, said Chicherin,

fully recognizes the special economic and commercial interests of Japan in the Far East, surpassing in some respects at present those of other Powers. It is equally interested in concluding an agreement on the subject which will be useful and beneficial to both parties. The Russian Soviet Government wishes to establish a *modus vivendi* guaranteeing peace between Russia and Japan, and the mutual benefits to the two governments of those relations which should be established between them.[12]

Here was an oblique reference to the buffer state the Soviet government wished to create in the Far East. Such a state, in the guise of a democratic republic, would serve as an ideal arena for the clash of Japanese and American economic interests and allow greater concessions to those interests than if its territory were included in the frontiers of Soviet Russia.

Moscow pressed ahead with its preparations for the creation of this state. These included the appointment of V.D. Vilenskii as the plenipotentiary of the Soviet government in the Far East[13] and the creation of a Far Eastern Bureau of the Communist Party to assume direction of its affairs east of Irkutsk. The formation of the Dalburo (as it became known) was attributed to "the complicated international situation in Transbaikal and the Far East which demands strict control of responsible party centres and strict co-ordination of local organizations with the directives of the central organs of the party." [14] In short, Moscow wished to reduce the possibility that local party organizations might undermine its own policies. It wanted no trouble in the Far East while dealing with the threatening European situation.

This aim clashed with the aspirations of local Bolsheviks who did not want the Far East excluded from Soviet Russia. As elsewhere, the approach of the Red Army raised hopes of imminent delivery from White oppression. With Kolchak beaten, local partisans quickly displaced his officers. The Whites were driven from Verkhneudinsk in early March, leaving Semenov with only the eastern portion of Transbaikal. Still earlier, White generals had been driven from power in most of the Amur and Maritime provinces, including Vladivostok where the hated Rozanov had been replaced by a provisional zemstvo government supported by the Bolsheviks. These accomplishments soon proved insufficient for local Bolsheviks who wished to press on towards expulsion of all foreign military forces, total sovietization, and inclusion of their regions in Soviet Russia. Spokesmen for Moscow's policy attempted to halt this process but only succeeded in slowing its development. At the end of March 1920 the Bolshevik insurgents in the Far East continued to move towards the confrontation with the Japanese which the Soviet government sought to avoid. [15]

The rapid development of the revolutionary process in the Russian Far East contributed to a hardening of the Japanese position there. For nearly two years they had been able to pursue their aims with the silent assent of the Whites. Now the local population had risen, and with arms in hand, demanded that Japan leave. The precariousness of the Japanese position was shown in mid-March when they attempted to crush Russian insurgents at Nikolaevsk, near the mouth of the Amur River, and failed. The Japanese, however, were not about to be turned out of Siberia by poorly armed partisans. In late February they had decided to remain in Vladivostok, the southern Maritime Province, and the Chinese-Eastern Railway zone in Manchuria. The general staff demanded a forceful policy and, in late-March, the government agreed. The Japanese army occupied northern Sakhalin and reinforcements were sent to Siberia. When the last American troops had left, the Japanese presented an ultimatum to the provisional government at Vladivostok. On 2 April they demanded that the new authorities accept all the agreements which Japan had concluded with the Whites, assume responsibility for provisioning the Japanese army in Siberia, suppress all activities threatening the safety of Japanese troops and "the public peace in Korea and Manchuria," and "insure the safety of life, property and other rights of [Japanese] subjects in the region." [16]

The Japanese military preparations had strengthened the hand of those Bolsheviks who supported Moscow's policy. They punctured the euphoria created by Kolchak's collapse and indicated that the Japanese were unlikely to be driven out of Siberia by locally generated pressure. Moscow sought to protect the Far East by protesting against the Japanese military preparations and bringing them to the attention of the western powers, especially the United States.[17] Primarily, however, it demanded greater discipline from the Bolsheviks in the Far East. Vilenskii laid down the party line in Vladivostok while Krasnoshchekov did the same in Verkhneudinsk.[18] Improved communications following the Soviet occupation of Irkutsk facilitated this task as it allowed them to appeal directly to the Central Committee for support. This brought a halt to spontaneous sovietization and a reluctant acceptance of the necessity of forming a buffer state. Even the Japanese ultimatum of 2 April did not shake this discipline. The Bolshevik-backed provisional government in Vladivostok agreed to negotiate and accepted the Japanese terms in principle. Even leading Bolsheviks who had previously favoured sovietization supported this decision. A formal agreement, embodying the Japanese demands, was to have been signed on 5 April.[19]

Such ready submission had no place in Japanese plans. Their army was coiled to strike, and they were determined to attack the partisan forces which the local Bolsheviks had begun to organize into a regular army. On the night of 4 April the Japanese army struck at Bolshevik bases in the Maritime Province. Fighting lasted several days with heavy Russian losses, especially at Khabarovsk. The Bolshevik party, which had functioned quite openly since January, hastily went underground but not before three of its leaders, including S.G. Lazo, a member of the Dalburo, were captured. All three were burned alive in a locomotive boiler. The Japanese attempted to form a new government in Vladivostok but failed. They, therefore, allowed a somewhat modified provisional government to resume some of its functions. The Japanese army, however, retained tight control over the principle centres of the Maritime Province.[20]

The Bolsheviks developed a multifaceted response. Where possible they defended themselves, inflicting heavy casualties on the Japanese at Nikolsk and Khabarovsk. They also brought the railroad workers out on strike and forced the Japanese to run the railway themselves. There was, however, no question of prolonged resistance. Local armed forces were insufficient, and there was no hope of reinforcement from elsewhere. The Bolshevik response, therefore, was primarily political. The provisional government in Vladivostok filed a sharp protest with the representatives of the western powers, reminding them that they had undertaken intervention jointly and, consequently, they were all responsible for the Japanese action. The Americans had already issued their own protest but took no concrete measures against the Japanese.[21] Washington was unwilling to go beyond public disapproval. The Bolsheviks, therefore, had to bargain alone with the Japanese. They still had a substantial basis from which to negotiate. The Japanese clearly feared the partisans and, in the absence of a negotiated agreement, would have to engage in a protracted struggle against them. The Japanese failure to find serious collaborators among the Russian population was also significant as, in the absence of an agreement, they would have to establish their own military administration of the province. Continuing warfare and a Japanese military government were certain to antagonize the Americans, whose forebearance was already stretched to the breaking point. Thus, the Bolsheviks bargained from some strength when they resumed talks. The terms they accepted accurately reflected the local balance of power. The agreement of 29 April barred all Russian armed forces from entering zones within thirty kilometres of all major railways and the borders of China and Korea. The provisional government was allowed to maintain a small militia to police the remainder of the province. The Japanese, therefore, controlled the principal cities and industries of the Maritime Province without having to fight the partisans. The Bolsheviks were left the rest with a somewhat reduced possibility of further hostilities.[22]

The Japanese offensive also accelerated the development of Bolshevik policy in Transbaikal. Throughout March opposition to the formation of a buffer state had remained strong and was fuelled by the continuing struggle against Semenov. When a Bolshevik-sponsored Congress of the Toilers of the Baikal Region met in Verkhneudinsk at the end of the month, Krasnoshchekov secured the passage of a resolution endorsing the formation of a buffer state but found no consensus concerning its structure. Most Bolsheviks wanted a thinly camouflaged Soviet state, while the Mensheviks and Socialist Revolutionaries demanded a genuinely democratic republic. Lenin instructed Krasnoshchekov to disregard the Mensheviks and Socialist Revolutionaries. "Either they will submit to us without any conditions or they will be arrested." On the other hand he would not permit the Transbaikal Bolsheviks to draw on the resources of Soviet Russia.[23] Transbaikal Bolsheviks, therefore, had to confront the Japanese challenge without outside assistance. The situation appeared all the worse because the Japanese also sent troops into the Chinese-Eastern Railway zone and rushed munitions to Semenov.

The Japanese offensive brought immediate action to appease Tokyo. On 6 April the Toilers Congress created a Far Eastern Republic and proclaimed its independence from Soviet Russia. The new state extended from Baikal to the Pacific and included the districts of Transbaikal, Amur, the Maritime Province, Sakhalin, Kamchatka, and the Chinese-Eastern Railroad zone. The Congress proclaimed the new state to be a democratic republic and offered amnesty to all officers and soldiers of the armies of Kolchak and Semenov. The Socialist Revolutionaries and Mensheviks initially refused to join the government but supported the creation of the new state. Moscow signalled its approval on 16 April when Karakhan wired Krasnoshchekov that the Soviet government saw the buffer state "as the single way out of the circumstances arising in the Far East." It is significant that this endorsement was communicated privately to Krasnoshchekov. Bolshevik counsels in Siberia remained divided and unable to formulate unified recommendations for Politburo consideration.

Moscow had provided the framework for Soviet policy but had left its development to the Siberian Buro and Dalburo. They in turn were hampered by

the chaotic conditions which still prevailed in eastern Siberia. Consultation with
the governments at Verkhneudinsk and Blagoveshchensk was difficult at best
and with that at Vladivostok frequently impossible. In addition, while Verkhneudinsk and Vladivostok had both accepted the necessity of a far eastern
buffer state, they disagreed as to where it was to be based. Vladivostok Bolsheviks thought their city should be the centre of the new state.[24] Until these
differences could be sorted out Moscow was reluctant to intervene.

The rapid development of events in the Far East forced this intervention. The
Japanese wanted to consolidate their hold on eastern Siberia, shape the emergence
of the buffer state in a manner favourable to themselves, and project their
influence as far towards Baikal as possible. The agreement of 29 April led them
to believe that they could base part of their plan on the provisional government
at Vladivostok. Unofficial talks with Vilenskii, who favoured Vladivostok as
the political centre of the Far Eastern Republic, contributed to this conclusion.
On 4 May the Japanese government decided to accept the concept of a buffer
state and try to bring it under their control. A week later General Morimoto Oi,
the Japanese military commander in Siberia, issued a declaration endorsing the
formation of an independent Far Eastern Republic and reaffirming an earlier
Japanese pledge to withdraw their troops as soon as circumstances in Siberia no
longer threatened Manchuria, Korea, or the lives and property of Japanese citizens. Oi wished to establish neutral zones in Transbaikal to prevent the clash
of Japanese and Russian armed forces. The following day he telegraphed Verkhneudinsk saying the Japanese would not impede "the birth of a united autonomous Far Eastern Russia."[25]

Oi's message received a mixed reception in Verkhneudinsk, where two of the
three members of the Dalburo based in that city dismissed it as a Japanese snare
and wanted to reject the overture. Krasnoshchekov disagreed and asked the Soviet
government "to clarify its relationship to the Far Eastern Republic in general
and to this question in particular, and to give [the government at Verkhneudinsk]
corresponding instructions."[26] When this message reached Moscow the Poles
had already occupied Kiev and the Soviet government lost little time in responding. On 14 May Chicherin, in the name of the RSFSR, officially recognized the
Far Eastern Republic and its provisional government. In conclusion he expressed
the wish that "the Far Eastern Republic flourish and maintain peaceful relations
with its neighbouring countries."[27] That same day Krasnoshchekov replied to
Oi that the Far Eastern Republic was prepared to open negotiations on the basis
proposed by the Japanese army.[28]

This exchange opened two months of extremely difficult negotiations. The
talks began on 24 May at Gongotta, a railway station one hundred kilometres
southwest of Chita, near the frontline separating the People's Revolutionary
Army, as the armed forces of the Far Eastern Republic had become known, and
that of Semenov. The two sides approached the talks with sharply conflicting
objectives. The Bolsheviks wanted to hasten the withdrawal of Japanese troops

from Transbaikal and thus lead to its unification under the authority of the Verkhneudinsk government. They proposed a general armistice throughout Transbaikal with narrowly defined demilitarized zones. This would allow the Japanese troops to withdraw safely but not encourage them to stay. Most of all, the Bolsheviks wanted Japanese recognition of the sovereignty of the Far Eastern Republic in the territories specified in the declaration of 6 April. The Japanese, on the other hand, wanted an agreement that would limit the authority of the existing Far Eastern Republic, recognize other governments in the region, and provide for the extension of Japanese influence throughout it. They proposed an armistice limited to the Chita front, immediate recognition of Semenov's authority over the larger part of Transbaikal, and the extension of broadly based neutral zones along the Trans-Siberian Railway to Lake Baikal. They refused to recognize the sovereignty of the Far Eastern Republic and said that any unified state would have to emerge from negotiations among the existing regimes. If accepted, these proposals would have allowed the Japanese to crush the Bolshevik partisans operating in eastern Transbaikal and the Amur district, shore up Semenov, and establish a protectorate over the entire area east of Baikal. No agreement was possible, and negotiations collapsed in early June. Hostilities resumed immediately, with Semenov attacking Bolshevik partisans in eastern Transbaikal while the Japanese presence west of Chita effectively prevented the People's Revolutionary Army from assisting them.[29]

The failure to extract any concessions from the Japanese, the weakened position of the party in the Maritime Province, and the threatening situation in Transbaikal served to discredit moderate Bolsheviks in both Vladivostok and Verkhneudinsk. The Siberian Buro grew increasingly impatient with the pretensions of Vladivostok Bolsheviks which seemed to invite Japanese interference in the political life of the region. The Siberian Buro wanted the Far Eastern Republic based near Irkutsk and condemned the refusal of Vladivostok to acknowledge the primacy of Verkhneudinsk. On 20 May they asked for the recall of Vilenskii, whom they believed was encouraging the opposition in Vladivostok. Eight days later they ruled that negotiations with the Japanese could only be conducted by the authorities at Verkhneudinsk with the advice of Moscow. This led Vladivostok to acknowledge the "important and difficult work" of the government at Verkhneudinsk but no unequivocal acceptance of its authority. Such acceptance would have invited Japanese retaliation and, by itself, this stiffened the determination of the Siberian Buro to base their policy in Verkhneudinsk.[30]

This did not mean that the Siberian Buro was satisfied with the way Krasnoshchekov was handling the affairs of the Far Eastern Republic. Far from it. They had supported him in opposing the sovietization of the Far East and had removed the advocates of this policy from the Dalburo, but a majority of the Siberian Buro believed he allowed the Mensheviks and Socialist Revolutionaries too much political freedom and overemphasized the independence of the Far Eastern Republic. Krasnoshchekov was summoned to Omsk to answer these charges, but the Siberian Buro were so badly divided they had to ask Moscow for instructions regarding the future development of the Far Eastern Republic. Krasnoshchekov was called to Moscow to present his own report to the Central Committee.[31]

The eclipse of Krasnoshchekov did not signal a change in the foreign policy of the Far Eastern Republic. This was directed by Moscow and aimed at a negotiated settlement with the Japanese. The People's Revolutionary Army and Bolshevik partisans successfully beat off the attacks launched by Semenov in early June, but as long as the Japanese remained in Transbaikal the Bolsheviks could not attempt to capture Chita. The Japanese, however, soon had to reassess their policy. They had failed to intimidate the Bolsheviks, and Semenov made no appreciable gains. Instead the partisans grew stronger, and the Japanese realized that if they wished results similar to those achieved in the Maritime Province they would have to employ their own armed forces. First, however, they would have to secure their lines of communication through the politically sensitive Chinese-Eastern Railroad zone and the formidably dangerous Amur region. They would have to send a force at least equal to their army in the Maritime Province and certainly excite American hostility. The risks were too great, and in early July the Japanese decided to withdraw from Transbaikal.[32]

This forced the Japanese to reopen negotiations with Verkhneudinsk. Only the Bolsheviks could assure them safe passage from Transbaikal, and on 5 July the Japanese commander asked for a new meeting at Gongatta. The talks began five days later and concluded successfully on 15 July. What emerged from the meeting is a curious document, because essentially it was an agreement to disagree. In it the Japanese recorded their view that the Far Eastern Republic was neither the sole nor even main government on the territory of the Russian Far East, and therefore they could not conclude an agreement with it ending military operations on all fronts in the region. The Russian delegation passed over this assertion in silence but agreed to a separate armistice with the Japanese on the Chita front. The Japanese promised that Semenov would abide by this decision.[33]

At first glance it would appear that the Japanese had wrung major concessions from the Bolsheviks, but this was not so. The Japanese, in fact, had yielded nothing in principle but everything in substance. They had negotiated a passport for their forces to leave Transbaikal. Once they left, Semenov would face the Bolsheviks alone. The Japanese refusal to acknowledge that the authority of Verkhneudinsk extended to all parts of the Russian Far East reflected the strong position they retained in the Maritime Province, but elsewhere the balance of power was clearly shifting to the Bolsheviks.

In the following month this process accelerated. Semenov's position deteriorated still further, and on 3 August the Japanese turned down his appeal for further assistance.[34] In addition, the Americans began to raise serious objections to the enlarged Japanese military presence in Siberia. On 11 July the acting secretary of state informed the British ambassador that the American government had originally intended only to inform Japan that they could not recognize her occupation of Russian territory but had since decided "that it was desirable to tell Japan definitely that she must evacuate these areas."[35] Five days later Secretary of State Colby wrote the Japanese ambassador expressing American "gratification" concerning Japanese withdrawal from Transbaikal, reserving judgment as to the necessity of the continued occupation of the Vladivostok region, but rejecting the explanation for the seizure of northern Sakhalin. He declared that the American government could not "participate in the announced decision of [the Japanese] government with regard to Sakhalin, nor can it recognize the occupation of the said territory by any non-Russian authority."[36] The Americans had not quite demanded Japanese withdrawal from the entire Russian Far East, but they were clearly moving in that direction.

The Japanese also had to consider the changing political situation in Europe. The British did not join the American protest but warned Tokyo that its action "would probably entail war between her and [the] future Russian Government if [the] Japanese occupation were to be permanent."[37] Until the summer this hardly seemed a serious concern, but in July, as Budenny's cavalry rode into Poland and the entire world appeared to witness the rebirth of Russia as a major power, Tokyo had to revise its calculations. Soviet Russia victorious in Europe might well turn to settle scores in the Far East. On 4 August Tokyo called a halt to further offensive operations in Siberia. The army in the Maritime Province would prepare fortified winter quarters and defend itself if attacked. For the moment Japan decided to rely on political action and attempt to influence the provisional government at Vladivostok.[38]

As the Japanese position weakened Moscow re-examined its own policy. It was twice debated by the Central Committee, who on 5 August submitted it to a special commission composed of Krestinskii, Preobrazhenskii, and Chicherin.[39] On 13 August they reported to the Politburo, who adopted their recommendations. The revised policy substantially strengthened central control over the party east of Baikal. Thus the concept of the Far Eastern Republic as a "bourgeois democratic," and not a soviet, state was confirmed. At the same time the Politburo agreed to preserve local forms of soviet government where they already existed. They also confirmed that the Communist Party was to retain its "directing role" and that no significant scope was to be given for the development of other political parties. "The bourgeois democratic character of the buffer state," decreed the Politburo, "is purely formal. The introduction of a parliamentary structure must not be permitted." Verkhneudinsk, or Chita after its liberation, was to serve as the capital. Vladivostok was said to be unsuitable because it was effectively controlled by the Japanese. All important questions of internal policy and every question of foreign policy of the Far Eastern Republic were to be determined in consultation with the central organs of the Soviet Russian government. To ensure this, the Dalburo was removed from the control of the Siberian Buro and subordinated directly to the Central Committee. The existing Dalburo was confirmed, including Krasnoshchekov who was sent back to Verkhneudinsk, presumably to serve as a rein on those who still desired full sovietization of the Far East.[40] Even at the height of Soviet victory in Poland, perhaps in part because of the great vistas suddenly opening in Europe, the Politburo wished to avoid any clash with Japan. Siberia remained at the very bottom of the lengthy list of Soviet priorities in August 1920.

These decisions and the changing balance of power in the Far East brought the Vladivostok Bolsheviks to heel. Throughout July they had persisted in pursuing a policy sharply at odds with Bolshevik objectives elsewhere. They had sought to organize a conference at Valdivostok of all far eastern Russian governments as a platform from which to summon a constituent assembly. They had even invited Semenov, and the state they foresaw emerging from the projected constituent assembly was far more pluralist than that taking shape in Verkhneudinsk. As a consequence, the government there had pointedly refused to answer the invitation from Valdivostok, and the Siberian Buro had issued a directive demanding that the Vladivostok Bolsheviks cancel their conference and agree to attend one held in Soviet-controlled territory. The Siberian Buro also ordered the Maritime Province party organization "to issue promptly a declaration affirming the organic tie of the Maritime Province with the Far Eastern Republic and its central government at Verkhneudinsk." Failure to do so would result in expulsion from the party. On 14 August local Bolsheviks issued a public statement containing the required statement. Ten days later the Vladivostok government openly defied the Japanese by adopting the Bolshevik position as their own. While all this took place a delegation from the Valdivostok popular assembly had journeyed to Verkhneudinsk where it had received a severe dressing down by Soviet officials. It returned to Vladivostok at the end of the month with an agreement calling for the constituent assembly to meet in Verkhneudinsk without the participation of Semenov. This too was promptly adopted by the government and popular assembly in Vladivostok.[41]

Verkhneudinsk Bolsheviks now began to tighten their grip on the Russian Far East. But not too quickly, because they did not wish to summon a constituent assembly until they controlled all governments in the region. Abandoned by Semenov, Chita had been occupied by the Kappelites. Although the latter feared Semenov more than the People's Revolutionary Army and had allowed the formation of a popular assembly at Chita, they were still unprepared to recognize the authority of Verkhneudinsk. They were primarily interested in reaching Vladivostok. Semenov had withdrawn to Dauria, near the Manchurian frontier, but remained the primary obstacle to Bolshevik goals. Neither the Kappelites nor Semenov posed an immediate threat to Verkhneudinsk, but their continued presence allowed the Japanese to ignore the claim of the Far Eastern Republic to speak for all Russians in Transbaikal and provided a ready-made base for further military operations should the Japanese choose to resume hostilities.

While maintaining momentum towards the unification of the Far East, therefore, the Bolsheviks had to tie it to the elimination of the Kappelites and Semenov. Thus, instead of issuing an immediate call for a Far Eastern constituent assembly, Krasnoshchekov, on returning from Moscow in early September, summoned the representatives of Chita, the Amur district, and the Maritime Province to yet another meeting in Verkhneudinsk. They decided on 26 September that a further conference including representatives from eastern Transbaikal and Sakhalin would meet the following month either at Chita or Verkhneudinsk to call a constituent assembly. The uncertainty of location for the October meeting clearly reflected the tenuous political situation at Chita. Much would depend on political and military developments in October. The direction in which these developments were moving, however, was clearly shown by the negotiations conducted by the Vladivostok delegation on their way to Verkhneudinsk: the Kappelites had asked permission to settle in the Maritime Province, while Semenov had sought recognition of his government. The delegation was prepared to consider the former but not the latter. Semenov still felt compelled to let them pass safely through his territory.[42]

Debate at Verkhneudinsk now focused on the most effective way of removing the Chita "stopper," as the territory still held by the Kappelites and Semenov had become known. G. Kh. Eiche, the commander of the People's Revolutionary Army, was confident he could crush the Whites in a single swift campaign. Krasnoshchekov was not so sure. He had no doubt that the People's Revolutionary Army could defeat the Whites, but he feared that this might provoke the Japanese. Smirnov, the chairman of the Siberian Buro, shared this concern. On 23 September he cabled Lenin: "Semenov is probably acting on the instruction of the Japanese H.Q., which is seeking an occasion for a new entry of Japanese troops into Chita." Instead of a purely military action, Smirnov suggested that "Semenov should be liquidated by eviction from within." By this he meant the frequently used Bolshevik tactic of instructing a local revolutionary committee to organize an insurrection and then appeal for the help of the nearest formation of the Red Army, in this case the People's Revolutionary Army. Lenin passed the telegram to Trotsky, who sought the advice of S. Kamenev. The Red Army commander-in-chief emphatically agreed with Smirnov. Trotsky's response is illuminating. "No one is to venture to begin without instructions (peace with Poland)."[43] By this he meant that the Far East would have to wait until Soviet Russia concluded peace in Europe. The Central Committee adopted this view on 29 September, and two days later Kamenev issued categorical orders that "at the present time it is necessary to abstain from any action which might lead to conflict with Japan."[44]

The plans of the People's Revolutionary Army were changed. Instead of a frontal assault on Chita, arrangements were made for a series of local insurrections. The partisans were told to avoid any appearance of belonging to the People's Revolutionary Army and issued strict orders to abstain from any kind of anti-Japanese agitation. Even so, the assault on Chita was delayed until the treaty of Riga was signed and the last Japanese troops had left Transbaikal. On 19 October the partisans took the offensive. The battle lasted two days, with the remnants of the Kappelites and Semenov's troops fleeing to the southeast.[45]

On 25 October Krasnoshchekov entered Chita. With him came representatives from every district of the republic, who promptly convened the conference foreseen at Verkhneudinsk in September. On 29 October they reaffirmed the independence of the Far Eastern Republic and its bourgeois-democratic character.[46] They chose a government headed by Krasnoshchekov and based at Chita, which claimed sovereignty over the entire far eastern territory of the former Russian empire. Elections for a constituent assembly were to be held in January. Problems arose at once. The sweeping jurisdiction claimed by the new government was not initially recognized in the Maritime Province. Not until 11 December did the Bolshevik-controlled popular assembly officially recognize the authority of the Far Eastern Republic. The Vladivostok government, however, was not dissolved. The Japanese had made it clear that they would not deal with Chita regarding the Maritime Province, and it was necessary to preserve a Russian administration in Vladivostok to conduct relations with the Japanese army. The functions of the new government, however, were greatly reduced and entrusted to V.G. Antonov, an old Bolshevik enjoying the confidence of the Dalburo and Moscow. In this way, a "buffer within a buffer" was created with Soviet-Japanese rivalry focused increasingly on Vladivostok and the Maritime Province.[47]

Tension increased sharply when the shattered remnants of the Kappelites and Semenov's troop arrived in the Vladivostok region. In November they had been driven out of Transbaikal into Manchuria. This eliminated the "Chita stopper" but not the problem of the remaining White forces. The Chinese did not want them in Manchuria and sent them by rail to the Maritime Province, where the Vladivostok government could not stop them from crossing the frontier. The Japanese took them under their protection and settled them in camps inside the zones allotted their army by the agreement of 29 April. The Vladivostok militia could not enter these areas, and the Whites remained a source of danger to Bolshevik authority in the Maritime Province.[48]

In December 1920, therefore, the Bolshevik position in the Far East remained tenuous but was certainly far better than in the spring, which encouraged local Bolsheviks to ask Moscow for permission to proceed to the full sovietization of their region. When Krasnoshchekov fell ill, Dalburo members favouring sovietization passed a resolution calling on the Central Committee to reconsider the far eastern policy adopted in August. On 20 December the Dalburo declared that the time had come to include the Far East in the RSFSR. Although the Siberian Buro endorsed this resolution, the Central Committee did not. At their meeting of 4 January 1921 they declared "the sovietization of the Far Eastern Republic unconditionally impermissible at this time" and banned "any violation of the [29 April] agreement with Japan."[49] Moscow felt unable to proceed any further towards the consolidation of Soviet power in the Far East.

This meant that far eastern Bolsheviks had to proceed to the construction of a theoretically liberal-democratic state and abstain from applying military pressure to force Japan out of the Maritime Province. The necessity for such quiescence increased in the spring when widespread peasant insurrections swept western Siberia, cutting the Trans-Siberian Railway and effectively severing the Far East from central Russia. Although the vital link was soon restored, its security was not assured until summer.[50] During this time Japanese determination to remain in the Maritime Province hardened and did not initially generate further American resistance. Thus, the Constituent Assembly elected in January produced a liberal-democratic, rather than soviet, constitution. Proclaimed on 27 April 1921, this constitution provided the façade of a non-Soviet government. Other socialist parties were tolerated, even unofficially required to sit in the popular assembly, but all power remained in Bolshevik hands. Despite the growing number of White troops and increased political activity of conservative groups at Vladivostok, the Bolsheviks could take no repressive action. Chita could only file diplomatic protests, which Tokyo pointedly ignored.[51] By the spring of 1921, therefore, the fate of the Maritime Province depended upon the willingness of either the Japanese or the Bolsheviks to disturb the armed truce observed at Vladivostok.

THE RECONQUEST OF SIBERIA and the establishment of the Far Eastern Republic created the necessary conditions for the Soviet government to seek a restoration of relations with China. These had been severed in the summer of 1918 when foreign intervention in Siberia had driven the Bolsheviks back to the Urals. China, although not a major participant, had sent troops to Vladivostok, crushed the Russian soviet in Harbin, and sanctioned the use of the Chinese-Eastern Railroad to support anti-Soviet forces. Peking had also refused to take official note of the first Soviet attempt to divest Russia of the special rights acquired by the tsarist empire in China during the previous century. For eighteen months Moscow and Peking had been separated by the hermetic seal of the Russian civil war. During that time no message passed between them, although Chicherin did exchange greetings with Sun Yat-sen, the leader of a revolutionary nationalist regime at Canton.[52] The rising ride of Chinese nationalism, however, was to shape these relations profoundly and when Soviet Russia again appeared in the Far East, Chinese politics had been shaken by the humiliation suffered at Versailles, the transfer of Shantung to Japan, the eruption of the May Fourth movement, and heightened anti-foreign, especially anti-Japanese, sentiment.[53]

These developments were all the more interesting because the Bolsheviks learned of them at exactly the time when revolutionary prospects in Europe had dimmed and the gaze of some Soviet leaders had turned towards Asia. Chinese nationalism, with its strongly anti-imperialist character, was clearly a potential ally. Bolshevik leaders wanted to attract Chinese attention and present their own anti-imperialist credentials, but they were not prepared to compromise fundamental Soviet interests. In the summer of 1919, however, those interests had not yet been defined. It was even unclear whether the Russian civil war would end decisively. If hostilities ended inconclusively, with Kolchak holding the Far East, Moscow would want to exacerbate his relations with Peking, possibly by abandoning all Russian claims on China. On the other hand, if the war ended with Moscow in control of the Far East, the Soviet government would have to be more circumspect. They could abandon all rights, privileges, and Russian-owned property in China, but they would have to ensure the security of the long frontier with China, prevent the Whites from using Chinese territory to continue hostilities, and reach some agreement concerning the future use of the Chinese-Eastern Railway. The strategic and economic importance of the railway could not be ignored. Not only did it provide the most direct route between Irkutsk and Vladivostok (the Amur route was nearly twice as long), it delivered grain from Manchuria to feed substantial portions of eastern Siberia. In addition, tens of thousands of Russians, many Soviet supporters, lived in the railway zone and could not easily be abandoned, especially if Peking could not keep the zone out of the hands of the Whites or Japanese.[54]

The capacity and policies of the Peking government raised additional questions. Chinese politics had become militarized, with Peking the prize of competing generals. In the midst of this chaos the foreign policy of the republic remained remarkably stable but, from the Bolshevik perspective, quite unsatisfactory because of its continuing anti-Soviet bias. The Wai-chiao Pu, as the Chinese Foreign Ministry was known, supported allied intervention throughout 1919. Moscow, therefore, could hardly afford a grand gesture divesting itself of tsarist rights to the Chinese-Eastern Railway when this action would legitimize its use against Soviet interests in the Russian Far East.

The Soviet government had to address these questions as they began to formulate a response to the rising wave of Chinese nationalism. A response was necessary, because a leading opponent of Versailles and the world's only Marxist power could hardly ignore the events shaking China in the summer of 1919. The exact process by which this response was formulated remains unclear, but it resulted in two separate, but closely related, approaches to the problem. Sow-Theng Leong, who has studied this question closely, speculates that the two approaches arose from the conflicting assessments of the situation made by different Soviet leaders. It is even possible, he continues, that these were not hardened positions but only "different states of mind shared by most, if not all, the policymakers at the time." Sow concludes that "the evidence points to what seems to have been the ultimate decision reached by the Narkomindel: that of adopting both positions and maneuvering between them with flexibility."[55] This conclusion fits the available evidence, is consonant with Bolshevik negotiating practices, and corresponds with subsequent events. The political dynamics of mid-1919 were simply too fluid, the unknowns too many, to allow the Soviet government to commit themselves to a single well-defined policy.

However formulated, the decision led to the preparation of a manifesto signed by Karakhan but issued in the name of the Sovnarkom. It exuded confidence in the success of Soviet arms and projected an image of the Red Army sweeping victoriously across Siberia to the frontiers of China. Karakhan carefully linked this advance to Chinese issues. Since November 1917, he said, the Bolsheviks had sought to open negotiations to annul the unequal treaties forced on China by the tsarist regime. This attempt had been thwarted by the allied powers, who had forced the Chinese government to ignore the Soviet overture. Karakhan then renewed Moscow's offer to renegotiate the basis of Sino-Russian relations. In one version of his manifesto this began: "The Soviet Government returns to the Chinese people without any compensation, the Chinese-Eastern Railroad and all the mining, timber, gold and other concessions seized by [Russia in the past]." In the second he omitted all reference to the Chinese-Eastern Railway, but renounced the indemnity due Russia as a result of the Boxer rebellion, all Russian economic concessions in China, and the right of Russians to extraterritoriality. In conclusion he invited the Chinese people "in the person of their government ... to enter right away into official relations with us and send their representatives to meet our army."[56] The Soviet government decided to proceed cautiously and chose to issue the version which did not mention the Chinese-Eastern Railway. Dated 25 July 1919, it was actually published a month later. This delay can possibly be attributed to a temporary halt in the Bolshevik advance in the late summer of 1919. It would not have done to issue such a triumphant declaration with the Red Army marking time in the forests of western Siberia.

The Red Army did not mark time for long, and Kolchak's retreat soon turned into a rout. Although Peking learned indirectly of the Karakhan manifesto, Moscow had no way of bringing it officially to the attention of the Wai-chiao Pu, and initially it made little impact on the Chinese government. The tumultuous events following the fall of Omsk, however, were followed closely in Peking. The collapse of tsarist authority had led the Chinese government to embark upon a program of recovering sovereign rights lost to Russia in the previous century. Soviet victory was viewed as an opportunity to accelerate this process. Peking had already reasserted its sovereignty over Outer Mongolia and breached the Russian monopoly of navigation on the Amur River, but the Wai-chaio Pu aimed at nothing less than the liquidation of the privileged position enjoyed by Russians in China. In particular they wished an end to Russian extraterritoriality and full control of the Chinese-Eastern Railway.

Soviet and Chinese policy, therefore, had much in common, but there were important differences. Peking sought to recover China's sovereign rights without giving anything in return. It would recognize the Soviet government but only in concert with the allied powers. Peking was not prepared to align itself with Soviet Russia against the allies and did not wish to exchange one set of treaties impairing Chinese sovereignty for new agreements amounting to the same thing. Moscow, on the other hand, wanted China to act independently and guarantee that its territory would not be used to attack Soviet Russia. Given Chinese disunity, there was no way Peking could assure Moscow that it could control Sinkiang, Outer Mongolia, and Manchuria. As these were the very regions which bordered Russia, the Bolsheviks were bound to seek some guarantee other than the promise of the Chinese government to secure Soviet territory from attack. Agreement, therefore, would not be easy.[57]

Everything went well at first. In early 1920 the Bolshevik-backed governments at Blagoveshchensk and Vladivostok entered into amiable relations with the Chinese authorities in Manchuria, and Peking agreed to withdraw the small force it had sent to Vladivostok a year before. Peking and Vladivostok also cooperated in driving General Dmitri Horvath, the long-time tsarist head of the Chinese-Eastern Railway, from Harbin. Horvath's command of five thousand Russian railway guards had given him effective control over the railway zone. He and his subordinates were intensely anti-Bolshevik, and the new government in Vladivostok saw them as a threat to their security. The Chinese wanted to get rid of them as a first step towards the elimination of Russian control of the railway. Chang Tso-lin, the chief Chinese military commander in Manchuria, commenced this process by appointing General Pao Kaui-ch'ing as president of the railway. Pao now demanded the reorganization of the railway, including the disbanding of the Russian guards. By the end of March civil and military authority had passed into Pao's hands, and Horvath was forced to leave Harbin.[58]

While these events took place, V. Vilenskii, the Narkomindel plenipotentiary, had arrived in the Far East bringing the Karakhan manifesto with him. In late February he delivered it to the Chinese consulate in Irkutsk. He then moved on to Vladivostok where he presented the document to the Chinese consul there and had it published by the local Bolshevik newspaper. In both instances it was the version which returned the Chinese-Eastern Railway to China without compensation. Was this a decision of the Soviet government taken before Vilenskii's departure from Moscow or one made on his own authority when he arrived? The evidence is unclear, and either interpretation is plausible. It was standard Soviet practice to open negotiations with a grand gesture and see where it would lead. Moscow may have instructed Vilenskii to publish the more generous version of the manifesto in the hope of accelerating the process of opening relations with China. On the other hand, given the fluidity and uncertainty of the far eastern political situation in February 1920, Moscow may have left the decision to Vilenskii's discretion. If so, the political situation he found on his arrival (the establishment of de facto Bolshevik governments and assumption of Chinese control over the Chinese-Eastern Railroad) would certainly have encouraged him to put forward the more generous of the two documents. If, as seemed possible in March, the Chinese could drive the Whites from the railway zone and the Japanese could be levered out of Vladivostok, then Soviet Russia could easily accept Chinese control of the railway. These were exactly the points Vilenskii made in a conversation with the Chinese consul in Vladivostok on 31 March. Soviet Russia, he added, "regards it a primary objective to seek a close relationship with China with the view that the two countries should stand together as allies."[59]

The events of April 1920 showed these expectations to be illusory. The Japanese offensive in the Maritime Province, the sending of Japanese troops into the railway zone, and Chinese acquiescence in the use of the Chinese-Eastern Railway to support Semenov demonstrated that, for the moment at least, the future of the railway could not be settled with China alone. The Chinese government, far from seeking negotiations with Soviet Russia, hoped to resolve the issues arising from the Karakhan manifesto in concert with the western powers. To make matters worse, the provisional government at Vladivostok headed by the socialist revolutionary A.S. Medvedev, opposed Russian abandonment of the Chinese-Eastern Railway. The United Conference, the Russian workers' organization formed in the railway zone, had recognized the authority of the Vladivostok government, and Medvedev now claimed to exercise existing Russian treaty rights in the zone. He even wanted to retain the extraterritorial rights of Russian citizens.[60] The fragmented political structure of the Russian Far East, therefore, made any simple solution of the Chinese-Eastern Railway problem impossible.

The proclamation of the Far Eastern Republic opened a new avenue for China and Soviet Russia to explore the reopening of relations, and Peking responded by sending a delegation headed by General Chang Ssu-lin to Verkhneudinsk. They were able to conclude an agreement allowing resumption of trade between western Transbaikal and China but lacked authority to discuss political questions. When Chang returned to Peking, however, he carried a letter from Krasnoshchekov calling for a meeting in the near future to restore political relations. Instead of waiting for a reply, Krasnoshchekov ordered I. Iurin to proceed at once to Peking. His mission left Verkhneudinsk on 7 June.[61] The moment was ill-chosen. Japanese intentions regarding Transbaikal remained unclear, and the future of Soviet Russia itself was shaken by the Polish invasion. Most important, Peking was temporarily paralysed by an armed clash between the ruling Anfu clique and its rivals in Fengtien and Chihli provinces. When Iurin reached the Chinese frontier, therefore, he was not allowed to continue until the international and Chinese political situations stabilized.[62]

In July they did. The Gongotta accord implied that Japan would soon evacuate Transbaikal, and the Soviet offensive in Poland seemed to confirm the re-emergence of Russia as a major power. In China the Fengtien and Chihli generals took control of Peking. They had accused the Anfu clique of insufficient vigour in pursuit of rights recovery, and the new foreign minister, Yen Hui-ch'ing, undertook a more forceful policy. In August he ceased payment of the Boxer indemnity to the Russian ambassador, and in September withdrew official recognition of the embassy itself and all Russian consulates in China. The abolition of Russian extraterritoriality was not mentioned, but as the embassy and consulates had exercised this right, their suspension had this effect. Yen decided to follow the British model of negotiating with the Bolsheviks. He did not mention political negotiations, but informed Iurin that his mission could conduct unofficial talks concerning the development of commercial relations between the Far Eastern Republic and China. Iurin arrived in Peking on 26 August.[63]

The link between Peking and the Far Eastern Republic would soon form the basis of Sino-Russian relations, but the Wai-chiao Pu first wanted a clarification of Bolshevik policy. This is hardly surprising given the variety of policies put forward by Soviet spokesmen. In late June the Wai-chaio Pu had sent Chang Ssu-lin back to Moscow. Had he gone as the official representative of the Chinese government Soviet leaders would have given him a warm reception, but as he arrived in Moscow without credentials, the Narkomindel could only conduct unofficial talks with him. These concluded on 27 September with Karakhan providing Chang with a clear statement of Soviet policy. Essentially it was a rewording of Karakhan's own manifesto of July 1919 and a tacit, but unstated, repudiation of the version circulated by Vilenskii in the spring. It called for the voiding of all existing Sino-Russian treaties, the end of Russian extraterritoriality in China, the return of all Russian economic concessions to China, and the termination of Chinese payment of the Boxer indemnity to Russia. The Soviet government proposed the immediate establishment of diplomatic and economic relations with both countries, promising to prevent their territory from being used to attack the other. The new manifesto left no doubt about what Moscow thought should be done with the Chinese-Eastern Railway. The two governments, it proposed, should "agree to conclude a special treaty to provide for the rules and regulation of the exploitation of the Chinese Eastern Railway *for the needs of the R.S.F.S.R.*"[64] This was a definitive statement of Soviet policy. The Bolsheviks were eager to liquidate the past but would not compromise the security of Russian frontiers or leave to chance the exploitation of such a major resource as the Chinese-Eastern Railway.[65]

Peking did not share these aspirations. Unilateral Chinese action had already voided those tsarist rights which Moscow proposed to relinquish. Moreover the Bolsheviks, far from abandoning the Russian claim to the Chinese-Eastern Railroad, were demanding that China agree to its use by Soviet Russia. Peking did not wish to conclude such an agreement or any accord which required it to assist the Bolsheviks in guaranteeing Soviet territory from attack. Nor did the Wai-chaio Pu want normal and continuous diplomatic relations. Any of the measures sought by the Bolsheviks might trigger a hostile Japanese (or even general allied) reaction. Chinese concern focused primarily on the Chinese-Eastern Railway. It was feared that Japan and the western powers might retaliate for the measures taken by General Pao in the spring by enforcing the "internationalization" of the railway. To avert this and prepare for future negotiations with a still undetermined Russian government, Peking sought to obtain the Russian shares in the railway. These were held by the Russo-Asiatic Bank which, under intense Chinese pressure, relinquished them in early October. This effectively converted the railway into a purely commercial venture and gave Peking an equal role in its management. The former judicial, administratives and police powers of the railway reverted to the Chinese authorities in Manchuria.[66] None of this bound the Soviet government, but it was a major step towards the restoration of sovereign rights lost in the previous century.

The Chinese had virtually used extortion to compel the Russo-Asiatic Bank to relinquish the Russian shares in the railway and, together with all the other measures of rights retrieval, this action was bitterly resented by the allied powers. Foreign criticism linked rights retrieval with the exchange of government missions with Moscow. The Chinese quickly saw that criticism of the former could be deflected by seeming to retreat from the latter. So, Chang was recalled from Moscow and the allied ministers in Peking were told that it was not China's intention to enter into normal relations with either Moscow or Verkhneudinsk. In reality the Chinese had little further to gain from developing these contacts and were once more content simply to observe the development of Russian affairs.[67]

This did not last long. The defeat of Semenov and the consolidation of the Bolshevik position in Transbaikal came at the same time as Moscow drove Wrangel into the sea. When Iurin took advantage of these victories to present his full set of credentials from the Bolshevik-backed governments of the Russian Far East, Yen told the American minister that the Chinese government would soon have to begin negotiations with Chita. "The very long common boundary, the absence of any means to protect the numerous unrepresented Chinese in Siberia and the need of commercial relations," he said "all made it imperative [that] something be determined upon." Without altering his basic policy, Yen had decided to move one step closer to the Bolsheviks. On 26 November he invited Iurin to his home for a private conversation. This emphasized the unofficial nature of the meeting but allowed Yen to inform Iurin that Peking was prepared to begin negotiations for the restoration of commercial relations.[68]

The Soviet envoy lost no time in submitting concrete proposals. On 30 November he sent Yen a declaration calling for the establishment of political and economic relations with China. It was based on the Soviet declarations of 25 July 1919 and 27 September 1920 but also dealt with the agreement just concluded between the Russo-Asiatic Bank and the Chinese government. Iurin said the pretensions of the bank were illegal and the agreement invalid. He declared that the question of the Chinese-Eastern Railway could only be settled through the negotiation of a Sino-Russian agreement.[69] This document went far beyond the framework suggested by Yen, and on 9 December he replied that the Chinese government were not yet ready to engage in political talks with the Far Eastern Republic. Peking would conduct commercial negotiations, but first the Russians had to promise to refrain from disseminating Bolshevik propaganda in China, compensate Chinese merchants for losses suffered as a result of the revolution, protect the lives and property of Chinese citizens living in Russia, and regulate past border incidents while avoiding others in the future. Such a limited agenda was disappointing, but Iurin did not wish to give Yen a pretext for breaking off the talks entirely. In accepting Yen's terms he added that all questions would have to be settled on the basis of strict reciprocity.[70]

Negotiations proceeded slowly. First the Wai-chiao Pu submitted claims which could not be resolved outside the context of a general settlement, and then simply refused to respond to repeated proposals that the two sides begin to examine the terms of a draft trade treaty. The Chinese would not move ahead of the western powers in negotiating with the Bolsheviks. The British minister reported in February 1921 that it was "unlikely that [China] will enter into serious negotiations until the anxiously awaited lead has been given her by one of the powers, or until her hand is forced by definite aggression on the part of Russia."[71]

Soviet Russia intended no aggression. China came under Russian attack but not from the Bolsheviks. Instead, one of the last remnants of Semenov's army, several thousand men led by Baron Roman Nikolaus von Ungern-Sternberg, fleeing from the People's Revolutionary Army, invaded Outer Mongolia in the fall of 1920. Ungern-Sternberg was seeking a base from which to continue the war against the Bolsheviks. China had only recently reasserted its sovereignty over this distant province and had been able to send only a small force to defend it. This garrison was strong enough to beat back the first attack which Ungern launched in October, but the Whites remained in the vicinity of Urga and were soon preparing for a further assault.[72]

The Soviet government viewed these developments with alarm. As the civil war came to an end, Moscow was determined to deny the territory of neighbouring states to the remnants of White armies as they were driven from Russia. Refuge was bad enough, but actual conquest, as seemed possible in Outer Mongolia, was far worse. When Chicherin learned of Ungern's presence in Mongolia, he wired Peking on 11 November describing the baron as a threat to both Soviet Russia and China and offering Soviet military aid "for the purpose of annihilating the White bands in Urga." Soviet troops would leave Mongolia as soon as Ungern was crushed.[73] Two weeks later, when informed that the Chinese had repulsed Ungern's forces, he sent congratulations to Peking but called on the Chinese to complete the liquidation of the White troops. He again offered Soviet assistance. Neither message reached Peking until mid-December, at which time Yen replied that China needed no assistance and warned that the movement of Soviet troops into Mongolia would violate Chinese sovereignty.[74] Nevertheless, Peking was made aware of the importance which Moscow attached to the elimination of Ungern's forces.

The situation was serious, for in reality the Chinese were unable to defend Outer Mongolia. The distance was too great, the terrain too difficult, and troops too few to reinforce the garrison at Urga. In February 1921 Ungern easily captured the city and installed a Mongolian government of his own choosing. Moscow renewed its offer of assistance, but China again refused.[75] The combination of Chinese impotence and unwillingness to accept help caused Moscow to alter its policy from cooperation with Peking to assistance for the Mongolian National

Party, a small group of Mongol intellectuals who had been in contact with the Bolsheviks since 1919. Moscow would clearly have preferred cooperation with Peking but was unable to ignore the danger posed by Ungern at Urga. Even so, the Bolsheviks hesitated to launch the type of military-revolutionary operation that they had conducted repeatedly across Eurasia in the previous three and a half years.[76] There were several reasons for this: Soviet military forces in the Far East remained small and scattered; the establishment of a Soviet-backed government in Mongolia would damage relations with China; and the reaction of the other powers, especially Japan, could not yet be calculated. Bolshevik policy was based essentially on their perception of the threat which Ungern posed to Soviet security. In the first months of 1921 that threat did not appear too great, but as Japanese hostility increased it began to take on a far different appearance. Rising tension between Japan and Soviet Russia served to paralyse China and compel the Bolsheviks to seek a favourable resolution of the Mongolian question.[77]

Japanese hostility also prevented China from conducting serious trade negotiations with the Far Eastern Republic. These had been delayed while China waited to see what action Britain would take. When London concluded a commercial pact with Moscow, the Bolsheviks hoped the Chinese would sign a similar agreement with Chita. Upon conclusion of the Anglo-Soviet treaty, the Far Eastern Republic issued an appeal to China for diplomatic recognition and negotiation of a trade treaty. Peking waited a month before acknowledging receipt of this message and then did so without comment. Iurin, however, was determined to force the issue and on 30 April, without waiting for a further response, presented the Wai-chiao Pu a draft trade treaty. Ten days later the Chinese responded that, although they sympathized with Chita's wish to restore diplomatic relations, they did not believe the time was ripe to do so. They said they wished to continue trade negotiations but made no reference to the Soviet proposal or any of their own. Prior to sending this note, Yen had consulted the allied ministers who unanimously advised him against any further development of relations with Chita. The Japanese had been the most emphatic, but even the British opposed this step, saying that none of the allied powers had recognized the Far Eastern Republic. The Chinese feared that Soviet-Japanese tension would lead to renewed hostilities, and, in that event, they wished to remain neutral. Given the strategic importance of the Chinese-Eastern Railway this would be difficult, if not impossible, and therefore they did not want to alienate the western powers at a time when they might urgently need their support against Japanese aggression in Manchuria.[78] Negotiations with the Bolsheviks would have to wait. The situation in China was so unpromising that in mid-May Iurin was recalled to Chita. Relations with China were not broken as he left his deputy in Peking, but the time had not yet come for fruitful negotiations. The complicated international situation in the Far East required further clarification before a Sino-Soviet settlement was possible.

THE BOLSHEVIK ACHIEVEMENT in Siberia and the Far East was quite substantial. In eighteen months they had defeated Kolchak and Semenov, regained almost all the territory previously held by the tsar, and organized it politically in a manner of their choosing. They certainly did not view the Far Eastern Republic as an ideal political structure, but it did correspond to the form of government which they then wanted in the Far East. Along the frontier of southern Siberia the Bolsheviks had concluded agreements with local authorities in Sinkiang and Uranchai, closing these territories to remnants of the White armies.[79] Further east, however, armed bands hostile to the Bolsheviks had taken refuge in Mongolia and near Vladivostok. Their elimination remained important items on the Bolshevik agenda. The achievement was far greater than could have been anticipated even as late as mid-1919. Earlier, the Bolsheviks would have settled for far less. The civil war might well have ended with the Whites in control of much of Siberia. This would have constituted a vast base from which Soviet Russia could have been attacked. Its elimination meant that European Russia could not easily be threatened from the Far East. The major centres of Bolshevik power and the economic raw materials on which they depended were, therefore, far more secure than if a hostile army held Siberia.

Bolshevik success was due not so much to the military superiority of the Red Army as to the political divisiveness and incapacity of their enemies. After smashing Kolchak's spring offensive in 1919 the Red Army ceased to attach a high priority to the eastern front. For the remainder of the civil war Lenin drew heavily on the military resources of the eastern front until it was nearly drained of men, equipment, and railway rolling stock. Even without a large army the Bolsheviks were able to establish and maintain their hold on most of the Russian Far East. Kolchak's regime was cordially hated and that of Semenov held in even lower esteem. They possessed no sanction other than force, and they were driven out at the first opportunity. Local Bolsheviks, speaking with the voice of the new all-Russian central authority, were able to organize the chaotic political situation left in the wake of the civil war. As elsewhere, the Bolsheviks were aided by their ability to forge temporary alliances with lesser enemies against major foes. At one time or another they were able to secure the cooperation of all their adversaries except Kolchak, Semenov, and the Japanese.

What role did the Far Eastern Republic play in the successful development of Soviet foreign policy? The idea of such a state originated with the Whites, was taken over by the Mensheviks and Socialist Revolutionaries, and was hated by most far eastern Bolsheviks. It came into its own when embraced by Lenin and Trotsky. The Soviet leadership found it attractive for exactly the same reason that far eastern Bolsheviks loathed it. It was a means of placing a certain political distance between Moscow and the Far East and institutionalizing the limitation of Bolshevik liabilities in the Far East. It served to reduce the political expectations of local Bolsheviks, provide a constant reminder of political realities, and erect an institutional barrier to the flow of men and material to the East.

The Far Eastern Republic was of less use internationally. No one was fooled by its thin bourgeois-democratic camouflage, and everyone was aware that first Verkhneudinsk and then Chita was a branch office of the Soviet government in Moscow. Lenin had hoped that foreign governments might find it easier to deal with a supposedly democratic, rather than openly soviet, regime, but this did not prove to be the case. The Chinese may have found it easier to receive Iurin as the representative of the Far Eastern Republic, rather than that of Moscow, but this cannot be established with any certainty. Ironically, the British were able to point to the "independence" of the Far Eastern Republic as sufficient reason for China not to recognize its government. The Far Eastern Republic might have attracted greater international interest if Moscow had not controlled it so closely, but the Soviet government was hardly interested in fostering a genuinely independent state. Their aim was to keep the Far East for Soviet Russia at the lowest possible cost.

The shadow of Japan fell darkly over the Russian Far East. Moscow never ceased to fear that Japan might embark on the conquest of the entire region. The Far Eastern Republic was created with such a possibility in mind. In a sense it defined what the Bolsheviks could surrender if necessary. They freely described the Vladivostok accord of April 1920 as a far-eastern Brest-Litovsk and, as in the case of the earlier agreement, they were well aware that they might have to surrender much more. This was why local Bolsheviks hated the Far Eastern Republic. It was a constant reminder that Soviet Russia might abandon them at any minute, and they could be forced underground to undergo another indeterminate period of savage struggle against a merciless foe. Time, however, was working for the Bolsheviks, and it soon became apparent that they would be able to hold most of the Far East. By early 1921 they had greatly strengthened their hold on the region; with the end of fighting in Europe they were in a position to strengthen it still further.

All the same, much remained to be done. In April 1921 the Japanese army remained in occupation of the southern Maritime Province and northern Sakhalin Island. The Japanese provided refuge for the last remnants of the White army, and Ungern Sternberg had seized Outer Mongolia. Although the consolidation of the Far Eastern Republic had been completed, it had not been recognized by any foreign power. Moreover, its boundaries remained unfixed; China would not establish regular relations and Japan adamantly refused to deal with it in any way. The entire picture appeared strikingly tentative, and the menace of renewed intervention hung heavily in the air. The Far East was the most threatened of all Soviet regions at the end of the civil war.

Conclusion

When the Tenth Congress of the Communist Party of Russia assembled in March 1921 the Soviet government was nearing completion of treaties effectively ending hostilities with Great Britain and Poland. In addition, Moscow had just or was about to sign agreements regularizing relations with Afghanistan, Persia, nationalist Turkey, and Germany. Peace had already been concluded with Finland, Estonia, Latvia, and Lithuania. In his opening address Lenin proudly proclaimed: "This is the first congress that is meeting without any hostile troops, supported by the capitalists and imperialists of the world, on the territory of the Soviet Republic."[1]

At one time the Bolsheviks had been driven back to a territory little larger than that of seventeenth-century Muscovy but had sprung back to reclaim virtually the entire empire of Nicholas II. The centre of the former empire had acted as a great magnet attracting all parts of the periphery, and economic necessity had proved to be a powerful force promoting the reassemblage of the dismembered state. The Bolsheviks had entrenched themselves in the economic fastness of old Muscovy, and their adversaries had been unable to root them out. Even when supplied from abroad, the periphery was an inadequate base from which to overwhelm the centre. Nor, in a short while, could it be geared to interact successfully with the outside world. The Ukraine, south Russia, and the Caucasus were glutted with grain and petroleum, commodities needed everywhere in Europe, but in the conditions of 1919 and 1920 they could not be transported to markets abroad. The several parts of the sundered economy could only rely on themselves. The unity of the prewar economy had been reinforced by the near autarchy imposed on Russia by the Great War and the civil conflict which followed. Wartime barriers and restrictions placed a hermetic seal on the economy, turning it ever inward to meet the insatiable demands of the Russian military. Although total production declined precipitously by 1919, the Red Army absorbed what was available. Once the Bolsheviks commanded a sufficient quantity of basic economic resources, they were able to break out of central Russia and follow the railways of the tsar to the former frontiers. The Whites were driven into exile never to return again.

The Bolsheviks could not have won the civil war with the lightly armed militia of 1917. The Red Guard was sufficient to withstand the initial armed challenge of Bolshevik adversaries, but the organization of White armies and the arrival of foreign troops in Russia required an equivalent force. This was the Red Army, which grew to more than two million men by the end of the civil war. But Bolshevik victory was not primarily military; it was profoundly political. The Soviet government acted decisively and effectively while their enemies, foreign and domestic, did not.

Their enemies were ineffective because they were badly divided and woefully misjudged the nature of the Russian civil war. The aspirations of the intervening powers clashed everywhere and served to hold each other in check. Two powers had the means to destroy the Bolsheviks – Germany in Europe and Japan in the Far East. Both would have been pleased to do so but were restrained by their primary adversaries, Germany by France and Japan by the United States. Neither would let their rival act freely (and thus grow stronger) in Russia, and both were ideally positioned to thwart their antagonists. France held the Ruhr hostage, and the United States had an equal grip on the Japanese economy. The rivalry between Britain and France was nearly as great, and both sought to prevent the other from securing an advantage anywhere. They could not cooperate in Russia, and "allied" policy there was a charade, a grotesque parody of the diplomatic art in which words were carefully chosen to shroud the nakedness of Anglo-French enmity.

During the critical year of 1919 it was of special importance that none of the intervening powers placed a solution of the Russian problem at the top of their political agenda. Russia, in fact, came nowhere near the top of anyone's agenda. The Japanese gazed greedily at China; the French and Germans warily circled one another; Woodrow Wilson pursued his League of Nations to the edge of the grave; and the British enlarged their empire and sought to resuscitate international trade. Even the Poles had other enemies to contend with before even reaching the territory in dispute with Russia. Moreover, Pilsudski hated the Whites even more than the Bolsheviks. The small nationalities originally feared the Bolsheviks more than the Whites, but soon discovered their error. In any case, they were too weak, divided, and bereft of foreign support to do much damage. By the end of the year Lloyd George had advised them to deal with Moscow. To be sure, Winston Churchill opposed this and every other concession to Moscow, and from beginning to end had wanted to mount a major military challenge to the Soviet government. His views were so extreme, however, that he could not secure the support of his colleagues, and they soon came to share the view of Lloyd George that the war secretary had "Bolshevism on the brain."

This relative indifference to the Bolsheviks was due not only to more pressing concerns but also to the deeply intrenched and widely held assumption that the life expectancy of the Soviet government was minimal. Bolshevism had not been expected to survive 1917, let alone a second year, and lengthy existence beyond the end of the Great War seemed entirely out of the question. Profound ignorance of Russian realities was widespread and actually deepened as a result of the severing of relations with the Bolsheviks. Foreign leaders forswore almost all first-hand knowledge of events in the heart of the former empire. This ignorance and belief in the ultimate victory of the Whites offered a certain degree of protection to the Bolsheviks. Until November 1919 it would have been difficult to find any foreign leader who believed the Bolsheviks would win the civil war. The only question was which White general would reach Moscow first. This by itself generated additional rivalry among the intervening powers, as each wished to back the winner and did not hesitate to cripple other candidates. Foreign leaders were shocked when they realized that the Soviet regime would survive indefinitely. Only Lloyd George had a real policy, and this helps to account for its success. It was difficult to oppose something with nothing, and that was about all his opponents had to offer. By early 1920 the intervening powers had few resources with which to continue armed intervention in Russia. Not only had their armies melted away, but most of their remaining military supplies had been scattered to diverse battlefields, many in fact in Russia. Allied weapons and military equipment had been delivered in large quantities to the Whites and, with their withdrawal from the field of battle, came into the hands of the Red Army. At the end of the civil war many Soviet troops were clothed in the best of British uniforms.

The Bolsheviks made the most of the time given them by their enemies. They were able to judge their strength, view their problems in perspective, plan realistically, set priorities, and maintain surprising flexibility in the pursuit of their aims. Much of their strength came from the ability to monopolize political power in Soviet Russia. By late 1919 membership in the Bolshevik Party had become a prerequisite for any kind of sustained political activity. Victory on the battlefield soon filled Bolshevik ranks and prompted many who had remained on the sidelines to rally to the party. Even before the Polish invasion, the Bolsheviks had become associated with a form of Russian nationalism, and their enemies were seen as somehow un-Russian and foreign. The Polish invasion completed this process, and not even the rising tide of peasant rebellion could reverse it. The importance of their political monopoly can be seen in the words of a Bolshevik representative identified only as M. Michalski, a "collaborator of Chicherin." In February 1921 he told a French agent in Berlin that the ardent hostility of the mass of Russian peasantry to the Soviet government was unimportant. The Bolsheviks would remain in power, because of the impossibility of other groups forming a government. "It is simple," he proclaimed: "Chaos exists. I do not deny it, but, in the midst of this chaos, only we are organized; the little which Russians get they receive from us."[2]

The Bolshevik political monopoly freed the Soviet government from serious criticism of their foreign policy. This allowed them to view their problems in a somewhat detached manner and make tactical sacrifices which other governments could not contemplate. Thus even such extortionate pacts as the treaty of Brest-Litovsk and its supplements were hailed as triumphs of Soviet foreign policy. And, viewed in the long run, they were, for they permitted the Bolsheviks to retain power in Russia. The alternative was destruction by the German army, and even a precarious survival was preferable. Although never forced to make such great sacrifices again, the Bolsheviks were always ready to yield territory to adversaries strong enough to take it. In the spring of 1919 they would gladly have settled with the allied powers on the basis of the terms negotiated with Bullitt. This would have left them only a small part of the former Russian empire and consigned the remainder to the clients of the allied powers. The terms were onerous but far preferable to waging a war they were uncertain of winning. As it turned out, the allies were unable to mount a full-scale attack, but in March 1919 the Bolsheviks did not know this. By contrast, at the end of the year they knew only too well that Pilsudski was eager and ready to attack. This sharpened their already keen desire to negotiate peace with their neighbours and caused them to offer Poland very generous frontiers. Not generous enough, however, to satisfy the marshal who, at this time, was unprepared to settle for anything less than the creation of a Polish client state in Ukraine. Another year of fighting was required before the Bolsheviks were able to bring the war with Poland to a close. Peace was then concluded on the basis of a frontier which, while still generous, was actually less favourable to Poland than that offered, without further fighting, in 1919. The same considerations governed Soviet policy in eastern Siberia, where the desire to avoid war with Japan led the Bolsheviks to establish the Far Eastern Republic. Although they actually controlled this theoretically independent state, its very existence indicated a probable willingness to surrender it to Japan if the island empire escaped the restraint of the United States.

All this speaks to the larger question of setting priorities, something which the Bolsheviks did so much better than their adversaries. Bolshevik priorities were defined in terms of economic resources. These were located along a line drawn from Petrograd through Moscow to Baku, and included the agricultural and mineral resources of Ukraine, the bread-basket of western Siberia, and the petroleum and mineral deposits of the Caucasus. All else and much of these could be and were sacrificed at one time or another to the simple necessity of holding power in the centre of Russia. Finland, the Baltic provinces, Belorussia, Poland, western Ukraine, the Crimea, central Asia, and the bulk of Siberia could all be left on the side while the Communist Party and Red Army did battle in the economically vital portions of the former empire. The Whites simply could not do this. They inscribed "Great Russia, one and indivisible" on their banners and meant it. They bridled over the smallest territory. They would not recognize the independence of Finland and the Baltic states; they would not negotiate with Pilsudski; they refused to cooperate with the independent states of the Caucasus.

Kolchak fought with the Czechs, Denikin with the Cossacks. Yudenich wished to arrest the nationalist governments of Finland and the Baltic states. All antagonized the only allies they had. In September 1920, when the handwriting was already on the wall, Wrangel refused to accept Pilsudski's terms for continuing the war against the Bolsheviks. The marshal had demanded a free hand in Ukraine, and although Wrangel had no hope of establishing himself there in the near future, he still would not satisfy Pilsudski. It should be noted that the French also spurned the proposal. They hoped to dominate Ukraine following a White victory and were unwilling to allow such an unpredictable figure as Pilsudski to get there first. Better it be left to the Bolsheviks from whom it could be more easily retrieved than from Poland. As Wrangel was the creature of France and could not exist without its assistance, he had no choice but to refuse the offer. Thus there was nothing for Pilsudski to do but to seek the best possible terms from the Bolsheviks who, as always, were eager to bargain for their own advantage. Small wonder that the Bolsheviks prevailed.

Brutal realism was a major feature of Bolshevik policy. Its practice had allowed the Soviet government to survive 1918, and it continued in the following years. In the interview noted above, Michalski declared that the Soviet government was "the most realist in the world." "We are able to adopt ourselves to all circumstances ... ," he said, "we are capable of assimilating perfectly all policies." A few weeks later Krasin said much the same thing, telling a different French representative that Soviet policy had already evolved a great deal. "A year ago I was able to make Lenin and Trotsky understand arguments to which they would have remained deaf, two years before. And I have just made them admit some considerations that only a year before they would have rejected with indignation."[3] Litvinov put it most succinctly when he told a British representative that the Bolsheviks "now realized that the world revolution was not coming off."[4] Chicherin, however, was closest to the mark when he told a Finnish representative in January 1921: "We have just concluded the first part of our action, the politico-military period; now the economic and social phase is going to begin, that is to say that we are going to attempt to adopt our communist principles to the material necessities of the life of a great people."[5]

This realism gave enormous flexibility to Soviet diplomacy. Michalski was right to emphasize the Bolshevik ability to assimilate other policies, because they excelled in identifying common interests with even their worst enemies. The Germans in 1918, Pilsudski in 1919, Lloyd George in 1920, and Kemal Ataturk in 1921 all attest to this ability. Open alliances were not possible, but de facto parallel actions (as Chicherin had described it to a surprised Helfferich in August 1918)[6] took their place. Moscow was nearly always ready to open negotiations with anyone. Negotiations might not initially succeed, but Moscow was determined to inform the world that it would rather bargain than fight. As a matter of policy the Bolsheviks would deluge their adversaries with peace proposals. Moscow's enemies found it difficult to frustrate the importunate Soviet willingness to open negotiations. Krasin's pursuit of French representatives into London's exclusive British Empire Club and the attempt to confront Millerand at Lympne testify to this difficulty. Moreover, when negotiations did begin, the Bolsheviks had a great deal to offer. To achieve their primary objectives of peace, regularization of relations, and opening of commerce they were prepared to offer a great deal. Russia was vast and its resources almost unlimited; the Bolsheviks could afford to be generous. Only the most determined opponents, motivated by deep-seated grievances and/or exaggerated fear of communist ideology, were able to refuse the Bolshevik call for a negotiated settlement of differences. By the spring of 1921 the Bolsheviks had secured their frontiers and established acceptable (if not wholly satisfactory) relations with their neighbours and two of the great powers in Europe. Soviet Russia had not risen into their ranks but it had emerged from the chaos of the Great War and its aftermath as the single greatest power in eastern Europe. It had, in Lenin's words, won "the right to an independent existence."

This was a wholly unexpected conclusion to the events of the previous three and a half years. Neither the Bolsheviks nor their enemies had anticipated such a possibility. As sincerely as the Bolsheviks celebrated the winning of the right to an independent existence, it had not been their initial aim. Far from it; in October 1917 they had believed that in taking power in Russia they were igniting the world workers' revolution and initiating a process which would not only eliminate the independence of all states but those very states themselves. "Proletarians of the world unite!" was an affirmation of internationalism and the interdependence of all peoples, not a call for the independent existence of a single, even Soviet, state. When their revolution did not ignite others and the Bolsheviks found themselves isolated in Russia, they altered their policy to one of survival until, in their words, "other revolutionary contingents [German, French, British] came up to them." Those contingents never arrived, and as late as November 1918 few Bolsheviks believed their regime could survive the failure of revolution to develop in the West. Lenin himself had affirmed at the end of the Great War that "world capital itself is now coming for us." In fact it was, but not as a single Beelzebub but as a pack of ravenous dogs each eager to carry off its share of the prey, and thus subject to being driven off separately with even the limited resources at the disposal of the Bolsheviks.

The possibility that the Bolsheviks might survive the western assault and yet remain isolated in Russia emerged only slowly. It took shape from the almost imperceptible restoration of peace in eastern Europe. Peace did not come easily because, unlike the West, there were no identifiable winners. Instead the sudden collapse of German power created chaos. Germany could no longer dominate the region but neither could the western powers, who proved unable to occupy the region militarily. As only insignificant allied forces arrived to replace the Germans, a kind of power vacuum came into existence. From the start, the Bolsheviks as heirs to the tsars and the strongest of the former German clients were major contenders, but they were soon joined by the Russian Whites, as well as the major centres of national authority (in particular Poland) which emerged in the wake of the German withdrawal. Eastern Europe was at its most plastic in December 1918, but after that the plasticity of the region diminished with each passing month. First it became unmalleable for the western powers, and then to the local centres of power which soon discovered that they could only change the emerging status quo marginally. They were able to consolidate power locally and prevent the intrusion of their territory by hostile forces, but they could not effect significant territorial or systemic changes beyond the areas of their primary authority.

The reciprocal and progressive inability to effect significant change was shown in the Soviet-Polish conflict. By late 1919 neither Moscow nor Warsaw were able to alter the strategic status quo. Pilsudski could not impose his will beyond the western fringes of the former tsarist marchlands, and the Bolsheviks were unable to impose their classic form of sovietization upon ethnic Poland. This was first recognized by the Bolsheviks, who hastened to negotiate a compromise with Pilsudski. When this was rejected and another year's fighting resulted, the stalemate became even clearer. Although Pilsudski was able to march hundreds of kilometres beyond the Polish ethnographic frontier, he could not shake the Soviet hold on Ukraine and overturn the strategic advantage enjoyed by the Bolsheviks. In March 1921 he had to make peace with Lenin on less advantageous terms than those offered him in late 1919.

Stasis in eastern Europe could have been overcome through Soviet-German cooperation, but this was prevented by the western powers. Although the allies were unable to bring their power to bear in eastern Europe, they were able to threaten decisive action against Germany in the west. Any attempt by Berlin to join Moscow in a fourth partition of Poland had to reckon with such a possibility. This accounts for the extreme caution displayed by the Reich in August 1920. Berlin had no choice but to allow Moscow to take the lead in destroying Poland, and it is impossible to say what France would have done if Germany and Soviet Russia had been able to carry their plan to completion. Instead, what followed was a revalidation of Versailles Poland, but no one, least of all Berlin and Moscow, lost sight of the potential of the Soviet-German combination for wreaking havoc in eastern Europe. European generals and politicians would spend the next generation contemplating just that potential.

If the ultimate fate of eastern Europe still hung in the balance, there was nothing inconclusive about the outcome of the Russian civil war. It had been long and destructive, but there was no question of who had won. The Whites had not simply been defeated, they had been killed, captured, or driven into exile. As a result of the Polish war many had even rallied to the Bolsheviks. Foreign support for the Whites, while prolonging the war, had also compromised them in the eyes of Russian public opinion. The Bolsheviks, past masters of sophisticated propaganda, were easily able to discredit their adversaries as the paid agents of foreign powers wickedly determined to cripple Russia. *Soviet* Russia to be sure, but Russia all the same. The battlefield had spoken. The Soviet government was free to speak in the name of Russia and most of its former empire.

This was surely not predetermined. The civil war could well have ended in 1919 without such a decisive result. The Far East with its multiple Russian regimes, phantom bourgeois-democratic republic, and ever-present fear of resumed hostilities suggests what might well have happened if the western powers had pursued intervention in European Russia in the manner which Japan did in Siberia. Had the British been able to leave a large force at Novorossiisk or the French an army at Sevastopol, it seems unlikely that the Bolsheviks would have chosen to confront them directly. Instead they would probably have sought to evict the British and French in the same way as they chose to drive the Japanese from the Maritime Province. It would probably have resembled a chess game, a series of indirect confrontations more political than military, with the interventionists being forced back towards the sea and "bourgeois-democratic" (but Bolshevik-controlled) regimes established to separate the Red Army from the main bodies of foreign troops. This could have continued for a longer or shorter period of time depending on the relative strength of the antagonists. In that event, Russia might have degenerated into something resembling warlord China, with large foreign enclaves and multiple centres of Russian authority. This did not happen because western intervention was never pursued with sufficient skill and vigour to produce such results and the Bolsheviks proved adept in sovietizing all territory (save ethnic Poland) which came into their hands.

Soviet Russia therefore survived into the postwar world, and Bolshevik policy imperceptibly changed from simple (almost day-to-day) assurance of that survival to one of consolidation – the uniting and strengthening of the territories subject to Moscow's control. Although Bolshevik spokesmen continued to mouth the rhetoric of 1917–18, there was no return to a genuinely revolutionary foreign policy. Foreign revolutionaries arrived in Moscow as Islamic pilgrims to Mecca and received encouragement and even some material assistance, but at no time did the Soviet state or Commmunist Party invest large sums or great hopes in their imminent success. Still less did they pursue policies posited on the widespread advance of the communist revolution. Far from it, they sought exactly the opposite, to build barriers between themselves and the outside world, to create defensible frontiers behind which the Soviet order could be nurtured.

Where were these frontiers to be placed, or put differently, what was to be consolidated? Not surprisingly, this question had no fixed answer but evolved with the international circumstances of Soviet Russia. August 1918 had marked the maximum compression of the Soviet state, but the question of what represented an absolute minimum of territory was never posed and the improved international environment of late 1918 spared the Bolsheviks from having to answer it. Certainly by the arrival of the Bullitt mission in Moscow the Soviets felt they had made sufficient gains to agree in principle to a cessation of hostilities. This was not feigned; the Bolsheviks would have been delighted to suspend military hostilities while being free to continue political warfare. The Whites realized their peril and refused to cooperate. Kolchak, Denikin, and Yudenich each made his separate bid for power and failed. This was the decisive moment in the civil war and, as victors, the Bolsheviks were more than ready to open negotiations with anyone ready to acknowledge their authority in Russia. A settlement at this point would have left Ukraine to Moscow but most of the borderlands beyond Soviet control. Lloyd George was eager to negotiate on this basis, but other western leaders were not.

The civil war continued, and the Bolsheviks benefited enormously. Against negligible resistance they invaded Azerbaidzhan and took the oilfields of Baku. There Lenin called a halt to the advance of the Red Army and again sought to open negotiations with the western powers. Neither France nor Pilsudski agreed. Nor did borderland Bolsheviks. The latter wanted no part of treaties based on the *uti possidetis* of April 1920. Such agreements would have denied them the protection of Soviet Russia. What resulted was a brutal dialectic between the central authorities and borderland Bolsheviks. The latter had before them the terrifying spectre of the Baltic Bolsheviks, who had already been sacrificed on the altar of the international well-being of Soviet Russia. Men of the stamp of Ordzhonikidze and Stalin would not tolerate being treated in this manner and used their high office in party and state to lever their homelands under the Soviet umbrella.

Poland was a special case. It was part of the process described above but, at the same time, much more. Originally Bolshevik policy towards Poland was little different from that pursued in relation to the other western borderlands. Throughout 1919, in fact, Moscow would have been delighted to acknowledge Poland's independence within its ethnographic frontiers (and a great deal more) in exchange for peace. This was especially true early in the year when it appeared as if Polish independence might form part of a larger peace package to be purchased from the allies. When this failed, Moscow opened direct (but secret and unofficial) negotiations with Pilsudski. The result was a bizarre agreement which allowed Pilsudski to take what he wanted in Belorussia and Ukraine in exchange for de facto parallel action against Denikin. Moscow hoped the agreement would lead to an eventual settlement with Poland. Unlike other areas of the former Russian empire, there was no large number of Bolsheviks in Poland summoning the Red Army to their rescue. Prior to Pilsudski's eastern campaign in the spring of 1920, therefore, there was little agitation for Soviet Russia to attempt to sovietize Poland. Many Polish Bolsheviks, Karl Radek for example, were entirely opposed to such an effort, knowing the nationalist outburst which was likely to follow. Denikin's defeat and Poland's refusal to make peace confronted Moscow with Pilsudski's actual challenge, a bid for hegemony in the borderlands. Russia without Ukraine could never regain its great power status (or even that of a major power), so the Bolsheviks had to fight.

War followed, and when Pilsudski failed to achieve his objectives the Bol-sheviks were free to re-examine their own priorities. Those who wished to adopt more ambitious aims were greatly aided by Pilsudski who, during the long march back to Warsaw, repeatedly refused to open peace negotiations. Still, the Bol-shevik decision to invade ethnographic Poland was not based on Polish intran-sigence. The very idea of allowing their enemies to force decision on them in this way was anathema to the Bolsheviks. The Politburo could have selected a convenient military frontier and ordered the Red Army to stop there. They did not, because they had rethought their entire foreign policy. In doing so, they did not consider a return to the revolutionary goals of 1917-18. Lenin knew full well that the halcyon days of the great "field revolution" were gone for good. Instead, the Politburo elaborated on their existing policy of consolidation. The question of what was to be consolidated was again posed and more ambitious answers were given. In 1919, and even early 1920, there had been no question of seeking major power status for Soviet Russia or posing more than a distant threat to the Versailles settlement. In the summer of 1920 the Soviet government took dead aim at both objectives. The liquidation of an independent Poland and the arrival of the Red Army on the frontiers of Germany would restore Russia as the single major power in eastern Europe and bring Versailles crashing to the ground. The order to cross the ethnographic frontier of Poland, therefore, was a summons to all those who hated Versailles to join Soviet Russia in its revision. This was not a revolutionary crusade but an exercise in armed revision of the still fluid status quo.

The historian will look in vain for a single document formulating the aims of the campaign in Poland. It may never have existed, as Soviet objectives remained largely in the hypothetical world of contingency. Still, the initial parts of the strategy emerge clearly from the myriad of documents generated in the tumul-tuous summer of 1920. There is no mystery about the first step, the frequently voiced determination to smash Pilsudski and install a Soviet government in Warsaw. Nor is the next step unclear. The arrival of Dzerzhinskii at the Belvedere was to be paralleled by the conclusion of a preliminary Soviet-German political pact of the nature outlined by Kopp and Chicherin in July and August. Soviet Poland was then to invite Germany to negotiate a revision of their common frontier. The Reich would regain the ethnically German territories lost to Poland at Versailles. This would be followed by the opening of talks to settle remaining Soviet-German political and economic differences. Lenin and Chicherin believed these agreements would improve the Soviet bargaining position in London. They wanted much more than the anemic trade treaty offered by Britain and hoped to obtain the necessary leverage in Berlin to force Lloyd George to conclude a full-blooded political agreement. As can be seen from Krasin's attempt to open negotiations with the French in early August, however, Moscow's ambitions reached to the Seine itself. Lenin and Chicherin hoped that the creation of a Soviet Poland, followed closely by the conclusion of political accords with Berlin and London, would force the French, if only to escape political isolation, to open negotiations with Soviet Russia. The financial inducements offered by Krasin were designed to loosen French lips and hasten the process of settling with Paris. Had the Bolsheviks achieved those aims they would have been well on their way to restoring Russia as a major power in Europe.

But what then? Can Soviet aims following the success sketched above be ascertained? They can in part, because they would have followed naturally from Moscow having regained its freedom of political action. For the other powers the most effective way of dealing with the explosive force let loose in eastern Europe would have been an international conference to regulate the affairs of the region. This was the course followed in 1922 when nationalist Turkey ripped up the treaty of Sèvres, and certainly would have been the choice of Lloyd George had Moscow succeeded in destroying Pilsudski's Poland. France would have opposed such a conference, but with Britain unwilling to fight to restore the former order in eastern Europe and nothing to bar Soviet-German cooperation, Paris may have had little choice. Moscow would certainly have agreed. Chicherin had repeatedly hinted at such a conference, and in the far more constrained circumstances of early 1922 Moscow was pleased to accept an invitation to the Genoa conference. If the Soviet objectives of August 1920 had been realized there is no reason such a conference could not have been held a year earlier, with Moscow enjoying a far greater status and, consequently, having a more ambitious agenda at hand. Much would have depended on how great a change had occurred as a result of the fall of Poland and the political agreements which followed. If Moscow had succeeded in reaching a preliminary accord with France, the conference might well have focused primarily on issues of European economic reconstruction. Had Moscow failed, as was probable, lengthy political hostilities were likely.

Political skirmishing in the wake of the fall of Poland would have been deeply marked by the Anglo-French split so clearly visible in early August. If Lloyd George had remained as prime minister and Millerand had not altered his fundamental policies, the earlier split might well have widened and served to promote an Anglo-Italian-German rapprochement. In late August Lloyd George, Giolitti, and Simons were all in Switzerland and, in the context of a Soviet triumph in Poland, it does not take much imagination to see them coming together to decide how best to deal with the new political circumstances in eastern Europe. The process might have begun with Lloyd George and Giolitti issuing an urgent appeal to Millerand and Simons to join them at Lucerne to formulate a "European" policy to deal with the crisis. To avoid isolation Millerand might have agreed, but had he refused, the remaining three, in the name of sparing European civilization from further ruin and devastation, could conceivably have invited Lenin to meet with them to seek ways of keeping the peace. At such a conference the Soviet delegation (led either by Lenin or Chicherin) would have sought much of what they did at Genoa eighteen months later with the subsequent "Rapallo formula" (de jure recognition and reciprocal cancellation of claims) as their primary objective. Moscow would also have wanted to free Germany from most of the restraints placed on it at Versailles. Most, but certainly not all, as with the liquidation of Pilsudski's regime and the creation of Soviet Poland, Moscow had little reason to want unlimited German rearmament. In fact, as Litvinov and Krasin had repeatedly told French representatives, Paris and Moscow had a common interest in restraining German militarism. How better to do this, in the context of treaty revision, than to have the other powers build their armed forces down to the German limit rather than vice versa. Chicherin's views on Japan, expressed to Kamenev in late August, suggest another aim of Soviet diplomacy at such a conference. Moscow had long contended that the western powers were in part responsible for Japanese aggression in Siberia and, in the context of treaty revision, would have wanted their assistance in expelling Japan from the Maritime Province, Manchuria, and Transbaikal. It is likely that Moscow would have been willing to offer some kind of compensation for this assistance, such as economic concessions in Siberia for Japan, recognition of Romanian sovereignty in Bessarabia and, perhaps most attractive, Soviet mediation of western differences with nationalist Turkey.

Some such arrangement would have been more stable than the Versailles settlement but would still have been marred by serious flaws. Treaty revision would not have been gladly accepted by France, and the attempt to force it might well have advanced the date of the French invasion of the Ruhr by two years. But would the French have attacked Germany in the teeth of British hostility and without a sympathetic Poland in the east? Would Paris have wanted to drive Berlin even further into the arms of Soviet Russia? Such questions cannot be answered, but they point to a still more serious flaw in treaty revision of the type outlined above. Would not a spectacular revision of this nature simply have whetted the already ravenous appetite of German chauvinists for still further change? If the Reich had escaped Versailles to this degree, why accept any restraint? The answer, of course, was to keep British and Soviet goodwill and not to do the work of the French for them, but that would hardly satisfy the right wing of German politics. The German and French flaws, however, were only part of the problem. There was also the Polish dimension. A Soviet regime in Warsaw might temporarily drive Polish nationalism underground, but would it stay there for long? Not likely. Here indeed was the Achilles heel of Soviet aspirations, because even Felix Dzerzhinskii would have found it difficult to hold power for long in a thoroughly enflamed Poland. Nor would other powers be long in seeking to exploit the boundless fury of enraged Polish nationalism. Obviously Paris, unless satisfied by some far-reaching settlement with Moscow, would have sought to set Poland alight. But within a very short time Germany could well have come to pose the greatest danger to a Soviet Poland. Although benefiting initially from Dzerzhinskii's regime, Berlin might soon have wanted still more from Poland. The Reich would have been the natural refuge for the most conservative Polish nationalists, who would have cooperated with anyone willing to assist them against the Bolsheviks. German revanchism could easily have come to focus on a further and more favourable partition of Poland. The inescapable truth was that Moscow was badly overextended. Nineteen twenty was not 1945 (or even 1939), and Soviet Russia simply could not have met a serious German challenge in Poland. At what point would Germany have sought revision? Would France have been prepared to help Russia? Or would Paris have sought to further its objectives by backing its own Polish clients based, perhaps, in Czechoslovakia and Romania? The grotesque possibilities that loom from these scenarios suggest that Pilsudski did the Bolsheviks a favour in driving them out of Poland in 1920.

In the long run Soviet Russia probably benefited from a territorial settlement which so accurately reflected the realities of power at that time. The existence of a Soviet Poland that could neither be sustained from within nor defended from external aggression would have been an enormous source of weakness, seriously endangering the internal stability and international security of Soviet Russia. Its inclusion in the Soviet Union at the time of its formation in 1922 would have been a tragedy.

An absolutely arresting feature of the far-reaching plans of the summer of 1920 was the breath-taking rapidity with which they were abandoned. It was done so quickly (three days after the débâcle on the Vistula) that it suggests that Politburo criticism of the Polish strategy had been intense and the alternative adopted on 19 August had been worked out well in advance of the actual defeat. It may be that Lenin had been able to convince his colleagues that in the circumstances of the summer of 1920 (the Anglo-French split, American withdrawal from Europe, and partial German disarmament) it was reasonably safe to seek maximum gains from the apparent victory over Poland. He may have presented them with one of his either/or hypotheses. Either Pilsudski's Poland would disappear under the hammer blows of the Red Army, he could have argued, or it would survive but because of the terrible exhaustion of several years of war be unable to do more than win back the territory lost since May. Any agreement made in the summer could also be concluded in the fall. To be sure it was a gamble, but one which Lenin gladly took. In late August it no longer looked like such a good idea, and Soviet diplomacy had to scramble to cope with the wreckage left in its wake. It took until November to clear away the debris and only then could progress be resumed towards the achievement of the earlier (now reinstated) priorities of Soviet foreign policy. These were finally achieved in the spring of 1921.

The trade agreements with Britain and Germany and the peace treaty with Poland each represented a major achievement, but the accomplishment as a whole was far greater than the sum of its parts. Only the treaty with Poland formally established peace, but the two trade agreements confirmed that armed hostilities, which had sputtered out over the previous two years, would not be resumed. The importance of this accomplishment arose from the threat these three states posed to Soviet Russia. Poland because of its size and propinquity, Germany because of its enormous military potential, and Great Britain because of its financial resources and vast political influence were all in a position to do great damage to Soviet Russia. Soviet security had increased as each of these adversaries left the field of battle, and the three agreements of the spring of 1921, taken together, made it unlikely that any would return in the near future. The treaties further enhanced Moscow's security by limiting, in varying degrees, the opportunity of White emigrés to utilize the territory of the three states to conduct operations hostile to Soviet Russia.

The three treaties also opened opportunities for the future. The treaty of Riga permitted Soviet Russia to demobilize the Red Army and concentrate scarce manpower and resources on economic reconstruction. The trade agreements with Britain and Germany allowed Moscow to re-enter the international marketplace. They also greatly simplified the task of concluding further trade agreements with other countries. In addition, the agreement with Germany held out the tantalizing possibility of developing a broadly based cooperation capable of further dividing the capitalist states.

The treaty with Poland possessed special symbolic significance. It completed the conclusion of peace with the five states that had arisen in the western borderlands. The process had begun with Estonia in 1919 and had been achieved entirely by Soviet diplomacy without external mediation and in the teeth of unrelenting French opposition. At Versailles the allied powers had redrawn the map of Europe; Soviet Russia had proved capable of negotiating the placement of almost the entire length of its European frontier. The one exception was the frontier with Romania, and Moscow had pointedly refused to recognize the allied right to dispose of Bessarabia. This refusal, and the successful negotiation of the remainder of its European frontier, marked the first steps in the re-emergence of Russia as a great power.

The success of early 1921 had its price, and this was paid primarily in terms of limiting Soviet ability to promote revolution abroad. In return for promises not to allow their territory to be used to attack Soviet Russia, Poland, Germany, and Great Britain required Moscow to pledge that Soviet territory would not be used for activities hostile to them. This certainly did not prevent such action, but it was bound to limit it seriously. To the extent that the Bolsheviks valued the benefits derived from the treaties, they would have to honour the non-intervention clauses contained in them. A further step back from the heady revolutionary days of 1917 had been taken. Given the hard-won nature of what had been gained over the previous years, caution was likely, at least in the immediate future.

The three sets of negotiations had been parts of a single process. The German agreement was dependent on the prior conclusion of the Anglo-Soviet treaty, which in turn was greatly facilitated by the conclusion of the preliminary peace of Riga in October 1920. The latter had demonstrated the Soviet desire for peace and willingness to abstain from armed force as a means of overturning the Versailles settlement. This, and Soviet acknowledgment of Britain's special interests in the Baltic and Asia, contributed substantially to London's de facto recognition of the Soviet government. The British treaty had a reciprocal impact upon the final Polish negotiations as, once it was clear that London would reach agreement with Moscow, the Poles did not want to remain in a state of war with Soviet Russia.

This international success was all the greater when viewed in the context of the enormous internal problems confronting the Soviet government in early 1921. Transport had virtually ceased to function, the economy was near collapse, and the countryside was torn by peasant rebellion. In these terms, Soviet Russia was weaker than at any time since the early fall of 1918. Why then did Poland, Germany, and Great Britain come to terms with Moscow? The Poles did so because they were just as weak as the Bolsheviks. Only substantial foreign assistance would have allowed them to continue the war against Soviet Russia, and in 1921 no major power, even France, was willing to provide it. The Germans clearly acted in reaction to allied sanctions. Although the commercial benefits of the Soviet trade agreement appeared doubtful, Berlin had little to lose from a restoration of relations with Moscow. For their part the British, especially Lloyd George, did not want eastern Europe plunged into total chaos. They sought to promote the pacification of the continent as a whole and this required as much stability in eastern Europe as circumstances would allow. Provided that the Bolsheviks would contribute to this stability, as seemed the case in early 1921, Lloyd George was prepared to deal with them. In an odd way this illustrates the degree to which Soviet Russia had become a part of the status quo and had begun to benefit from it.

The Soviet diplomatic achievement was not unblemished. Neither Romania nor France, despite Soviet urging, had come to terms. Worse still, the United States remained hostile to any settlement and, in the Far East, Japan grew more recalcitrant with every passing day. The Romanians, because of their own weakness and vulnerable frontiers, had to feign interest in negotiation but were determined not to restore relations with Soviet Russia. The French and Americans, far distant and secure, could afford to be brutal in their refusal to negotiate. But none were likely to attack Soviet Russia. The Romanians had no such inclination, and, in any case, could not act without foreign assistance. The French would have liked to continue armed hostilities but did not have the means to do so. As the Americans had largely withdrawn from European affairs, they posed little threat to Soviet security. The immediate danger appeared greatest in the Far East. The Japanese army remained entrenched in the Maritime Province and did not seem likely to be dislodged in the near future. The very existence of the Far Eastern Republic was threatened, and there was little Moscow could do about it.

Failure to reach agreement with Romania, France, the United States, and Japan was disturbing to Moscow but, with the exception of the Far East, tolerable. On balance, the achievements of 1921 were far more significant. They marked that which could be obtained from military victory in the civil war and the patient pursuit of realizable objectives. Future success would depend on what the Bolsheviks could do to heal the wounds of the civil war and revitalize the Soviet economy.

Abbreviations

RUSSIAN SOURCES

BSV-Bel   Institut istorii partii pri TsK KPB, *Bor'ba za Sovetskuiu Vlast' v Belorussii, 1918–1920gg. Sbornik Dokumentov i Materialov*

BZPSVA   Institut Istorii Partii pri TsK KP Azerbaidzhana, *Bor'ba za pobedu Sovetskoi vlasti v Azerbaidzhane, 1918–1920:* Dokumenty i Materialy

BZPSVG   Akademiia Nauk Gruzinskoi SSR, *Bor'ba za Pobedu Sovetskoi vlasti v Gruzzi. Dokumenty i Materialy (1917–1921gg)*

BZUiUSVD   Institut Istorii, *Bor'ba za ustanovlenie i Uprochenie Sovetskoi Vlasti v Dagestane 1917–1921gg. Sbornik dokumentov i materialov*

BZVSVPRi   Arkhivnyi otdel Upravleniia MVD, *Bor'ba za vlast' sovetov v Primor'e (1917–1922 gg). Sbornik Dokumentov*

CW   Lenin, *Collected Works*

DGKKA   Glavnoe arkhivnoe upravenie pri sovete ministrov SSSR, *Direktivy Glavnogo Komandovaniia Krasno Armii (1917–1920). Sbornik Dokumentov*

DiM SCh   Akademiia nauk SSSR, *Dokumenty i Materialy po istorii sovetsko-chekhoslovatskikh otnoshenii*

DiM SPO   Akademiia Nauk SSSR, *Dokumenty i Materialy po istorii sovetskogo Pol'skikh Otnoshenii*

DKFKA   Glavnoe arkhivnoe upravlenie pri sovete ministrov SSSR, *Direktivy Kommandovaniia Frontov Krasnoi Armii (1917–1920 gg.) Sbornik Dokumentov*

DVP   Ministerstvo inostranykh del SSSR, *Dokumenty vneshnei politiki SSSR*

GVU   Arkhivnoe upravlenie pri sovete ministrov UkSSR, *Grazhdanskaia voina na Ukraine*

IIGVII   Akadmiia Nauk SSSR, *Iz istorii grazhdanskoi voiny i interventsii 1917–1922 gg. Sbornik statei*

IIGV	Institut Marksizma-Leninizma pri TsK KPSS, *Iz Istorii grazhdanskoi voiny v SSSR: 1917–1922: Sbornik dokumentov i materialov*
IVIiGVUSAIK	Arkhivnye upravleniia pri sovete ministerov i TsGA Kazakhskoi, *Inostranniai voennaia interventsiia i grazhdanskaia voina v Srednei Azii i Kazakhstane*
KVR	Trotsky, *Kat Vooruzhulas' Revoliu*
PSS	Lenin, *Polnoe Sobranie Sochinenii*
PS TsK	Institut Marksizma-Leninizma pri TsK KPSS, *Perepiska Sekretariata TsK RKP(b): Sbornik dokumentov*
PSVUZ	Akademiia Nauk Azerbaidzhanskoi SSR, *Pobeda Sovetskoi vlasti v Zakavkaz'e*
SGO	Ministertvo inostrannykh del SSSR, *Sovetsko-Germanskie Otnosheniia. Sbornik dokumenty*

BRITISH SOURCES

DBFP	Woodward and Butler, *Documents on British Foreign Policy*
FO	Foreign Office Papers

FRENCH SOURCES

MAE	Ministère des Affaires étrangères Archives

GERMAN SOURCES

ADaP	Bundesrepublik Deutschland, *Akten zur deutschen auswartigen Politik, 1918–1945*
ARK	Archiv des Reichskanzlei [Archive of the Reichs Chancellory]
DSB	Ministerium fur Auswartige Angelegenheiten der DDR, *Deutsche-Sowjetische Beziehungen von den Verhandlungen in Brest-Litowsk*
PAAA	Politisches Archiv des Auswärtigen Amtes
RFDOH	*Die Rückführung des Ostheeres*

ITALIAN SOURCES

IDDI	Ministero degli Affari Esteri, *I documenti diplomatici italiani*

UNITED STATES SOURCES

FRUS	United States, Department of State, *Foreign Relations of the United States, 1918, Supplement I*

Notes

PREFACE

1 Zarnitskii and Sergeev, *Chicherin*, 120.
2 Lenin, *CW*, 31:411–12.
3 Ibid., 441.

1. INTRODUCTION

1 For the transformation of the party, state, and army, see: Service, *The Bolshevik Party in Revolution;* Rigby, *Lenin's Government*; and Kliatskin, *Na zashchite Oktiabria.*
2 Harding, *Lenin's Political Thought, Vol. 2: Theory and Practice in the Socialist Revolution.*
3 Debo, *Revolution and Survival*; 381–2.
4 PRO FO371/3344/184126/ Cecil Minute, 6 November 1918.
5 "Sur l'action qu'il convient d'exercer en Russie," 10 décembre 1918, MAE/Russie/219/63–7.
6 "Les conséquences de l'ouverture des détroits pout la solution du probléme russe," 18 octobre 1918, MAE/Russie/208/187–190.
7 CAB 24/68/GT. 6100, "The Growing Danger of Bolshevism in Russia."
8 Mayer, *Politics and Diplomacy of Peacemaking*; 94–5.
9 See Kennan, *Soviet-American Relations, 1917–1920; Vol. 2: The Decision to Intervene*; and Maddox, *The Unknown War with Russia.*
10 CAB 24/66/GT 5995, Minutes of Supreme War Council, 7 October 1918.
11 CAB 23/8, War Cabinet 481, 2 October 1918.
12 See DBFP, III: 369–70. See Ullman, *Anglo-Soviet Relations, 1917–1921: Vol. I: Intervention and the War*, 54–5.

13 CAB 23/8, War Cabinet 502, 14 November 1918.

14 See Carley, *Revolution and Intervention*. See also MG/16N/3026/68/1; 14.476 BS/ 3, 21 November 1918, and Pichon to Clemenceau, 26 November 1918, MAE/Russie/224/255–255bis.

15 See CAB 23/8, War Cabinet 481, 2 October 1918; and War Cabinet 511, 10 December 1918.

16 See Kenez, *Civil War in South Russia*.

17 CAB 23/8, War Cabinet 502, 14 November 1918.

18 Fleming, *The Fate of Admiral Kolchak*, 112–7. See also Ullman, I: 279–83, and Livshits, "Kolchakovskii perevorot," 79–90.

19 Ironside, *Archangel*, 37ff; MAE/Russia/210/91–2, 121, 136–7; FO 371/3346/1 69701/210762.

20 *DVP*, I: 565–7.

21 Lenin, *PSS*, 37: 188–97.

22 Iakovlev, "V.I. Lenin ob otnoshenii k mel'koi burzhuazii derevni i goroda v kontse 1918 g. i nachale 1919 g," 93–101.

23 Dallin, "The Outbreak of the Civil War," 186.

24 See, for example, Steklov's lead article in *Izvestiia*, 26 November 1918, "Better late than never."

25 Lenin, *PSS*, 37:207–24 (emphasis added).

26 Dallin, "Outbreak," 186.

2. "WE ARE NOT ACCUSTOMED TO WAITING"

1 See Lösche, *Der Bolschewismus im Urteil der deutschen Sozialdemokratie*.

2 See Debo, *Revolution and Survival*, 195–229, 300–55.

3 Baumgart, *Deutsche Ostpolitik, 1918*, 330, n. 104.

4 Baumgart, ed., *Von Brest-Litovsk zur deutschen November-revolution*, 198, 206.

5 Lenin, *PSS*, 50: 194–5.

6 Baumgart, *Deutsche Ostpolitik*, 329.

7 Lenin, *PSS*, 50: 195.

8 *Izvestiia*, 6 November 1919.

9 Fischer, *Men and Politics: An Autobiography*, 26. See also Debo, *Revolution and Survival*, 390–2.

10 Lenin, *PSS*, 37: 110.

11 Miller, *Die Bürde der Macht. Die deutsche Sozialdemokratie, 1918–1920*, 193ff.

12 See Morgan, *The Socialist Left and the German Revolution; Wheeler, U.S.P.D. und Internationale*; and Badia, *Les Spartakistes*.

13 Miller, *Die Bürde der Match*, 193ff. See also Mayer, *Politics and Diplomacy of Peacemaking*, 90ff.

14 Larsons, *Im Sowjet-Labyrinth*, 31.

15 Lenin, *PSS*, 37: 150, 184.

16 Zarnitskii and Sergeev, *Chicherin*, 108.

17 T-136, reel 102, PA AA Deutschland Nr. 131/Band 54/129/A.48288. Aufzeichnung von L.R. Thermann, 12 November 1918.

18 *DVP*, I: 564–5.

19 *SGO*, I: 677. These documents are reproduced in a German edition: see *DSB*, 2 vols.

20 Nadolny, *Mein Beitrag*, 64.

21 *Izvestiia*, 12 November 1918.

22 *DVP*, I: 658–60; Radek "Noiabr," (Stranichka iz vospominanii), 142.

23 For a full examination of this exchange, see Debo, "The 14 November 1918 Teleprinter Conversation of Hugo Haase with Georgii Chicherin and Karl Radek;" 513–34.

24 Chicherin, "Lenin i Vneshniaia Politika," 7.

25 PA AA Deutschland Nr. 131/56/106–108/zu A. 49029 and A. 49041; *DVP*, I: 578; *SGO*, I: 683–4; *DSB*, I: 818–19.

26 Lenin, *PSS*, 50: 211.

27 PA AA Deutschland 131/56/143–144/A.50516; *DVP*, I: 576–7; *DBS*, I:823–5; *SGO*, I: 687–8. Solf to Chicherin, 2 December 1918, PA AA Deutschland 131/57/16. A.50516; *DSB*, I:828; *SGO*, I:691.

28 *DSB*, I:826, 829.

29 PA AA Deutschland NR. 131/57/71/zu A. 52036.

30 PA AA Friedens-verhalndlungen/Abteilung II, W./Russland NR. 4/Band 8, Russland 2921.

31 Radek, "Noiabr."

32 Kriegsminsterium Deutschlands, Forschungsanstalt für Kriegs-und Heeresgeschichte, *Darstellungen aus den Nachkriegskämpfen deutscher Truppen und Freikorps*, I: *Die Rückführung des Ostheeres*, 23, 112–13, 158–60; Linke, *Deutsch-sowjetische Beziehungen bis Rapallo*, 65; *DSB*, I: 835–6. See also Elben, *Das Problem der Kontinuitat in der deutschen Revolution*.

33 *DKFKA*, I: 174–7.

34 Winnig, *Am Ausgang der deutschen Ostpolitik*, 40–4. See also Martna, *Estland, die Esten und die Estnische Frage*, 174–5.

35 *DKFKA*, I: 475–7.

36 See Bienhold, *Die Entstehung des litausichen Staates*; Volmann, "Probleme des deutsch-lettischen Verhältnisses zwischen Compiegne und Versailles," 713–26.

37 Koch, *Der deutsche Bürgerkrieg*.

38 See Adams, *Bolsheviks in the Ukraine*; Borys, *The Russian Communist Party and the Sovietization of Ukraine*; Borowsky, *Deutsche Ukrainepolitik 1918*; Pipes, *The Formation of the Soviet Union*; rev. ed.; and Suprunenko, *Ocherki istorii grazhdanskoi voiny i inostrannoi voennoi interventsii na Ukraine*.

39 *GVU*, I:pt. 2, 16–17.

40 Ibid., pt. 1, 449–50.

41 Antonov-Ovseenko, *Zapiski o grazhdanskoi voine*, III: 27. *DGKKA*, 198. See also *GVU*, I:pt. 1, 478–9.

42 *DVP*, 1:582–6; *GVU*, 1:pt. 1, 459–62.

43 *GVU*, 1:pt. 1, 493–4. *PS TSK*, V:51.

44 *RFDOH*, 52.

45 *DKFKA*, 1:553–7, 557–60; *GVU*, 1:pt. 1, 527.

46 Pipes, *Formation*, 141.

47 Antonov-Ovseenko, *Zapiski* III:111–14.

48 Matthias, *Die Regierung der Vb*, II:39–51.

49 Schwabe, *Deutsche Revolution und Wilson-Frieden*.

50 See Golbach, *Karl Radek und die deutsch-sowjetischen Beziehungen*.

51 Weber, ed., *Der Gründungsparteitag der K.P.D*, 94–113. See also Trotnow, "Karl Liebknecht und die russische Revolution," 379–97.

3. AUDIATUR ET ALTERA PARS

1 FO 371/3344/186867; MG, Campagne contre Allemagne GN/237, military attaché to Clemenceau, Stockholm, 10 October 1918.

2 MAE/Russie/6/37–40.

3 Gromyko and Ponomarev, *Istoriia vneshnei politiki SSSR*, I:101.

4 Cited in Gorokhov, Zamiatin and Zemskov, *G.V. Chicherin – Diplomat Leninskoi Shkoly*, 47–8.

5 FO 371/3344/175192. See also FO 371/3321/179604.

6 *DVP*, 1:549; FO 371/3344/184126. See also *DVP*, 1:556.

7 FO 371/344/184126.

8 *IDDI*, 1:29, *FRUS*, 1:488; MAE/Russie/154/10; FO 371/3344/188836.

9 See especially Radek, "Vilson i Lenin," *Pravda*, 6 November 1918, 2. See also Trotsky, *KVR*, 1:375–98.

10 *Izvestiia*, 15 October 1918; 12 and 16 November 1918.

11 Trotsky, *KVR*, 1:375–98. See also *Izvestiia*, 14, 19, 20 and 24 November 1918; Bukharin, "Konetz imperialisticheskoi voiny i mirovaia revoliutsiia," *Pravda*, 24 November 1918.

12 Trotsky, *KVR*, 1:331–41.

13 *DKFKA*, 1:597–611; *DGKKA*, 249; Trotsky, *KVR*, 1:354–6.

14 *DGKKA*, 285–5. See Lenin, *PSS*, 50:220–1; *DGKKA*, 288ff; Stalin, *Works*, IV:202–32. See also WO33/962 and FO 371/3989/2409/2409.

15 MAE/Russie/224/226; Russie/225/23–26, 29–31/37; Russie/225/168–178. See also Carley, *Revolution and Intervention*, 105–22.

16 *DVP*, 1:593–4; FO 371/3345/169701/202541.

17 FO 371/3594/3863/3863; MAE/Russie/210/53–4.

18 *DVP*, 1:626–7.

19 Ibid, 628–30.

20 Imperial War Cabinet, 23 and 29 December 1918, minutes, CAB 23/42.

21 FO 371/3346/169701/211538.

22 MAE/Russie/154/41–42.

23 See in particular MAE/Russie/211/61–2.

24 CAB 23/42, Imperial War Cabinet, 30 December 1918.

25 Ullman, *Anglo-Soviet Relations*, II:95.

26 FO 371/3954/91/1347.

27 MAE/Russie/154/58.

28 *IDDI*, I:415; *FRUS*, 1919, Russia, 6–7; FO 371/3954/91/3253.

29 Link, ed., *The Papers of Woodrow Wilson*, 53:588.

30 FO 371/3954/91/7567; *DVP*, II:28–9.

31 *DVP*, II:29.

32 Debo, "The Manuilskii Mission: An Early Soviet Effort to Negotiate with France, August 1918 – April 1919," 214–35.

33 MAE/Russie/130/145–148.

34 FO 371/3955/91/13344, 18287.

35 "Notes by W. H. Buckler of conversations with Mr. L. in Stockholm January 14th to 16th 1919," Buckler Papers, Yale University Library.

36 *FRUS*, 1919, Russia, 15–18.

37 Dockrill and Steiner, "The Foreign Office at the Paris Peace Conference in 1919," 55–86.

38 *FRUS*, Paris Peace Conference, 1919, III:490–1.

39 Ibid., 581–4.

40 Ibid., 623–46.

41 FO 800/215/103–105; *FRUS*, Paris Peace Conference, 1919, III:647–9.

42 *FRUS*, 1919, Paris, Peace Conference, III:649–69.

43 Ibid., 686, 691–2.

44 FO 371/3955/91/11972.

4. "CONCESSIONS TO IMPERIALISM"

1 *DGKKA*, 142.

2 Trotsky, *Sochineniia*, 17:67–96.

3 *DGKKA*, 142.

4 Lenin, *CW*, 29:30–1.

5 Lenin, *PSS*, 37:473, 620. For the early development of Soviet concession policy, see Shishkin, *Sovetskoe Gosudarstvo i strany zapada v 1917–1923 gg*, 97–103.

6 Reports of these interviews appeared in the Oslo press in early March 1919 and translations were forwarded to the Foreign Office from the British minister in Norway. See FO 608/293/452ff.

7 Iakovlev, "V.I. Lenin ob otnoshenii k mel'koi," 96–7. Also see Anikeev, *Deiatel'nost' TsK RKP(b) v 1918–1919 godakh*, 175.

8 Golinkov, *Krakh vrazheskogo podpol'ia*, 186–7. See also Lenin, *CW*, 28: 447–8.

9 Lenin, *CW*, 29:151.

10 FO 608/203/452.

11 Lenin, *CW*, 29:31.
12 *Pravda*, 22 December 1918.
13 Lenin, *CW*, 29:31.
14 *DVP*, II:24–6, 33–4.; Lenin, *PSS*, 50:247–8; Trotsky, *Trotsky Papers*, I:258–61.
15 *Trotsky Papers*, I:260–3.
16 *DVP*, II:42–8.
17 Ibid., II:41–2. See also MAE/Russie/161/10; *Le Temps*, 26 January 1919; *Le Populaire*, 27, 31 January 1919.
18 MAE/Russie/90/06–106; FO 371/3955/91/14851.
19 FO 608/179/21; Akademiia nauk SSR: Institut slavianovedeniia i balkanistiki, *Dokumenty i materialy po istorii sovetsko-chekhoslovatskikh otnoshenii. Tom 1: Noiabr' 1917g. – avgust 1922 g.*, 208–9.
20 Trotsky, *KVR*, II, ii:225–6.
21 FO 371/3958/91/36690.
22 Lenin, *CW*, 29:149.
23 *DVP*, II:52, 54–5.
24 *FRUS*, Paris Peace Conference, 1919, III:835–6.
25 *DVP*, II:57–60.
26 Kerr to Lloyd George, 11 February 1919, Lloyd George Papers, F/89/2/7
27 Lloyd George to Kerr, 13 February 1919, ibid., F/89/2/8. See also *FRUS*, 1919, Russia, 38.
28 Mayer, *Politics*, 442ff. For a recent examination of the American side of these developments, see Walworth, *Wilson and his Peacemakers*, 132ff.
29 Nabokov to Sazonov, 5 February 1919. Glavnoe Arkhivnoe Upravlenie. Tsentral 'nyi gosudarstvenny arkhiv sovetskoi armii. *Severnyi Front: Bor'ba sovetskogo naroda protiv inostrannoi voennoi interventsii i belogvardeishchiny na sovetskom severe (1918–1920): Dokumenty*, 47. See also: Schmid, *Churchills privater Krieg*.
30 CAB 23/9, War Cabinet 531, 12 February 1919; CAB 23/15, War Cabinet 532A, 13 February 1919.
31 Lloyd George Papers, F/202/1/1.
32 *FRUS*, 1919, Russia, 56–9.
33 Kerr to Lloyd George, 13 February 1919, Lloyd George Papers F/89/2/10.
34 Ibid., 15 February 1919, Lloyd George Papers, F/89/2/16.
35 Jones, *Whitehall Diary*, I:77.
36 *FRUS*, 1919, Russia, 56–67.
37 Kerr to Lloyd George, 15 February 1919, Lloyd George Papers, F/89/2/16.
38 Mayer, *Politics*, 454–5; Thompson, *Russia, Bolshevism, and the Versailles Peace*, 140–1.
39 Gilbert, *Churchill Documents*, IV, i:533–4.
40 "Memorandum on Russian Situation," 15 February 1919, Balfour Papers, British Museum, Add. Mss. 49751.
41 Gilbert, *Churchill Documents*, IV, i:534.
42 Ibid., 537.

43 Ibid., 538–9.
44 Kerr to Lloyd George, 17 February 1919, Lloyd George Papers, F/89/2/22.
45 Gilbert, *Churchill Documents*, IV, i:540–6; Mayer, *Politics*, 458–9; Thompson, *Russia*, 143–4.
46 *FRUS*, 1919, Russia, 71–2; *Woodrow Wilson Papers*, 55, 229–30.
47 Mayer, *Politics*, 461ff; Thompson, *Russia*, 178ff.
48 "Supplies for General Denikin's Force," GT. 6867, CAB 24/75; War Cabinets of 26 February and 6 March 1919, CAB 23/9; War Cabinet 541A, 4 March 1919, CAB 23/15; Gilbert, *Churchill Documents*, IV, i:570–5.
49 Kerr to Lloyd George, 17 February 1919, Lloyd George Papers, F/89/2/21.
50 Ibid., 18 February 1919, Lloyd George Papers, F/89/2/23.
51 Bullitt, *The Bullitt Mission to Russia*, 36–7. See also Farnsworth, *William C. Bullitt and the Soviet Union*, 32–54, and Walworth, *Wilson and His Peacemakers*, 137ff.
52 Bullitt, *The Bullitt Mission*, 4. On the role of Colonel House, see Floto, *Colonel House in Paris*, 112–16.
53 Steffens, *Autobiography*, 791, 793.
54 *FRUS*, 1919, Russia, 77.
55 Ibid., pp. 81–4.
56 In fact the Central Committee of the Russian Communist Party. See Anikeev, *Deiatel "nost,"* 251.
57 *FRUS*, 1919, Russia, 77–80.
58 *Trotsky Papers*, 1:303–5.
59 Fischer, *Men and Politics*, 132.
60 Lenin, *CW*, 29:30–1.
61 Ibid., 149.
62 *FRUS*, 1919, Russia, 76.
63 Bullitt, *The Bullitt Mission*, 66, 73; *FRUS*, 1919, Russia, 85.
64 Trotsky, *KVR*, II, i:50–2.
65 Blair to War Office, telegrams 1670–1, WO 33/966.
66 See Carley, *Revolution and Intervention*, 142–81.
67 MAE/Russie/226/142–3.
68 MAE/Russie/665/un, Lestchenko to Tchekovski, 23 January 1919.
69 Majstrenko, *Borot'bism. A Chapter in the History of Ukrainian Communism*, 115–19.
70 *DVP*, II:61–4.
71 MAE/Russie/226/192–221, 173, 304; Russie/227/141–2.
72 MAE/Russie/227/59–63, 134, 154; FO 371/3963/93/41562.
73 Fischer, *Deutsche Truppen und Entente-Intervention in Südrussland*, 135ff.
74 MAE/Russie/227/164, 180–4.
75 Ibid.
76 Berthelot to War Ministry, telegrams 398–402, 12 March 1919, MG/CCA/16N/3172/un. See also Torrey, ed., *General Henri Berthelot and Romania*.

77 MAE/Russie/227/186, 199.

78 MAE/Russie/228/6-10.

79 MAE/Russie/228/64-8; Russie/229/77, 84, 92; Mantoux, *Les Deliberations du Conseil du Quatre*, 18–23, 57–8.

80 See Akademiia Nauk Moldavskoi SSR – Institut Istorii, *Bor'ba Trudiashchikhsia Bessarabii za svoe Osvobozhdenie i Vossoedinenie s Sovetskoi Rodinoi (1918–1940 gg), 119–65. See also Karchmar, "Communism in Romania 1918–1921" in Banac, ed., *The Effects of World War I*; 153ff.

81 *DVP*, II: 64–6.

82 R. de Flers to Foreign Ministry, telegram 234, 13 March 1919. MG/CcA/16N/3171/un; MAE/Russie/228/101; Mantoux, *Deliberations*, I:52–7; Clemenceau to Franchet d'Esperey, #3226 BS/3, 29 March 1919, MG/CCA/16N/3028.

83 Pastor, *Hungary between Wilson and Lenin*. See also Tökes, *Bela Kun and the Hungarian Soviet Republic*, 123ff.

84 Lenin, *CW*, 29:226.

85 *DGKKA*, 219.

86 Mantoux, *Deliberations*, I:52–7; Franchet d'Esperey to War Ministry, #7284/3, 28 March 1919, MG/CCA/20N/234.

87 Cited in Nezhinskii, 'Iz istorii sovetsko-vengerskikh otnoshenii (mart-avgust 1919 g.), 3–22.

5. DEFENCE AGAINST "DISGUISED INTERVENTION"

1 See above, chapter 2.

2 *AdaP*, I:142. See also Wengst, *Graft Brockdorff-Rantzau und die aussenpolitischen Anfänge der Weimarer Republik*.

3 See, for example, *DSB*, II:51–3.

4 Linke, *Deutsch-sowjetische Beziehungen*, 38; Von Rabenau, *Seeckt, Aus seinen leben, 1918–1936*, 120; and Meier-Welcker, *Seeckt*, 202.

5 *DGKKA*, 188–9; Akademiia Nauk SSSR, *Bor'ba za sovetskuiu vlast' v Pribaltike*, 524.

6 *DVP*, II:32–3; Chicherin to Auswärtiges Amt, 16 January 1919, PA, AA Deutschland NR. 131/bd. 59.

7 Angress, *Stillborn Revolution*, 29–31. See also Carsten, *The Reichswehr and Politics*; Diehl, *Paramilitary Politics in Weimar Germany*; Schulze, *Freikorps und Republik* and Goldbach, *Karl Radek*.

8 *DSB*, II:42.

9 Lenin, *CW*, 28:411; *DVP*, II:40–1.

10 Radek, "Noiabr," 146; Schumacher and Tych, *Julian Marchlewski–Karski*, 272–4.

11 Lenin, *CW*, 29:30.

12 *Trotsky Papers*, I:260–3.

13 See Davis, *God's Playground*, vol. II; Leslie, et al., *The History of Poland since 1863*; and Watt, *Bitter Glory*.

14 *DIM SPO*, II:34–5.

15 Ibid., 40–2, 48–9, 58–60.
16 Ibid., 43–8, 60–1. See also Szafar, "The Origins of the Communist Party in Poland, 1918–1921" in Banac, ed., *Effects of World War I. The Class War after the Great War*. All but one member of the mission were subsequently murdered by the Polish police assigned to expel them from Poland.
17 *FRUS*, PPC, 1919, II:424–5; FO 371/3896/73/660, 1244.
18 WO 33/962, Colonel Wade to DMI, 3 and 5 January 1919.
19 FO 371/3897/73/17226; FO 608/266/2136/206; MAE/Pologne/130/15–16; MG/CCA/6N/215/sn.
20 *RFdOH*, 26, 63–4. Also see *DSB*, II:58–9.
21 *DVP*, II: 68–70, 78–9; *DiM SPO*, II:105–7.
22 FO 371/3957/91/30876; FO 608/203/3392; FO 608/63/4129.
23 *DiM SPO*, II:161–2. See also Leinwand, *Polska Partia Socjalistyczna Wobec Wojny Polsko-Radzieckiej 1919–1920*.
25 Lenin, *PSS*, 50:266; *DiM SPO*, II:192–3, 197.
25 For established views on the founding of Cominterm, see: Carr, *The Bolshevik Revolution*, vol. III; Lazitch and Drachkovitch, *Lenin and the Cominterm*; and Ridell, ed., *The Communist International in Lenin's Time*. For a dissenting view, see Melograni, *Lenin and the Myth of World Revolution*.
26 See Debo, *Revolution and Survival*, chapters 3–7.
27 *DiM SPO*, II:210–12, 221.
28 Lundgreen-Neilsen, *The Polish Problem at the Paris Peace Conference*.
29 Schumacher and Tych, *Marchlewski*, 289–90. See also: Tampke, *The Ruhr and Revolution*; Gostynska, "Rola Juliana Marchlewsgiego w tajnych Rokowaniach Polsko-Radzieckich," 23–40; and Chernykh, "Iu. Markhlevskii o sovetskoi vneshnei politike," 12–22.
30 *Bor'ba za pribaltike*, 418–19. Sipols, *Die ausländische Intervention in Lettland, 1918–20*, 111ff. Kriegsministerium Deutschlands, Forschungsanstalt für Kriegs- und Heeresgeschichte, *Darstellungen aus den Nachkriegskämpfen deutscher Truppen und Freikorps*, II: *Die Feldzug im Baltikum*, 1–10.
31 Rabenau, *Seeckt*, 126; Meier-Welcker, *Seeckt*, 205; *RfdOH*, 126–7; *Feldzug im Baltikum*, 19–20, 36–7; FO 371/3624/95380/124023.
32 Latvijas Padomju Socialistiskas Respublikas, Zinatnu akademija Vestures instituts, *Sotsialisticheskaia Sovetskaia Respublika Latvii v 1919 g. i inostrannaia Interventsiia*, II:100–1. See also *DGKKA*, 361, 402.
33 *DVP*, II:71–3; Linke, *Deutsch-sowjetische Beziehungen*, 70–1.
34 *DVP*: II, 70–1.
35 Jääskeläinen, *Die Ostkarelische Frage*, 175.
36 FO 371/3738/26579, 39580, 40991. The director of naval intelligence described Mannerheim's plan as madness in as much as sentiment in the country and the Finnish Diet were opposed to it and would be likely to provoke "another bloody civil war." The French, on the other hand, feared that Finland would seek to keep any Russian territory it took from the Bolsheviks. MAE/Russie/341/13–14, 15–16.

37　See, for example, PAAA Deutschland NR. 131/Band 59/passim.

38　Meier-Welcker, *Seeckt*, 207–8; Sipols, *Lettland*, 108–9; *Die Feldzug in Baltikum*, 39–50; DSB, II:77; Linke, *Deutsch-sowjetische Beziehungen*, 39.

39　*IIGII*, 255; Kliatkin, *Na Zashchite Oktiabria*, 364–77.

40　Stalin, *Works*, IV:254–7.

41　*IIGII*, 256–7.

42　Huerten, ed., *Swischen Revolution und Kapp-Putsch*, 81–5.

43　*Ada P*, I:421–2.

44　Mayer, *Politics and Diplomacy*; and Walworth, *Wilson and his Peacemakers*. See also Haupts, *Deutsche Friedenspolitik 1918–1919*.

45　Degras, ed., *The Communist International*, I:50.

46　DVP, II:131–5.

47　*Das Kabinett Scheidemann*, 204–5, 220–25; Meier-Welcker, *Seeckt*, 219.

48　Mordacq, *Le Ministère Clemenceau*; III:263; Cahen, *Der Weg nach Versailles*; 313.

49　*Das Kabinett Scheidemann*, 305.

50　*Die Feldzug in Baltikum*, 117.

51　Koch, *Der Deutsche Burgerkrieg*, 152ff; Volkmann, "Probleme des deutsch-lettischen Verhältnisses zwischen Compiegne und Versailles," 713–26; Sullivan, "The German Role in the Baltic Campaign – Spring 1919," 40–62; *Die Feldzug in Baltikum*, 117–28; *Bor'ba za vlast'v pribaltike*, 434–5; *Das Kabinett Scheidemann*, 311.

52　*Trotsky Papers*, 1:458–63; Kriegsministerium Deutschlands, Forschungsanstalt für Kriegs- und Heeresgeschichte, *Die Kämpfe im Baltikum nach der sweiten Einnahme von Riga*, 6–10. See also Thompson, *Russia, Bolshevism and the Versailles Peace*, 338.

53　*Das Kabinett Scheidemann*, 361–2; *Bor'ba za vlast'v pribaltike*, 450–2.

54　PAAA Deutschland NR. 131/Bd. 60/A. 14867.

55　PAAA Russland NR. 61/Bd. 174.

56　Senn, *Diplomacy and Revolution*, 89–90.

57　Schüddekopf, "Deutschland zwischen Ost und West," 260–1.

58　Ibid., 239.

59　Ibid., 262–3.

60　PAAA Russland Nr. 61/Band 174/A.13324, Schmidt to Rantzau, 11 June 1919; DSB, II:135–7.

61　Himmer, "Harmonicas for Lenin?"

62　Linke, *Deutsch-sowjetische Beziehungen*, 88.

6. "THE INTRUDER"

1　Ullman, *Anglo-Soviet Relations*, II: 150–2; Mayer, *Politics*, 471ff; Thompson, *Russia*, 237ff; Bullitt, *The Bullitt Mission*, 65–6; *Woodrow Wilson Papers*, 56; 279–80, 309–10, 335–7; Walworth, *Wilson*, 236–7.

2 *Woodrow Wilson Papers*, 56: 337, 375–8; Walworth, *Wilson*, 241; Thompson, *Russia*, 230ff; Mayer, *Politics*, 471ff.

3 *Woodrow Wilson Papers*, 56:575–6.

4 Ibid., 57:93–4; Thompson, *Russia*, 251–4; Bullitt, *The Bullitt Mission*, 79–96; *FRUS*, 1919, Russia, 103–7; Mayer, *Politics*, 479ff.

5 MAE/Russie/407/sn, "Ravitaillement de la Russia," 13 April 1919.

6 Ibid., "Note: Ravitaillement de la Russie," 14 April 1919.

7 Ibid., Pichon to Hoover, 16 April 1919.

8 Ibid., Berthelot to Kammerer, 15 April 1919.

9 Mayer, *Politics*, 484–5; Walworth, *Wilson*, 242–3; *Woodrow Wilson Papers*, 57:438–40.

10 114 HC, 2939–61.

11 MAE/Russie/407/sn, Martel to Pichon, tels. 222–3, 15 April 1919.

12 *FRUS*, Russia, 1919, 331–6.

13 FO 608/188/598/2/1/7649.

14 CAB 24/78/GT 7717; FO 608/188/598/2/1/7649.

15 *Churchill Documents*, IV, i:640–1.

16 WO 33/966, Blair to War Office, tel. 2244, 24 April 1919.

17 *Churchill Documents*, IV, i:pp. 619–20.

18 MAE/Russie/407/sn, Martel to Pichon, tels. 247–9, 26 April 1919.

19 FO 608/204/1 and 3, Lindley to Curzon, tel. 144, 21 April 1919.

20 Lenin, *PSS*, 50:304–6 (emphasis in original).

21 *DVP*, II:154–60; *FRUS*, Russia, 1919, 111–15.

22 For Soviet concern, see Trotsky, *Ecrits militaires*, 801ff; Trotsky, *Sochineniia*, XVII:99–112, 112–32, 132–35; Lenin, *CW*, 29:276–9; for Soviet evaluation of the situation in the east, see *DGKKA*, 548–50, 550–3, 553–5, 556–8.

23 Mantoux, *Deliberations*, II:109.

24 MAE/Russie/408/sn, 14 May 1919; *FRUS*, Russia, 1919, 111, 115.

25 *Churchill Documents*, IV, i:645, 647.

26 *FRUS*, Russia, 1919, 341–2.

27 Ibid., 351–4; Mantoux, *Deliberations*, II:127–9; Walworth, *Wilson*, 243–5; Thompson, *Russia*, 296–8.

28 Mantoux, *Deliberations*, II:179, 190–2, 203–4; *FRUS*, Russia, 1919, 354–60, 360–6, 367–70; Thompson, *Russia*, 298–303.

29 Mantoux, *Deliberations*, II:203–4.

30 See Lenin, *PSS*, 50:309, and *Trotsky Papers*, 1:483.

31 *Trotsky Papers*, 1:546–9; Lenin, *PSS*, 50:354–5, 491.

32 *DBFP*, III:339; WO 33/967/40; MAE/Russie/212/154.

33 *DBFP*, III:342; Mantoux, *Deliberations*, II:387–9, 453–5; *DBFP*, III:376–7; Thompson, *Russia*, 303–8; Walworth, *Wilson*, 245–6.

34 *Churchill Documents*, IV, i:678, 685–8, 690–1, 698; FO 371/3960/91/92860, WO to Knox, 18 June 1919.

35 CAB 23/15, War Cabinet 580A, 18 June 1919.

36 CAB 23/15, War Cabinet 585B, 27 June 1919; Ullman, *Anglo-Soviet Relations*, II:185–90.

37 CAB 23/11, War Cabinet 598, 23 July 1919; Ullman, *Anglo-Soviet Relations*, II:190ff; Ironside, *Archangel*, 144ff. The normally calm secretary of the war cabinet, Maurice Hankey, even compared the situation to that of the British débâcle at Khartoum in 1885. "The Government could not afford another General Gordon incident," he wrote Lloyd George, "and, *prima facie*, there seems to be some points of resemblance between the two." Lloyd George Papers, F/24/1/4, Hankey to Lloyd George, 28 July 1919.

38 Lenin, *CW*, 29:527–8.

39 Chicherin, *Stat'i i Rechi po voprosam mezhdunarodnoi politiki*, 67–86. Chicherin is referring to the play, *The Intruder*, by Maurice Maeterlinck.

7. SOVIET NATIONALITIES POLICY AND THE BALTIC

1 Akademiia Nauk SSSR, Institut Istorii, *Ocherki Istorii Leningrada*, IV:159–80. For an eyewitness account, see Serge, *Memoirs of a Revolutionary*, 70–4.

2 See, for example, *FRUS*, 1919, Russia, 674.

3 Rintala, *Three Generations: The Extreme Right Wing in Finnish Politics*, 71–121. See also Jääskeläinen, *Die Ostkarelische Frage*, 18–40; Amburger, *Ingermanland*, Matley. "The Dispersal of the Ingrian Finns," 1–16.

4 See, for example; MAE/Russie/211/67, 219–20; MAE/Estonie/2/30; MG/CCA/6N/232; FO 371/3959/91/45414; FO 608/183/4508.

5 Jääskeläinen, *Die Ostkarelische Frage*, 168ff; Kholodkovskii, *Finliandiia i Sovetskaia Rossiia*, 73–4.

6 Maynard, *The Murmansk Venture*, 216ff, 251ff.

7 Ibid., 228ff, 255ff; Jääskeläinen, *Die Ostkarelische Frage*, 184; WO 33/967, Maynard to FO, 30 June 1919.

8 Akademiia Nauk SSSR, Institut Istorii SSSR. *Pogranichnye voiska SSSR*, 296–8; *DVP*, II:124–6.

9 *DVP*, II:143–5.

10 Maynard, *Murmansk Venture*, 258–9ff.

11 MAE/Russie/221/362–3.

12 Smith, Jr., *Finland and the Russian Revolution*, 134–5; Page, *The Formation of the Baltic States*, 128–9; Bennett, *Cowan's War*, 105.

13 MAE/Russie/280/sn, Gendre to MG, dispatches #104 and 121, 3 and 9 May 1919.

14 See FO 371/3968/140/passim for continuing reports of Estonian political life in early 1919.

15 FO 371/3968/140/74113.

16 FO 371/3967/140/60297 and 60899.

17 FO 371/39671/140/60779 and 66509.

18 FO 608/186/9050/597/1/7; FO 371/3968/140/77122.

19 FO 371/3624/95380/124023; Ullman, *Anglo-Soviet Relations*, II:254ff; FO 371/

3959/9/71756; Glavnoe arkhivnoe upravlenie, *Severnyi Front*, 57–60; Bennett, *Cowan's War*, 105ff; ADM 116/1864, Bell to Admiralty, telegram 82, 13 May 1919.

20 Ullman, *Anglo-Soviet Relations*, II:256ff; Bennett, *Cowan's War*, 115ff; Tipner, *V Ogne Revoliutsii*, 200ff; MAE/Russie/212/154–8; Tsentrarkhiv Leningradskoe Otdelenie tsentral'nogo istoricheskogo arkhiva RSFSR, *Baltiiskii Flot v Oktiabr'skoi Revoliutsii i Grazhdanskoi Voine*, 175–80; Institut Marksizma-Leninizma pri TSK KPSS, *Istoriia Grazhdanskoi Voiny v SSSR*, IV:149–56.

21 *DGKKA*, 367–8; Anikeev, *Deiatel 'nost Tsk*, 407. See also Stalin, *Works*, IV:275–81.

22 *DKFKA*, II:80–2. See also *Ocherki Istorii Leningrada*, IV:180–93; Stalin, *Works*, IV:268–70.

23 Ulam, *Stalin*, 182–3.

24 *DKFKA*, II:75. See also Leggett, *The Cheka*, 1284–5; Sofinov, *Ocherki istorii Vserossiiskoi Chrezvychainoi komissii*, 156–62; Golinkov, *Krakh Vrazheskogo Podpol'ia*, 190–5.

25 Lenin, *CW*, 29:54; *PSS*, 50:325.

26 Lenin, *CW*, 29:403.

27 Lenin, *PSS*:50, 331, 334–5, 343, 489–90.

28 *DKFKA*, II:97.

29 Lenin, *PSS*, 50:343–4; *CW*, 29:407; *Trotsky Papers*, I:546–7.

30 Golikov, *Krakh Vrazheskogo Podpol'ia*; Lenin, *PSS*, 50:347–8; *Baltiiskii Flot*, 186–204.

31 Stalin, *Works*, IV:272–4, 275–81.

32 MAE/Russie/281/sn, Delavaud to Pichon, tels. 978–9, 6 July 1919; MAE/Russie/341/104.

33 *DVP*, II:169–71, 186–7, 192–3; see FO 371/3738/26579/79125.

34 *DBFP*, III:382, n.2. See also MAE/Russie/280/sn, Gendre to MG dispatch 172, 25 May 1919; Ullman, *Anglo-Soviet Relations* II;262–5.

35 *DBFP*, I:29–30.

36 Mannerheim, *Memoirs*, 211.

37 "The Germans cannot be made use of with impunity," wrote Lord Balfour on 10 June, "and these compacts with the Devil are apt to turn out ill in the end" (FO 608/189/599/2/1/12,600). A few months later the Foreign Office was still of the same opinion (*DBFP*, III:140–3). For a full examination of the question, see Hovi, *The Baltic Area in British Policy*, 110–63. Churchill, *Documents*, IV, ii:726–31; CAB 23/5, War Cabinet 588A, 4 July 1919; *DBFP*, III:430.

38 Trotsky, *Sochineniia*, XVII:191–9.

39 Bennett, *Cowan's War*, 134; Agar. *Baltic Episode*, 126–79; *DVP*, II:230–2.

40 *Trotsky Papers*, I:600–3; *DVP*, II:219–20; *DGKKA*, 385–6.

41 Carr, *History of Soviet Russia*, I:260–85; Pipes, *Formation of the Soviet Union*; 34–49. See also: Stetten, "The National Question and the Russian Civil War"; Iroshnikov, Kovalenko, and Shishkin. *Genesis of the Soviet Federative State*; Kuli-

chenko, *Bor'ba kommunisticheskoi partii za reshenie natsional'nogo voprosa v 1918–1920 godakh*; and Makarova, *Oslushchestvlenie Leninskoi Natsional'noi Politiki v pervye gody sovetski vlasti.*

42 Lenin, *CW*, 29:127.

43 Institut Marksizma-Leninizma pri TSK KPSS, *Vos'moi S"ezd RKP(b): Protokoly*, 47ff, 78ff, 85ff.

44 Lenin, *CW*, 29:174, 194–5.

45 *Vos'moi S"ezd*, 331, 337–8.

46 Kliatskin, *Na Zashchite Oktiabria*, 378ff.

47 Selivanov, *Voennoe Stroitel'stvo v Belorussii v period Razgroma Pokhodov Antanty*, 94–5.

48 *DGKKA*, 310–12.

49 *BSV-Bel*, II:268–9.

50 Lenin, *PSS*, 50:287–8 (emphasis in original); Selivanov, *Voennoe stroitel'stuo v Belorussii*, 96–7.

51 Kliatskin, *Na Zashchite Oktiabria*, 388.

52 See *GVU*, II:62–3; *BSV-Bel*, II:119.

53 Degras, ed. *Soviet Documents on Foreign Policy*, 1:158–9.

54 *Trotsky Papers*, 1:496.

55 *IIGVII*, 89. See also Tipner, *V Ogne Revoliutsii*, 206–7.

56 *IIGVII*, 95; *Bor'ba za sovetskuiu vlast'v Pribaltike*, 437; *BSV-Bel*, II:122; See also final chapters of Tipner, *V Ogne Revoliutskii.*

8. THE END OF "SPONTANEOUS VICTORIES"

1 See Carley, *Revolution and Intervention.* See also Munholland, "The French Army and Intervention in Southern Russia," 43–66; Masson, *La Marine française et la mer noire*; and Hogenhuis-Seliverstoff, *Les Relations franco-sovietiques.*

2 Trousson to Bouchez, Sevastopol, 6 April 1919, MG/CCA/20N/273. It is worth noting that d'Anselme, who had commanded at Odessa, shared Trousson's negative view. In his final report to Berthelot, written on 20 May 1919, he wrote: "The Volunteer Army is an army of emigrés who have learned nothing and forgotten nothing; they have taken the revolution to be a revolt; between the Volunteers and the people there is a true and savage hatred." The Volunteers, d'Anselme said, "excel in retreat, they are able to run 25 kilometres in a day." MAE/Russie/230/123–140. See Carley, *Revolution and Intervention*, 154–7.

3 MAE/Russie/229/103.

4 Franchet d'Esperey to Foch, 13 and 15 April 1919, MAE/Russie/229/159, 195–6. See also Defrance to MAE, 9 April 1919, MAE/Russie/91/230 and Amet to MM, MAE/Russie/229/115.

5 MG/CCA/16N/3028.

6 MAE/Russie/229/198.

7 PRO Adm 137/1734, "Report of Lieutenant L.H. Ashmore, R.N.," undated; MAE/Russie/229/225, 226.

8 MAE/Russie/229/267–8; GVU, I, ii:348–9.

9 See, for example, Franchet d'Esperey to Clemenceau, tels 992–4, 7 April 1919, MAE/Russie/229/94.

10 Note de Renseignement, 13 April 1919, MAE/Russie/229/330–2.

11 MG/CCA/16N/3028, 4068 BS/3.

12 MAE/Russie/229/272.

13 Adm 137/1734, Report of Lt. L.H. Ashmore, R.N., undated; Adm 137/1734. Black Sea Letter o Proceedings – Events at Sebastopol, 22 April 1919–29 April 1919. See also Carley, *Revolution and Intervention*, 174–181, and Masson, *La marine française*.

14 See MAE/Russie/229/272 and Mordacq, *Le Ministere Clemenceau*, III:234; FO 371/3964/93/62817, 63230, 64575 and MAE/Russie/229/313, 325.

15 Adm 137/1734/unnumbered. Black Sea Letter of Proceedings – Events at Sebastopol, 22 April–29 April 1919. Also see FO 371/3964/93/62817.

16 Given these events, the words of Sir Henry Wilson, written on 31 October 1918, are ironic. "It can certainly be assumed that Romania can produce sufficient troops to garrison a greater Romania, but she may ask for a stiffening of Allied troops to avoid the infection of Bolshevism." FO 371/3344/169701/188552. See also MG/CCA/16N/3172/80, 83, 96; MG/CCA/20N/234, Franchet d'Esperey to MG, EMG 3, no. 7587; MG/CCA/20N/720, D'Anselme to Berthelot, 13 and 15 April 1919; MAE/Russie/229/197. On Soviet awareness of French and Romanian problems, see Akademiia nauk moldavskoi SSR, Institut Istorii, *Bor'ba trudiashchikhsia Moldavii protiv interventov i vnutrennei kontrrevoliutsii*, 266ff.

17 In addition to Pastor, *Hungary between Wilson and Lenin*, Tökes, *Bela Kun and the Hungarian Soviet Republic*, and Nezhinskii, "Iz istorii sovetsko-vengerskikh otnoshenii," see Hajdu, *The Hungarian Soviet Republic*; Volgyes, ed., *Hungary in Revolution*; Janos and Slottman, eds., *Revolution in Perspective*; Pastor, "One Step Forward, Two Steps Back" in Banac, ed., *Effects of World War I*; Nezhinskii, "U istokov sovetsko-vengerskoi druzhby"; and, most recently, Pastor, ed., *Revolutions and Interventions in Hungary and its Neighbor States*.

18 Nezhinskii, "Iz istorii sovetsko-vengerskikh otnoshenii," 6; Kholodkovskii, 'V.I. Lenin i zarozhdenie mezhdunarodnykh otnoshenii novogo, sotsialisticheskogo tipa," 90. See also Bak, "Aus dem Telegrammwechsel zwischen Moskau und Budapest," 187–224.

19 DGKKA, 219, 220–1.

20 Nezhinskii, "Iz istorii sovetsko-vengerskikh otnoshenenii," 15; GVU, I, i:726–7.

21 Stachiw and Sztendera, *Western Ukraine. At the Turning Point of Europe's History*; and Cienciala and Komarnicki, *From Versailles to Locarno. Keys to Polish Foreign Policy*, 151ff.

22 Doroshenko, *A Survey of Ukrainian History*, 644.

23 Reshetar, *The Ukrainian Revolution 1917–1920*, 278–80.

24 Lenin, PSS, 50:282–3. See also Lenin, CW, 29:327, and Majstrenko, *Borot'bism*, 126–7.

25 *Trotsky Papers*, 1:370–3, 380; Lenin, PSS, 50:285–6; DGKKA, 224.

26 Kholodkovskii, "Lenin i zarozhdenie mezhdunarodnykh otnoshenii," 93, DVP, II:148.

27 Conte, *Christian Rakovski*, I:240ff; GVU, I, ii:303–6.

28 GVU, I, ii:312–13; Adams, *Bolsheviks in the Ukraine*, 260ff.

29 DVP, II:148–52; GVU, I, ii:404–6.

30 Antonov-Ovseenko, *Zapiski*, IV:196; Stachiew, *Western Ukraine*, II, 131ff; Borys, *The Russian Communist Party and the Sovietization of Ukraine*, 220–3; MAE/Russie/229/273–4; MAE/Russie/230/5–6; DGKKA, 230–1; GVU, II:783–4; *Trotsky Papers*, I, 387–95.

31 Adams, *Bolsheviks in the Ukraine*, 284ff; GVU, II:783–4.

32 Adams, *Bolsheviks in the Ukraine*, 354ff; GVU, I, ii:350–2; DGKKA, 222–3, 229–30; Kenez, *Civil War in South russia*, 27–36.

33 *Trotsky Papers*, I:364–5, 372–5.

34 Antonov-Ovseenko, *Zapiski*, IV:48; Hajdu, *The Hungarian Soviet Republic*, 128–9; Shumikhim, "Trassa proletarskogo internatsionalizma," 183–7. See also Nezhinskii, "U istokov sovetsko-vengerskoi druzhby," 26, and Böhm, *Im Kreuzfeuer zweier Revolutionen*, 387–8.

35 Adams, *Bolsheviks in the Ukraine*, 352ff; Mawdsley, *The Russian Civil War*, 161–72.

36 Lenin, PSS, 50:324; DGKKA, 236–7.

37 DGKKA, 238–9.

38 MG/CCA/16N/3171, Petin to MG, 5 and 23 June 1919.

39 MG/CCA/16N/3171, Petin to MG, 1 June 1919; MAE/Pologne/84/45–7, 55–7, 70–1; Stachiew, *Western Ukraine*, II:151–5, 247–9.

40 DBFP, III:851–61; MAE/Pologne/84/58, 97–8, 100–2, 150; Lundgreen-Nielsen, *The Polish Problem at the Paris Peace Conference*, 217–24, 385–8; Cienciala and Komarnicki, *From Versailles to Locarno*, 160–4.

41 The Poles felt the Romanians were too sympathetic to the Ukrainian population of Bukhovina and Ukrainian nationalists in general. The Romanians regarded the Directory as a more desirable neighbour than Soviet Ukraine and were prepared to aid Ukrainian nationalists in their struggle against the Bolsheviks. As the Ukrainians also continued their struggle against the Poles, this served as a constant irritant in relations between Warsaw and Bucharest. See MG/CCA/16N/3171, Petit to MG, 24 June 1919; MAE/Pologne/84/133–5, 214–15; MAE/Romania/33/37–9; MAE/Russie/670/215–16.

42 Lenin, *Sbornik*, 36; 79; cited in Tökes, *Bela Kun and the Hungarian Soviet Republic*, 202–3.

9. THE PEACE OF DORPAT

1 Trotsky, *Sochinenia*, XVII:188–90.

2 Lenin, CW, 29:456–69.

3 Ibid., 547–50.

4 *Trotsky Papers*, 1:621–9.

5 Kenez, *Civil War in South Russia*, 37ff; Mawdsley, *Russian Civil War*, 166–72; Brinkley, *The Volunteer Army and Allied Intervention in South Russia*, 186ff.

6 DGKKA, 591–2.

7 Institut Marksizma-Leninizma pri Tsk KPSS, *Vladimir Il'ich Lenin*, 7:350–1.

8 *Trotsky Papers*, 1:590–5; DGKKA, 429ff.

9 Trotsky, *My Life*, 453–4. See also Erickson, *The Soviet High Command*, 66ff; Adams, *Bolsheviks in the Ukraine*, 376–7; *Trotsky Papers*, 1:606.

10 War Office to Denikin Missi, #79307, 28 June 1919, WO 33/967; *Churchill Documents*, IV, ii:757–64, 766–74, 786–90; War Office to British Mission, Vladivostok, #80251, 5 August 1919, WO 33/967.

11 MAE/Russie/231/69–72; MAE/Russie/233/passim. Also MG/CCA/16N/3030/sn, War Minister to d'Esperey, #7798, 19 August 1919.

12 MAE/Russie/233/141–2.

13 *Trotsky Papers*, 1: 644–59; Lenin, PSS, 51:33–4; Kenez, *Civil War in South Russia*, 43.

14 Egorov, *Razgrom Denikina*, 120–1; Denikin Mission to War Office, Ekaterinodar, 19 August 1919, WO 33/967; Kenez, *Civil War in South Russia*, 44. See also MAE/Russie/233/216; Trotsky, *Sochinenia*, XVII:199–205.

15 *Trotsky Papers*, 1:658–60; ibid., 660–3; Lenin, PSS, 51:39–41.

16 MG/CCA/16N/3256/sn, "Considerations sur le front polono-bolcheviste," 28 July 1919.

17 Lenin, PSS, 51:17–18.

18 MG/CCA/16N/3256/sn, Henrys to War Ministry, tels. 487–9, 12 August 1919.

19 Stalin, *Works*, 4:282–4; *Trotsky Papers*, 1:654.

20 Debo, *Revolution and Survival*, 338ff.

21 Schumacher and Tych, *Marchlewski*, 187–90; Leinwand, *Polska Partia Socjalistyczna*, 86; Wandycz, "Secret Soviet-Polish Peach Talks," 428.

22 Wandycz, "Secret Soviet-Polish Peace Talks," 429–31; DiM SPO, II:282–3; Schumacher and Tych, *Marchlewski*, 290–1. See also MAE/Pologne/69/239; MAE/Pologne/70/16–17.

23 DiM SPO, II:283; Ibid., 294–5; DVP, II: 235; Lenin, *Biograficheskaia Khronika*, 7:457.

24 DiM SPO, II:307–8; Wandycz, "Secret Soviet-Polish Peace Talks," 431–2.

25 DiM SPO, II:308–9, 312–13. See also MG/CCA/6N/214/sn, Fouchet to Foreign Ministry, tels. 251–3, 22 August 1919; MAE/Russie/670/297–8.

26 MG/CCA/6N/214/sn, Fouchet to Foreign Ministry, tel. #213.

27 MAE/Pologne/85/38–9; MG/CCA/6N/214/sn, Fouchet to Foreign Ministry, tel. #235; MG/CCA/16N/sn, Henrys to War Ministry, tel. #734/2B, 11 September 1919.

28 See above, chapter 8.

29 Libman, 'Deiatel'nost' kommunisticheskoi organizatsii na territorii Estliandskoi Trudovoi Kommuny' in *IIGVII*, 89.

30 *Bor'ba zaa Sovetskuiu vlast' v Pribaltike*, 236–7; see also Lenin, *Sbornik*, 34:169.

31 Kingisepp, *Bor'ba protiv inostrannykh imperialistov i ikh posobnikov*; 74–6.

32 *Bor'ba za Sovetskuiu vlast' v Pribaltike*, 237–8.

33 Kingisepp, *Bor'ba*, 83–7. See also Akademiia Nauk Estonskoi SSR. Institut Istorii, *Istoriia Estonskoi SSR*, III:182–8.

34 Kingisepp, *Bor'ba*, 87.

35 *FRUS*, 1919, Russia, 380–1.

36 FO 371/3968/140/97149, Bosanquet to Foreign Office, tel. #144, 30 June 1919.

37 "Obrazovanie severo-zapadnago pravitelstva," *Arkhiv Russkoi Revoliutsii*, I:306–8.

38 *DBFP*, III:500–6.

39 Ibid. See also Ullman, *Anglo-Soviet Relations*, II: 266ff.

40 FO 608/200/607/4/1/18209, Curzon to Balfour, #5574, 21 August 1919; *DBFP*, III: 508–9; *DBFP*, I:446–50.

41 Ibid., III:86–9. See also Avalov, *Im Kampf gegen den Bolschewismus*, 174ff.

42 *DBFP*, III: 86–7. See also: Sullivan, "The 1919 German Campaign in the Baltic," 35–42.

43 Lenin, *PSS*, 37:165; ibid., 51:28.

44 Cowan to Admiralty, #525/3, 19 August 1919, ADM 137/1679. See also Agar, *Bartic Episode*, 126–79.

45 Lenin, *Biograficheskaia Khronika*, 7:473; DGKKA, 389.

46 *Trotsky Papers*, I:620; Lenin, *Biograficheskaia Khronika*, 7:440, 457.

47 Goode, *Bolshevism at Work*, 21. See also Lenin, *Biograficheskaia Khronika*, 7:460, and Lenin, *Sbornik*, 37:166–7.

48 Goode, *Bolshevism at Work*, 23–7.

49 FO 371/3616/61232/134859; FO 371/3960/91/127799; Tipner, *V Ogne Revoliutsii*, 221–2.

50 Trotsky, *Sochineniia*, 17:239–40.

51 Kingisepp, *Pod igom nezavistimosti*, 199ff; *Bor'ba za sovetskuiu vlast' v Pribaltike*, 238; WO 33/975, British Mission Helsingfors to War Office, 4 September 1919. See also *Istoriia Estonskoi SSR*, III:195–7.

52 Lenin, *PSS*, 39:180.

53 *DVP*, II:242–3.

54 FO371/3618/67181/125511; FO 371/3619/67181/134103; MAE/Estonie/2/173–4.

55 MAE/Estonie/2/149–50, 158, 160; FO 371/3618/67181/127198, 130081; WO 33/975, British Mission Helsingfors to War Office, 7 September 1919.

56 MAE/Estonie/2/159; *DVP*, II:244.

57 Schumacher and Tych, *Marchlewski*, 291–2; Lenin, *PSS*, 51:42, 383; DKFKA, II:118–19, 120–1, 122; Lenin, *Biograficheskaia Khronika*, 7:484–5; *Bor'ba za sovetskuiu vlast' v Pribaltike*, 533; MG/CCA/5N/183/sn, Pujol to War Ministry, tels. 214, 216, 4 and 10 September 1919.

58 FO 371/3619/67181/134103. See also Hovi, "Die Randstaatenkonferenzen," 94–5.

59 MAE/Estonie/2/158; FO 371/3618/67181/129884, 130216; *DVP*, III:543–5, 553–4.

60 *DVP*, II:247–8.

61 MG/CCA/5N/183, Hurstel to War Ministry, tels. #122–3, 21 September 1919; See also Lenin, *Biograficheskaia Khronika*, 7:497; Taigro, *Bor'ba trudiashchikhsia Estonii za sovetskuiu vlast'*, 123–5; FO 371/3618/67181/131941.

62 *DBFP*, III:554.

63 FO 371/3616/61232/132916.

64 FO 371/3616/61232/137119.

65 FO 371/3739/132785/132785; *DBFP*, III:564; MG/CCA/5N/183, Douparquet to War Ministry, tels. #57–9, 23 September 1919.

66 MAE/Estonie/2/149–50, 160.

67 MAE/Estonie/2/173–4 (emphasis in original).

68 MG/CCA/16N/3030, Clemenceau to Etievant, #8429, BS/3–2.

69 MAE/Russie/272/sn, Pichon to Fabre, tel. 226, 27 September 1919.

70 Curzon to Lloyd George, 2 September 1919, Lloyd George Papers F/12/1/39.

71 *Churchill Documents*, IV, ii:848–54; FO 371/3618/67181/130081.

72 FO 800/15a, "The Baltic States and Peace Negotiations with the Bolsheviks," 20 September 1919.

73 CAB 23/12, WC 623, 24 September 1919; CAB 23/12, WC 624, 25 September 1919, Appendix II.

74 CAB 23/15, WC 624A, 25 September 1919. See also Ullman, *Anglo-Soviet Relations*, II:220.

75 *DBFP*, III:569–70.

76 FO 371/3616/61232/136761.

77 MAE/Russie/272/sn, Delavaud to Foreign Ministry, tels. #1295–1303, 30 September 1919.

78 MG/CCA/5N/183, du Parquet to War Ministry, tels. #75–7, 5 October 1919.

79 FO 371/3619/67181/141623. See also MAE/Estonie/2/1919 and Hovi, 'Randstaatenkonferenzen,' 95–6.

80 *DGKKA*, 461–8; *Trotsky Papers*, I:665–9; Lenin, *PSS*, 51:45.

81 Lenin, *PSS*, 51:26, 61; *Trotsky Papers*, I: 695–7. See also Trotsky, *My Life*, 423ff.

82 MAE/Russie/183; Trotsky, *My Life*, 427ff; *Trotsky Papers*, I:792–801; *DGKKA*, 394–6.

83 FO 371/4027/116696/155479.

84 FO 371/4027/116692/148809.

85 *Trotsky Papers*, I:696–9, 700–7.

86 Ibid., 719–21.

87 Ibid., 716–19. Lenin, *PSS*, 51:69 (emphasis in original).

88 *Trotsky Papers*, I:731.

89 FO 371/3619/67181/143530; *DVP*, II:256.

90 *Trotsky Papers*, I:741, 43, 45.

91 Kholodovskii, *Finliandiia i Sovetskaia Rossiia*, 131–3; FO 371/4038/144099/144099, 144570, 144514, 145193, 145267.

92 *Trotsky Papers*, I:735, 737–9; Ibid., 737–9.

93 Ibid., 710; *Bor' ba za sovetskuiu vlast' v Pribaltike*, 444; Tipner, *V Ogne Revoliutsii*, 246; Kenez, *Civil War in South Russia*, 165–6; Mawdsley, *The Russian Civil War*, 202–15.

94 Lenin, *PSS*, 51:391–2; *DVP*, II:286–7.

95 WO 33/975, Haking to War Office, 12 November 1919; *DBFP*, III:658–60; FO 371/3619/67181/152447; *Bor' ba za sovetskuiu vlast' v Pribaltike*, 239–40. Sipols, *Tainaia Diplomatiia*, 47–8.

96 Bicknell, *With the Red Cross in Europe*, 311; *Bor' ba za sovetskuiu vlast' v Pribaltike*, 454; FO 371/4038/144099/147947 and FO 371/4041/148009/148009.

97 MG/CCA/5N/183, Hurstel to War Ministry, tel. #222, 24 November 1919; *DVP*, II:291–3; *DBFP*, III:652–3.

98 Oznobishin, *Ot Bresta do Iur'eva*, 287–8, 296; Sipols, *Tainaia Diplomatiia*, 48.

99 *DVP*, II:299–305; *DBFP*, II:439.

100 FO 371/3619/67181/159778, 161120, 161892. See also Oznobishin, *Ot Bresta do Iur'eva*, 295–6.

101 FO 371/3619/67181/160764; see also MAE/Russie/703/25.

102 FO 371/3619/67181/161138, 161139, 161517, 161521; see also MAE/Russie/703/26, 29–30, 33, 35, 36, 37.

103 FO 371/3619/67181/160764, 165803.

104 FO 371/3619/67181/163454, 163553, 164232; *DVP*, II:310–11.

105 WO 106/604, "Agent's Report," Reval, 19 December 1919, 2 January 1920.

106 Taigro, *Bor'ba*, 133.

107 *DVP*, II:313–19. See also FO 371/3619/67181/164968, 165074, 167824.

108 FO 371/3611/140/175870.

109 See chapter 10.

110 *DBFP*, II: 678, 689–90; WO 33/996/3, War Office to Turner, 3 January 1920.

111 *FRUS*, 1920, III:644.

112 For the role of Poland, see Gostynska, "Konferencja Panstw Baltychich i Polski w Helsinkach 1920 roku," 77–94; MAE/Russie/704/67–72; and FO 371/4044/165013/171655, 171830.

113 FO 371/4044/165013/passim.

114 MAE/Russie/704/120–2; FO 371/3617/61232/173315.

115 *DVP*, II:323–5; Chicherin, *Stat'i*, 135–43; Lenin, *Sbornik*, 37:192–3.

116 For the treaty, see *DVP*, II:339–54; WO 33/996/3–4, Turner to War Office, 4 January 1920.

117 MAE/Russie/703/12, 13, 28; MAE/Russie/704/17, 18, 23, 24, 29; MG/CCA/125, Binet to Foreign Ministry, tels. 114–115, 26 December 1919. See also FO 371/3619/67181/159818.

118 Sipols, *Tainaia diplomatiia*, 50–2.

119 FO 371/3630/167566; FO 371/3912/40430/168188; WO ee/966/8, Turner to War Office, 8 January 1920; War Office 106/968, de Wiart to War Office, 12 January 1920; MAE/Russie/286/90–1, 97.

120 Hunczak, "'Operation Winter' and the Struggle for the Baltic," 48.

121 MAE/Russie/703/72; *DIM SPO*, II:479–81; *DVP*, II:320–1.
122 *Bor'ba za sovetskuiu vlast'v Pribaltike*, 456; *DVP*, II:323–5, 333–9.
123 FO 371/3612/855/175153; FO 371/3630/167566/177709.
124 Lenin, *CW*, 30:216, 315–20.
125 Chicherin, "Der Volkskommissar des Auswärtigen über den Frieden und über die Lage in Russland," 1.
126 Chicherin, *Stat'i*, 135–43.
127 Kingisepp, *Bor'ba*, 100.
128 MAE/Russie/156/5.

10. "CO-EXISTENCE OF SOCIALIST AND CAPITALIST STATES"

1 *DBFP*, I:88–92, 98–100; *FRUS, 1919, Russia*, 151–3. See also Gaworek, "From Blockade to Trade;" 36–69.
2 *FRUS, 1919, Russia*, 153–7, 159–60; *DBFP*, I:188–90, 193–4, 824–6.
3 Lucius to A.A., Nr. 2051/580, Stockholm, 20 September 1919, PA, AA, Russland Nr. 61/Bd. 178/A.27977.
4 Haniel to Lersner, Berlin, 11 October 1919, PA, AA, Russland Nr. 61/Bd. 178/A.26721.
5 Lucis to A.A., 12 October 1919; Mutius to A.A., 12 October 1919; Neurath to A.A., 13 October 1919; Adolf Muller to A.A., 21 October 1919, PA, AA, Russland Nr.61/Bd. 178/A.26900, A.27042, A.27747.
6 *DSB*, II:157–8. See also Linke, *Deutsch-sowjetische Beziehungen*, 85–6, and PA, AA, Russland Nr.61/Bd. 178/A.27903, zu A.28109, A.28426.
7 *DBFP*, VI:293–4.
8 Maddox, *The Unknown War with Russia*, 117–25; *FRUS, 1919, Russia*, 119–20.
9 See, for example, *FRUS*, 1919, *Russia*, 441–2. On Wilson, see Park, *The Impact of Illness on World Leaders*, 3–76.
10 Lloyd George Papers, F/89/23. See also George W. Egerton, "Britain and the 'Great Betrayal';" 885–911.
11 CAB 23/35/11–12.
12 Regarding the reduction of the French role in Russia, see MAE/Russie/231/388–9, 277–8; MAE/Russie/233/passim; MAE/Russie/212/193–4; MG/CCA/16N/3029. For the more general French economic problems, see Silvermann, *Reconstructing Europe after the Great War*, 93ff.
13 Goode, *Bolshevism at Work*, 20–7.
14 Lenin, *CW*, 30:38–9.
15 Ibid., 50–1.
16 *The Times* (London), 17 September 1919:10.
17 See Debo, "Prelude to Negotiations," 58–75; FO 371/3942/9/131991, 136734, 138714; and *DBFP*, III:597.
18 FO 371/4031/136152/136152; *DBFP*, III:670–2.
19 MAE/Russie/160/24–8.

20 FO 371/4043/153757/153757; *Times*, 4 December 1919:14; *DBFP*, III:738–40.

21 *Churchill Documents*, IV, ii:963–5; CAB 24/94/CP 293, "M. Savinkov and Russian Policy;" Lloyd George Papers F/9/1/51; CAB 23/35/11–13.

22 CAB 23/35, 11 December 1919.

23 *DBFP*, II:735–7, 744–8, 764–5, 773–8, 872.

24 *FRUS*, 1920, III:444–5; MAE/Russie/160/passim.

25 *DBFP*, II:867–70. Regarding Wise, see Harris, "Bureaucrats and Businessmen in British Food Control," 151. On the Russian cooperative societies, see Blanc, *The Co-operative Movement in Russia*. For the outline of an earlier plan to use the Russian cooperatives against the Bolsheviks, see Conty to MAE, Copenhagen, 10 April 1919, tels. 305–6; and MAE/Russie/121/58–61.

26 *DBFP*, II:866–75, 911–12, 894–6.

27 Jones, *Whitehall Diary*, I:97; *Times*, 16 January 1920:10–11 and 17 January 1920:10.

28 *Churchill Documents*, IV, ii:1010.

29 CAB 23/20, 29 January 1920; Jones, *Whitehall Diary*, I:103.

30 Cited in Oznobishin, *Ot Bresta do Iur'eva*, 294.

31 *DVP*, II:315–16, 320.

32 MAE/Russie/68/14–15, 20–1.

33 Shishkin, *Sovetskoe gosudarstva i strany zapada*, 157–8.

34 FO 371/4032/142549/173925; *DVP*, II:327–9, 358.

35 *DBFP*, III:762–3, 821–4.

36 Cmd. 587 (Russia No. 1 [1920]) *Agreement between His Majesty's Government and the Soviet Government of Russia for the Exchange of Prisoners*.

37 *FRUS*, 1920, III:702.

38 Sherwood, *George Mandel and the Third Republic*, 53. On Millerand, see Farrar, "Victorious Nationalism Beleagured," 481–519.

39 See MAE/Russie/68/23, 83, 89–90; MAE/Russie/214/58–64, 159–60; MAE/Estonie/3/21.

40 FO 371/3619/67181/176885.

41 FO 371/3961/91/178568; MAE/Grande Bretagne/60/533–4.

42 MAE/Russie/68/115–17; MAE/Russie/160/196.

43 On Nitti, see Coppa, "Francesco Saverio Nitti," 211–19. For the changing nature of Italian policy toward Soviet Russia at this time, see Petracchi, *La Russia Rivoluzionaria nella Politica Italiana*.

44 *DBFP*, VII:140ff, 194ff, 206ff, 217–18.

45 Lenin, *CW*, 30:365–7, 368–9; *DVP*, II:379–84. See also Berkman, *The Bolshevik Myth*, 50ff.

46 *DVP*, II:387–8; *FRUS*, 1920, III:447.

47 Lenin, *CW*, 30:374–5; *DVP*, II:391–2.

48 Lenin, *CW*, 30:491–3.

49 Shishkin, *"Rol' V.I. Lenina v Razvitii Mezhdunarodnikh ekonomicheskikh sviazei Sovetskogo Gosudarstva,"* 199–200. See also Lenin, *Sbornik*, 37:196.

50 Zarnitskii and Sergeev, *Chicherin*, 120.

51 Zarnitskii and Trofimova, *Sovetskoi Strany Diplomat*, 70–1.

52 FO 371/4032/142549/183226. For characterizations of Litvinov, see Debo, "Lloyd George and the Copenhagen Conference," 440.

53 MAE/Russie/69/106–9.

54 *FRUS*, 1920, III:703–8; *DBFP*, VII:502–5; *DBFP*, XII:686–7.

55 *DVP*, II:424–6.

56 MAE/Russie/347/19–23.

57 MAE/Russie/69/83–91, 106–9, 136–40; MAE/Russie/70/90–5; MAE/Russie/156–59; MAE/Russie/160/220; MAE/Russie/214/173.

58 MAE/Russie/71/9; MAE/Russie/69/218, 221; MAE/Russie/156/44–5.

59 Zarnitskii and Trofimova, *Sovetskoi Strany Diplomat*, 65–6, 69–70; FO 371/4033/142549/189508, 190538; FO 371/4052/188432/189666; MAE/Russie/70/2, 25–8, 82–3. On Krasin, see also Karpova, *L.B. Krasin*, and Kremnev, *Krasin*.

60 FO 371/4034/142549/194885, 196438; FO 371/4033/142549/190737,190774.

61 See Ullman, *Anglo-Soviet Relations*, III:114–16; and Andrew, *Her Majesty's Secret Service*, 259ff.

62 FO 371/4033/142549/190774; FO 371/4034/142549/192083.

63 Karpova, *Krasin*, 63–4. See also Zarnitskii and Trofimova, *Sovetskoi Strany Diplomat*, 73–4.

64 FO 371/4034/142549/192062, 192083.

65 *DBFP*, III:822, 825–6.

66 See also Chicherin's response to a subsequent British query concerning the fate of certain White officers captured in north Russia. The foreign commissar agreed to investigate, but only, as he said, "in order to respond to the desires of the British government." This was noted with satisfaction in the Foreign Office; FO 371/3994/3669/189704; *DVP*, II:439.

67 Kenez, *The Civil War in South Russia*, 253, and Mawdsley, *The Russian Civil War*, 219–25. See also WO 158/746 and 747/passim.

68 *Churchill Documents*, IV, ii:1061; *DBFP*, XII:691–2.

69 *DBFP*, XII:696–7; MAE/Russie/238/174–7; MAE/Russie/239/42, 56–7, 63, 90. See also Kenez, *Civil War in South Russia*, 259ff, and Mawdsley, *The Russian Civil War*, 262–7.

70 *DBFP*, XII:698–9.

71 FO 371/3981/1089/190125.

72 *DVP*, II:453–4; Degras, *Soviet Documents*, I:184–5 (emphasis added).

73 *DBFP*, XII:700–1; FO 371/3981/1089/193046.

74 FO 371/3981/1089/192770.

75 *DVP*, II:470–1.

76 FO 371/3981/1089/192952, FO 371/4935/I/E.3768,E.2845,E.2938. For a detailed examination of events along the eastern coast of the Black Sea at this time, see Voronovich, "Mezh dvukh ognei," VII:113ff.

77 FO 371/3981/1089/193304.

78 FO 371/4034/142549/193988.
79 FO 371/4054/193185/193248, 197592; DBFP, VIII:152–3, 182–5.
80 DVP, II:474–5; DBFP, VIII:230–1 (emphasis added).
81 DBFP, XII:711.
82 MAE/Russie/240/112.
83 See FO 371/3981/1089/195172, minute of R. Hoare.
84 FBFP, XII:713; DVP, II:490–2.
85 FO 371/3981/1089/194211. See also Kenez, Civil War in South Russia, 293ff.
86 DBFP, XII:714.
87 Lenin, CW, 30:380, 451.

11. "WE SHOULD TAKE BAKU"

1 See Debo, Revolution and Survival, 370ff; Zürrer, Kaukasien, 221; Kashkaev, Grazhdanskaia Voina v Dagestane, 163–77; Suny, The Baku Commune.
2 WO 33/965, WO to CIC Salonika, 11 December 1918.
3 BZPSVA, 266–7.
4 PSVVZ 380ff; Tokarzhevskii, Iz Istorii Inostrannoi Interventsii i Grazhdanskoi Voiny v Azerbaidzhane, 192ff; Kashkaev, Grazhdanskaia Voina v Dagestane, 180ff.
5 PSVVZ, 416ff. Swietochowski, Russian Azerbaidjan, 139–50.
6 CAB 45/107, "Appreciation of the Situation as it was when I left it – May 13th, 1919."
7 CAB 45/107, "Situation on arrival in Transcaucasus."
8 See chapter 7 above, and Blank, 'Bolshevik Organizational Development in early Soviet Transcaucasia;' 305–38.
9 BZPSVA, 138–9.
10 PSVVZ, 392ff, and Surguladze, Zakavkaz'e v bor'be za pobedu sotsialisticheskoi revoliutsii, 380.
11 Lenin, PSS, 50:288, BZUiUSVD, 212–14; Kashkaev, Grazhdanskaia voina v Dagestane, 184ff.
12 Kashkaev, Grazhdanskaia Voina v Dagestane, 199ff; Tokarzhevskii, Iz Istorii, 213ff; PSVvZ, 402ff; Zürrer, Kaukasien, 311.
13 Zürrer, Kaukasien, 313; PSVVZ, 402–3; DBFP, III:603–4; Azizbekova and Mnats'akanian, Sovetskaia Rossiia i Bor'ba, 116ff.
14 DBFP, IV:1000–4, 1232–5, 1241–4.
15 Trotsky Papers, 1:621–9.
16 Chicherin, Stati i Rechi, 86–98.
17 BZPSVA, 257.
18 BZPSVG, 467–8.
19 Cited in Zürrer, Kaukasien, 361.
20 Degras, Soviet Documents, 1:161–7; DVP, II:238–42.
21 MAE/Russie/233/181.
22 DGKKA, pp. 5513–16; Lenin, PSS, 51:56.

23 Lenin, *CW*, 30:151–62; Garibzhanian, *V.I. Lenin i Bolshevistskie Organizatsii*, 420.

24 *DBFP*, II:321.

25 *BzPSVA*, 289–92, 311–12; Garibzhanian, *Lenin i Bolshevistkie Organizatsii*, p. 407; Kashkaev, *Grazhdanskaia Voina v Dagestane*, 228; *BzUiSVD*, 330–43; Kol'tsov, "Rol' Leninskoi Vneshnei Politiki v Obespechenii Pobedy Sovetskoi Vlasti v Zakavkaz'e," 106.

26 Lenin, *PSS*, 51:106, 399; *BzPSVG*, 527; *BzPSVA*, 367; Azizbekova and Mnat'akanian, *Sovetskaia Rossiia i Bor'ba*, 144; Zürrer, *Kaukasien*, 329ff; Swietochowski, *Russian Azerbaijan*, 174ff.

27 *DBFP*, III:747–8, 753; FO 371/4932/E.776/1/53.

28 Lenin, *Sbornik*, 36:91; *BzPSVG*, 534–5; *PSVVZ*, 424.

29 Lenin, *PSS*, 40:52.

30 MAE/Russie/236/240–1; MAE/Russie/237/2–4, 11–13; *Churchill Documents*, IV, ii:996.

31 *DBFP*, II:688–9, 796–7, 896, 915–27; MAE/Levant/Caucase/6/2–5.

32 Azizbekova and Mnat'akanian, *Sovetskaia Rossiia i Bor'ba*, 149–51.

33 Kadishev, *Interventsiia i Grazhdanskaia Voina v Zakavkaz'e*, 231; *BzUiSVD*, 344–5.

34 *Trotsky Papers*, II:81.

35 Lenin, *PSS*, 51:171, 420. Kashkaev, *Grazhdanskaia Voina v Dagestane*, 256–7; *DGKKA*, 738; Zürrer, *Kaukasien*, 362–3.

36 FO 371/4932/E.1171/1/58; MAE/Russie/648/330.

37 Kadishev, *Interventsiia i Grazhdanskaia Voina*, 236; *BzPSVA*, 419–20; *BzPSVG*, 543–6; *DBFB*, XII:570.

38 FO 371/4932/E.1227/1/58.

39 See, for example, MAE/Russie/648/330, 331–2; FO 371/4935/E.3344/1/58.

40 *DBFP*, XII:574–6, 580.

41 *BzPSVG*, 549–50.

42 *Trotsky Papers*, II:126–7; *DGKKA*, 732.

43 *DGKKA*, 733–7; *Trotsky Papers*, II: 140–3; *DGKKA*, 740.

44 *Istoriia Grazhdanskoi Voiny v SSSR*, 5:224. Azizbekova and Mnats'akanian, *Sovetskaia Rossiia i Bor'ba*, 153–4; *DKFKA*, 309–10.

45 FO 371/4937/E.4868/1/58.

46 *DBFP*, XII:593; FO 371/4935/E.3616/1/58; Azizbekova and Mnats'akanian, *Sovetskaia Rossiia i Bor'ba*, 154.

47 Zürrer, *Kaukasien*, 391–3; Swietochowski, *Russian Azerbaijan*, 180–4; Bechhofer-Roberts, *In Denikin's Russia and the Caucasus*, 316–17; FO 371/4938/E.55326–7/1/58; FO 371/4939/E.5777/1/58; MAE/Russie/639/13, 25; MAE/Russie/644/30; MAE/Levant/Caucase/7/71–82.

48 Lenin, *CW*, 31:121.

49 Guliev, *Bor'ba Kommunisticheskoi Partii*, 546; Zürrer, *Kaukasien*, 393–5; Swietochowski, *Russian Azerbaijan*, 184ff.

50 Lenin, *PSS*, 51:424.

51 See above, chapter 10; *DBFP*, XII:714.

52 *DVP*, II:501-2.

53 Lenin, *CW*, 31:135.

54 Lenin, *PSS*, 51:191, 195, 424-6.

55 MAE/Russie/648/333, 349. See also FO 371/4939/E.5778/1/58.

56 FO 371/4934I E.3014/1/58; FO 371/4935/E.3154, E.3676/1/58.

57 Lenin, *PSS*, 51:178, 191, 424; Lenin, *Sbornik*, 34:292; Lang, *A Modern History of Soviet Georgia*, 225. See also Kazemzadeh, *The Struggle for Transcaucasia*.

58 FO 371/4942/E.7446/1/58.

59 See Hovannisian, *The Republic of Armenia, Vol. II*; Suny, *Armenia in the Twentieth Century*; Nassibian, *Britain and the Armenian Question*; Galoian, *Bor'ba za Sovetskuiu Vlast' v Armeniia*.

60 MAE/Russie/648/390-1; FO 371/4939/E.5778/1/58.

61 See Azizbekova and Mnats'akanian, *Sovetskaia Rossiia i Bor'ba*, 182-5.

62 Ibid. See also FO 371/4959/E.10734/13458; *Trotsky Papers*, II:160-3; *DGKKA*, 744-5, 678-9; *GVU*, III:110-12.

63 FO 371/3872/150/199102; *Trotsky Papers*, II:146.

64 Kadishev, *Interventsiia i grazhdanskaia voina*, 262, 264.

65 CAB 23/21/151-2.

66 CAB 23/21/153-7, 193; *Churchill Documents*, IV, ii:1102-5; *DBFP*, XIII:487-8.

67 *DVP*, II:542-3; *Trotsky Papers*, II:178-81.

68 Kheifets, *Sovetskaia Rossiia i Sopredel'nye Strany Vostoka*, 235-6.

69 See Ravasani, *Sowjetrepublik Gilan*; Zabih, *The Communist Movement in Iran;* Tagieva, *Natsional'no Osvoboditel'noe Dvizhenie v Iranskom Azerbaidzhane*, Blank, "Soviet Politics and the Iranian Revolution," 173-94.

70 Kheifets, *Sovetskaia Rossiia i Sopredel'nye Strany Vostoka*, 244; Eudin and North, eds., *Soviet Russia and the East*, 95-8.

71 See Zürrer, *Persien zwischen England und Russland*; and Abrahamian, *Iran Between Two Revolutions*.

72 Kheifets, *Sovetskaia Rossiia i Sopredel'nye Strany Vostoka*, 179ff; Kapur, *Soviet Russia and Asia*.

73 *DVP*, II:198-200, 238-42; Kheifets, *Sovetskaia Rossiia i Sopredel'nye Strany Vostoka*, 209.

74 FO 371/3864/150/168496; see also *DBFP*, III:752-3; *DBFP*, XIII:433-5, 438-40, 449-50.

75 *DBFP*, XIII:457-8, 462-3, 467, 469-72; FO 371/3869/150/184917.

76 *DVP*, II:535-8.

77 Kheifets, *Sovetskaia Rossiia i Sopredel'nye Strany Vostoka*, 236-55.

78 *DVP*, II:556. See also Tamkoc, *The Warrior Diplomats;* Sonyel, *Turkish Diplomacy*, Dumont, "L'Axe Moscou-Ankara;" 165-93.

79 *DVP*, II:554-5; Sonyel, *Turkish Diplomacy*, 35-41; Kapur, *Soviet Russia and Asia*, 87-93; Kheifets, *Sovetskaia Rossiia i Sopredel'nye Strany Vostoka*, 80-112.

80 Cited in Kheifets, *Sovetskaia Rossiia i Sopredel'nye Strany Vostoka*, 109-110.

81 *DBFP*, XIII:487–8.

82 *Trotsky Papers*, II:208.

83 FO 371/3982/1089/199283.

12. "ASTOUNDINGLY ATTRACTIVE OFFERS"

1 For a clear and detailed presentation of Pilsudski's views, see CAB24/97/CP511. See also Dziewanowskii, *Joseph Pilsudski*.

2 *DBFP*, I: 694, 696–8, 689–91, 701–5; *DiM SPO*, II:339–43.

3 *DiM SPO*, II:331, 336–7; MG/CCA/16N/3526; FO 371/3900/73/145576; MAE/Pologne/70/76–8; MAE/Pologne/85/59–63; MAE/Pologne/137/17–8.

4 *DiM SPO*, II:366–70, 372–4, 393.

5 Ibid., 308–9; MG/CCA/5N/190, Henrys to War Ministry, tels. 651–2, 10 September 1919; MG/CCA/16N/3526, Fouchet to Foreign Ministry, tel. 276, 4 September 1919; and Henrys to War Ministry, 11 September 1919, 734/2B.

6 Wandycz, "Secret Soviet-Polish Peace Talks in 1919," 435–45. See also Wandycz, *Soviet-Polish Relations*, 129–31; and Davies, *White Eagle, Red Star*, 71–3.

7 *DGKKA*, 346, 483–4.

8 MG/CCA/16N/214/, Pralon to Foreign Ministry, tel. 396, 21 November 1919; MAE/Russie/286/18–20.

9 *DiM SPO*, II:376–8, 388–92; *Trotsky Papers*, I:759.

10 *DiM SPO*, II:427–8; Schumacher and Tych, *Marchlewski*, 294; and *Trotsky Papers*, I:767.

11 FO 688/1/F, Savery to H. Rumbold, 2 November 1919; *DBFP*, III:630, 633–6. For Rumbold, see Gilbert, *Sir Horace Rumbold*.

12 MG/CCA/6N/214, Pralon to Foreign Ministry, tels. 405–7, 26 November 1919.

13 MAE/Russie/664/21; MAE/Pologne/85/239; *DBFP*, III:908–9; *DBFP*, II:581–2, 735–7; MAE/Pologne/70/115; MG/CCA/6N/72, "Notes of a Conversation at Downing Street, 11 December 1919."

14 MG/CCA/6N/214, Pralon to Foreign Ministry, tel. 465, 29 December 1919.

15 MAE/Pologne/9/12. See also FO 371/3900/73/168049, 168049; MAE/Pologne/85/215–16 and Watt, *Bitter Glory*, 105.

16 *DiM SPO*, II:442–4.

17 The Twelfth Army lay at the hinge between the western and southern fronts, and in mid-October it had been transferred from the former to the latter. It would be the first threatened by any Polish attack. *Trotsky Papers*, I, 801.

18 *DVP*, II:312–13; Degras, *Soviet Documents*, I:177–8.

19 *DiM SPO*, II:449–52.

20 MG/CCA/6N/214, Pralon to Foreign Ministry, tel. 1, 3 January 1920; and *DBFP*, III:745; MAE/Russie/704/21.

21 MAE/Russie/284/, Pralon to Foreign Ministry, tel. 2, 3 January 1920.

22 *DVP*, II:320.

23 *DiM SPO*, II:451 (emphasis in original); *DGKKA*, 495–6; *GVU*, II:655.

24 MAE/Russie/286/117; *DBFP*, III:759–60.

25 *DVP*, II:331–3; Degras, *Soviet Documents*, I:178–80.

26 MAE/Russie/236/190, 231; MAE/Russie/236/55; MAE/Russie/286/5a; *FRUS*, 1919, *Russia*, 777.

27 MAE/Russie/286/78–84; MAE/Russie/236/290; MAE/Russie/237/2–4, 10; *DBFP*, II:683ff.

28 MG/CCA/6N/213, Henrys to War Ministry, tels. 971–2, 30 December 1919; MG/CCA/6N/214, Pralon to Foreign Ministry, tel. 5, 5 January 1920; MAE/Russie/286/90–1, 98.

29 MG/CCA/6N/214, Pralon to Foreign Ministry, tels 434, 466–7, 9 and 30 December 1919; MAE/Pologne/137/35–40.

30 MAE/Pologne/70/119–20; FO 371/3731/4/159966, 162298; MAE/Russie/213/185–6; MAE/Russie/286–69.

31 MG/CCA/6N/215, note, 31 December 1919; MAE/Russie/286–108.

32 MAE/Russie/286/200. See also the highly persuasive and well-argued examination of this question by Carley, "The Politics of Anti-Bolshevism," 163–89.

33 Lloyd George Papers, F/201/1/9. See also Wandycz, *Soviet-Polish Relations*, 161–2; *DBFP*, III:803–5; and CAB 23/20/Cab 6(20), 29 January 1920.

34 *DBFP*, XI:202; FO 688/3/78, 82–8.

35 MAE/Russie/286/147.

36 *DVP*, II:359; FO 371/3913/40430/176646; FO 371/3913/40430/179589; MAE/Russie/286/155, 161–2; MAE/Pologne/137/41–2.

37 FO 371/3913/40430/176418, 176646.

38 *DiM SPO*, II:601–2; *DBFP*, XI:243–5; FO 371/3913/40430/185749.

39 FO 688/3, Rumbold to Parodi, 13 February 1920. See also FO 371/3913/40430/179901 and Gilbert, *Rumbold*, 193ff; MAE/Russie/286/201–6, 217–19; *DBFP*, XI:245–6; MAE/Russie/156/170.

40 MAE/Pologne/70/139–42. See also Zamoyski, *The Battle for the Marchlands*, 16–35; Wandycz, *Soviet-Polish Relations*, 168–9; and Watt, *Bitter Glory*, 113–15.

41 Carley, "The Politics of Anti-Bolshevism," 172. For the subsequent arming of the Poles, see *DiM SPO*, II:591–6.

42 Lenin, *CW*, 30:350, 315–29, 345, 347–9; Lenin, *PSS*, 40:113–21.

43 Lenin, *CW*, 30:365–7, 394–5; Lenin, *PSS*, 40:379.

44 *DVP*, II:370–1.

45 Ibid., II:397–8.

46 *Trotsky Papers*, II:118, 122, 132; Lenin, *CW*, 30:453.

47 See *DKFKA*, II:404–5, 410, 412–13; *DGKKA*, 673; *IIGV*, III:253–7.

48 *Trotsky Papers*, II:75, 98–9.

49 MG/CCA/6N/212, 213, Henrys to War Ministry, 13 and 15 March 1920; *GVU*, III:3–9; Lenin, *PSS*, 51:155; *DKFKA*, II:176–7; Zamoyski, *Battle for the Marchlands*, 36–8; Wandycz, *Soviet-Polish Relations*, 168.

50 Lenin, *PSS*, 51:159; *DGKKA*, 733–5, 735–7, 676–7; *DKFKA*, II:423.

51 MAE/Russie/664/60–3; *GVU*, II:770–1 and III:9; MAE/Russie/156/54–5; *DBFP*, XI:250; MAE/Pologne/70/199.

52 FO 371/3630/165045/1886881; MAE/Russie/704/15; Varslavan, *Politika angli-iskogo imperializma v otnoshenii burzhuaznoi Latvii*, 71–2.

53 FO 371/3757/16086/184335. See also Jaaskelainen,·*Die ostkarelische Frage*, 227–8, and Holsti, "The Origins of Finnish Foreign Policy," 209ff.

54 *DVP*, II:393–5; MAE/Russie/342/64, 65–7.

55 *Trotsky Papers*, II:118. On the crisis and its resolution, see Holsti, "The Origins of Finnish Foreign Policy," 213–15.

56 *DVP*, II:406–7; French translation in FO 371/3737/16086/188901.

57 MAE/Russie/342/72; Kholodkovskii, *Finliandiia i Sovetskaia Rossiia*, 182–5.

58 FO 371/3737/16086/188901; MAE/Russie/342/76–9.

59 FO 371/3737/16086/191469; *DVP*, II:421–2; Jaaskelainen, *Die ostkarelische Frage*, 229; *DVP*, II:429–30, 434; MAE/Russie/342/89–90; Holsti, "The Origins of Finnish Foreign Policy," 216.

60 *DVP*, II:430–1; MAE/Estonie/3/73–5; FO 371/3611/140/185382.

61 *DVP*, II: 377–8; FO 371/3630/167566/177709; Sipols, *Tainaia Diplomatiia*, 56; *DVP*, II:423; MAE/Russie/704/21.

62 *DBFP*, XI:239–40, 246–7; FO 371/3620/67181/189278.

63 FO 371/3620/67181/190433, 191593. See also *DVP*, II:438, 450–1, 482, and *DBFP*, XI:305–6.

64 MAE/Roumanie/34/74.

65 MAE/Roumanie/34/54–61; MAE/Roumanie/55/3–5; MAE/Pologne/70/150, 160–2; MAE/Russie/286/170–1.

66 *DVP*, II:390 (emphasis added). Litvinov conveyed the same message in more precise terms to a Romanian representative in Copenhagen. "Within the framework of a Soviet-Romanian conference and according to the principle of self-determination the recognition of Bessarabia's union with Romania would be possible," he said (cited in Lungu, "Soviet-Romanian Relations and the Bessarabian Question," 29–45).

67 Lloyd George Papers, F/16/7/8; MAE/Roumanie/55/6, 7, 8; *DBFP*, VII:379–80; *DVP*, II:402–3, 409–10.

68 *DVP*, II:390–1.

69 FO 371/4050/18165/184821 and FO 371/4050/183165/183168; MAE/Tchechoslo-vaquie/63/2–3.

70 FO 371/4050/183165/193860; *DiM Sch*, I:332–4; *DVP*, II:476–7.

71 MAE/Roumanie/55/10–11.

72 *DiM SPO*, II:615; see also Wandycz, *Soviet-Polish Relations*, 180–2.

73 MAE/Russie/287/63–4; *DVP*, II:427–8; English translation in Degras, *Soviet Documents*, I:183–4; and *DiM SPO*, II:634.

74 *Trotsky Papers*, II:138–41.

75 FO 371/3913/40430/189700.

76 MAE/Russie/306/67–8; MAE/Russie/287/81, 100–2.

77 MAE/Russie/287/72–3; *DiM SPO*, II:636.

78 *DVP*, II:444–8, 451–3; *DiM SPO*, II:643.

79 FO 371/3913/40430/191156; *DBFP*, XI:287; MAE/Russie/287/100–2.

80 MAE/Russie/287/112–14, 117–18; MAE/Russie/317/170–2; MAE/Pologne/70/218–21; FO 371/3914/40430/194114. See also Wandycz, *Soviet-Polish Relations*, 185–7.

81 *DiM SPO*, II:656–8, 660–4. See also MAE/Pologne/137/69–71 and MAE/Pologne/70/117–31; Wandycz, *Soviet-Polish Relations*, 189–93, and Davies, *White Eagle, Red Star*, 100–4.

82 Jaaskelainen, *die ostkarelische Frage*, 230–1; MAE/Russie/704/19; MAE/Pologne/70/209; Holsti, "The Origins of Finnish Foreign Policy," 217ff.

83 FO 371/3737/16086/191089.

84 Kholodkovskii, *Finliandiia i Sovetskaia Rossiia*, 186–93; Jaaskelainen, *Die ostkarelische Frage*, 231–2; MAE/Russie/342/126–7; MAE/Russie/343/20; *DBFP*, XI:293–8, 303–5; FO 371/3737/16086/190776, 192086, 194228, 194370, 194916; *DGKKA*, 405, 630–1.

85 MAE/Russie/287/126–8; MG/CCA/6N/213, Henrys to War Ministry, tels. 526, 530–33, 16 April 1920; MAE/Russie/287/145, 151.

86 *DGKKA*, 629–30, 742–3; *DKFKA*, II:424–5; *DKFKA*, III:14–17, 178; MG/CCA/6N/213, Henrys to War Ministry, tel. 553, 16 April 1920.

13. SOVIET POLICY IN EASTERN EUROPE

1 FO 371/3914/40430/196783; MAE/Russie/672/2–3.

2 MAE/Russie/287/161; MAE/Russie/306/77–8, 82–4; MG/CCA/6N/212, 213, 215. See also Davies, *White Eagle, Red Star*, 130ff; Zamoyski, *Battle for the Marchlands*, 38ff.

3 *DGKKA*, 678–80; *DKFKA*, III:139–44.

4 Lenin, *CW*, 31:119ff; Trotsky, *KVR*, II, ii:102–5.

5 Lenin, *CW*, 31:131.

6 Trotsky, *KVR*, II, ii:94; Lenin, *CW*, 31:121.

7 *DVP*, II:501–2.

8 Ibid., 759; Lenin, *CW*, 31:131.

9 Riddell, *Lord Riddell's Intimate Diary of the Peace Conference*, 191–9.

10 FO 371/3914/40430/197470.

11 *The Times*, 10 May 1920; Ullman, *Anglo-Soviet Relations*, III:48ff. FO 688/3/1485/236–7; *DVP*, II:513–14.

12 FO 371/3914/40430/198285; MAE/Russie/672/30–1.

13 *IIGV*, III:285; *DGKKA*, 633–5; MAE/Russie/288/51–2, 70, 93–4, 98–9; MAE/Russie/306/97. See also Davies, *White Eagle, Red Star*, 133.

14 *IIGV*, III: 288–9, 289–90, 296–7; *DGKKA*, 685–94; Erickson, *The Soviet High Command*, 90–1; *GVU*, III:166–7; *Trotsky Papers*, II:176–9, 196–9, 206–7, 210–15; Lenin, *PSS*, 51:205ff. See also Zamoyski, *Battle for the Marchlands*, 49–74.

15 *DBFP*, VIII:281ff; Lloyd George Papers, F/58/1/14.

16 Lloyd George Papers, F/58/1/15.

17 FO 371/4036/142549/205118.

18 Zarnitskii and Trofimova, *Sovetskoi strany diplomat*, 82–3, 87–8.

19 Lenin, *Sbornik*, 38:317.

20 *DVP*, II:562; Lenin, *CW*, 31:169–70; Lloyd George Papers, F/12/3/50.

21 Lenin, *CW*, 31:173.

22 *DBFP*, XI:363. *FRUS*, 1920, III:384–5. MAE/Pologne/71/9–11; MAE/Russie/288/111; *DBFP*, XI:325–8; MAE/Russie/672/237; *GVU*, III:173–229; *DGKKA*, 636–8, 694–701.

23 Cited in Narkiewicz, *The Green Flag*, 157. See also Wandycz, *Soviet-Polish Relations*, 209–10.

24 *DiM SPO*, III:111–13; *DBFP*, XI:371–2; MAE/Russie/289/50–3.

25 Wilson diary, cited in Ullman, *Anglo-Soviet Relations*, III:140; *DBFP*, XI, 370; *Churchill Documents*, IV, ii:1134; Roskill, *Hankey*, II:176.

26 *DBFP*, VIII:441–2; *DiM SPO*, III:128–31.

27 *DiM SPO*, III:133–5, 151–3; *DBFP*, VIII:490–1, 502–6.

28 *DVP*, III:16–17; Roskill, *Hankey*, II:172; *DBFP*, VIII:490–1.

29 *DBFB*, VIII:513–16.

30 Ibid., 524–30; *DiM SPO*, III:151–3.

31 *DBFP*, VIII:517.

32 Lenin, *PSS*, 51:237; *Trotsky Papers*, II:228–31; Trotsky, *My Life*, 455–7.

33 Lenin, *PSS*, 51:238. On Soviet decision-making, see Lerner, "Attempting a revolution from without: Poland in 1920," 94–107; Davies, "The Missing Revolutionary War," 178–95; Fiddick, "The 'Miracle of the Vistula'," 626–43; Wandycz, *Soviet-Polish Relations*, 213–22, and Davies, *White Eagle, Red Star*, 136–41.

34 *DGKKA*, 610–12.

35 Zetkin, *Reminiscences of Lenin*, 20.

36 Leinwand, *Polska Partia Socjalistyczna*, 184.

37 Trotsky, *My life*, 457; Lenin, *CW*, 31:205, 560; *Lenin Biograficheskaia Khronika*, 9:105.

38 Significantly the final clause appears to have been added by Lenin; see Lenin, *Sbornik*, 39:237.

39 Degras, *Soviet Documents*, I:194–7; *DVP*, III:47–53. See Chapter 15.

40 *DGKKA*, 613–15, 639ff, 703ff; *GVU*, III:251ff. Davies, *White Eagle, Red Star*, 145–52; Zamoyski, *Battle for the Marchlands*, 77–102.

41 *DBFP*, XI:318, 338–40; FO 371/3620/67181/20296, 207092, 208935, 209876; FO 371/3621-part 1/67181/9205; *DVP*, III:28–40. See also FO 371/3915/40430/208682.

42 CAB 23/22, Cabinet 41(20), 20 July 1920.

43 Lenin, *PSS*, 51:242–3.

44 FO 371/4058/207846/209307; *DVP*, III:61–2.

45 FO 371/4036/142549/209364; *DBFP*, VIII:662, 668. See also Jones, *Whitehall Diary*, I:118–19.

46 MG/CCA/6N/214, Panafieu to Foreign Ministry, tels. 294–302, 15 and 19 July 1920; *DBFP*, XI:386–8.

47 *DiM SPO*, III:190–2.

48 FO 371/3916/40430/209868; *DBFP*, XI:396.

49 *DiM SPO*, III:196–202; *DVP*, III:60–1, 64–5; Wandycz, *Soviet-Polish Relations*, 222ff.

50 *Trotsky Papers*, II:226–9; Schumacher and Tych, *Marchlewski*, 301–2.

51 *DiM SPO*, III:221–5.

52 *DBFP*, XI:392; Roskill, *Hankey*, II:181.

53 CAB 1/29/18, Hankey to Lloyd George, 21, 22 and 24, July 1920; Hankey to Wilson, 23 July 1920. For the same view, see D'Abernon, Warsaw Diary, 26 July 1920, British Museum, D'Abernon Papers, Add. Mss. 48923.

54 *DBFP*, XI:4200–3; FO 371/3916/40430/210181; MAE/Russie/291/62–3.

55 D'Abernon, Diary, 27 July 1920; MAE/Russie/291/111–12.

56 *DGKKA*, 631; FO 371/3737/16086/195709, 197621; MAE/Russie/343/1–3, 9.

57 FO 371/3737/16086/198953; MAE/Russie/343/11–13.

58 *DVP*, II:511–12.

59 Kholodkovskii, *Finliandiia i Sovetskaia Rossiia*, 191–2. Holsti, "The Origins of Finnish Foreign Policy," 224ff; MAE/Russie/343/39–41.

60 Kholodkovskii, *Finliandiia i Sovetskaia Rossiia*, 204–8; MAE/Russie/288/139; FO 371/3737/16086/208754; FO 371/3743/199306/201261; FO 371/4058/207846/208421.

61 FO 371/3737/16086/207363; Holsti, "The Origins of Finnish Foreign Policy," 232ff.

62 Kholodkovskii, *Finliandiia i Sovetskaia Rossiia*, 193–8.

63 Jaaskelainen, *Die ostkarelische Frage*, 235; MAE/Russie/703/143–7; MAE/Russie/343/83.

64 MAE/Russie/343/110–11; Holsti, "The Origins of Finnish Foreign Policy," 238ff, 246ff; FO 371/3737/16086/210863; Kholodkovskii, *Finliandiia i Sovetskaia Rossiia*, 211–12; *DVP*, III:124–9.

65 Sipols, *Tainaia diplomatiia*, 56–8; MAE/Lettonie/2/242, 246, 268, 269; FO 371/4004/67181/198897; FO 371/3630/167580/195704; WO 33/996/116–18.

66 *DVP*, III:101–16.

14. THE END OF THE POLISH EPHEMERON

1 *DVP*, III:79–80; *DiM SPO*, III:244–7.

2 MAE/Russie/289/195–200; FO 371/4037/142549/211006.

3 MAE/Russie/307/3. This message was intercepted by the Poles and passed on to the French. Regarding Polish success in deciphering Soviet radio traffic, see Rohwer, "Der Einfluss der allierten Funkaufklarung auf den Verlauf der Zweitern Weltkrieges," 334–5.

4 *DBFP*, XI:435–6; MAE/Russie/291/95–7.

5 *DiM SPO*, III:253–8, 262–3; *DBFP*, XI:435–6, 441.

6 FO 371/3916/40420/210451.

7 *DBFP*, VIII:670–80. See also Ullman, *Anglo-Soviet Relations*, III:193ff; *DBFP*, XI:436.
8 MAE/Russie/291/91–2, 122; *Churchill Documents*, IV, ii:1159–60.
9 Lloyd George Papers, F/203/1/10 and F/203/1/7; Ullman, *Anglo-Soviet Relations*, III:208.
10 Lloyd George Papers, F/203/1/7.
11 Tanin, *Desiat let vneshnei politiki SSSR*, 85.
12 *DBFP*, VIII:681–708; CAB 24/110/CP 1752.
13 Lloyd George Papers, F/203/1/10.
14 FO 371/3916/40430/210843.
15 *DBFP*, VIII:709–55.
16 Ullman, *Anglo-Soviet Relations*, III:220–8. See also Macfarlane, "Hands off Russia in 1920," 126–52, and White, "Labour's Council of Action 1920," 99–122.
17 Lloyd George Papers, F/203/1/10.
18 FO 371/3917/40430/211548; Ullman, *Anglo-Soviet Relations*, III:225ff; *DBFP*, XI:411, 455–6.
19 CAB 21/180, D'Abernon to Hankey, 12 August 1920; FO 371/3918/40430/212514. See also Gilbert, *Rumbold*, 208–9; MG/CCA/6N/214, Jusserand to Foreign Ministry, tels. 149–50, 11 August 1920; MAE/Russie/308/92–5; and Wandycz, *Soviet-Polish Relations*, 236ff.
20 *DBFP*, XI:462; MAE/Russie/293/26–8, 89.
21 Lenin, *PSS*, 51:254–5.
22 This was the first indication many members of the British Foreign Office had seen suggesting such a condition of peace, and one wrote with evident confusion: "This seems to refer to some further terms with which we are unacquainted. The statement about arming the workers refers presumably to the annual contingent of 50,000 which the Polish army is to consist of." FO 371/3917/40430/211450.
23 Lloyd George Papers, F/203/1/1, F/203/10, F/203/1/9.
24 Ibid., F/31/1/39, F/203/1/10.
25 Ibid., F/203/1/1, F/203/1/10.
26 Lenin, *PSS*, 51:259–60; Lloyd George Papers, F/203/1/10.
27 Zamoyski, *Battle for the Marchlands*, 98–110, 125ff; Davies, *White Eagle, Red Star*, 148–50.
28 MG/CCA/6N/213, Henrys to War Minister, tels. 160–2, 13 August 1920; MAE/Russie/293/48–9, 104–5; CAB 21/180, D'Abernon Diary, 7 August 1920. See also Zamoyski, *Battle for the Marchlands*, 111ff; Davies, *White Eagle, Red Star*, 195ff; and Gervais, "Le général Weygang," 115–23.
29 See Fiddick, "The Miracle of the Vistula," Zamoyski, *Battle for the Borderlands*, 120ff; and Davies, *White Eagle, Red Star*, 212ff.
30 Lenin, *PSS*, 51:247; *IIGV*, III:336–41.
31 *IIGV*, III:342–4, 346, 348–50; *DGKKA*, 650–4, 707–12.
32 See the admirable analyses in Davies, *White Eagle, Red Star*, 207ff, and Zamoyski, *Battle for the Marchlands*, 125–40.

33 MAE/Russie/307/59; MAE/Russie/3808/101–3; MG/CCA/6N/213, Henrys to War Ministry, tels. 263–71, 300–307, 24 and 29 August 1920; and Zamoyski, *Battle for the Marchlands*, 141ff.

34 *DGKKA*, 657–9.

35 *Trotsky Papers*, II, 254, 256 (emphasis in original).

36 *DGKKA*, 620.

37 Lenin, *PSS*, 51:348–9, 349–50, 467–8.

38 Ibid., 263–4; *Trotsky Papers*, II:264–7.

39 *Trotsky Papers*, II:260–1, 266–7; Lenin, *PSS*, 51:266.

40 MAE/Russie/308/101–3; MG/CCA/6N/214, Jusserand to Foreign Ministry, tels. 177–80; MAE/Pologne/137/95–6; *DBFP*, XI:536.

41 MAE/Pologne/71/91–4.

42 "Bear in mind," Chicherin had told Krasin on 15 August, "that we reckon to take Warsaw on the 16th instant." Lloyd George Papers, F/203/1/9.

43 *DVP*, III:137–9. English text in Degras, *Soviet Documents*, I:201–2.

44 Lenin, *PSS*, 51, p. 261.

45 *DiM SPO*, III:318–23; FO 371/3320/40430/214700.

46 MG/CCA/6N/214, Jusserand to Foreign Ministery, tels. 179–82, 20 August 1920; CAB 21/180, D'Abernon to Hankey, 20 August 1920; MAE/Russie/294/131–2; British Museum, D'Abernon Mss, Add. Mss 48923, D'Abernon to Lloyd George, 21 August 1920.

47 Lloyd George Papers, F/203/1/11, F/203/1/9, F/203/1/10.

48 *DBFP*, XI:448–9, 507–8; MAE/Russie/241/257–8; MAE/Grande Bretagne/45/100; Lloyd George Papers, F/13/1/11; Roskill, Hankey, II:187–8.

49 *DBFP*, VII:756–75. See also CAB 21/180, Hankey to D'Abernon, 20 August 1920; Ullman, *Anglo-Soviet Relations*, III:262ff.

50 *DBFP*, VIII:777–81.

51 FO 371/3919/40430/213192. It is worth nothing that Dr Simons, the German foreign minister, was also vocationing in Switzerland at this time. On 22 August he sent Lloyd George a memorandum proposing Anglo-German cooperation in re-opening trade with Russia. Although he explicitly denied that he was seeking an interview with the British prime minister, it is unlikely, had circumstances developed differently (a Soviet victory in the battle of Warsaw and/or an even greater split in the entente cordiale), that he would have refused an invitation to meet with Lloyd George and Giolitti at Lucerne. See Lloyd George Papers, F/203/1/4.

52 Ibid., F/9/2/13, F/203/1/11; MAE/Russie/294/161–2.

53 Cited in MAE/Russie/74/70.

54 Lloyd George Papers, F/9/2/42, FO 371/3919/40430/213179; published in *DVP*, III:144–49, and Degras, *Soviet Documents*, I:203.

55 Lloyd George Papers, F/203/1/9.

56 Ibid., F/203/1/10.

57 *DVP*, III:150–1, 156–9.

58 *DiM SPO*, III:299. For the Revkom and its problems, see Lerner, "Attempting a Revolution from without"; Davies, *White Eagle, Red Star*, 152–7; and Wandycz, *Soviet-Polish Relations*, 226ff.

59 MAE/Russie/294/176–9.

60 Zetkin, *Reminiscences of Lenin*, 20.

15. SEEKING A "SUBSTITUTE FOR PEACE"

1 See Ullman, *Anglo-Soviet Relations*, III:89–316, 397–421; White, *Britain and the Bolshevik Revolution*, 1–54; Glenny, "The Anglo-Soviet Trade Agreement," 63–82; Shishkin, *Sovetskoe gosudarstvo i strany zapada*, 177ff; Lavrov, "Bor'ba v politcheskikh krugakh Velikobritanii vokrug anglo-sovetsikh peregovorov," 59–80; and Garamvolgyi, *Aus den Anfängen sowjetischer Aussenpolitik*.

2 See above, chapter 10.

3 *DVP*, II:506–7. English translation in Degras, *Soviet Documents*, I:186–7, but misdated as 13 May 1920; FO 371/4048/180988, 200234.

4 *DVP*, II:516–30. See also Karpova, *Krasin*, 57–9; Zarnitskii and Trofimova, *Sovetskoi strany diplomat*, 77–8; and MAE/Russie/71/156–64.

5 Lenin, *PSS*, 51:341. The British, in fact, did keep a very careful watch on the extent of Soviet trade with Sweden. See FO 371/4037/142549/passim.

6 FO 371/4034/142549/1347445, 197720; Lloyd George Papers, F/90/1/6–7.

7 Lloyd George Papers, F/202/3/5.

8 CAB 24/106/145–53.

9 CAB 24/105/1284; CAB 23/21/28(20).

10 CAB 24/106/171–5, published in *DBFP*, XII:723–6.

11 CAB 23/21/191–200.

12 *DBFP*, XII:726–7; MAE/Russie/72/7–9, 38, 55–6; *DBFP*, XII:743; FO 371/4035/142549/201229.

13 CAB 24/105/168; Lloyd George Papers F/58/1/11, 14.

14 *DBFP*, VIII:280ff.

15 Ibid., XII:720; *DVP*, II:513–14, 538; *DGKKA*, 683.

16 *DBFP*, XII:718–20; Ullman, *Anglo-Soviet Relations*, III:60–88.

17 MAE/Russie/240/2, 27; *DBFP*, XII:722.

18 MAE/Russie/240/102–4, 111–15; MAE/Russie/288/127–8bis. See also Kenez, *Civil War in South Russia*, 300ff, and Mawdsley, *The Russian Civil War*, 268ff.

19 *DBFP*, XII:728.

20 CAB 23/21/276–80; *DBFP*, XII:733.

21 *Trotsky Papers*, II:196–9.

22 Lenin, *PSS*, 51:203 (emphasis in original).

23 Ibid., 205; *Trotsky Papers*, II:198–201.

24 *Trotsky Papers*, II:206–17; *IIGV*, III:378.

25 *DVP*, II:564–5.

26 *Trotsky Papers*, II:216–19.

27 Lenin, *PSS*, 51:214–15 (emphasis in original).

28 Lloyd George Papers, F/203/1/10; *DVP*, II:566–8.

29 FO 371/3982/1089/203949.

30 Lloyd George Papers, F/202/3/19.

31 Ibid., F/203/1/10.

32 *DBFP*, VIII:380–8; FO 371/4036/142549/207569.

33 Zarnitskii and Trofimova, *Sovetskoi strany diplomat*, 88, 97–8.

34 *DVP*, III:16–17.

35 Lenin, *PSS*, 51:236, 438 (emphasis in original).

36 Ibid., 235.

37 *Trotsky Papers*, II:228–31; Lenin, *PSS*, 51:237.

38 *DVP*, III:47–53; Degras, *Soviet Documents*, 1:194–7.

39 *DVP*, III:61–2.

40 Jones, *Whitehall Diary*, I:118–19.

41 *DBFP*, VIII:662, 678.

42 Jones, *Whitehall Diary*, I:118; *DBFP*, VIII:650–61, 663–4; *DVP*, III:86.

43 *DBFP*, VIII:670–708; *DVP*, III:83–6.

44 Lloyd George Papers, F/203/1/1.

45 MAE/Russie/95/100–11.

46 Lloyd George Papers, F/31/1/39.

47 MAE/Russie/74/45; MAE/Russie/421/passim; *DVP*, III:99–100.

48 Ibid.

49 MAE/Russie/241/238–9.

50 See Radosh, "John Spargo and Wilson's Russian Policy," 548–65; Smith, *Aftermath of War*.

51 *FRUS*, 1920, III:463–8. For the Soviet response to the Colby note, see *DVP*, III:171–7. English translation in Degras, *Soviet Documents*, 1:207–11.

52 MAE/Russie/241/256, 268–70; *DBFP*, XI:465ff, 483.

53 Lloyd George Papers, F/203/1/1.

54 Degras, *Soviet Documents*, 1:197–200; FO 371/3984/1089/211164.

55 For this support, see Andrew, *Her Majesty's Secret Service*, 262–8; Ullman, *Anglo-Soviet Relations*, III:270–3; and Kendall, *The Revolutionary Movement in Britain*, 253–6.

56 Lloyd George Papers, F/203/1/10; F/203/1/11.

57 Ibid., F/9/2/42.

58 CAB 23/22/237; Lloyd George Papers, F31/1/43–4.

59 CAB 23/22/185–6; *DBFP*, VIII:783–91.

60 Karpova, *Krasin*, 93, 98–9.

61 *DVP*, III:208–10; Degras, *Soviet Documents*, 1:211–12.

62 CAB 24/111/610–18; CAB 23/22/157, 197–8, 205.

63 FO 371/4037/142549/215561.

64 *DVP*, III:228–32; FO 371/5434N.4512/207/38.

65 *DVP*, III:233–4 (emphasis added); FO 371/5431/N.70/70/38.

66 Lloyd George Papers, F/13/1/25; FO 371/5431/N.243/70/38; MAE/Russie/74/161.

67 Karpova, *Krasin*, 103, 96ff.

68 CAB 21/200.

69 *DVP*, III:314–16, 320–4; *DBFP*, XII:795–801.

70 CAB 21/200; Lloyd George Papers, F/103/1/11.

71 CAB 21/200.

72 Roskill, *Hankey*, II:210; *Churchill Documents*, IV, i:1241–2.

73 *Churchill Documents*, IV, i:1241.

74 CAB 23/23/92–8, 102–8.

75 CAB 23/23/106 (emphasis added).

76 MAE/Russie/175/10; FO 371/5420/N.3004/30/38; MAE/Russie/175/31–2.

77 Lenin, *Sbornik*, 36, p. 143; *DBFP*, XII:647, 650.

16. FINAL FRENCH FAILURE

1 See Carley, "Anti-Bolshevism in French Foreign Policy," 410–31.

2 MAE/Russie/156/165–7.

3 MAE/Grand Bretagne/45/passim; Russie/74/passim.

4 MAE/Russie/162/44.

5 MAE/Russie/187/sn.

6 MAE/Russie/242/184, 194–6, 213–14.

7 MAE/Russie/242/251; *IIGV*, III:150–2; MAE/Russie/242/404, 412.

8 MAE/Russie/242/445 (emphasis in original).

9 CAB 63/29; *DBFB*, XII:463–6.

10 MAE/Roumanie/55/24–31; MAE/Roumanie/35/6.

11 MAE/Russie/295/83; MAE/Russie/242/220, 255.

12 MG/CCA/6N/213, Henrys to War Ministry, tels. 347–53, 3 September 1920; MAE/Russie/295/116–21.

13 MAE/Russie/243/4–6, 35–6.

14 MAE/Russie/243/23–6.

15 MAE/Russie/162/60–3, 71–4.

16 Lloyd George Papers, F/9/2/42.

17 *DVP*, III:210–11; MAE/Russie/188/28–31, 45.

18 See Carley, "Anti-Bolshevism in French Foreign Policy," 416–18; and Bonnefous, *Histoire politique de la Troisieme Republique*, III:158ff.

19 *DiM SPO*, III:379–70; MG/CCA/6N/214, Panafieu to Foreign Ministry, tels 339–42, 31 August 1920; FO 371/3919/40430/214135.

20 *DiM SPO*, III:379–80. See also Wandycz, *Soviet-Polish Relations*, 250ff; MAE/Russie/295/126–9.

21 *DBFP*, XI:558; FO 371/3920/40430/215362.

22 FO 371/3920/40430/214804.

23 Lenin, *PSS*, 51:282–3.

24 FO 371/3920/40430/215371.
25 Zetkin, *Reminiscences of Lenin*, 26.
26 Lenin, *PSS*, 51:285–6; FO 371/3920/40430/215433.
27 MAE/Russie/295/116–21.
28 FO 371/3920/40430/215705.
29 See reports of the British military mission in Warsaw, WO 106/972/passim, and those of the French military mission in MAE/Russie/307/passim.
30 FO 371/3920/40430/215171, 215252; *DVP*, III:212.
31 MAE/Russie/295/167–9, 171; MAE/Russie/296/1; FO 371/3920/40430/215463.
32 Lenin, *CW*, 31:304; *DGKKAA*, 670–1.
33 *DiM SPO*, III:423.
34 See Senn, *The Great Powers, Lithuania and the Vilna Question;* and Cienciala and Komarnicki, *From Versailles to Locarno*, 131ff.
35 See Wandycz, *Soviet-Polish Relations*, 270–1.
36 *DVP*, III:245–58.
37 *FRUS*, 1920, III:621–2; MAE/Russie/296/45–6.
38 FO 371/5396/N.61/1/55; *DiM SPO*, III:426.
39 FO 371/5396/N.153/1/55.
40 Lenin, *CW*, 31:318–19.
41 MAE/Russie/96/196.
42 FO 371/3732/4/213150; cf. MAE/Russie/704/142–3. See also Holsti, "The Origins of Finnish Foreign Policy," 250ff.
43 Kholodkovskii, *Finliandiia i Sovetskaia Rossiia*, 225–6; Holsti, "The Origins of Finnish Foreign Policy," 258ff.
44 MAE/Russie/344/35–8, 47, 57.
45 *DVP*, III:265–82.
46 See Kenez, *Civil War in South Russia*, 304ff; Mawdsley, *Russian Civil War*, 269–71; and Ageev and Solonitsyn, "Razgrom Vrangelia," 9–16.
47 MAE/Russie/242 and 243/passim.
48 *DGKKA*, 760–1; *IIGV*, III:398–9.
49 *Trotsky Papers*, II:327.
50 Ibid., 322–5. See also Lenin, *PSS*, 51:293, 295; *DGKKA*, 769.
51 Lenin, *PSS*, 51:298.
52 *Trotsky Papers*, II:331; *DGKKA*, 626–8; Lenin, *PSS*, 51:301.
53 *DGKKA*, 772–3; Lenin, *PSS*, 51:307.
54 Lenin, *PSS*, 51:315; FO 371/54524/N.4317/46/38.
55 MAE/Russie/244/29–31; *Trotsky Papers*, II:343; Lenin, *PSS*, 51:321.
56 MAE/Russie/245/177–83; FO 371/5424/N.4317/46/38.
57 MAE/Russie/244/238, 243–4; MAE/Russie/244/249–50.
58 *DBFP*, XII:797, 802.
59 MAE/Russie/244/269–72.
60 *GVU*, III:729–30; *Trotsky Papers*, II:357.
61 MAE/Russie/245/passim.

62 MAE/Russie/244/288–9; MAE/Russie/245/4–7; *FRUS*, 1920, III:625–6; *DGKKA*, 789–90.

63 MAE/Russie/244/264.

64 *DGKKA*, 790.

65 MAE/Russie/75/11–14.

17. "GETTING POLAND AWAY FROM THE ENTENTE"

1 PAAA, Deutschland NR. 131/61/A.19325.

2 Linke, *Deutsch-sowjetische Beziehungen*, 76–7.

3 Ibid., pp. 77, 83.

4 Himmer, "Harmonicas," D1244.

5 ARK 130/Russland Ausw. Angel./I/ZURK 7578; L.617/120/4765/L.193183–5.

6 PAAA, Frieden Verhandlungen, Abteilung II W/Russland NR.4/10/I WK Russland 3478; T–120 4061/L.157/L.038987–9. See also Rosenfeld, *Sowjetrussland und Deutschland*, 251.

7 ARK 130/Russland Ausw.Angel./I/ZURK323;W/L.617/120/4765/L.193187.

8 ARK 130/Russland Ausw.Angel./I/ZURK84558; L.617/120/4765/L.193190.

9 Von Blücher, *Deutschlands Weg nach Rapallo*; 94–6.

10 Ibid., pp. 52–3.

11 Von Blücher, *Deutschlands Weg nach Rapallo*, 96–7; Linke, *Deutsch-sowetische Beziehungen*, 240, fn 91.

12 PAAA, Deutschland NR. 131/63/no number.

13 *DVP*, II:297–8; PAAA, Deutschland NR. 131/63/no number; and NR. 131/64/A.31643.

14 PAAA, Deutschland NR. 131/64/A.61.

15 Linke, *Deutsch-sowjetische Beziehungen*, 240, fn 91.

16 See Schüddekopf, "Karl Radek in Berlin," 87–166; Lerner, *Karl Radek*, 84ff; and Goldbach, *Karl Radek und die deutsch-sowjetischen Beziehungen*, 44ff.

17 ARK 130/Russland Ausw.Angel./I/AS 74/L.617/120/4765/L.193234–8.

18 Radek, "Der Friede und die Aussichten der Sowjetrepublik," 44–52.

19 PAAA, Abteilung A., Geheim Akten; T–136/33/Aufzeichnung Maltzans, 17 January 1920.

20 "Dokumenty o sovetsko-germanskikh otnosheniiakh," 67–8.

21 PAAA, Deutschland NR. 131/Geheim Band 20; T–136/33/Aufzeigchnung Maltzans, 20 January 1920; PAAA, Deutschland NR. 131/Band 65/Aufzeichnung Haniels, 9 February 1920.

22 Golecki, ed., *Das Kabinett Bauer, 21 June 1919 bis 27 März 1920*, 602–3.

23 PAAA, Deutschland NR. 131/Band 65/A.2646 and zu A.2659/T–136/103.

24 Schlesinger, *Erinnerungen eines Aussenseiters im diplomatischen Dienst*, 116.

25 Schlesinger, *Erinnerungen*, 117.

26 Lenin, *PSS*, 40:235–6; Lenin, *CW*, 30:366.

27 *Izvestiia*, 16 March 1920; Angress, *Stillborn Revolution*, 45.

28 PAAA, Abteilung IV.A Russland, Po 2 – Russland/1/ L.625/L.198914–18. See also Eliasberg, *Der Ruhrkrieg von 1920*, I:82–5.

29 PAAA, Abteilung IV.A. Russland, Po 2 – Russland/1/L.625/L.198914–18.

30 K.281/95851–3, AA. IV Ru 1171.

31 PAAA, Abteilung IV.A. Russland, Po 2 – Russland/1/L.625/L198922.

32 *FRUS*, 1920, III:311–14; Ibid., 300–3; *DBFP*, IX:180ff.

33 See Himmer, "Soviet Russia's Economic Relations with Germany," 179ff.

34 *DBFP*, IX:406–7; K.281/958511–3, Abteiling IV.A. Russland 1171.

35 *DSB*, II:207.

36 Williams, "Russian War Prisoners and Soviet-German Relations," 292.

37 For the original treaty see *DVP*, II:459–62, and *DSB*, II:207–10. For the July supplementary agreement, see *DVP*, III:14–16, and *DSB*, II:223–5.

38 Von Riekhoff, *German-Polish Relations*, 23ff; PAAA, Geheim Akten, Polen, Po 2/1/IV PO.3145.60160/K.170/K.023960–3.

39 Wagner, *Deutschland und der Polnisch-Sowjetische Krieg*, 27–39.

40 Rabenau, *Seeckt*, 252; Meier-Welker, *Seeckt*, 294–5.

41 Golecki, *Das Kabinett Bauer*, 603, fn. 8; PAAA, Deutschland NR. 131/65/AS 312/T-136/103.

42 *DBFP*, IX:122–5. A member of the Foreign Office Northern Department commented on one such proposal: "Stripped of all verbiage this amount to the offer of an offensive and defensive alliance with the object of enslaving Russia."

43 *DVP*, II:370–1.

44 Himmer, "Soviet Policy toward Germany," 671–2.

45 PAAA, Deutschland NR. 131(Geheim)/20/AS261 and 272b/St. Anthony's Reel 33.

46 PAAA, IV Ru 1171/K.281/K.95851–3.

47 PAAA, Referat Deutschland/Po I NR. I/I/Ref D.No. 723/T-120/5660/L.1757/L.512056–9. See also Himmer, "Soviet Russia's Economic Relations with Germany," 196–8; Carsten, *Reichswehr and Politics*, 135.

48 *DSB*, II:214–15.

49 Ibid., 215–16; PAAA, Abreilung IV – Russland, Po I/IV Ru 3599/L.614/L.197860.

50 PAAA, Referat Deutschland/Po I Nr I/I/Ref D. NO. 841/T–120/5660/L.1757/L.512062–5.

51 *DVP*, III:14–16. See also Stamm, "Der Bela-Kun Zwischenfall im Juli 1920," 365–85.

52 Wulf, *Das Kabinett Fehrenbach*, vii-xxxiv.

53 See *DBFP*, VIII; Wulf, *Das Kabinett Fehrenbach*, 41ff.

54 Linke, *Deutsch-sowjetische Beziehungen*, 107.

55 PAAA, Abteilung IV.A. Russland, Po 2, NR. 3(Kopp)/I/IV. Rus. 3359/L.671/L.211949; Linke, *Deutsch-sowjetische Beziehungen*, 107.

56 PAAA, Geheime Akten, Po 2 – Russland/I/K.281/ K.095871–2/IV. Rus. 4294.

57 See Debo, *Revolution and Survival*, 316–17.

58 *DSB*, II:229–30.

59 Wulf, *Das Kabinett Fehrenbach*, 74–5.

60 MAE/Russie/318/163–4; *DBFP*, X:361–2.

61 Wulf, *Das Kabinett Fehrenbach*, 79; MAE/Russie/290/41–2.

62 *DSB*, II:232–4.

63 Von Blücher, *Deutschlands Weg nach Rapallo*, 101; Rosenfeld, *Sowjetrussland und Deutschland*, 297; Helbig, *Die Träger der Rapallo-Politik*, 43–5; Wagner, *Deutschland und der Polnish-Sowjetische Krieg*, 89.

64 PAAA, Geheim Akten, Po 2 – Russland/1/K.281/K.905858–65 and K.096011.

65 Lenin, *PSS*, 51:242; *DSB*, II:231–2.

66 PAAA, Geheim Akten, Po 2 – Russland/1/K.281/K.095936–8. This is the original document signed by Chicherin. A version of this document appears in *DSB*, II:253–5, but it is worded entirely differently, as it appears to be a German translation from the Russian translation of the original document (almost surely written originally by Chicherin in German) printed in *DVP*, III:75ff.

67 PAAA, Geheim Akten, Po 2 – Russland/1/K.281/ K.095929–31.

68 Meinhardt, "Deutschland und Westpreussen im russisch-polnishchen Krieg," 22–3.

69 See the many reports on this subject in PAAA, Abteilung IV.A. Russland/Po 2 – Russland/1/L.6.25, and PAAA, Geheim Akten 139/1/Polen-Russland Po 23/1/ K.195.

70 PAAA Geheim Akten 139/1/Polen-Russland Po 23/1/ K.195/K.037914–15, 037920; Referat Deutschland/Po 1 Nr 1/1 Ref D.No.1108/T–120/5660/L.1858/ L.512076–8. See also Linke, *Deutsch-sowjetische Beziehungen*, 113.

71 PAAA, Geheim Akten, Po 2 – Russland/1/K.281/ K.095945–50.

72 Ibid., K.095920–3, K.095958ff, K.096029, K.096044–6.

73 See Trotsky Papers, II:250.

74 *DSB*, II:266–8, 270.

75 PAAA, Geheim Akten, Po 2 – Russland/1/K.281/K.096055–7; PAAA, Geheim Akten/ Polen/Russland/Po 23/1/T–120/3762/K.195/K.037948–50; Lloyd George Papers, F/203/1/14.

76 *DBFP*, X:300–1; FO 371/4826/C.5115, 5230/1897/18.

77 PAAA, Abteilung IV.A. Russland Po 2/2L.625/ L.625/ L.199074–84; ibid., Russland Po 5/1C/IV Ru 5727/T–120/5199/K.1865/K.469994–470011.

78 *DSB*, II:278–9, 289–90.

79 Wulf, *Das Kabinett Fehrenbach*, 231; Angress, *Stillborn Revolution*, 70–1.

80 See PAAA, Abteilung IV. A. Russland Po 2/2/passim; also PAAA, Buro des Reichsminister/Akten betreffend Russland/1/passim.

81 See Himmer, "Soviet Russia's Economic Relations with Germany," 239–41, 258–61.

18. "THE RIGHT TO AN INDEPENDENT EXISTENCE"

1 Lenin, *CW*, 31:347, 410.

2 Ibid., 411–12.

3 Ibid., 412–13, 441.

4 Ibid., 442–50, 475.

5 Ibid., 468.

6 *DVP*, III:338–9; Degras, *Soviet Documents*, II:220–1; Shishkin, *Sovetskoe gosudarstvo i strany zapada*, 229–39.

7 *DVP*, III:376–7, 377–8.

8 Lenin, *CW*, 31, 442ff, 464ff.

9 Ibid., 432, 441, 457; Lenin, *PSS*, 42:124–5.

10 Lenin, *CW*, 31:452.

11 CAB 24/115/165–70, 291–3.

12 CAB 23/23/179.

13 CAB 24/115/272–6.

14 CAB 23/23/149–50.

15 Lenin, *CW*, 31:445.

16 Lenin, *PSS*, 52:20–1, 350–1.

17 Ibid., 54:435, 718.

18 Lloyd George Papers, F/203/1/11.

19 Ibid.; Lenin, *PSS*, 54:435, 728–30.

20 CAB 24/116/320.

21 *DVP*, III:367–9; *DBFP*, XII:820–2; Zarnitskii and Trofimova, *Sovetskoi strany diplomat*, 109–11.

22 FO 371/5432/N.3839/70/38; FO 371/5432/N.4645/207/38.

23 FO 371/5434/N.4547/207/38; FO 371/5434/N.4546/207/38; FO 371/6878/N.86/86/38.

24 FO 371/5434/N.4037, 43334, 4715/207/38; Zarnitskii and Trofimova, *Sovetskoi strany diplomat*, 111–12.

25 Lloyd George Papers, F/13/1/42.

26 *DBFP*, VIII:879–92; Zarnitskii and Trofimova, *Sovetskoi strany diplomat*, 111–12.

27 CAB 23/23/75 (20)/282–4; 136 House of Commons, *Debates*, col. 1876.

28 FO 371/6877/N.505, 506, 527, 867, 2690/69/38; *DBFP*, XII:823–5.

29 Lloyd George Papers, F/203/1/11.

30 FO 371/6853/N.460/5/38.

31 *DVP*, III:440–1, 458–61; FO 371/6853/N.5 and N.461/5/38.

32 *DiM SPO*, III:448–9; *GVU*, III:653–5; and MAE/Russie/224/309, 673/passim.

33 *DGKKA*, 672; *GVU*, III:639; MAE/Russie/673/263–5.

34 *Trotsky Papers*, II:346–7; *GVU*, III:630–2; *DVP*, III:298–9, 305–9.

35 *DKFKA*, III:136, *GVU*, III:700, 718–19.

36 *DiM SPO*, III:469–75.

37 *DVP*, III:332–4; MAE/Russie/297/18; FO 371/5397/N.3319/1/55.

38 *DiM SPO*, III:484.

39 *BSV-Bel.*, II:522–52; *GVU*, III:775–83; MAE/Russie/309/56–9, 63–4, 69, 72–81; FO 371/5414/N.3122, 3313/3122/55.

40 FO 371/5397/N.2873–74/1/55; FO 371/5399/N.3383/236/55.

41 MAE/Russie/297/39–40; FO 371/5397/N.3749/1/55.

42 *DVP*, III:355–56; FO 371/5397/N.3314, 3519, 3749, 3818/1/55.

43 *DVP*, III:353–6; FO 371/5397/N.3799, 3861/1/55; MAE/Russie/297/3.

44 Lenin, *PSS*, 51:316, 463; *DVP*, III:295–6, 359–61; MAE/Russie/3244/122; MAE/Lettonie/3/136–8; MG/CCA/6N/125/passim.

45 Senn, *The Vilna Question*, 50.

46 FO 371/6720/N411/49/59.

47 MAE/Russie/297/14, 16; FO 371/5397/N.3467/1/55; MAE/Lettonie/3/212; CAB 1/29/234.

48 FO 371/5397/N.3574/1/55; FO 371/5405/N.3550/272/55.

49 *DVP*, III:380–1.

50 FO 371/5398/N.4891/1/55 (translation as in document).

51 Senn, *The Vilna Question*, 57; FO 371/5397/N.4682.

52 *DVP*, III:385–7.

53 FO 371/5397/N.4274/1/55.

54 FO 371/5406/N.4674/272/55; published in *DBFP*, XI:700–1.

55 FO 371/5447/3124/passim; MG/CCA/6N/125/passim; *FRUS*, 1920, III:666–8. See also Bicknell, *With the Red Cross*, 335–9.

56 MAE/Russie/297/75–6.

57 FO 371/6830/N.808/808/55; MAE/Russie/132/215–18; MAE/Russie/133/6–13.

58 Lenin, *CW*, 31:323–4; MAE/Russie/381/153–4.

59 *DVP*, III:446–7.

60 MAE/Russie/692/145; *DVP*, III:454–5; MAE/Russia/97/13–15.

61 *DBFP*, XII:499–500; FO 371/5413/N.1648, 2005/1648/55.

62 *DVP*, III:312; English translation in Degras, *Soviet Documents*, I:219.

63 *DVP*, III:340–1.

64 Ibid., 383–4; English translation in Degras, *Soviet Documents*, I:224–5.

65 MAE/Roumanie/55/38–41, 44–5, 54–5, 58–9.

66 MAE/Roumanie/63/10–12, 14, 15–17, 20.

67 MAE/Russie/132/215–18, 224–5, 242–9; FO 371/5444/N.4908/1322/38; FO 371/6884/N.217/217/38.

68 FO 371/5444/N.4909/1322/38.

69 MAE/Roumanie/55/75; *DVP*, III:431–3.

70 Lenin, *PSS*, 52:43–4, 357, fn. 64; *DVP*, VIII:736.

71 *DVP*, III:454–5, 474–5 (emphasis added).

72 FO 371/6884/N.1533/217/38; MAE/Russie/133/57; MAE/Russie/134/23; MAE/Russie/157/99–100; MAE/Roumanie/55/114/15.

73 FO 371/6830/N.3313/1014/55; FO 371/6831/N.8790/1074/55; MAE/Roumanie/63/42–4, 46–8.

74 *DVP*, III:510–12, 525–6; MAE/Roumanie/55/143–4, 148–9, 162; FO 371/6887/N.4983/217/38.

75 FO 371/6877/N.968/69/38; MAE/Russie/321/287–8. See also *New York Times*, 29 January 1921.

76 PAAA, Geheim Akten Po 2 – Russland/2/IV Ru 599, T–120/3925/K.281/K096222. See also MAE/Russie/321/285–6.

77 MAE/Russie/76/89–93, 121–3.

78 Zarnitskii and Trofimova, *Sovetskoi strany diplomat*, 112–13; Lenin, *Biograficheskaia Khronika*, X:13–14; Chicherin, *Stati i Rechi*, 284; PAAA, Abteilung IV Russland Po 13, Nr 6/11/IV Ru 603/K.1751/K.429120–1.

79 Akademiia Nauk SSSR, Institut Istorii SSSR, *Velikii Oktiabr' i zashchita ego zavoevanii*, 299–354; Lenin, CW, 32:170ff.

80 FO 371/6853/N.1665/5/38.

81 FO 371/6272/E.1905/116/38.

82 FO 371/6853/N.1997/5/38; published in DBFP, XII:832–4; DVP, III:530.

83 PAAA, Geheim Akten Po 2 – Russland/2/O.N/T.120/3925/K.281/K.096205–8.

84 FO 371/6847/N.2755/4/38; on Kronstadt, see Avrich, *Kronstadt*; Getzler, *Kronstadt*; Semanov, *Likvidatsiia antisovetskogo kronshtadtskogo miatezha 1921 goda*.

85 FO 371/6878/N.4046/69/38; Lloyd George Papers, F/38/3/34.

86 CAB 23/24/153–6; FO 371/6878/N.4032/69/38. Both the treaty and letter are reproduced in Ullman, *Anglo-Soviet Relations*, III:474–82.

87 Lenin, CW, 32:181.

88 DVP, IV:10–12; III:582–8, 594–5, 615.

89 Ibid., IV:13–14.

90 DBFP, XII:832–3.

91 DVP, IV:11.

92 Eudin and Fisher, eds., *Soviet Russia and the West*, 65–6.

93 Lenin, CW, 32:181.

94 See Wandycz, *Soviet-Polish Relations*, 281–90, and Davies, *White Eagle, Red Star*, 259–63.

95 FO 371/5398/N.4993/1/55; Ol'shanskii, *Rizhskii dogovor*, 171–2, 183.

96 Ibid., 78–9; FO/371/6813/N.116/116/55.

97 On Upper Silesia, see von Riekhoff, *German-Polish Relations*, 39–47; Cienciala and Komarnicki, *From Versailles to Locarno*, 52–7; and Campbell, "The Struggle for Upper Silesia," 361–85.

98 FO 371/6813/N.781, 784/116/55; MAE Russie/297/146–7.

99 DBFP, XI:725; FO 371/6813/N.2359/116/55.

100 Ol'shanskii, *Rizhskii dogovor*, 195; DiM SPO, III:502–14; DBFP, XI:182.

101 PAAA, Geheim Akten Po 2 – Russland/2/O.N./T–120/3925/K.281/K.096205–8.

102 DVP, III:555; Ol'shanskii, *Rizhskii dogovor*, 196–7.

103 FO 371/6817/N.3269/123/55; FO 371/6847/N.3074/4/38.

104 DVP, III:618–58.

105 MAE/Pologne/27/6–26; FO 371/6829/N.3271/514/55; FO 371/6814/N.6552/116/55.

106 See Linke, *Deutsch-sowjetische Beziehungen*, 118ff; Himmer, "Soviet Russia's Economic Relations with Germany," 230–303.

107 PAAA, Büro des Reichsminister/Russland/Band 2/RM758/2860/D.551948–51.

108 PAAA, IV.A Russland/Po 2/3/IV Ru 7810/L.625/L.199192–5.

109 PAAA, Büro des Reichsministers/Russland/Band 2/RM865/2860/D.551986–9;
     PAAA, IV.A Russland/Po 2/3/IV RU 7810/L.625/L.199198–9.

110 DSB, II:305; PAAA, Geheim Akten/Po 2 – Russland/2/0.N/T–120/3925/K.281/
     K.096160–2, 64. See also Himmer, "Soviet Russia's Economic Relations with
     Germany," 266ff.

111 DSB, II:317–18; PAAA, Geheim Akten/Po 2 – Russland/2/0.N./T–1203925/
     K.281/K.096184–9/K.096197–8.

112 PAAA, Geheimakten/Po 2 – Russland/Band 2/0.N./T–120K.281/K.096179–83.

113 Schlesinger, Erinnerungen, 165; PAAA, Abteilung IV Russland/Po 11 #3[Kopp]/
     2/IV Ru 365/T–120/L.167/L.212090.

114 Schlesinger, Erinnerungen, 183–4; DSB, II:340–1; DVP, III:495.

115 "Dokumenty o sovetsko-germanskikh otnosheniiakh," 72–3; PAAA, Büro des
     Reichsministers 9/Russland/3/1405/2860/D.552179.

116 Schlesinger, Erinnerungen, 185–93. See also Linke, Deutsch-sowjetische Bezie-
     hungen, 126–9; Himmer, "Soviet Russia's Economic Relations with Germany,"
     277–81; PAAA, Abteilung IV Russland/Po 2A/1/passim/T–120/4782/L.639/pas-
     sim.

117 PAAA, Abteilung IV Russland Po 2A/1/zu IV Ru 1204/T–120/4782/L.639/
     L.203068.

118 PAAA, Geheim Akten Po 2 – Russland/2/0.N./T–120/3925/K.281/K.096205–8.

119 Bariety, Les relations franco-allemandes apres la premiere guerre mondiale, 64–
     76; McDougall, France's Rhineland Diplomacy, 139–57; Dohrmann, Die en-
     glische Europapolitik in der Wirtschaftskrise, 55–70.

120 FO 371/6880/N.3594/105/38; PAAA, Abteilung IV Russland/Po 2/4/IV Ru 1746/
     T–120/4775/L.625/L.199280.

121 For an examination of this question and the März Aktion, see Angress, Stillborn
     Revolution, 105ff; Golbach, Karl Radek, 85–94; Lazitch and Drachkovitch, Lenin
     and the Comintern, 470–527.

122 Wulf, Das Kabinett Fehrenbach, 605–11.

123 PAAA, Büro des Reichsministers 9/Russland/3/RM.2377/T–120/1405/2860/
     D.552215–16; PAAA, Abteilung IV Russland/Po 2A/1/ zu Ru 1797, IV Ru 2075/
     T–120/4782/L.639/L.203108–10, 203241–3; PAAA, Referat Deutschland/Po 1
     No 1/2/Ref D.766/T–120/5660/L.1757/L.512203–8.

124 Trotsky Papers, II:440–3. For the origins of Soviet-German military collabora-
     tion, see Gatzke, "Russo-German Military Collaboration," 565–97; Carsten, The
     Reichswehr and Politics, 135–7; and Linke, Deutsch-sowjetische Beziehungen,
     152–7. For a differing view, see Mueller, "Rappalo Re-examined; 109–17.

125 Lenin, PSS, 43:188.

126 DSB, II:379–80; Lenin, Sbornik, 39:283; PAAA, Abteilung IV/0 2A/2/0. N./T–
     120/4782/L.639/L.203255.

127 *DBFP*, XV:579–80.
128 PAAA, Abteilung IV Russland/Po 2A/2/O.N./T–120/4782/L.639/L.203381–2;
   DVP, IV:99–105; Wulf, *Das Kabinett Fehrenbach*, 669–70.
129 *Izvestiia*, 14 May 1921.
130 FO 371/6880/N.5773/105/38 and MAE/Russie/322/156–7, 178–9.

19. FEDERATION AND ALLIANCE

1 Lenin, *CW*, 31:144–51, 240–5. See also Lazitch and Drachkovitch, *Lenin and the Comintern*, 381–96.
2 Eudin and North, *Soviet Russia and the East*, 65–7; Roy, *Memoirs*, 368–82.
3 Degras, *The Communist International*, 1:141.
4 White, "Communism and the East," 492–514; and Chabrier, "Les delegues au Premier Congress des Peuples de l'Orient, Bakou," 21–42.
5 Pipes, *Formation of the Soviet Union*, 174–83; Park, *Bolshevism in Turkestan*, 1–42.
6 See Clayton, *The British Empire as a Superpower*, 160–73; Stewart, *Fire in Afghanistan*, 41ff; and Poullada, *Reform and Rebellion in Afghanistan*.
7 Kheifets, *Sovetskaia Rossiia i sopredel'nye strany vostoka*, 273–81; *DVP*, II:174–5, 204.
8 Pipes, *Formation of the Soviet Union*, 183; Kheifets, *Sovetskaia Rossiia i sporedel'nye strany vostoka*, 281–76; *DVP*, II:261–2; FO 371/3991/191281/3267/38.
9 FO 371/3991/191281/3267/38.
10 Kheifets, *Sovetskaia Rossiia i sopredel'nye strany vostoka*, 287; FO/371/3991/ 191281/3267/38.
11 Kheifets, *Sovetskaia Rossiia i sopredel'nye strany vostoka*, 292–6; Park, *Bolshevism in Turkestan*, 42–7; Pipes, *Formation of the Soviet Union*, 176–82.
12 Park, *Boshevism in Turkestan*, 42–4; IVIIGVVSAIK, II:495–507.
13 Kheifets, *Sovetskaia Rossiia i sopredel'nye strany vostoka*, 292; IVIIGVVSAIK, II:514–15; 518ff; Park, *Bolshevism in Turkestan*, 48–9; Pipes, *Formation of the Soviet Union*, 184.
14 Ademec, *Afghanistan*, 148–57.
15 FO 371/3991/191281/3267/38; Lloyd George Papers, F/12/3/50.
16 *DVP*, II:550–1; III, 139–40.
17 FO 371/3992/202951/3267/38.
18 Ademec, *Afghanistan*, 157–8.
19 Kheifets, *Sovetskaia Rossiia i sopredel'nye strany vostoka*, 301–6; *DVP*, III:193–4.
20 *DVP*, IV:663.
21 Ibid., III:199–200.
22 Ademec, *Afghanistan*, 158–9; *DVP*, III:193–4; Lloyd George Papers, F/203/1/11.
23 Ademec, *Afghanistan*, 160–1; *DVP*, IV, 655.
24 *DVP*, III:550–3.
25 Ademec, *Afghanistan*, 161.

26 Ibid., 191.

27 See Zürrer, *Kaukasien*, 413–24; Kadishev, *Interventsiia i grazhdanskaia voina*, 289–310; *Trotsky Papers*, II:200–5; DGKKA, 668.

28 MAE/Levant/Caucase/7/3–5, 39–40, 63, 90–1; MAE/Russie/242/33–6; FO 371/4944/E.9478/1/58; IIGV, III:382–3, 390–1; Lenin, *PSS*, 51:254; *Trotsky Papers*, II:249–51.

29 *Trotsky Papers*, II:284–5, 316–21; DGKKA, 763; Lenin, *PSS*, 51:281.

30 *Trotsky Papers*, II:107–11.

31 FO 371/4959/E.11703/134/58. Significantly this document is not included in DVP. For the circumstances leading to the armistice, see FO 371/4940/E.6039/1/58; FO 371/4944/E.9344/1/58; FO 371/4959/E.10343, 10378–9, 10734/134/58; MAE/Russie/644/51–2; MAE/Russie/639/106–7; BZPSVG, 612–18.

32 DBFP, XII:633–4.

33 Sonyel, *Turkish Diplomacy*, 41–8.

34 Ibid., 48–50; Vartamian, *Pobeda sovetskoi vlasti v Armenii*, 198–205; FO 371/4959/E.11868, 12317, 13194/134/58.

35 Kheifets, *Sovetskaia Rossiia i sopredel'nyi strany vostoka*, 130–2.

36 Lenin, *Sbornik*, 31:131.

37 Kheifets, *Sovetskaia Rossiia i sopredel'nyi strany vostoka*, 133.

38 Ibid., 137; DBFP, XII:638; Zürrer, *Kaukasian*, 424–55.

39 Ibid., 134; Lenin, *PSS*, 54:432, 716–17.

40 FO 371/4962/E.13496/134/58; Kheifets, *Sovetskaia Rossiia i sopredel'nyi strany vostoka*, 140–2.

41 DVP, III:325; Kheifets, *Sovetskaia Rossiia i sopredel'nyi strany sostoka*, 142–5; Sonyel, *Turkish Diplomacy*, 52–3; FO 371/4966/E.15222/134/58.

42 Azizbekov, et al., *Sovetskaia Rossiia i Bor'ba*, 191–4; Lenin, *PSS*, 52:14–15; Lloyd George Papers, F/203/1/11.

43 Lenin, *Sbornik*, 36:144; 39:260; *PSS*, 52:14–15, 347; *Trotsky Papers*, II:364–5.

44 FO 371/4965/E.15081/134/58; see also DBFP, XII:648–9.

45 Kheifets, *Sovetskaia Rossiia i sopredel'nyi strany vostoka*, 145.

46 Ibid., 150–2; Vartamian, *Pobeda*, 322ff; IIGV, III:496–7, 503; DBFP, XII:655; FO 371/4965/E.15290, 15415/134/58.

47 Kheifets, *Sovetskaia Rossiia i sopredel'nyi strany vostoka*, 151; Sonyel, *Turkish Diplomacy*, 53–4.

48 Kheifets, *Sovetskaia Rossiia i sopredel'nyi strany vostoka*, 159–63; Sonyel, *Turkish Diplomacy*, 54.

49 BZPSVG, 579–99.

50 See Rose, "Batum as Domino," 266–87.

51 Sonyel, *Turkish Diplomacy*, 83–5.

52 FO 371/4948/E.15488/1/58.

53 DBFP, XII:641–2; see also FO 371/4947/E.13161/1/58 and MAE/Russie/526/299–301.

54 FO 371/4947/E.13195/1/58.

Notes to pages 359–68

55 Lenin, *PSS*, 51:51.
56 FO 371/6271/E.56/56/58 (emphasis added); see also FO 371/4947/E.13311/1/58.
57 *DVP*, III:330; FO 371/6271/E.56/56/58. See also *Izvestiia*, 18 November 1920, and *DBFP*, XII:650, 651.
58 Sonyel, *Turkish Diplomacy*, 86–8.
59 Eudin and North, *Soviet Russia and the East*, 187–8; Kheifets, *Sovetskaia Rossiia i sopredel'nyi strany vostoka*, 161–2; *DVP*, III:364–5.
60 Kheifets, *Sovetskaia Rossiia i sopredel'nyi strany vostoka*, 162; *DVP*, III:373–4, 380.
61 See the interesting reports of A. Chevailley, the French representative in Tiflis, based on secret talks with Mosline Israfiloff, the representative of Soviet Azerbaijan in Georgia, MAE/Russie/632/179–80, 189–91.
62 MAE/Russie/649/57–8, 81–2, 106–7; FO 371/4948/E.15476/1/58, FO 371/49049/E.16137/1/58, FO 371/6268/E.299/55/58; *BzPSVG*, 640–4.
63 Azizbekov, et al., *Sovetskaia Rossiia i Bor'ba*, 217.
64 Zhvaniia, "V.I. Lenin i partiinaia organizatsii Gruzii."
65 Azizbekov, et al., *Sovetskaia Rossiia i Bor'ba*, 218; Lenin, *PSS*, 54:437, 719.
66 Lenin, *PSS*, 52:66; Lenin, *Biograficheskaia Khronika*, X:87.
67 Lenin, *PSS*, 52:69–70; also see *Trotsky Papers*, II:374–5 (Emphasis in original).
68 Kadishev, *Interventsiia i grazhdanskaia voina*, 368–73.
69 Lenin, *PSS*, 52:71; *Trotsky Papers*, II:376–7.
70 *IIGV*, III:508.
71 Kadishev, *Interventsiia i grazhdanskaia voina*, 380–6, 421–31.
72 Lenin, *PSS*, 32:137; *IIGV*, III:533; *DBFP*, XII:676.
73 MAE/Russie/649/225; MAE/Russie/649 and 650/passim; FO 371/6268/E.2273/55/58; MAE/Russie/633/7–19; MAE/Russie/650/2–9, 29–50; Kadishev, *Interventsiia i grazhdanskaia voina*, 401ff.
74 *DBFP*, XII:666–7; MAE/Russie/649/216.
75 MAE/Russie/650/59–60, 69–70.
76 MAE/Russie/650/73, 82, 94.
77 *BzPSVG*, 702–7; MAE/Russie/650/120–33, 173–85; Kadishev, *Interventsiia i grazhdanskaia voina*, 412ff.
78 For the background of these events, see Dumont, "L'Axe Moscou-Ankara" and the additional articles by the same author: "La fascination du Bolchevisme," 141–66; "Bolchevisme et Orient," 377–410; and "La revolution impossible," 143–74. See also *The Origins of Communism in Turkey*.
79 Lenin, *PSS*, 52:392–6, 479, 484–8; *DVP*, III:391–2, 435–6, 468. See also MAE/Russie/632/196–7.
80 Sonyel, *Turkish Diplomacy*, 90–2; FO 371/6465/E.1710/1/44.
81 *DVP*, III:556.
82 Lenin, *PSS*, 52:92; Soneyl, *Turkish Diplomacy*, 64, 98–100.
83 *DVP*, III:597–607. (English translation in Degras, *Soviet Documents*, I:237–42).
84 Kheifets, *Sovetskaia Rossiia i sopredel'nyi strany vostoka*, 237–44; Kapur, *Soviet Russia and Asia*, 172–6.

85 Kheifets, *Sovetskaia Rossiia i sopredel'nyi strany vostoka*, 250–1.
86 *DBFP*, XIII:598–600; *Trotsky Papers*, II:306–7.
87 Kheifets, *Sovetskaia Rossiia i sopredel'nyi strany vostoka*, 258–9; *DVP*, III:153.
88 FO 371/6399/E.515/2/34; Lloyd George Papers, F/203/1/71.
89 FO 371/6401/E.2124/2/34; Kheifetz, "Leninskaia vneshniaia politika i strany vos-toka," 141–2.
90 FO 371/6402/E.3491/2/34; *DBFP*, XII:680–1.
91 *DBFP*, XIII:672–4, 682.
92 FO 371/6402/E.3495/2/34.
93 *DBFP*, XIII:679–80, 684–5, 691, 696.
94 *DVP*, III:491–3; *DBFP*, XIII:718–19, 728–31.
95 FO 371/6401/E.3993/2/34.
96 *DVP*, III:536–44 (English translation in FO 371/6403/E.4270/2/34).

20. "NOT A STEP FURTHER TOWARDS THE EAST"

1 Fleming, *Admiral Kolchak*, 163ff; *Istoriia Grazhdanskoi voiny v SSSR*, IV:350ff; *Trotsky Papers*, I:768–71; Pereira, "White Power during the civil War in Siberia, 45–62; and White, *The Siberian Intervention*, 343–4.
2 Fleming, *Admiral Kolchak*, 174–88; White, *Siberian Intervention*, 343; Footman, *Civil War in Russia*, 211–30; Parfenov, *Bor'ba za Dalnii Vostok*, 17ff.
3 Footman, *Civil War in Russia*, 233; Papin, *Krakh kolchakovshchiny i obrazovanie Dalnevostochnoi Respubliki*, 101–2.
4 Papin, *Krakh*, 102; Shereshevskii, *V bitvakh*, 52–3; *DGKKA*, 598; *Trotsky Papers*, II:9.
5 Lenin, *PSS*, 51:334; Papin, *Krakh*, 104–5; Shereshevskii, *V bitvakh*, 54.
6 Footman, *Civil War in Russia*, 236–41; White, *Siberian Intervention*, 343; Papin, *Krakh*, 105–6; *Istoriia grazhdanskoi voiny v SSSR*, IV:355.
7 Shereshevskii, *Razgrom semenovshchiny*, 58–9.
8 *Trotsky Papers*, II:40, 51–3.
9 Lenin, *PSS*, 51:137.
10 *DGKKA*, 600; *Istoriia grazhdanskoi voiny v SSSR*, VI:355.
11 *FRUS*, 1920, III:486–502.
12 *DVP*, II:387–9.
13 Smith, *Vladivostok under Red and White Rule*, 23.
14 *IIGV*, III:708–9. See also Shurygin, "Dalburo TSK RKP(b) v gody grazhdanskoi voiny," 55–62.
15 White, *Siberian Intervention*, 118–19, 266–9, 285–6; Smith, *Vladivostok*, 10–17; Papin, *Krakh*, 116–20; Parfenov, *Bor'ba*, 165–7; *Istoriia grazdanskoi voiny v SSSR*, IV:355ff.
16 Smith, *Vladivostok*, 32ff; White, *Siberian Intervention*, 358ff.
17 *DVP*, II:409, 414–17.
18 *DBFP*, VI:1055–6; Shereshevskii, *Razgrom*, 75ff.
19 Smith, *Vladivostok*, 40–1; Nikiforov, *Zapiski Prem'iera DVR*, 190.

20 Smith, *Vladivostok*, 32ff; Svetachev, *Imperialisticheskaia interventsiia v Sibiri*, 223ff.

21 *DVP*, II:441–3; *FRUS*, 1920, III:507, 512–13.

22 Smith, Vladivostok, 43–4; *FRUS*, 1920, III:510–13; *DVP*, II:496–8.

23 Eudin and North, *Soviet Russia and the East*, 209–10; Shereshevskii, *Razgrom*, 78ff; Lenin, *PSS*, 51:136; Shereshevskii, *Razgrom*, 60.

24 *DVP*, II:444–5; Svetachev, *Interventsiia*, 232; *IIGV*, III:720–2.

25 Smith, *Vladivostok*, 46ff; Shereshevskii, *Razgrom*, 137–8; *FRUS*, 1920, III:548.

26 Shereshevskii, *Razgrom*, 138–9.

27 *DVP*, II:514; Eudin and North, *Soviet Russia and the East*, 210.

28 Shereshevskii, *Razgrom*, 139–40.

29 Ibid., 140–2, 147–50; Shishkin, *Grazhdanskaia voina na Dalnem Vostoke*, 162–6.

30 Shereshevskii, *Razgrom*, 143–6.

31 Ibid., 158–64.

32 *FRUS*, 1920, III:516–17.

33 *DVP*, III:44–7.

34 *BzVSvPri*, 512.

35 *FRUS*, 1920, III:513–16; *DBFP*, XIV:70–1.

36 *FRUS*, 1920, III:517–19.

37 *DBFP*, XIV:70–1, 76–7.

38 *BzVSvPri*, 513–14.

39 Shereshevskii, *Razgrom*, 164.

40 *Istoriia grazhdanskoi voiny v SSSR*, V:343–4; Shereshevskii, *Razgrom*, 180–1; Svetachev, *Interventsiia*, 235.

41 Shereshevskii, *Razgrom*, 179ff; Smith, *Vladivostok*, 55ff.

42 Shereshevskii, *Razgrom*, 189ff; Smith, *Vladivostok*, 60ff.

43 *Trotsky Papers*, II:300–3.

44 Shereshevskii, *Razgrom*, 207; *IIGV*, III:734.

45 Shereshevskii, *Razgrom*, 206, 214–20; *IIGV*, III:734–5; *FRUS*, 1920, III:544.

46 *IIGV*, III:735–7.

47 Smith, *Vladivostok*, 65ff; Shereshevskii, *V bitvakh*, 28ff.

48 Smith, *Vladivostok*, 72ff; Shereshevskii, *Razgrom*, 224ff.

49 *IIGV*, III:744–5; Shereshevskii, *V bitvakh*, 55.

50 *Trotsky Papers*, II:384–7.

51 Shereshevskii, *V bitvakh*, 60–7; Svetachev, *Interventsiia*, 240ff; *DVP*, III:447, 479–84; *BzVSvPri*, 551–5.

52 *DVP*, I:415–16.

53 See Tse-tsung, *The May Fourth Movement*; Pye, *Warlord Politics*; and Sheridan, *China in Disintegration*.

54 Quested, *"Matey" Imperialists*.

55 Leong, *Sino-Soviet Diplomatic Relations*, 134.

56 *DVP*, II:221–3; Degras, *Soviet Documents*, I:158–60.

57 On Chinese policy, see Leong, *Sino-Soviet Diplomacy*, 60–92, 140–1.

58 Kheifets, *Sovetskaia Rossiia i sopredel'nye strany*, 376ff; Leong, *Sino-Soviet Diplomatic Relations*, 93ff.

59 Leong, *Sino-Soviet Diplomacy*, 142.

60 Ibid., 143–5.

61 *DVP*, II:498–9. See also Persits, *Dalnevostochnaia Respublika i Kitai*, 97ff.

62 Persits, *Dalnevostochnaia Respublika i Kitai*, 101ff. See also Kazanin, *Zapiski sekretaria missii.*

63 Leong, *Sino-Soviet Diplomacy*, 117ff, 153ff; Persists, *Dalnevostochnaia Respublika i Kitai*, 116ff.

64 *DVP*, III:213–16; Degras, *Soviet Documents*, I:212–15 (emphasis added).

65 Persits, *Dalnevostochnaia Respublika i Kitai*, 100, 109; Kurdiukov, Nikiforov, and Perevertailo, eds. *Sovetsko-Kitaiskie Otnosheniia*, 51ff.

66 Leong, *Sino-Soviet Diplomacy*, 103–6.

67 *DBFP*, XIV:155; Persits, *Dalnevostochnaia Respublika i Kitai*, 110, 117–25; Leong, *Sino-Soviet Diplomacy*, 156–7.

68 *FRUS*, 1920, I:779; Leong, *Sino-Soviet Diplomacy*, 159; Persits, *Dalnevostochnaia Respublika i Kitai*, 136.

69 Persits, *Dalnevostochnaia Respublika i Kitai*, 137–41.

70 Ibid., 141–2; Leong, *Sino-Soviet Diplomacy*, 160.

71 Cited in Leong, *Sino-Soviet Diplomacy*, 161.

72 Shereshevskii, *V bitvakh*, 92–3; Nislov, *Razgrom Ungerna*, 11–15; Brown and Onon, *History of the Mongolian People's Republic*, 84–6; Ewing, *Between the Hammer and the Anvil?* 194–7; Smith, "Atamanshchina in the Russian Far East," 57–67; Smith, "The 'Ungernovshchina'" 590–5.

73 *DVP*, III:324; Eudin and North, *Soviet Russia and the East*, 200–1.

74 *DVP*, III:345–6; Leong, *Sino-Soviet Diplomacy*, 173.

75 Brown and Onon, *History of the Mongolian People's Republic* 87–8; Ewing, *Between the Hammer and the Anvil'*, 197–201; Kislov, *Razgrom Ungerna*, 15–17; Leong, *Sino-Soviet Diplomacy*, 174.

76 Ewing, *Between the Hammer and the Anvil?* 159–87; Brown and Onon, *History of the Mongolian People's Republic*, 49–83; Isono, "The Mongolian Revolution of 1921," 375–94; Isono, "Soviet Russia and the Mongolian Revolution of 1921," 116–40.

77 Ewing, *Between the Hammer and the Anvil?*, 222 8.

78 *DVP*, IV:19–21; Persits, *Dalnevostochnaia Respublika i Kitai*, 142ff.

79 *DVP*, II:546–9; Carr, *The Bolshevik Revolution*, III:498–500; Whiting, *Soviet Policies in China*, 141; *Trotsky Papers*, II:16–19; Ochur, *Velikii Oktiabr' i Tuva.*

CONCLUSION

1 Institut Marksizma-Leninizma pri TSK KPSS, *Desiatyi S'ezd RKP, (b): Protokoly*, 1.
2 MAE/Russie/157/102–9.
3 MAE/Russie/157/113–16.
4 FO 371/6854/N.3573/5/38.
5 MAE/Russie/133/15–16.
6 Debo, *Revolution and Survival*, 339–40.

Bibliography

UNPUBLISHED DOCUMENTS AND PAPERS

FRANCE
Archives of:
  Ministère des Affaires étrangères
  (MAE), Paris.
  Ministère de la Guerre, Vincennes.

GERMANY
Microfilmed records of:
  Auswärtiges Amt.
  Reichskanzlei.

GREAT BRITAIN
British Museum
  Balfour Papers

Library, House of Lords
  Bonar Law Papers
  Lloyd George Papers
Public Record Office
  Admiralty Papers
  Cabinet Papers
  Foreign Office Papers
  War Office Papers

UNITED STATES
National Archives
  Records of Department of State
  Yale University: Buckler Papers

PUBLISHED DOCUMENTS AND PAPERS

– . "Dokumenty o sovetsko-germanskikh otnosheniiakh (1919–1921 gg)." *Sovetskie Arkhivy* 2 (1971): 60–78.

Akademiia Nauk Azerbaidzhanskoi SSR, Armianskoi SSR, Gruzinskoi SSR. Instituty Istorii. *Pobeda Sovetskoi vlasti v Zakavkaz'e*. Tbilisi: Izdatel'stvo "Metsniereba" 1971.

Akademiia Nauk Gruzinskoi SSR, Gruzinskii Filial Instituta Marksizma-Leninizma pri TSK KPSS, Arkhivnoe Upravlenie Gruzinskoi SSR. *Bor'ba za Pobedu Sovetskoi Vlasti v Gruzii. Dokumenty i Materialy (1917–1921 gg)*. Tbilisi 1958.

Akademiia Nauk SSSR. Institut Istorii SSSR. *Pogranichnye voiska SSSR 1918–1928*. Moscow: Izdatel'stvo Nauka 1973.

– .Institut slavianovedeniia i balkanistiki; Chekoslovatskaia Akademiia nauk – chekhos-
lavatsko-sovetskii institut; Slovatskaia Adademiia nauk – Institut istorii evropeiskiikh
sotsialisticheskikh stran. *Dokumenty i Materialy po istorii sovetsko-chekhoslovatskikh
otnoshenii* Tom I. Noiabr' 1917g.-avgust 1922 g. Moscow: Izdatel'stvo "Nauka"
1973.

– .Institut slavianovadeniia i pol'sko-sovetskikh otnoshenii. *Dokumenty i Materialy
po istorii sovetskogo-pol'skikh otnoshenii.* 6 vols. Moscow: Izdatel'stvo Nauka
1963–69.

Anikeev, V.V. *Deiatel'nost' TsK RKP(b) v 1918–1919 godakh: (Khronika sobytii).*
Moscow: Izdatel'stvo "Mysl" 1976.

Arkhivnyi otdel Upravleniia MVD Primorskogo kraia Primorskii Kraevoi Gosudarstvennyi
Arkhiv. *Bor'ba za vlast' sovetov v Primor'e (1917–1922 gg).* *Sbornik Dokumentov.*
Vladivsotok: Primorskoe Knizhnoe Izdatel'stvo 1955.

Arkhivnye upravleniia pri sovete ministerov i TSGA Kazakhskoi, Uzbekskoi, Tadzhikskoi,
Turkmenskoi SSR, et al. *Inosrannaia voennaia interventsiia i grazhdanskaia voina v
Srednei Azii i Kazakhstane.* 2 vols. Alma-Ata: Izdatel'stvo Akademii Nauk Kazakhskoi
SSR 1963–64.

Arkhivnoe upravlenie pri sovete ministerov UKSSR, Tsentral'nyi Gosudarstvennyi Arkhiv
Oktiabr'skoi Revoliutsii Sotsialisticheskogo Stroitel'stva UKSSR, Institut Istorii AN
UKSSR. *Grazhdanskaia voina na Ukraine.* 3 vols. in 4. Kiev: Naukova dumka 1967.

Bak, Janos M. "Aus dem Telegrammwechsel zwischen Moskau und Budapest, März-
August 1919." *Vierteljahreshefte für Zeitgeschichte* 19 (1971): 187–224.

Baumbart, Winfried, ed. *Von Brest-Litovsk zur Deutschen November-Revolution: Aus
den Tagebüchern, Briefen und Aufzeichnungen von Alfons Paquet, Wilhelm Groener
und Albert Hopman, März bis November 1918.* Deutsche Geschichtsquellen des 19
und 20 Jahrhunderts, Band 47. Göttingen: Vandenhoeck und Ruprecht 1971.

Bundesrepublik Deutschland. Auswärtiges Amt. *Akten zur Deutschen Auswärtigen Politik
1918–1945. Serie A: 1918–1925.* 4 vols. Göttingen: Vandenhoeck und Ruprecht 1982–
86.

Chicherin, G.V. *Stat'i i rechi po voprosam mezhdunarodnoi politiki.* Moscow: Izdate-
l'stvo sotsial'no-ekonomicheskoi literatury 1961.

– "Der Volkskommissar des Auswärtigen über den Frieden und über die Lage in Russland." *Russische Korrespondenz* 4 (Februar 1920): 1.

Commission Nationale Pour la Publication de Documents Diplomatiques Suisses. *Documents Diplomatiques Suisses 1848–1945.* 7 vols. 1918–20. Tome I, 11 novembre
1918–28 juin 1919. Bern: Benteli Verlag 1979.

Degras, Jane, ed. *Soviet Documents on Foreign Policy, 1917–1941.* 3 vols. London:
Oxford University Press 1951–53.

– , ed. *The Communist International, 1919–1943.* 2 vols. New York: Oxford University
Press 1956–60.

Eudin, Xenia J. and Robert C. North, eds. *Soviet Russia and the East, 1920–1927: A
Documentary Survey.* Stanford, California: Stanford University Press 1957.

– and Harold H. Fisher, eds. *Soviet Russia and the West, 1920–1927: A Documentary
Survey.* Stanford, California: Stanford University Press 1957.

Gilbert, Martin. *Winston S. Churchill*. Vol. 4, pts. I and 2, *Documents (January 1917–March 1921)*. London: Heinemann 1977.

Glavnoe arkhivnoe upravlenie pri sovete ministrov SSSR, Tsentral'nyi Gosudarstvenny Arkhiv Sovetskoi Armii, Institut Voennoi Istorii Ministerstva Oborony SSSR. *Direktvy Glavnogo Komandovaniia Krasnoi Armii (1917–1920)*. *Sbornik dokumentov*. Moscow: Voennoe Izdatel'stvo Ministerstva Oborony SSSR, 1969.

– Insitutut Voennoi Istorii Ministerstva Oborony SSSR, Tsentral'nyi Gosudarstvennyi Arkhiv Sovetskoi Armii. *Direktivy Kommandovaniia Frontov Krasnoi Armii (1917–1922 gg)*. *Sbornik dokumentov*. 4 vols. Moscow: Voennoe Izdatel'stvo Ministerstva Oborony SSSR 1969.

Glavnoe arkhivnoe upravlenie. Tsentral'nyi gosudarstvenny arkhiv sovetskoi armii. *Severnyi Front: Bor'ba sovetskogo naroda protiv inostrannoi voennoi Interventsii i Belogvardeishchiny na Sovetskom severe (1918–1920): Dokumenty*. Moscow: Voennoe Izdatel'stvo Ministerstva Oborony Soiuza SSSR 1961.

Golecki, Anton, ed. *Das Kabinett Bauer, 21 Juni 1919 bis 27 März 1920. (Akten der Reichskanzlei Weimarer Republik)*. Boppard an Rhein: Harald Boldt Verlag 1980.

Hunczak, Taras, ed. *Ukraina i Pol'shcha v dokumentakh 1918–1922*. Chastyna I and II. New York 1983.

Institut Istorii, Iazyka i literatury Dagestanskogo filiala Akademii Nauk SSSR; Institut Istorii Partii pri Dagestanskom Obkome KPSS; Filial Instituta Marksizma-Leninizma pri TSK KPSS; Arkhivnyi Otdel MVD DASSR. *Bor'ba za ustanovlenie i uprochenie Sovetskoi vlasti v Dagestane 1917–1921 gg*. *Sbornik dokumentov i materialov*. Moscow: Izdatel'stvo Akademii Nauk SSSR, 1958.

Institut istorii partii pri TSK KP Azerbaidzhana – filial instituta Marksizma-Leninizma pri TSK KPSS; Institut Istorii AN Azerbaidzhanskoi SSR – Arkhivnoe Upravlenie pri Sovete Ministerov Azerbaidzhanskoi SSR. *Bor'ba za pobedu Sovetskoi vlasti v Azerbaidzhane, 1918–1920: Dokumenty i Materialy*. Baku 1967.

Institut Marksizma-Leninizma pri TSK KPSS. *Desiatyi S'ezd RKP(b): Protokoly*. Moscow: Gosudarstvennoe Izdatel'stvo politicheskoi literatury 1963.

– *Iz Istorii grazhdanskoi voiny v SSSR: 1917–1922: Sbornik dokumentov i materialov*. 3 vols. Gosudarstvennoe Izdatel'stvo politicheskoi literatury 1960–61.

– *Perepiska Sekretariata TsK RKP(b): Sbornik dokumentov*. 8 vols. Moscow: Izdatel'stvo politicheskoi literatury 1966–74.

– *Vladimir Il'ich Lenin. Biograficheskaia Khronika, 1870–1924*. 12 vols. Moscow: Izdatel'stvo Politicheskoi Literatury 1970 82.

– *Vos'moi S'ezd RKP(b): Protokoly*. Moscow: Gosudarstvennoe Izdatel'stvo politicheskoi literatury 1959.

Institut istorii partii pri TsK KPB – filial Instituta Marksizma-Leninizma pri TSK KPSS. *Bor'ba za Sovetskuiu Vlast' v Belorussii 1918–1920 gg*. *Sbornik dokumentov i materialov*. 2 vols. Minsk: Izdatel'stvo "Belarus" 1971.

Italy. Ministero degli Affari Esteri. *I documenti diplomatici Italiani*. Series 6. Rome, 1952–.

Jeffery, Keith, ed. *The Military Correspondence of Field Marshal Sir Henry Wilson 1918–1922*. London: Bodley Head for the Army Records Society 1985.

Kingisepp, V. *Bor'ba protiv inostrannykh imperialistov i ikh posobnikov: Sbornik statei i listovok*. Tallin 1956.

Kriegsministerium Deutschlands. Forschungsanstalt für Kriegs-und Heeresgeschichte. *Darstellungen aus den Nachkriegskämpfen deutscher Truppen und Freikorps*. 3 vols: I, *Die Rückführung des Ostheeres* (1936); II, *Die Feldzug im Baltikum bis zur zweiten Einnahme von Riga* (1937); III, *Die Kämpfe im Baltikum nach der zweiten Einnahme von Riga, Juni bis Dezember 1919* (1938). Berlin: Verlag von E.S. Mittler und Sohn.

Kurdiukov, I.F., V.N. Nikiforov, and A.S. Perevertailo, eds. *Sovetsko-Kitaiskie otnosheniia 1917–1957. Sbornik dokumentov*. Moscow: Izdatel'stvo Vostochnoi literatury 1959.

Latvijas Padomju Socialistiskas Respublikas. Zinatnu akademija vestures instituts. *Sotsialisticheskaia Sovetskaia Respublika Latvii v 1919g. i inostrannaia interventsiia. Dokumenty i materialy*. 2 vols. Riga 1959.

Lenin, V.I. *Leninskii Sbornik*. 40 vols. Moscow 1924–85.

– . *Polnoe Sobranie Sochinenii*. 5th edition, 55 vols. Moscow: Izdatel'stvo Politicheskoi Literatury 1958–66.

McNeal, Robert H., ed. *Resolutions and Decisions of the Communist Party of the Soviet Union*. 4 vols. Toronto: Toronto University Press 1974.

Mantoux, Paul. *Les Délibérations du Conseil de Quatre (24 mars–27 juin 1919): Notes de l'Officier Interprète*. 2 vols. Paris 1955.

Matthias, Erich. *Zwischen Räten und Geheimräten: Die Deutsche Revolutionsregierung, 1918/19*. 2 vols. Düsseldorf: Droste Verlag 1969.

Ministerium für Auswärtige Angelegenheiten der DDR und Ministerium für Auswärtige Angelegenheiten der UdSSR. *Deutsche-Sowjetische Beziehungen von den Verhandlungen in Brest-Litowsk bis zum Abschluss des Rapallovertrages*. 2 vols. Berlin: Staatsverlag der Deutschen Demokratischen Republik 1967–71.

Ministertvo inostrannykh del SSSR. *Sovetsko-Germanskie Otnosheniia. Sbornik dokumenty*. 2 vols. Moscow: Politizdat 1968–69.

– *Dokumenty vneshnei politiki SSSR*. 21 vols. Moscow: Izdatel'stvo Politicheskoi Literatury 1959–.

O'Brien, Francis William, ed. *Two Peacemakers in Paris. The Hoover-Wilson Post-Armistice Letters 1918–1920*. College Station, Texas: Texas A & M University Press 1978.

Riddell, Lord. *Lord Riddell's Intimate Diary of the Peace Conference and after, 1918–1923*. London: Gollancz 1933.

Schulze, Hagen, ed. *Das Kabinett Scheidemann: 13 Februar bis 20 Juni 1919. (Akten der Reichskanzlei Weimarer Republik)*. Boppard am Rhein: Harald Boldt Verlag 1971.

– . *Friekorps und Republik, 1918–1920*. Boppard am Rhein: Harald Boldt Verlag 1969

Stalin, Joseph V. *Works*. 13 vols. New York: Progress Publishers 1952–55.

Trotnow, Helmut. "Karl Liebiknecht und die russische Revolution: Ein unveröffentlicher Diskussionsbeitrag Karl Leibknechts zu Karl Radeks Rede auf dem Gründungsparteitag der KPD 1918/19." *Archiv für Sozialgeschichte* 13 (1973): 379–97.

Trotsky, Leon. *Écrits militaires*. Paris: Éditions de l'Herne 1967.

– . *Kak Vooruzhulas' Revoliutsiia.* 3 vols. Moscow 1923–25.

– . *The Trotsky Papers.* Edited by Jan M. Meijer. 2 vols. The Hague: Mouton & Co. 1964–71.

– . *Sochineniya.* 21 vols. Moscow: Gosudarstvennoe Izdatel'stvo 1925–1927.

Tsentrarkhiv Leningradskoe Otdelenie tsentral'nogo istoricheskogo arkhiva RSFSR. *Baltiiskii flot v oktiabr'skoi revoliutsii i grazhdanskoi voine.* Moscow, Leningrad: Partiinoe Izdatel'stvo 1932.

United States. Department of State. *Foreign Relations of the United States.* Washington, DC.

Vogt, Martin, ed. *Das Kabinett Müller I: 27 März bis 21 Juni 1920. (Akten der Reichskanzlei Weimarer Republik).* Boppard am Rhein: Harald Boldt Verlag 1971.

Weber, Hermann, ed. Der Gründungsparteitag der K.P.D.: Protokoll und Materialien. Frankfurt am Main: Europäische Verlagsanstalt 1969.

Woodward, E.L. and R. Butler, eds. *Documents on British Foreign Policy, 1918–1945.* 1st series. London: HMSO 1947–.

Wulf, Peter, ed. *Das Kabinett Fehrenbach: 25 Juni 1920 bis 4 Mai 1921. (Akten der Reichskanzlei Weimarer Republik).* Boppard am Rhein: Harald Boldt Verlag 1972.

NEWSPAPERS

Izvestiia (Moscow)
New York Times
Le Populaire (Paris)
Pravda (Moscow)
Le Temps (Paris)
The Times (London)

AUTOBIOGRAPHIES AND MEMOIRS

Antonov-Ovseenko, V.A. *Zapiski o grazhdanskoi voine.* 4 vols. Moscow: Gosvoenizdat 1924–33.

Avalov, Pavel Mikhailovich. *Im Kampf gegen den Bolschewismus.* Glückstadt: J.J. Augustin 1925.

Bechhofer-Roberts, C.E. *In Deniken's Russia and the Caucasus, 1919–1920.* London: W. Collins and Co. 1921.

Berkman, Alexander. *The Bolshevik Myth (Diary 1920–1922).* London: Hutchinson 1925.

Bicknell, Ernest P. *With the Red Cross in Europe, 1917–1922.* Washington, DC: The American National Red Cross 1938.

Blücher, Wipert von. *Deutschlands Weg nach Rapallo: Erinnerungen eines Mannes aus dem zweiten Gliede.* Wiesbaden: Limes Verlag 1951.

Böhm, Wilhelm. *Im Kreuzfeuer zweier Revolutionen.* Münich: Verlag für Kulturpolitik 1924.

Bullitt, William C. *The Bullitt Mission to Russia.* New York: B.W. Huebsch 1919.

Cahén, Fritz Max. *Der Weg nach Versailles: Erinnerungen 1912–1919. Schicksalsepoche einer Generation.* Boppard am Rhein: Harald Boldt Verlag 1963.

Chicherin, Georgii. "Lenin i Vneshniaia Politika." *Mirovaia Politika v 1924 godu (sbornik statei pod redaktsii F. Rotshteina).* Moscow: Izdatel'stvo kommunisticheskoi akademii 1925.

Fischer, Louis. *Men and Politics: An Autobiography.* New York: Duell, Sloan and Pearce 1941.

Goode, William T. *Bolshevism at Work.* New York: Harcourt Brace & Howe 1920.

Ironside, E. *Archangel, 1918–1919.* London: Constable 1953.

Jones, Thomas. *Whitehall Diary.* 3 vols. London: Oxford University Press 1969–71.

Kazanin, Mark I. *Zapiski sekretaria missii: stranichka istorii pervykh let sovetskoi diplomatii.* Moscow: Izdatel'stvo vostochnoi literatury 1963.

Kingisepp, V. *Pod igom nezavistimosti.* Tallin 1955.

Larsons, M.J. *Im Sowjet-Labryrinth.* Berlin: Transmane 1931.

Mannerheim, Carl Gustav Emil. *The Memoirs of Marshal Mannerheim.* London: Cassell 1953.

Maynard, Major-General Sir Charles. *The Murmansk Venture.* London: Hodder and Stoughton 1928.

Mordacq, General Jean Jules Henri. *Le Ministère Clemenceau: Journal d'un Temoin.* 3 vols. Paris 1930–31.

Nadolny, Rudolf. *Mein Beitrag.* Wiesbaden: Limes Verlag 1955.

Nikiforov, P.M. *Zapiski Prem'era DVR.* Moscow: Izdatel'stvo politicheskoi literatury 1974.

Radek, Karl. "Noiabr." (Stranichka iz vospominanii). *Krasnaia Nov'* 10 (1926).

Roy, Manabendra Nath. *M.N. Roy's Memoirs.* Bombay: Allied Publishers 1964.

Schlesinger, Moritz. *Erinnerungen eines Aussenseiters im dipomatischen Dienst.* Köln: Verlag Wissenschaft und Politik 1977.

Serge, Victor. *Memoirs of a Revolutionary, 1901–41.* New York: Oxford University Press 1963.

Steffens, Lincoln. *Autobiography of Lincoln Steffens.* New York 1931.

Stevenson, Frances. *Lloyd George: A Diary.* London: Hutchinson & Co. 1971.

Torrey, Glenn E., ed. *General Henri Berthelot and Romania: Memoires et Correspondence, 1916–1919.* Eastern European Monographs 219. Boulder, Colorado: East European Monographs 1987.

Trotsky, Leon. *My Life.* New York: Charles Scribner 1930.

Voronovich, N. "Mez dvukh ognei." *Arkhiv Russkoi Revolutsii* 7 (1922): 53–184.

Winnig, August. *Am Ausgang der deutschen Ostpolitik.* Berlin 1921.

Zetkin, Klara. *Reminiscences of Lenin.* London: Modern Books 1929.

BOOKS, ARTICLES, AND DISSERTATIONS

– . 'Obrazovanie severo-zapadnago pravitelstva.' *Arkhiv Russkoi Revoliutsii* 1 (1922): 295–308

Abrahamian, Ervand. *Iran between Two Revolutions*. Princeton: Princeton University Press 1982.

Adamec, Ludwig W. *Afghanistan, 1900–1923: A Diplomatic History*. Berkeley: University of California Press 1967.

Adams, A.I. *Bolsheviks in the Ukraine: The Second Campaign*. New Haven: Yale University Press 1963.

Agar, Augustus. *Baltic Episode: A Classic of Secret Service in Russian Waters*. London: Conway Maritime Press 1983.

Ageev, A., and G. Solonitsyn. "Razgrom Vrangelia." *Voenno-Istorii Zhurnal* 11(1980): 9–16.

Akademiia Nauk moldavskoi SSR. Institut Istorii. *Bor'ba trudiashchikhsia Bessarabii za svoe osvobozhdenie i vossoedinenie s sovetskoi rodninoi (1918–1940 gg.)*. Kishinev: Izdatel'stvo "Kartia Moldoveniaske" 1970.

– *Bor'ba trudiashchikhsia Moldavii protiv interventov i vnutrennei kontrrevoliutsii v 1917–1920 gg*. Kishinev: Izdatel'stvo "Kartia Moldoveniaske" 1967.

Akademiia Nauk Estonskoi SSR. Institut Istorii. *Istorii Estonskoi SSR*. 3 vols. Tallin: Izdatel'stvo "Eesti Raamat" 1974.

Akademiia Nauk SSSR. Institut Istorii Oktiabr' i grazhdanskaia voina v SSSR. *Sbornik statei k 70 letiiu akademika I. I. Mints*.

– . *Bor'ba za sovetskuiu vlast" v pribaltike*. Moscow: Izdatel'stvo "Nauka" 1967.

– . *Iz istorii grazhdanskoi voiny i interventsii 1917–1922 gg. Sbornik statei*. Moscow: Nauka 1974.

– . Institut Istorii. *Ocherki istorii Leningrada*. 4 vols. Moscow: Izdatel'stvo Nauka 1955–64.

– . Nauchnyi sovet po kompleksnoi probleme "istoriia velikoi oktiabr'skoi sotsialisticheskoi revoliutsii." *Iz istorii grazhdanskoi voiny i interventsii. 1917–1922 gg. Sbornik statei*. Moscow: Nauka 1974.

– . Institut Istorii SSSR. *Leninskaia vneshniaia politika sovetskoi strany 1917–1924*. Moscow: Izdatel'stvo Nauka 1969.

– . Institut Istorii SSSR. *Velikii Oktiabr' i zashchita ego zavoevanii*. 2 vols. Moscow: Nauka 1987.

Akademiia Nauk UkSSR. Institut Istorii. *Istoriia gorodov i sel Ukrainskoi SSR. Zakarpatskaia oblast'*. Kiev: Institut Istorii Akademii Nauk UkSSR 1982.

Ambrosius, Lloyd E. "Woodrow Wilson's Health and the Treaty Fight, 1919–1920." *International History Review* 9, no. 1 (February 1987): 73–84.

Amburger, Erik. *Ingermanland. Eine junge provinz Russlands im Wirkungsbereich der Residenz und Weltstadt St. Petersburg-Leningrad*. 2 vols. Koln: Boehlau 1979.

Andrew, Christopher. *Her Majesty's Secret Service. The Making of the British Intelligence Community*. New York: Viking 1986.

Angress, Werner T. *Stillborn Revolution: The Communist Bid for Power in Germany 1921–1923*. Princeton: Princeton University Press 1963.

Avrich, Paul. *Kronstadt 1921*. Princeton: Princeton University Press 1970.

Azan, General Paul. *Franchet D'Esperey*. Paris: Flammarion 1949.

Azizbekova, P.A., and A.N. Mnats'akanian. *Sovetskaia Rossiia i bor'ba za ustanovlenie i uprochenie vlasti sovetov v Zakavkaz'e*. Baku 1969.

Badia, G. *Les Spartakistes: 1918, l'Allemagne en Revolution*. Paris: Gallimard 1973.

Balogh, Eva S. "Nationality Problems of the Hungarian Soviet Republic." Ivan Völgyes, ed. *Hungary in Revolution 1918–1919. Nine Essays.*

Banac, Ivo, ed. *Effects of World War I. The Class War after the Great War: The Rise of Communist Parties in East Central Europe 1918–1921*. East European Monographs 137. Boulder, Colorado 1983.

Bariéty, Jacques. *Les relations franco-allemandes après la première guerre mondiale.* Paris: Éditions Pedone 1977.

Baumgart, Winfried. *Deutsche Ostpolitik, 1918*. Oldenbourg: Wien und München 1966.

Bennett, Geoffrey. *Cowan's War: The Story of British Naval Operations in the Baltic 1918–1920*. London: Collins 1964.

Benvenuti, Fancesco. *The Bolsheviks and the Red Army, 1918–1922*. Cambridge: Cambridge University Press 1988.

Bienhold, Marianne. *Die Entstehung des litauischen Staates in den Jahren 1918–1919 im Spiegel deutscher Akten*. Bochum: Studienverlag Dr. N. Brockmeyer 1976.

Blanc, Elsie Terry. *The Co-operative Movement in Russia*. New York: Macmillan 1924.

Blank, Stephen. "Soviet Nationality Policy and Soviet Foreign Policy: The Polish Case 1917–1921." *International History Review* 7, no. 1 (February 1985): 103–28.

– . "Soviet Politics and the Iranian Revolution of 1919–1921." *Cahiers du monde russe et soviétique* 21, no. 2 (1980): 173–94.

– . "Bolshevik Organizational Development in early Soviet Transcaucasia: Autonomy vs. Centralization 1918–1924." In Suny, *Transcaucasia*, 305–38.

Blobaum, Robert. *Feliks Dzierzynski and the SDKPil: A Study of the Origins of Polish Communism*. East European Monographs 154. Boulder, Colorado 1984.

Bonnefous, Georges. *Histoire politique de la troisième République*. 7 vols. Paris: Presses universitaires de France 1956–.

Borowsky, P. *Deutsche Ukrainepolitik 1918*. Lübeck: Mattiesen 1970.

Borys, J. *The Russian Communist Party and the Sovietization of Ukraine*. Stockholm: Kungl. Boktryckereit P.A. Nortedt & Soner 1960.

Brinkley, G.A. *The Volunteer Army and Allied Intervention in South Russia, 1917–1921*. Notre Dame: Notre Dame University Press 1966.

Brown, William A., and Urgunge Onon. *History of the Mongolian People's Republic*. Cambridge, Mass: East Asian Research Center, Harvard University 1976.

Busch, Briton Cooper. *Hardinge of Penshurst: A Study in the Old Diplomacy*. Manden, Conn: Archon 1980.

Campbell, F. Gregory. "The Struggle for Upper Silesia, 1919–1922." *Journal of Modern History* 42, no. 3 (September 1970): 361–85.

Carlbäck-Isolato, Helene. "Pengar eller politik. Ekonomiska forbindelser mellan Sverige och Sovjet 1917–1924." *Historisk Tidskrift* 2, (1985): 187–233.

Carley, Michael. "Anti-Bolshevism in French Foreign Policy: The Crisis in Poland in 1920." *International History Review* 2, no. 3 (July 1980): 410–31.

– . *Revolution and Intervention. The French Government and the Russian Civil War, 1917–1919.* Kingston: McGill-Queen's University Press 1983.

– . "The Politics of Anti-Bolshevism: The French Government and the Russo-Polish War, December 1919 to May 1920." *Historical Journal* 19, no. 1 (1976): 163–89.

Carr, Edward Hallett. *A History of Soviet Russia: The Bolshevik Revolution.* 3 vols. London: Macmillan 1950–53.

Carsten, Francis Ludwig. *The Reichswehr and Politics, 1918–1933.* Oxford: Oxford University Press 1966.

Chabrier, Edith. "Les delegues au premier congres des peuples de l'orient, Bakou." *Cahiers du monde russe et soviétique* 26, no. 1 (1985): 21–42.

Chernykh, M. "Iu. Markhlevskii o sovetskoi vneshnei politike." *Sovetskoe Slavianovedenie* 2 (1979): 12–22.

Cienciala, Anna M., and Titus Komarnicki. *From Versailles to Locarno. Keys to Polish Foreign Policy, 1919–1925.* Lawrence, Kansas: University Press of Kansas 1984.

Clayton, Anthony. *The British Empire as a Superpower, 1919–1939.* London: Macmillan 1986.

Conte, Francis. *Christian Rakovski (1873–1941). Essai de Biographie Politique.* 2 vols. Lille: Atelier Reproduction des Thèse, Université Lille III 1975.

Coppa, Frank John. "Francesco Saverio Nitti: Early Critic of the Treaty of Versailles." *Risorgimento* 2 (1980): 211–19.

Cornebise, Alfred E. *Typhus and Doughboys: The American Polish Typhus Relief Expedition 1919–1921.* Newark, Delaware: University of Delaware Press 1983.

Dallin, D. "The Outbreak of the Civil War." L. Haimson, ed. *The Mensheviks: from the Revolution of 1917 to the Second World War.* Chicago: University of Chicago Press 1974.

Davies, Norman. *God's Playground: A History of Poland.* 2 vols. New York: Columbia University Press 1982.

– . "The Missing Revolutionary War. The Polish Campaigns and the Retreat from Revolution in Soviet Russia 1919–1921." *Soviet Studies* 27, no. 2 (April 1975): 178–95.

– . *White Eagle, Red Star. The Polish-Soviet War, 1919–1920.* London: Macdonald 1972.

Debo, Richard K. "Lloyd George and the Copenhagen Conference of 1919–1920: The Initiation of Anglo-Soviet Negotiations." *Historical Journal* 24, no. 2 (1981): 429–41.

– . "Prelude to Negotiations: The Problem of British Prisoners in Soviet Russia November 1918-July 1919." *Slavonic and East European Review* 58, no. 1 (1980): 58–75.

– . "Lockhart plot or Dzerzhinskii plot?" *Journal of Modern History* 43, no. 3 (September 1971): 413–39.

– . *Revolution and Survival: The Foreign Policy of Soviet Russia 1917–1918.* Toronto: Toronto University Press 1979.

– . "The 14 November 1918 Teleprinter Conversation of Hugo Haase with Georgii Chicherin and Karl Radek: Document and Commentary." *Canadian-American Slavic Studies* 14, no. 4 (Winter 1980): 513–34.

– . "The Manuilskii Mission: An Early Soviet Effort to Negotiate with France, August 1918-April 1919." *The International History Review* 8, no. 2 (May 1986): 214–35.

Dennis, Alfred L.P. *The Foreign Policy of Soviet Russia.* New York: E.P. Dutton 1924.

Diehl, James M. *Paramilitary Politics in Weimar Germany.* Bloomington, Ind.: Indiana University Press 1978.

Dobson, Christopher, and John Miller. *The Day They Almost Bombed Moscow: The Allied War in Russia, 1918–1920.* New York: Atheneum 1986.

Dockrill, Michael L., and J. Douglas Goold. *Peace Without Promise: Britain and the Peace Conferences, 1919–1923.* London: Batsford Academic and Educational Ltd. 1981.

– and Zara Steiner. "The Foreign Office at the Paris Peace Conference in 1919." *The International History Review* 2, no. 1 (January 1980): 55–86.

Dohrmann, Bernd. *Die englische Europapolitik in der Wirtschaftskrise 1921–1923. Zur interdependenz von Wirtschafts interessen und Aussenpolitik.* München: R. Oldenbourg Verlag 1980.

Doroshenko, Dmytro. *A Survey of Ukrainian History.* Winnipeg: Humeniuk Publication Foundation 1975.

Dumont, Paul. "Bolchevisme et Orient. Le Parti Communiste Turc de Mustafa Suphi, 1918–1921." *Cahiers du monde russe et soviétique* 18, no. 4 (octobre-decembre 1977): 377–410.

– . "La fascination de Bolshevisme: Enver Pacha et le Parti de Soviets Populaires, 1919–1922." *Cahiers de monde russe et soviétique* 16, no. 2 (avril-juin 1975): 141–66.

– . "La Révolution impossible: Les courants d'opposition en Anatolie 1920–21." *Cahiers du monde russe et soviétique* 19, nos. 1–2 (janvier-juin 1978): 143–74.

– . "L'Axe Moscou-Ankara: Les relations turco-soviétiques de 1919–1922." *Cahiers de monde russe et soviétique* 18, no. 3 (juillet-septembre 1977): 165–93.

Dziewanowskii, M.K. *Joseph Pilsudski: A European Federalist, 1918–1922.* Stanford: Stanford University Press 1969.

Egerton, George W. "Britain and the 'Great Betrayal': Anglo-American Relations and the Struggle for United States Ratification of the Treaty of Versailles, 1919–1920." *Historical Journal* 21, no. 4 (1978): 885–911.

Egorov, A.I. *Razgrom Denikina.* Moscow: Gosvoenizdat 1931.

Elben, Wolfgang. *Das problem der kontinuität in der deutschen revolution. Die Politik der Staatssekretara und der militarischen Fuhrung vom November 1918 bis Februar 1919.* Beitrage zur Geschichte des Parlamentarismus und der politischen Parteien, 31. Düsseldorf: Droste Verlag 1965.

Eliasberg, George. *Der Ruhrkrieg von 1920.* Bonn-Bad Godesberg: Verlag Neue Gesellschaft GmbH 1974.

Erger, Johannes. *Der Kapp-Lüttwitz-Putsch. Ein Beitrag zur deutschen Innenpolitik 1919/20.* Düsseldorf: Droste Verlag 1967.

Erickson, John. *The Soviet High Command. A Military-Political History, 1928–1941.* London: Macmillan 1962.

Ewing, Thomas E. *Between the Hammer and the Anvil? Chinese and Russian Policies in Outer Mongolia, 1911–1921.* Bloomington, Ind.: Research Institute for Inner Asian Studies, Indiana University 1980.

Farnsworth, Beatrice. *William C. Bullitt and the Soviet Union.* Bloomington, Ind.: University of Indiana Press 1967.

Farrar, Marjorie. "Victorious Nationalism Beleagured: Alexandre Millerand as French Premier in 1920." *Proceedings of the American Philosophical Society* 126, no. 6 (1982): 481–519.

Fiddick, Thomas. "The 'Miracle of the Vistula': Soviet Policy versus Red Army Strategy." *Journal of Modern History* 45, no. 4 (December 1973): 626–43.

Fischer, Kurt. *Deutsche Truppen und Entente-Intervention in Südrussland 1918/19.* Boppard am Rhein: Harald Boldt Verlag 1973.

Fleming, P. *The Fate of Admiral Kolchak.* London: Rupert Hart-Davis 1963.

Floto, Inga. *Colonel House in Paris.* Aarhus: Universitetsforlaget 1973.

Footman, David. *Civil War in Russia.* New York: Praeger 1961.

Galoian, G.A. *Bor'ba za sovetskuiu vlast' v Armenii.* Moscow: Gosudarstvennoe izdatel'stvo politicheskoi literatury 1957.

Garamvölgyi, Judit. *Aus den Anfängen sowjetischer Aussenpolitik. Das britisch-sowjetrussische Handelsabkommen von 1921.* Köln: Verlag Wissenschaft und Politik 1967.

Gardner, Lloyd C. *Safe for Democracy: The Anglo-American Response to Revolution 1913–1923.* New York: Oxford University Press 1984.

Garibzhanian, G.B. *V.I. Lenin i Bolshevistskie organizatsii Zakavkaz'ia (1893–1924).* Erevan 1967.

Gatzke, Hans W. "Russo-German Military Collaboration during the Weimar Republic." *American Historical Review* 63 (1958): 565–97.

Gaworek, Norbert H. "From Blockade to Trade: Allied Economic Warfare against Soviet Russia, June 1919 to January 1920." *Jahrbücher für Geschichte Osteuropas* 23, no. 1 (1975): 39–69.

Gervais, Céline. "Le général Weygand, la question du commandement polonais et la bataille de Varsovie." In Céline Gervais, ed., *La Guerre Polono-Soviétiques de 1919–1920.* Paris: Institut d'etudies slaves 1975.

Getzler, Israel. *Kronstadt 1917–1921. The Fate of a Soviet Democracy.* New York: Cambridge University Press 1983.

Gilbert, Martin. *Sir Horace Rumbold: Portrait of a Diplomat 1869–1941.* London: Heinemann 1973.

– . *Winston S. Churchill. Vol. IV: The Stricken World 1916–1922.* Boston: Houghton Mifflin 1975.

Glenny, M.V. "The Anglo-Soviet Trade Agreement, March 1921." *Journal of Contemporary History* 5, no. 2 (1970): 63–82.

Goldbach, Marie-Luise. *Karl Radek und die Deutsch-Sowjetischen Beziehungen, 1918–1923.* Bonn: Verlag Neue Gesselschaft GmbH 1973.

Golinkov, D.L. *Krakh vrazheskogo podpol'ia. (Iz istorii bor'by s kontrrevoliutsiei v sovetskoi rossii v 1917–1924 gg.).* Moscow: Izdatel'stvo politicheskoi literatury 1971.

– . *Krushenie antisovetskogo podpol'ia v SSSR (1917–1925 gg)*. Moscow: Politizdat 1975.

Gorokhov, I., L. Zamiatin, and I. Zemskov. *G.V. Chicherin – Diplomat Leninskoi Shkoly*. Moscow: Izdatel'stvo politicheskoi literatury 1966.

Gostynska, Weronika. "Konferencja Panstw Baltyckich i Polski w Helsinkach 1920 roku. (Sprawa Stosunka do Rosji Radzieckiej)." *Zapiski Historyczne* 42, no. 4 (1977): 77–94.

– . "Rola Juliana Marchlewskiego w tajnyuch Rokowaniach polsko-radzieckich (Czerwiec-Lipiec 1919 r.)." *Z Pola Walki* 34, no. 2 (1966): 23–40.

Gromyko, A.A., and B.N. Ponomarev. *Istoriia vneshnei politiki SSSR*. 2. vols. Moscow: Izdatel'stvo Nauka 1980.

Gründer, Horst. *Walter Simons als Staatsmann, Jurist und Kirchenpolitiker*. Neustadt an der Aisch: Verlag Ph. C. W. Schmidt 1975

Guliev, Dzhamil' B. *Bor'ba kommunisticheskoi partii za osushchestvlenie Leninskoi natsional"noi politiki v Azerbaidzhane*. Baku: Azerbaidzhanskoe Gosudarstvennoe Izdatel'stvo 1970.

Harding, Neil. *Lenin's Political Thought*. 2 vols. New York: St Martin's Press 1981.

Harris, George S. *The Origins of Communism in Turkey*. Stanford, California: Hoover Institution 1967.

Harris, José. "Bureaucrats and Businessmen in British Food Control, 1916–1919." In Kathleen Burk, ed., *War and the State: The Tranformation of British Government, 1914–1919*. London: Allen and Unwin 1982.

Haupts, Leo. *Deutsche Freidenspolitik 1918–1919. Eine Alternative zur Machtpolitik des ersten Weltkrieges*. Düsseldorf: Droste Verlag, 1976.

Helbig, Herbert. *Die Träger der Rapallo-Politik*. Veröffentlichungen des Max-Planck-Instituts für Gexchichte 3. Göttingen: Vandenhoeck & Ruprecht 1958.

Hajdu, Tibor. *The Hungarian Soviet Republic*. Budapest: Adademiai Kiado 1979.

Himmer, Robert. "Harmonicas for Lenin? The Development of German Economic Policy toward Soviet Russia, December 1918 to June 1919." *Journal of Modern History*, Supplement to 49, no. 2 (June 1977): D.1221–D.1247.

– . "Soviet Russia's Economic Relations with Germany, 1918–1922." Johns Hopkins University: PH D dissertation 1972.

– . "Soviet Policy toward Germany during the Russo-Polish War, 1920." *Slavic Review* 35, no. 4 (December 1976): 665–82.

Hogenhuis-Seliverstoff, Anne. *Les relations franco-soviétiques, 1917–1924*. Paris: Publications de la Sorbonne Serie internationale 17, 1981.

Holsti, Kalevi Jacque. "The Origins of Finnish Foreign Policy, 1918–1922. Rudolf Hosti's Role in the Formulation of Policy." Stanford University: PH D dissertation 1961.

Hovannisian, Richard G. *The Republic of Armenia*. Berkeley: University of California Press 1982.

Hovi, Kalervo. *Alliance de Revers: Stabilization of France's Alliance Policies in East Central Europe, 1919–1921*. Turku, Finland: Turku University 1984.

—. *Interessenspharen im Baltikum: Finnland im Rahmen der Ostpolitik Polens, 1919–1922.* Helsinki: Suomen Historiallinen 1984.

—. "Polish-Finnish Cooperation in Border-State Policy, 1919–1922." *Journal of Baltic Studies* 14, no. 2 (Summer 1983): 121–27.

—. "Die Randstaatenkonferenzen 1919 bis 1927." In J. von Hehn and Cs. J. Kenez, eds., *Reval und die Baltischen Länder. Festschrift für Helmuth Weiss zum 80. Geburtstag.* Marburg/Lahn: Verlag J.G. Herder-Institut 1980.

Hovi, Olavi. *The Baltic Area in British Policy, 1918–1921.* Helsinki: The Finnish Historical Society 1980.

Huerten, Heinz, ed. *Zwischen Revolution und Kapp-Putsch. Militaer und Innenpolitik 1918–1920.* Düsseldorf: Droste Verlag 1978.

Hunczak, Taras. "'Operation Winter' and the Struggle for the Baltic." *East European Quarterly* 4, no. 1 (March 1970): 40–57.

Iakovlev, B.M. "V.I. Lenin ob otnoshenii k mel'koi burzhuazii derevni i goroda v kontse 1918 g. i nachale 1919 g." *Voprosy Istorii KPSS* 7 (1972): 93–101.

Institut Marksizma-Leninizma pri TSK KPSS. *Istoriia grazhdanskoi voiny v SSSR 1917–1922.* 5 vols. Moscow: Gosudarstvennoe Izdatel'stvo politicheskoi literatury 1938–1960.

— *Istoriia Kommunisticheskoi Partii Sovetskogo soiuza.* Vol. III, 3 pts. Moscow: Izdatel'stvo politicheskoi literatury 1968.

Iroshnikov, M., D. Kovalenko, V. Shishkin. *Genesis of the Soviet Federative State (1917–1925).* Moscow: Progress Publishers 1982.

Isono, Fujiko. "The Mongolian Revolution of 1921." *Modern Asian Studies* 10, no. 2 (July 1976): 375–94.

—. "Soviet Russia and the Mongolian Revolution of 1921." *Past and Present* 83 (May 1979): 116–40.

Jääskeläinen, Mauno. *Die ostkarelische Frage. Die Entstehung eines nationalen Expansionsprogramms und die Versuche zu seiner Verwirklung in der Aussenpolitik Finnlands in den Jahren 1918–1920.* Helsinki: Finnish Historical Society 1965.

Janos, Andrew C., and William B. Slottman, eds. *Revolution in Perspective. Essays on the Hungarian Soviet Republic of 1919.* Berkeley: University of California Press 1971.

Jeffrey, Keith. *The British Army and the Crisis of Empire, 1918–1922.* Manchester: Manchester University Press 1984.

Jones, Stephen. "The Establishment of Soviet Power in Transcaucasia: The Case of Georgia, 1921–1928." *Soviet Studies* 40, no. 4 (October 1988): 616–39.

Kadishev, A.B. *Interventsiia i grazhdanskaia voina v Zakavkaz'e.* Moscow: Voennoe Izdatel'stvo 1960.

Kapitsa, M.S. *Sovetsko-Kitaishie Otnosheniia.* Moscow: Gospolitizdat 1958.

Kapur, Harish. *Soviet Russia and Asia, 1917–1927.* Geneva: Michael Joseph 1966.

Karchmar, Lucien. "Communism in Romania, 1918–1921." In Ivo Banac, ed., *The Effects of World War I.*

Karpat, Kemal H. "The Personality of Ataturk." *American Historical Review* 90, no. 4 (October 1985): 893–99.

Karpova, R. *L.B. Krasin. Sovetskii Diplomat.* Moscow: Izdatel'stvo sotsial'no-ekonomicheskoi literatury 1962.

Kashkaev, B.O. *Grazhdanskaia voina v Dagestane. 1918–1920 gg.* Moscow: Nauka 1976.

Kazemzadeh, Firuz. *The Struggle for Transcaucasia, 1917–1921.* New York: Philosophical Library 1951.

Kendall, Walter. *The Revolutionary Movement in Britain 1900–1921. The Origins of British Communism.* London: Weidenfeld and Nicolson 1969.

Kenez, Peter. *The Birth of the Propaganda State. Soviet Methods of Mass Mobilization, 1917–1929.* Cambridge: Cambridge University Press 1985.

– . *Civil War in South Russia, 1918.* Berkeley: University of California Press 1971.

– . *Civil War in South Russia, 1919–1920. The Defeat of the Whites.* Berkeley: University of California Press 1977.

Kennan, George F. *Soviet-American Relations, 1917–1920.* 2 vols. Princeton: Princeton University Press 1958.

Kennedy, Paul. *The Realities Behind Diplomacy: Background Influences on British External Policy, 1865–1980.* London: George Allan & Unwin 1981.

Kettle, Michael. *The Road to Intervention. March to November 1918.* London: Routledge 1988.

Kheifetz, A.N. "Leninskaia vneshniaia politika i strany vostoka." In Akademiia Nauk SSSR Institut Istorii SSSR, *Leninskaia venshniaia politika sovetskoi strany,* 122–65.

– . *Sovetskaia Rossiia i sopredel'nye strany vostoka v gody grazhdanskoi voiny (1918–1920).* Moscow: Izdatel'stvo Nauka 1964.

Kholodkovskii, Viktor Mikhailovich. *Finliandiia i Sovetskaia Rossiia 1918–1920.* Moscow: Izdatel'stvo Nauka 1975.

– . "V.I. Lenin i zarozhdenie mezhdunarodnykh otnoshenii novogo, sotsialisticheskogo tipa." Akademiia Nauk SSSR. Institut Istorii SSSR, *Leninskaia vneshniaia politika sovetskoi strany 1917–1924.* Moscow: Izdatel'stvo Nauka 1969.

Kislov, A.N. *Razgrom Ungerna.* Moscow 1964.

Kliatskin, Saul Markovich. *Na zashchite Oktiabria: Organizatsiia reguliarnoi armii i militsionneo striotelstvo v sovetskoi respublike, 1917–1920.* Moscow: Nauka 1965.

Koch, Hannsjoachim W. *Der Deutsche Bürgerkrieg: Eine Geschichte der Deutschen und Osterreichischen Freikorps, 1918–1923.* Frankfurt am Main: Verlag Ullstein 1978.

Kol'tsov, P.S. "Rol' Leninskoi vneshnei politiki v obespechenii pobedy sovetskoi vlasti v Zakavkaz'e (1920–1921 gg.)." *Iz istorii grazhdanskoi voiny i interventsii 1917–1922 gg. Sbornik statei.* Moscow: Izdatel'stvo Nauka 1974.

Kremnev, Boris Grigor'evich. *Krasin.* Moscow: "Mododaia Gvardiia" 1968.

Kulichenko, M.I. *Bor'ba kommunisticheskoi partii za reshenie natsional'nogo voprosa v 1918–1920 godakh.* Karkhov: Izdatel'stvo khar'khovskogo ordena trudovogo krasnogo znameni gosudarstvennogo universiteta im. A.M. Gor'kogo 1963.

Kunz, Hans Beat. *Weltrevolution und Völkerbund: Die Schweizerische Aussenpolitik unter dem Eindruck der Bolschewisteschen Bedrohung, 1918–1923.* Bern: Verlag Stämpfli & Cie AG 1981.

Lahey, Dale Terence. "Soviet Ideological Development of Coexistence: 1917–1927." *Canadian Slavonic Papers* 6 (1964): 80–94.

Lang, D.M. *A Modern History of Soviet Georgia*. New York: Grove Press 1962.

Lavrov, S.V. "Bor'ba v politcheskikh krugakh Velikobritanii vokrug anglo-sovetskikh peregovorov 1920–1921 godov." *Voprosy Istorii* 6 (1977): 59–80.

Lazitch, Branko, and Milorad M. Drachkovitch. *Lenin and the Comintern*. Stanford: Hoover Institution Press 1972.

Leggett, George. *The Cheka: Lenin's Political Police*. Oxford: Clarendon Press 1981.

Leinwand, Artur. *Polska Partia Socjalistyczna wobec Wojny Polski-Radzieckiej 1919–1920*. Warsaw: Panstwowe Wydawnictwo Naukawe 1964.

Leong, Sow-Theng. *Sino-Soviet Diplomatic Relations, 1917–1926*. Honolulu: University Press of Hawaii 1976.

Leslie, R.F., Antony Polonsky, Jan M. Ciechanowski, Z.A. Pelczynski. *The History of Poland Since 1863*. London: Cambridge University Press 1980.

Lerner, Warren. *Karl Radek. The Last Internationalist*. Stanford: Stanford University Press 1970.

– . "Poland in 1920. A Case Study in Foreign Policy Decision Making under Lenin." *South Atlantic Quarterly* (Summer 1973): 406–14.

– . "Attempting a Revolution from Without: Poland in 1920." *Studies on the Soviet Union* 1, no. 4 (1971): 94–107.

Libman, A.B. "Deiatel'nost' kommunisticheskoi organizatsii na territorii Estliandskoi Trudovoi Kommuny." *Iz istorii grazhdanskoi voiny i interventsii*: 85–104.

Linke, Horst Günther. *Deutsch-Sowjetische Beziehungen bis Rapallo*. Köln: Verlag Wissenschaft und Politik 1970.

Livshits, S.G. "Kolchakovskii Perevorot." *Voprosy Istorii* 3, (1983): 79–90.

Long, John W. "American Intervention in Russia: The North Russian Expedition 1918–1919." *Diplomatic History* 6, no. 1 (Winter 1982): 45–68.

Löshe, Peter. *Der Bolshewismus im Urteil der Deutschen Sozialdemodratie, 1903–1920*. Berlin: Colloquium Verlag 1967.

Lundgreen-Nielsen, Kay. *The Polish Problem at the Paris Peace Conference: A Study of the Policies of the Great Powers and the Poles, 1918–1919*. Odense, Denmark: Odense University Press 1979.

Lungu, Dov B. "Soviet-Romanian Relations and the Bessarabian Question in the Early 1920's." *Southeastern Europe* 6, no. 1 (1979): 29–45.

Lungu, V.N. "Ustanovlenie v Bessarabii okkupatsionnogo regima korolevskoi Rumynii." *Voprosy Istorii* 10 (1982): 18–30.

McDougall, Walter A. *France's Rhineland Diplomacy, 1914–1924. The Last Bid for a Balance of Power in Europe*. Princeton: Princeton University Press 1978.

Macfarlane, L.F. "Hands Off Russia in 1920." *Past and Present* 38 (December 1967): 126–52.

McNeal, Robert H. *Stalin. Man and Ruler*. New York: New York University Press 1988.

Maddox, Robert. *The Unknown War with Russia: Wilson's Siberian Intervention*. San Rafael: Presidio Press 1977.

Majstrenko, Iwan. *Borot' bism. A Chapter in the History of Ukrainian Communism.* New York 1954.

Makarova, G.P. *Osushchestvlenie leninskoi natsional' noi politiki v pervye gody sovetskoi vlasti (1917–1920 gg.).* Moscow: Izdatel'stvo Nauka 1969.

Malet, Michael. *Nestor Makhno in the Russian Civil War.* London: London School of Economics and Political Science 1982.

Marks, Sally. *Innocents Abroad: Belgium at the Paris Peace Conference of 1919.* Chapel Hill, NC: University of North Carolina Press 1981.

Martna, Mikhel. *Estland, die esten und die estnische frage.* Olten 1919.

Masson, Philippe. *La Marine française et la mer noire 1918–1919.* Paris: Publications de la Sorbonne 1982.

Matley, Ivan M. "The Dispersal of the Ingrian Finns." *Slavic Review* 38, no. 1 (March 1979): 1–16.

Mawdsley, Evan. *The Russian Civil War.* Boston: Allen and Unwin 1987.

Mayer, Arno J. *Politics and Diplomacy of Peacemaking: Containment and Counter-Revolution at Versailles, 1918–1919.* New York: Knopf 1967.

Meier-Welcker, Hans. *Seeckt.* Frankfurt am Main: Bernard und Graefe 1967.

Meinhardt, Günter. "Deutschland und Westpreussen im russisch-polnischen Krieg von 1920." *Westpreussen Jahrbüch* 20 (1970): 16–26.

Melograni, Piero. *Lenin and the Myth of World Revolution: Ideology and Reasons of State, 1917–1920.* Humanities Press International Atlantic Highlands, NJ 1989.

Miller, S. *Die Bürde der Macht. Die Deutsche Sozialdemokratie 1918–1920.* Beiträge zur Geschichte des Parliamentarismus und der politischen Partien. Band 63. Düsseldorf: Droste Verlag 1978.

Morgan, David W. *The Socialist Left and the German Revolution: A History of the German Independent Social Democratic Party 1917–1922.* Ithaca, NY: Cornell University Press 1975.

Morgan, Kenneth O. *The Age of Lloyd George.* London: Allen and Unwin 1971.

Mueller, Gordon H. "Rapallo Re-examined: A New Look at Germany's Secret Military Collaboration with Russia in 1922." *Military Affairs* 40 (October 1976): 109–17.

Munholland, J.R. "The French Army and Intervention in Southern Russia, 1918–1919." *Cahiers du monde russe et soviétique* 22, no. 1 (janvier-mars 1981): 43–66.

Musialik, Zdislaw. *General Weygand and the Battle of the Vistula, 1920.* London: Jozef Pilsudski Institute of Research 1987.

Narkiewicz, Olga A. *The Green Flag: Polish Populist Politics, 1867–1970.* London: Croom Helm 1976.

Nassibian, Akaby. *Britain and the Armenian Question 1915–1923.* New York: St Martin's Press 1984.

Nezhinskii, L.N. "U istokov sovetsko-vengerskoi druzhby." *Voprosy Istorii* 3, (1969): 18–31.

– . "Iz istorii sovetsko-vengerskikh otnoshenii (mart-avgust 1919g.)." *Istoricheskie Zapiski* 77 (1965): 3–22.

Ochur, V. Ch. *Velikii Oktiabr' i Tuva.* Kyzyl: Tuvinskoe knizhnoe Izdatel'stvo 1967.

O'Connor, Timothy Edward. *Diplomacy and Revolution. G.V. Chicherin and Soviet Foreign Affairs, 1918–1930.* Ames, Iowa State University Press 1988.

Ol'shanskii, P.N. *Rizhskii Dogovor i razvitie Sovetsko-Pol'skikh Otnoshenii 1921–1924.* Moscow: Izdatel'stvo Nauka 1974.

Oznobishin, D.V. *Ot Bresta do Iur'eva.* Moscow: Izdatel'stvo Nauka 1966.

Page, Stanley, W. *The Formation of the Baltic States.* Cambridge: Harvard University Press 1959.

Papin, Leonid M. *Krakh Kolchakovshchiny i obrazovanie Dalnevostochnoi Respubliki.* Moscow: Izdatel'stvo Moskovskogo Universiteta 1957.

Park, Alexander Garland. *Bolshevism in Turkestan, 1917–1927.* New York: Columbia University Press 1957.

Park, Bert Edward. *The Impact of Illness on World Leaders.* Philadelphia: University of Pennsylvania Press 1986.

Pastor, Peter, ed. *Revolutions and Interventions in Hungary and its Neighbor States, 1918–1919.* War and Society in East Central Europe, vol. 20. Boulder, Colorado: Social Science Monographs 1988.

– . "One Step Forward, Two Steps Back: The Rise and Fall of the First Hungarian Communist Party, 1918–1922." In Ivo Banac, ed., *The Effects of World War I.*

– . *Hungary Between Wilson and Lenin: The Hungarian Revolution of 1918–1919 and the Big Three.* East European Monographs 20. Boulder, Colorado: European Quarterly 1976.

Pease, Neal. *Poland, the United States, and the Stabilization of Europe, 1919–1933.* New York: Oxford University Press 1986.

Pereira, N.G.O. "White Power during the Civil War in Siberia (1918–1920): Dilemmas of Kolchak's 'War Anti-Communism'." *Canadian Slavonic Papers* 29, no. 1 (March 1987): 45–62.

Parfenov, P. *Bor'ba za Dalnii Vostok.* Moscow: Moskovskoe Tovarishchestvo Pisatelei 1931.

Persits, Moisei A. *Dalnevostochnaia Respublika i Kitai: Rol DVR v bor'be sovetskoi vlasti za druzhbu s Kitaem v 1920–1922 gg.* Moscow: An SSSR, Institut narodov Azii, Izdatel'stvo vost. lit., 1962.

Petracchi, Giorgio. *La Russia Rivoluzionaria nella politica italiana: La relazioni italo-sovietche, 1917–1925.* Rome: Laterza 1982.

Petsalis-Diomidis, N. "Hellenism is Southern Russia and the Ukrainian Campaign: Their Effect on the Pontus Question." *Balkan Studies* 13, no. 2 (1972): 233–37.

Pipes, R.E. *The Formation of the Soviet Union: Communism and Nationalism, 1917–1923.* Cambridge: Harvard University Press 1964.

Poullada, Leon B. *Reform and Rebellion in Afghanistan, 1919–1929. King Amanullah's Failure to Modernize a Tribal Society.* Ithaca, NY: Cornell University Press 1973.

Pye, Lucian W. *Warlord Politics.* New York: Praeger 1971.

Quested, R.K.I. *"Matey" Imperialists: The Tsarist Russians in Manchuria 1895–1917.* Hong Kong: University of Hong Kong Press 1982.

Rabenau, Friedrich von. *Seeckt, Aus seinen Leben, 1918–1936.* Leipzig: Hase und Koehler 1940.

Radek, Karl. *Die auswärtige Politik Sowjet-Russlands.* Hamburg: Carl Hoym 1921.

Radosh, R. "John Spargo and Wilson's Russian Policy, 1920." *Journal of American History* 52 (December 1965): 548–65.

Rakenius, Gerhard W. *Wilhel Groener als erster General-Quartiermeister. Die politik der Obersten Heeresleitung 1918/1919.* Boppard am Rhein: Harald Boldt Verlag 1977.

Ravasani, Schapour. *Sowjetrepublik Gilan: Die sozialistische Bewegung in Iran seit Ende des 19. Jahrhundert bis 1922.* Berlin: Basis-Verlag 1973.

Reshetar, John S. *The Ukrainian Revolution 1917–1920: A Study in Nationalism.* Princeton: Princeton University Press 1952.

Rezun, Miron. *The Soviet Union and Iran. Soviet Policy in Iran from the Beginnings of the Pahlavi Dynasty until the Soviet Invasion in 1941.* Alpheen aan den Rijn: Sijthoff & Noordhoff International Publishers 1981.

Riekhoff, Harald von. *German-Polish Relations, 1918–1933.* Baltimore: Johns Hopkins Press 1971.

Rigby, T.H. *Lenin's Government: Sovnarkom 1917–1922.* New York: Cambridge University Press 1979.

Rintala, Marvin. *Three Generations: The Extreme Right Wing in Finnish Politics.* Bloomington, Ind.: Indiana University Publications 1962.

Rohwer, Jurgen. "Der Einfluss der allierten Funkaufklarung auf den Verlauf der Zweitern Weltkrieges." *Vierteljahreshefte für Zeitgeschichte* 27, no. 3 (Juli 1979): 325–69.

Rose, John D. "Batum as Domino 1919–1920." *International History Review* 2, no. 2 (April 1980): 266–87.

Rosenfeld, Günter. *Sowjetrussland und Deutschland, 1917–1922.* Berlin: Akademie Verlag 1960.

Röskau-Rydel, Isabel. "Polnisch-litauische Beziehunger zwischen 1918 und 1939." *Jahrbücher für Geschichte Osteuropas* 35, no. 4 (1987): 556–81.

Roskill, Stephen. *Hankey, Man of Secrets.* 3 vols. New York: St Martin's Press 1970–74.

Ross, Nikolaj. *Vrangel v Krymu.* Frankfurt: Possev 1982.

Rumbold, Algernon. *Watershed in India 1914–1922.* London: Athlone Press 1979.

Sboichakov, M.I., S.I. Tsybov, N.F. Chistiakov. *Mikhail Sergeevich Kedrov.* Moscow: Voennoe Izdatel'stvo Ministerva Oborony SSSR 1969.

Scheibert, Peter. *Lenin an der Macht: Das russische Volk in der Revolution 1918–1922.* Weinheim: VCH Verlagsgesellscht 1984.

Schmid, Alex P. *Churchills Privater Krieg. Intervention und Konterrevolution im russischen Bürgerkreig, November 1918-März 1920.* Zurich and Freiburg: Atlantis Verlag 1974.

Schüddenkopf, Otto-Ernst. "Karl Radek in Berlin: Ein Kapitel deutsch-russischer Beziehungen im Jahre 1919." *Archiv für Sozialgeschichte* 2 (1962): 87–166.

– . "Deutschland zwischen Ost und West. Karl Moor und die deutsch-russischen Beziehungen in der ersten Häfte des Jahres 1919." *Archiv fur Sozialgeschichte* 3 (1963): 223–63.

Schumacher, Horst, and Feliks Tych. *Julian Marchlewski-Karski: Eine Biographie.* Berlin: Dietz 1966.

Schwabe, Klaus. *Deutsche Revolution und Wilson-Frieden. Die Amerikanische und Deutsche Friedenstrategie zwischen ideologie und Realpolitik. 1918/19.* Düsseldorf: Droste Verlag 1971.

— . *Woodrow Wilson, Revolutionary Germany and Peacemaking, 1918–1919. Missionary Diplomacy and the Realities of Power.* Chapel Hill, NC: University of North Carolina Press 1985.

Selivanov, Panteleimon Alekseevich. *Voennoe stroitel' stvo v Belorussii v period pokhodov Antanty.* Minsk: Izdatel'stvo "Nauka i tekhnika'" 1973.

Semanov, S.N. *Likvidatsiia Antisovetskogo Kronshtadtskogo Miatezha 1921 goda.* Moscow: Izdatel'stvo Nauka 1973.

Senn, Alfred E. *The Great Powers, Lithuania and the Vilna Question.* Leiden: Brill 1966.

— . *Diplomacy and Revolution: The Soviet Mission to Switzerland, 1918.* Notre Dame, Ind.: University of Notre Dame Press 1974.

Service, Robert. *The Bolshevik Party in Revolution: A Study in Organizational Change, 1917–1923.* New York: Barnes and Noble 1979.

Shereshevskii, Boris Mikhaikovich. *Razgrom Semenovshchiny.* Novosibirsk 1966.

— . *V Bitvakh za Dal'nii Vostok 1920–1922.* Novosibirsk 1974.

Sheridan, James E. *China in Disintegration.* New York: The Free Press 1975.

Sherwood, John M. *George Mandel and the Third Republic.* Stanford: Stanford University Press 1970.

Shishkin, S.N. *Grazhdanskaia voina na Dalnem Vostoke 1918–1922.* Moscow: Voenizdat 1957.

Shishkin, V.A. "'Rol' V.I. Lenina v razvitii mezhdunarodnikh ekonomicheskikh sviazei sovetskogo gosudarstva. " *Leninskaia vneshniaia politika sovetskoi strany 1917–1924.*

— . *Sovetskoe gosudarstvo i strany Zapada v 1917–1923 gg. Ocherki Istorii stanovleniia ekonimicheskikh otnoshenii.* Leningrad: Izdatel'stvo Nauka Leningradskoe Otdelenie 1969.

Shumikhim, V.S. "Trassa proletarskogo internatsionalizma." *Voprosy Istorii* 6 (1979): 183–87.

Shurygin, A.P. "Dalburo TSK RKP(b) v gody grazhdanskoi voiny 1920–22 gg.' *Voprosy Istorii KPSS* (August 1966): 55–62.

Silverman, Dan P. *Recontructing Europe after the Great War.* Cambridge: Harvard University Press 1982.

Sipols, V. Ia. *Tainaia Diplomatiia.* Riga: Izdatel'stvo Liesma 1968.

— . *Die Ausländische intervention in Lettland, 1918–1920.* Berlin: Rütten & Loening 1961.

Sirotkin, Vladlen. "The Riga Peace Treaty." *International Affairs* 9, (1988): 128–43.

Smith Daniel. *Aftermath of War: Bainbridge Colby and Wilsonian Diplomacy, 1920–1921.* Philadelphia: American Philosophical Society 1970.

Smith, Caufield F. "The 'Ungernovscina' – How and Why." *Jahrbücher für Geschichte Osteuropas* 28, no. 4 (1980): 590–95.

— . "Atamanshchina in the Russian Far East." *Russian History* 6, no. 1 (1979): 57–67.

– . *Vladivostok under Red and White Rule: Revolution and Counterrevolution in the Russian Far East, 1920–1922.* Seattle and London: University of Washington Press 1975.

Smith, Jr, C. Jay. *Finland and the Russian Revolution 1917–1922.* Athens: University of Georgia Press 1958.

Sofinov, P.G. *Ocherki istorii Vserossiiskoi chrezvychainoi komissii (1917–1922 gg).* Moscow: Gosudarstvennoe izdatel'stvo politicheskoi literatury 1960.

Sonyel, Salahi Ramsdan. *Turkish Diplomacy 1918–1923. Mustafa Kemal and the Turkish National Movement.* London: Sage Publications, 1975.

Spirin, Leonid Mikhailovich, and Alter L'vovich Litvin. *Na zashchite revoliutsii. V.I. Lenin, RKP(b) v gody grazhdanskoi voiny (Istoriograficheskii ocherk).* Leningrad: Lenizdat 1985.

Stachiw, Matthew, and Jaroslw Sztendera. *Western Ukraine. At the Turning Point of History 1918–1923.* 2 vols. New York: The Shevchenko Scientific Society 1969.

Stamm, Christoph. "Der Bela-Kun Zwischenfall im Juli 1920 und die deutsch-sowjetischen Bezhiehungen." *Jahrbücher für Geschichte Osteuropas* 31, no. 3 (1983): 365–85.

Stankevich, N.S. *Prigovor Revoliutsii: Krushenie antisovetskogo dvizhenia v Belorussii 1917–1925.* Minsk: 1985.

Stetten, Nancy. "The National Question and the Russian Civil War, 1917–1921." University of Chicago, Ph D dissertation 1977.

Stewart, Rhea Talley. *Fire in Afghanistan 1914–1929. Faith, Hope and the British Empire.* Garden City, New York: Doubleday, 1973.

Sullivan, Charles L. "The 1919 German Campaign in the Baltic: The Final Phase." In Stanley Vardys and Romauld J. Misunas, eds., *The Baltic States in Peace and War 1917–1945.* University Park, Penn.: Pennsylvania University Press 1978.

– . "The German Role in the Baltic Campaign – Spring 1919." *Baltic Review* 36 (October 1969): 40–62.

Suny, Ronald G. *Armenia in the Twentieth Century.* Chico, California: Scholars Press 1983.

– . ed. *Transcaucasia: Nationalism and Social Change.* Ann Arbor: University of Michigan Press 1983.

– . *The Baku Commune 1917–1918.* Princeton: Princeton University Press 1972.

Suprunenko, N.I. *Ocherki istorii grazhdanskoi voiny i inostrannoi voennoi interventsii na Ukraine.* Moscow: Nauka 1966.

Surguladze, A.N. *Zakavkaz'e v bor'be za pobedu sotsialisticheskoi revoliutsii.* Tbilisi: Izdatel'stvo Tbilisi Universiteta 1971.

Svetachev, M.I. *Imperialisticheskaia interventsiia v Sibiri i na Dal'nem Vostoke (1918–1922 gg).* Novosibirsk: Izdatel'stvo Nauka Sibirskoe Otdelenie, 1983.

Swietochowski, Tadeusz. *Russian Azerbaidjan 1905–1920. The Shaping of National Identity in a Muslim Community.* Cambridge: Cambridge University Press 1985.

Szafar, Tadeusz. "The Origins of the Communist Party in Poland, 1918–1921." In Banac, ed. *Effects of World War I.*

Tagieva, Sh.A. *Natsional'no osvoboditel'noe dvizhenie v Iranskom Azerbaidzhane v 1917–20 gg.* Baku: Izdatel'stvo Akademia Nauk AZSSR 1956.

Taigro, Iulo. *Bor'ba trudiashchikhsia Estonii za sovetskuiu vlast' i za mir gody grazhdanskoi voiny (1918–1920).* Tallin 1958.

Tamkoc, Metin. *The Warrior Diplomats: Guardians of the National Security and Modernization of Turkey.* Salt Lake City: University of Utah Press 1976.

Tampke, Jügen. *The Ruhr and Revolution: The Revolutionary Movement in the Rhenish-Westphalian Region, 1912–1919.* London: Croon Helm 1979.

Tanin, M. *Desiat let vneshnei politiki SSSR, 1917–1927.* Moscow: Gosizdat 1927.

Tipner, Johannes. *V ogne revoliutsii.* Tallin 1964.

Thompson, John M. *Russia, Bolshevism, and the Versailles Peace.* Princeton: Princeton University Press 1966.

Tokarzhevskii, E.A. *Iz istorii inostrannoi interventsii i grazhdanskoi voiny v Azerbaidzhane.* Baku: Izdatel'stvo Akademii Nauk Azerbaidzhanskoi SSR 1957.

Tökes, Rudolf L. *Bela Kun and the Hungarian Soviet Republic.* New York: Praeger 1967.

Trush, M.I. "Problemy sovetskoi vneshnei politiki v Sochineniiakh V.I. Lenina." *Leninskaia vneshniaia politika sovetskoi strany 1917–1924.*

Tse-tsung, Chow. *The May Fourth Movement.* Cambridge: Harvard University Press 1960.

Ulam, Adam B. *Stalin: The Man and His Era.* New York: The Viking Press 1973.

Uldricks, Teddy J. *Diplomacy and Ideology. The Origins of Soviet Foreign Relations 1917–1930.* London and Beverley Hills: Sage Publications 1979.

Ullman, R.H. *Anglo-Soviet Relations, 1917–1921.* 3 vols. Princeton: Princeton University Press 1961–1972.

Varslavan, A. *Politika angliiskogo imperializma v otnoshenii burzhuaznoi Latvii (1920–23).* Riga: Zvaigzne 1967.

Vartamian, S. *Pobeda sovetskoi vlasti v Armenii.* Erevan: Gosudarstvennoe Izdatel'stvo Armenii 1959.

Vincent, C. Paul. *The Politics of Hunger: The Allied Blockade of Germany, 1915–1919.* Athens: Ohio University Press 1985.

Völgyes, Ivan, ed. *Hungary in Revolution 1918–1919. Nine Essays.* Lincoln: University of Nebraska Press 1971.

Volkan, Vamik D. *The Immortal Ataturk: A Psychobiography.* Chicago: University of Chicago Press 1986.

Volkmann, H.E. "Probleme des deutsch-lettischen Verhältnisses zwischen Compiegne und Versailles." *Zeitschrift für Ostforschung* 4, (1965): 713–26.

Wagner, Gerhard. *Deutschland und der Polnisch-Sowjetische Krieg, 1920.* Wiesbaden: Franz Steiner Verlag 1979.

Walworth, Arthur. *Wilson and His Peacemakers. American Diplomacy at the Paris Peace Conference, 1919.* New York: W.W. Norton 1986.

Wandycz, Piotr S. *Soviet-Polish Relations, 1917–1921.* Cambridge: Harvard University Press 1969.

– . "Secret Soviet-Polish Peace Talks in 1919." *Slavic Review* 24, no. 3 (September 1965): 425–49.

Watt, Richard M. *Bitter Glory: Poland and its Fate 1918–1939*. New York: Simon and Schuster 1979.

Wengst, Udo. *Graf Brockdorff-Rantzau und die Aussenpolitischen Anfänge der Weimarer Republik*. Bern: Herbert Lang 1973.

Wheeler, Robert F. *U.S.P.D. und Internationale: Sozialistischer Internationalismus in der Zeit der Revolution*. Frankfurt am Main: Ullstein 1975.

White, John A. *The Siberian Intervention*. Princeton: Princeton University Press 1950.

White, Stephen. *Britain and the Bolshevik Revolution. A Study in the Politics of Diplomacy, 1920–1924*. London: Macmillan 1979.

– . "Communism and the East: The Baku Congress, 1920." *Slavic Review* 33, no. 3 (September 1974): 492–514.

– . "Labour's Council of Action 1920." *Journal of Contemporary History* 9, no. 4 (October 1974): 99–122.

Whiting, Allen S. *Soviet Policies in China, 1917–1924*. New York: Columbia University Press 1953.

Williams, Robert. "Russian War Prisoners and Soviet-German Relations: 1918–1921." *Canadian Slavonic Papers* 9, no. 2 (1967): 270–95.

Wilson, Michael. *Baltic Assignment: British Submariners in Russia 1914–1919*. London: L. Cooper-Secker 1985.

Zabih, S. *The Communist Movement in Iran*. Berkeley: University of California Press 1966.

Zapantis, Andrew. *Greek-Soviet Relations 1917–1941*. New York: 1982.

Zarnitskii, S., and A. Sergeev. *Chicherin*. Moscow: Molodaia gvardiia 1968.

– and L.I. Trofimova. *Sovetskoi strany diplomat*. Moscow: Izdatel'stvo politicheskoi literatury 1968.

Zhvaniia, G. "V.I. Lenin i partiinaia organizatsii Gruzi v period bor'by za sovetskuiu vlast." *Zaria Vostoka* (Tiflis) 21 (April 1961).

Zürrer, Werner. *Kaukasien 1918–1921*. Düsseldorf: Droste Verlag 1978.

– . *Persien zwischen England und Russland 1918–1925. Grossmachteinflüsse und nationaler Wiederaufstieg am Beispiel des Iran*. Bern: Peter Lang 1978.

Index